D0026085

Content Area Reading
A Heuristic Approach

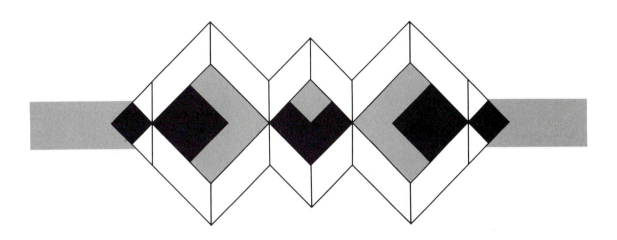

Anthony V. Manzo
Professor and Director of the Center
for Studies in Higher Order Literacy
University of Missouri—Kansas City

Ula Casale Manzo
Coordinator of Language Arts, K–12
School District of Kansas City, Missouri

LB
1050.455
.M36
1990

Macmillan Publishing Company
NEW YORK
Collier Macmillan Canada
TORONTO
Maxwell Macmillan International
NEW YORK OXFORD SINGAPORE SYDNEY

AKP9603

INDIANA-
PURDUE
LIBRARY

WITHDRAWN

FORT WAYNE

To all who labor so that all may learn
and
''Lenny,'' our labor and our love

Cover Art: Marko Spalatin

Macmillan Publishing Company
866 Third Avenue, New York, New York 10022

Macmillan Publishing Company is
part of the Maxwell Communication
Group of Companies.

Maxwell Macmillan Canada, Inc.
1200 Eglinton Avenue East
Suite 200
Don Mills, Ontario M3C 3N1

This book was set in Meridien.

Administrative Editor: Jeff Johnston
Developmental Editor: Linda James Scharp
Production Editor: Linda H. Bayma
Art Coordinator: Vincent A. Smith
Cover Designer: Brian Deep
Text Designer: Connie Young

Copyright © 1990 by Macmillan Publishing Company. "Merrill" is an imprint of Macmillan
Publishing Company. All rights reserved. No part of this book may be reproduced in any form,
electronic or mechanical, including photocopy, recording, or any information storage and
retrieval system, without permission in writing from the publisher.

Library of Congress Catalog Card Number: 89–64397
International Standard Book Number: 0–675–20652–9
Printed in the United States of America
2 3 4 5 6 7 8 9—94 93 92 91

Heuristic: self-educating, or learn-by-doing, strategies for improving comprehension, cognition, content, comportment, and communication across grades, subjects, and conditions.

Preface

What will you have in common with other teachers of mathematics, English, art, history, science, or health? No matter what content area subject you teach, every teacher teaches students. Teaching students as well as content is what content area reading is all about. Content area reading means, among other things,

- Starting instruction where *students* are, not where the textbook or curriculum guide begins
- Modeling, or demonstrating, the processes necessary for reading and learning concepts in a subject area
- Instructing students in ways that will enable them to become successful independent learners.

If this sounds complicated, keep in mind the basic theme of this book: The *best* strategies for teaching students also tend to be the most self-instructive, or heuristic. As you use these strategies, you will discover more and more about how students learn and therefore about how you can teach more effectively.

This book also has a strong emphasis on the professional development of teachers. The first chapter emphasizes the strong connections between the roles of teacher and learner. The next chapter provides you with a solid background in the historical roots of teaching reading. Subsequent chapters outline where the field of reading is today as well as where it seems to be headed in the future. Your participation as learner, critic, and explorer is welcome throughout.

Several features are built into the text to help you read and study the book more effectively.

- Each chapter begins with a focus statement and outline.
- Each chapter ends with a graphic organizer which serves as a visual chapter summary, and a critique and anticipation section which both summarizes the current chapter and previews the next chapter.
- A special feature called Trade Secret (also found at the end of each chapter) offers teaching tips and other "insider" information based on "real world" experiences.
- Throughout the text you will find Concept Clarification Boxes. These boxes invite you to explore and apply key ideas.
- Key terms are boldfaced throughout the text.
- The glossary at the end of the book defines all key terms.

Both students and professors will find the Nested Chapters Index useful. This index provides page references for important topics that are integrated throughout the text, rather than collected in a single chapter. It may be useful to think of these topics as "nested chapters," or chapters within chapters. The topics included in this index are vocabulary, questioning, writing, and life management. The Nested Chapters Index precedes the author and subject indexes.

Finally, because there are so many acronyms and abbreviations for the topics and strategies used in content area reading, you will find a list of the most commonly used acronyms and their "full names" identified inside the front and back cover for easy reference.

To get the most from the text, we suggest that you begin to keep notes on what you do and think as a student while you are reading. For example, do you reread some sections to increase your comprehension? Do you underline? Make notes in the margin? Do you use chapter outlines? Do you relate ideas to your own personal experience? By reflecting on how you learn, you will find that you already know how to be an effective model and how to promote literacy. Many of the methods you will read about in this book will refine strategies you already use and show you how to teach students to think and construct meaning from the printed page.

ACKNOWLEDGMENTS

We are indebted to our reviewers, who kept us humble by making many valuable suggestions. We incorporated as many as we could, and some we will try to implement in the next edition.

George Cabrera, Oregon State University/Western Oregon State College
Karen S. Daves, University of Northern Colorado
Bonnie O. Ericson, California State University-Northridge
Cindy Gillespie, Ball State University
Urich H. Hardt, Portland State University
Michael McKenna, Wichita State University
Karen L. Parker, Liberty University, Virginia
Don Richardson, University of Kansas
Randall L. Ryder, University of Wisconsin-Milwaukee

Carol M. Santa, San Diego State University
Albert J. Shannon, St. Joseph's University, Philadelphia
Lana Smith, Memphis State University
James E. Walker, Clarion State College, Pennsylvania
Liane H. Willey, Central Missouri State University

The staff at Merrill Publishing Company have been of great assistance. We are especially grateful to Jeff Johnston, executive editor; Linda James Scharp, developmental editor; Linda Bayma, production coordinator; and Vince Smith, art coordinator.

Contents

x CONTENTS

9
Study Skills and Habits: Preface, Notetaking, Memory Training, Test Taking, Speed Reading, and Life Management 270

PART FOUR
Compensatory and Content Reading Programs 305

10
Special-Needs Students 306

11
Schoolwide Programming: Elements, Hubs, and Other Catalysts 338

PART FIVE
Content Area Applications 361

12
English and Mathematics: Writing and Notation 362

13
Biological-Physical and Social Sciences: Scientific and Executive Thinking 396

PART ONE

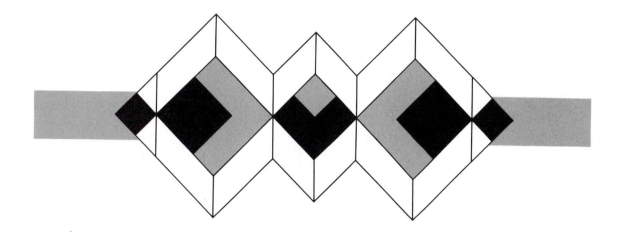

Foundations of
Content Area Reading

Content Area Reading

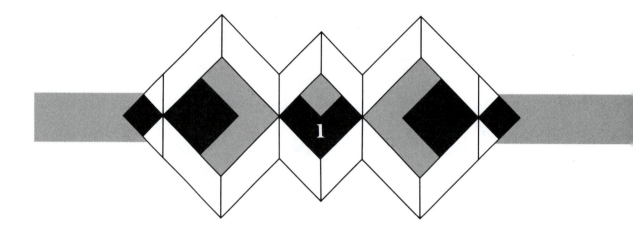

For Teachers and for Students

Let no one imagine that they are without influence. The person who thinks becomes a light and a power.

— *Henry George (paraphrase)*

FOCUS

Teaching students to master content and reading skills requires teaching methods that will empower students and ignite self-exploration and self-education in both students and teachers. This chapter presents ideas and a graduated ladder of methods that will permit teachers and students to meet the challenges of various textual materials.

OUTLINE

QUESTIONS ARE THE ANSWER

When a teacher faces a class or a student opens a book, elaborate and well-conceived answers often unfold. Unfortunately, students rarely know what the questions are and therefore often cannot understand or relate to the answers. This text is about the teaching of reading, thinking, and study skills across the curriculum. Much of its content was developed in response to a handful of pivotal questions. It is these questions, most of which originated from teachers, that launched the field now called **content area reading (CAR).**

There are several reasons for opening this text with a brief look at the questions that first attracted attention and interest to the CAR field. The first reason is simple enough: When you can grasp such basic questions or problems, you often can share in the wonder and intrinsic motivation of its founders. Second, when learners understand these pivotal questions, they are more likely to develop possible resolutions on their own, both inside and outside the classroom. Finally, it is useful to initiate a new area of study with an overview of its basic issues. An overview, almost by definition, sets up categories that greatly enhance comprehension of the relevance and place of incoming information. This becomes the basis for sound concept formation, improved long-term memory, and application of new knowledge to other learning and doing opportunities.

To use a play on an old analogy, being given a *fact* is like being given a fish, but being given a *question* is like being given a fishing pole, a hook, and some lures. This theme runs throughout the field of content area reading. Indeed, this field could be subtitled "Helping Readers to Help Themselves."

Organizing Questions

The content area reading movement has evolved largely in response to middle and secondary school teachers' desire to help students better read and learn from their textbooks. From its inception in the 1930s, several pivotal questions have impelled its development. Try your hand at answering and discussing each of the following questions from your current perspective. Then compare your answers with those the CAR field now offers. (See Appendix A for a brief synopsis of these.)

1. Haven't students learned to "read" by the time they finish grade school?
2. In the past, few students were taught "reading" after grade school. Doesn't reading improve naturally and, more or less, *as a result of* reading?
3. If reading instruction is still needed, why can't it just be taught in a separate class by a reading teacher?
4. How can content teachers be expected to have time to teach reading when most school districts have stringent policies that mandate teacher responsibility for students' (including mainstreamed students') mastery of specific content objectives?
5. Some content areas, such as physical education, art, music, and math, involve little or no reading. *What* should teachers in these disciplines know about content area reading, and *why?*

6. What skills and abilities can content teachers expect students to bring to class? How can these be assessed?
7. How can students of varying ability levels be helped to read and learn content from a common classroom text? Are there practical alternatives to the single-text model?
8. How can students' independent reading and learning strategies be improved?
9. What does a content area reading program look like?

Nourishing Teachers and Students

As you can see, many questions underlying the CAR movement have been brought to light and addressed. The goal of working toward reading improvement in every class, however, has yet to be reached. Recent efforts to gain perspective on this problem have yielded a striking insight. Previous CAR research and methodology as represented by the organizing questions above were concerned almost exclusively with the art and science of teaching youngsters. We have since learned a great deal about student needs and teacher responsibilities. What we haven't learned much about are the learning and developmental needs of *teachers*. You might say we've spent all day in the classroom when we should have spent a period or two in the teachers' lounge. The following section explores two "new" pivotal questions from this perspective.

"New" Questions and Emerging Answers

1. *What classroom dynamics tend to interfere with effective teaching, and what can be done about them?* There are personal problems to face and resolve at every stage of human development, particularly in the early career stages. Doing so before a class of youngsters who are similarly preoccupied—and rarely aware of adults' personal problems—can be trying.

The high potential for stress and job frustration that can exist when youngsters with "growing pains" are brought together with young professionals who are also feeling their own way suggests the need to nourish teachers so that they can effectively nourish students. In a typical classroom setting, teachers must continually evaluate progress toward instructional goals and make many complex "in-flight" decisions based on their perceptions (Padak, 1986). In an effort to assist teachers during these difficult decision-making periods, several educators, ourselves included, advocate strategic teaching. **Strategic teaching** is based on the regular use of teaching procedures or relatively precise external guides by which to teach and manage a class.

Strategic teaching procedures provide a well-thought-out and predictable, but not confining, teaching-learning environment. They help keep instruction and learning on course through most student disruptions as well as during teacher lapses resulting from inexperience and personal problems. Strategic teaching also can reduce lesson-planning time, because it offers a basic formula that can be easily adapted to different materials and needs. Equally important, tried and tested teaching procedures often are designed to encourage greater student participation. When student participation is high, teachers tend to be more responsive and empathetic, and teaching and learning become crisp and uplifting.

2. *Why do teachers, regardless of their training, tend to teach the way they were taught rather than employing a strategic approach?* There is a predictable pattern of events in the early years of teaching that can impede professional growth and turn teachers away from strategic teaching prematurely. A novice teacher will select an approach to teaching that is too idealistic for the situation and/or too far a stretch for the unseasoned professional. The personal and classroom management problems that result from early misguided decisions cause the inexperienced teacher's future decisions to be somewhat more defensive—that is, designed to avoid negative outcomes rather than to produce positive ones. In due course, a teaching style evolves that is tied to initial personal and classroom management needs. The two become so tightly interwoven that to change one is to unravel the other.

Take, for example, the teacher who builds a class around seatwork, or "auto-instructional," self-pacing, and self-scoring material. In such a situation, the teacher tends to talk little to avoid unruly responding. This defensive posture then becomes the centerpiece around which the class is organized, structured, managed, and therefore taught. On the other hand, consider the lecture-based class. This teaching approach, in which the teacher talks a great deal, can also be a defensively selected management style. The teacher simply could be trying to limit students' opportunity for disruptive talk. The teacher also may not feel secure enough in his or her knowledge of the field to depart from notes and risk looking up at what is happening in the classroom.

In any case, whenever *instructional* decision making becomes inseparable from naive and defensive *management* concerns, the results are likely to be costly in terms of learning outcomes and teacher growth. Regrettably, this "defensive-choice" scenario will probably be magnified in difficult school situations, particularly since new teachers often receive the most difficult teaching assignments. Those who manage to survive the challenge "escape" (understandably) as soon as opportunity or seniority permit, and the cycle is perpetuated.

Sometimes there is an almost indistinguishable line between defensive and responsive teaching. It can be natural and efficient to shape one's teaching style "responsively," or adaptively, around classroom management and personal needs as well as student needs. The problem arises when *most* decisions become subconscious reactions formed too quickly, too rigidly, and, most of all, too defensively. When decisions are made this way repeatedly, the teacher loses self-esteem and is unable to adapt and grow professionally. Such fears have slowed the implementation of content area reading methods. However, the field has been pioneering several means of dealing with this problem. Most notable is the development of a class of teaching strategies expressly designed to permit teachers to make more mature decisions about how they will teach and manage and be known professionally. These teaching strategies, which we shall call *heuristics,* are discussed more fully later.

Heuristic strategies cannot completely solve the complex paradox of being a "responsive" teacher without becoming an overly "defensive" teacher. But, as you shall see, content area reading methods offer several advantages that can help meet the obligations and demands of modern-day teaching while leaving the teacher with the energy, the will, and the way to fashion a plan for professional growth and development.

To aid you in selecting and acquiring teaching practices that will best serve your personal professional growth, most of the teaching strategies presented in this chapter are organized by their relative degree of difficulty in implementation. The actual level of difficulty and effect on classroom climate of a given teaching procedure cannot be known for certain, of course, since it will vary greatly with the personality, strengths, and weaknesses of each teacher, each class, and, as every teacher knows, the dynamics of any given day. In Appendix B, we provide a format for recording and planning various aspects of your career. One item you may wish to refine now for this "Personal Recorder and Professional Planner," because it has strong implications for employment, promotion, and teaching style, is your evolving answer to the question most frequently asked in job interviews: "Why did you choose to become a teacher?" This question is only slightly less unsettling than "What is your philosophy of education?" The purpose of these questions is (or should be) to get a clue as to how you will interpret—and therefore either benefit from or be diminished by—your teaching experiences. Your answers to such questions will also affect what and how much you will learn in your courses or from your professional reading. In either case, it is a good idea to consider some pragmatic and uplifting reasons for being a teacher. The introspective mindset necessary for doing so also dovetails nicely with the next portion of this chapter, which urges you to undertake certain "heuristic" teaching exercises designed to help you discover the security and benefits of becoming a "strategic teacher" of reading and content in your chosen field.

Guardian of the Past, Trustee of the Future

There probably are as many reasons for being a teacher as there are teachers. No doubt you already are aware of some of your own reasons, and others will reveal themselves to you as you mature in your profession. In all probability, your immediate reasons for wishing to teach are very practical considerations related to finances, time frame, and opportunities. Later you probably will find that certain personal character traits have played a larger role than you now think.

One of the authors once asked a psychology major who was close to completing her degree why she wanted to change direction and become a teacher when that would require her to "start all over again." She had no sensible answer to offer at that time, at least none that this author could discern. Some time later, while watching her at work with kindergarten children in a year-long study of children's curiosity that we were conducting, the answer became obvious: She was instinctively nurturing, especially of children with special needs. Her intuitive recognition of this innate characteristic surely was what had led her to teaching. This instinct to teach was so much a part of her, in fact, that anyone watching her teach became enchanted by how natural and uncomplicated teaching could be. Not surprisingly, she went on some years later to become an equally effective professor of education.

Of course, there are other less flattering but equally valid reasons for wanting to be a teacher. Over 50 years of psychological studies of the characteristics of persons in various professions have shown that teachers are almost as high in "dominance" needs as they are in "nurturance" needs. This means that we tend to really like being in control. The realities of teaching, however, soon convince us that no one really "controls" anyone else, nor is it desirable to do so. The wise soon learn that teaching essentially is modeling, guiding, and explaining consequences.

No matter what your initial reasons for becoming a teacher, you will be a stronger one if you forge a personal philosophy or guiding ideology for yourself. You can find some very noble elements of an ideology among the purposes for which schools were founded. For example, education is expected to provide society with continuity and stability by passing along all that has been learned from the past. Also, schools serve as "advocates" for the young. For this reason, we as teachers constantly must remind ourselves, one another, and the lay public that those "antsy," sometimes obstreperous, and occasionally charming youngsters sitting before us will inherit the future and that the effort and expense—in both dollar and human terms—invested in them are always worthwhile. In this sense, it strikes us that a reasonable ideology for a teacher is to see oneself as a guardian of the past and a trustee of the future. And, while that doesn't always "spend" well in our highly materialistic world, it is equally difficult to buy.

Box 1.1 illustrates an activity designed to clarify the concept of professional growth as change and describes the factors that help and hinder it. The next section of this chapter focuses on the concept of heuristics as a valuable means of facilitating growth throughout your career.

Heuristics Meet Teacher and Student Needs

Although content area reading had its inception in the 1930s, it didn't really get perking until the 1970s. Content area reading specialists, as relative newcomers to the educational scene, have had to figure out the best ways to familiarize educators at all levels with the rudimentary principles and practices of the field. In the process of teaching teachers and teacher trainers about this new technology, much has been and is being learned about teaching effectiveness and what it takes to get it. Researchers have learned, for example, that it can take up to three years of teacher training to produce expert content reading "decision makers" able to use appropriate strategies flexibly and effectively (Conley, 1986). Further, successful acquisition of such teaching strategies is profoundly related to the strategies' compatibility with teachers' and, to a great extent, students' prior conceptions and experiences (Duffy & Anderson, 1982).

In an effort to accelerate this process for teachers, a rigorous hands-on approach to teaching and learning has evolved. This process, which we have referred to as **heuristics,** takes a more developmental approach to professional growth. Heuristic teaching strategies meet teachers as well as students "where they are" and permit them to grow and be shaped gradually in the effective use of CAR teaching and learning strategies. This gradual, process approach to becoming a strategic teacher

BOX 1.1

CONCEPT CLARIFICATION
Professional Growth

The following force field analysis form is useful in considering how to bring about change of any form (Schmuck & Runkel, 1985). Work with a small group of classmates to determine factors that promote or inhibit change in the form of teachers' individual professional growth. You can derive these from the material you have just read or from your own experience.

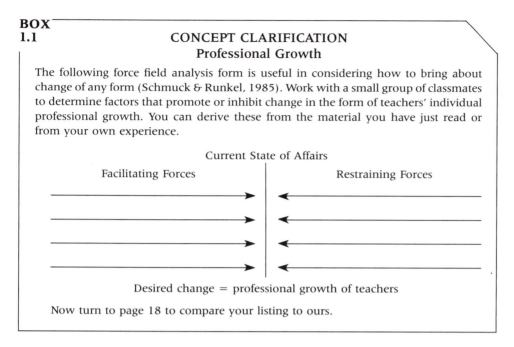

Current State of Affairs

Facilitating Forces   Restraining Forces

Desired change = professional growth of teachers

Now turn to page 18 to compare your listing to ours.

is especially appealing under the current convention of giving an individual full responsibility for a class after only a single semester of "student teaching."

The concept of heuristics has a long history in education. Why, then, you might ask, is this term unfamiliar? The answer is simply that the design of methods that effectively employ this approach has lagged far behind the ideal. A **heuristic approach,** according to *Webster's New Collegiate Dictionary* (1968), is one that involves "exploratory problem-solving" and "self-educating techniques." Harold Herber, a major contributor to the CAR movement, uses an aspect of the heuristic approach to teacher training when he has teachers construct "reading guides" for textbook reading assignments. In the process of developing questions to help students with a text's vocabulary load, idea density, sentence complexity, and assumptions of prior knowledge, a teacher begins to realize how difficult the text might be for students. Additional problems usually become apparent when the teacher uses the reading guide with the class. Once the teacher has a clearer sense of why students are having difficulty, he or she is better positioned to provide effective instruction.

The term *heuristic* as used in this text refers to methods that have been carefully constructed to cause teachers and students to *behave* differently, which in turn leads them to begin to *feel* and *think* differently. Heuristics are a special means of promoting strategic teaching: Teachers and students are procedurally led to do certain things that, *through their doing,* initiate a spiraling effect that reinforces and extends some behaviors and diminishes others. In this climate, "defensive" teaching is reduced and more strategic means of *teaching* and *learning* are unearthed.

**BOX
1.2**   CONCEPT CLARIFICATION
         The Heuristic That Imparted What Could Not Be Taught

Jonas Salk, the famous medical researcher, told of a very powerful heuristic discussed on a late-night television talk show about 10 years ago. Despite huge expenditures, the government of India had for many years been singularly unsuccessful in educating its poorest classes on the benefits of birth control. It seemed to be paddling upstream against a strong current of tradition, religious belief, and simple habit.

Working on your own or with classmates, think of all the possible suggestions you might have made to the government for educating its people on the benefits of birth control. Then turn to page 18 to see how an incidental occurrence ultimately solved the problem. In what way was this solution a heuristic? Were any of your own suggestions similarly heuristic in nature?

To be effective, a teaching heuristic must be simple and compatible with what we already do as teachers. Ideally, when carried from concept into practice, it will have a "time-release" effect: In the process of using it, more and better ways of teaching will continue to occur to the teacher and more and better ways of learning will occur to students. Thus, good teaching heuristics are strategies one can adopt to "learn more about how to teach" rather than methods one must "learn in order to teach." They are, in effect, a conscious form of "learning from doing." Box 1.2 further clarifies the concept of heuristics.

Many high-quality teaching strategies contain a heuristic element. The one described in the following section, however, was designed primarily for this purpose. The strategy attempts to introduce the teacher to the values and "feel" of content area reading methodology in a conceptual, hands-on way. This heuristic is particularly suitable for the content area teacher, because it is most compatible with the lecture mode used most frequently to impart basic information and knowledge.

A PLACE TO START: THE LISTEN-READ-DISCUSS HEURISTIC

Effective learning, including learning how to be an effective teacher, needs something to get it started, something to keep it going, and something to keep it from becoming random or misguided (Bruner, 1971). The Listen-Read-Discuss (L-R-D) heuristic (Manzo & Casale-Manzo, 1985) meets these requirements for teachers and students. It offers a simple lesson design that can be tried almost immediately and provides several elaborations on the basic design that can be phased in as necessary and appropriate. This is one way to develop a personal program of professional development.

First we will examine the guidelines for using the L-R-D heuristic. Then we will see some of the teaching behaviors the L-R-D induces and the benefits to students, teachers, and the school program that it offers.

Guidelines for Use of the L-R-D Heuristic

Following are the recommended guidelines for using the L-R-D heuristic:

1. Select a portion of a text to be read.
2. Present the information from that portion of the text in the customary lecture style for about half the class period.
3. Have the class read the textbook version of the same material. Students will then be "empowered" to read material with which they have some familiarity.
4. Discuss the material students have heard and read.

The following three questions, adapted and extended from Frank Smith (1978), are recommended for provoking a fruitful discussion following reading:

1. What did you understand most from what you heard and read?
2. What did you understand least from what you heard and read?
3. What questions or thoughts did this lesson raise in your mind about the content and/or about effective reading and learning?

Nested Values of the L-R-D Heuristic

Use of the L-R-D heuristic benefits teachers, students, and the school program in ways that are not immediately apparent. The benefits are nested, one inside another, like sets of Chinese boxes. An overview of these nested values, shown in Figure 1.1, illustrates how the L-R-D can provide a sound foundation for effective teaching, learning, and schoolwide programming.

One important nested value of the L-R-D begins to emerge in the lesson-planning stage. When teachers select textual material for use in an L-R-D lesson, they find themselves looking at the textbook more carefully and from more points of view than they might otherwise. They begin, quite naturally, to sense where students' comprehension is likely to falter and to better align the phrasing, facts, and organization of the lecture material they are preparing with the textbook material that students will read. With better alignment and organization, teachers automatically begin to heed a basic dictum of effective reading instruction: "Preteach" key terms, pivotal questions, and new concepts prior to reading. Better organization and alignment also are likely to raise teachers' levels of tolerance for reasonable digressions in the form of student and teacher comments about how the new information relates to real-life events and experiences. In so doing, teachers help students to better recall and develop relevant background information and appropriate anticipation, both of which have been shown to be of great value in effective comprehension (Crafton, 1983; Harste, 1978; Stevens, 1982).

Careful preparation of this type raises students' ability to read a particular piece beyond their normal reading and thinking performance levels. This can be a positive "enabling experience" that can become a new benchmark to strive for in both teaching and learning from text.

Figure 1.1   Nested Values of the L-R-D

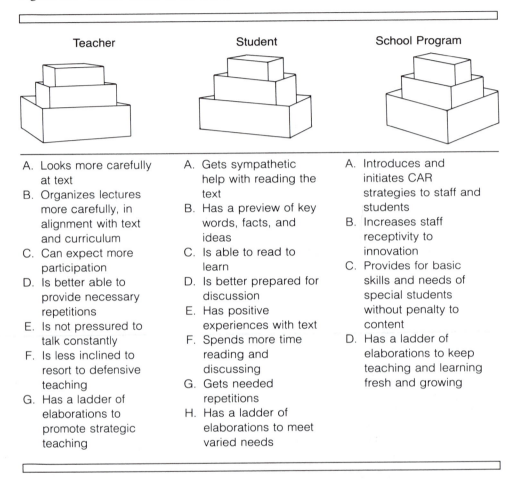

Teacher	Student	School Program
A. Looks more carefully at text	A. Gets sympathetic help with reading the text	A. Introduces and initiates CAR strategies to staff and students
B. Organizes lectures more carefully, in alignment with text and curriculum	B. Has a preview of key words, facts, and ideas	B. Increases staff receptivity to innovation
C. Can expect more participation	C. Is able to read to learn	C. Provides for basic skills and needs of special students without penalty to content
D. Is better able to provide necessary repetitions	D. Is better prepared for discussion	D. Has a ladder of elaborations to keep teaching and learning fresh and growing
E. Is not pressured to talk constantly	E. Has positive experiences with text	
F. Is less inclined to resort to defensive teaching	F. Spends more time reading and discussing	
G. Has a ladder of elaborations to promote strategic teaching	G. Gets needed repetitions	
	H. Has a ladder of elaborations to meet varied needs	

Following the lecture and empowered reading, the lesson design calls for discussion, providing a third repetition and elaboration of the material. This built-in redundancy factor is the most basic—and probably most often overlooked—principle of good teaching.

Finally, a teacher who follows the L-R-D guidelines will have begun to restructure class time and expectations from a typical 90% lecture format to one containing greatly increased proportions of purposeful reading and *informed* discussion. This achieves yet another important precept of all effective teaching-learning: increased "time on task." Some have argued that the simple lack of attention to reading in content classes accounts for a great part of the current literacy crisis in the schools. This conclusion seems justified by the fact that several observational studies of content area courses have revealed that virtually no purposeful reading goes on during class time (Feathers & Smith, 1987; Greenewald & Wolf, 1980; Mikulecky, 1982; Ratekin, Simpson, Alvermann, & Dishner, 1985).

Other incidental benefits to schoolwide programming are advanced through use of the L-R-D heuristic. The L-R-D provides a simple, hands-on way to introduce and initiate a staff to the principles and practices of content area reading. The reapportioning of class time offers teachers with defensive teaching styles—who overuse either lectures or seatwork—an opportunity to experiment with modulated alternatives. This tends to leave teachers with more energy and a greater willingness to try still more sophisticated teaching strategies and potentially benefit more fully from in-service workshops, consultations, and graduate coursework.

L-R-D Ladder of Elaborations

To help teachers ease into the actual use of more sophisticated, strategic teaching approaches, we have developed a ladder of elaborations on the basic L-R-D heuristic. You can use L-R-D elaborations to explore and develop your skills as a strategic teacher. These are described in the following list in order of increasing difficulty for teachers and/or students. Try ascending this ladder as your own readiness and students' needs suggest. It's a good idea to keep notes of your thoughts and questions as you try each elaboration. Your notes and thoughts will be useful in discussions with your instructor and coursemates and in your own processing of your teaching experiences.

1. Have students reread the information covered in the L-R-D format rapidly to increase their speed of reading and thought processing. Reading speed tends to rise as a result of increases in prior knowledge, although it can also be easily improved simply by systematic attention and practice.
2. Inform the class that you will lecture, intentionally omitting a few important details that they will need to read their texts to discover. This gives practice in recognizing what is not yet known and experience in careful reading and knowledge seeking.
3. Inform the class that your lecture will cover all the details of a lesson but that they will need to read to discover what questions these details answer. This is one way to teach students to actively seek an understanding of the concept base, or central question around which an area of study is focused.
4. Inform the class that a quiz will follow the L-R-D sequence. Allow a short study period. This is recommended to activate a high level of focused attention, give practice in test taking, and set the stage for questions and discussion about how to study effectively.
5. Invert the core process *occasionally* by having the class R-L-D, or *r*ead (for about 15 minutes), then *l*isten, and finally *d*iscuss. This variation tends to focus and improve listening attention and the ability to learn from an effective lecture. This effect can be further heightened when joined with the other listening training and note-taking techniques covered in Chapter 9.
6. Watch a videotape or educational film on a text topic before reading. Such visual representations are compatible with the habits of contemporary youngsters and can help build new bridges to print.

7. Ask students which portions of the text struck them as "inconsiderate," that is, too presumptive, poorly written, or poorly organized. This activity can help students learn when to ask for help with textual and class material. It also helps the teacher become more aware of student learning needs. Analysis of the writing in texts is also a good way to informally teach some of the basics of effective writing.

8. Provide the class with a definitive purpose for reading and discussing that will require critical and/or creative expression or application. State that purpose clearly on the chalkboard for easy reference, e.g., "As you read this section on the steam engine, try to determine why it was bound to be replaced by the gasoline engine." This will serve as a reminder to read analytically and with reference to real-life problem solving. A good deal more will be said about how to do this in each content area.

9. Hold postreading discussions on teaching and learning strategies. Make the discussion positive by asking students what they or you may have done that resulted in solid learning. Such discussion gives credit to student intuition and develops "metacognitive" processing, or thinking about thinking—an idea that is developed more fully in several places later in the text.

10. Create research teams, and provide time for students to delve into a topic in greater depth. One group could simply see what other textbooks say on the topic. Another could check with other authoritative references—persons and books. Another could write their best estimate of which real-life problems the information learned might help solve or answer. Still another group, where appropriate, could try to identify and discuss theme-related stories, poetry, music, or art. Activities such as these provide links between text topics and nonprint resources and among school learning, artistic expression, and the real world.

Figure 1.2 gives an example of elaboration 6. See Chapter 7 on postreading for another example of the L-R-D.

Again, each of the above "heuristics" offers a way to begin self-exploring ideas and bases for methodologies more fully developed throughout the text. Now here are some further thoughts on how you might maximize the benefits of planning and examining your experiences as a teacher.

Guided Self-Examination

Profound learning and insights often must be coaxed along by notes and reflections. Box 1.3 provides some ideas for reflecting on the L-R-D.

One teacher-in-training gave this personal account after using the L-R-D. He had selected and used elaboration 2, in which a lecture is presented omitting several significant details that students must then read to discover. Initially he felt he had learned little about teaching from the experience. When he made notes for our course discussion, however, he began to realize that he probably had left out too many details and that the content of his lecture was so thin that it was virtually

Figure 1.2 Illustration of L-R-D Elaboration 6: Viewing a Videotape or Film Prior to Reading, World Geography Class

Purposes for Viewing

Teacher: Today we are going to continue our study of Kenya by focusing on the Maisi tribe of Southern Kenya. First, we will watch a 20-minute National Geographic tape on this most unusual tribe of people. Listen carefully as you watch for two things, which you will then read about: the diet of the Maisi and the names of three other tribes of the north whom few people know of but who figure in Kenyan life in a big way.

Brief Review Following Viewing

Teacher: OK, what were the two points we listened for?

Student: The Maisi basically live off their cattle, eating meat and drinking their blood and raw milk.

Teacher: And?

Student: Well, there were three other tribes mentioned, but I can't remember any of them.

Teacher: OK, read pages 66–71 in your text now to learn more about the Maisi diet, and let's get the names of those tribes. If you happen to finish reading early, there are a few copies of a recent magazine report on cholesterol here on my desk that might help answer the question "Why aren't the Maisi dying of clogged arteries and heart failure from their high-fat diet?"

Postreading Discussion

Teacher: What did you understand best from what you watched and read about?

Student: The names of the three other tribes.

Teacher: Say and spell them, and I'll write them on the board.

Student: Samburu, Turkana, and Hamitic.

Teacher: What did you understand least from what you watched and read about? [When students have understood what they have viewed and read, they will take this question to mean pretty much the same thing as the next one: What questions or thoughts did this lesson raise in your mind?]

Student: I pretty much understood what was said, but I don't understand why the Maisi don't raise things the way the other tribes do.

Teacher: The land they live on is not arable. There is poor topsoil and little water. But that really doesn't explain why they don't move to where there is arable land.

Student: I was wondering about their high-fat diet, so I read fast to get to the article you talked about. It seems that there are at least two reasons why they don't have high blood cholesterol. The raw milk has enzymes that break down fat in the blood. Also, they lead very active lives. They burn off the fat as fast as they put it on.

Teacher: If raw milk is so good for you, why do we homogenize and pasteurize ours, I wonder? Why don't you ask Mrs. Shell in science today if she can help us out with this?

BOX 1.3

CONCEPT CLARIFICATION
Discovering Your Style

Look back over the ladder of elaborations. Pick the two or three elaborations *you* would use first with students in *your* content area. Try to visualize yourself doing these. If you like what you see in your mind's eye, according to research on the psychology of change, you probably will do it—and do it well. Compare your choices with those of your classmates. Are there similarities and/or differences?

meaningless to students who had little prior knowledge on the subject. More important, he discovered that the text itself offered little in the way of relevant details and that a naive reader could hardly reconstruct the central concepts from the textual information. From this he concluded that contrary to popular belief, textbooks probably contain too *little* information rather than too much. He resolved to provide students with more complete details and facts before and after having them read from their textbooks.

The wisdom in this "cadet" teacher's insight is verified by recent studies that point to two related findings. One recurring finding is that "prior knowledge" is the best predictor of how well one will understand, or be able to reconstruct meaning from, text. The second is that "elaborated" text can be easier to follow than some "controlled" forms edited to contain fewer facts and an oversimplified vocabulary (Jonassen, 1985a, 1985b).

CHAPTER TIE-UPS

♦♦♦   *Graphic Organizer*

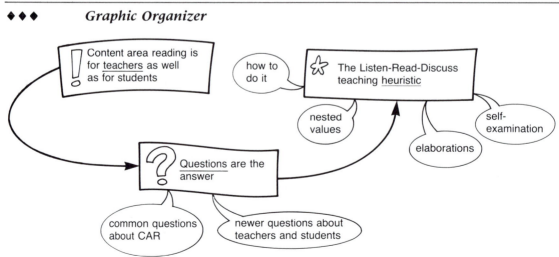

Critique and Anticipation   ◆◆◆

This chapter dealt first with the concept of pivotal questions and their value in guiding reading and learning. Then it presented nine frequently asked questions in the field of content area reading. You were invited to try to anticipate how these questions might be answered.

Next, the chapter struck a strong note for the importance of developing a plan for professional and student growth. It suggested that at least two important features of the content area reading movement are making this more attainable: an emphasis on *strategic teaching*—direct and guided teaching—and the special benefits of *heuristics*—self-discovery procedures.

Finally, the chapter proposed the Listen-Read-Discuss (L-R-D) heuristic as a means of preparing yourself for understanding and being able to use many of the other teaching strategies that have evolved from the CAR movement. It further suggested and illustrated the value of self-examination of teaching and learning experiences.

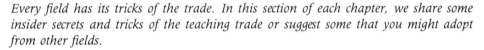

TRADE SECRET

Teacher Lesson Prompters

Every field has its tricks of the trade. In this section of each chapter, we share some insider secrets and tricks of the teaching trade or suggest some that you might adopt from other fields.

Television personalities use teleprompters, or "idiot cards," to help keep them on track during TV shows. Master musicians and conductors follow musical scripts. Commercial pilots rely on looseleaf binders containing step-by-step instructions to help them get huge planes off the ground and navigators to guide them once they are aloft. Nonetheless, as teachers we tend to make many difficult "in-flight" decisions with no map or on-board navigator to guide us.

You will find it valuable to construct, and even laminate, a set of cards outlining the procedural steps of acknowledged and published lesson designs (as well, eventually, as those of your own creation). Prop these up on your desk to guide you as you teach. The security they provide will make it easier for you to digress from a lesson plan and attend to student needs and/or seize a propitious moment to pursue a point that may be incidental to the lesson but nevertheless important and timely. You can collect these "lesson prompters" in a looseleaf binder or a computer and share them with other teachers.

Now make a lesson prompter on the L-R-D heuristic. It is a good idea to use a large-print typewriter or a photocopy machine with enlargement capability if one is available.

The next chapter offers a "primer" on many of the most basic concepts and practices in the field of reading, from kindergarten through adulthood. Armed with this foundation of "prior knowledge," you will be able to more fully appreciate the remainder of this text.

Continuation of Box 1.1

Facilitating Forces:	*Restraining Forces:*
Guiding ideology	Teaching like we were taught
Heuristic methods	Inadequate teacher training
Strategic teaching	Defensive teaching
Teacher support from administration	Distress, frustration
Concurrent methods	Time demands

Continuation of Box 1.2

A sharp decline was noticed in the birth rate of those poor families who had been moved into new high-rise dwellings. No one could figure out why until government officials interviewed the occupants. It made sense, they said, to have fewer children. Each apartment, you see, had its own bath and toilet—but only one. With the great outdoors eliminated as an option, the father and other family members hastened to this realization as the line formed each morning. Noting this, the wise officials designed a conscious, concurrent program of housing and education. They diverted much of their educational fund to their building fund and greatly accelerated housing construction.

Think about other social, economic, and educational changes this self-educating process must have set into motion.

Primer on Reading

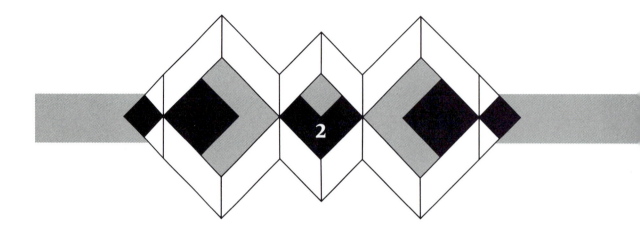

Foundations, Elementary, Content

Too much new information can drive knowledge out of circulation. Knowledge is orderly and cumulative, an enduring treasure.
— *Dan Boorstin, Librarian of Congress, 1987*

FOCUS

Even a cursory study of the foundations of reading instruction can provide an informed basis for knowing where we have been, where we are, and where we might go. Time spent acquiring a solid background in any field helps reduce random errors and adds to future time savings.

OUTLINE

FOUNDATIONS OF READING

The Reading Process: Definition and Models ◆ Practical Partitions: Literacy's Four Estates ◆ Developmental Progress: Stages of Literacy

ELEMENTARY, OR READING-BASED, INSTRUCTION

The Plan: Scope and Sequence ◆ The Premises ◆ The Practices

CONTENT AREA READING INSTRUCTION

The Plan ◆ The Premises ◆ The Practices: Four Universal Strategies in Content Area Reading

CHAPTER TIE-UPS

Graphic Organizer ◆ Critique and Anticipation ◆ Trade Secret: Notes and Memoranda

FOUNDATIONS OF READING

This chapter introduces the field of reading. It presents the stepping stones from the foundations of the field across the plans, principles, and practices of elementary reading to those of content area reading. The chapter draws heavily from both classical and contemporary works, with some emphasis on theory and a great deal on curriculum and methodology.

The Reading Process: Definition and Models

Definition

Reading, simply put, is the unlocking and construction of meaning from a coded message through the use of four acquired skills: symbol decoding, vocabulary, comprehension, and reflection. Each of these functions may be known by other names, and each has several components. But more important than these components themselves, which one may know intuitively from being a reader, is an understanding of the many ways in which they interrelate and function in the "process" of reading. What do we *do* when we read? Why does one student accurately decode a page and comprehend 95% of the information while another student accurately decodes the same page but comprehends only 60%? To help the second student achieve better comprehension, it is logical to consider what the first student does in more detail. However, what this student does—and what you do—when reading is very complex. Although the reading process generates thought, much of it is performed subconsciously. The more we find out about this process, it seems, the more we need to know. Theories of the reading process typically are presented in the form of "models" that describe or illustrate, in flowchart form, the sequence in which various subskills are activated and the ways in which they interrelate.

Models

Harris and Sipay (1985) suggest that most reading models can be categorized as primarily bottom-up, top-down, or interactive. *Bottom-up* models build from details and specifics toward a global concept. *Top-down* models start with a global concept and use reading to clarify details and specifics. *Interactive* models explain the reading process as partly top-down and partly bottom-up. Each of these three categories of models has distinct implications for how reading should be taught.

Bottom-Up Models. Bottom-up models define reading as a text-driven process that begins with perception and recognition first of letters, then of phonetic elements, then of words, then of word groups, and ultimately of sentence meaning and passage meaning. The reader's role is to process these units accurately and rapidly, building meaning from the smaller to the larger units—that is, from the bottom up. It is assumed that if children master each successive reading subskill, they eventually will attain overall reading competency (Gough & Cosky, 1977). This assumption has been challenged, however, mostly by psycholinguists and cognitive psychologists, who tend to advocate top-down models (Goodman, 1984; Smith, 1979).

Top-Down Models. Top-down models describe reading as a meaning-driven process. The reader starts with prior knowledge, which he or she actively applies and compares to the material being read. Top-down models imply that reading instruction should deemphasize subskills and focus on prereading activities that develop students' background of information and on spending more time reading. One theorist believes that comprehension instruction is valueless and only time spent reading accounts for reading gains (Carver, 1985).

Interactive Models. Interactive models propose that readers employ both top-down and bottom-up processing, using information gleaned from one process to inform and advance the other (Rumelhart, 1977). For example, when reading material on a familiar topic, the reader is able to use top-down processing: reading quickly to check the information against prior understandings. When the material moves into unfamiliar territory, the reader may need to switch to bottom-up meaning-constructing strategies. Other factors that may cause difficulty for the reader and require him or her to switch from top-down to bottom-up strategies can be viewed as *external*—outside the reader's head—and *internal*—inside the reader's head (Schell, 1988). Figure 2.1 lists the primary factors that influence reading in each of these categories.

The interactive model views reading as an active, *strategic* process of questioning, predicting, confirming, and self-correcting. Good readers have a variety of such strategies at their disposal and are able to apply them as needed to accommodate any internal and external factors that may be contributing to the difficulty of a given reading selection. The implications of this model for effective teaching of reading are only recently being recognized. Schell (1988) gives the clearest summarization of these implications that we have encountered:

> An interactive view of reading comprehension minimizes or ignores some aspects we have long focused on, such as levels of comprehension (literal, inferential, and critical) and comprehension skills (main idea, sequencing, drawing conclusions, etc.). Instead, it emphasizes aspects such as the reader's oral language, prior knowledge of the topic, and ability to reason. It focuses more on causes than on symptoms and deemphasizes the

Figure 2.1 Factors Influencing Interactive Reading Strategies

External	Internal
Size of print	Linguistic competence
Text format	Word meaning
Clarity of writing	Prior knowledge about topic
Distractions	Goal/purpose for reading
Interest of material	Interest in the topic
Text topic	Reasoning ability
	Ability to attend
	Strategies for "fixing up" (correcting misunderstandings)

role of reading tests in comprehension diagnosis and increases the importance of the teacher as gatherer of information.

In general, interactive models appear to hold the most promise as a basis for developing effective instructional strategies. Bottom-up models tend to be too narrow: They describe only what novice readers do when first learning to read or what skilled readers do when facing difficult material. Top-down models also have a shortcoming: They tend to describe what skilled readers do when reading familiar material, in which case they already have a good schema, or sense of what they are reading about, but fail to explain how this familiarity can be developed through reading. Interactive models tend to describe what readers must do to "construct," as opposed to simply deriving, knowledge from the printed page.

For further information on models of reading, see Geyer (1972), Harker (1972–73), Lovett (1981), Mitchell (1982), Samuels (1977), Singer (1976), Singer and Ruddell (1976), and Williams (1973).

Practical Partitions: Literacy's Four Estates

The term *literacy* recently has acquired various technical nuances in the field of reading. Four sociopolitical domains, or estates, in which it is specifically defined include *emergent, developmental, functional,* and *higher-order* literacy. An overview of these key concepts should prove valuable in comprehending and classifying information and connecting past reports and research with current social, political, and educational efforts.

Emergent Literacy: Early Reading

The term **emergent literacy** recently has been popularized by the federally funded Reading Research and Education Center at the University of Illinois. Studies and efforts reported under this label are a continuation of research formerly aimed at "reading readiness," "early reading," and "reading in kindergarten." This research has attempted to get a better grasp on how children gain the knowledge and skills that contribute to learning to read in school. This understanding, in turn, has made it possible to design more appropriate "prereading" experiences and educational opportunities. Several familiar contemporary movements have been influenced by this line of research. Among the most visible are:

1. Preschools with a "reading readiness" emphasis
2. The popularity of children's literature so that children can be read to and have interesting things to read themselves
3. Widespread efforts to gather home support for literacy
4. Extensive prekindergarten screening to identify and assist youngsters with high risk of reading failure
5. Kindergartens with actual reading instruction
6. Early reading programs that emphasize both phonics instruction and language enrichment

7. Recent efforts to note and monitor children's "emergent knowledge" of how to read (Mason, 1980; Mason, Stuart, & Dunning, 1986).

Also worth noting here, for its historical impact, is an "early" reading issue that dominated the field for many years. In 1955, Rudolph Flesch's book *Why Johnny Can't Read* brought widespread public attention to the trend away from teaching phonics in most elementary schools. This trend was real, but it was also part of a larger movement away from a "lockstep" approach to education that demanded that every student move through the curriculum at an established pace. Elementary teachers were being urged toward alternative approaches. These approaches included some contemporary mainstays such as providing for each child as an individual; considering students' "readiness" for each aspect of learning; and a shift in emphasis from memorization to concept development. Such innovations were unfamiliar and probably somewhat awkward to implement at first. As a result, Flesch and other critics found a favorable audience in the public.

What was the *best* way to teach children to read? Even professional educators had little firm evidence, even though hundreds of research studies had been done and many more were subsequently undertaken. Chall's book *Learning to Read: The Great Debate* (1967) and its revision (1983) summarized the controversy and the research. At about the same time, the U.S. Office of Education funded 27 "first-grade studies" on the issue (see Dykstra, 1968). In the final analysis, the answer was clear: Aside from some commonsense guidelines, there was no one "best" way to teach beginning reading.

In fact, classroom observations disclosed that few teachers employed any single teaching approach. Instead, they tended to improvise on and combine approaches. Among the many approaches to teaching beginning reading, the only distinction discernible among actual classroom practices was that some teachers used a "code-emphasis" approach while others used a "meaning-emphasis" approach. Thus, the question of whether to use a decoding-only or meaning-only approach remained largely theoretical; most teachers already employed both, varying only in their emphasis on one or the other. Common sense and later research further supported this eclectic approach. It is notable, however, that Chall's 1967 research synthesis did indicate that among groups of children taught with a code-emphasis approach, there were fewer cases of severe reading problems than among groups taught with a meaning-emphasis approach.

In general, experience more than research has shown that emergent-literacy programs that stress either a highly structured phonics curriculum or a context-only approach produce students who are ill prepared to make the transition to content area study reading. Children taught—or, more precisely, raised—in an eclectic reading-language-thinking environment are likely not merely to learn how to read but to lay the foundation for becoming lifelong readers. This is the important contribution of the emergent-literacy estate to developmental literacy.

One other commonsense guideline that survived this period of scrutiny and continues in practice today is a selective use of "look-say," or whole-word, training. This approach is used with phonetically irregular words, such as "night" for "nite" and "talk" for "tauk." About 250 of these words need to be taught in the early grades, because they have the highest frequency of occurrence in the English language. A method of teaching in which the content teacher occasionally reads orally to the class is described later as one way to help upper-grade students deal with phonetically irregular and foreign words (e.g., *chauvinism, coup d'état, leitmotif*).

Developmental Literacy: Study-Type Reading

The term **developmental literacy** refers to research and efforts aimed at keeping reading on track and growing after initial decoding and basic comprehension skills have been acquired. The key feature of this estate is the transition from "learning to read" to "reading to learn." Instruction geared toward assisting students in this transition tends to focus on dictionary, library reference, verification, and textbook usage skills. In today's school systems, developmental literacy tends to be the responsibility of intermediate and junior high school content teachers. "Developmental reading" courses, taught by reading specialists, often provide a further means of corrective reading instruction for those in need. Reading instruction for above-average students sometimes falls into this category as well.

David Russell, a pioneer in the field of reading, offers these six principles regarding the concept of and need for a developmental literacy program:

1. Reading abilities develop gradually over the years.
2. Reading achievement is closely related to school success in both upper elementary and secondary schools.
3. Reading abilities are significant in the personal and social adjustment of individuals and their contributions to the group at all ages.
4. Reading abilities vary as much as two or three grades in primary classes and five or six grades in higher classes. Accordingly, many pupils need guidance in their reading activities at all school levels.
5. Reading is a complex process that requires substantially different abilities in different situations. For example, a good reader of historical or literary materials may be a poor reader of scientific materials in the intermediate or upper grades. Accordingly, reading may be profitably stressed in the various subject matter fields.
6. Most children do not acquire new reading abilities automatically. Because both good and poor students meet new materials and read for new purposes, some teacher help on a preventive rather than remedial level is desirable. (Russell, 1949, pp. 166–167)

Until recently, the issue of functional literacy logically preceded developmental literacy in consideration. Today, as you shall see, it incorporates it and even extends beyond it.

Functional Literacy: Everyday Reading

The term **functional literacy** simply means the ability to read and write well enough to "function" in society: read the newspaper, tend to daily work requirements, keep records, and write an occasional letter. Fifty years ago, this required a fourth-to-sixth-grade level of proficiency; thirty years ago, it meant an eighth-to-tenth-grade level. More recently, estimating the level required for full functional literacy has been like trying to hit a moving target. Most people today, no matter how well schooled, have some areas of their daily lives in which they do not function well in reading or function only marginally. Few individuals can "read" and comfortably comprehend their various insurance policies, tax forms, or even the financial section of the daily newspaper. One generation ago, we would have labeled such people "functionally illiterate." Today we accept this shortcoming as a necessary by-product of the complexity of modern life: language peppered with hi-tech words and phrasings convoluted to avoid legal challenges in a heavily litigious society (Kirsch & Guthrie, 1977–78).

Regardless of its causes, functional illiteracy has serious consequences. For one thing, it causes many individuals to feel out of touch, at sea in their own society. For another, it actually deflates the value of education, particularly for the 50% of the population with IQs below 100. One pursues personal education to open doors; the inflated demands of society slam doors. There is little point in raising aspirations with expensive and enlightened school programs if upon completion a young person can hardly expect to tend to his or her affairs with competence and dignity. It is this feeling of being thwarted before one even gets started, more than a lack of quality instruction, that is creating the American "illiteracy problem." In reality, probably few people are illiterate in the classical sense of the term. Most simply have stopped reading—and therefore suffer reversals in previously attained levels of reading proficiency—because of simple atrophy and loss of hope. In general, it simply is not true that today's schools are not doing their job and that we are graduating large numbers of illiterates. It is more realistic to say that the requirements of a "basic" education have risen astronomically. The task of meeting the new demands of these "astrobasics" can heighten anyone's level of anxiety and confusion. Some initially experience shock, followed by silent rage. The (then) young American writer Stephen Crane, after barely escaping from a capsized boat, expressed similar shock and rage when he wrote of his experience, "If I'm going to be drowned, why, in the name of the seven mad gods who rule the sea, was I allowed to come thus far and contemplate sand and trees?" (*The Open Boat,* 1919). This is likely analogous to going to school for 13 years (K–12) only to be confronted with one document after another noting issues and other life demands that one can barely grasp, let alone select from and decide upon.

Several national and school-based efforts to quell some of the confusion and silent rage engendered by contemporary functional illiteracy already are under way. There are national (mostly volunteer) programs to find the victims of this isolation—as well as those few who never learned to read—and, through tutoring and human contact, bring them back into the mainstream. In addition, federally funded programs have been initiated to simplify the language of materials produced by commercial and government institutions and agencies ("Simply Stated," Document Design Center, 1055 Jefferson Street N.W., Washington D.C. 20007). The intent of the latter effort is to discover ways to write text more plainly so that readers will not be overwhelmed with unnecessarily complex words, sentence structures, and faulty assumptions of prior knowledge. We will examine this emerging "text technology" in Chapter 6 when we discuss guiding silent reading and acquiring self-guided reading strategies.

The related efforts of the schools to combat functional illiteracy have tended to center on three fronts: the developmental thrust noted earlier, in which reading and study skills support is being offered from the intermediate grades through college and even professional school levels; a corrective effort, in which instruction in specific skill deficiencies is being provided by content teachers and/or reading resource teachers; and a remedial effort, in which reading specialists and community volunteers are helping to provide a "safety net" by monitoring student progress and working individually and in special classes with those who are not achieving. Ironically, the increased attention to students who are failing has tended to come from legal actions against the schools for graduating persons who cannot read.

At present, students identified for special corrective and remedial assistance come from one or both of two groups: those whose low reading skill is within the range of expectancy for their measured IQs and those whose reading skill deficiency is inconsistent with IQ-based expectancy. We believe a third category should be identified: those who are good to excellent at literal and even inferential reading but cannot read effectively at critical, evaluative, or applied levels—"higher illiterates," as Chase (1961) calls them. The following section discusses the many efforts currently under way in this long recognized but little addressed estate.

Higher-Order Literacy: Productive Reading

Higher-order literacy is the stage of reading maturity reached through the fine-tuning of critical, evaluative, and (often forgotten) *constructive* thinking skills. The distinction between simple literacy and higher-order literacy is the difference between being *schooled,* or trained for a specific purpose, and being *educated.* It implies that one can not only "read the lines" (what is written) and "read between the lines" (what is inferred) but "read beyond the lines," that is, at critical, evaluative, and applied levels. This issue is rapidly becoming a national priority, as evidenced by the increasing federal funding of research into higher-order literacy.

Developmental Progress: Stages of Literacy

It is always helpful for a teacher to have a gestalt, or larger picture, of the normal staging of a developmental process. Such information can serve as a general guide to effective "kid watching"—informal observation and evaluation of students' individual growth and development. This section provides a larger picture of the developmental process in the form of an integrated sketch of language, thinking, social-emotional, and literacy development at successive school grade and age levels. Of course, not everyone who passes through this chronology benefits or grows to the same extent. Some carry immature patterns into adult life. For example, every child has a "view of the world" that he or she uses to read and think with "a minimum of personal bewilderment" (Smith, 1978). This primitive structure, however, only vaguely resembles the highest stage of reading, which Jeanne Chall (1983) calls "world view," or the complex value system and experiential bases on which mature readers rely to interpret, judge, and apply what they read.

Stages of Reading, Language, Thinking, and Social-Emotional Development

Preschool to Primary Grades (Ages 4–8).   Most children are learning how to decode (decipher) letters into sounds and sounds into words. They are mastering very basic concepts (e.g., small-medium-large) and acquiring vocabulary at a rate that will be unparalleled in subsequent grades. Thinking, however, is largely egocentric and focused around self and home. Toward the end of this period, a great deal of personal effort goes into trying to be "good" and obeying stated rules.

Middle Grades, 4–6 (Ages 9–12).   Most students have mastered the fundamentals of word attack skills, recognition of high-frequency vocabulary, and most basic language patterns. Their reading interests tend to move from one area to another as their funds of knowledge continue to grow. Thinking begins to change dramatically. At first very concrete, it moves quickly to more refined forms of categorization, generalization, and abstraction. Most youngsters begin to transfer learning from one context to another. This springs from a primitive form of abstract thinking that Piaget calls "conservation," that is, realization that things may change in form though not in substance—physically, a piece of clay is the same weight whether in the shape of a ball or a platter; verbally, something may be said in several different ways, including figuratively, and have essentially the same meaning. The child continues to abide by adult rules, although the peer group plays an increasingly influential role in values, self-image, and behavior.

Grades 7–10 (Ages 13–16).   Reading patterns and behaviors are equal to the requirements of most schoollike textual materials, although guidance and assistance often may be required. Peer influence and rapid hormonal and other physical changes tend to disrupt and distract from school and home. Ironically, thinking sharpens as the teen mind struggles to understand the role of the self in the social group. Critical-evaluative thinking, however, remains relatively primitive, because it is uninformed by knowledge gained from experience and is subject to distortion by a growing desire to become more of a "rule maker" than "rule abider."

Grades 10–College (Ages 17–25).   Comprehension, vocabulary, and study habits grow and are honed in direct relationship to career interests and social and educational opportunities. Without specific training, thinking and general knowledge are analogous to those of the 9–11 period, though at a higher level. Thinking appears to be effective and well informed, but it still is somewhat two-dimensional. The rapid changes and tough choices of adolescence have given way to slower changes and more binding, and therefore stabilizing, choices. This process can easily continue for 10 or more years in contemporary societies where entrance into responsible adult life is delayed by the demands of higher levels of education and greater financial "start-up" costs. Forced delays in ability to accept the responsibilities of adult life can impede development of realistic views of society and world forces. Ironically, this creates a need for even more education. Continuing education for adults is justified in these times on the grounds that society itself is volatile. Even the best trained and educated can, and likely will, be displaced during a normal lifetime.

Postschooling (Ages 26 and Older).   Reading grows insightful and is routinely applied to a wide range of human affairs. Life experiences round out formal education. Some previous notions are validated and others dispelled, but mostly there is a growing sense that life is composed of paradoxes and that quality of life means reading, writing, and doing things that are meaningful, creditable, and, ideally, durable. To paraphrase Benjamin Franklin, "If you would not be forgotten as soon as you are dead and rotten, either write things worth reading or do things worth writing."

Next, we will consider how elementary schools plan, organize, and conduct instruction. From this basis, it will be easier to judge what can be transferred, or continued, to the upper grade levels, what can be adjusted, and where new levels of problem-solving or educational engineering are called for. The activity in Box 2.1 offers an aid to clarifying your current schema for elementary reading instruction.

ELEMENTARY, OR READING-BASED, INSTRUCTION

The following discussion of elementary reading would be presented quite differently in a textbook intended for use in training elementary reading teachers. For purposes of this text, an overview of elementary reading is intended to serve as a point of reference for elementary teachers and provide secondary teachers with a general sense of where their students have been.

We use broad brush strokes to cover what the elementary teacher-in-training would need to know in much greater detail. Those of you who are familiar with the material summarized in this section will realize that there are exceptions and qualifications to almost every possible rule or generalization. We attempt to provide *general* concepts and discuss most typical practices, realizing that for the elementary teacher the exception could be more important than the rule in dealing with

---

BOX 2.1

CONCEPT CLARIFICATION
Initial Reading—A Personal Retrospective

To get a firmer sense of how many ways there are to be taught how to read and how differently young minds can perceive them, take a moment to jot down what *you* remember most about being taught to read. Compare your thoughts with those of others. Use these questions to guide your reflections:

♦ What do you remember with positive feelings?
♦ What do you remember with negative associations?
♦ What remains vague or neutral?
♦ What do you remember about phonics instruction?
♦ What do you remember about story writing and reading?
♦ What else stands out in your mind, such as being read to, exercise books, grouping, and so on?

Calling up some of your prior experience and knowledge, or schema, in this way should help you read and discuss this section more thoughtfully and critically.

individual students in individual school districts. These exceptions are within the domain of other courses.

Currently elementary education offers many innovations and alternative programs that also are outside the realm of this primer overview of a complex field. It is likely, however, that this overview will provide you with a useful schema for recognizing and understanding these programs as you encounter them in the future.

The Plan: Scope and Sequence

The general plan, or curriculum, of the elementary reading program is referred to as the program's **scope and sequence.** A scope and sequence provides detailed instructional objectives (the *scope*) and indicates at what point in the program (the *sequence*) each will be introduced, practiced, mastered, and reinforced. As you review these core instructional elements, note the gradual shift from factors associated with learning to read toward those that contribute to reading to learn.

Core Scope and Sequence of Elementary Reading

Preprimer
- A. Language development and basic concept of reading taught
- B. 200–300 frequently used sight words (including many phonetically irregular words) taught with a "look-say" approach
- C. Training in auditory and visual discrimination
- D. Writing taught through teacher recording of students' stories

Grades 1–2
- E. Children's literature introduced through teacher's oral reading
- F. Additional sight words taught and practiced
- G. Phonic generalizations for word discrimination

Grades 3–4
- H. Specific comprehension training introduced
- I. Word study emphasizes learning meanings of new words
- J. Oral reading fluency practiced

Grades 5–6
- K. Emphasis on independent reading, writing, study, and reference skills
- L. Word analysis instruction continues to decrease, while emphasis on content and vocabulary instruction increases

This basic plan has remained remarkably constant for about 40 years, although emphasis areas and approaches have varied. In some "mastery learning" programs, hundreds of specific skills are listed and tested. Other programs tend to take a more whole-language approach, and objectives tend to be less specific. Almost all basal reader programs, however, cover at least the elements described in the above core scope and sequence. The next section describes three basic concepts of basal reading instruction.

The Premises

Most fields of endeavor are organized around a few informally agreed-upon premises or conditions. In the case of elementary reading instruction, there are essentially three such premises: (1) Reading is *focal;* (2) learning occurs best with materials at the student's *instructional level;* and (3) *graded readers* are available to accommodate students at different reading levels.

Reading Is Focal

The first premise is that the essential purpose of the primary grades is to teach youngsters to read. Nothing is put above it, and everything is organized around it. In this environment, students, teachers, parents, and curriculum are all aligned to the same expectation. Nowhere else in the school program does such uniformity of purpose exist.

Instructional Level

The second premise is that learning is most effective when the student is provided with reading materials that are at his or her **instructional level.** Material is said to be at a particular student's instructional level when that student can decode 95% of the words *and* comprehend about 75% of the text without assistance. Within this range, teacher guidance is most likely to enrich learning and keep the student positively disposed toward the task (see Figure 2.2).

The term **frustration level** applies when the material is too difficult for a student even with teacher guidance. The student reaches this level when he or she can no longer decode with at least 90% to 95% accuracy and comprehension falls below 50%. At this level, it is assumed that instruction cannot be successfully provided because the student is too overwhelmed by the task.

Conversely, in the case of materials that a student reads with 99% to 100% decoding (word-deciphering) accuracy and 90% to 100% comprehension, the student is said to be operating at an **independent level.** At this level, the student no longer is distracted by words and literal comprehension and therefore can read and learn from the material without teacher guidance. (Techniques and instruments for determining each reader's three levels are discussed in the next chapter.)

As we consider these three levels, we can easily see why many students have difficulty reading and learning from content textbooks. Even when the book's difficulty level matches the student's reading skill level, the student is often expected to learn independently from material that is at his or her instructional level. For this reason alone, it is necessary that every content teacher, from the middle grades onward, expect to provide some instructional assistance in reading even where a

Figure 2.2   Reader Levels

Level	Decoding Accuracy	Comprehension
Independent level	99% or higher	90% or higher
Instructional level	At least 95%	At least 75%
Frustration level	Below 90%	Below 50%

"grade-level" text is available. In order for most students in a typical classroom to learn independently from a text, the text would have to have a difficulty level of two to three years below that of the grade for which it is intended. There are no such textbooks on the market, and it is doubtful that there ever could be. Each content area has its own inherent set of specialized terms and ideas that inflate the difficulty level of the material beyond easy control.

Graded Readers

The basic vehicle for implementing the reading curriculum at the elementary level is the *basal reading program.* This is a series of graded books, workbooks, practice exercise sheets, and teacher resources designed to systematically increase difficulty at a carefully controlled and sequenced pace. Multilevel reading books and supplements allow the teacher to work with students in small groups. The typical elementary classroom has from three to five "reading groups," each working on material at an appropriate level of difficulty and progressing at a suitable pace. Basal reading books begin with narrative, story-type material using words that are part of most children's oral language. Material of a more expository, fact-based nature is introduced gradually, along with words of increasing difficulty.

All in all, the basal reading program, despite much of the criticism leveled at it, is a rather ingenious and highly honed device for structuring and teaching reading. The teacher receives clear guidelines on how to proceed and has several options suitable for varied student backgrounds and needs.

We will now look at the three most basic lesson designs used at the early grade levels in a conventional basal reading program.

The Practices

A basal reading program essentially consists of three activity strands: one to promote word decoding, one to guide comprehension, and one to build related language skills. These may be combined and overlapped for maximum reinforcement. Secondary education majors rarely get an opportunity to see just how these skills are taught initially; thus, it all appears rather vague. To overcome much of this ambiguity, we discuss the three basic lesson designs in detail in the following sections. As you study these, you should come to appreciate the concept that "today began yesterday" and that time-tested ideas are always worth our attention and consideration.

Word Decoding

The classic method of teaching word decoding was defined by William S. Gray, known by many as the "founder of modern reading instruction." Many variations on this method exist—so many, in fact, that few reading specialists would recognize the method in the basic form we present. We should note here that while this approach to teaching decoding is the one most widely adopted and adapted for elementary reading instruction, you may find that a different method, developed

William S. Gray, founder of modern reading instruction

Source: Cover illustration, *Journal of Reading,* October, 1987. Reprinted with permission of Dave Bailey and the International Reading Association.

by Gerald Glass (1973), is more appropriate for teaching decoding to older, remedial students. Glass's approach is detailed in Chapter 10.

Gray's basic **paradigm,** or lesson design, calls for teaching each phonic element—a letter or a cluster of letters—in a four-step fashion. The first step is intended to focus students' attention visually and aurally (through hearing) on the element to be taught. The second step is to "fix" students' attention visually and aurally on discrimination of the new element with similar-looking and sounding elements. The third step teaches students to blend the newly learned phonic element with other, known elements. The final step is to recognize and use the new element in context (Gray, 1948). Figure 2.3 illustrates how these steps would unfold in teaching the phonic element *squ*, one that often must be retaught to intermediate-grade and secondary school disabled readers.

Story Comprehension

The most basic lesson design for teaching story comprehension is the *Directed Reading Activity (DRA)*. The DRA is often attributed to Emmett Betts. Actually, Betts merely pulled it together from the teachers' manuals accompanying the basal readers in use in the 1930s and 1940s. Here is how he stated this basic idea in his popular text, *Foundations of Reading Instruction:*

> In general, the lesson plans in most teachers' manuals are organized as follows:
>
> I. Developing readiness
>   A. Insuring an adequate background of experience
>   B. Developing working concepts
>   C. Stimulating interest and identifying a general motive for the reading
> II. Guiding the first silent reading
> III. Developing word-recognition skills and comprehension
> IV. Rereading
> V. Following up the book reading (Betts, 1946, p. 491)

We will say considerably more about this very important foundational design in other chapters. While the DRA is still the basic instructional plan of most basal reading programs, many of these programs have begun to include more innovative strategies that reduce the strongly teacher-directed nature of instruction. An early and still popular innovation developed to produce student-centered lessons is the Language Experience Story, discussed next.

The Language Experience Story

The most common means of introducing young children to basal reading—and subsequently enriching the basal reading program with the children's own pro-ductions—is through language experience activities. The idea of *language experience activities* is less to teach reading skills than to create a literate environment in which these skills are acquired as a natural extension of language learning. The elementary form, the *Language Experience Story* (Allen, 1976), begins with the teacher writing down short stories or experiences dictated by the children. These are written as dictated and not corrected in any way. It is important that children see their *own* language in print before being introduced to textual materials, which often represent unfamiliar language forms. The Language Experience Story teaches children the fundamental concept "What I can say, I can write, and what I can write, I can read." The children's stories are then used in several ways: to teach and/or reinforce and extend word recognition and analysis skills; to build familiarity with various story plot lines (or "story grammars," as they are now called); and to help young-sters cope better with the transition from oral to written language forms. Often other educational objectives can be achieved incidentally. For example, children can learn to work cooperatively in recounting experiences and comparing per-

Figure 2.3 Gray's Paradigm for Teaching Phonic Elements

Sample sound: *squ* blend

Step 1: Visual and Aural "Fixing"

a. Recognizing visual similarities: Words are written on the board. The student circles the part(s) that all the words have in common:

squirrel   squeeze   squeak   square   squaw

b. Recognizing aural similarities: Using the same list as above, the teacher reads each word from the board, giving only slight emphasis to the *squ* sound. The students try to identify the sound that each word has in common. The auditory step may precede the visual step if the student tends to have an auditory orientation.

Step 2: Visual and Aural Discrimination

a. Visual discrimination: Presenting words in groups of three, the student first underlines *squ* in each word in which he or she finds it. Next, the student attempts to say only those words containing the *squ* sound:

queen	require	squirrel	shrimp
squat	squirt	squirm	spring
whom	whenever	sprint	squeaky

b. Auditory discrimination: The teacher says three (3) words. Without seeing the words, the student identifies the word(s) containing the *squ* sound:

squeal	squash	shield	squelch
spur	squid	square	squeak
dig	send	squash	squat

Step 3: Blending (Substitution)

The teacher shows the student how to blend and substitute sounds to form new words. Example: Substitute the *squ* sound for the existing sound at the beginning of each word.

ball − b = all + squ = squall   wire − w = ire + squ = squire
what − w = at + squ = squat   tint − t = int + squ = squint

Step 4: Contextual Application

The student underlines words containing the *squ* sound, which are embedded in sentences:

1. He led a *squad* of men into battle.
2. He leads a *squadron* in the army.
3. Try not to *squash* it, please.

spectives. At the intermediate levels, language experience activities can be used to help children reprocess science experiments, social studies simulations, and field trip experiences. At the upper grade levels, student-developed compositions can be used to develop and refine language skills. See the Language Shaping Paradigm in Chapter 12 for an example.

The importance of mastering basic reading skills in a timely manner cannot be overstated. By about the third grade, students are expected to be able to apply their reading skills to learn new information. Box 2.2 illustrates how frustrating it can be to try extracting information while still struggling to decipher print.

BOX 2.2

CONCEPT CLARIFICATION
What's It Really Like to Try to Read to Learn
While Having to Learn to Read?

What is it like to try to glean information from text without efficient decoding skills? Try it.

Study the alternate letters you'll need below. Notice that most of the new letters are very similar to the ones you already know. Then read the simple definition for the word *xenophobia*.

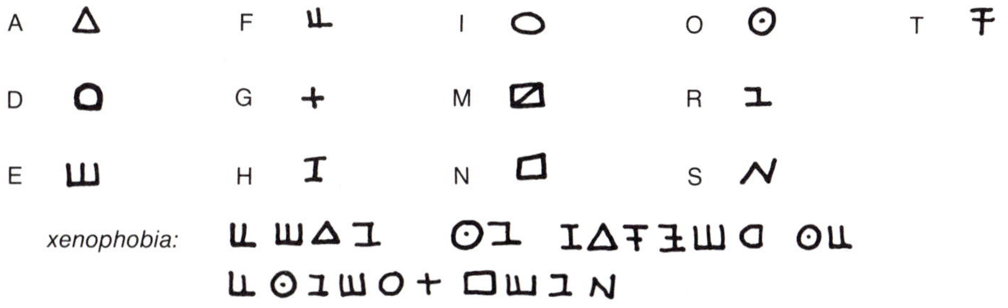

A	△	F	�	I	○	O	☉	T	∓
D	◖	G	+	M	⊠	R	⅃		
E	Ш	H	I	N	◻	S	∧		

xenophobia: Ш Ш △ ⅃   ☉ ⅃   I △ ∓ Ш ◖ ◻Ш   Ш ☉ ⅃ Ш + ◻ Ш ∧

CONTENT AREA READING INSTRUCTION

Now that you have a grasp of the magnitude of the concepts of literacy from its emergence to its maturity, let's try to tie these more explicitly to the content area reading movement.

In its earliest days, content area reading instruction essentially focused rather exclusively on improving comprehension. During this period, however, research and thought in related areas of higher-level processing began to merge with content area reading efforts. Today, while there still is no official content area reading curriculum, or scope and sequence chart, there is a set of ''characteristics'' that serves this purpose.

The Plan

The reading curriculum for the upper grades is composed of two overlapping sets of objectives: those related to the development of mature readers and those related to the information and skills of each subject area. The latter subject area concerns, which have been called the *content processing model* of a discipline (Peters, 1982; Steinley, 1983) are addressed in Chapters 12 through 14.

The curriculum that resulted from studies of the characteristics of mature readers is informal and therefore rarely found collected and stated together as it is here. Nonetheless, the elements of this "nested curriculum" are very much a part of the purpose of schooling and can be found in the curriculum guides for most subject areas.

The characteristics described in this section have been compiled from several sources: from the classical research on mature (adult) readers by William S. Gray and Bernice Rogers (1956); from Jeanne Chall, who has described six stages in the quest for higher-order literacy (1983); from efforts to define and measure "progress toward reading, language, thinking, and social-emotional maturity" (Manzo & Casale, 1979; Casale, 1982); and from the work of members of the Center for the Study of Reading between 1975 and 1987 (now newly organized as the Center for Reading and Educational Research).

For the sake of convenience, this informal curriculum is divided into two types of characteristics: (1) those that are *text-bound* (i.e., one must actually be reading to do them) and (2) those that are *non-text-bound* (i.e., are general functions of mature thinking and development that can occur before, during, or following reading). The former group tends to vary from subject area to subject area, while the latter group tends to be common across disciplines. Review these characteristics carefully, because they are repeatedly referenced and developed thoroughly throughout the remainder of the text. You might try listing as many characteristics of the mature reader as you can before you read the following lists. In this way, your mind will be actively engaging the words with "yeah's" ("I thought of that"), "uh-huh's" ("I knew that but forgot to mention it"), and "huh's" ("there's something I hadn't thought about"). You might even have an occasional "uh-uh" ("I disagree"). In any case, you will read, analyze, and recall better for having raised your arousal and attention levels above the sleepy thresholds we tend to reserve for textbook reading. In so doing, you also will be adding introspectively to the level of consciousness you need to attain to understand and better guide the reading demands your students face.

Text-Bound Characteristics
The mature reader (have you listed your characteristics first?)

1. Has achieved high accuracy in decoding, or word recognition and analysis
2. Has a rich vocabulary and a genuine interest in words
3. Is able to read with purpose and sustained attention
4. Reads to comprehend rather than merely to recall

5. Automatically adjusts reading rate and thinking to the various content and language demands of text
6. Uses reading strategies appropriate for the nature of the learning task
7. Has the inclination and ability to monitor independent reading and engage in self-correction
8. Is an interactive reader—relates what has been experienced to what is read and what is read to what has been experienced

Non-Text-Bound Characteristics

The mature reader (have you listed your characteristics first?)

1. Has the inclination and ability to think abstractly
2. Has a rich fund of general information, or prior knowledge
3. Is able to speak and write cogently and reflectively
4. Has the inclination and ability to deal with ambiguities and to reach critical judgments
5. Has the inclination and ability to think constructively or creatively
6. Is continuously involved in a process of personal self-examination
7. Is constantly growing in comprehension and understanding of larger structures and ideas, such as basic life forces, societal dynamics, and historical movements

These mature-reader characteristics can be thought of as the cross-disciplinary objectives of content area reading.

The next section describes some of the basic concepts of instructional and program design.

The Premises

Traditional Premises

Essentially there are five traditional premises of content area reading instruction. Each premise is briefly described in the following paragraphs and will be elaborated on throughout the text.

Reading Is Developmental.   Reading is an open-ended process that can (and should) grow and change throughout one's lifetime (Holmes, 1953; Russell, 1949). Therefore, reading instruction should continue well past the sixth grade.

Communality of Reading and Content Objectives.   A careful review of the characteristics of the mature reader, particularly those that are non-text-bound, reveals that they are virtually identical to the objectives of most school subject areas. Therefore, subject and reading objectives are compatible and can and should be pursued together.

Teachable-Moment Hypothesis.   Under the **teachable-moment** hypothesis, the content teacher is the person present when the obstacles to textual reading arise and the student is developmentally ready for more instruction. Therefore, it is logical for the subject teacher to provide both content and reading instruction at this most propitious, or teachable, moment.

Concurrent Methods, or "Go-for-it" Hypothesis.   Experience and research have shown that when objectives are compatible and student needs are most strongly felt, it is possible to concurrently, or simultaneously, teach toward more than one objective efficiently and effectively. In *The Artistry of Teaching,* Rubin (1984) refers to a similar idea, which he calls *collateral teaching,* as the critical factor that distinguishes superior from mediocre teachers. Therefore, it is sensible to continue to develop and use **concurrent methods** of teaching in place of content-only or reading-only methods or, as Rubin suggests, to go for as many *incidental benefits* as the teacher can inventively pursue.

Process and Product Hypothesis.   The *process and product* premise is the one that makes the others work. The simplest form of this complex idea holds that content should be taught in a "language-rich environment" (Readence, 1984). In such an environment, the deep processes of thinking, reading, writing, speaking, and comportment are acquired along with the products, or facts, rules, and ideas of a content-based curriculum. Therefore, this "deep processing" objective should mark all content instruction. In practical terms, *deep processing* means that students' learning of new words and ideas should be marked by four characteristics:

1. Students should be able to *compare* new words and ideas. This might be exhibited by recountings of related personal experiences or knowledge of synonyms and/ or ability to see analogies.
2. Students should be able to *contrast* new words and ideas with one another and with previous learnings. This might be evidenced by statements of antonyms and dissimilar ideas.
3. Student learning becomes *generative.* This might be expressed through self-induced thinking and by transfer, or application, of new words and ideas to appropriate situations.
4. Students should begin to show some social and developmental indications of how the new words and learnings are touching them in personal-behavioral terms. Thus, their **comportment**—the manner in which they conduct themselves—should begin to reflect the changes, or enhancements, of their minds. This might be exhibited in the form of reduced levels of impulsivity, greater capacity to accept constructive criticism, an increased willingness to try to see other points of view, and a growing capacity for self-examination.

Languaging in the Content Areas (LICA)

Languaging is the chief instrument for teaching deep processing. Languaging itself is a complex and therefore somewhat elusive concept. It is a mechanism for helping one to form a concept or reach a thoughtful position. Because attempts at conventional definition sometimes yield a result too abstract to be useful, we will rely instead on an alternative form of definition: consideration of the features of languaging, followed by examples of some of the forms it has assumed in actual teaching practices.

Languaging, according to Postman and Weitgartner (1969), is simply a way of promoting inner speech: a means of getting students to "talk through" and more precisely label and codify their experiences and thoughts. The idea is that when vague feelings, experiences, and new learnings are "languaged through" in this way, they are more deeply felt and can more easily be examined and applied (Manzo & Sherk, 1978). For example, it is a good idea for educators to construct their own "models" of reading to promote inner speech and through this vehicle come to grips with what they really know, think, and believe about the reading process and reading instruction. The additional acts of writing, speaking, and answering questions on this personal model of reading, or *externally* languaging it through for others to scrutinize, permit even deeper examination and reflection. By subsequently studying, comparing, and contrasting the model with other models, one can reasonably expect to gain even greater clarity and insight. These analytical acts are then expected to change one's comportment, or the way one acts and teaches. As you can see, languaging activities are an effort to drive one's actions by one's thoughts and values rather than merely by instincts and defensive reactions. Whether one applies this model to teacher growth or to student learning enhancement, the effect is the same: greater self-control and progress toward maturity.

In practical content reading terms, **LICA (Languaging in the Content Areas)** lessons add another level of symbolic processing to prereading, postreading, and/or silent reading; in other words, reading instruction is supplemented with instruction in speaking, listening, writing, and comportment. In general, a good LICA lesson tends to follow a sequence that closely parallels the way language and most behavioral expressions develop. In this vein, Sticht, Beck, Hauke, Kleiman, and James (1974) have said that literacy would be achieved more easily if the content teacher taught youngsters to listen and speak in each new field before reading and writing in it. Listening and speaking precede reading and writing in normal language development and therefore constitute a more familiar means for assimiliating new information and acquiring greater dexterity with the more demanding symbolic systems of reading and writing. You will recall that the L-R-D heuristic follows this pattern on a daily lesson basis and thus is an exemplary languaging-based lesson.

Four other conditions, also drawn primarily from the way in which language is learned, have strong implications for conducting effective LICA instruction. Briefly stated, these conditions are:

1. That perspectives on or scrutiny of the content material be conducted in a thorough, or dialectical, way, giving fair consideration even to extreme positions (the term *dialectical* is further developed in Chapter 7)
2. That a highly competent model of language use (i.e., the teacher) be present to be strategically drawn into the examination and therefore observed engaging in the desired level of "symbolic processing," whether it be speaking, listening, reading, or writing. See Chapter 5 for a further explanation of this point.

3. That some well-thought-out teaching heuristic be employed to draw attention to that model and to the particular competencies that students are expected to note and emulate
4. That the content, or the material to be read, listened to, spoken, or written about, be sufficiently relevant and valuable to warrant careful analysis (you can't improve your racquetball game by hitting a ball into a pillow!)

To get a sense of its living form, picture a typical languaging lesson as an "apprenticeship" in which complex analytical skills are transferred to students primarily by a teacher thinking aloud rather than by one making pronouncements. It is believed that when student-teacher and student-student interactions contain this feature, more will be "caught" than could ever be explicitly taught, as Durkin (1978–79) put it. See the discussion of modeling in Chapter 5 for an elaboration of the notion of apprenticeship teaching.

We use the term *languaging* sparingly—and parenthetically—throughout the remainder of the text. While your understanding of the term will grow with repeated exposure to it, the concept may temporarily hinder your comprehension of the methodologies—which probably illustrate the concept better than descriptive words do anyway. For this reason, we use more familiar terms that hint at deep processing, such as *speaking, listening, writing, discussing,* and *behavior* (or *comportment*) in place of *languaging*. These lay terms can introduce problems, however, primarily because they carry nontechnical connotations that can distort the intended message. The term *discuss,* for example, suggests a polite, almost directionless interaction among peers of equal authority. When a teacher leads a *discussion,* however, he or she has (or should have) a clear purpose in mind. Unfortunately, the educational device of discussion can be considerably diminished because some students, their parents, and even some teachers think of the term in the more familiar lay context of opinion, or the very casual, content-deficient way it is sometimes employed in primary school language arts activities. In content classes, a languaging approach is used to gain more precise insight into content, language, and idea structures, not merely as an incidental vehicle for teaching the surface features of reading, writing, speaking, and listening.

Figure 2.4 summarizes the synergistic property of languaging, or process-oriented instruction. In a **synergistic** combination, the addition of some things produces an effect that may be greater than the simple sum of its parts. The combination of exercise and diet, for example, has a greater impact on health and well-being than the sum of these elements would indicate (you look better, feel better, and live longer). A similar effect occurs with languaging lessons: When the four deep-processing elements of languaging are added to some or all of the four surface-processing elements of the language arts, the learning outcomes appear much greater than the sum of those elements would suggest.

An example of a synergistic outcome is an entire class that becomes enamored of a subject because of the way it is being taught or because of who is teaching it. Another synergistic outcome occurs with the student who assumes a lifelong in-

Figure 2.4 Synergistic Effect of Languaging

The four language arts (surface-processing) features of language learning	Reading
	Speaking
	Listening
	Writing
The four languaging (deep-processing) features of language learning	Scrutiny (dialectical thinking)
	Competent model present
	Attention drawn to model
	+ Compelling content
	Total learning outcome = *greater than 8,* or beyond information acquisition to critical/creative thinking and productive applications

terest or even chooses a career as a result of class activities. Less dramatic but equally important is the student who comes to think about a subject or idea outside of class, thereby transporting it to other contexts to which it could contribute or from which it could grow. Such generative—synergistic—outcomes are the crowning purpose of effective schooling.

Let us now consider some additional concrete examples of how these abstract and theoretical issues are being translated into teaching practices. The methods presented in the next section address some of the most fundamental objectives of effective deep processing in the content areas: helping students (1) deal with the language and phrasing characteristics of a new field; (2) read with a minimum of word recognition problems; and (3) become familiar with a field's most basic concepts, terms, and underlying questions.

The Practices: Four Universal Strategies in Content Area Reading

The term *universal strategies* simply means teaching methods that are broadly applicable and accessed relatively easily by content teachers. These methods require little preparation, although they require more than those presented in Chapter 1. They also contain some valuable heuristic properties that should provoke some quality interactions with your students. These particular methods are supported mostly by inferences drawn from related research and from field experiences. You will have to rely a good deal on your own judgment to determine the appropriateness of these strategies for you and your students.

Universal Strategy 1: Content-Cloze (Languaging) Procedure

By fifth grade, most students are quite competent linguistically. They have been exposed to virtually all of the complex sentence structures in the English language. The structures they encounter in basal reading, however, are intentionally kept simple and tend to carry relatively uncomplicated ideas; the exceptions are few and far between. For this reason, we still need methods at the upper grade levels to help students meet the challenge of new levels of linguistic, factual, and ideational intensity. The *Content-Cloze procedure* is one such strategy.

The Content-Cloze *teaching* procedure is based on the **cloze testing** procedure, a concept covered more fully in the next chapter. Cloze exercises for teaching have students attempt to replace words deleted from sentences or brief passages. As students try to deduce the word that best fits in each blank, they are drawn into careful analysis of the linguistic and contextual elements of each sentence: its syntactical structure, word choices, tone, phrasing, verb tenses, and message. For this reason, properly constructed and conducted cloze lessons are considered a good way to help students acquire familiarity with the characteristic language patterns of each content area.

Discussion of appropriate replacement words creates a teaching heuristic that requires no special reading, training, or background on the teacher's part. As teacher and students language through their choices for replacement words, they are led to observe and comment on several subtleties of language and elements of context that are peculiar to the content area and even to the particular textbook from which the exercise was drawn. Notice too as you study this strategy that the teacher is little more than a wiser party in this particular discussion and that students can generate considerable insights from one another.

Here are some steps for this "quick form" of content-cloze. These steps are drawn from the suggestions of several writers and researchers (Martin, 1968; Meeks & Morgan, 1978; Hayes & Tierney, 1982). *Note:* If you substitute the words *language-through* or *languaging* wherever you see the words *internal dialog* or *discussion,* you will see how the concept of carefully processing and reprocessing in dialog with others improves thinking and learning.

Steps in the Quick-Form Content-Cloze

1. The teacher prepares a cloze passage training exercise by deleting every ninth word from a passage. The first and last sentences should be left intact, with deletions starting with any word in the second sentence. (A typical cloze exercise should contain 5 to 25 deletions.)
2. Students initially conduct an *internal dialog* within themselves while attempting to replace deleted terms (to reduce frustration-level responding, the teacher should tell students that correct replacement of as few as 60% of the words is a very good performance for this type of task).
3. Students are formed into groups of five to *discuss* their replacement decisions.
4. The entire class *discusses* the groups' findings.

5. The teacher lists a set of class-generated replacements on the chalkboard.
6. Feedback on the deleted words is provided.
7. The teacher encourages *discussion* of which words suggested by the class are precise replacements and which are plausible synonyms.

Following is a sample cloze passage:

Monoclonals: The Super Antibodies
When 67-year-old Philip Kau of Santa Barbara, California, failed to respond to a number of both conventional and experimental drugs for his lymphatic cancer, researchers at Stanford University Medical Center tried a new treatment with a twist. They injected him with specially _____ proteins, called monoclonal antibodies, that had been created _____ a process that involved his own cancer cells _____ cancer cells from a mouse. Kau received eight intravenous injections of monoclonals over a four-week period.

[Replacement words: 1. tailored; 2. in; 3. and]

Note that the blank spaces in the above passage are uniform in length so as to provide no extraneous clues to the correct replacements.

Quick-Form Options.   There are several optional ways to do a quick-form cloze. Here are three widely used methods:

1. Delete words only from the first paragraph or two of a longer passage; discuss replacements; continue reading the remainder of the selection silently; discuss full selection, deleted and intact portions.
2. After steps 1 through 7 have been completed, have the class continue to read the next 500 words or so. Follow this with a "comprehension check" made up of a few (about five) deletions selected for their value as key content terms.
3. Offer two choices of terms for each deletion, or make the blank space conform to the size of the missing word and/or have the initial letter of the word at the beginning of the space. These are good ideas for using cloze with slower students or as an introduction to the cloze process.

The term *quick form* probably suggests that there is a longer version—and there is. The *Elaborated Content-Cloze Exercise Format* is quite a bit more demanding, but it also has a much greater payoff. Dewitz, Carr, and Patberg (1987) found this form to be highly effective in improving literal and inferential comprehension as well as heightening students' abilities to monitor and correct their own thinking while reading (an idea discussed more fully in Chapter 4). This method recently has been republished and renamed the *Inferential Training Technique* by its authors (Carr, Dewitz, & Patberg, 1989).

Steps in the Elaborated-Form, or Inferential Training, Technique

1. Students are taught essential vocabulary.
2. The teacher demonstrates to students how to infer a correct word replacement by using semantic (context) clues, syntactic (sentence structure) clues, and stu-

dents' previous background knowledge. This is done progressively over several lessons, first with a single sentence, then groups of sentences, and finally paragraphs and first as teacher-directed work and then as individual student work.

3. While doing the cloze exercises, students are expected to follow a self-monitoring checklist developed by Cambourne (1977):
    a. Does the answer make sense?
    b. Does the answer make sense in the sentence?
    c. Is the answer based on a combination of knowledge you had before you read the passage and the clues in the passage?
    d. Is there a forward clue in the same sentence, paragraph, or passage?
    e. Is there a backward clue in the same sentence, paragragh, or passage?
    f. Did the clue make you change your answer, or is your answer the same?
4. The teacher goes over answers with students and explains why a particular answer is correct.
5. The teacher asks inferential questions about the completed passage.
6. The teacher asks students to read a second (usually a continuing) passage of intact text.
7. The teacher attempts to ensure transfer of learning by again asking a few inferential questions (Dewitz, Carr, & Patberg, 1987).

The next strategy builds on the somewhat forgotten value of having a teacher, at any level, read to a class. It can be entertaining, relaxing, and instructive.

Universal Strategy 2: Oral Reading (and Languaging) Strategy

The *Oral Reading Strategy* (Manzo, 1980b) is a simple way to impart complex processes. The teacher reads content-rich material to students, pausing at logical points to comment or pose simple translation questions. In effect, the teacher models the deep-processing dialog of a mature reader and urges the student reader to come along.

Several concurrent objectives are met in this simple lesson design. Students are introduced to correct pronunciations of new words in a straightforward, informal manner. Moreover, the strategy builds familiarity with the cadence and patterns of language and thought peculiar to each content area. When the teacher reads aloud, both students and teachers become more alert to obstacles to comprehension in specific textual material. This creates a valuable teaching/learning heuristic: The teacher models and provides assistance with words, phrasing, missing facts, and thought obstacles to reading, while students learn how to read more fluently and to detect and deal with typical textual obstacles.

Steps in the Oral Reading Strategy

1. The teacher reads the first few pages of a selection to the class while they follow along in their texts. In preparation for this step, the teacher should always preread the selection. At the most basic level, the teacher should be certain about how to pronounce all the words; silent prereading makes oral reading more fluent and poignant. It also is helpful, especially the first few times the

teacher uses this strategy, to jot down some personal notes about comments or questions to raise during this step.

2. The teacher pauses periodically and comments or asks a few simple, translation-level questions on the text: "What do you suppose this word means here?" or "Tell in your own words what point was just made here." (At first, the teacher may have to answer his or her own questions, because students are unaccustomed to translating what they read and could have difficulty understanding what they are being asked to do.)

Example   ◆ ◆ ◆

Teacher reading from text: The Jura (*joo'-ruh*) is a mountain range that lies between two rivers, the Rhine and the Rhone.

Teacher question to class: What do you picture when you hear that the Jura lies between two rivers?

Teacher reading from text: The Jura forms part of a natural boundary between Switzerland and France. The Jura extends from the northeast to the southwest in parallel ridges.

Teacher question to class: What other kinds of "natural boundaries" do you know of? Can someone define "parallel ridges?"

3. The teacher reads the next page or so with fewer questions and comments. Students are told to listen for cadence, pronunciation, and questions they might wish to raise before they begin silent reading.

4. The teacher tells the class to read the next portion of the selection silently (or for homework).

5. When content acquisition is the goal, the teacher should conduct a postreading oral comprehension check. Questions that necessitate use of new language and verification of answers from text, and therefore some limited oral reading by students, are preferable.

Oral Reading Considerations.   Oral reading to a class from supplements to the text can be done without interruption, although generally not for more than 15 minutes at a time or more than twice a week. Again, remember to practice reading silently the material you will read orally. Oral reading has a large performance component: Elocution and phrasing are essential to effective communication of the words, the message, and the process.

With the next universal strategy, the teacher shows students a way to analyze textbook information. It requires a shift in emphasis from *information* to the *question(s)* the information answers.

Universal Strategy 3: C/T/Q (Languaging) Strategy

With the *C/T/Q strategy*, teacher and students identify the most uncluttered versions possible of key *c*oncepts, *t*erms, and *q*uestions around which units of information are built (Manzo, 1980b). The C/T/Q strategy has a strong heuristic element. Teachers come to better understand, anticipate, and provide for the idea load students face when reading content material. Students are led to observe and practice what expert readers do to construct meaning, namely combine textual information with prior knowledge and experience.

The discussions (or languaging interactions) that occur between teacher and class contain the basic ingredients necessary for students to "catch on" to this process and begin to do it for themselves rather than being explicitly instructed in how to do it. In going through the C/T/Q process, the teacher effectively repeats important overlapping facts and ideas in three different ways: as concepts, as terms, and as questions. This redundancy effect alone can justify the effort. Other means of analyzing and structuring content information with students, such as "semantic mapping," are developed elsewhere in the text.

Steps in the C/T/Q Lesson

1. The teacher selects three brief selections of text for analysis.
2. The teacher notes and "talks through" the key concepts, terms, and questions underlying the first selection. A visual representation should be provided on the overhead, on the chalkboard, or in a handout.

◆ ◆ ◆   *Example*

Key concept: Rivers often are found at the bases of mountain ranges.
Key terms: Jura mountains; parallel ridges
Key question: How did Switzerland's geography help Switzerland to form itself into a country separate from France, Germany, and Italy?

3. The class reads that portion of the text. A brief discussion follows to determine that comprehension, or alignment, between the passage and the C/T/Qs presented occurred. The best way to do this is to begin with the key question.
4. The teacher asks the class to read the second selection and to construct along with him or her a second set of C/T/Qs for that portion. This can be done first in small groups and then with the teacher.
5. Students are instructed to independently isolate and identify the C/T/Qs of the third selection without peer discussion or teacher assistance.
6. The teacher again displays his or her rendition of the C/T/Qs on the chalkboard, on an overhead, or in a handout, and the students compare their versions with the teacher's.
7. Discussion of similarities and differences between the teacher's and students' renditions follows.

C/T/Q Options

1. The teacher can develop C/T/Qs for use as guides to homework reading and/or as summary notes following weighty reading assignments.
2. As a cooperative learning experience, student groups can be directed to prepare C/T/Qs for various assigned portions of a text, which are then reproduced and shared with the rest of the class. Ideally, the teacher leads a discussion that attempts to correlate the parts to the larger, or macro-organizational, structure of the unit.

The next universal strategy is an exciting, high-participation heuristic. It engages students in the active questioning process—the mark of an expert reader.

Universal Strategy 4: The Question-Only Strategy
The *Question-Only strategy* evolved from a cluster of studies on why children slowly but surely cease to express curiosity and possible remedies for this problem (Manzo & Legenza, 1975; Legenza, 1978). Research and field experience have revealed that with thoughtful human engineering, students from kindergarten through medical school can be roused to raise incisive and systematic questions on even the most seemingly mundane topics. The enthusiasm students have shown for this strategy arises, we suspect, because the strategy offers them an assertive but non-belligerent means of "poking back," or reciprocally influencing lesson activity. It also helps students to incidentally discover and provide for their own learning needs by stimulating them to ask questions about the things that most befuddle them in an upbeat and ego-protective atmosphere.

The only time this sometimes rousing but always highly analytical activity may go stale is when the teacher becomes overwhelmed by the rapidity with which the day's material is being covered. The teacher may react by slowing down the lesson, taking the winds of enthusiasm out of the students' sails in the process. Before using this strategy, therefore, the teacher should be prepared to cover a good deal of information quickly and with considerable depth.

Steps in the Question-Only Strategy

1. The teacher announces a topic to the class and explains that they must learn about it solely through their questions and will be tested on the topic. The test will cover all the information the teacher considers important, whether or not the students actually extract the information with their questions.
2. The class questions and the teacher answers fully, but without telling more than anyone logically would need to know and at the same time taking care not to miss a teachable moment for telling all that the question logically entails.
3. The teacher gives the test.
4. Class discussion follows. Here teacher and students note which questions were raised and which should have been raised.
5. Students are directed to read their texts carefully or listen to a short lecture to discover what they failed to learn through their initial questions.

Example   ◆ ◆ ◆
Teacher: The topic today is the Jura. Any questions?
Student: You said *the*—does that mean Jura is a thing?
Teacher: Yes.
Student: This is geography, so is it a country?
Teacher: No.
Student: A river?
Teacher: No.
Student: Mountains?

Teacher: Yes.
Student: It sounds foreign. Is it in India?
Teacher: No.
Student: South America?
Teacher: No.
Student: Eastern Europe?
Teacher: No, but close.
Student: Western Europe?
Teacher: Yes.

Ten minutes later, students will have deduced facts such as that the Jura is between Switzerland and France and its highest peak is 6,000 feet. The quiz that follows should teach the class more about the topic, but also more about how to inquire.

Quiz Questions:

1. Does the Jura serve as a natural boundary?
2. What does it divide?
3. What happened to the valuable forests that once covered the mountainsides?
4. What do you suppose is the relationship between mountains and rivers?

Check your text now for answers to those questions you didn't anticipate.

Question-Only Options

1. The teacher can add a five-minute period of "comments-only," encouraging students to say what they feel they learned about the topic and/or about asking questions from the Question-Only format.
2. The teacher can have students use the Question-Only strategy to "interrogate" other students on a report or term paper previously prepared as a class requirement.

CHAPTER TIE-UPS

♦♦♦   *Graphic Organizer*

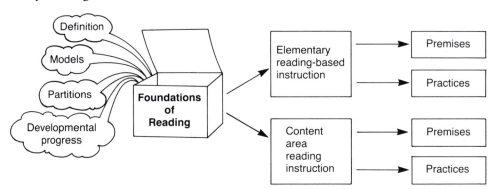

Critique and Anticipation

This chapter reviewed foundational concepts related to the "inner workings" of the reading process, four literacy domains, and stages in a developmental process toward higher-order literacy. From this springboard, it described elementary reading instruction in terms of the most commonly used curriculum, rationale, and practices. These elementary-level plans, premises, and practices, in turn, served as a stepping stone to those of secondary and content area reading. The chapter concluded on a practical note, illustrating how a number of the conceptual premises of content area reading can be implemented through the use of four teaching strategies that are universal in that they are applicable to any content area.

The next chapter details several content-teacher-oriented strategies for assessing students' reading skills. You will find that your own definition of reading figures largely in how you evaluate various assessment strategies. Evolving models of the reading process currently are being translated into several classes of "emerging assessment options."

TRADE SECRET

Notes and Memoranda

Sooner than you expect, you will be writing notes and memoranda to students, parents, colleagues, and your principal. Here are some simple guidelines to keep in mind:

1. Check your spelling.
2. Check your punctuation.
3. Watch your penmanship in handwritten notes.
4. Ask a colleague to read and react to notes that will leave the school building.
5. Hold a note for a day if you wrote it in anger.
6. Picture everything you write being reprinted in the evening newspaper.
7. Reread your note as though you were the recipient.
8. After rereading your note, rewrite it.

The value of these tips is easily tested. One day ask colleagues in the teacher's lounge whether any of them has had a bad experience with a note he or she wrote hurriedly. You may well hear the reply "I haven't, but you should hear what happened to one teacher I used to work with. . . ."

Traditional and Emerging Assessment Options

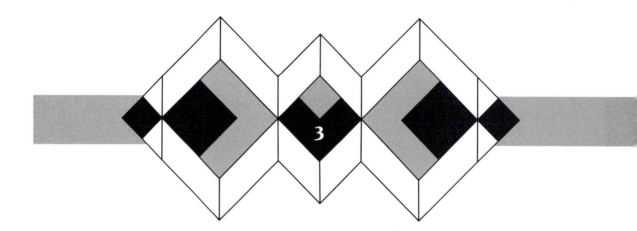

3

Reading, Writing, and Readability

We have to remember that what we observe is not nature herself, but nature exposed to our methods of questioning.
— Werner Heisenberg, 1985, Nobel prize–winning physicist

FOCUS

Why assess? What to assess? How to assess? This chapter considers these questions from several points of view.

OUTLINE

WHY ASSESS?

There is a reticent group of authorities in the reading field who secretly believe that testing, particularly of the diagnostic variety, is essentially a waste of precious time. The first author initially discovered this some time back while visiting the reading clinic of an eminent behavioral psychologist at a major university accompanied by a fellow graduate student. This professor was the former mentor of our major doctoral adviser and therefore something of an academic grandfather to us. It was easy to respect him, because he had a well-deserved reputation for coming up with elegant solutions to perplexing problems.

Two days into our visit, my fellow student and good friend Tom Estes (now at the University of Virginia) asked the question that was puzzling us. "We must be missing it," he ventured politely, "but where, when, and how do you do diagnostic workups on these kids?" Without a hint of defensiveness or apology, the professor replied, "We don't do that stuff anymore!" He went on to explain that after years and years of testing people in every conceivable fashion, he came to realize that he actually had only one "treatment" and that it systematically retaught everything he felt a failing student would need to know. Therefore, he reasoned, why waste time on a battery of tests to deduce the origins and nature of a problem when he could immediately get on with correcting it?

Other reading professionals feel likewise, and, while they are less candid, this sentiment is implicit in their writings and practices. Some popular content area reading textbooks, for example, do not have a section devoted to assessment, and those that do often seem uncomfortable with the topic. One introduces it with "Just say 'ah!' "—humorous, perhaps, but more than a bit cavalier for a professional text.

In contrast, this chapter does not rush to answer the opening question "Why assess?" Rather, it begins with a section filled with what many believe are practical and useful assessment instruments and practices. The chapter then returns to the issue of "why assess?" and how it is affecting and being affected by "mastery learning" programs. Next, it takes up some pioneering, or "emerging," assessment ideas and measures that are being developed in response to current thinking on the nature of the reading process and the problems and paradoxes associated with attempting to address higher-order literacy skills.

The final section of the chapter turns from assessment of the student's reading skill to assessment of the difficulty of the text material. It offers several practical ways to estimate the extent to which a particular text or selection is appropriate difficultywise for your class. Keep an open mind as you consider the opportunities and issues covered in this chapter. See if you come to believe, as most professionals do, that there are great benefits to be reaped from some time spent in classroom-based assessment.

INSTRUMENTS AND PRACTICES
SUITABLE FOR THE CONTENT CLASS

Standardized Reading Test Scores

In most schools, content teachers have access to their students' scores on standardized reading tests. There are several basic facts regarding standardized reading tests that content teachers should recall, as well as some limitations on the practical utility of these test scores for content teachers' purposes. This section briefly reviews these basic facts and limitations. Then it provides some suggestions for using standardized test scores to meet some of the requirements of content area instruction.

Basic Facts

The first basic fact to note about standardized reading tests is that scores are norm-referenced. This means that a student's raw score, or percentage of correct answers, is compared to the raw scores of a sample group of students and then converted into a standardized score. Information about the sample group of students is available in the test manual. Test developers attempt to identify a sample group that approximates nationwide demographics: percent urban/rural, percent minority/nonminority, and percent of students from various geographical regions of the country.

The second point is that the most commonly used norm-referenced scores are grade equivalents, percentiles, and stanines. A *grade equivalent* score indicates that a student's raw score is the same as the average score of the sample students in a certain grade level, usually reported to the nearest 10th (e.g., grade 9.3). A *percentile* score indicates that a student's raw score is higher than the raw scores of a certain percentage of the sample students at his or her grade level. For example, a ninth grader's score of 87th percentile means that that student's raw score is higher than those of 87% of ninth graders in the sample group. A *stanine* (or *standard nine*) score indicates that a student's raw score is equal to the scores of sample group students in one of nine segments of rank-ordered scores. Stanine scores range from a low of 1 to a high of 9. For instance, a 10th grader's score of 7th stanine means that his or her raw score is the same as that of the 10th-grade sample of students in the 7th group of raw scores—or 2 stanines above the 5th stanine, which is the standardized average score for stanine rankings.

The third point to note is that there are two marks of a good standardized test. First, a good test is *valid*, meaning that it accurately measures what it says it measures. Second, a good test is *reliable*, that is, yields scores that reflect actual attributes of the student rather than chance circumstances. Reliability generally is indicated when a student scores the same on the test (or different forms of the test) on more than one occasion. Test manuals typically provide extensive evidence of these two criteria.

Limitations

There are several limitations associated with standardized tests. First, norm-referenced scores often are misinterpreted. Grade equivalent scores in particular tend to be overgeneralized and taken to mean that a student's overall achievement and experience level are equal to the grade equivalent score. In content area reading, this assumption can be especially misleading. A ninth grader with a score of 7.5 may have a great deal more science knowledge and experience to draw on to read a ninth-grade science textbook than would a seventh grader with a score of 9.5. For this reason—and other, more technical ones—the International Reading Association (1982) has called for a discontinuance of the use of grade equivalent scores.

Percentile scores also pose a problem. *Percentile* scores are sometimes mistakenly interpreted as *percent* scores. For example, a percentile rank of 50 means that a student's score is equal to the average score of the sample group; it does not mean that the student answered 50% of the items correctly.

The second limitation of standardized tests is that scores do not represent equal raw score intervals. In general, more raw score points are associated with standardized score points within the middle range of scores. This means that it takes fewer test items to get a higher or lower standardized score at the upper and lower extremes of the scale than it does in the middle range.

Third, standardized reading test scores do not necessarily indicate a student's ability to read at a certain level in a particular content field. Factors such as background knowledge, motivation, and interest in the subject often are as important as general reading level to comprehension of text material.

Finally, standardized reading test scores may indicate that a student has a reading problem but give no indication of *why*. Some tests do provide a way to analyze a student's performance on an item-by-item basis to pinpoint areas of strength and weakness, such as main idea, literal, or interpretive items. This more diagnosis-related information, however, usually is not included in students' records and is time consuming to calculate. In any case, the reliability and validity of such item analyses usually are questionable, because the subcategories contain so few items.

More important, standardized test scores do not explain whether a low score is the result of poor word attack, or decoding, skills or poor thinking and comprehension. This is an important distinction. Students with poor decoding skills are difficult to help in the content classroom setting. On the other hand, students with adequate decoding but poor comprehension skills can be more easily empowered to read content materials. It is true that a skillful teacher can partially meet both needs, but it is a very taxing process. See Chapter 10 for ideas on helping the neediest students.

Suggested Uses

Despite the limitations just described, standardized reading tests scores can be worthwhile tools for assessing students' abilities and needs if you follow certain guidelines:

1. Obtain students' test scores from office files, including item analysis information if available.

2. Make a note of students with scores below your grade level, or the 40th percentile rank, or the 4th stanine. Try to determine whether a low score is due to a decoding deficit.

   a. See if the school reading specialist has additional information for answering this question.

   b. If no such information is available, ask the student, in private, to read a brief portion of the text out loud. Open one hand as the student begins to read 100 words. Close one finger for each word error. If you have a fist before the oral reading is completed, the student has a decoding deficit at that level.

   c. If you wish to obtain more precise information, administer the San Diego Quick Test described later in this chapter. This simple individualized test can indicate the grade level at which the student will be able to read at instructional and independent levels, as well as his or her frustration reading level.

3. When you identify a decoding deficit, refer the student to the reading specialist or counselor. If these resources are unavailable, consult with the student's parents. The objective is to obtain individual or small-group remedial assistance for the student as soon as possible. The amount of assistance you can provide such a student in the content classroom will be limited. If all content teachers collected and reported such information, principals would have a strong justification for expanding remedial resources and programs. See the section on "decoding stations" in Chapter 10 for one possible way to assist these students.

4. For students with low reading scores who do not have decoding deficits, keep in mind that the standardized scores are not infallible. This is also true for students with average and above-average reading scores. It is useful to compare these students' scores with their performances on other instruments that measure content area reading abilities. Several such instruments are described in this chapter, including the Informal Textbook Inventory, Free-Associational Assessment, and the Standard Cloze Passage test. Each of these instruments is based on the classroom textbook to yield a more accurate assessment of reading ability in a particular area.

5. You can use accurate information on your students' general and content-related reading levels in several ways in your instructional planning:

   a. To group students of mixed ability levels for cooperative learning activities. The better readers will be able to assist and support the poorer readers in their group.

   b. To determine how much assistance and direct instruction a particular class will need in the prereading, guided silent reading, and postreading stages of instruction.

   c. To develop individualized assignments or unit projects.

   d. To select appropriate supplementary instructional materials at varying levels of difficulty.

Informal Textbook Inventory (ITI)

A "new" idea over 60 years old, the *Informal Textbook Inventory (ITI)* essentially is a clever open-book test designed to familiarize students with using one of the most basic learning tools: their textbooks. The strategy sometimes is attributed to Betts (1946), who described it as the content textbook portion of the Informal Reading Inventory, an assessment scheme described more fully later in this chapter. In fact, we have seen an excellent 10-question version of the ITI called "Getting Acquainted with Your Book" built into a fifth-year study reader by Walker and Parkman (1924). Most texts currently on the market do not contain a ready-made ITI; in all likelihood, you will need to construct your own. First, however, let us examine the why and wherefore of the ITI.

The Informal Textbook Inventory is a group-administered, diagnostic-teaching device that is highly compatible with three aspects of content area reading:

1. It is *concurrent:* It tests and teaches simultaneously.
2. It is *heuristic:* The guidelines naturally draw teacher and student into self-evaluation through discovery and use of text parts, text aids, and related references.
3. It has a rich *languaging* component: It provokes poignant discussion of text features at three levels of interaction—with self, with classmates, and with the teacher.

When used early in the school year, while student attitudes and expectations are still being formed, the ITI also can provide an excellent means of establishing a disciplined, well-managed classroom tone. Class can begin in a purposeful and well-structured but nonthreatening way. Also, by simply tallying the results of the inventory (see Figure 3.2), the teacher can obtain a precise record of each student's ability to deal with the text as well as a clue to the potential benefits and shortcomings of the text itself.

The ITI takes considerable time to prepare, but it also stores well and improves with age and use. It is the type of activity that is the mark of a professional teacher. Students appreciate the help, and supervisors rarely fail to take note. The second and subsequent times you use it, you will be even more pleased because you will have refined it and will know better what to expect and how to orchestrate the full activity. In the version shown in Figure 3.1, the item "Evaluating and Judging" and the suggestion to integrate other options are peculiar to the form we recommend. The combination of the basic and optional parts provides the teacher with an especially good database for lesson planning, for pointing up issues to supervisors, for talking to parents at fall "open house," and for formulating questions to reading resource teachers and other potential consultants.

Constructing the ITI
The following outline illustrates the general form of the Informal Textbook Inventory:

   I. Organization and Structure of the Text
     A. Understanding the Textbook Organization
        Develop three to five straightforward questions about how the text is

structured and how to use the comprehension aids provided within the text.

    B. Using the Text Organization Effectively

    Develop three to five questions that students can answer by referring to the index, table of contents, glossary, appendices, or other text sections and/or aids.

II. Basic Comprehension

Select a short portion of the text that contains an *important concept* with supporting details and at least one graph, chart, or picture. (The same selection can be used in the following section on applied comprehension.)

    A. Comprehending the Main Idea

    Develop one or two fill-in or multiple-choice questions that direct students to state or select the main idea of the material read.

    B. Noting Supporting Details

    Develop three or more fill-in, multiple-choice, or matching questions about specific facts or ideas in the selection.

    C. Understanding Vocabulary in Context

    Develop three or more fill-in, multiple-choice, or matching questions that direct students to state or select a definition for key terms used in the selection.

    D. Understanding Information Presented in Graphic or Pictorial Form

    Develop one or more questions requiring students to state or select an interpretation of a graph, chart, or picture that adds information not explicitly stated in the selection.

III. Applied Comprehension

Questions in these sections can be based on the same text selection used above.

    A. Drawing Conclusions and Critical Thinking

    Develop one or more questions that require students to draw valid conclusions based on the information presented.

    B. Evaluating and Judging

    Develop one or more questions that require students to evaluate and apply information from the text in terms of their own experiences, values, and existing knowledge base.

    Option 1: Assess special requirements of the discipline. (This could mean understanding geographical directions in social studies [see Figure 3.1], a section on understanding style or mood in literature, or a section on applying symbols in mathematical formulas. More is said about this shortly.)

    Option 2: Assess language features with a Standard Cloze Passage test (discussed shortly).

    Option 3: Assess perspective and depth of comprehension with Free-Associational Assessment (discussed shortly).

Several of the optional categories listed in the above outline are described later in the chapter.

Figure 3.1 presents a sample ITI that the first author created and used to introduce seventh graders to a good but most unusual book (actually it was two "separate" books under one hard cover). Additional examples of specialized questions appropriate for each discipline are presented in Chapters 12, 13, and 14.

Administering the ITI

Before asking students to tackle the ITI, explain some of its features and purposes. It is not a "test" in the usual sense of the word; every text differs slightly from every other, and this is a way to find out how well students will be able to use this particular text. Also, point out that answers will be discussed as a group, but each student should attempt to complete the worksheets as thoroughly and accurately as possible in order to yield a quality assessment of the appropriateness and value of the text.

Provide adequate time for all students to complete the inventory. It may take two or more class periods, and students who finish early should be provided with an alternate activity.

Evaluating Results of the ITI

After all students have finished their ITIs, collect and score the tests. A "total score" need not be recorded on the students' papers, since the purpose of the test is to identify strengths and weaknesses in the various subsections. For diagnostic purposes, any error is taken as a sign of need in that category.

Much of the diagnostic value of the inventory comes from the group discussion of the items when the tests are returned to the students. Compare and contrast student strengths and weaknesses among the various categories of questions. Review and discussion of the ITI with the class can take from one-half to three full class periods depending on individual students' abilities, the difficulty of the text, and the objectives you wish to achieve.

Results of the ITI can be used as a part of school- or districtwide diagnostic survey evaluation as well as at the classroom level.

Recording Results of the ITI

ITI results should be recorded in a way that will permit easy reference. Figure 3.2 shows a sample summary sheet format.

The Informal Textbook Inventory provides useful information for determining how much assistance your students will need to use their textbooks effectively. The next assessment instrument, the Standard Cloze Passage test, is also constructed from the class textbook.

Standard Cloze Passage Test

The *Standard Cloze Passage test* has an interesting history. It is useful to know a little of its evolution to understand its power and pitfalls. Some have said that cloze was first developed by a Russian around 1890. For our purposes, we can pick up the story with Wilson Taylor in the 1950s. Taylor originally set out to study "closure" but discovered cloze. In 1953, he developed a simple technique, which he called "cloze" passages, for studying the effect on comprehension of a psychological trait called *closure:* the tendency to fill in the missing elements of an incomplete stimulus and recognize it as a meaningful whole. The cloze passage test Taylor developed, which this section describes in detail, is essentially a written passage with random words blanked out to be filled in by the reader. Even when this test proved to be a poor measure of closure, Taylor continued to study it. Upon discovering that this "fill-in-the-blanks" task is highly correlated with reading and listening ability, he used it to study aspects of "communication theory" and labeled it cloze to avoid its confusion with *closure* in the research literature.

The value of cloze in this regard was pursued by John Bormuth (1965), who was able to show that correlations of cloze passage testing with reading comprehension were very high and consistent across age and most grade levels. Following a format originally laid out by Betts, though in a more scientific manner, Bormuth then developed a standard form of cloze test with criteria for evaluating students' comprehension levels. A subsequent study by Weaver and Kingston (1963) shook confidence in the measure when they found that contrary to prevailing belief, cloze is a direct measure not of reading comprehension but of a shadow that it casts, namely familiarity with the "language redundancy patterns" in prose. In other words, there were two things—comprehension and familiarity with language patterns—that had only a little in common but were both strongly related to a third thing (probably verbal reasoning), and therefore one could be used to infer the other.

Culver, Godfrey, and Manzo (1972) verified the ambiguity of this relationship and cast some new doubts. They found that cloze scores did not correlate as well as did conventional measures of comprehension with two other skills that are part of the very structure of effective reading: vocabulary and rate of reading. Nonetheless, this study could not refute the fact that the cloze test was a quick and fairly accurate indicator of comprehension. This and related work did, however, add several points to our understanding of cloze passage testing:

1. Cloze is a good strategy for sampling students' ability to handle the language vagaries of different types of content material (and therefore can profitably be added to an Informal Textbook Inventory).
2. Cloze underestimates the comprehension abilities of students with weak standard English backgrounds.
3. Cloze tends to penalize students who are divergent thinking, impulsive, or perfectionistic. Even the best students tend to find the task rather tedious and the error rate higher than what they are used to. This is because some answers scored as incorrect are perfectly legitimate synonyms (see justification for this shortly) and because sometimes it simply is impossible to know which word was deleted from available clues.

Preparation of the Standard Cloze Passage Test
To prepare a Standard Cloze Passage test, select a passage of about 300 words from a textbook. Copy the first sentence with no deletions. Then select a word at random

Figure 3.1   Informal Textbook Inventory: Social Studies Text: *New York State in Story* by Jeanne Schwarz and Minerva Goldberg (Phoenix, NY: Frank E. Richards, 1962)

I. Organization and Structure of the Text

Understanding the Textbook Organization

1. If you wanted to know if your textbook covered the *what, why,* and *who* of New York State government, you would check the:

(x) a. Table of contents
      b. Index
      c. Chapter headings
      d. Publisher

2. Which one of the following would you first turn to if you wished to read a book about one of the topics in your text?

      a. Librarian
      b. Table of contents
(x) c. Your teacher
      d. Bibliography

3. Check the following statements by studying the design of this book. If you find a statement to be true, mark it with a plus (+) sign; if false, a minus (−) sign:

    The book has:

(−) a. a very complete bibliography
(+) b. two major parts; really two books in one
(+) c. good charts, pictures, and maps
(+) d. a good description of the authors and their backgrounds
(+) e. a glossary
(+) f. a brief outline of the material covered before each chapter
(+) g. follow-up activities after each chapter
(+) h. a storylike style
(−) i. beautiful color illustrations
(+) j. a comfortable, compact look
(+) k. easily visible printing

Using the Text Organization Effectively

See how quickly you can answer the following questions using the parts of your book to their best advantage (based on the first half of the book).

4. How long is the term of office of the Attorney General?
5. a. What is the meaning of the word *almshouse?*
   b. Where did you find the answer to 5a?
6. What are the three divisions of Chapter 1?

II. Basic Comprehension

New York State is our home. Carefully read the section called "Where is it?" beginning on page 3 and ending on page 4. See how much you can read about our state. Answer the following questions based on your reading. You may look in the book.

Figure 3.1 *continued*

Comprehending the Main Idea

7. Which of the following best expresses the author's purpose for this brief selection?
   a. Show the friendliness of New York people
   b. Show the boundaries of New York State
(x) c. Show where New York is in relation to the other states and the world
   d. New York State lies between the parallels of 40–31 and 45 north latitude

Noting Supporting Details

8. New York State is bounded by five states, three lakes, three rivers, one foreign country, and one ocean. Name them.

9. New York State most resembles a:
   a. hexagon
(x) b. triangle
   c. circle
   d. rectangle

Understanding Vocabulary in Context

10. Match the following based on their use in context:

Column A	Column B
_____ latitude	a. circular lines running east and west around the globe designed to measure distances north and south
_____ prime meridian	b. first line of longitude
_____ equator	c. imaginary lines designed to measure distance east and west on the globe
_____ province	d. a region of a country
_____ longitude	e. the center latitudinal line around the earth

Understanding Information Presented in Graphic or Pictorial Form

To answer questions 11–13 below, study the illustration on the page specified and answer each question based on that illustration.

11. Illustration—Page 3
   a. The point of this illustration is that:
      (1) We have neighbors to the north.
      (2) Different countries are represented by different flags.
   (x) (3) We have good relations with our northern neighbors.
      (4) People are the same around the world.
   b. What symbol in this illustration shows the major difference between the two groups of people shown?
      (1) people
      (2) names
   (x) (3) flags
      (4) boundaries

Figure 3.1   *continued*

12. Illustration—Page 2

    Study the three illustrations on page 2 carefully. What is the major relationship among the three separate items?
    a. They are all maps.
    b. They focus on the relative size and place of New York State.
    c. They show the size of New York State.
    d. They show the population density of New York State.

13. Illustration—Page 5

    The two pictures on page 5 tell us that New York State has *two* features. They are:
    (x) a. seashores and rolling hills
    b. good natural resources
    c. high population density
    d. good industry

III. Applied Comprehension

Drawing Conclusions and Critical Thinking
14. Which of the following is a reasonable conclusion that can be drawn from just pages 3 and 4?
    a. New Yorkers must be fine people.
    (x) b. New York must have extremely long boundaries.
    c. New York is probably one of the largest states in the Union.
    d. New York is probably sparsely populated.

Evaluating and Judging
15. If you were the governor of New York and you wished to raise the educational level of its citizens, which three things would you consider most important to do? Why?

in the second sentence. Delete this word and every fifth word thereafter until 50 words have been deleted. Finish the sentence containing the 50th blank, and copy the next sentence with no deletions. The blanks should be typed lines five spaces long and numbered from 1 to 50. Students record their responses on numbered answer sheets.

Administration of the Standard Cloze Passage Test

When ready to give the test, inform students that the task will be difficult but that 60% accuracy is a good score. Demonstrate the task itself with examples on the chalkboard. You may want to assure the class that the scores will be used to group students for class activities and parent conferences but not as part of their course grades. Consequently, scores will be recorded but papers will not be returned. This

Figure 3.1 *continued*

a. Build more schools
b. Hire more teachers
c. Find a new tax source
d. Borrow money from the government
e. Build more libraries
f. Establish adult education courses
g. Raise teachers' salaries and attract the best teachers from other states
h. Develop a slum-clearing project
i. Study the problem more carefully
j. Try out varied approaches in different parts of the city

Social Studies: Understanding Directions

16. Below is a circle that represents the earth. Study the key below and mark the spaces with the direction of the arrows in the circle.

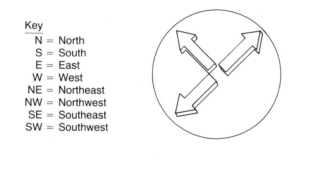

Key
N = North
S = South
E = East
W = West
NE = Northeast
NW = Northwest
SE = Southeast
SW = Southwest

introduction will encourage students to do their best while reducing some of the frustration associated with the task.

Scoring the Standard Cloze Passage Test

To begin scoring, count the number of actual words filled in correctly; do not count synonyms. Multiply this number by 2 (since there are 50 items) to get the percent correct. This score can be entered as a supplement to the Informal Textbook Inventory or used to group students as shown in Figure 3.3.

Why Synonyms Won't Do

One typical concern of teachers is the fact that only exact answers are counted correct in scoring the test. There are three sound reasons why synonyms should not be

Figure 3.2 ITI Classroom Summary Sheet

Name of Book _____   Class _____
Edition _____   Teacher _____
Author(s) _____

Student	Text Organization		Basic Comprehension				Applied Comprehension		Optional Tests/Measures				
	A	B	A	B	C	D	A	B	Content	Cloze	Writing	FAA/	Other

Figure 3.3 Reference Worksheet for Class Cloze Scores

Material Used: _____

Class Period: _____

Date Given: _____

Independent-Level Readability (above 60%)	Instructional-Level Readability (40%–60%)	Frustration-Level Readability (below 40%)

Record students' names in appropriate columns

counted in cloze testing. First, the assessment format was standardized according to exact-word scoring; therefore, the evaluation criterion cannot be used if synonyms are accepted. Second, the rank ordering of students does not change appreciably when synonyms are accepted; everyone simply has a higher score. Finally, if synonyms are allowed, scoring becomes a longer and more tedious process.

What to Do

For those students who score within the instructional and frustration ranges on the Standard Cloze Passage test, here are some general options:

1. Try to verify findings with standardized test scores already on record and/or with results of other assessment instruments such as the comprehension section of the Informal Textbook Inventory.
2. Refer the lowest-scoring students to the school reading specialist for further evaluation and/or remediation. Review the section on standardized testing earlier in this chapter for some criteria for determining which students may need this level of assistance.
3. Use prereading strategies (see Chapter 5).
4. Use guided silent reading strategies (see Chapter 6).
5. Use postreading strategies (see Chapter 7).
6. Use cooperative learning strategies (see Chapter 4).
7. Build better independent learning and study habits (see Chapter 9).
8. Consider using special methods for improving thinking and language skills (see Chapter 10).
9. Build meaning vocabulary (see Chapters 5 and 7).

The remainder of the text offers a variety of resources for using these options.

Rubric Evaluation of Student Writing

Writing is a learning tool that can be used in inventive ways to enrich instruction in any class. Simply put, "any time students must process information and facts, then they can write. This writing, in turn, can serve as a catalyst for further study and reflection on a topic, as opposed to being an end in itself'' (Pearce, 1987). This text emphasizes the importance of writing as a learning tool, particularly Chapter 7 on postreading comprehension development. However, teachers' enthusiasm about activities that involve student writing often is dampened by the prospect of piles of papers to be painstakingly graded. Fortunately, the recent renovation of an old idea called *rubric evaluation* of student writing cuts down on such paper load. As a result, it makes student writing a more attractive option for any teacher.

Using Rubric Evaluation to Enhance Writing Activities

A *writing rubric* is a set of guidelines for holistic scoring of compositions. It is a teacher-constructed list of characteristics of high-, medium-, and low-quality papers (or up to six quality levels for finer distinctions). The teacher uses a rubric to grade student compositions by simply determining which rubric level each composition best matches. Grading compositions thus becomes a speedy process of categorizing papers by level rather than a tedious chore of red-penciling each and every error and composing brief but time-consuming written comments on students' papers (that are seldom read in any case).

Typically the teacher gives the rubric for a writing assignment to students along with the topic. Then the students' working drafts are read by other students, in small groups, using the rubric to make editorial suggestions. As the teacher drops in on these small-group formative editing sessions, his or her suggestions are more meaningful than written comments on the final product would be. Used in this way, rubrics provide a valuable heuristic for stimulating individual and peer revision of compositions.

Depending on the importance or the objective of the writing assignment, the rubric may be simple or quite complex. Figures 3.4, 3.5, and 3.6 present three sample rubrics with increasing levels of detail.

Sample rubric 1, shown in Figure 3.4, describes quality levels for an assignment intended to teach students to include examples and illustrations in a composition. Papers are scored 1, 2, or 3 according to the descriptors shown.

Sample rubric 2, presented in Figure 3.5, is a more content-specific set of descriptors developed for a major paper on civil rights. Papers are rated high, medium, lower, or lowest. This rubric combines evaluation of several elements, including specific content objectives, use of examples and comparison-contrast, and mechanical elements of writing. A persistent problem in evaluating student writing is that some compositions will be organizationally, structurally, and mechanically perfect but lack originality and richness of thought, while others will have distracting errors in form but contain striking expressions and/or fresh conceptual approaches. A popular solution to this problem has been a dual-grade system—one grade for ideas and one for mechanics. Unfortunately, this system tends to widen the schism between writing and content (Tchudi & Huerta, 1983). A rubric that combines mechanics and content, such as sample rubric 2, provides guidelines for students to assist one another in working toward effective combination of both aspects of a quality composition.

Sample rubric 3, shown in Figure 3.6, describes high-, medium-, and low-quality papers in terms of six key factors of effective writing: focus, organization, devel-

Figure 3.4   Sample Rubric 1: Using Examples and Illustrations

3   The topic sentence is clearly written and strongly supported by lucid and interesting examples. Transitions tie the paper together in a fluid manner. Mechanical errors are slight.

2   The topic sentence is present, but support from the examples needs to be stronger and better organized. Transitions are used but need polishing. There are some mechanical errors.

1   The paragraph lacks a clear topic sentence. Examples are few in number and inadequately explained. Transitions are lacking, and mechanical errors are frequent.

Source: Adapted from *The Double Helix: Teaching the Writing Process,* edited by P. Behle, 1982, Florissant, MO: Ferguson-Florissant Writers Project.

opment, mechanics, sentence structure, and diction. This rubric is easily adaptable for a variety of uses. Any of these factors, or combination of them, could be used to compose a separate, more specific rubric.

As these three samples demonstrate, rubrics can vary in content and format based on the importance and/or objectives of a particular assignment. The initial planning time necessary for preparing the rubric, however, tends to enhance the quality of student products and simplify grading. A rubric-guided writing assignment at the beginning of the school year can provide a valuable addition to the ITI summary sheet of student reading and learning skills.

The next assessment instrument, Free-Associational Assessment, puts a heavy emphasis on factual learning and recall as the bases for effective reading, writing, and content mastery.

Free-Associational Assessment

Wood's *Free-Associational Assessment* (1985), or *FAA,* is a classroom-based strategy that offers a way to deal with the problem of students who know a good deal more than they show by their performances on typical tests. Free-Associational Assessment makes an especially good addition to an Informal Textbook Inventory, because it involves writing and offers a less restricted means of viewing students who typically receive short shrift by conventional and even cloze-passage-type assessment instruments. In the tradition of diagnostic teaching, FAA is as much a method of *teaching* as it is a means of *testing.*

Development and Administration

1. Identify the key concepts and details of a chapter of text. Use these to prepare a study sheet for students in the form of a handout or notes to be copied from

Figure 3.5   Sample Rubric 2: A Specific Content Assignment

Paper topic: 1960's approaches to civil rights in the U.S.

High quality papers contain:
An overview of civil rights or their lack during the 1960's, with 3 specific examples
A statement defining civil disobedience, with 3 examples of how it was used and Martin Luther King's role
At least one other approach to civil rights, with specific examples, and a comparison of this approach with King's civil disobedience that illustrates differences or similarities in at least 2 ways
Good organization, well developed arguments, few mechanical errors (sentence fragments, grammatical errors, spelling errors)

Medium quality papers contain:
An overview of Black civil rights during the 1960's with 2 specific examples
A statement defining civil disobedience, with 2 examples of its use and Martin Luther King's involvement
One other approach to civil rights, with examples, and a comparison of it with King's civil disobedience by their differences
Good organization, few mechanical errors, moderately developed arguments

Lower quality papers contain:
A general statement defining civil disobedience with reference to Martin Luther King's involvement and at least 1 example
One other approach to civil rights and how it differed from civil disobedience
Fair organization, some mechanical errors

Lowest quality papers contain:
A general statement on who Martin Luther King was or a general statement on civil disobedience
A general statement that not all Blacks agreed with civil disobedience
A list of points, poor organization, many mechanical errors

Source: From "Guidelines for the Use and Evaluation of Writing in Content Classrooms" by Daniel L. Pearce, 1983, *Journal of Reading, 27,* p. 215. Copyright 1983 by the International Reading Association. Reprinted with permission of Daniel L. Pearce and the International Reading Association.

the chalkboard (see Figure 3.7). The key concepts and details should be organized in the same sequence as they occur in the text.
2. Have students read their texts to discover relationships among the details and major concepts listed on the study sheet. On separate sheets of paper or in their notebooks, students write notes about how the details and concepts are related and elaborated on in the text. Save the teacher-prepared study sheet for the next step.

3. Have students close their textbooks and check their recall using the study sheet. For each word on the study sheet, students should recall relationships to the other concept and detail terms and make other relevant associations.
4. Have students split up into pairs and discuss how they conceptualized and recalled each concept term and detail (this is called *associational dialog*).
5. Test learning outcomes by giving students a list of some major concepts and/or terms and having them write *everything they can remember* about each by defining, using specific examples, and showing relationships among terms (see Figure 3.8).

Figure 3.6 Sample Rubric 3:   Six Factor Appraisal

High

Focus:	Has clear controlling idea and sense of direction; responds directly to topic
Organization:	Includes logical progression of ideas and coherence; contains evident beginning, middle, and end
Development:	Contains strong support, many specifics
Mechanics:	Has good to excellent mechanics; contains no distracting errors
Sentence structure:	Possesses sentence clarity, complexity, and variety
Diction:	Includes mature and appropriate vocabulary and diction; freshness of expression

Medium

Focus:	Has a controlling idea and sense of direction, though may be less evident than in higher categories
Organization:	Includes a generally logical progression of ideas and paragraphing where appropriate, though may occasionally show lapses in coherence and less fully developed sense of beginning, middle, and end
Development:	Contains details for support, but these may lack specificity, or the paper may lack generalizations to frame the details
Mechanics:	Has fair to excellent mechanics
Sentence structure:	Possesses clear sentences, though they may lack variety and complexity
Diction:	Includes appropriate vocabulary and diction, though these may lack freshness and variety

Low

Focus:	May possess a controlling idea or may lack a controlling idea altogether
Organization:	May lack coherence; may be characterized by digressions or irrelevancies; may have little sense of beginning, middle, end
Development:	May have little support or development, or support may be irrelevant
Mechanics:	Has poor to good mechanics; often has distracting mechanical errors
Sentence structure:	May have immature sentences that lack clarity, complexity, and/or variety
Diction:	Has relatively unsophisticated vocabulary and diction

Source: Adapted from the Missouri Department of Elementary and Secondary Education, 1986, pp. 145–146.

Figure 3.7   Excerpt of List from a Chapter on "Perception" from a Psychology Text

Directions: Read this chapter with these concepts in mind. Take notes, but not on this sheet. Use this sheet for study purposes: Look at each word and try to associate all the information you can with it by mentally or subvocally recalling the content. In class we will work in pairs to engage in an "associational dialogue" surrounding these concepts.

Selection	Organization	Interpretation
intense		past experience
repetitions		assumption
contrast/change		expectations
motives		knowledge
		personal

Source: From "Free Associational Assessment: An Alternative to Traditional Testing" by K. D. Wood, 1985, *Journal of Reading, 29,* p. 108. Copyright 1985 by the International Reading Association. Reprinted with permission of Karen D. Wood and the International Reading Association.

Figure 3.8   Sample Recalls on the Perceptual Selection

Student A: We do not notice every stimulus available. Four conditions cause us to select data to attend to: (1) intense—loud, bright, large objects stand out; (2) repetitions—hear messages again and again; (3) contrast/change—notice when things are different; (4) motives—we perceive when we have a drive to notice.

Student B: It would be impossible for us to notice everything in our environment, so we select things to notice. Objects (or people) that are loud and dress in bright colors or that we encounter again often catch our attention. Likewise, we become aware when change occurs. Perhaps a friend treats us differently or a bank opens a new branch office. Also, we notice things for a reason like the person who wants to buy a new jeep notices that type of vehicle on the highway.

Student C: There are many types of stimuli to select from: (a) intense; (b) repeating; (c) compare and contrast and motives. This occurs when someone who is getting married notices all the married people.

Note how the recall of students A and B, while different, are still acceptable, since both have captured the concept's essence. If the question asked them specifically to "List and explain the four causes of perceptual selection," student B's response would be considered insufficient. . . . [A]lthough . . . exact textbook terminology may be forgotten, it is obvious that student B has a thorough understanding of the concept. The responses of student C, in contrast, suggest an inadequate understanding or recall of this particular topic.

Source: From "Free Associational Assessment: An Alternative to Traditional Testing" by K. D. Wood, 1985, *Journal of Reading, 29,* p. 109. Copyright 1985 by the International Reading Association. Reprinted with permission of Karen D. Wood and the International Reading Association.

Scoring

If the student's responses demonstrate ample knowledge of the topic, give a plus (+); if sketchy and incomplete, give a minus (−). Do this for each concept term. Using this deceptively simple scoring protocol, you will discover that you are still working from the traditional basis of starting with a preconceived idea of what constitutes a correct answer; however, you also will easily recognize and be able to reward reasonable variations on it. Another advantage of this approach is that the student who would have answered a conventional question correctly generally will have no difficulty with this format, but considerable latitude is granted to the divergent-thinking youngster for whom conventional questions typically are quite confining. Also, test preparation takes a fraction of the time, and test scoring only a bit longer. To derive a conventional grade, simply determine the proportion of pluses to minuses, such as 10 terms with 9 pluses equals 90% (see Figure 3.8).

Now let us consider some instruments and practices suitable for informal individual administration or referral when information on basic comprehension and word recognition skills is required.

Informal Reading Inventory

Recall from Chapter 2 that Betts delineated three levels at which each person reads: an independent, an instructional, and a frustration level. We have seen how these levels can be approximated with a group-administered cloze test of familiarity with language patterns using Bormuth's criteria. What we have not explained is how Betts recommended that teachers assess students to arrive at these levels. We shall briefly describe his recommendation because, while not very practical at upper grade levels, it sets the stage for a more reasonable option for teachers interested in individualized assessment.

Betts (1946) designed the *Informal Reading Inventory (IRI)* and related guidelines for interpretation to be used with passages from available basal, or graded, readers. Since the readers already are constructed at levels of increasing difficulty, it is a relatively simple matter to select brief portions and infer students' reading levels from how well they handle materials at representative levels.

Administering an IRI can be quite complicated. It involves having each student read some paragraphs orally while the teacher carefully notes various types of errors with a special marking system. Then the teacher asks an assortment of comprehension questions on the passages just read. Children usually are quite anxious when reading orally, which makes it difficult for them to think about *what* they are reading while worrying about *how* they are reading. More recent IRI protocols have students read additional graded passages silently and then answer comprehension questions. Finally, the IRI specifies that a student listen to, and then answer questions on, other paragraphs of increasing difficulty. This helps ascertain the student's listening comprehension and, therefore, reading capacity, or potential to comprehend beyond one's immediate reading level.

As you can see, effective administration of an IRI requires some degree of training and practice. The results of this individually administered test, however, usually are more valid than those of group-administered standardized tests.

The next assessment instrument, the San Diego Quick Test, also is individually administered, but it does not require extensive training.

The San Diego Quick Test

For the teacher who wishes to get a "close-up" of a student's reading skill on an individualized basis, there is a simple instrument that yields an approximation of the diagnostic information an IRI provides, but in a fraction of the time. Reading specialists to whom you might refer a student sometimes will use this instrument, the *San Diego Quick Test* (LaPray & Ross, 1969)—named after its authors' home institution, the University of San Diego—in conjunction with an Informal Reading Inventory. Content area teachers, however, may wish to combine San Diego Quick Test scores with the Informal Textbook Inventory data.

The San Diego Quick Test is based on graded word lists. Its validity has been verified by comparing the grade-level reading score yielded by the test for sample groups of students with those students' scores on comprehension of a series of graded passages.

Steps in the San Diego Quick Test

1. Type up each list of 10 words on an index card (see the following section on word card lists).
2. Begin with a card that is at least two years below the student's grade placement.
3. Ask the student to read the words aloud to you. If he or she misreads *any* words on the list, drop to easier lists until the student makes *no* errors. This indicates the base reading level.
4. Write down all incorrect responses, or use diacritical marks on your copy of the test. For example, *lonely* might be read and recorded as *lovely* or *apparatus* as *a-per'-a-tus.*
5. Encourage the student to read words he or she does not know so that you can identify the techniques used for word identification.
6. Have the student read from increasingly difficult lists until he or she misses at least three words on one of the lists.
7. Identify the student's independent, instructional, and frustration levels using the following interpretation criteria:

   Independent level = no more than one error on a list
   Instructional level = two errors on a list
   Frustration level   = three or more errors on a list

Word Cards
Prepare a set of word list cards by typing the words for each grade-level list on a large index card. Leave several spaces between words so that you can easily point

to each word as you administer the test. Type the grade-level designations on the *back* of each card for your reference only. The word list cards can be laminated for durability.

Preprimer	Primer	Grade 1	Grade 2	Grade 3
see	you	road	our	city
play	come	live	please	middle
me	not	thank	myself	moment
at	with	when	town	frightened
run	jump	bigger	early	exclaimed
go	help	how	send	several
and	is	always	wide	lonely
look	work	night	believe	drew
can	are	spring	quietly	since
here	this	today	carefully	straight

Grade 4	Grade 5	Grade 6	Grade 7	Grade 8
decided	scanty	bridge	amber	capacious
served	certainly	commercial	dominion	limitation
amazed	develop	abolish	sundry	pretext
silent	considered	trucker	capillary	intrigue
improved	behaved	elementary	blight	immaculate
certainly	splendid	comment	wrest	ascent
entered	acquainted	necessity	enumerate	acrid
realized	escaped	gallery	daunted	binocular
interruption	grim	relatively	condescend	embarkment

Grade 9	Grade 10	Grade 11
conscientious	zany	galore
isolation	jerkin	rotunda
molecule	nausea	capitalism
ritual	gratuitous	prevaricate
momentous	linear	risible
vulnerable	inept	exonerate
kinship	legality	superannuate
conservatism	amnesty	piebald
inventive	barometer	crunch

A student's score on this test answers the important question "How much of this student's apparent reading problem is caused by lack of word decoding skills?" Students whose instructional levels are well below their school grades should be referred for remediation. If no such services are available in the school, parents should be consulted. Chapter 10 provides several activities for working with such students. Too often reading problems go unnoticed in middle and senior high school simply because they are misinterpreted as lack of basic ability, poor motivation, or behavior problems. If students' instructional levels on this task are at or above their grades—meaning that their decoding skills are adequate—the teacher can refer to the suggestions for instruction listed in the discussion of the cloze test.

In the next section, we turn from teachers' assessments of students to students' self-assessments. It has been said that the mark of an educated person is his or her willingness to lead an "examined" life. The next strategy, self-appraisal, helps foster this introspective attitude in students in a nonthreatening way.

Self-Appraisal

Self-appraisal cannot substitute for formal testing. Jason and Dubnow (1973) compared the scores on the Self-Report Reading Scale and subtests of the Iowa Tests of Basic Skills. The results indicated statistically "significant, although not high, relationships between self-perceptions of reading abilities and 'vocabulary' and 'comprehension.' " Nonetheless, self-appraisal seems justified as a complementary form of testing, because it draws attention to self-examination and evaluative thinking, two critical elements in promoting progress toward reading maturity. Figure 3.9 presents a sample self-appraisal inventory.

Figure 3.9   Reading Self-Appraisal Inventory

	Always	Most of the Time	Seldom	Never
1. I understand most of what I read in my textbooks.				
2. I can usually understand new words in my textbooks.				
3. It is easy for me to pronounce new words.				
4. I read my textbook as rapidly as I think I should.				
5. I read as well as most of my classmates.				
6. I read more books than most of my classmates.				
7. It is easy for me to learn new ideas by reading.				
8. I easily remember information I have read.				
9. I can locate information I need by using library sources.				
10. Most people understand what I write				

Source: Betty L. Criscoe/Thomas C. Gee, *CONTENT READING: A Diagnostic/Prescriptive Approach,* © 1984, p. 83. Reprinted by permission of Prentice-Hall, Inc., Englewood Cliffs, New Jersey.

WHY ASSESS? (THIS TIME SERIOUSLY)

A Basic Rationale

If you've been forming some thoughts about "why assess?", you should be ready to hear some of the classical and contemporary reasons for doing so. The traditional—and current—reason for assessment, blunt as it may sound, is to grade and classify students into As, Bs, Cs, and so on. Formerly, the purpose of assessment was to try to predict those students who were most likely to fail and, therefore, were not worth the time, energy, and resources it would take to educate them. Fortunately, contemporary educators have tended to focus on more enlightened objectives. Bloom, Hastings, and Madaus (1971) have pointed out five goals of assessment:

1. To acquire and interpret evidence needed to improve learning and teaching
2. To obtain process information to be added to the usual final (or product-oriented) examination
3. To clarify the significant goals and objectives of education as reflected in student progress
4. To obtain a quality control measure to determine whether each step of the instructional process has been working or needs to be changed
5. To acquire a way to compare and contrast alternative teaching procedures

Do these sound like the ideas you came up with? If so, you are thinking very soundly when compared with this professional standard. These five reasons for assessment were considered progressive in the 1960s and 1970s and in fact formed the basis for the "mastery learning" movement. Because this notion still holds considerable sway, we will now consider it in greater detail.

Mastery Learning: Testing the Limits of Testing?

Prior to the advent of **mastery learning,** the prevailing sentiment was that "not *all* students could learn what schools and teachers desire to teach or achieve" (Levin & Long, 1981, p. 561). Bloom's (1976) more progressive view was simple and hope inspiring: If teachers or curriculum developers could identify the cognitive prerequisites (skills and knowledge) and "affective entry" characteristics (attitudes, interests, and level of self-concept) necessary for learning, they could ensure that all students would possess these and, therefore, a "greater majority (75% by one estimate) could be expected to achieve at roughly the same high levels attained by only the best students" (Bloom, Hastings, & Modares, 1971, p. 47).

Frequent assessment became the hallmark of mastery learning. The supportive "how-to's," however, have been less publicized. Following are the key instructional operations that are as essential as assessment to a successful mastery learning program:

1. Thoughtful *selection* of instructional areas
2. Adequate and sensitive use of *alternative patterns* of instruction

3. Appropriate *sequence* of instruction
4. Timing of *transition* from one activity to the next
5. Rational and sensitive definition of the *performance standard*
6. Careful use of *reinforcements* and rewards
7. *High expectations* among teachers that students will achieve

Bloom and his followers believed, in sum, that the key to teaching anything effectively is to have a view of the final model and to pursue it *one step at a time*, checking the results of each instructional step and *reteaching* each step as needed until it has been mastered. Bloom points out that one gets a "glimpse of the great power of pedagogy" when one realizes that every day millions of students are taught ideas such as Einstein's theory of relativity and DNA genetic coding that but a generation ago only a few could understand.

Some professionals strongly believe that in practice, Bloom's mastery learning principles have tended to reduce instructional goals to product-oriented objectives to the detriment of process-oriented instruction. Bloom certainly did not—and does not—intend this, but such programs often seem to produce this effect. Many educators feel that the problem with current assessment practices is simply that we test too much and place too much emphasis on testing. Another view, discussed in the following section, is that currently we test, and therefore emphasize, the wrong things.

EMERGING ASSESSMENT OPTIONS

> The examiner pipes and the teacher must dance—and the examiner sticks to the old tune. If the educational reformers really wish the dance altered they must turn their attention from the dancers to the musician. (H. G. Wells, 1892, in Valencia & Pearson, 1987, p. 382)

The power of the examiner is a long-standing and deeply rooted issue in education. In this section, we present a few recent efforts that address this problem. With the magnitude of such efforts rapidly increasing, it seems wise for the young professional to be alerted and for the veteran teacher to begin to formulate an informed and thoughtful position on these matters.

Toward the Measurement of Strategic Reading

Valencia and Pearson (1987) have emphasized that the influence of testing is greater now than at any time in history. As evidence, they point to the "accountability" movement and the fact that effective school research focuses almost exclusively on standardized test scores, with a proportionate increase in minimum competency and norm- and criterion-referenced testing. They note that at least 40 states have instituted competency testing programs on top of the thousands of locally regulated criterion-referenced tests that accompany basal reading programs and countless school and teacher tests.

This morass of testing would be less disturbing were it not for the fact that our understanding of the reading process has taken on a new dimension. The logic of mastery learning, which so strongly influenced teaching and testing in the 1960s and 1970s, is rapidly being replaced with the interactive model of the reading process. Where mastery learning stresses careful selection of content, the interactive model emphasizes the active role of readers as they use print to construct meaning. In this latter view, effective readers use personal strategies to make use of available resources such as text markers, prior knowledge, environmental clues, and other potential cue options to make sense out of text. Effective assessment, according to Valencia and Pearson, should reflect this view of reading as an interactive process by checking students' use of reading strategies rather than continuing to base assessment solely on students' ability to respond accurately to factual and simple inferential questions about a short passage.

Formats for Testing Strategic Reading

Drawing on the resources of the Center for the Study of Reading and their pilot work with 15,000 students, Valencia and Pearson are developing a variety of novel test formats. One distinguishing feature of these tests is that students read entire sections excerpted from authentic text rather than short passages. Following are some of the test formats they are developing at the time of this writing.

Summary Writing.   Students read summaries of the same selection written by other students and pick the one they think is best. In one version of this format, they get a list of features of summaries and check off the reasons for their choice.

Metacognitive Judgments.   Students are asked to perform a task associated with the selection they have read, such as retelling it to different audiences (peer, younger child, teacher). Or they may be asked to rate the helpfulness of several different retellings for a certain audience.

Question Selection.   Students pick 10 out of 20 questions that they think will help a peer best understand the important ideas about the selection.

Multiple Acceptable Responses.   In a discussion format, students select all responses to questions that they find plausible. In a related format, they grade responses as "really complete," "on the right track," or "totally off base" (much as a teacher grades short-answer or essay responses).

Prior Knowledge.   Two machine-scorable formats are used to assess prior knowledge. In one, students predict (yes/no/maybe) whether certain ideas are likely to be included in a selection on a specified topic. In the other, they rate the relevance of vocabulary terms to a central concept of the selection.

To date, the most ambitious effort to change conventional assessment currently is taking place in Michigan. In a rare spirit of cooperation among educational entities, the State Education Association and the Michigan Reading Association have jointly adopted a revised position on reading testing and developed a set of innovative testing formats.

New Directions in Statewide Reading Assessment

The rationale behind Michigan's innovative testing program is that reading tests should conform to a new definition of the reading process, namely that "reading is the process of constructing meaning through the dynamic interaction among the reader, the text, and the context of the reading situation" (Wixson, Peters, Weber, & Roeber, 1987, p. 750). This new definition "is in contrast to the view implied by Michigan's previous objectives and tests that reading is a series of sequential and hierarchial skills" (Wixson et al., 1987). Accordingly, the new Michigan tests measure objectives in three categories: constructing meaning, knowledge about reading, and attitudes and self-perceptions.

There are three particularly striking and refreshing features of the Michigan blueprint. One is that the difficulty level of the test selections will be determined not by a simple formula (the currently prevailing method) but by factors such as how well the text is structured, its literary merit, the print aids provided (headings, illustrations, etc.), and the consistency of the text with the knowledge area it represents. The second noteworthy innovation concerns students' perceptions of the task. Students are asked to describe the difficulty of the material and its questions, as well as how well they think they understood the selection and answered the questions. The third feature—and potentially the one of most practical value—is that the new tests are slated to be reported in a way that describes each reader's performance under specified conditions: the reader's familiarity with the topic, the type of text, and the reader's level of interest.

The authors of this text also have participated in research and efforts to more appropriately measure reading progress. To enable you to follow the logic of these efforts, it is necessary to say something about our frame of reference. You will not be surprised to find that it is quite consistent with the other educational goals and methods you are reading about in this text.

Toward Broad-Spectrum Assessment

The authors' efforts have been based largely on the need for a means to gain a more comprehensive view of the *reader* as well as of his or her reading ability. Simply stated, our position is that a broad spectrum of factors can inhibit or promote progress toward language, reading, thinking, and social-emotional maturity. Assessment of these factors should be laid out in profile fashion so as to permit a more holistic look at how a student is developing in reading and related areas. To this end, we have assembled an array of 15 experimental subtests called the *ALARM (Assessment of Language and Reading Maturity) battery.*

The development of broad-spectrum assessment has been delayed by technical and logistical problems despite the fact that it has been done informally, mostly through teachers' anecdotal records, in years past. Criticisms, again by measurement specialists (who rarely work in school settings), of the "subjectiveness" of anecdotal information have obscured the valuable insights such information offers. Further, professionals in the mushrooming fields of "psychometrics" and counseling have insisted that teachers should not dabble in the complex issues of assessing social-emotional development (which makes one wonder how such information will in fact be used). Still another roadblock has been the warnings of test specialists and psychologists that intelligence cannot be measured precisely and therefore we certainly cannot assess the even more elusive factors of critical-creative thinking and cultural advantage and disadvantage. All of these barriers have left educators, since the days of anecdotal records, with little more than standardized measures such as the Iowa Test of Basic Skills as the only tune to which to dance.

Dangers of a Single Tune

There are dangers in single-factor testing, which are best illustrated with another analogy: assessing the fitness of the family car by checking only the oil. A car's oil level can be measured quite accurately by inserting an oil stick into the pan below the engine block. This measurement gives a reasonably accurate diagnosis of the auto's "health." Given a large sample of cars, it correlates well with the car's age, performance, and even looks, although strictly speaking these factors are not related. Due to the strength of this correlation, we might conclude that more standard and precise measurements of the same type would increase accuracy even further in assessing and caring for the family car. More care might include procedures such as noting the car's last oil change and/or making sure to check the oil only after the engine has been shut down for several minutes to allow the oil to settle in the pan. Further, more sophisticated oil sticks could be designed. For example, they could contain more and finer lines to more accurately measure smaller quantities of oil loss. Or state-of-the-art engineering could be called upon to produce an electronic digital readout stick. However, it would take a much more elaborate and expensive piece of equipment to indicate the next most evident thing about oil: that it is dark and dirty. This simple observation, which most car owners could make, attains an even higher level of value in the hands of a competent service attendant. This person can tell from touch such things as whether the oil has lost its viscosity (slipperiness) and whether the dirt contains grit and possibly metal and therefore indicates dangerous engine wear. However, even an expert mechanic's observations of the oil would not reveal whether the brakes might soon fail, or the transmission begin to slip, or the radiator overheat, or the carburetor sputter.

The premise of broad-spectrum assessment, then, is simply that some youngsters "drive through" school with carefully and regularly measured "oil levels," but their "brakes" or "transmissions" may be failing, and even a cursory look at these, especially by a teacher with a keen eye, is better than no look at all.

Recently a major publisher made funds available to the Center for Studies in Higher Order Literacy at the University of Missouri–Kansas City to continue development of more sensitive, process-oriented reading tests such as those in the ALARM experimental battery, described next.

ALARM Experimental Battery

The *ALARM battery* has been administered and partially normed on approximately 800 urban and suburban youngsters between grades 6 and 12. The tests were designed to permit group administration. The current battery requires approximately 2¼ hours to administer. To avoid unnecessary redundancy, virtually any standardized reading test can be used in place of the explicit measures of reading—subtests 1, 2, and 6.

Overview.   The 15 subtests and total score in the current ALARM battery can be clustered in a variety of ways to answer questions from different perspectives. Figure 3.10 illustrates how these subtests can be clustered to obtain subscores for functional literacy, developmental literacy, and higher-order literacy. It also provides a brief description of each subtest. For more complete information about the ALARM subtests, as well as sample items, see Appendix C.

Chapter 8 on critical-creative reading looks at four common reader profiles that can be identified through use of the ALARM battery. To provide the teacher with additional help in seeing into and beyond the most superficial features of students, some educators—ourselves included—are beginning to believe that it may be necessary and proper for teachers to delve more deeply into students' personality organizations and motivational sets. This interest is intensifying with the increasing incidence of violence and suicide among school-age youngsters.

Personality and Motivation

Murky Matters

In general, many educators have been reluctant to assess—and, in some cases, even discuss—deeper elements of human motivation such as those derived from temperament and personality. This stems in part from our having come through a long period of domination of the allied field of psychology by cognitive and operant-conditioning psychologists with a penchant for writing entire books on human learning without reference to motivation, personality, or temperament.

Cognitive and operant-conditioning psychologists view these factors as "murky" and attempt to avoid them in experimental research. It is difficult, however, to evaluate research about human learning that ignores personality and motivational factors, for it is impossible to ignore them in real-life school situations. "Real" youngsters simply will not be treated as though they were heads suspended in beakers.

In writing about the "psychology of tomorrow," the preeminent motivational researchers Atkinson and Raynor (1978) noted that experimental psychology has managed to survive "with a white labcoat and without either noticing or doing much about the fact that 'people often react in diametrically opposite ways, not merely in different degrees, to the same . . . treatments' " (p. 240). They went on to say that they expect psychology eventually will reintegrate the "study of individual differences and basic behavioral processes."

There are three rather compelling reasons to know something about individual student differences from the personality/temperament point of view:

• Such factors influence how one understands and interprets what one reads, hears, and experiences.

Figure 3.10 ALARM Subtest Descriptions in Three Literacy Domains

Functional Literacy

Three ALARM subtests measure basic reading skills:

Subtest 1:   *Word Recognition.* Show recognition of simple words by picking an opposite word.

Subtest 2:   *Vocabulary.* Identify more difficult word meanings by selecting synonyms.

Subtest 6:   *Comprehension.* Read a passage silently, and answer questions about its content.

Developmental Literacy

Three ALARM subtests measure basic thinking skills:

Subtest 3:   *Analogies.* Select the best words to fill blanks in incomplete analogies.

Subtest 8:   *Abstract Comprehension.* Select the most general meanings of proverbs.

Subtest 9:   *Elaborative Thinking.* Rate the degree to which you prefer each of several critiques of a short passage.

Two ALARM subtests measure language sophistication:

Subtest 4:   *Complex Sentences.* Identify the meanings of syntactically difficult sentences.

Subtest 5:   *Modified Cloze.* Select the best words to fill blanks in a passage.

One ALARM subtest measures prior knowledge:

Subtest 7:   *Fund of Information.* Select the best answers to general-information-type questions.

Higher-Order Literacy

Three ALARM subtests measure nonintellective factors:

Subtest 10: *Self-Construct Inventory.* Rate the degree to which you would most like to be various animals.

Subtest 11: *Teaching/Learning Range.* Rate the degree to which you would like to learn in different classroom situations.

Subtest 12: *School Compatibility.* Rate the degree to which you agree with statements about school, family, and students.

Three ALARM subtests measure critical-evaluative thinking:

Subtest 13: *Critical Judgments—Useful Information.* Judge the value to society of given facts.

Subtest 14: *Critical Judgments—Reasonableness.* Judge the reasonableness of given opinions.

Subtest 15: *Critical Judgments—Appreciation.* Make a variety of judgments about facts and phrases in a continuous passage.

Total ALARM score = index of progress toward reading, language thinking, and personal-social maturity

♦ An adjustment in teaching methodology may be called for to optimize, or at least correct, a serious inhibition to student learning.

♦ Classroom sanity and discipline are always at stake when you are in an environment in which a gentle stroke to one student can be a sharp poke to another.

If and when you are personally ready to begin collecting information on your students, you might to look into two easy-to-administer instruments: the Luscher Color Test (tr. by Scott, 1969) and the Bestiary (animal identification) Inventory (Manzo, 1975).

A Word of Caution

Should you decide to talk to youngsters or their parents or other teachers about your findings, be sure to stress that you used these instruments as eye-opening tools to get a purchase on students and their needs. Clearly you will need to further verify, refute, or add to your test findings with specific examples of observed behavior and/or with information derived from other tests and other persons.

Some individuals are far more adept than others at characterizing and understanding human behavior. If this is not your long suit, it's fine to just forget about affective measurement. It would be better, however, to solicit the views of other teachers—and, of course, professional counselors and psychologists—in attempting to understand your students and their needs. In any case, one need not be trained in psychology to teach and provide for students in ways that are both academically and emotionally nourishing. Later in this chapter, we present several methodologies that put this objective within easy reach of almost any caring teacher.

Turning now from the difficult issue of personality assessment, the complex but far more manageable matter of assessing the difficulty level of textual material will appear refreshingly simple. When text difficulty level is known, it is easier to decide whether or not a textbook is appropriate for a certain group of students and which level of instructional assistance will best help students learn from a particular text.

ASSESSING TEXT DIFFICULTY

Readability Formulas

The difficulty level of a text is referred to as the text's **readability.** Historically junior and senior high school texts have been written with more concern for content than for difficulty level. A 10th-grade American history text, for example, might have a readability of grade 12. This has begun to change in recent years as members of school district text selection committees have started including readability as a major criterion by which to evaluate potential new textbooks.

Readability depends on a number of factors, including the influence of print size, number and quality of pictures, and even an individual student's level of interest in the subject area. The greatest influence by far, however, comes from two simple factors: average sentence length and word difficulty. The most commonly used procedures for estimating readability are formulas that employ these two factors in one way or another.

The earliest procedures developed for estimating readability with formulas were based on the number of words in a given 100-word passage that were not on a list of "easy words." This "hard-word" count was entered into a mathematical formula along with the average sentence length and several "constant numbers" (numbers that were provided with the formula). Solution of the formula yielded a grade level readability index (Dale & Chall, 1948; Spache, 1953).

Simplified readability procedures, such as those described in the following section, eliminated the need to compare every word in a passage against an "easy-word" list. This painstaking process of word comparison was shown to have a strong correlation with the results of simpler measures of word difficulty such as total number of syllables in a passage (Fry, 1968, 1977), number of words of three syllables or more (Gunning, 1979; McLaughlin, 1969), or simply number of words containing six or more letters (Raygor, 1977).

Two commonly used readability formulas are detailed next, primarily to illustrate the process rather than suggest that teachers should regularly undertake even these abbreviated analyses by hand. It can be enlightening, however, to do a text analysis by hand, especially if no other means is available. The second author was surprised when first applying a readability formula to samples from a seventh-grade literature textbook. The selections varied widely in difficulty, and some were far above the students' level.

Raygor's Readability Graph

Alton Raygor (1977) provided a reliable simplification of Fry's earlier graph-based technique. Raygor's procedure, illustrated in Figure 3.11, uses the number of words containing six or more letters and the average sentence length of three passages of 100 words each to estimate a text's difficulty. Baldwin and Kaufman (1979) found the Raygor formula faster than and as accurate as the Fry formula. (The Fry formula is available on computer disk from Jamestown Publishers, Rhode Island.)

Gunning's FOG Index

In another simple procedure for estimating readability, Gunning (1979) used the average number of words per sentence and number of words of three or more syllables. Figure 3.12 illustrates the step-by-step procedure.

However, even these simplified formulas for estimating readability are time consuming to do manually. Fortunately, a wide variety of computer software is now available for obtaining readability estimates on textbook excerpts. This is much more realistic in terms of time and elimination of the "human error" inevitable with lengthy syllable/word counting and calculating. For more information on commercially available computer readability programs, see Mason and Blanchard (1979) and Mason, Blanchard, and Daniel (1987).

Subjective Readability Measures

Experienced teachers' judgments generally differ little from readability estimates obtained from using formulas, whether hand calculated or computer generated. A

Figure 3.11   Raygor's Readability Graph Technique

1. Count out three 100-word passages at the beginning, middle, and end of a selection or book. Count proper nouns but not numerals.
2. Count sentences in each passage, estimating to nearest the tenth.
3. Count words with six or more letters.
4. Average the sentence length and word length over three samples, and plot the average on the graph.

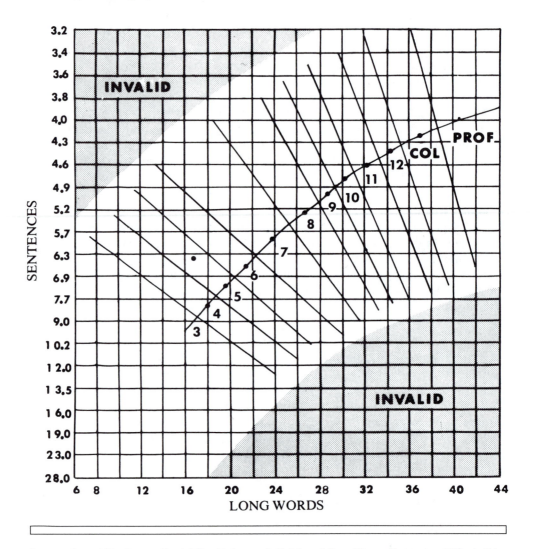

Source: From ''The Raygor Readability Estimate: A Quick and Easy Way to Determine Difficulty'' by A. L. Raygor, in *Reading: Theory, Research and Practice*, edited by P. D. Pearson, 1977, Clemson, SC: National Reading Conference.

Figure 3.12 Steps in Obtaining a FOG Index

1. Select a sample of 100 words.
2. Find the average sentence length (100 divided by number of sentences).
3. Count the number of words of three syllables or more. (Do not count proper nouns, easy compound words like *bookkeeper*, or verb forms in which the third syllable is merely the ending, for example, *directed*.)
4. Add average sentence length to the number of hard words.
5. Multiply the sum by .4. This gives the FOG index.

Summary: FOG = number of hard words + average words per sentence × .4

veteran teacher's subjective assessment of text difficulty has the added advantage of drawing on a range of very important factors that mathematical formulas do not account for. Concept density, for example, may make a passage quite difficult even if it uses short sentences and easy words. Poetry, plays, science fiction, and legal documents are just some writing forms that require a high proportion of think time relative to read time. The particular interests of a grade level or group of students is another factor that teachers can account for in their subjective readability assessments. The content area teacher will also recognize that students will already have encountered certain difficult or multisyllabic words. These and other even more subtle language factors can be synthesized subjectively to estimate difficulty level. Two techniques in particular have been developed to guide such analyses: readability checklists and passage comparisons.

Readability Checklists
Checklists to guide subjective readability estimates do not necessarily yield a grade level readability estimate. They do, however, indicate whether a given book is appropriate for a particular group of students. Checklists are most effective when several teachers rate the same material and then average (or otherwise compare) their judgments. A group of teachers from a given content area may wish to develop their own checklist that addresses specific content concerns.

One general list by Harker (1977) includes the following items, to which the rater responds with a particular group of students in mind:

1. Are the concepts far beyond the students' direct experiences?
2. Are abstract concepts linked to examples and situations that are familiar to students?
3. Are technical terms defined in context as they appear?
4. Does one idea lead logically to another?
5. What does the author assume about the students' previous learning experiences?
6. Are textbook aids provided?

7. Is the material appealing, or does it look too "textbookish"?
8. Is the writing brief, concise, and to the point?

A second subjective readability checklist is presented in Chapter 6 on guiding silent reading. It is offered at that point to help you pull together some further technical information on understanding, appraising, and dealing with text difficulty.

Passage Comparisons

Passage comparison techniques also can be used to estimate the readability level of materials. The material to be rated is simply compared with a set of sample passages that exemplify typical material for a particular grade level. Two of the better known passage comparison instruments are Carver's Rauding Scale (1975–76) and Singer's (1975) SEER (Singer Eyeball Estimate of Readability). Each of these instruments provides a set of graded sample passages and directions for their use. The directions for using Carver's Rauding Scale, for example, specify three factors to be considered when comparing passages: (1) how common the words are; (2) how complex the ideas are; and (3) how involved the sentences are. Singer suggests that at least two raters' estimates should be averaged to determine a reliable readability level.

Each of the readability techniques described so far—formulas, checklists, and passage comparisons—can be used to *indirectly* match students with reading materials by comparing students' test scores with readability results. The Standard Cloze Passage test described earlier can provide a *direct* measure of student/text compatibility.

Direct Matching of Student Reading Ability with Text Difficulty: Cloze (Again!)

The Standard Cloze Passage test described earlier in the chapter is as much a readability strategy as it is a measure of students' reading ability. It does not yield a grade level estimate of the difficulty of a given text, but it does predict how well a particular student or group of students will be able to read and learn from it. Hittleman (1978) pointed out that "cloze measures readability whereas other means predict text difficulty." He also noted that "the cloze procedure is the only available procedure which can take into account, in a natural setting, the constraints of the language system of the reading matter, the reading ability and other characteristics of the reader, and the background information needed by the reader." In other words, there are two ways to compare your students' reading levels with your textbook's readability level. One is to compare students' standardized reading test scores to a formula-based readability estimate on the text. Another is to give a Standard Cloze Passage test using a portion of the text. The Standard Cloze Passage test permits a direct comparison using a single measure.

CHAPTER TIE-UPS

Graphic Organizer   ◆◆◆

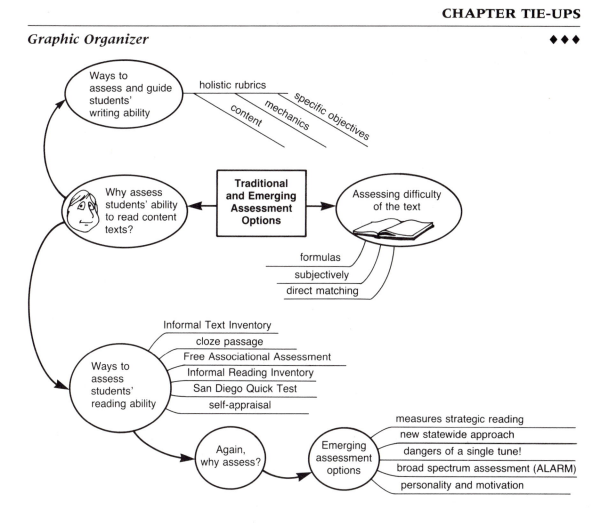

TRADE SECRET

Know Thyself

It is an axiom of professional education that to know others, you must first know yourself. To reach this lush island of self-knowledge, however, one must navigate through the reefs of self-examination. This can be particularly formidable because, as the German writer Herman Hesse put it, "Nothing . . . is so distasteful to man as to go the way which leads him to himself" (1949).

When you are up to facing this lifelong process (or, dare we say, struggle), you might wish to try the impulsivity-stability scale. This instrument is particularly useful for revealing factors that bear on teaching and learning.

The Impulsivity-Stability Scale originally was abstracted by Smith (1967) from two scales of the widely used Minnesota Multiphasic Personality Inventory. This author used it as a learning styles inventory in his college developmental reading text *Learning to Learn*. Figure 3.13 presents a slightly modified version of the Impulsivity-Stability Scale and a scoring guide.

Figure 3.13   Impulsivity-Stability Scale and Scoring Guide

Directions: There are no right or wrong answers to the following questions. Indicate your responses by marking Y (yes), N (no), or ? (not sure) in the space before each question. A few questions require an "a" or "b" answer. Do not spend time "pondering" questions. You should mark an item ? (not sure) only when it is impossible to say yes or no. Be sure to answer every question.

_____ 1. Are you good at repartee, quick retorts, and snap judgments?
_____ 2. When you meet someone new, do you usually start the conversation?
_____ 3. Are you inclined to express your thoughts without much hesitation?
_____ 4. Are you apt to say things you may regret later rather than keep still?
_____ 5. Do you think much and speak little?
_____ 6. Do you get very excited by new ideas and new people?
_____ 7. Would you say that you have (a) many friends or (b) just a few friends?
_____ 8. Do you often find yourself making comments to a friend while listening to a lecture or watching a movie?
_____ 9. In discussion, do you think better when you are challenged to defend your position?
_____ 10. Would you rather take (a) an oral test or (b) a written test?
_____ 11. Does it irritate you to listen to someone who speaks slowly?
_____ 12. Do you recover your emotions rapidly after a sudden upset?
_____ 13. Are you inclined to be quick and a little careless in your actions?
_____ 14. Would you rather talk than listen in a social situation?
_____ 15. Can you turn out a large amount of work in a short time if you are under pressure?
_____ 16. Do you usually start to work on a new academic subject with a great amount of enthusiasm?
_____ 17. Do you hesitate to volunteer remarks in class?
_____ 18. Do you quickly form larger concepts from a few disconnected ideas?
_____ 19. Do you find that your recall of past conversations is more accurate than that of most of your friends?
_____ 20. Do you usually find that you understand a complex situation with a minimum of explanation?
_____ 21. Do you tend to be submissive and apologetic (a) often or (b) seldom?
_____ 22. Are you likely to complain about your suffering and hardships?
_____ 23. Do you sometimes have a feeling of fear as though you had done something wrong?
_____ 24. Do you often have trouble falling asleep at night?
_____ 25. Do people tell you you worry unnecessarily?

_____ 26. Do you become discouraged when things go wrong?
_____ 27. Are you usually tired when you get up in the morning?
_____ 28. Do you have nightmares (a) seldom or (b) often?
_____ 29. Do you usually have a feeling of being able to handle minor crises?
_____ 30. Do you sometimes feel that life would be happier if people only treated you better?
_____ 31. Do you sometimes perspire or feel tense without any reason?
_____ 32. Do you think of yourself sometimes as neglected and unloved?
_____ 33. Would you say that one is wise to be very careful about whom one trusts?
_____ 34. Are your ideas generally well organized and systematic?
_____ 35. Are you frequently troubled by pangs of conscience?
_____ 36. Are you often concerned that you may not have done right in social situations?
_____ 37. Do you feel sometimes that people disapprove of you?
_____ 38. Is the control of your emotions (a) easy or (b) difficult?
_____ 39. Are you easily discouraged when people make fun of you?
_____ 40. Are there times when you can't help feeling sorry for yourself?

Impulsivity-Stability Scoring Guide

Stability Scale

	I	II
	high stability high impulsivity	high stability low impulsivity
Impulsivity Scale	low stability high impulsivity IV	low stability low impulsivity III

Key: These are not "right" answers, but just put a check beside the numbers where this answer is the same as yours. A total score of 0 to 8 is considered a "low" score; 9 to 11 is "moderate"; 12 to 20 is "high."

1. Yes	11. Yes	21. b	31. No
2. Yes	12. Yes	22. No	32. No
3. Yes	13. Yes	23. No	33. No
4. Yes	14. Yes	24. No	34. Yes
5. No	15. Yes	25. No	35. No
6. Yes	16. Yes	26. No	36. No
7. a	17. No	27. No	37. No
8. Yes	18. Yes	28. a	38. a
9. Yes	19. No	29. Yes	39. No
10. a	20. Yes	30. No	40. No

Total, Items 1–20 _____   Total, Items 21–40 _____
   (Impulsivity Score)   (Stability Score)

Interpretation of the I-S Scale

With no other factors taken into account, here is what placement in each quadrant tends to mean:

Quadrant I: High stability/high impulsivity. Quick thinking; secure; gregarious; appetitively or intrinsically motivated; executive type; tends to like social studies

Quadrant II: High stability/low impulsivity. Secure; reserved and methodical; accountant type; tends to like math, grammar, and literature

Quadrant III: Low stability/low impulsivity. Worries a great deal; tends to be fear motivated (motivated by what you don't want to happen); also may appear either apathetic or standoffish; librarian type; tends to like literature, art history, crafts, and repetitive tasks

Quadrant IV: Low stability/high impulsivity. Worries a great deal; given to exaggeration; driven but seldom able to satisfy needs; salesperson type; preference for subject is greatly influenced by who is teaching it

In general, scores between 9 and 11 constitute an indefinite range. In all probability, the two factors this scale measures simply are not critical factors in your life. But that's the way it is with most learning-style factors: important when they are definitive and largely meaningless otherwise.

♦ ♦ ♦   *Critique and Anticipation*

This chapter offered a broad range of options for considering and conducting assessment in the context of the content area classroom. It described traditional options for assessing students' reading, text management, and writing skills. These were followed by two categories of emerging options: (1) test formats for assessing students' strategic reading skills and (2) a broad-spectrum battery of tests for assessing students as readers and thinkers as well as accumulators of skills. Finally, the chapter turned from student assessment to text assessment and provided a tour of available means for assessing the difficulty level of printed material.

This chapter concludes Part One. The next chapter begins the core section, which includes four chapters on the comprehension process. Reading comprehension is one of the most complex areas of human learning. As you read more about this process and how to promote it, you will likely come to a fuller appreciation of the emerging efforts to develop more insightful models and instruments for comprehension assessment that this chapter described.

PART TWO

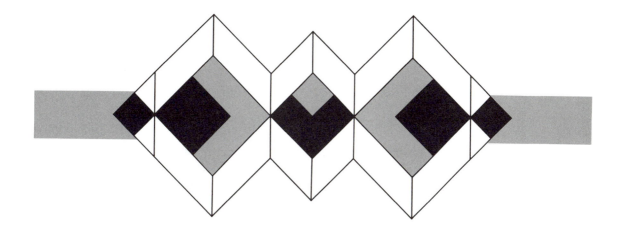

Instructional
Framework for
Comprehending Text

Total Lesson Designs

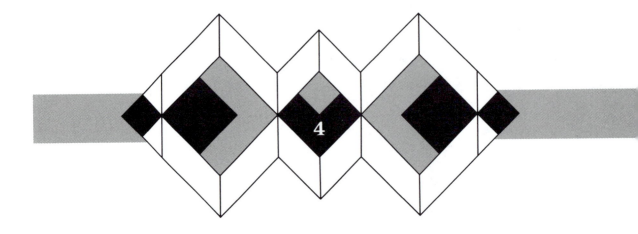

Theories of Comprehension and Cooperative Lesson Designs

Great discoveries and improvements invariably involve the cooperation of many minds.

— Alexander Graham Bell

FOCUS

Mature comprehension, the focus of this and the next five chapters, refers to the attainment of full understanding from text—from literal-level understanding to interpretive levels to critical, applied, and creative levels. This chapter presents eight theories of comprehension and six general principles of quality instruction. Then it offers six Total Lesson Designs. One of these, the Directed Reading-Thinking Activity, is acknowledged as a master plan for most other strategies and practices in content area reading. Two of the other designs are based on cooperative learning approaches.

OUTLINE

THEORIES OF COMPREHENSION

The Value of Theories ◆ Background: Comprehension as Guided Problem Solving ◆ Eight Constructs That Guide Efforts to Improve Reading Comprehension ◆ Overarching Features of Quality Instruction

TOTAL LESSON DESIGNS

An Instructional Framework: Prereading, Guided Silent Reading, and Postreading ◆ Medial Checkup and Review ◆ Design 1: The Directed Reading-Thinking Activity ◆ Design 2: Structured Overview ◆ Design 3: The Guided Reading Procedure ◆ Design 4: K-W-L Plus

COOPERATIVE LEARNING DESIGNS

Fostering Cooperative Learning ◆ Guidelines for Small-Group Work in the Classroom ◆ Design 5: The Group Reading Activity ◆ Design 6: Cooperative DR-TA

CHAPTER TIE-UPS

Graphic Organizer ◆ Trade Secret: Insider Information

THEORIES OF COMPREHENSION

The Value of Theories

If there is a single element of student progress that all educators agree is important, it is reading comprehension. As youngsters learn to comprehend, they gain the ability to learn from printed material as well as from spoken language. This gives them access to an infinite number of "teachers." It also permits them to verify and extend what they are taught.

Effective reading comprehension is as much an end product of doing things correctly in school as it is a means of getting things done, or learned, correctly. The next four chapters deal with comprehension instruction in some very explicit and practical ways. This chapter begins with a brief account of some of the theoretical issues regarding how we comprehend and how to teach comprehension. Good theory is always practical. Often good theory is simply the articulation of understandings that have evolved from effective practices, that is, taken a "bottom-up" route. At other times, theoretical ideas have suggested new and effective practices—a "top-down" route. In either case, the ideas will be helpful to you in applying the instructional tools of the trade.

The purpose and power of an effective theory can be illustrated with a real-life example. Some time ago, the first author became acquainted with a fellow junior high school teacher, Frank, who had a side business as an air conditioning and refrigerator repairperson. Frank was respected, if not revered, by a large and wealthy clientele on Long Island's North Shore because he often could "fix" air conditioning problems that were not covered in the manufacturer's repair manual or lay not in the machine itself but somewhere in its operating environment. You see, Frank was a science teacher. He understood the theoretical underpinnings of cooling in addition to the mechanics of coolers. Let's now examine the comprehension process and how to "fix" poor comprehension so that we may become more than manual-controlled repairpeople.

Background: Comprehension as Guided Problem Solving

The scientific basis for the study of the comprehension process began around World War I with a study designed to demonstrate that acquiring understanding from reading was far more than the simple act of reading words. Edward L. Thorndike, one of the most eminent educational psychologists of the twentieth century, made the following observation:

> Understanding a paragraph is like solving a problem in mathematics. It consists in selecting the right elements of the situation and putting them together in the right relations, and also with the right amount of weight or influence or force for each. The mind is assailed as it were by every word in the paragraph. It must select, repress, soften, emphasize, correlate and organize, all under the influence of the right mental set or purpose or demand. (Thorndike, 1917, pp. 327–328)

In this single paragraph, Thorndike makes it clear that comprehension is a process of interacting with text and that to do so effectively the reader must be attentive, analytical, purposeful, flexible, self-aware, world-aware, and socially and emotionally sound. The following section briefly summarizes some theories of reading comprehension that Thorndike's work set in motion. Before you review these theories, however, you may wish to attempt the activity described in Box 4.1. This activity illustrates the concept of a seemingly simple and natural process that has many contributing factors and is not easily explained.

Eight Constructs That Guide Efforts to Improve Reading Comprehension

There are eight *constructs,* or sets of ideas, that strike us as especially relevant to promoting effective comprehension in the content areas. Some of these are held by their major proponents as being at odds with certain others. We, however, view these constructs as mutually compatible, differing mainly in their emphases and perspectives on developing effective comprehenders. Each has been mentioned previously in some way, and each will be mentioned again in other portions of the text. These are complex ideas, and you probably will need to derive their meanings through repeated exposures in different contexts. The process you will go through in absorbing and trying to apply these ideas is analogous to what we ask students to do to master the rudiments of social studies, science, industrial arts, mathematics, literature, and so on. Again, use this opportunity to discover what *you* do to comprehend and learn. You might also think about what we as authors might reasonably have done to make things clearer—please feel free to write and tell us.

Psycholinguistic Theory
The *psycholinguistic theory* holds that all learning is driven by human beings' innate capacity to speak, reflect, and therefore seek meaning in everything they feel, see, and do. According to this idea, youngsters learn best when they are offered mean-

---

**BOX
4.1**

CONCEPT CLARIFICATION
The Comprehension Process

Why are there so many complex theories regarding reading comprehension? One way to get a sense of why comprehension development is complex (although manageable when you understand it) is to consider a metaphor: a simple plant.

Try to list everything you can think of as essential to raising a single, lush, *flowering* plant. Then check your list against the essentials listed at the end of this chapter. See if it doesn't suggest to you why it is necessary to know as much as possible about theories of comprehension even though your goal is simply to grow a few healthy plants.

ingful material, language experience stories, and opportunities to write rather than merely "sequentially ordered" skills exercises. Many researchers adhere to this theory structure, but Kenneth Goodman (1984) and Frank Smith (1978) have been its leading proponents. In some ways, the concept of "languaging in the content areas" is an upward extension of this initial reading approach to the intermediate, secondary, college, and adult levels.

Psycholinguistic theory should not be confused with linguistic theory. *Linguistic theory* deals primarily with how children learn to decode words. Contrary to psycholinguistic theory, it places a strong emphasis on phonics instruction and mastery learning. We discuss mastery learning next.

Reading Skills or Mastery Learning Theory

The **mastery learning theory** proposes that reading comprehension consists almost entirely of hierarchical sets of basic reading-specific skills such as word knowledge, organizational skills, use of context clues, and the ability to draw inferences (Davis, 1944). The theory suggests that reading maturity is attained by the sequential mastery of these basic skills objectives (Bloom, 1971). Early basal reader approaches were based on this view of comprehension and study skills instruction. Most modern basals have incorporated a greater emphasis on psycholinguistic theory and approaches. This is reflected in the fact that they tend to be literature based and closely integrated with the other language arts.

Substrata Factor Theory

The *substrata factor theory* holds that different "working systems" (skills, subskills, abilities, and inclinations) are called into play as one encounters material at various levels of difficulty and, therefore, at different levels, or stages, of progress in learning to read and then reading to learn. The authors of this theory (Holmes, 1953; Holmes & Singer, 1961) estimate that subtle factors such as attitudes, beliefs, and inclinations constitute approximately 30% of overall "power of reading." No single approach to reading embodies this theory, but the theory lends strong support to the need for continuous instruction throughout all stages of human development.

Content Area Reading Theory

Content area reading theory addresses the comprehension skills needed beyond the elementary grades for continued reading growth. The basis for this theory is an early study (Artley, 1944) that found a high correlation among 11th-grade students between general reading and social studies reading. Artley concluded that general reading skills would continue to improve if instruction were continued in each content area. The timing was right. This conclusion was waiting to be drawn, since an earlier meeting of leading educators had endorsed the proposition that "each teacher become a teacher of reading" (Gray, 1925).

Schema Theory

Schema is more a fundamental principle of knowing than a theory. It is referred to in various forms in the works of Aristotle, Plato, and Thomas Aquinas. The plural is *schemata,* but this form is seldom used in comtemporary writing. The developmental psychologist Piaget popularized the term *schema* in psychology and education: "Schemata are internal cognitive structures representing the real world. They have *concrete-sensory* and *motor* properties and *abstract relational* properties" (in Bourne, Eckstrand, & Dominowski, 1971, p. 251).

In terms of reading, schema theory proposes that one comprehends best what one already has understood and experienced in some way. One's "schemata" are the general theories of the world that one carries in his or her head and uses to interpret events (Smith, 1978). It includes prior knowledge (Anderson, 1970) and a sense of the language forms, logic, and organizational patterns that permit us to anticipate meaning from print. In narrative reading, for example, a child first learns to expect a story to contain a beginning, a middle, and an end. By the intermediate level, the student anticipates plot, theme, setting, and character. By the secondary level, the student typically can differentiate such complex structures as flashbacks, symbolism, irony, and satire (Tonjes & Zintz, 1987). The application of schema theory to reading has tended to exclude reference to its "concrete-sensory" and "motor" properties. We believe, however, that these are important dimensions of schema theory. To understand their potential practical implications for instruction, keep this idea in mind when you reach the sections on Motor Imaging (for vocabulary), Thinking Hats (for cognitive enrichment), and Note Cue (for comprehension and classroom participation training) in later chapters.

Metacognitive Theory

Metacognition simply means contemplating one's own thinking processes. It is based on self-knowledge, task knowledge, and self-monitoring, or "knowing when you know," "knowing what you know," "knowing what you need to know," and "knowing what can be done to improve the comprehension process" (Brown, Campione, & Day, 1981; Sanacore, 1984). Evidence in favor of this precept is strong though not unequivocal. Erickson, Stahl, and Rinehart (1985) report at least one researcher who has cast doubts on the strategic value of metacognition for reading. They found no differences between good and poor sixth-grade readers on three measures of metacognitive functioning. The application of the term *metacognitive* to reading, as defined above, is a relatively new one, probably created by researchers at the Center for the Study of Reading. The classical meaning of the term denotes transcending conventional thought to reach intuitive, or even metaphysical, levels of thinking.

Cognitive Processing Theory

Cognitive processing theory examines reading from the standpoint of systems for information acquisition and concept formation. The idea is to build thinking minds that read more than readers who think. With this reasoning, most reading problems are the result of cognitive dysfunctions rather than linguistic difficulties. Thus, you "fix" reading problems by first fixing cognitive processing difficulties. Word decoding problems, for example, stem from "successive processing" deficiencies and comprehension problems from "simultaneous processing" deficiencies (Leong &

Haines, 1978; Leong, 1980). In other words, reading skills are viewed as part of a broader class of cognitive skills (Crowder, 1982). Many of the methodologies recommended in this text line up comfortably within this model, although the theory does not fully explain the choices of methods offered. Because the reading process still is something of a mystery, it seems best to continue to construct and select methods from a combination of theoretical perspectives, experiences, ideologies, empirical findings, and a fair measure of intuition.

Trace Elements Theory

The **trace elements** theory says that progress toward reading maturity is best achieved when the educational "diet" includes nourishment in a wide array of subtle skills, abilities, attitudes, and inclinations. Many of these elements might seem unimportant in a quantitative analysis of reading comprehension, but they are essential to high-level functioning. "Trace elements" in education are viewed as being roughly analogous to the trace-level quantities of certain minerals, such as potassium and zinc, essential for healthy operation of the body and mind. Examples of specific educational trace elements include effective inquiry skills; abstract and elaborative thinking; ability to give and receive criticism; appropriate introspection, or self-examination; ability to work cooperatively with as well as against peer pressure; and social-emotional adjustment (Manzo & Casale, 1983). This theory suggests that every teacher should be as much a teacher of people as of content and/or reading or, continuing the metaphor, teach in ways that are academically, socially, and emotionally nourishing. See Chapter 14 on the "minor area" subjects for an example of the significance of this idea at a more general, curricular level.

You will find periodic reference to several of these theories when we discuss the various teaching strategies. Their significance should become clearer as you reconsider the theories in the context of practical applications. The same will be true for the overarching features of instruction, discussed next.

Overarching Features of Quality Instruction

There are several overarching features of effective general instruction that also apply to content area reading instruction. Six of these features are particularly relevant:

- Direct explanation
- Fading
- Engagement
- Modeling
- Reciprocity
- Cooperative learning

The **direct explanation** feature (Berliner & Rosenshine, 1976; Roehler & Duffy, 1984) is best summarized as four things a teacher must do to ensure effective instruction:

1. Explain the purpose of the procedure
2. Model its use
3. Provide opportunities for practice and feedback
4. Encourage independent transfer of the skill to new learning situations

Fading aids in building independence and transferring learning. The teacher accomplishes this by planning for the gradual "release of responsibility" for learning from the teacher to the student (Campione, 1981; Valencia & Pearson, 1987).

Engagement, modeling, and reciprocity are detailed further in the next chapter. Briefly, **engagement** is a concept derived from motivational and learning theories and involves getting and holding students' attention during instruction. **Modeling** is a means of teaching by "showing." It is particularly useful for teaching thinking behaviors employed before, during, and after effective reading. **Reciprocity** is a term used to describe teaching interactions in which students and teacher are encouraged to influence one another's thinking and the direction of instruction.

Cooperative learning is a means of encouraging collaboration among students. This idea is treated more fully later in the chapter.

These features of quality instruction have been woven into a number of effective strategies for prereading, guided silent reading, and postreading instruction. Figure 4.1 illustrates their relationships with a typical sequence of instruction.

The Total Lesson Designs described in the next section illustrate how these features have found expression in teaching practices and designs. You might wish to try the activity in Box 4.2 before turning to them. It will also be helpful to reread some of these ideas and theories after you have studied some of the applications covered later in the chapter.

Figure 4.1 Features of Quality Instruction

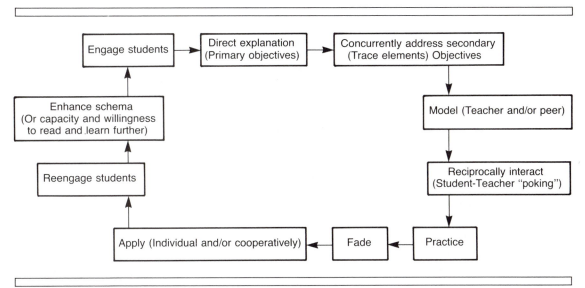

BOX 4.2

CONCEPT CLARIFICATION

Help with Content Area Reading—When and How Much?

To get a firmer grasp on the organization of the field of content area reading, ask yourself the following questions. Jot down and discuss your answers with a partner or group of classmates.

♦ In what subjects or realms do you read easily?
♦ Which subjects are troublesome and/or uninviting?
♦ Why do you feel the way you do?
♦ What could textbooks and teachers do to make reading in these realms more inviting?
♦ When and where would you like help with reading?
♦ Can you do anything to help yourself?

Now read on to see what options exist for providing help with text while teaching students to help themselves.

TOTAL LESSON DESIGNS

An Instructional Framework: Prereading, Guided Silent Reading, and Postreading

The simple instructional framework on which this text is built is useful in planning content area comprehension instruction. Instructional strategies can be categorized according to emphasis on one of the three stages of the reading process: prereading preparatory activities, guided silent reading support, and postreading reflection and skill development. Some instructional strategies, which we will call *Total Lesson Designs,* incorporate all three stages. Instructional strategies in each category involve students in activities that parallel the strategic reading behaviors that ''expert'' readers perform at that stage (see Figure 4.2). Pragmatic considerations such as time available for instruction, the nature of student needs, and the difficulty level of the textual material are some of the factors to consider in deciding which strategy or combination of strategies to select. Each strategy is based on the assumption that the *other* stages are being provided for in some way.

Medial Checkup and Review

This is an opportune time to check how well you are grasping the ideas and methods presented so far. Match the teaching method in the first column of Figure 4.3 with the reading stage you think it emphasizes in the next column. (Note that a strategy may emphasize behaviors from all three stages, in which case it would be classified as a Total Lesson Design.)

Figure 4.2   Strategic Reading Processes of Expert Readers in the Three Stages of the Reading Process

Reading Phase	Strategic Reading Process of Expert Readers
Prereading	Look for organizing concepts Recall related information/experiences/attitudes/feelings Decide how easy or difficult the reading will be Set a purpose for reading Try to develop a personal interest
Guided silent reading	Fluent subvocalization Translate ideas into own words Compare ideas to personal experience Try to identify main ideas—stop and question when this is unclear Note important detail Reread whenever necessary for clarification Consolidate ideas into meaningful groups Notice unfamiliar vocabulary Form mental pictures Evaluate the author's purpose, motive, or authority when appropriate Invent study strategies as needed Manage time to sustain concentration
Postreading	Check basic comprehension by reciting ("What did I learn?") Organize information into "chunks" of manageable size ("How can I remember it?") Decide what is important ("How much should I understand this?") Try to clarify ambiguous ideas ("Did I really understand this?") Evaluate new information in terms of previous knowledge and experience ("Does this make sense?") Develop study strategies according to class demands or personal purposes ("What should I do to remember this?") Review material periodically ("How much do I remember now?")

Figure 4.3

Teaching Method	Reading Stage Emphasis
Chapter 1	
1. _____ Listen-Read-Discuss Heuristic	A. Prereading
Chapter 2	B. During reading
2. _____ Content/Cloze Languaging Procedure	
3. _____ Concepts/Terminology/Questions	C. Postreading
4. _____ Oral Reading Strategy	
5. _____ Question-Only	D. Total Lesson Design

Answers are at the end of the chapter.

The remainder of this chapter details variations on Total Lesson Designs, including cooperative learning approaches. The first design we will consider, the Directed Reading-Thinking Activity, is the source of the organizational format for comprehension lessons and the basis for the structure of the next four chapters.

Design 1: The Directed Reading-Thinking Activity (DR-TA)

The *Directed Reading-Thinking Activity,* or *DR-TA* (Stauffer, 1969), provides the master lesson structure for many methods and designs used in education. It resembles the Directed Reading Activity (DRA) that Betts found to be in use in various forms in the 1930s.

The DR-TA is a form of guided problem solving. Several studies have shown that it improves purpose setting (Henderson, 1963), critical thinking (Petre, 1970; Davidson, 1970), and personal-social adjustment as measured by increases in constructive verbal responses during lessons (Grobler, 1971). The procedural outline presented in Figure 4.4 is a version developed by David Shepherd (1978) for content area use.

The DR-TA and the earlier DRA undoubtedly have provided much of the framework for the eight-step lesson design popularized by Madeline Hunter (1980). Hunter's model is outlined in Figure 4.5.

In our judgment, the DR-TA and the Hunter model contain two weaknesses. First, both methods are relatively imprecise regarding how to achieve the described objectives. Second, neither approach offers a "reciprocal" feature to enable students to signal the direction they need a lesson to take. These two needs have prompted the development of many parallel and complementary methods.

On a more positive note, the DR-TA is an artfully constructed framework for instruction. In the procedural outline presented in Figure 4.4, note the symmetry

Figure 4.4   Procedural Outline: DR-TA for Content Area Use

Step 1: Preparation for Reading

A. Investigating and expanding the background of student experience
B. Previewing the reading material
C. Introducing the vocabulary pertinent to the fundamental concepts
D. Evolving purposes for reading

Step 2: Reading the Material Silently

A. Noting the students' ability to adjust their reading to the purposes set up and to the material
B. Observing students to note specific areas of need

Step 3: Developing Comprehension

A. Discussing answers to purpose questions
B. Clarifying and guiding further development of the concepts and vocabulary, introducing new vocabulary if needed
C. Assisting the student in noting organization of information and in recall of pertinent facts
D. Noting need for further information from text and/or other source books
E. Redefining purposes; setting new purposes for reading

Step 4: Rereading (silent and/or oral, in part or in entirety)

A. Clarifying further the essential pertinent information and concepts
B. Giving specific skills training in comprehension as indicated by student needs

Step 5: Following up the Information

A. Setting up problems requiring further information
B. Choosing supplementary reading related to the topic to develop and extend interests, attitudes, and appreciations
C. Extending further understanding and clarifying additional concepts as necessary
D. Analyzing the information and helping students relate it to their own lives

Source: From *Comprehensive High School Methods* by D. Shepherd, 1978, Columbus, OH: Merrill.

Figure 4.5   Madeline Hunter Model

Step 1: Anticipatory set
Step 2: Objective/purpose
Step 3: Instructional input/development
Step 4: Modeling
Step 5: Checking for comprehension
Step 6: Guided practice
Step 7: Independent practice
Step 8: Evaluation

between the first objective—calling up students' prior knowledge of and experience with the topic to be read—and the last step—relating what was called up, read, and learned back to the students' own lives.

Stauffer himself saw the DR-TA as being built around three key "problem-solving" actions by the teacher and three key actions by students. These can be done in sequence after a few paragraphs, pages, or the entire selection, as suggested by need:

Teacher actions
1. What do you think you will find in the text? *(activate thought)*
2. Why do you think so? *(agitate thought)*
3. Prove it! *(require "evidence")*

Student actions
1. Predict *(set purposes)*
2. Read *(process ideas)*
3. Prove *(seek verification in text)*

This more simplified translation of the DR-TA is a useful formula for approaching prereading, guided silent reading, and postreading. The next strategy offers another practical way to do so.

Design 2: Structured Overview

The **Structured Overview** is a graphic organizer initially presented by the teacher prior to silent reading, then referred to by students during silent reading, and finally referred back to by the teacher to guide postreading discussion. This strategy is primarily the product of the research and development of Richard Barron (1969). See the Trade Secret at the end of the chapter for more details.

Alvermann and Boothby (1983) found Structured Overviews especially useful in helping the reader deal with what they called "inconsiderate" text, that is, textual material that is too difficult due to poor writing and/or faulty assumptions about the reader's level of familiarity with the topic. The Structured Overview tends to lend unity to such material by providing a graphic connector that highlights important ideas and plays down irrelevant and distracting points.

Alvermann and Boothby went on to say that there are many other means of achieving this same end. Further, they suggested that some of these other methods may be better because they are designed to teach students strategies for organizing text themselves rather than having the teacher do it for them. Structured Overviews, with the addition of a fourth "follow-up" step (see Figure 4.6), can be a satisfactory application of the spirit of the DR-TA.

Notice how each example in Figure 4.6 is arranged in a hierarchical order. The tiers clarify concepts by showing relationships among classes, properties, or elements. Each idea can be easily seen in terms of its relative position as superordinate, subordinate, or coordinate to the other ideas presented. Notice how example B, for instance, clarifies the idea that none of the government branches stands above the power of the people. Example C makes it clear that triangles and quadrilaterals are subordinate to polygons, coordinate to each other, and superordinate to certain of their respective subtypes. The same approach can be used with a chapter or even an entire book.

The acts of resorting and recategorizing information as new information is added are among the most fundamental learning operations. Using them with students improves their basic thinking skills as well as reading and content mastery. The Structured Overview nonetheless is only one form of **graphic organizer,** that is, pictorial representation of meaning. Several other forms of graphic organizer are presented in later chapters.

The next Total Lesson Design also offers a systematic means for teaching students how to collect, sort, and organize information so that they can develop their own Structured Overviews. More important, it addresses several essential "trace element" attitudinal factors involved in effective content area reading, including valuing of factual information, confidence in one's ability to recognize and recall important facts, and determination to read with understanding. In effect, this strategy focuses as much on the reader as it does on reading.

Design 3: The Guided Reading Procedure (GRP)

In the *Guided Reading Procedure,* or *GRP* (Manzo, 1975), students are told, in effect, to read and to recall everything they can. The first author initially issued this unusual directive to inner-city youngsters to help them learn how to self-intensify their efforts, especially in content reading. The fundamental purpose of the lesson is to bring students to the firm conviction that they determine within themselves the outcomes of the time spent reading and learning.

The GRP is highly structured and gives students a valuable opportunity to learn from one another. It has students retrace and restructure the material read in several ways, thus providing ample opportunity for review and repetition. It also provides for improvement in studying and test taking. For these reasons, the strategy can be especially useful in working with unmotivated, learning-disabled, and minority group students whose fading hopes of keeping up with their subjects have hindered their progress in school. Figure 4.7 illustrates the steps in the GRP.

In a typical GRP lesson, students may say little or nothing on the first invitation to recall and recite what they have read. As teachers, we tend to have great difficulty dealing with silence. If you can force yourself to wait silently for a few (seemingly interminable) seconds, the flow of language and thought will begin. The first few— and probably labored—responses will lead to corrections, reflections, and associations. These will generate still more recollections and responses. The result will be a spiraling effect that may draw in even the most reticent students.

Aptly characterized as a "teacher-directed but student-dominated" strategy (Tierney, Readence, & Dishner, 1985), the GRP has been called a "bottom-up" strategy. Recall from our look at models of the reading process that "bottom-up" reading is detail rather than concept driven. The GRP begins with an emphasis on

Figure 4.6   Procedural Outline: Structured Overview

1. *Preparation:* The teacher selects words and concepts that students should know by the end of a reading selection and arranges them into a diagram, or overview, that illustrates their interrelatedness. The easiest way to do this is to first organize ideas into a conventional outline of bigger to lesser and then convert it into a word display (see examples below).
2. *Presentation:* The teacher talks students through the overview while presenting it on a chalkboard or overhead projector.
3. *Read:* During reading, students may refer back to the SO for guidance and integration (assuming it is still visible or was copied into notes).
4. *Follow-up:* The teacher and class use the Structured Overview as a heuristic to pose questions, consider different impressions of what was read, and relate the new information to prior experiences and learnings. The teacher may also use the SO as a bridge to the next topic.

Some applications lend themselves especially well to display as Structured Overviews. This is particularly true when SOs are used to clarify technical concepts and key terms, in which case they may be referred to as *semantic mapping* or *semantic webbing.*

Following are three examples that explain the process through illustration. Example A (Alvermann & Boothby, 1983) summarizes information about Structured Overviews. Example B parallels information on the branches of U.S. government frequently found in social studies texts. Example C uses an SO to clarify an extended unit in geometry.

Example A: Structured Overview of the Structured Overview

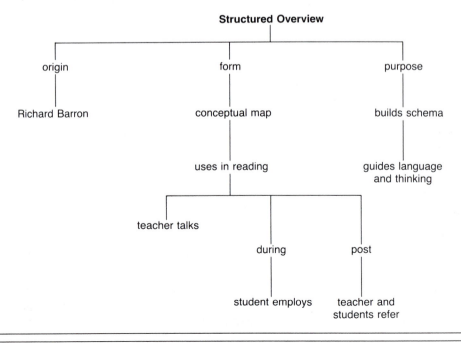

Figure 4.6 *continued*

Follow-up questions:

1. Who typically constructs Structured Overviews?
2. When may students use Structured Overviews?

Example B: Branches of the U.S. Government

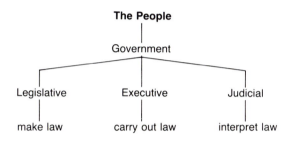

Follow-up questions:

1. How is the legislative branch further divided?
2. Why do you suppose the President needs to be commander in chief of all the armed forces?
3. Can the judicial branch give an order to the executive branch? Must the executive branch follow that order?

Example C: Two-Dimensional Shapes

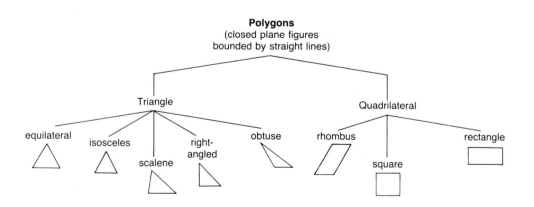

Follow-up activity: Draw and write a brief description of each polygon shown above.

Figure 4.7 Procedural Outline: Guided Reading Procedure

Step 1: Teacher Preparation. Identify a selection to be read, or listened to, of moderate to high difficulty and not exceeding 2,000 words for a senior high class, 900 words for a junior high class, and 600 words for an intermediate class. Prepare a 10-to-20-item test on the material to be given at the end of the class period (a multiple choice test is best). As the lesson proceeds, make sure that the test items are given fair coverage.

Step 2: Student Preparation. Two purposes for reading are established. One is content specific and arrived at with the class. The second is more of a mindset: Direct the group to "read to remember all you can, and after you have read, I will record what you remember on the chalkboard just as you state it to me."

Step 3: Reading and Recalling. After approximately 15 minutes of reading, begin asking for free recall. Record all information on the chalkboard until students have expressed everything they can remember. Difficulties in remembering and differences in what students do remember will form implicit questions that impel the next step.

Step 4: Self-Monitoring/Self-Correcting. Instruct students to review the material read and self-correct inconsistencies that arose in their attempts to recollect. Students may also wish to add information previously overlooked. Note such changes and/or additions on the chalkboard.

Step 5: Restructuring. Encourage students to organize their recollections into outline form to be recorded in their notebooks. The outline can be as simple or elaborate as age and grade level permit. You may ask nonspecific questions at this time, such as "What was discussed first?"; "What details followed?"; "What was brought up next?"; and "What seems to be the main idea?" Avoid specific and leading questions.

Step 6: Teacher Monitoring and Correcting. If it appears that students have overlooked any critical ideas or inappropriately equated them with other ideas, raise guiding questions about these points, such as "What do you suppose is the most important of these five points made by the author?"; "How does this information relate to what we studied last week?"; or, more specifically, "Do you see any ideas here that could be connected to the article we read last week, 'Man and the Moon?'"

Step 7: Evaluation. Give the test prepared in step 1. A score of 70% to 80% should be required for a "pass."

Step 8: Introspection. Discuss any insights students may have reached about their own learning processes as a result of the GRP experience. The chief point to be made is that accuracy in comprehension and recall can be improved to a great degree by an act of will.

Step 9: Optional Study Step. Several days later, give a second test on the same material. Allow students about 15 minutes prior to the test to review material from their notes. The exam can be a multiple choice test or a simple "unaided recall" test such as Wood's Associational Test, which simply has students write down all they can remember of what they read in response to certain key terms.

Source: From "Guided Reading Procedure" by A. V. Manzo, 1975, *Journal of Reading, 18,* pp. 287–291.

recalling, but it is concept driven in a different sense. The driving concept is the charge to be *self-determinedly* accurate, focused, purposeful, and aggressive in *discerning details* from a page of print. The subsequent act of reconstructing information into a meaningful outline, along with short- and long-term tests, also provides practice in forging information into conceptual bundles for long-range storage and in recalling information under high-stress, testlike conditions.

The GRP has been studied by several researchers and has collected strong empirical validation (Culver, 1975; Bean & Pardi, 1979; Ankney & McClurg, 1981). Its effectiveness is most clearly established at the intermediate and junior high levels with science and social studies material. It also has achieved strong endorsements as a listening activity (Cunningham & Cunningham, 1983) and as a suitable method for learning-disabled adolescents (Alley & Deshler, 1980; Maring & Furman, 1985). Several other adaptations of the GRP have been developed by Spiegel (1980), Eanet (1983), and Hayes (in press). These versions, discussed elsewhere in the text, involve use of the basic paradigm in science, social studies, lecture learning, and, especially, writing. The distinctive feature of the GRP and its adaptations is an initial emphasis on accurate recall, followed by a restructuring of the organization of the material read and recalled.

The next strategy begins with an emphasis on students' background knowledge and inquiry skills.

Design 4: K-W-L Plus

The *K-W-L Plus* strategy, developed by Carr and Ogle (1987), follows the general format of the Directed Reading-Thinking Activity but contains some of the outlining, or restructuring, and attitude-stressing features of the Guided Reading Procedure. It also has an element of the Structured Overview in the form of a map that students construct of their progress in understanding a piece of textual material.

The strategy moves from what the student *k*nows to what the student *w*ants to know to what the student has *l*earned to the *plus* feature: conceptual mapping and summarizing. Carr and Ogle's key educational concern in constructing this strategy was that readers "fail to realize that good reading means asking questions and thinking about ideas while they read" (1987, p. 626). Figure 4.8 describes the steps in the K-W-L Plus strategy. Figure 4.9 illustrates a K-W-L worksheet, and Figure 4.10 presents a K-W-L concept map.

K-W-L Plus has not yet been fully tested, but it contains a strong ring of good sense. An earlier version, which did not contain the mapping or summarizing step, did not fare well. Reading resource teachers in particular seem to like this method because demonstration lessons are active and have clear and identifiable steps. Teachers sometimes have trouble, however, with the "thinking aloud" step. Some better mechanism for drawing out effective teacher modeling may be called for.

Now we shall pause to examine some valuable ideas on cooperative learning. Then we will conclude by illustrating how "active comprehension," the fundamental element of all quality instruction, can best be served in this way.

Figure 4.8 Procedural Outline: K-W-L Plus

Before Reading

1. Students "brainstorm" and note on individual worksheets what they think they know about a topic. (See Figure 4.9 for an example of a K-W-L worksheet.) Ogle recently suggested to us that the best way to direct this step is to ask, "How is/should this content be *structured?*"
2. Students categorize information they have generated and anticipate categories of information that they may find in the selection.
3. The teacher models categorizing by "thinking aloud" while combining and classifying information (Davey, 1983).
4. Students generate a list of questions they want answered as they read.

Silent Reading

5. During reading, students pause to answer the questions raised in the "want to know" list. (New questions can be added as they read.)
6. Students list things they have learned while reading.

Postreading

7. Discussion of what was learned takes place, and questions raised before reading are reviewed to determine whether they were resolved.

Follow-up

8. Students are encouraged to map and/or summarize the information from their "learned" list (see Figure 4.10).

Source: From "K-W-L Plus: A Strategy for Comprehension and Summarization" by E. Carr and D. Ogle, 1987, *Journal of Reading, 30,* pp. 628–629. Copyright 1987 by the International Reading Association. Reprinted with permission of Eileen Carr and the International Reading Association.

COOPERATIVE LEARNING DESIGNS

Fostering Cooperative Learning

Morton Deutsch (1962) identified *cooperative learning* as an alternative to competitive and individualistic learning. In cooperative learning situations, each student's achievement depends on the achievement of his or her group. This creates a classroom learning environment that is less brutalizing than typical *competitive* learning situations, in which achievement is defined in relation to someone else's failure. Such an environment is also more lively than *individualistic* learning situations, in which each student's achievement is unrelated to the others'. Of these three basic approaches to teaching, Deutsch suggested that only cooperative learning fosters the important secondary objectives of education. David Johnson, a former student of Deutsch, has continued this line of research along with his brother and coworker Roger Johnson.

Cooperative learning, as the term suggests, occurs in small groups. However, it entails more than simply sorting students by age, interest, or compatibility. It is group activity designed to encourage students to support and depend on one another and to develop a group identity. As David and Roger Johnson (1985) put it, cooperative learning creates "positive interdependence."

In a review of the literature on cooperative learning, Wood (1987) summarized the fundamental value of the approach and its relationship to content reading and languaging:

> Giving students the opportunity to share what they have learned, to hear the opinions of their peers, and to teach and be taught by fellow students is essential to the lifelong process of learning and socialization. In fact, the act of verbalizing newly learned information, if only to oneself, is according to Pauk (1974) the most powerful study technique known to psychologists. (p. 10)

Figure 4.9 Ninth Grader's K-W-L Worksheet for "Killer Whales"

K (Know)	W (Want to Know)	L (Learned)
They live in oceans. They are vicious. They eat each other. They are mammals.	Why do they attack? How fast can they swim? What kind of fish do they eat? What is their description? How long do they live? How do they breathe?	D—They are the biggest members of the dolphin family. D—They weigh 10,000 pounds. F—They eat squid, seals, and other dolphins. A—They have good vision underwater. F—They are carnivorous (meat eaters). A—They are the second smartest animal on earth. D—They breathe through blow holes. A—They do not attack unless they are hungry. D—They are warm-blooded. A—They have echo-location (sonar). L—They are found in the oceans.

A = Abilities; D = Description; F = Food; L = Location

Source: From "K-W-L Plus: A Strategy for Comprehension and Summarization" by E. Carr and D. Ogle, 1987, *Journal of Reading, 30,* pp. 628–629. Copyright 1987 by the International Reading Association. Reprinted with permission of Eileen Carr and the International Reading Association.

Figure 4.10   Ninth Grader's Concept Map

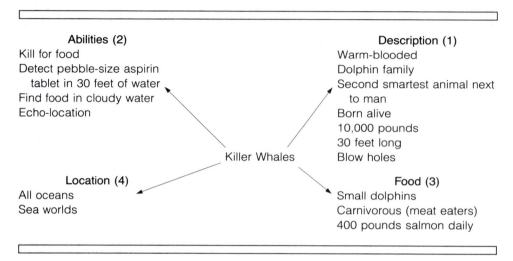

Meta-analyses—that is, studies of studies—by Johnson, Maruyama, Johnson, Nelson, and Skon (1981) and reviews of research by Pepitone (1980) and Lehr (1984) reveal that the overwhelming majority of studies indicate that cooperative learning approaches result in significant gains in achievement as well as substantial improvement in the all-important secondary "trace element" factors. Specifically,

1. Students develop greater confidence and self-esteem.
2. Students tend to like one another more.
3. When groups include students of different ethnic backgrounds, both prejudice and disparagement practically disappear.
4. Students develop a higher regard for school, the subject learned in the cooperative setting, and their teachers.
5. Students come to depend less on the teacher.
6. Students develop greater motivation to learn and greater appetitive (intrinsic) motivation.
7. The more complex the learning task, the greater the advantage of a cooperative learning approach.

Johnson and Johnson (1985) estimated that only 7% to 20% of class time currently is being spent on cooperative learning strategies. In Chapter 11, we return to this topic to offer some practical ways to urge teachers and even community members to come together in the same spirit.

Guidelines for Small-Group Work in the Classroom

The core of all cooperative learning efforts is the group. Figure 4.11 lists Lordon's (1981) guidelines for both teachers and students to follow in promoting effective group work. Note these carefully, and see if they are reflected in the cooperative lesson designs offered next. These teaching strategies are firmly rooted in the tradition of cooperative learning. They also heavily emphasize content mastery.

Design 5: The Group Reading Activity

The *Group Reading Activity* (Manzo, 1974b) combines several elements of the Directed Reading-Thinking Activity with the values and benefits of cooperative learning. It was created to foster more effective languaging—speaking, writing, and reading—among racially integrated groups of students and to build their ability to learn how to critique and be critiqued and to work harmoniously in groups. Figure 4.12 describes the steps in the Group Reading Activity.

Several facets and features of the Group Reading Activity deserve mention. For example, students tend to assume required roles in a surprisingly adult manner. Their language and thinking seem to rise to the occasion. When a "student critic" is intellectually unequal to the task, the group tends to note the difficulties he or she may have had in following the presentation and alter their presentation to the class accordingly. Students naturally tend to criticize in constructive and intelligent ways, probably to reduce the likelihood of being treated shabbily when they are critiqued in turn. Also, the teacher's emphasis on "constructive criticism" appears to have a penetrating effect. Baker and Schutz (1972) reported a relevant study in their textbook on instructional research. This was a problem-solving experiment that used engineers as subjects. When the subjects were asked to evaluate (critique) solutions to certain problems "constructively," they tended to produce much better solutions to subsequent problems than did those who had been asked to simply provide critical reviews of the other subjects' work (p. 71). Keep this finding in mind when you read about critical and constructive reading in chapter 8.

Design 6: Cooperative DR-TA

Debbra Uttero (1988) has defined a teaching strategy, the *Cooperative DR-TA*, that also follows the structure and achieves most of the benefits of the Directed Reading-Thinking Activity through a cooperative learning approach. The strategy is based on a three-phase system designed to promote active comprehension through *connection, guided independent reading,* and *follow-up*. Familiar options for carrying out each phase are available. Figure 4.13 presents some examples suggested by Uttero and elaborated on by the authors. See also Figure 4.14 for a graphic representation from Uttero (1983) of the connection between cooperative learning and active comprehension.

Uttero's (1988) reports of her field exercises with this approach include the important observation that students seem to internalize the value of cooperative learning. Some students, she says, progress to the point where they independently "formed study groups which met during recess or after school" (p. 394). This is a

Figure 4.11   Guidelines for Small-Group Work

Guidelines for Teachers

1. Provide specific goals and objectives for each group. It is important for the students to know exactly what they are to do and why they are doing it.
2. Provide written instructions for each group, particularly when tasks for various groups are different. Written instructions should be clear, explicit, and easy to follow step by step.
3. Establish and enforce some commonsense guidelines for student behavior in the group situation (see Guidelines for Students).
4. Set up procedures to evaluate both individual and group work.
5. Time allocation for group tasks is an important factor. Some groups will need more time than others, but teachers should be alert for those who are wasting time.
6. Plan your own time in detail. Decide what groups you will work with; what the other students will be doing; and how much time you will spend with each group. Be active. Circulate, monitor, assist, direct, and evaluate.
7. Use a variety of types of groups. Do not let your groupings become permanent and static.

Guidelines for Students

1. Conversation: Conversation must be on the topic. Keep your voice low. Communicate with your own group, but do not distrub other groups.
2. Stick to the Task: The work you do with your group is just as important as your individual work. It is important that you learn to stay on the job, to work hard. Group work is not an excuse to goof off! Time is all we have; we must use it well.
3. Responsibility: All your life you will have to work with others. You have a responsibility to yourself, but also to others in your group. You should help, not hinder, the progress of your group toward its goals.

very poignant outcome, because it suggests that students not only have been engaged momentarily but remain motivated and eager to reengage.

It seems that the finer the instruction provided, the more compelling it is in itself and, conversely, the poorer the instruction, the more heavily must the teacher rely on external means such as grades and threats to compel students to participate. Cooperative learning approaches do not require that teachers compel students to participate, but, when properly implemented, these methods can be quite compelling in their own right.

Figure 4.11 *continued*

4. Movement: Your movement around the classroom must be restricted to movement necessary to get the job done. For example, if you need material, get it quickly and quietly, without disturbing others. On the other hand, do not visit other groups to see what they are doing.
5. Cooperation: Working in groups requires you to be independent, mature, and cooperative. Group tasks are designed to help you learn. The teacher will not always be at your shoulder. You must be mature enough to cooperate with others in your group to ensure the orderly progress of the group toward completing the task.
6. Evaluation: You will be evaluated not only on the product of your group's efforts but on the process your group uses. In other words, the teacher will constantly check to see if you are on the task, cooperative, mature, and responsible. The degree to which you measure up to the guidelines for good group work will be reflected in your grades.
7. Sharing: Since the group process is a cooperative one, you must learn to share. You should share materials, ideas, tasks, and responsibility.
8. Listening: You must learn to be a good listener. Everyone in the group has something to contribute. Listen carefully and respectfully to others in the group and to the teacher. A good listener is a mature person.
9. Self-discipline: Working in groups demands accepting responsibility for your own behavior. You must learn to accept this responsibility, especially when your teacher is occupied with other students. Your goal, remember, is to become an independent, self-directed learner who makes the best possible use of class time.
10. Respect: Any cooperative endeavor is based on respect. You must respect yourself, the other students, and the teacher. This respect is reflected in your quiet, diligent, determined efforts to do your best on every learning task assigned.

Source: From "Small Group Instruction: To Make It Work" by J. Lordon, 1981, *The Clearing House, 54* pp. 265–266. Reprinted with permission of the Helen Dwight Reid Educational Foundation. Published by Heldref Publications, 4000 Albemarle St., N.W., Washington, D.C. 20016. Copyright © 1981.

It should be noted that this endorsement of cooperative learning does not mean that there is no value in certain aspects of competition as well. See the Cultural-Academic Trivia strategy in Chapter 7, a vocabulary enrichment game, for an example of one way to harness the human craving for competition as well as for cooperation.

Figure 4.12   Procedural Outline: Group Reading Activity

Step 1. The teacher identifies a unit of text to be analyzed. Then the teacher poses a larger question or directive to guide reading and problem solving.

> *Examples:* Let's see if we can learn from our textbooks how plants grow.
> Let's see how our textbook described the historical events that have come to be called the "Age of Exploration and Discovery."

Step 2. The teacher divides the text into subsections of a few pages each and assigns each selection to a small group (five per group is best).

Step 3. Initially, each group member is required to read silently and record his or her findings and thoughts on the larger directive. A (dittoed) worksheet should be provided with guiding questions and statements such as:

  a. What question does this section answer?
  b. Write a statement of the main idea(s) of this section. Support it with direct quotes or paraphrased facts and points found in the text.
  c. Comment on the quality of the ideas and supporting statements: Do these seem true? Complete? Biased?
  d. What other things, ideas, and facts have you learned in the past that seem to relate strongly to what you have read? (Several illustrations by the teacher over time seem to be necessary before students handle this last question effectively.)

Step 4. As members of the group become ready—though not before at least 10 to 15 minutes—they should begin to share their individual thoughts with one another and to create a single group rendition on a separate sheet.

Step 5. As each group becomes ready, a student critic chosen by the teacher from one of the other groups is sent to see and hear the group's collective rendition. He or she is expected to react with constructive criticism: "That sounds fine"; "That doesn't seem to make much sense"; "Perhaps you should have . . ."

Step 6. The group is permitted time to rework their rendition, drawing on the feedback provided by the student critic.

Step 7. The teacher consults with each group for a few minutes, helping them resolve remaining conflicts, and then schedules them to present their findings to the class. One of the best ways to learn is to teach.

Step 8. Each group presents their findings to the class. The class and teacher comment and question during the presentation. The teacher or a designated member of the group lists important findings on the chalkboard.

Step 9. To build a sense of reading with power and fluency, the class is told to "rapid read" each section covered with an eye toward verifying details and main points.

Source: From "The Group Reading Activity" by A. V. Manzo, 1974, *Forum for Reading, 3,* pp. 26–33.

Figure 4.13   Phases in a Cooperative DR-TA

Phase 1: Connection

In this prereading phase, students work cooperatively in small groups to activate and extend their prior knowledge. Sample options include:

1. *Brainstorming:* Students generate ideas related to a few key words provided by the teacher. They do this first in small groups, then as groups to the class.
2. *Semantic mapping:* The ideas generated in response to the words provided by the teacher are arranged into a semantic map. Each group presents their map on the chalkboard or an overhead. (See the example of pre- and postreading semantic maps in Chapters 5 and 7.)

Phase 2: Guided Independent Reading

In this phase, activities rather than the teacher guide silent reading. Sample options include:

1. *Guiding questions:* Students answer questions (either prepared by the teacher or generated by students from previewing the material and formulating questions in groups) druing reading.
2. *Outlining:* Students complete partial outlines prepared by the teacher.
3. *Paraphrasing:* Each student paraphrases a section of text. Then the groups coordinate the results to produce a new rendition of the entire selection in their own words.

Phase 3: Follow-up

This phases involves summarizing, application, and test preparation. Sample options include:

1. *Summarization:* Students collectively construct a summary from the original text and/ or the paraphrased renditions.
2. *Memory training:* Students apply memory strategies to mastery of the content (see Chapter 9 for several examples of these strategies).
3. *Test making:* Each group constructs a test on the material. Groups can be urged to take one another's tests and then discuss differences in their questions, question types, and answers.
4. *Inferring:* Actually more like conjecturing than inferencing, this invaluable critical-thinking activity encourages students to speculate about the thoughts, motives, and personalities of people connected to the information, including the authors.
5. *Semantic remapping:* Students construct a postreading semantic map that reflects new information acquired and corrected misconceptions (see Figure 4.14).

Figure 4.14   Active Comprehension through the Cooperative Learning Model

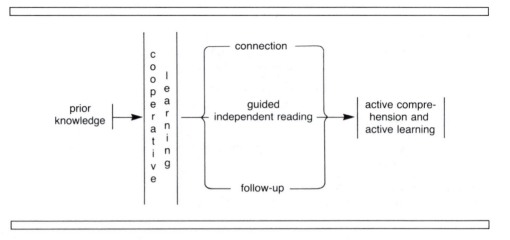

Source: From ''Activating Comprehension through Cooperative Learning'' by D. A. Uttero, 1988, *The Reading Teacher, 41,* p. 392. Copyright 1988 by the International Reading Association. Reprinted with permission of Debbra A. Uttero and the International Reading Association.

CHAPTER TIE-UPS

◆◆◆   *Graphic Organizer*

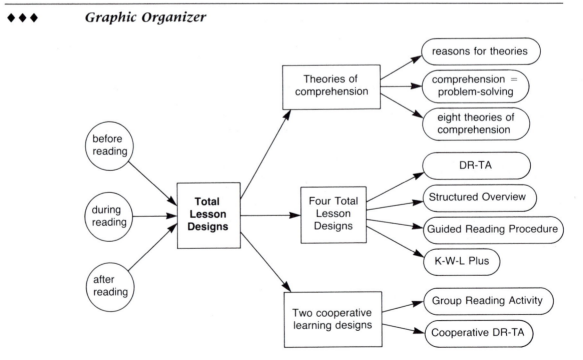

Critique and Anticipation ◆◆◆

This chapter described eight theories of the comprehension process. The precepts associated with four of these approaches—content reading, schema, cognitive processing, and trace elements—are especially valued in this text. Then the chapter presented several other overarching features of quality instruction, including the concepts of direct explanation, fading, and cooperative learning. Next, the chapter described an instructional framework, with options for prereading, guided silent reading, postreading, and total lesson activity, as a master plan for most of the other comprehension strategies. The Total Lesson Designs described included Structured Overviews, the Guided Reading Procedure, K-W-L Plus, the Group Reading Activity, and the Cooperative DR-TA.

The next chapter homes in on prereading, or "front-loading," designs. It also elaborates on several aspects of questioning and on three other overarching attributes of quality instruction: engagement, modeling, and reciprocity.

TRADE SECRET

Insider Information

There have been so many references to Structured Overviews in the literature that it is difficult to decide to whom to attribute this idea. The first author decided to write to Dick Barron, remembering his pioneering work on this approach when we were graduate students together. His response provides a valuable historical perspective, a candid insight into the creative process, and a reminder of a growing problem in education and most other professions. The following excerpts are printed with his permission.

> With respect to your question about who deserves "credit" for techniques involved with various forms of semantic mapping, I'm not sure what to say. I guess I deserve some, but how much I'm not sure. . . .
>
> The idea of what has been labeled a "structured overview" first came to me in 1968. It did not arise from anything I saw, read, or heard about as an instructional procedure—rather it came out of fear, anxiety, and desperation. You'll recall that when Hal Herber received his initial grant for a research and demonstration project in secondary reading, he recruited a group of "interns": Tom Estes, Judy Thelen, Pete Sanders, Dick Earle, and me. Our task, among other things, was to do iterative research in the schools while engaged in graduate work. I was paired with two science teachers from Jamesville-Dewitt High School and, not knowing much that first semester about science, secondary reading, high schools or adolescents (I really was a "mess"), decided the best way to proceed would be to actually take courses with the high school students while we were trying out, observing, and studying existing procedures for teaching reading through content. I ended up in a tenth grade biology class taught by a super-serious, dedicated young fella named Dan Mills.

Things went swimmingly for the first two months or so. I didn't have a tremendous amount of time to devote to the course, but I did O.K.—until we hit a unit on biochemistry, which Dan announced was the foundation for the remainder of the year. At this point I started flunking the course! I failed two quizzes and two or three days before the unit exam was still completely lost.

To make things even worse, the tenth grade kids had begun to like me—and take pity on me. The attitude was "let's help the old guy out" and I was invited to several study sessions. My peers were really "supportive." It was either Judy or Hal who cracked, "Aw, Dick, maybe after you get the Ph.D., you can go for a high school equivalency diploma."

Anyhow, a night or two before the unit exam, I was studying and struggling with the chapters, and as I did so, I began to almost absentmindedly jot terms on a sheet of paper (the vocabulary load in the unit was unbelievable!). I was on the verge of quitting when I looked at my scribbling and began to see relationships, first among a few and then among almost all of them. Serendipity! I "nailed" the unit test with the highest grade in the class! Although I was pleased with this, there was a negative consequence—the kids stopped talking to me! . . .

Insofar as the proliferation of various types of mapping techniques since then, I believe I can describe the process for you. My best guess is that perhaps a couple of us did what you term "pioneering" work, but what happened later was probably best described by Donald Campbell in a brilliant synthesizing paper in psychology—"Social Attitudes and Other Acquired Behavioral Dispositions," written in, I believe, the early sixties. Campbell prefaced the paper by questioning the knowledge explosion in psychology. He suggested that perhaps there was not so much a proliferation of knowledge as there was a proliferation of psychologists—many engaged in attempting to publish and gain recognition.

He suggested that there really weren't very many "new" ideas, processes, or techniques. Rather, there were many similar, if not identical, ones with different names or labels. What happens, according to Campbell, is that psychologists, and I guess anyone else, take an existing idea, change it or view it with a twist or a hook, and then label it. The "new" name . . . the "new" label means they become associated with it—they "own" it. He termed this process—you're gonna love this, Tony!—ready?—*Narcissistic Pseudo-Innovation.* Isn't that great?!

I may be seeing things unfairly, my perceptions may be warped, but I believe this is what has occurred vis-à-vis the spread of mapping techniques, visual learning strategies, or whatever. . . .

Warmest regards,
Dick Barron

You will find other references to Structured Overviews in the text. These are provided in deference to the different ways this story might be told and the other persons who may have independently developed the idea.

Continuation of Box 4.1

Essentials for growing a healthy plant: soil, light, adequate watering, soil aeration, drainage, moderate temperatures, bees and flying insects for pollination, resistance to other insects and systemic diseases, proper nutrients, protection from excessive direct ultraviolet rays, and lots of tender, loving care.

Continuation of Figure 4.3

1. D; 2. B; 3. A; 4. B; 5. A

Prereading Designs

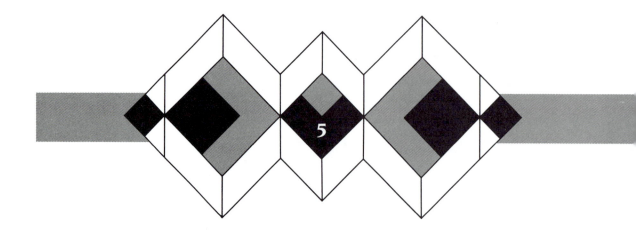

5

Questioning, Vocabulary Introduction, and Other Strategies to Launch Effective Reading

People see only what they are prepared to see.

— *Ralph Waldo Emerson*

FOCUS

Experience and evidence suggest that well-designed and implemented prereading instruction can effectively prepare students for subsequent silent reading of difficult material. Several options are now available for providing this crucial element of content area instruction.

OUTLINE

WHY PREREADING INSTRUCTION?

Effective comprehension depends largely on "readiness," that is, proper anticipation. A law school class we once observed demonstrated this principle in rather dramatic fashion. The class met in a large lecture hall. Midway through the lecture, someone burst into the hall, drew a pistol, and "shot" the professor. The professor fell down, helplessly grasping at the lecturn. The intruder dashed out. Within just a few moments, to the stunned astonishment of the class, the professor got up and calmly announced that this was a mock reenactment of a real-life event. He then instructed the class to write a description of the intruder. A discussion of the validity of eyewitness accounts ensued.

The students' written descriptions of the intruder, of course, varied widely. We see what we are prepared to see, and the students had not been prepared to see an intruder. Thus, their perceptions of the event were shaped from their preconceived notions of what an intruder might look like rather than from accurate observations. As the cartoon in Figure 5.1 illustrates, one often interprets experience in terms of highly personalized, preconceived notions rather than objective, impersonal observation.

It follows, then, that a roomful of students reading an assigned section of a textbook may come away from their reading with understandings that vary almost as widely as the possible interpretations of the characters in the cartoon. These diverse understandings likewise are based more on personal preconceptions than on accurate interpretations of the author's message or of an event. A basic goal of content area reading is to ensure that accurate comprehension forms the basis for subsequent interpretation, application, and evaluation.

Instruction aimed at improving basic comprehension begins *before* having students read. Consider, for example, what might have happened had the professor in the above illustration announced to the students that he had reason to believe a crank would interrupt the class that day and therefore it would be wise for them to observe the intruder carefully so as to provide campus police and school authorities with an accurate description. Undoubtedly there would have been much less variance among the students' descriptions, because the students would have been prepared to watch for pertinent facts. Similarly, in a content area lesson involving a reading assignment, the "readiness" portion of the lesson prepares students for what is coming. This enables them to perceive more of what they read without the interference of preconceived and possibly incorrect ideas. In a recent survey of teaching practices (Gee & Rakow, 1987), professors specializing in content area reading ranked prereading methods as the best techniques content teachers can use to help students read effectively and learn from text.

PREREADING COMPONENTS AND THEORETICAL ISSUES

The prereading, or "readiness," phase of reading instruction, as found in the Directed Reading Activity, typically includes three instructional components: proper

Figure 5.1   We See with the Mind, Not the Eye

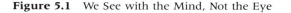

Source: Reprinted with permission of John Jonik.

attitude, schema activation, and reading "set." Figure 5.2 outlines these components and their chief characteristics.

The Directed Reading Activity addresses each of these "readiness" components in a one-by-one manner. This approach is adequate, but it can become protracted and tedious. The prereading strategies presented here permit several of these components to be addressed concurrently. These "compressed" methods appear better suited to the content classroom for several reasons:

1. They take less time, making more class time available for reading.
2. They keep the focus on idea and knowledge objectives.
3. They tend to contribute to other important educational objectives, such as inquiry training, at no additional cost in materials or human terms.

The following sections present four basic elements of prereading instruction: schema enhancement, motivation, questioning, and modeling. Note that we separate these elements only for discussion purposes. Later in the chapter, we bring them together in the form of recommended teaching practices.

Schema Aids That Transform as Well as Inform

In the previous chapter, we defined *schema* as the sum of one's prior knowledge, experience, sensory-motor learnings, and inclinations. In this section, we will discuss schema in terms of its functional value.

Figure 5.2 Prereading Components of the Directed Reading Activity

Attitude Orientation
1. Raise *attention* and reduce distractions.
2. Pique *interest* in the topic and the task.
3. *Motivate* for sustained effort.

Schema Orientation
1. Activate *relevant background* knowledge.
2. *Correct* misapprehensions.
3. Provide necessary *new ideas and facts*.
4. Establish a sense of *organization and sequence* of text.

Reading Orientation
1. Establish a *purpose* for reading.
2. Remove *word recognition obstacles*.
3. Preteach *key concept terms*.
4. Alert and alleviate other *vocabulary, graphic, and/or syntactic* hurdles.
5. Lay the necessary foundation for further *specific skills* development (e.g., inquiry, prediction, connection to prior readings, and evaluative thinking).

The primary role of schema is to provide the "grid" for receiving and ordering information. The ability of an individual's schema, or grid, to assimilate information is directly proportionate to its compatibility with that information. It is difficult to assimilate information that one does not already know, feel, and believe in some way. In fact, when we read or hear "new" information that is incompatible with our prior knowledge and experience, our first reaction is to handle it in one of three ways: (1) subconsciously block it out; (2) reduce it, or change it into something we already know; or (3) reject it. Only if our *cognitive dissonance* (Festinger, 1957)—that is, discomfort with the mismatch between the facts and our expectation—is kept at some optimal level do we finally attempt to adjust our schema structure to the demands of the new information. In other words, it is difficult even to perceive, let alone comprehend, what we are not in some way prepared to accept. For example, the Scandinavian researcher Elizabeth Waern (1977a) found that on first reading, 70% of "comprehension" consists only of facts and ideas that are compatible with the reader's prior knowledge and expectations, no matter what the author actually said. Fortunately, this level tends to fall to about 40% upon a second reading. Lipson (1983) found a similar effect with very bright Jewish youngsters attending a yeshiva (Jewish parochial school). When required to read material about the Holocaust, these students had considerable difficulty wading through the turbulent emotional waters surrounding this issue to the author's actual message. This admittedly extreme example makes the point for the more typical case, in which emotions constantly interact with cognition. A good deal of what is called *comprehension* training really comes down to *apprehension* training—teaching students how to overcome inappropriate anticipation and permit new information to alter preconceived thoughts and feelings. For this reason, it is sometimes said that the purpose of a quality education is to *transform*, or broaden and alter receptivity and thinking, as well as inform.

Transformation is a paradox, however. How does anyone ever come to think beyond his or her current wisdom and thereby grow and change? This puzzling question is the focus of a branch of philosophy called *epistemology.* Piaget, the renowned zoologist-turned-developmental psychologist, used the language of epistemology to discuss the psychology of learning. The term he used to explain how new learning occurs is **accommodation.** In this process, each time a schema structure is inadequate to the task of assimilating incoming information, it adapts by reforming itself into new cognitive structures that can receive and process the previously overlooked, blocked, or rejected information and viewpoints. If this sounds like a circle of words, it is because it is in a way. Although accommodation occurs every day in a variety of learning situations, we really don't know *how* it occurs. It is a mysterious phenomenon: It happens because it happens.

Fortunately, even though no one knows how accommodation occurs, years of research and experience have revealed how to facilitate its occurrence. Sometimes, as Waern (1977b) has illustrated, it is as simple a matter as having students read an emotion-charged selection more than once. Other times, discussion and guided reanalysis are required. Still other situations call for more "high-impact" methodology involving sensory-motor or simulation experiences. Finally, some cases require methods that develop students' metacognitive reading strategies, such as self-monitoring. These active, strategic reading habits tend to make the mind more alert and receptive to accommodation. Successful implementation of any prereading strategy often depends on how well other situational factors are dealt with. A key situational factor, motivation to learn, is the next topic.

Engagement Theory of Motivation

There are many different aspects of motivation, and each is addressed by several different theories. To strengthen your understanding of your goals in prereading instruction, we have compressed several of these theories into a single motivational precept for guiding reading. We refer to this amalgam here as **engagement** theory. Three key ideas underlying this theory are relevant to prereading practices:

1. Prediction-based techniques tend to have positive but sometimes limiting effects on reading comprehension. Only those that actively involve (engage) students in making predictions or setting purposes appear to be routinely effective (Shanahan, 1986).
2. Wherever possible, student engagement should be active, involving body and behavior as well as mental patterns. Body involvement permits **proprioceptive** (sensory-motor) **learning** to occur. Proprioceptive learning is self-stimulating and habit forming: Once it gets into the nervous system, it tends to close out other distractions and to be self-perpetuating. See the section on Motor Imaging in this chapter for a vivid example of how to promote this type of engagement.
3. Academic "engaged time" (Rosenshine, 1984) is a key ingredient and in itself a solid predictor of gain in reading achievement (Samuels & Turnure, 1974). Learning is a function primarily of "time spent on the learning task" and, more specifically, of the quality, intensity, and benefits (or relevance) of that time to students' personal-emotional objectives.

One means of motivating students to achieve school objectives such as effective reading and language skills is through the judicious use of modeling, or apprenticeship-based strategies of teaching, discussed next.

Modeling

Apprenticeship Training Goes to School
Apprenticeship training is an ancient and highly effective form of teaching and learning. Until fairly recently, its role in formal schooling was limited to training children and adults to perform complex gross and fine motor tasks. The chief characteristic of apprenticeship training is **modeling:** the demonstration of a particular behavior by a competent user (see Box 5.1 for an introduction to this concept). Thus, this teaching/learning design formerly was used for teaching ob-

BOX
5.1   CONCEPT CLARIFICATION
                          Learning from Modeling and Imitation

We tend to forget how influential modeling and imitation have been in our lives. Once we have incorporated a lesson into our personal way of operating, we forget where we learned it.

   Think back to who influenced your current thinking and behavior at some time in the past. Try to recall both positive and negative models. Think of peers, older individuals, and perhaps some younger persons. Were you able to interact with them or only to observe them?

   Now read on to learn more about the theory and practice of modeling as an element of effective teaching.

servable behaviors, such as those employed in arts and crafts, in highly individualized settings. It was difficult to imagine how it could be otherwise.

Modeling was first introduced as a means of teaching "mental" operations in the form of the ReQuest Procedure, discussed later. The ReQuest Procedure made it possible to implement modeling in a traditional academic classroom and bring to that setting many of the benefits of individualized apprenticeship training. This was achieved simply by creating a procedure that challenged teachers and students to produce an externalized version of a behavior that otherwise would be internal and unobservable. In this case, the behavior was setting a purpose for reading: a complex mental process essential to effective reading comprehension. Today modeling is widely considered a key element of effective instruction.

A closer look at this process will help explain the effectiveness and popularity of modeling-based instructional strategies for classroom use.

Modeling: A "Natural" for Language Learning.   Human beings' inclination to observe and imitate one another is the most familiar and frequently used mode of human learning outside of school. A prime example of its use is in language acquisition. Only a very small percentage of the words and language forms we know did we acquire as a result of direct instruction. A mother may teach her child to say some important words like "mommy," "hot," "chair," and so on, but the child picks up an enormous number of words on his or her own. A parent or teacher may remind the child to say "he ran" instead of "he runned," but the majority of what the child learns about word order and language structures is learned incidentally. The way we speak, the words we use, and the way we feel when using these words are the direct result of the speech patterns and concerns of the models to whom we were exposed and with whom we have interacted.

The fact that various language forms evoke strong feelings suggests that our models of language learning are also our guides to the ways we come to structure and interpret the world around us. From the models we select to emulate, we learn motives and attitudes as well as words and actions. Thus, inquiring minds can beget inquiring minds. In any situation, however, there are various models available from which to choose. We make our selections based on our subjective assessments of the degree to which those around us appear to have mastery over the situation. In school settings, the student does not automatically choose the teacher as a model. Instructional strategies that employ modeling must include devices for winning students' attention to the desired models and behaviors.

Modeling: The Objective Is the Tip of the Iceberg.   Modeling of mental operations has its rational basis in social and imitation learning theory (Bandura & Walters, 1963; Miller & Dollard, 1941). Simply put, the idea is that we tend to copy and internalize a larger array of a model's behaviors than merely those traits that are essential to the task at hand. By taking advantage of this additional, "incidental" learning dimension, it becomes possible to teach very complex and subtle behaviors along with key target behaviors, and in a much shorter period of time. Further, the mental image of the model serves as a mental "template," or set of guidelines, that the novice can use to evaluate subsequent attempts to apply and refine the new behavior in different situations. Thus, modeling becomes an ideal way to teach secondary and subtler (trace element) objectives as well as primary objectives.

Modeling: The Essence of Concept-Based Instruction.   A commonly cited flaw in traditional instruction is that concepts too often are presented as abstract ideas isolated from any appropriate context. Instead of teaching students about reading skills, modeling permits the teacher to coach students while they read.

Modeling: Whole-Student Instruction.   An additional—and often overlooked—benefit of modeling is that when students imitate the desired behaviors, these new learnings are physically, or proprioceptively, embedded. This increases the probability that the new behaviors will recur. It's a little like riding a bike: Once you've learned how, you need not think about it; you just do it.

Conditions for Effective Modeling

The efficiency of modeling as a basis for the teaching/learning of mental behaviors can be amplified under certain conditions:

1. Drawing the student's attention to the desired model
2. Strengthening the impression that the model is doing something masterful and desirable
3. Reducing social risks entailed in copying the desired behavior
4. Making the new behavior appear "doable" (such as letting the student observe competent models from his or her peer group)
5. Permitting the student to interact with the desired model in an affective (feeling) manner as well as in a contrived, "schoollike" way
6. Encouraging **reciprocity,** that is, giving the student the opportunity to both influence and be influenced by the model

The last element, reciprocity, serves another critical purpose in effective teaching: It invites the student's individuality to emerge. The student comes to learn the heuristic, or general guidelines for effective learning, rather than continuing merely to copy the examples offered by the model. On this point, Weinstein (1987) notes that "allowing students to practice with feedback is a more powerful teaching method than presenting many examples. Heuristics require . . . effective feedback."

As you study the teaching methods that feature modeling, remember to look for the *enabling action(s)* that might attract students' attention to, and active engagement with, the desired models. The ReQuest Procedure described later, for example, combines modeling with a strong emphasis on reciprocity into a procedure designed to improve purpose setting and comprehension by enhancing student and teacher *questioning*—our next topic.

Questioning

Inhibitions to Questioning

Research and intuition both suggest that the key to getting students to question is less a matter of teaching them to inquire than it is a process of enabling them to overcome several social-psychological inhibitions to their otherwise natural inclination to inquire. Two studies in particular lead to the conclusion that subtle social inhibitions tend to slowly accumulate into a dense blanket that muffles, and in some cases totally suffocates, student curiosity and questioning. In one of these studies (Manzo & Legenza, 1975), the researchers crawled around on the floor to observe the questioning behavior of kindergarten children for an entire school year. In the other (Legenza, 1978), the researcher observed and interviewed several classes of junior high students. Here, in brief, are some of the things we now conclude about sources of inhibitions to classroom questioning.

The Squelch.   Teachers understandably feel obliged to squelch passive-aggressive questions that students raise when they are fearful or annoyed. Before a test, for example, teachers often observe this flurry of questions: "Do we have to skip a line after every answer?"; "Do you want last names first?"; "Can we use notebook paper?"; "Can we use pencils?" This problem is not easily overcome, but it is useful to remember the advice of the Roman orator Publius Syrus: "Every question does not deserve an answer."

The Sting.   As teachers, we ourselves occasionally use questions in ill-advised, ambiguous, and even sarcastic ways. When a student persists in talking while we are trying to explain a point to the class, we might resort to saying something like: "Well, maybe you can explain this to the rest of the class better than I, since you don't seem to value my explanation." After a simple stare, and/or moving closer to the offender to quiet him or her down, you might try a more direct but less sarcastic statement that corrects and explains: "When you talk during class you distract yourself, me, and the class. Please try to save your enthusiasm for later."

The Void.   "Any questions?" is a popular teacher tool for inviting clarifying inquiries. When students are asked this question in this form, however, they feel, as did a student in an algebra class Legenza (1978) interviewed, a sinking sense of

"Oh, if only I knew what I don't know!" A better approach is to say something that will guide questioning into an area where there is often confusion in the topic at hand: "Can someone ask a good question to clarify when we need to change signs in an equation?"; then "What other questions could be asked about signs?"; finally, "Any other questions about anything discussed today?"

The Social Graces.   Even when students "know what they don't know," they often are (1) at a loss for the words to frame and articulate that vague thought into a question; (2) unsure of how to win the teacher's empathy with the question; and (3) wondering what needs to be done to get a response they can understand. On these points, several students have said things amounting to "I hate when the teacher answers my question with another question or says things to me that are even more confusing than my original question." Students often need assistance in how to better direct their initial questions and/or ask necessary follow-up questions. For considerable help with this problem, see the Ask-It-Rite procedure in Chapter 10 and Enabling Questions in Chapter 9.

The Ego Defense.   Asking a question in class sometimes feels like a public admission of ignorance. Subordinating oneself to another who is perceived as smarter is always difficult for delicate egos. This text offers several methods for reducing fear of expressing ignorance or subordination. In particular, see the Question-Only strategy in Chapter 2, the ReQuest Procedure in this chapter, and Ask-It-Rite and Note Cue in Chapter 10. See also the Nested Chapters Index for other hints on questioning.

Question Types
Effective teacher questioning can do much to overcome some of the inhibitions to student wonder and questioning. We will now consider some of the questions that you might reasonably model and use. Then we will detail several prereading methodologies with built-in heuristics for eliciting such questions from you and your students.

The most widely used system for characterizing questions is based loosely on a hierarchy of difficulty called the *Taxonomy of Educational Objectives: The Cognitive Domain* (Bloom, 1956). Here are eight cognitive domain question types selected from this and several other authoritative sources (Ashner, Gallagher, Perry, Afsar, Jenné, & Farr, 1962; Barrett, 1967; Sanders, 1969).

Eight Cognitive Domain–Type Questions

1. *Recognition questions.* Recognition questions require identifying the answers from available choices (e.g., multiple choice questions).
2. *Recall questions.* Recall questions require remembering the answers with little prompting and no clues ("When was the Battle of Hastings?").
3. *Translation questions.* Translation questions entail transferring something from one symbolic form to another ("Can you describe this picture?"; "Can you tell in your own words what the author said in this paragraph?"; "Can you say what you just heard in your own words?").

4. *Inference questions.* Inference questions have the reader combine available textual information to reach an answer that is logical but not explicitly stated in the text ("What is the relationship between Jack and Joseph in this story?").

5. *Conjecture questions.* Conjecture questions involve an inferential leap, because all the information is not yet, or may never be, available ("As we read ahead, do you suppose that Jack's life will rise above his father's?").

6. *Explanation questions.* Explanation questions require verification of a previous point. They may involve reference to the text and/or to other sources ("Why do you think Jack's life will rise above his father's?").

7. *Application questions.* Application questions require critical and constructive thinking and problem solving ("In similar circumstances, how might a person like Jack avoid hurting his father?").

8. *Evaluation questions.* Evaluation questions are a specialized type of application question that requires critical thinking, aesthetic sense, and personal judgment ("How do you feel about the story? The characters? The style of writing? The moral to be drawn?").

Patterns of Teacher Questioning.   Guszak (1967) found that teachers tend to ask too few translation-type questions—generally fewer than 1% of the total number of questions in instructional situations. This is unfortunate, because translation questions offer several advantages:

1. They offer an easy way to keep students engaged and attentive.
2. They urge students to listen to one another ("Can you tell in your own words what Mary just said?").
3. They provide a useful bridge to aid gradation of questions from literal to higher-order thinking.

Observational studies also reveal that teachers ask evaluative-type questions less than 13% of the time (Durkin, 1978–79; Guszak, 1967; Manzo, 1969a, 1969b). This also is unfortunate, since this type of question places a high value on student judgment and tends to draw pupils into schoolwork in a more thoughtful and engaging way. Ironically, this type of question is valuable for classic underachievers as well as for overachievers (or higher-order illiterates). Underachievers tend to have weak literal comprehension and be emotionally dependent; this is evident diagnostically in the frequency with which they reply "I don't know" to simple personal-judgment questions. More frequent use of such questions would tend to stimulate underachievers to fall back on their own resources and to read more carefully and thoughtfully. Overachievers—those with solid literal and inferential comprehension—have an analogous problem. They too can be emotionally dependent in a different sense: They will read and absorb but prefer not to think and relate. Evaluation questions coax this type of student into a more reflective mode. This causes such students to draw upon their own experiential resources and incorporate academic learnings into their social-emotional growth and maturity.

There are other less orderly but equally valuable ways to generate effective questions. Teachers who have used the ReQuest Procedure, for example, have created some very inventive questions during their interactions with students. Let us now examine the ReQuest Procedure in detail and see how it leads students and teachers into self-discovery of effective means of questioning.

PREREADING STRATEGIES

Design 1: ReQuest Procedure

Prior to the development of the Reciprocal Questioning, or ReQuest, Procedure (Manzo, 1969b), the common practice was for the teacher to try to anticipate and provide the necessary background information and purpose for reading. The ReQuest Procedure takes a different tack: It permits the teacher to model good prereading questioning behavior and encourages students to develop their own purposes for reading by reducing many of the "risks," or inhibitions, involved in class participation.

ReQuest first was developed as a remedial reading procedure for one-on-one teaching. It soon became evident, however, that it could be equally effective in regular classroom situations with heterogeneous groups. Early research indicated that its use tended to stimulate sensitive teaching and attentive, adultlike student responding. The inherent language development and "therapeutic" properties of ReQuest have led to its use in programs to promote personal-social adjustment in juvenile delinquents (Kay, Young, & Mottley, 1986), in mainstreaming learning-disabled students (Alley & Deshler, 1980; Hori, 1977), in content classrooms (Manzo, 1973), and with second-language students (McKenzie, Ericson, & Hunter, 1988). ReQuest also has become the basis for a larger movement in education called *Reciprocal Teaching* (Palinscar & Brown, 1984).

Steps in the ReQuest Procedure

1. Teacher and students should have copies of the selection to be read before them. The teacher states the basic goal: "Our intent in this lesson is to improve your skill in setting a purpose for reading."
2. The teacher guides the students through as many sentences (or, in time, short paragraphs) of the selection as seem necessary to formulate a logical purpose to continue reading silently. This is achieved in the following way:
   a. Students and teacher silently survey the selection and then read the title and first sentence. Students are first permitted to ask the teacher as many questions as they wish about that sentence (see Figure 5.3). Students are told that they should try to ask the kinds of questions the teacher might ask and in the same way.
   b. The teacher answers each question as fully as possible without intentionally withholding information, asking questions back, or elaborating unnecessarily.
   c. Once students have asked all their questions, the teacher asks as many questions as seem appropriate to focus attention on the purpose for which the selection was written or the key question that it answers.

Figure 5.3   The ReQuest Procedure: Sample Student Questions/Teacher Answers (Seventh-Grade Level)

First sentence of the selection: "The katydid is any of several large, green, American, long-horned grasshoppers usually having stridulating organs on the forewings of the males that produce a loud, shrill sound!"

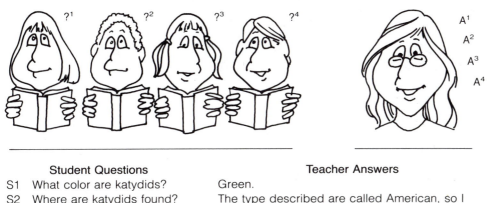

Student Questions	Teacher Answers
S1 What color are katydids?	Green.
S2 Where are katydids found?	The type described are called American, so I suppose they can be found in America, though perhaps elsewhere as well.
S3 What family are katydids in?	Grasshoppers, though I'm sure they have some scientific name as well (*Tettigoniidae!*).

d. When students encounter a teacher-generated question that they feel they cannot answer, the teacher encourages them to explain why they cannot do so.

e. The pattern used to review the first sentence—silent reading, followed by student questions, followed by teacher questions—is continued through the second and subsequent sentences of the first paragraph(s).

f. Beginning with the second or third sentence, the teacher, mindful of serving as a model of questioning behavior, begins to ask questions that require integration of units from the earlier sentence(s), for example, "Judging from the first two sentences, why do you suppose this selection about the history of architecture has been titled 'The Arches versus the Domes'?" (see Figure 5.4).

g. Throughout the interaction, students are reinforced for imitating the teacher's questioning behavior. Reinforcement can be direct or indirect: a socially approving comment ("That's a good question") or an empathetic and complete answer to the question—a natural, powerful, and often overlooked means of reward.

Figure 5.4   The ReQuest Procedure: Sample Teacher Questions/Comments and Student Answers

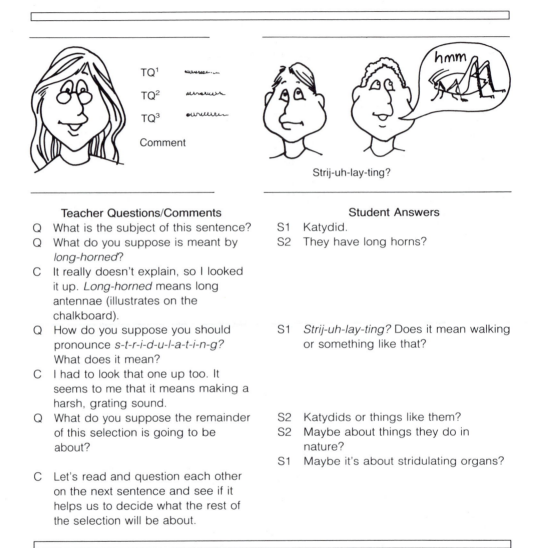

Strij-uh-lay-ting?

Teacher Questions/Comments	Student Answers
Q What is the subject of this sentence?	S1 Katydid.
Q What do you suppose is meant by *long-horned*?	S2 They have long horns?
C It really doesn't explain, so I looked it up. *Long-horned* means long antennae (illustrates on the chalkboard).	
Q How do you suppose you should pronounce *s-t-r-i-d-u-l-a-t-i-n-g*? What does it mean?	S1 *Strij-uh-lay-ting?* Does it mean walking or something like that?
C I had to look that one up too. It seems to me that it means making a harsh, grating sound.	
Q What do you suppose the remainder of this selection is going to be about?	S2 Katydids or things like them? S2 Maybe about things they do in nature? S1 Maybe it's about stridulating organs?
C Let's read and question each other on the next sentence and see if it helps us to decide what the rest of the selection will be about.	

3. The ReQuest procedure should continue until students can:
    a. Decode and derive proper meanings for all the words in the initial paragraph(s).
    b. Demonstrate a thorough understanding of the sentences read.
    c. Formulate a reasonable ''purpose,'' preferably stated as a question, for silently reading the remainder of the selection. The teacher can help with this process

by first urging students to frame thoughts and hypotheses into questions ("What question do you suppose this article will answer regarding the relationship between arches and domes?"). Then the teacher can guide students into reading by saying, "Now please read the remainder of this selection silently, and see if we have identified a good purpose for reading." (Note: On some occasions, more than one legitimate purpose for reading may evolve. Depending on the group's ability level, they may all be asked to test both purposes, or the class can be divided such that different groups of students test each prediction.)

4. Following silent reading, the teacher's first question should be "Did we identify the best purpose for reading this selection?" The next question should be the actual "purpose" question that was to guide silent reading (Manzo, 1985).

Done in this way, ReQuest is an effective means of preparing students for a difficult home reading assignment as well as for immediate classroom reading and discussion.

Peer Modeling: Can Anyone Ask Another Question Like That One?

A sixth-grade student named Clarence taught us a valuable way to bring about effective peer modeling during a ReQuest interaction. Clarence was one of several students the second author had invited to participate in a demonstration lesson of the ReQuest Procedure. Everyone was a little hesitant about including Clarence, because you never knew quite what to expect from him. He was a very active youngster and liked to be the center of attention. He also was characteristically disorganized and unconcerned about schoolwork.

As we began the ReQuest Procedure, Clarence immediately caught on to the idea of students asking questions. In fact, we found ourselves so mesmerized by the demonstration Clarence was providing that we let the lesson go on much longer than it should have. What captivated us was the nature of the questions Clarence asked and the compelling effect they seemed to have on the other youngsters. Here is how the lesson unfolded.

The reading selection used for the demonstration was a passage from a sixth-grade social studies text, which began as follows:

Discontent Turns to Revolution

Paris, July 1789: French people everywhere watched the events at Versailles with great interest. To most of them, the members of the Third Estate were heroes. Soon all kinds of wild rumors began to spread. Troops were gathering to murder the people of Paris! Assembly members were going to be killed!

Prior to beginning the ReQuest Procedure, the group had been given some background related to the text, including labels for the three "Estates" that comprised the Estates General of Paris and the fact that at the time representatives of the Third Estate (peasants, laborers, and professionals) were gathered in Versailles for the purpose of writing a constitution for France.

Once the ReQuest Procedure began, Clarence proceeded to ask five to six unusual questions about each sentence. The other students noticed the uniqueness of Clarence's questions: Each time he asked a question, they tended to follow with similar questions. On the first sentence, he asked, "What does 'watched' mean here?" Other students then asked, "What does 'turns to' mean here?"; "What does 'everywhere' mean here?" On the second sentence, Clarence asked, "Did the king think they were heroes?" Other students asked, "Did the clergy think they were heroes?"; "Did *all* the people in the Third Estate think they were heroes?"; "Did *they* think they were heroes?"

From this simple heuristic experience, we all learned that whenever a student asks an interesting question, the teacher can reinforce it simply by responding, "Can anyone ask another question *like that one?*" See Figure 5.5 for other question types that have been generated through use of the ReQuest Procedure for use in ReQuest interactions. The questions are described with respect to the instructional objectives they best serve.

Research Findings

An initial study of the ReQuest Procedure (Manzo, 1969a) compared the technique with a full Directed Reading Activity. The DRA contained vocabulary enrichment, purpose-setting, silent reading, question training, and follow-up activities. The subjects were severe remedial readers ranging in age from 7 to 25 and attending a university reading clinic. Various data analyses led to the following findings and conclusions:

1. ReQuest students asked many more questions (a ratio of 23 to 1) during lesson activities than did DRA-trained students (who were regularly urged to ask questions). This suggests that the ReQuest students were in a learning environment that made them more activated, assertive, and curious.
2. ReQuest students' questions were found to be equal in sophistication to those of their teachers. This suggests that students were emulating their teachers' thought processes.
3. ReQuest students had higher levels of "congruent" ("on-target") oral communications with their teachers during lesson activities. This implies that they had improved levels of listening comprehension and therefore were more thoroughly "engaged" in the teaching/learning activity.
4. ReQuest students made significantly greater gains on standardized measures of reading comprehension. This suggests that quality student involvement in purpose setting is beneficial to comprehension.
5. DRA students made significantly greater gains in vocabulary (although both groups made substantial gains—over three months in six weeks of instruction). This implies that students learn what we teach them; the DRA stresses vocabulary study.
6. ReQuest teachers and students seemed to have touched one another in some deep and personal ways. This suggests that the reciprocal—give-and-take—interaction among them offered a sound way for students to express, and teachers to diagnose and extemporaneously provide for, students' reading, learning, and growing needs.

Figure 5.5 Other ReQuest-Invoked Questions (Generated by ReQuest Users for a Variety of Purposes)

Cunning questions designed to get students' attention and engage them in the lesson: "Now that you have carefully read the first sentence and asked me all the questions you care to about it, I have some for you. But first, are you sure that you don't want to reread that sentence or ask any additional questions? OK, turn your books face down. Now what was the fifth word in that first sentence?" (turn to page 142 to see how this teacher answered this question when students turned it on him) or "What is the title of this piece?" and/or "Who is the author?"

Predictable questions intended to calm: Typical *what, why, who, when, where,* and *how* questions will do this. Students generally are ready for these and can feel successful and involved when they are asked them.

Mind-opening questions designed to stir wonder, connections, and stimulate further questioning: "Turn your books face up and study that first sentence for a moment. Why do you suppose there is a comma after the fourth word in that sentence?" Hearing no answer, "Let's read it orally with the comma after the third word. Now after the fifth word." The answer may never become vivid, but the youngsters who struggled with this question seemed to come to a fresh sense, perhaps for the first time, that there is a profound relationship between punctuation and communication. Awareness and effective use of such print markings are characteristic of expert readers. (To dramatize this point, show sentences under different punctuation conditions: "A woman without her man has no reason for living" can become "A woman: without her, man has no reason for living," or "Call me fool if you wish" can become "Call me, fool, if you wish.")

Introspective questions, which tend to induce "metacognitive" or introspective-type thinking: "Did we raise a good question (purpose) to guide our reading of this selection?"; "What have you learned about 'proper reading' from this lesson?"; "What meaning did you give to the word _____?"

Common-knowledge questions, which tap into and develop "cultural literacy" by cultivating awareness of the "information" that surrounds us: "What kinds of buildings typically are of Gothic design in American cities?" This was followed by these prompts: "Picture in your mind some older courthouses and state buildings you have seen. Can you describe some of their features?"

Elaborative-knowledge questions designed to stimulate a taste for additional potentially relevant information: "Do you know how architectural arches are supported? . . . Well, I just happen to have read that . . ."

Ponderable questions for which neither the teacher nor the selection has a "right" answer but nonetheless are worth discussing: "Why do you suppose certain forms of architecture have developed and flourished in some countries rather than in others?"

Personalized questions of the evaluative type that only the student can answer: "Do you think you would enjoy being an architect?" or "What style of architecture do you suppose you would lean toward if you were an architect?"

Overcoming Inhibitions to Curiosity, Responding, and Mature Behavior
In general, the ReQuest Procedure is most notable because it can be counted on to make inroads into overcoming the collection of inhibitions that otherwise tend to smother natural expressions of curiosity, purposeful responding, and mature behavior. It improves questioning because students come to better understand what it is that they do not comprehend and the teacher incidentally comes to serve as a model of appropriate and socially sensitive ways to phrase questions. Further, students do not have to admit ignorance.

The last point is worth dwelling on. During ReQuest interactions, we have observed students "safely" asking questions such as "How is this word pronounced [pointing to it or spelling it]?" and "What does this word mean?" In no other situation have we seen students willing to ask questions so basic to effective reading and learning.

In a related way, confused, ego-defensive, and sometimes tactless student responses that often can crush teacher enthusiasm for further questioning also are reduced during ReQuest interactions. Students slowly begin to emulate the more poised ways teachers *answer* as well as ask questions. In one incident, a student turned around and asked the teacher the "cunning" question "What was the fifth word in that sentence?" The teacher smiled and reflectively responded, "I thought you might ask me that, but with 17 words in this sentence, I knew I'd miss the whole sense of it if I tried to remember them in sequence, so I don't know." The stunned student leaned back, half-smiled, and said, "A minute ago, I felt stupid for not being able to answer that question. Now you don't know the answer either, and you sound smart!" This is the sort of effective use of modeling that makes concurrent teaching practical. In this case, students were led to see, value, and emulate complex and mature thinking and behaving as well as to acquire targeted content objectives and reading skills.

Now let us consider another approach to teaching that attempts to take full advantage of the byplay between modeling and reciprocity.

Design 2: Reciprocal Teaching

Reciprocal Teaching is an attempt to amplify and elaborate the fundamental elements of the ReQuest Procedure into a more broadly based educational approach. Annemarie Palincsar and Ann Brown of the Center for the Study of Reading have been responsible for this development. A summary of their thoughts, research, and recommended practices follows.

According to Palincsar and Brown (1984), much of what is called "reading" in the later grades actually is critical thinking and studying. Further, they feel that the rigorous thinking and reading demands of our technology-oriented society make reliance on remembered facts and fallacies from school an inadequate model for education. A more appropriate model would focus on development of "intelligent novices": students who may not possess necessary background knowledge in a new field but know how to acquire it—students who have learned how to learn.

Question, Summarize, Predict, Clarify

As a first step toward developing "intelligent novices," Palincsar and Brown (1986) selected four reading strategies frequently employed by "expert readers":

- *Questioning:* Framing main-idea questions and avoiding detail questions.
- *Summarizing:* Identifying or forming topic sentences; developing labels for lists given in the text; and deleting unimportant or redundant information.
- *Predicting:* Making predictions which can serve as purposes for reading. These may be text based (keyed to specific information given) or content based (based on the topic but not specified in the text).
- *Clarifying:* Identifying sections of text which may be unclear: "Is there anything in the third paragraph that makes it hard to understand?"

The goal of Reciprocal Teaching is not merely to teach an isolated skill; rather, it is for students to eventually take individual initiative for summarizing, questioning, clarifying, and predicting. Therefore, the teacher does not merely instruct and then leave students to work unaided; instead, he or she develops an "interaction" in which teacher and students work together toward developing good questioning, summarizing, predicting, and clarifying statements. As students voluntarily take on more of this responsibility, the teacher acts less as a model and more like a sympathetic coach. To make this transition, the teacher must engage in "on-line" diagnosis, continuously evaluating and revising his or her impression of each student's competence. Palincsar and Brown call this *expert scaffolding:* The teacher provides support when and where it is needed, moving toward a gradual transfer of control (fading) from the expert (teacher) to the intelligent novices (students). The expert's encouragement and direction form the scaffold that supports the novices' initial efforts. The scaffold is gradually removed as student competence grows.

Reciprocal Teaching begins with a class discussion of why we sometimes experience difficulties in reading text. The concepts of questioning, summarizing, clarifying, and predicting are introduced as activities helpful in attending, understanding, and remembering.

The next phase of Reciprocal Teaching is explicit instruction in each of the four concepts. This is done not in isolation but through teacher modeling and examples based on a meaningful context. When students are comfortable with the four processes, they and the teacher begin to take turns assuming the role of teacher to elicit questions, summaries, clarifications, and predictions from the class. The one playing the role of teacher is responsible for leading the dialog (or languaging interaction) in examining the reading selection. Figure 5.6 presents an example of questioning, summarizing, and predicting from an actual classroom dialog that occurred just 10 days into training with a group of children (Palincsar & Brown, 1986).

Teachers using Reciprocal Teaching have run into problems similar to one that Manzo and Legenza (1975) encountered about 10 years earlier when using the ReQuest Procedure with kindergarten children to analyze pictures. It was not

Figure 5.6   Illustration of Reciprocal Teaching

Student 1 (in role of "teacher"): My *question* is, what does the aquanaut need when he goes under water?
Student 2: A watch.
Student 3: Flippers.
Student 4: A belt.
Student 1: Those are all good answers.
Teacher: Nice job! I have a question too. Why does the aquanaut wear a belt? What is so special about it?
Student 3: It's a heavy belt and keeps him from floating up to the top again.
Teacher: Good for you.
Student 1: For my *summary* now: This paragraph was about what aquanauts need to take when they go under the water.
Student 5: And also about why they need those things.
Student 3: I think we need to clarify gear.
Student 6: That's the special things they need.
Teacher: Another word for *gear* in this story might be equipment—the equipment that makes it easier for the aquanauts to do their job.
Student 1: I don't think I have a prediction to make.
Teacher: Well, in the story, they tell us that there are "many strange and wonderful creatures" that the aquanauts see as they do their work. My *prediction* is that they'll describe some of these creatures. What are some of the strange creatures you already know about that live in the ocean?
Student 6: Octopuses.
Student 3: Whales?
Student 5: Sharks!
Teacher: Let's listen and find out. Who would like to be our teacher?

Source: From "Interactive Teaching to Promote Independent Learning from Text" by A. S. Palincsar and A. L. Brown, 1986, *The Reading Teacher, 39,* pp. 771–777. Copyright 1986 by the International Reading Association. Reprinted with permission of Annemarie S. Palincsar and the International Reading Association.

reported in the original Manzo and Legenza study, but there was one little girl who seemed devoid of curiosity. She would not ask a single question. Palincsar and Brown (1986) reported that they too had several students who could not quite get the "hang" of what it meant to lead a discussion. The solution hit upon by both sets of researchers was to have the children simply repeat what the teacher modeled. The little girl in the Manzo and Legenza classroom moved to the average for her class on the questioning scale in just two instructional periods. Palincsar and Brown's results were equally remarkable: The students who had been reluctant to talk suddenly began to lead organized discussions. Palincsar and Brown came to call this useful repetition strategy "mimicing." We have come to refer to it as "strategic parroting." A classroom strategy designed to capitalize on strategic parroting is called *Note Cue* and is described in Chapter 10.

Content Reading Reciprocal Teaching

Palincsar and Brown also have experimented with more content-area-based and peer-oriented versions of Reciprocal Teaching. Students are grouped by twos in what the authors call a peer "dyad" version and instructed to ask each other questions about the material to be read. The content area variation has five steps and is described in Figure 5.7.

Research Findings

In view of the broad applications of Reciprocal Teaching currently being developed, it seems appropriate to review a critique of related research findings. Reeve, Palincsar, and Brown (1985) report 10 main outcomes from studies using Reciprocal Teaching with students who were classified as good decoders but poor comprehenders:

1. There was clear improvement in students' ability to paraphrase, question, clarify, and predict.
2. Most students learned to lead (languaging) dialogs independently.
3. There was substantial quantitative improvement in performance on teacher-constructed comprehension tests (improvements ranged from 20% to 80% in various studies).
4. Effects were durable. No drops were noted over an almost eight-week period and only a small drop after six months.
5. Effects could be generalized to classroom settings: Poor students often reached or surpassed the average of their classmates.

Figure 5.7 Reciprocal Teaching for Content Area Reading

1. Students convert subheadings in text into two written predictions of what they think they will read about.
2. The class discusses these.
3. Following reading of a segment of material (usually four paragraphs), students write "two questions and a summary reflecting the information in that segment."
4. Students write examples of "any information which require(s) clarification."
5. The class discusses their written questions, summaries, and clarifications.

Source: From "Interactive Teaching to Promote Independent Learning from Text" by A. S. Palincsar and A. L. Brown, 1986, *The Reading Teacher, 39,* pp. 771–777. Copyright 1986 by the International Reading Association. Reprinted with permission of Annemarie S. Palincsar and the International Reading Association.

6. Effects could be transferred to other types of comprehension assessment tasks, such as writing summaries and questions and detecting anomolous sentences in texts.
7. Standardized comprehension test scores improved an average of two years.
8. The full four-phase strategy was more effective than any variations tried.
9. Given training, regular teachers were able to use the strategy effectively.
10. Teachers were enthusiastic about the strategy and planned to incorporate it into their daily routines.

There are two notable differences between ReQuest and Reciprocal Teaching. First, ReQuest is an incisive prereading procedure, while Reciprocal Teaching attempts to do much more. Second, Reciprocal Teaching requires considerable teacher and student training *prior to use,* whereas ReQuest is a heuristic for *providing* considerable teacher and student training *with* use.

The next prereading design also has a strong heuristic element. It is more a general approach than a specific teaching technique.

Design 3: Mindset Approach

The *mindset* approach to prereading attempts to provide students with a perspective for reading. This is done by offering an analogy that can serve as a mold into which raw textual information can be poured and shaped to some specific purpose.

Pichert and Anderson (1977) demonstrated the force of this approach. They had two groups read an identical passage from two different perspectives: a burglar and a home buyer. Predictably, each group came away with different information; the "burglars," for example, were much more likely to recall an open window than were the "home buyers."

When a certain outcome is strongly desired, the teacher should identify a role, or perspective, from which to ask students to read. To stimulate interesting discussion, the teacher can create a few different perspectives. These can be described on slips of paper and passed around to students before they read. Examples might be "Read this selection on Iran as if you were an Iranian religious fundamentalist; a westernized Iranian; an American oil driller; a Soviet citizen; an automaker." Students will not always fully grasp the perspectives offered, but they will be ready to hear and learn more about those perspectives from the teacher and other class members immediately following reading.

On a personal note, the first author once tried a misdirected variation on this approach with a graduate research seminar. It fell on its face! However, some of the mistakes made are worth noting. The students were asked to study certain leading figures in world history, from John Dewey to Napoleon, and then try to read and critique the reading research literature from the perspective of that individual. The process was too obscure and drawn out, however. It took the students so long to figure out the perspective(s) of the historical figures that they were stranded reading difficult research material from an even more ambiguous, rather than clarifying, perspective. A critique of each person and the nature and relevance of his or her perspective to the reading material probably would have helped. For discussions and examples of how this "mindset" approach can be made to work much more effectively, see Note Cue (Chapter 10), the Parallel Form strategy (Chapter 13), Communal Poetry (Chapter 12), and DeBono's Thinking Hats (Chapter 8).

The next strategy focuses on eliciting students' background knowledge. It has many advocates and a few critics. See what you think.

Design 4: Prereading Plan (PreP)

The *Prereading Plan (PreP)* is recommended by Judith Langer (1981), its developer, as a means of simultaneously providing effective assessment and quality instruction. The method is intended to foster group discussion and topic awareness. In this three-phase process, the teacher first identifies key terms. Then the teacher

1. Asks students about their associations with the terms
2. Leads a discussion about "what made you think of that association?"
3. Prompts further discussion and "reformulation of knowledge" by asking, "Now that we have discussed this, have you any new ideas before we read?"

PreP tends to be well received by teachers and some teacher trainers, but some valid criticisms also exist. Critiques by teachers following simulations of this method have brought out the following praise and concerns:

1. PreP gets students talking and contributing as few methods can.
2. PreP calls up a lot of irrelevant as well as relevant information.
3. It is not clear whether or not the teacher should suppress irrelevancies and correct misconceptions prior to reading.
4. If the teacher should suppress irrelevancies and/or correct misconceptions, how and when should this be done?

The purpose of prereading strategies is to activate and build background knowledge for reading (Holbrook, 1984). Langer and Nicholich (1981) have demonstrated that the level of prior knowledge exhibited by students in a PreP lesson is an excellent predictor of how well they will subsequently comprehend that passage. This study frequently is cited as supporting the efficacy of PreP. In reality, however, it does not. The study merely shows that PreP elicits background knowledge; it does not demonstrate that the strategy effectively empowers students with weak background knowledge or reading skills.

PreP certainly has value as a diagnostic teaching strategy, especially for beginning teachers. It readily reveals which students have much, some, or little prior knowledge. Beyond this, however, PreP is rather limited. Since it seems to activate but not necessarily build background knowledge, it probably should be used in conjunction with other prereading strategies for empowering students to read content text. Semantic Mapping, for example (discussed next), is quite compatible with Langer's PreP strategy and offers greater opportunity for schema building as well as a richer context for engagement, modeling, and reciprocity.

Design 5: Preliminary Semantic Mapping

You have read about Structured Overviews, a form of graphic organizer of text. The **Semantic Mapping** strategy (Hanf, 1971) uses a graphic organizer to structure students' *background information.*

Semantic Mapping is used prior to reading to draw out and organize students' background information pertaining to an upcoming reading topic. The teacher writes the title or main idea of the lesson on the chalkboard. Then, using students' associations and other labels acquired during PreP or by skimming the reading selection, teacher and students construct a partial *Semantic Map*, or graphic organizer (see Figures 5.8 and 5.9). Then *each* student completes and/or reorganizes the Semantic Map following silent reading.

If reading *builds* schema and *requires* schema, it follows that there should be value in reading to improve subsequent reading. This is the basis of the next strategy.

Design 6: Reading-before-Reading

There are at least four ways to build readiness to read with actual reading: Annotation Exchanges, Digest Versions, Advance Organizers, and Crafton's Reiterative

Figure 5.8   Prereading Semantic Map for "Sea Otters"

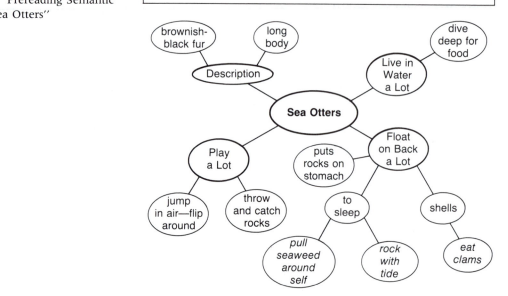

Source: From *Semantic Mapping: Classroom Applications* (pp. 4–5) by J. E. Heimlich and S. D. Pittleman, 1986, Newark, DE: International Reading Association. Copyright 1986 by the International Reading Association. Reprinted with permission of Joan Heimlich and the International Reading Association.

Figure 5.9   Postreading Semantic Map for Sea Otters

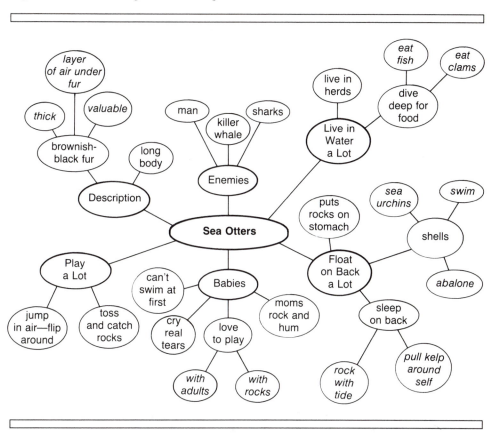

Source: From *Semantic Mapping: Classroom Applications* (pp. 4–5) by J. E. Heimlich and S. D. Pittleman, 1986, Newark, DE: International Reading Association. Copyright 1986 by the International Reading Association. Reprinted with permission of Joan Heimlich and the International Reading Association.

Reading. The Annotation Exchange system is described in Chapter 7 on postreading and Chapter 11 on schoolwide programming, because it is valuable in teaching writing as well as reading readiness.

Digest Versions
The idea of *reading-before-reading* started as a popular movement. In the 1950s, Cliff Notes (book digests) and even comic-book versions of the classics became familiar means of making the classics more palatable and giving the reader a leg up on the unabridged versions. Not surprisingly, these mechanisms received a black eye when many students began using them as surrogates rather than supplementals. Open resentment against digests and abridged materials was reversed shortly thereafter, however, when a research-based system called "Advance Ideational Organizers" restored credibility to the intuitive value of reading-before-reading.

Advance Organizers

In a classic study, learning theorist David Ausubel (1960) had college students read a "prestructured" statement (500 words) before reading a longer (2,500-word) selection in science. The Advance Ideational Organizers clearly improved student comprehension. Subsequent studies by several other researchers produced results that sometimes replicated this finding but at other times did not. The difference in these outcomes was traced primarily to the quality of the prereading passage. It had to impart a sense of structure but not be too abstract.

It is difficult to say precisely how abstract is *too* abstract. Accordingly, instructors in the college reading program at the University of Missouri–Kansas City have adapted this prereading strategy in a way that combines abstract and literal versions. An Abstract Organizer is pasted to the inside front cover of a book and a Literal Organizer to the inside back cover. Then students are encouraged to use both organizers as frequently as they wish while reading the larger work. Figures 5.10 and 5.11 provide examples of each type of organizer for *The Old Man and the Sea*.

Abstract and literal Advance Organizers can be provided for especially difficult textbook chapters. Students should be encouraged to read and ask questions about these before reading and reminded to refer to them as needed during reading.

The next strategy illustrates how an entire field can sometimes overlook the obvious.

Crafton's Reiterative Reading

Linda Crafton's *Reiterative Reading* (1983) is based on the proposition that students can independently acquire relevant background information through the reading process itself. In her study of this approach, Crafton found that simply having 11th graders read two different articles on the same topic "dramatically improved students' comprehension of the second article and the cognitive level at which they processed it" (1983, p. 587). Crafton went on to say that her study supports three assertions: (1) "the common view of reading as a natural knowledge-generating activity"; (2) the belief that "text on an unfamiliar topic can serve as cognitive preparation for the next"; and (3) the observation that experimental subjects who read two forms of the same material "were more active during the reading process and personalized information to a greater degree than did subjects who read unrelated materials" (1983, p. 590).

Our personal experience tends to validate and extend Crafton's findings. The first author once taught world geography to a difficult, sometimes unruly class of low-achieving ninth graders. We had a new, slick, black-covered text that was impossible in almost every way: The print was small, information was dense, and sentence structures were complex beyond reason. In short order, we found 20 copies of a very old geography text in the district's attic. We read both books, alternating the order according to fancy more than to any deep analysis of textual value. In addition to the obvious benefits of seeing most things twice, and in different words, we often were challenged and amused by diverse perspectives, sometimes contrary information, and changing and often bewildering facts. For example, we puzzled over how a then obscure and backward Iran could have been

Figure 5.10 *The Old Man and the Sea:* Literal Organizer

The Old Man and the Sea tells of an extremely poor old fisherman, SANTIAGO, who fishes alone in the Gulf Stream, and of MANOLIN, a boy who had fished with him until the man's luck had gone bad. The boy still had deep respect and affection for him, however, and brought him food and other things he needed.

The book opens in September as the old man decides to go far out into the Gulf Stream to take advantage of a strong current. He rowed out in the dark, lowered his bait and began drifting with the current. When the sun was high, the bait was taken by a large fish. The man tried to pull the fish up, but it was too big and simply began towing the boat out to sea. All afternoon and all night the fish pulled the SKIFF, with the old man resolutely straining against the line to insure that the fish did not break it.

About sunrise, the fish gave a lurch, which cut the man's hand. Santiago ate strips of raw tuna to keep up his strength, and he wished the boy were with him. Finally, the fish surfaced, and it was the biggest fish the man had ever seen—longer than the skiff. But it dove again and continued towing the boat the rest of that day and into the night.

The old man was suffering greatly by now but was still resolved to bring the fish in. He tried to sleep, still standing and holding the line, but woke as the fish again surfaced and pulled him down into the boat, where the line cut into his hands and his back. He got up and fought the fish to try and tire it. As the sun rose on the old man's third day at sea, the fish began to circle, and the man was able to pull in some line. After several hours, feeling dizzy and faint, the old man pulled the fish near enough to the boat to harpoon it. Since the fish was larger than the boat, the man lashed it alongside, rigged the sail, and, exhausted, set sail for home.

But it was too good to last. Sharks had caught the scent. From sunset until after midnight, the old man fought the sharks, first with his harpoon, then his knife, and finally a club. But it was no use—they had cleaned his fish, and he was beaten.

He arrived in the harbor and managed to reach his shack before he collapsed with fatigue. In the morning, the fishermen were astounded at the 18-foot skeleton lashed to the boat. When the old man awakened, the boy heard of his ordeal and tried to console him.

Figure 5.11 *The Old Man and the Sea:* Abstract Organizer

The Old Man and the Sea tells of a fisherman's struggle with the elements while trying to hook and kill a huge fish, only to have it eaten by sharks.

The story basically is a testament to humankind's unconquerable spirit—to our ability to achieve dignity in the face of defeat. Humans are shown to be noble because of their willingness to struggle and persevere against the hardships in life. The man tells the fish, "I will show him what a man can do and what a man endures" (p. 66) and "Man is not made for defeat . . . a man can be destroyed, but not defeated" (p. 103).

The book also shows the author's view of humankind in relation to the physical universe: The fisherman refers to both the stars and the fish as "my brother." This is taken to mean that we should respect and love our natural environment even as we strive to carve existence out of it and conquer it.

the seat of the great Persian Empire. There were many times when we wished we had a third- or fourth-grade text to explain some things in even greater detail. We never could quite get a conceptual fix, for example, on how maps were made in times past when map makers could not get up high enough to see. A recent docudrama on PBS television made this clearer than any text could and made a further point in support of reiteration.

A monthly look at public television offerings can provide some wonderful opportunities for nontextual reiteration or previewing and reviewing of topics in literature, science, social studies, and the arts. See the section on media and microcomputers in Chapter 11 for more information on the value of nonprint media.

The next and final strategy for facilitating the prereading stage of comprehension is based on a special kind of teacher-prepared worksheet. Its unique feature is that students complete the first part of the worksheet *before* they read.

Design 7: Anticipation-Reaction Guides

Anticipation-Reaction (A-R) guides are a means of eliciting students' prior knowledge of and attitudes toward a topic in a more guided way than tends to occur in the open-ended format of strategies such as PReP. The A-R guide typically is a series of three to five teacher-prepared statements that students react to before and after reading. Prior to reading, students agree or disagree with the statements and discuss the reasons for their responses. After reading, the statements are reconsidered as a guide for structuring oral and written reactions.

The primary purpose of the A-R guide is to encourage students to be active and therefore interactive and constructive readers. Structuring statements such as those in Figure 5.12 tend to reduce irrelevant comments when background knowledge

Figure 5.12 Anticipation-Reaction Guide Based on the Short Story "Caged" by Lloyd E. Reeve

---

Directions: Read each statement below. If you agree, put a check in the "Before Reading" blank. If you do not agree, do not put a check in the blank. Directions for the "Author's Ideas" column will be given later.

Before Reading		Author's Ideas
_____	The creatures in pet stores are happy and contented.	_____
_____	People sometimes commit cruel acts without realizing that they are cruel.	_____
_____	Freedom is more valuable than money.	_____
_____	Unusual behavior sometimes frightens people.	_____
_____	Two people can be a part of the same event yet have totally different understandings of it.	_____

Figure 5.13   Anticipation-Reaction Guide Based on a Selection Entitled "Ranchers and Cowboys"

Directions: Read each item and decide if you agree with it or disagree. Put a "yes" on the line next to the item labeled "Before Reading" if you agree, a "no" if you disagree. Think about how you would defend your point of view.

Before Reading	After Reading	
_____	_____	Cattle raising techniques were developed by American ranchers (p. 513).
_____	_____	You would enjoy life as a cowboy (p. 514).
_____	_____	You would not mind a cattle drive going through your land (pp. 515–516).
_____	_____	You would have a comfortable life as the wife of a cowboy (pp. 520–521).
_____	_____	Overstocking cattle and overgrazing resulted in the end of open range ranching (p. 523).

Source: From "Increasing Critical Reading in Junior High Classrooms" by B. Ericson, M. Hubler, T. W. Bean, C. C. Smith, and J. V. McKenzie, 1987, *Journal of Reading, 30,* p. 434. Copyright 1987 by the International Reading Association. Reprinted with permission of Bonnie Ericson and the International Reading Association.

is solicited, thus leading students into rather than away from the text. After reading, students are directed to consider the same questions from the author's point of view and to reconsider their initial judgments in light of the information and perspectives presented in the selection.

A-R guide statements should be designed to alert students to points on which their ideas or attitudes may conflict with those in the reading selection. The process of acknowledging and engaging such points of conflict has been called the key to critical reading (Frager & Thompson, 1985). A-R guides encourage this process before reading by having students identify existing ideas and attitudes. This alerts students to related information in the text. Their efforts to resolve these conflicts lead to an accommodation that expands on previous schema. After reading, the A-R guide reinforces and extends schema development (Head & Readence, 1986). Students who used the A-R guide in Figure 5.13, for example, discovered that it was Mexican ranchers who developed the cattle-raising techniques used in the United States (Ericson, Hubler, Bean, Smith, & McKenzie, 1987).

Duffelmeyer, Baum, and Merkley (1987) emphasized the power of A-R guides (which they call "Extended Anticipation Guides") for schema development. Note that their guide on planarians (flatworms) in Figure 5.14 includes two separate worksheets for the anticipation and reaction stages. The reaction worksheet asks for specific information to clarify anticipation statements that were not supported by the selection.

Figure 5.14   Extended Anticipation Guide

Part 1—Before Reading

Directions: Read each statement below. If you believe that a statement is true, place a check in the Agree column. If you believe that a statement is false, place a check in the Disagree column. Be ready to explain your choices.

Agree	Disagree	
_____	_____	Worms die when they are cut in half.
_____	_____	Some living things don't need sunlight.
_____	_____	Some animals can grow a new body part after it has been cut off.
_____	_____	Animals that don't have noses can't smell.
_____	_____	Laying eggs and giving birth are the only ways that animals can reproduce.
_____	_____	All worms have round bodies.

Part 2—After Reading

Directions: Now you will read information related to each of the statements in Part 1. If the information you read supports your choices above, place a check in the Support column. If the information does not support your choices above, place a check in the No Support column and write what the selection says in your own words.

Support	No Support	In Your Own Words
_____	_X_	Some flatworms split apart and become two flatworms.
_X_	_____	_____
_____	_X_	If you cut off a flatworm's head, it will grow a new one.
_____	_____	_____
_____	_____	_____
_____	_____	_____

Source: From "Maximizing Reader-Text Confrontation with an Extended Anticipation Guide" by F. A. Duffelmeyer, D. D. Blum, and D. J. Merkley, 1987, *Journal of Reading, 31,* pp. 146–150. Copyright 1987 by the International Reading Association. Reprinted with permission of Frederick Duffelmeyer and the International Reading Association.

Anticipation-Reaction guides tend to spark lively prereading discussions and promote active, empowered reading. Another key to empowered reading is vocabulary knowledge. In the next section, you will find strategies for introducing meanings of key vocabulary terms and research-based principles for guiding vocabulary instruction.

PREREADING VOCABULARY STRATEGIES

Vocabulary preparation and enrichment form an important traditional part of the prereading phase of content and reading instruction. The term *vocabulary* has been

Source: From *The Study Readers—Fifth Year* (p. 85), by Alberta Walker and Mary R. Parkman, 1924. Merrill.

alternatively used to refer to basic decoding—that is, word recognition and analysis—as well as to vocabulary meaning. A simple strategy for introducing and teaching students how to decode words is presented shortly (see Glass Analysis in Chapter 10).

This section offers five methods for introducing and teaching vocabulary meanings. They are built around four functions. Two of them, the Frayer model and Typical to Technical Meaning, take a strongly cognitive approach. The third, Subjective Approach to Vocabulary, takes a primarily affective approach. The fourth, Motor Imaging, is deeply rooted in that often forgotten aspect of schema, physical-sensory learning. The fifth, morpheme analysis, relies on the linguistic structure of words. Several other vocabulary approaches more suitable for postreading or separate enrichment are covered elsewhere.

Design 1: Frayer's Cognitive Approach

The *Frayer model* (Frayer, Frederick, & Klausmeir, 1969) is intended to provide a thorough basis for understanding words. The method resembles Gray's paradigm for teaching phonic elements in both structure and sequence. McNeil (1987) describes the steps in the process this way:

1. Discriminating the relevant qualities common to all instances of the concept. For example, the relevant attribute of "globe" is "spherical."
2. Discriminating the relevant from the irrelevant properties of instances of the concept. For example, "large" or "small" is an irrelevant attribute for "globe."
3. Providing an example of the concept, such as a classroom globe.

4. Providing a nonexample of the concept, such as a chart (nonspherical).
5. Relating the concept to a subordinate concept, such as "ball."
6. Relating the concept to a superordinate term, such as "global."
7. Relating the concept to a coordinate term, such as "map." (McNeil, 1986, p. 116)

According to McNeil, the Frayer model is "very useful in preparing pupils for reading." He describes the lesson in this way: "The teacher identifies new words critical to the topic . . . for the words. . . . [T]hen, pupils try to provide both examples and non-examples." Applying the Frayer model to vocabulary, however, strikes us as being a rather tedious method that may be necessary only with the slowest learners or with very difficult concepts not supported by a reinforcing context. A similar but more concise method, called *Semantic Feature Analysis* (Pearson & Johnson, 1978), exists and is described and illustrated in Chapter 7. The next strategy has more general applicability.

Design 2: Typical to Technical Meaning Approach

Often the most common words will have a special, technical application in a particular content area. For example, the word *true* is used in mechanics to indicate that gears are well synchronized, and *untrue* means poorly synchronized. The *Typical to Technical Meaning Approach*, developed by Pearson and Johnson (1978), is based on a prereading discussion designed to clear up the confusion that sometimes occurs when words have both familiar and technical meanings.

This method requires considerable preparation time. The time will be well spent, however, because a "strategic learning" benefit can be derived by referring back to these lessons as examples of how terms can have both typical and technical meanings. After just a few tries with this method, a teacher can simply ask, "Do we have any terms in today's material for which there is a common as well as a technical meaning?" and the rest of the lesson will unfold from previous practice.

Steps in the Typical to Technical Meaning Approach

1. Discuss a term's common meanings, then introduce its technical definition.
2. Have students do word-to-meaning exercises, matching each term with both definitions (see the examples in Figure 5.15).
3. Using a variation of the cloze technique, have students fill in blanks where the terms are used in either the typical or the technical manner.

The examples shown in Figure 5.15 are from a published account of junior high teacher William Welker (1987). Welker's example uses the mathematics terms *acute, complementary, angle,* and *supplementary.*

The Typical to Technical Meaning Approach highlights several pesky problems associated with teaching vocabulary in a content class. It can take years for students to fully assimilate word meanings. It is difficult to determine how much class time to give to vocabulary instruction. Finally, it is unclear when and how to teach

Figure 5.15   Typical to Technical Meaning Exercises

Exercise 1
Select the correct common and mathematical definitions for each term. Write the letter of each definition in the appropriate column for common or technical meaning.

Definitions:

A. Point of view
B. Making whole; completing
C. Supplying what is lacking; additional
D. Space between two lines or surfaces that meet
E. Having a sharp point
F. Either of 2 angles that combine to equal 90 degrees
G. An angle which is less than 90 degrees in value
H. Either of 2 angles that together form exactly 180 degrees

Terms	Common Meaning	Technical Meaning
acute	_____	_____
supplementary	_____	_____
complementary	_____	_____
angle	_____	_____

Exercise 2
Select the best word to complete each sentence below. Each word will be used twice.

Words: complementary, acute, angle, supplementary

1. The sword had a very _____ cutting edge.
2. The _____ angle for a 50-degree angle is a 40-degree angle.
3. Our reading textbook comes with _____ materials such as workbooks and ditto sheets.
4. If an angle is 55 degrees, it is called an _____ angle.
5. A black tie with a white shirt would be considered a _____ match.
6. Now that I have given my thoughts on the subject, what is your _____ (or opinion) on the matter?
7. A pie can be sliced into pieces with many different _____.
8. Two angles that together equal 180 degrees are _____ angles.

---

vocabulary in the middle of a content-based reading lesson. What *is* clear is that vocabulary instruction in a content class should be done quickly in order for it to be facilitating without being distracting. It also should be done with an eye toward building on what students already know, as well as laying a foundation for what they will be expected to learn. Words are building blocks for schema.

The next method illustrates how to introduce vocabulary terms quickly without losing students in the process.

Design 3: Subjective Approach to Vocabulary (SAV)

The affectively based SAV procedure (Manzo, 1983) is "fast food" but not "junk food." It builds on what students already know by urging them to find personal experiences or other associations with which to anchor the sometimes ethereal dictionary definitions of new terms. The method helps students remember meanings of important content-related terms while illustrating how they might use the same strategy in self-directed word learning. The *Subjective Approach to Vocabulary (SAV)* draws heavily upon the languaging process: The teacher guides students in a "talk-through" designed to make them better strategic readers by learning how to use their own and other students' experiences and tellings as a foundation for acquiring some of the many aspects of meaning in "new" words. In this way, the biographies of individual lives become part of the biography of the words and ideas offered in school. Learning is made more real and relevant.

Research Findings
In a study with sixth-grade subjects (Casale & Manzo, 1983), SAV was found to be considerably better than traditional (dictionary "look-up" and sentence-writing) approaches to vocabulary instruction. However, it was slightly less effective than the "motor"-based approach described later. A study with remedial readers (Manzo, 1984) showed that SAV provided some positive incidental benefits to two other important areas of comprehension: improved attention span and higher levels of abstract thinking.

SAV lends itself better than most vocabulary strategies to the preteaching of difficult words prior to a reading assignment. It also is useful in postreading vocabulary instruction and in concentrated vocabulary acquisition programs.

Steps and Options in the SAV Procedure
Step 1: The teacher identifies two to four words to be "pretaught" before reading.

Step 2: The teacher explains the contextual meaning of a word up front, then writes it on the chalkboard with an example or two, much as one would find in a dictionary. In this way, the teacher establishes the "objective"— or dictionary meaning of the word.

Step 3: The teacher asks the students, "What does this word remind you of?" The class briefly discusses and clarifies these experiences, thoughts, or images. (When using the method for the first time, the teacher might add, "It will be easier for you to learn and remember this new word if you can think of some personal 'mental pictures' or experiences that you can connect with it.")

Step 4: The teacher directs students to record the word, the objective meaning given, and some "subjective" association, either students' own or one offered by another class member that they find particularly vivid.

Step 5: (Added since initial publication) The teacher asks, "Now that you have a dictionary definition and a first reaction or association, what new associations or meanings do you have for this term?"

Step 6: The class reads the selection to build further contextual meaning of key words. (Context can be useless without some prior knowledge of a word's meaning.) Also, the teacher asks students whether they encountered other words of which they were unsure. The class lists and discusses such words as the need arises using the same basic approach.

Option 1: Students keep a glossary of objective, subjective, and "new" meanings for words covered in this way. It is best that they start their glossaries in the backs of their content class notebooks and work forward so as not to interfere with other class notes and to keep terms separate and easily available. This word listing can offer an excellent means of studying for exams in that almost all subjects can be reduced to a set of concept terms. Several studies have found that simple knowledge of key terms has a very high correlation with other, more elaborate forms of testing, such as multiple choice, fill-ins, and even essays.

Option 2: This SAV option has been suggested by primary and intermediate-grade teachers. Students divide a page into four equal parts and create an alphabetical, looseleaf-bound dictionary with illustrations of their own choosing. The word is placed in quadrant 1 along with its phonetic pronunciation; the dictionary meaning(s) goes in quadrant 2; a picture of the student's association with the word is drawn in quadrant 3; and one or two sentences containing subjective and/or new insights are written in quadrant 4. Quadrants 3 and 4 can be reversed if the teacher wishes to have students' illustrations "cap off" their best new interpretations of the words rather than serve as an exploration for meaning.

Figure 5.16 presents an example from an actual SAV lesson.

SAV: Problems and Promise

It is hard to tell how readily a class will take to an SAV lesson on its initial presentation. Group size may be an important factor. For example, the second author recently used SAV with a tenth-grade English class of only nine students. When asked for associations with five words (*adipose, adage, accrual, agape, alimentary*), the students stared at me as though I had asked them to drink hemlock. The very next hour, with some trepidation but little to lose, I trotted out the same five words and another tenth-grade class of 15 students was off and running. Soon they were *composing* as well as *associating*: "I picture Royal Stadium [home of the Kansas City Royals] when we were down but not out and came back to win the pennant and the Series; it's not over 'til the 'adipose' lady sings." A larger group sometimes may be necessary to increase the chance of at least one extrovert stirring the class's imagination and responding.

SAV can be particularly useful for providing multicultural outlooks and for working with second-language students. It gives teacher and students access to the alternative ways students may be processing and interpreting the world around them. It also provides students with a template, or mental model, illustrating how words are learned, thereby enabling them to become independent and strategic-word learners (see Figure 5.17).

Figure 5.16   Example from a SAV Lesson

The word was *arboreal*. It was in a seventh-grade science text. The teacher gave the meaning: "The word *arboreal* means 'having to do with trees or living in trees.' " A few examples were given: "Monkeys are arboreal animals"; "The word *arboreal* comes from the word *arbor*, as in Arbor Day, the day put aside to plant trees." The subjective-based aspect of the lesson began at this point. Explaining her question, the teacher added, "It will be easier for you to learn and remember this new term if you can think of some personal images or experiences which you can picture with it."

One student suggested, "The word reminds me of how my mother killed my peanut tree that we brought home from Georgia by overwatering it." To this, another student added, humorously, "That sounds like a 'tragic arboreal' experience." In that same humorous vein, another student asked, rhetorically, "Did you say that *arboreal* means 'living and swinging' in trees (?), 'cause I think my little brother is arboreal!"

The teacher then asked if anyone had formed a new meaning for *arboreal*. "It sounds to me like 'anything to do with trees,' " one student volunteered. The teacher then directed the class to record the word *arboreal* in their notebooks with the objective meaning she had provided and a parenthetical note on their initial and subsequent personal associations with the word.

The next strategy is subjective in another sense. It urges teacher and students to employ physical, or *motor*, associations to a greater extent than is usual in the sedentary context of schooling.

Design 4: Motor Imaging

Motor Imaging (Casale, 1985) may be unique among classroom strategies in that it draws on the physical-sensory as well as cognitive and affective domains of learning. The underlying principle of this strategy is akin to an expression in classical studies, "Nothing is in the intellect which was not first in the senses."

Motor Imaging is a form of "proprioceptive learning," that is, learning that "incorporates muscle movements to supplement visual and auditory stimuli" (Bush & Waugh, 1982). Developmental psychologists have observed that young children first respond to a stimulus with gross motor movements that signify (i.e., stand for) that stimulus. Over time, the motor movements become increasingly refined until the "motor meaning" is internalized as a "symbolic meaning," as Piaget refers to it. In this way, the meaning for the word has an internal, and potentially self-stimulating, counterpart to the cognitive association.

Apparently our initial schema consists almost exclusively of tactile and sensory-motor learnings. While this is no surprise, since that is all babies can do, we seem to have overlooked the fact that this aspect of schema may remain an active element of human learning even after other aspects of schema are added. Having students

Figure 5.17 Strategic Use of Personal Associations

Source: From "Subjective Approach to Vocabulary Acquisition (or 'I Think My Brother Is Arboreal!')" by A. V. Manzo, 1982, *Reading Psychology*, 3 (no. 2), p. 158. Copyright 1982 by Anthony V. Manzo. Reprinted by permission.

express words in physical terms seems to effect a stronger association, thereby improving the speed and depth with which they learn and recall words and their associated concepts.

Steps in Motor Imaging

1. The teacher takes a difficult word from the text, writes it on the chalkboard, pronounces it, and tells what it means.
2. The teacher asks students to imagine a simple pantomime for the word meaning ("How could you 'show' someone what this word means?").
3. When the teacher gives a signal, students do their "pantomimes" simultaneously.
4. The teacher selects the most common expression observed. He or she then demonstrates it to all the students, who then say the word and make the corresponding gestures.
5. The teacher repeats each new word, directing the class to do the pantomime and simultaneously recite a brief meaning or synonym.
6. The students' next encounter with the word is in the assigned reading material.

Figure 5.18 presents some examples from a Motor Imaging lesson.

A Hole in the Darkness

Manzo and Casale (1983) compared a cognitive (dictionary), an affective (subjective association), and a physical-sensory (motor) based approach to vocabulary. The motor-based strategy proved significantly better on several kinds of vocabulary measures. It appears that this methodology "punches a hole in the darkness" in

Figure 5.18   Motor Imaging Examples

New Word	Language Meaning	Motor Meaning
Appropriate	Right or fit for a certain purpose	Both palms together, matching perfectly
Convey	Take or carry from one place to another	Both hands together, palms upward, moving from one side to the other
Woe	Great sadness or trouble	One or both hands over the eyes, head slanted forward
Dazzle	Shine or reflect brightly	Palms close together, facing outward, fingers spread
Utmost	The very highest or most	One or both hands reaching up as far as possible
Abode	Place where you live	Hands meeting above the head in a triangular "roof" shape

terms of understanding and appreciating the need for some level of physical-kinesthetic involvement in the learning process. The highest forms of learning seem to have the most primitive foundations.

Among the more promising features of this observation is the fact that students at every level of intellectual ability seem to share a capacity for physical-associative learning. This makes Motor Imaging, and possibly other motor-based strategies, a potentially significant breakthrough, especially for heterogeneously grouped students from diverse cultural and linguistic backgrounds. For more information on Motor Imaging, see the section on English as a second language in Chapter 10.

Design 5: Incidental Morpheme Analysis

Eighty percent of the words in the English dictionary contain Greek or Latin prefixes, suffixes, or roots. These word parts, called *morphemes,* are units of language that cannot be further divided without losing meaning. Some morphemes have meanings only when attached to other word parts. Examples of such *bound morphemes* include *ed, ing, tele,* and *cide.* Other morphemes, such as *cover, graph,* and *stand,* called *free morphemes,* can stand alone, that is, are words in themselves.

Most expert readers and language users use morphemes to make sense out of and remember new words. The *Incidental Morpheme Analysis* strategy, a method fashioned by the authors for this book, teaches students to apply existing knowledge or morphemes to new words encountered in content reading.

Steps in Incidental Morpheme Analysis
As preparation for using the Incidental Morpheme Analysis approach, watch for words in reading assignments that probably are unfamiliar to students but have familiar word parts, or morphemes. Use the following steps to preteach these terms.

1. Write the term on the chalkboard or overhead, and underline meaningful word parts, or morphemic elements, that might help students understand the word's concept base.

    Example: <u>seis</u> mo <u>graph</u>

2. Ask students if they can use the underlined parts to grasp the word meaning, and why. If the word meaning is predicted correctly, write it under the word and proceed with steps 3 and 4 as reinforcement.
3. Tell students you will give them additional clues for predicting (or remembering) the word meaning. Beneath the underlined word parts, write "level one" clues, which are other, easier words using those morphemes. If students have not yet correctly predicted the word meaning, continue to ask for predictions.
4. Beneath the "level one" clues, write "level two" clues, which are word part meanings, and continue to ask for predictions until the correct definition is reached and written below the clues.

Example:

	seis	mo	graph
Level one clues: familiar words containing the underlined morphemes	seizure		telegraph graphic
Level two clues: word part meanings	to shake		written
Definition:	An instrument that records the direction, time, and intensity of earthquakes		

See Appendix D for a listing of Latin and Greek morphemes. See also the section on memory training in Chapter 9 for an interesting complementary means of introducing morpheme study.

We have now considered five methods for introducing key vocabulary terms. Several additional means of reinforcing vocabulary knowledge are developed in Chapter 7. The next section summarizes some important principles for guiding vocabulary instruction.

Principles for Guiding Vocabulary Efforts in Content Classes

Vocabulary acquisition, like reading comprehension, is an ongoing, lifelong process. There has been a wealth of research on how we learn words and how to best promote vocabulary development. The following list of principles is an abridged and updated version of an earlier review of 50 years of literature on vocabulary acquisition (Manzo & Sherk, 1971–72). While interest in vocabulary has been on the rise for some time, we are not aware of a more recent comprehensive review of this literature. Oddly enough, even the *Handbook of Reading Research* (Pearson, 1984) does not contain one.

1. The difficulty of the vocabulary in text affects students' ability to comprehend. Preteaching selected vocabulary terms improves comprehension.
2. Students develop an abiding interest in word acquisition primarily through interaction with teachers who are excited about words and are themselves "students of language."
3. Vocabulary is best taught at the teachable moment, when need arises. However, it also must be taught regularly and systematically for significant growth to occur.

4. It is necesssary to develop a rich "community of language" within the school to encourage continued vocabulary reinforcement and use outside the classroom.
5. Effective vocabulary instruction is best anchored in affective, cognitive, and physical experiences, more so than in word manipulation activities and games.
6. The study of morphemes—prefixes, suffixes, and roots—has a positive effect on learning the many words in our language with Greek and Latin roots.
7. When a student asks for the meaning of a word, provide a meaning at that time rather than saying "look it up." Referring the student to the dictionary at the moment of greatest need tends to discourage inquiry. However, where there is doubt about a word's meaning, there is no better arbiter than the dictionary. Show students that *you* use it.

There is a great deal to know about vocabulary acquisition that is interesting as well as useful. For example, did you know that vocabulary level tends to remain relatively intact following most neurological trauma and therefore is a good measure of intellectual potential following trauma? The following brief postscript on context cues is another interesting and useful concept for guiding instruction.

Postscript: Context Clues

A popular idea is that it is desirable to teach students how to use context to determine a word's meaning. This can be a misguided practice, however. Context is useful for determining the various shades of meaning for known words and reminding one of meanings previously learned and partially forgotten. But context is almost never sufficient to reveal the meaning of an *unknown* word. In fact, the meanings of most sentences (and therefore the context) often are determined by the very words we expect students to use context to define.

The purpose of vocabulary instruction is to build greater precision in comprehension, thought, and expression. Context-based word learning can have the opposite effect. All of us have words in our lexicons to which we have attributed slightly incorrect or totally oppositional meanings. These mislearnings can travel with us for years, distorting context, comprehension, and communication. Context tends to reinforce the meanings (correct or incorrect) we already have for words rather than impart new meanings. Almost every word that has been mislearned was "learned" from context. When evaluating vocabulary instruction strategies, keep in mind that good strategies for teaching vocabulary will involve getting precise meanings for words. Use of context most often parallels the way we *mislearn* words.

CHAPTER TIE-UPS

♦♦♦   *Graphic Organizer*

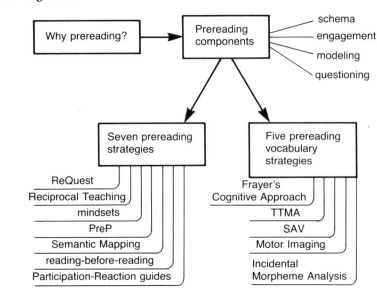

♦♦♦   *Critique and Anticipation*

This chapter showed that prereading instruction involves calling up appropriate prior experiences, providing relevant knowledge and vocabulary, raising a compelling question or purpose for reading, and teaching students how to achieve each of these objectives independently and strategically. The chapter presented seven prereading designs for these purposes: (1) ReQuest; (2) Reciprocal Teaching; (3) mindset approach; (4) PreP; (5) preliminary Semantic Mapping; (6) reading-before-reading (Digest Versions, Advance Organizers, and Reiterative Reading); and (7) Anticipation-Reaction guides. Next, the chapter presented five methods for "preteaching" relevant vocabulary: (1) the Cognitive Approach; (2) the Typical to Technical Meaning Approach; (3) the Subjective Approach to Vocabulary; (4) Motor Imaging; and (5) Incidental Morpheme Analysis. The chapter concluded with a summary of seven principles for guiding vocabulary learning and a strong suggestion to reconsider the popular, and perhaps misguided, use of context clues to teach new word meanings.

The next chapter details efforts to handle the elusive job of guiding silent reading. It opens with a brief description of what "expert readers" do during silent reading to remind us of what we are striving to teach all readers to do.

TRADE SECRET

Dealing with a Variety of QACs

There are numerous ways for students to QAC—*question, answer,* and *comment*—during classroom interactions. Some of these are facilitating and productive, and others are quirky and difficult to handle. Start a personal journal of "useful verbal protocols," or "things to say when . . ."

Here are some typical problem situations that tend to arise during questioning, answering, and commenting and some techniques we have seen veteran teachers use to deal with them. A few of these are repeated or expanded in other portions of the text.

Problem: Students can't seem to think without talking. They are not really disrespectful but garrulous or irrepressibly talkative. They begin to answer every question whether or not they know the answer.
Remedies:

1. Avoid eye contact with them.
2. Occasionally turn your back to them and ask a question while walking away from them so that they can't quite hear it thus preventing them from answering before others can.
3. Call a name or a row before asking a question.
4. Strictly enforce a rule of raising a hand before talking.
5. Find a reason to talk about the different ways people think and talk. Be sympathetic, but point out that "compulsive talkers" tend to disrupt the teacher, dissuade others from speaking up, overly dominate a discussion, close out opportunities to listen and learn, appear boorish, and anger others. Stress that this is a problem that can plague a person for the rest of his or her life if not curtailed early.

Problem: Students raise the same question repeatedly.
Remedy: Ask "Does anyone recognize this question?" If no one responds, you have strong evidence that you need to raise and probably answer the question again. If the question or the answer has more than one part, write out key words on the chalkboard.

Problem: A student characteristically speaks too low to be heard.
Remedy: Begin walking to the other side of the room so that the student must project to you, and in the process speak loudly enough for others to hear.

Problem: Disruptive sounds, such as heating or cooling systems, prevent class members from hearing one another.
Remedies:

1. Have students arrange desks so that they face one another.
2. Repeat students' questions and answers (despite the usual prohibition against doing so).

3. Explain the problem to the class, and say that you frequently will be calling on someone else to repeat questions and answers to ensure that everyone hears. This also can keep students more alert the first time.

Problem: Students fail to participate in responding to recitation-type questions.
Remedies:

1. Examine your questions. You might be asking "guess what I'm thinking" questions. All teachers occasionally lapse into this routine.
2. Provide more "wait time": Count to five to yourself before saying another word, then ask students if they want the question repeated or explained further.

Problem: Students do not pay attention or participate in discussions or other class activities.
Remedies:

1. Reassess what you are asking students to do. Is it meaningful, clear, and "doable" in the time you are allowing?
2. Use a "polling" technique to warm up your "audience" and get them involved. The most popular method is to ask questions that require one of two choices, such as those asked in television polls in which one calls a given phone number for each choice. You can also offer more elaborate, content-related choices. Here is an example: "Some people think *The Merchant of Venice* is a put-down of Jews, others think it is a put-down of Christians. Who thinks it is a put-down of Jews? Who Christians? Who is undecided? Let's continue to analyze this play and see whether Shakespeare tips his hand one way or the other."

Problem: A student asks a question, gives an answer, or makes a comment that is "out in left field."
Remedies:

1. Simply say, "I don't quite see the relevance of that. Can you explain further?" Where such responses clearly are characteristic of a certain student and it is clear to the class that you are not being arbitrary, omit the request for further explanation.
2. Ask if another student can help explain or clarify the question, answer, or comment.
3. Try to get things going in another direction by simply accepting the response and saying, "OK, does anyone else have a different point of view or way of answering this question?"
4. Don't forget the power of a stare—or simple silence.

Guided Silent Reading Designs

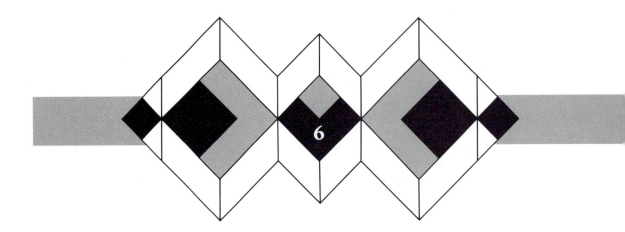

Strategic Reading, Adjunct Aids, and Text Modifications to Keep Effective Reading Going

Reading taste and ability are always tethered to past experience. But reading itself is one way of increasing this capital fund of past experience.

— *Edgar Dale*

FOCUS

The aspect of reading comprehension we know least about is guiding the reader's silent incursion into print. This area of research and development, however, is expected to achieve considerable growth. This chapter presents the ideas and prototype methods available for addressing this objective. These range from attempts to teach the reader to follow the structure of a text to means of restructuring the text to the reader's needs.

OUTLINE

"Expert readers," according to Baker and Brown (1984), are readers who

- Clarify and focus their purposes for reading
- Identify the important aspects of a message
- Separate relevant from irrelevant details
- Monitor their ongoing efforts to comprehend
- Engage in self-questioning to determine whether they are meeting their goals
- Take corrective action, that is, use "fix-up" strategies, when their failure to understand becomes evident

This chapter reports on some traditional and emerging means and methods of helping students achieve this level of "metacognitive" control over their reading. First, it briefly examines what it means to think while one reads. Next, it homes in on conventional means and methods of guiding silent reading. Finally, the chapter describes some emerging innovations in the technology of writing and text construction that some predict will ultimately render all books as extinct as the dinosaur.

TEACHING STUDENTS TO THINK WHILE THEY READ

Once a student begins to read silently, something is needed to keep the process going and to keep it focused. The teacher cannot physically follow the student on this silent incursion into print. How, then, can teachers help students practice the subtle, metacognitive habits of focusing attention, drawing on prior knowledge and experiences, self-monitoring and self-questioning, and, most of all, sustaining these efforts in a sea of other competing interests and needs? Indeed they can, though not easily, and certainly not for all students all of the time. This is important to remember, because teachers can easily get discouraged by the din of competing forces such as the need to "cover the curriculum."

The last chapter described prereading activities designed to "prime" reading by calling up relevant background, establishing the appropriate mindset and purpose, and removing potential word obstacles or converting them into facilitators of comprehension. Realistically, however, we as teachers know that within moments of guiding students back into their own minds, each one's unique personal mental agenda begins to add some static interference to the author's voice and to our instructions. The object of guiding silent reading is to permit the author to be heard, to allow our curriculum objectives to be met, but also to permit, and even encourage, students to be active readers, able to pursue and fulfill personal interests and objectives as well. For these reasons, we need a subtle combination of static suppressors and voice amplifiers.

This chapter examines three classes of "suppressors" and "amplifiers": those that can be "implanted" in students, those that provide external cues, and those that can be built into the text.

STRATEGIC IMPLANTS TO AID SILENT READING

Strategic implants are teacher-taught but student-controlled strategies for increasing self-monitoring and self-fixing—in other words, things to do when reading comprehension begins to falter. In this section, we will consider three classes of strategic implants. The first—and simplest to use—is various forms of "guiding questions" designed to get students to think along certain lines while they read. The second is "marking systems" intended to keep reading active and alert. The third is based on a controversial approach that emphasizes identifying basic organizational patterns of paragraphs and text to improve comprehension of text. A fourth approach, which attempts to teach students formulas for guiding reading, notetaking, and studying, is discussed in Chapter 8.

Guiding Questions

Rationale and Basic Examples

The wise teacher always looks for the easiest way to meet a given set of student needs. Several researchers recently have shown that students can easily be trained to ask themselves some simple guiding questions while they read (Baker & Brown, 1984; Meichenbaum & Asarnow, 1979; Singer & Dolan, 1980). Here are three simple questions that students have been taught for guiding story-type reading:

1. What is the main idea?
2. What are the important details?
3. How do the characters feel, and why? (Meichenbaum & Asarnow, 1979)

The first two questions can be used to guide the reading of expository textbook material. This simple approach can be enhanced by having students pause after about 10 minutes of reading and asking them these questions. This reminds them to ask the questions on their own and helps them clear up any misapprehensions that might be impairing their silent reading comprehension.

The next method we will discuss is one you have seen before. See how you can use this familiar strategy to implant an appropriate mindset for guiding silent reading.

The Oral Reading Strategy Revisited

The Oral Reading Strategy described in Chapter 2 is a simple and basic method for teaching students to think while they read. The teacher reads a brief portion of the selection to the class, making a conscious attempt to think aloud—that is, model the metacognitive thought processes good readers might use to focus attention, develop and maintain interest, and monitor comprehension.

Recall that the Oral Reading Strategy calls for the teacher's oral reading to be brief and for students to have an immediate opportunity to read silently. Much of the teacher's "think-aloud" will consist of guiding questions such as these:

1. What is this about?
2. Do I know anything about this already?
3. Can I summarize that paragraph in my own words?
4. Do I know what that word means in this context?
5. Can I make any predictions about where this is going?

The Oral Reading Strategy gives students a feel for how to use guiding questions while reading. The next method also encourages students to pause periodically while reading to question and translate.

About-Point

About-Point (Martin, Lorton, Blanc, & Evans, 1977) is an easy-to-remember guide for silent reading. Students are instructed to pause at logical points, such as at the ends of paragraphs or text subsections, and complete the following two phrases:

> This section is *about* _____; *and*
> the *point* is _____.

Here is an example:

This section is about the characteristics of plains; and the point is that while plains may have different weather and vegetation characteristics, the key characteristics are their altitude and their flatness.

Steps in Teaching About-Point

1. Instruct students to read the first paragraph of a selection.
2. Put three possible "about" statements on the overhead or chalkboard. Ask students to choose the best "about" statement and discuss the reasons for their selection. Follow the same procedure for a "point" statement for the first paragraph.
3. Instruct students to read the second paragraph of the selection.
4. Ask students to suggest a good "about" statement for that paragraph. Have them discuss their suggestions and develop an "about" statement. Then write that statement on the overhead or chalkboard. Follow the same procedure for developing a "point" statement for the second paragraph.
5. Instruct students to read the third paragraph of the selection and work with a partner to develop an "about" statement and a "point" statement.
6. Discuss the statements developed by the student pairs.
7. Instruct students to read the remainder of the selection and write their own "about-point" statements for all the paragraphs or selected paragraphs.

Suggestions for Using About-Point

1. Be sure to suggest to students that "about-point" is a study strategy they should use when they read difficult material and it will improve their recall of information.
2. Periodically, when giving reading assignments, assign certain paragraphs for students to write "about-point" statements on. Students can turn in these state-

ments, or you can start a class discussion by asking students to read their statements.

3. From time to time, include an "about-point" item on tests. Give students a paragraph from the material tested, and ask them to write "about-point" statements.

Postreading Reinforcement of Guiding Questions

The use of guiding questions can be enhanced with postreading discussion focused on additional questions designed to make students more process aware:

1. What cues in the text helped you determine what was important?
2. What cues helped you determine what was unimportant?
3. How did things you knew previously help you skip over or perhaps read more thoroughly than you might have?
4. Do you have a personal goal or interest that drew your attention in this piece that you would like to share?

The Oral Reading Strategy, About-Point, and Guiding Questions are good examples of how strategic teaching promotes strategic reading. The next method is another example of a teaching strategy that engages students in active reading behavior often demonstrated by expert readers.

Text Marking and Responding Systems

Text Marking Strategy

Readers have been marking books for hundreds of years. *Text marking* strengthens comprehension, impresses key ideas, and triggers personal associations. Interacting with the author can tell readers a good deal about themselves. According to McNeil, (1987) the following metacognitive questions tend to arise while one reads:

- What is your own background and purpose?
- Did you recognize ways and means by which the author could have improved the text, making it more considerate?
- Were you concerned with style, practical application, or criticism?
- Did you try to unify or to fragmentize the passage? (p. 176)

Figure 6.1 presents an example of text marking as applied to a passage titled "Teacher questioning."

Steps in the Text Marking Strategy

1. Show the opening section of the text assignment on the overhead.
2. Read aloud, pausing to jot down questions, challenges, translations of key ideas, and associations.
3. Ask students whether they would have made other notations in the above list.

Figure 6.1 Textbook Marking: "Teacher Questioning" Passage

There are two ways teacher questions

What are the two ways?

can be effective in improving children's

comprehension. First, teacher questions

Effective in what way: motivating, mastering a concept, creating cognitive dissonance?

can direct the child's attention to what

is important. By emphasizing certain

information, teacher questions help

students focus upon the information they

must learn and recall. Second, teacher

How long will they recall it if it is not related to their own lives?

questions can serve as models of the

comprehension process, showing the children

How do different kinds of questions relate to the process of comprehension?

the qualities of fruitful questions.

The effective teacher uses questions

to activate children's relevant background

The procedure seems similar to authors' ETR method.

knowledge, to elicit comparisons of

personal experiences with what the text

says, and to help children integrate the

new information of the text with what

Although this procedure helps children create meaning from a particular text, will it develop independent readers?

they already know.

First in sequential order, priority, or merely first in the sense of enumeration?

Important to whom?

Does this procedure develop active readers who generate their own questions and a sense of what is important?

Does the child always have the relevant background to be activated?

Source: From *Reading Comprehension: New Directions for Classroom Practice*, 2/e, by John D. McNeil. Copyright © 1987, 1984 by Scott, Foresman and Company. Reprinted by permission.

176

4. Show the next short section of text on the overhead. Ask that a student volunteer to read the first paragraph and comment on it. Ask different students to do the same with the next few paragraphs.
5. Immediately following this preparation, have students continue to read silently in their texts. Encourage them to note their own questions, comments, translations, and associations.

Often students are not permitted to write in schoolbooks. If this is the case, distribute 8½" × 2" slips of paper to insert between the pages. Instruct students to simply write the page numbers on the tops of the slips and jot down their notes roughly alongside the text material.

Textbook marking has its shortcomings. First, it tends to support excessive written responding that takes up a lot of time and space. Second, it can divert the reader from the writer's expository format, which in good time might well deal with many of the concerns the reader is painstakingly reacting to and noting. Finally, the strategy provides no entry-level step for the reader who tends to leave no footprints, whose book and pages never show signs of human exploration. The next strategy offers a simplified system for converting such a nonresponder into a responsive reader willing to leave behind some material evidence of the struggle to map new ideational land.

Comprehension Monitoring Strategy

Richard J. Smith and Velma Dauer (1984) recommend a textbook marking strategy that they have field tested with 40 high school teachers in home economics, social studies, and biology. In *Comprehension Monitoring,* students use a code to record their cognitive and affective responses to materials they read. The code may vary according to the characteristics of the material and the teachers' curriculum objectives. Smith and Dauer devised these codes for social studies and science. The code they suggest for social studies reading is as follows:

A = Agree
B = Bored
C = Confused
D = Disagree
M = Main idea

The code they suggest for science reading is:

C = Clear
D = Difficult
I = Important
S = Surprising

Students are given the code on a handout sheet before reading and asked to record their responses as they read on narrow strips of paper affixed to the margins of the pages they are reading.

The Comprehension Monitoring strategy offers guidance in *how* to respond to text. However, students often need additional guidance in when to respond. The next strategy offers this assistance.

Free Response

The *Free Response* strategy (Santa, Dailey, & Nelson, 1985) uses a premarked, reproduced section of a reading assignment to encourage active reading. Free Response involves preparation, direct instruction, and follow-up and offers several ''elaboration'' options.

Preparation

1. Start with a selection that is likely to generate emotional reactions and diverse opinions.
2. Underline for students key vocabulary terms and ideas in the text that are likely to stimulate thought.
3. Reproduce and distribute this material to the class.

Direct Instruction

4. Begin with a few questions to help students use their own background knowledge and thinking with the selection.
5. Examine the title of the selection to predict the direction of the material.
6. Have students read the selection, stopping to react to the underlined words and ideas in the margins of the reproduced form.
7. Discuss students' free responses. Encourage divergent opinions, but remember to instruct students to always answer why they think or feel as they do.
8. Discuss the effectiveness and purpose of free responding. The key idea to develop here is that free response encourages active reading and integration of students' own background knowledge with the selection.

Follow-up

9. After students have practiced the above steps with three or four selections, instruct them to read in their unmarked texts and jot down four or five reactions to what they are reading.
10. Instruct students to respond without the constraint of underlined words and the requirement of a specific number of responses.

Elaboration

11. Develop with the class some criteria for guiding free responding and reacting to textual materials. Santa et al. (1985) provide these guides to reacting while reading:
    a. Things that I like or dislike about a character or event
    b. Situations that make me angry or sad
    c. Questions about things I do not understand
    d. Comments about what I think an unfamiliar word means
    e. Events from my life that come to mind as I read

   f. Situations or events with which I do not agree

   g. Can I make predictions?

   h. What will happen next?

   i. Is the author giving me a clue here?

Santa et al. report that they typically have used Free Response in conjunction with three other postreading activities: Opinion-Proof, Writing, and Peer Editing (discussed in Chapter 7). Free Response works well alone or in combination with many of the other postreading strategies described in the next chapter.

Now that we have considered several strategic implants to silent reading, let us turn to a different type of implant. This one is based on the controversial proposition that teaching students how text is structured will enhance their text comprehension. Before reading ahead, try to anticipate why this might be a controversial approach.

Text Structure

Some reading educators contend that an effective way to improve silent reading comprehension is to teach students about text structure. This belief is based on the widespread research finding that a strong relationship between reading comprehension and knowledge of text structure exists (Meyer, 1975). This implies that teaching poorer readers about the structure of writing will result in improved comprehension. Those who interpret this research finding in this way propose that the form and format of a communication are integral parts of its message. This is akin to, albeit less powerful than, Marshall McLuhan's assertion that "the medium is the message."

Interest in text structure dates back to ancient history, when it was studied first as an extension of rhetoric, or logic, persuasion, and argument. In more contemporary times, early writers in reading education such as Rachel Salisbury (1934), Nila Banton Smith (1964a, 1964b), and James McCallister (1964) have defined and delineated various paragraph patterns that they felt readers should be taught to recognize. Modern linguists such as Kintsch (1977) and Meyer (1975) have raised such study to a keener scientific level, but they have been unable to provide convincing evidence of its value in guiding silent reading.

In general, advocates for the study of text structure are not reading educators but theorists. They tend to venture into classrooms to study theories of learning and language more so than theories of teaching. For this reason, it is difficult to take their admonitions about how to teach too seriously. In one recent study (Gee & Rakow, 1987), reading specialists ranked text structure instruction 14th out of 23 teaching practices for comprehension improvement.

One basic objection to text structure study was raised some time ago by Olive Niles, a school-based scholar. Niles (1965) stated that elaborate instruction in classification schemas such as paragraph patterns is not only unnecessary but potentially counterproductive. The reason is simple: The number of paragraphs that follow a clearcut pattern is low, but the number of paragraphs that combine a variety of patterns into one paragraph is high (Niles, 1965).

In general, experience and research suggest that text structure theorists probably have inverted the meaning of their data: They have interpreted their research to mean that if youngsters are taught structure, they will learn to comprehend better and therefore should be taught further how to identify structures. A more plausible interpretation, however, is that when students are taught to read for meaning, their awareness of text structure also increases, but when they are taught to identify text structure, comprehension growth does not follow to the same extent. In other words, reading for meaning seems to reveal form, but reading for form appears to reveal little about meaning.

Having addressed both sides of the issue, it seems only fair to offer you the opportunity to consider for yourself the educational value of teaching paragraph patterns. In this section, we describe a traditional strategy for teaching text structure and a list of the types of paragraph patterns that typically are taught. Then we turn to two more contemporary approaches that attempt to overcome the criticism leveled at teaching paragraph patterns for their own sake.

Expository Patterns Activity

In the *Expository Patterns Activity* (Tonjes & Zintz, 1987), the teacher collects a stack of old newspapers and labels each of 12 envelopes for a specific type of expository paragraph. Then the students, working in pairs, search the newspapers for appropriate samples of each paragraph type. Students cut out the sample paragraphs and place them in the appropriate envelopes. Finally, the groups decide which is the best example of each paragraph type. This discussion is the critical (languaging) element in this lesson.

The 12 expository paragraph patterns are as follows:

1. *Introductory.* The introductory paragraph often appears at the beginning of a selection. It introduces the topic and gives the reader a mental set, or focus, by previewing the ideas and imparting the author's purpose and organizational plan.
2. *Definition.* The definition paragraph defines technical terms or explains concepts. Terms and concepts sometimes are printed in italics or underlined the first time they occur. This paragraph provides the reader with a foundation for later comprehension.
3. *Transitional.* The transitional paragraph helps shift the reader's attention from one aspect of a topic, point of view, or time frame to another. It often contains one sentence that signals the upcoming change.
4. *Illustrative.* The illustrative paragraph attempts to make an abstract process or principle more concrete by giving examples or illustrations. Sometimes, however, readers will confuse the examples with the principle because the language used in examples often is easier to understand, more interesting, and more concrete. Therefore, it is important to point out the difference between the thought and the illustration of that thought.
5. *Summary.* The summary paragraph reinforces and summarizes the main ideas. Generally it comes at the end of the chapter or a section of a long chapter.

However, since David Ausubel's writings on advance organizers, summaries increasingly are being presented as introductory-type paragraphs.

6. *Main ideas supported by details or examples.* The most common type of general paragraph structure is that in which one sentence states the topic and the rest of the sentences in the paragraph support that main idea. The topic sentence usually appears at the beginning or the end of the paragraph, although sometimes it falls in the middle. When no main idea is explicitly stated, the reader must put all the examples together to infer one.

7. *Chronological order.* Chronological order is one form of sequential ordering. Such paragraphs put events in perspective relative to what occurred before or after, thus organizing information for easy anticipation.

8. *Comparison/contrast.* Comparison/contrast paragraphs describe similarities and differences among various ideas. Generally they follow the format of the Frayer model of teaching discussed in Chapter 5.

9. *Cause and effect.* Cause-and-effect paragraphs attempt to show relationships among facts and outcomes. However, such paragraphs are not always labeled as cause and effect, so the reader must be especially alert.

10. *Problem/solution.* Problem/solution paragraphs present problems and then offer solutions. The reader needs to (1) identify the problem and realize that the solutions suggested are those of the author and (2) look for evidence that the problem exists and that there is support for the proposed solutions.

11. *Descriptive.* Descriptive paragraphs attempt to evoke a mental picture of what the writer is trying to convey. Descriptions may be used to set the mood or tone for forthcoming events. Such paragraphs often do not contain a topic sentence but merely describe settings and conditions.

12. *Narrative.* Narrative, or story-type, paragraphs relate anecdotes or logical sequences of events. Often they are used to capture attention and, like descriptive paragraphs, frequently contain no topic sentence.

The next two text structure methods hold to the more popular proposition that teaching students to identify the structure of expository writing should not be, as Horowitz (1985) puts it, an end in itself.

Four-Pronged (Languaging) Approach
Junior high teacher Nancy J. Farnan (1987) has devised the *Four-Pronged approach* to increasing students' awareness of text structures. This approach stresses application of text structure knowledge using all four language skills areas. Students (1) read and discuss model texts; (2) write similar texts; (3) organize and present their texts in verbal form; and (4) listen critically, aiming for constructive evaluation of the speeches presented. Figure 6.2 presents a sample Four-Pronged lesson.

Text Connecting Questions
The *Text Connecting Questions* method, developed by Denise Muth (1987), demonstrates how teachers can achieve a focus on text structure just by asking the "right"

Figure 6.2   Farnan's Four-Pronged Approach to Text Structure: Sample Lesson

As a model, students first read and discussed Daniel Mannix's intriguing and informative biographical sketch of Grace Wiley, a renowned herpetologist who specialized in handling the deadly King Kobra (in *Adventures for Readers, Book Two,* Harcourt Brace Jovanovich, 1979). As they read, we discussed features of this type of writing.

Students could clearly see both narration and exposition in Mannix's style. They could note his "attention-getter" in the beginning; his selective use of physical description, detail and dialogue; and his skillful use of figurative language to spark the reader's imagination.

Next, students each chose a subject and wrote their own biographical sketches. Building on what they had learned, the additional discussion and sharing of information during the writing process provided students with further insights into this type of writing.

My district has made a strong commitment to incorporating speech into the curriculum . . . so, after completing their written work, students prepared speeches to present to the class.

As they gave their speeches, students in the audience functioned as critical listeners, evaluating each speaker's delivery as well as the speech's organization and content. These evaluations were then given to the speakers, providing them with immediate peer feedback.

By the time a class has gone through this process with one type of discourse, students have had the opportunity to concentrate on both its form and content through reading, writing, speaking, and listening.

Source: From "All the Language Arts for Reading Comprehension" by N. J. Farnan, 1987, *Journal of Reading, 31,* pp. 274–275. Copyright 1987 by the International Reading Association. Reprinted with permission of Nancy J. Farnan and the International Reading Association.

questions. The teacher's questions prompt students to see meaningful connections among internal structural elements and external ideas that they already know.

The basic way to achieve this focus, according to Muth, is to simply construct questions whose format parallels that of the text. These questions will not always seem different from those one might typically ask except that they will be organized and sequenced in this parallel form. To ensure that the "lesson" or point is not missed, the teacher draws students' attention to "why you are asking a particular question and how you developed it" (Muth, 1987, p. 259). Figure 6.3 illustrates the approach for "compare-contrast" and "cause-effect" questions. Many of these question types also work with process-oriented reading guides, discussed in the next section.

Muth's Text Connecting Questions and Farnan's Four-Pronged approach provide several valuable ingredients of quality content area reading instruction quite apart from their concern with paragraph patterns:

1. They are *concurrent:* They simultaneously teach author's craft (i.e., thinking like a writer), comprehension skills, and paragraph patterns.
2. They are *heuristic:* They offer a self-exploration strategy for teachers and students to examine textual material in an interesting way.
3. They are *metacognitive:* Proficient readers clearly, though subconsciously, rely on such analyses during silent reading.
4. They involve *modeling* and *integrative functioning:* The language and thought processes of teachers and exemplary students become natural models for peer participants to observe and emulate.

ADJUNCT AIDS TO SILENT READING: TEXT EXTERNAL AND TEXT INTERNAL

When a coach shouts commands during an athletic event, he or she is attempting to remind the athlete of what has already been taught and practiced in a less competitive situation. Such cuing would be distracting were it not for the extensive prior training. The same general principle appears to apply to written aids to text comprehension, or **adjunct aids.** These aids work best when students have been taught to use them and are given ample opportunity for practice.

Adjunct aids fall into two classes: those that are external to the text and those that are built into the text. Research findings on the merit of both external and internal aids is mixed but generally positive. The problem, however, is that there is no theory structure to provide a set of simple guidelines for constructing aids that will always be effective. Essentially it is a matter of hit-or-miss engineering. This would be tolerable in the case of a teaching method being delivered extemporaneously and therefore easily adaptable to the situation. Adjunct aids, however, require considerable preparatory work and expense and thus require a greater degree of assurance to match their built-in permanence.

Support for adjunct aids stems as much from their face value as it does from empirical evidence. Written guides, either alongside or built into the text, appear to offer obvious and ready assistance in silent reading. Moreover, written guides tend to match most teachers' expectations of what it means to ingest and learn textual material in an attentive, orderly manner.

Reading Guides: Text External

Vacca and Vacca (1986) describe **reading guides** as "teacher-made instructional materials which accompany reading assignments." Such guides somewhat resemble old-fashioned workbook exercises, but they can be used *before* reading (as illustrated in Chapter 5), *during* reading (as demonstrated in this chapter), or *after* reading (as illustrated in Chapter 7).

The idea of reading guides, according to Harold Herber (1978), their chief contemporary proponent, is to simplify difficult material. Reading guides are designed to teach reading processes as well as to improve information acquisition: The

Figure 6.3   Internal and External Connecting Questions

Compare-Contrast

People who want to buy a horse for pleasure riding usually choose between the Quarter horse and the Saddle horse. The Quarter horse has a thick mane and tail. It is strong and is able to carry heavy riders over rough trails for several miles. It is also very healthy and does not catch diseases easily. However, the Quarter horse is not comfortable to ride. It has a jerky walk, which bumps its rider up and down. Also, it is nervous and is hard to control when something unexpected happens.

The Saddle horse is usually brown with dark eyes. It has a steady walk, which is comfortable for riding. It is also easy to control. It responds instantly to commands and is always ready for unexpected things that might lie in its path. The Saddle horse is not very healthy though, and it tends to catch diseases easily from other horses. Also, it is not strong enough to carry heavy loads.

Teachers' questions should focus on helping students understand the author's purpose for using the compare-contrast structure and on the relationships among the ideas in the passages. Here are some questions [and possible student answers] which could help students build "internal connections" among the ideas in the passage.

1. What is the author comparing and contrasting? (Answer: the Saddle horse and the Quarter horse.)
2. Why is the author comparing and contrasting these two types of horses? (So we can decide which horse is best for pleasure riding.) This clearly is the key question, since it encompasses most others.
3. Why did the author use the compare-contrast structure in this particular passage? (To show us that each type of horse has advantages and disadvantages for pleasure riding.)
4. What are the advantages of the Quarter horse for pleasure riding? (Strong and healthy.)
5. What are the advantages of the Saddle horse? (Comfortable and easy to control.)
6. What are the disadvantages of the Quarter horse for pleasure riding? (Uncomfortable and hard to control.)
7. What are the disadvantages of the Saddle horse? (Not healthy or strong.)
8. What other characteristic of the two horses does the author include in the passage? (Physical apearance.)
9. Is the appearance of the horses important in determining which horse is best for pleasure riding? (No.)
10. According to the passage, which of the two types of horses is best for pleasure riding? (There is no clear-cut answer.)
11. How would someone decide which of the horses to buy based on what he or she read in this passage? (They would have to decide which horse is best for their particular needs.)

Here are some questions which could help students build "external connections":

Figure 6.3 *continued*

1. Which of the two horses would you pick, and why? (Answer: I'd pick the Saddle horse because I'm light and wouldn't be carrying heavy loads. Also, I don't have any other horses, so it would be hard for my Saddle horse to catch a disease if there aren't any other horses around.)
2. Do you know anyone who might be concerned with the appearance of the horses? (My aunt would. She participates in horse shows, and appearance is very important for show horses.)

Cause-Effect

Why do some things rust? Perhaps you found out if you left a shovel or rake out overnight. When you picked them up a few days later, you might have seen rough, brown spots of rust on them. Air is composed partly of oxygen. Oxygen combines with iron to make rust. Moisture or water helps to bring about the change. Tools like rakes and shovels are made of iron, and they rust quickly if they are left out in wet or damp air. If you left them out long enough, they would rust completely and crumple away.

Again, teachers' questions should focus on helping students understand why the author used the cause-effect structure and how the ideas in the passage are related to each other.

Here are some questions which could help students build "internal connections" among the ideas:

1. Why did the author use the cause-effect structure for this passage? (Answer: to describe a process; to show us that in this case one thing causes something else to happen.)
2. What is the cause-effect process that the author is describing? (How things rust.)
3. Describe the process of how some things rust. (Oxygen and moisture in the air combine with the iron in the objects to cause rust.)
4. What causes the process? (The oxygen and the moisture combining with the iron.)
5. What is the effect of this combination? (Rust.)
6. What are the three necessary "ingredients" for rust? (Oxygen, moisture, and iron.)

These questions could help students build "external connections":

1. Why don't most things usually rust inside your house? (Answer: There's not enough moisture.)
2. When do you think things might rust in your house? (When the humidity is very high.)
3. Can you think of some things that might rust in your house? (The scale in the bathroom, the pipes in the basement.)
4. Can you think of some things that you own that might rust if you left them outdoors long enough? (Bicycle, wheelbarrow, car.)
5. Can you think of some things that you own that won't rust if you leave them outdoors? (Basketball, book, sweatshirt.)

Source: From "Teachers' Connecting Questions: Prompting Students to Organize Text Ideas" by K. D. Muth, 1987, *Journal of Reading, 31*, pp. 254–259. Copyright 1987 by the International Reading Association. Reprinted with permission of K. Denise Muth and the International Reading Association.

student is expected to refer to the guide while reading, then back to the text, then back again to the guide. Often a guide amounts to a written-out version of the DR-TA. It can contain vocabulary and concept preparation as well as guiding questions (see Figure 6.4). The most significant advantages of guides, in our judgment, are that they permit the teacher to focus student attention on key elements in a passage and that they require every student to attempt some type of reflective response to those points.

Three studies (Armstrong, Patberg, & Dewitz, 1988; Berget, 1973; Sanders, 1969) have found reading guides to have positive effects on comprehension. Other studies (Estes, 1973; Maxon, 1979; Riley, 1979a, 1979b; Thelen, 1977; Vacca, 1973) have found reading guides to have positive effects for some variables but not for others. Still other studies (Berget, 1977; Carney, 1973; Estes, 1969; Hash, 1974; Phelps, 1979; Thelen, 1969) have found no positive effect. Despite these mixed findings, however, the popularity of reading guides is evidenced in the numerous versions that have been developed. Some of the most commonly used formats for reading guides and some recent innovations in them are described ahead.

Three-Level Guides

A *Three-Level Guide* is designed to lead students from basic to more advanced levels of comprehension of textual material (Herber, 1978). The first section in the guide contains questions at a literal level: What did the author *say*? The next section contains interpretive questions: What did the author *mean*? The third section contains application questions: How can you *use* this information?

To construct a Three-Level Guide, Vacca and Vacca (1986) suggest that the teacher follow this procedure:

1. Begin by deciding which applications are appropriate to the material, and develop questions for *part three* of the guide.
2. Next, determine what information is needed to make these applications, and whether it is explicitly stated in the text or must be inferred. Information which must be inferred in order to make the level-three applications is used to develop questions for *part two* of the guide.
3. Finally, the necessary literal information is used to develop questions for *part one* of the guide.

There is no firm evidence to suggest whether Three-Level Guides are better used during or after reading. A reasonable procedure would be to have students look for the answers to the literal questions while they are reading and complete the interpretive and applied questions after reading.

Process Guides

Robert Karlin (1984) makes a distinction between Process Guides and Content Guides. A *Process Guide* is intended to teach the skills needed to derive meaning from text, while a *Content Guide* focuses primarily on identifying particular facts and ideas that the teacher deems important. A Process Guide essentially is a reading guide, while a Content Guide is a traditional worksheet aimed at fact identification. These differences are exemplified in the Process Guide questions in Figure 6.4.

Figure 6.4 Examples of Activities Used in Process Guides

1. Identification of Key Terms

Terms are noted by page and by category. Readers are encouraged to note these while they read and to study them afterward.

Directions: Check off the terms listed below as you come to them in reading. Review them after reading to see what you can remember about each.

Page	Reading Vocabulary	Social Studies Terms	People, Places, Events
166	stealthily summit	regulars redcoats	Bunker Hill Breed's Hill
175	ill-matched	tactics Tories tarred and feathered	continental army man-of-war

2. Categorization

Directions: Use the context in which you encounter the above terms in your text to place them in one of the categories listed below.

A. Categories (not all words fit these categories):
    1. Words that describe an action or state of being (verbs)
    2. Words that modify (adjectives and adverbs)
    3. Words that name persons, places or things (nouns)
B. Should you finish early, try recategorizing the above terms in the following ways:
    1. Words related to war
    2. Words that describe strong feelings
    3. Words that describe the English and their sympathizers

3. Text Structure

Directions: Chapter 9 answers three basic questions. The first and third are listed below. What is the second question this chapter addresses?

A. Why did the Thirteen Colonies decide to declare their independence?
B. _____
C. How did the Thirteen Colonies win their independence?

4. Identification of Important Details

Directions: As you read, mark each statement as true (T) or false (F). Where a statement seems false, cross out the incorrect information and replace it with the correct information.

_____ A. The Battle of Bunker Hill actually was fought on Breed's Hill.
_____ B. Breed's Hill is in Pennsylvania.
_____ C. The "Continental Army" was made up largely of Europeans against England.

5. Process Questions

Review Muth's strategy (see Figure 6.3) for examples of process-oriented questions that can be used to draw attention to the author's craft and organization.

As the examples in Figure 6.4 show, there are many kinds of Process Guides. The best way to learn how to construct them is simply to try it. Here are some suggestions to guide your efforts:

1. Pick an *important* section of text. Process guides are time consuming to construct, so you will want to spend your efforts on something of value.
2. Read the selection carefully, putting yourself in your students' place: "If I didn't know much about this, what would I need to do?"
3. Refer to the sample activity types in Figure 6.4 to determine which activity or combination of activities is best suited to the material.
4. Remember that the purpose of a Process Guide is not to elicit *facts* but to engage students in active thinking *processes* as they read.

Even with guidance, some students find it difficult to relate to textbook material. This is particularly true of students who have experienced significant failure in deciphering their texts. The next strategy puts the students' own words into a reading guide. This makes the text more inviting to poor readers and helps them over the initial barrier that the mere sight of a textbook poses.

Student-Generated Anticipation-Reaction Guides

Mary Morin, a Kansas City public school teacher, has developed a variation on Anticipation-Reaction Guides (described in Chapter 5). Morin's *Student-Generated Anticipation-Reaction Guide* involves students in developing their own reading guides (see Figure 6.5).

Steps in Development and Use of Student-Generated Anticipation-Reaction Guides

1. Prior to the class period, the teacher previews the reading selection and develops several incomplete sentences designed to elicit student predictions.
2. The teacher writes the incomplete sentences on the chalkboard or overhead. Then the teacher directs the class to preview the reading selection briefly and complete the sentences, indicating their predictions. They may also write additional predictions of their own.
3. The teacher collects the students' written predictions and after class uses them to prepare the Anticipation-Reaction Guide.
4. The teacher distributes the Anticipation-Reaction Guide the following day, prior to reading. Students complete the prereading column, then read the selection, then complete the postreading column.
5. Class discussion typically begins with the question "Did you change your mind about any of your prereading predictions after reading the selection?"

This strategy has been particularly effective in generating interest among moderate- to low- achieving urban students. Students look forward to seeing their own and their classmates' predictions in print. These more personalized predictions, in turn, stimulate interest in reading the material to test predictions, and a lively postreading discussion tends to follow completion of the postreading section of the guide.

Figure 6.5 Example of Student-Generated Anticipation-Reaction Guide

---

Incomplete Sentences Used to Develop Guide

1. When the main character turns 16, _____.
2. To get a driver's license, he will have to _____.
3. The main character may have trouble _____.
4. To get a job, he may have to _____.

Your own predictions:

_____

_____

Student-Generated Anticipation-Reaction Guide

Directions: Before reading, read each statement and check if you "agree" or "disagree" with each of the statements (use the "Before Reading column"). Leave the "After Reading" column blank until we have read the selection.

| Before Reading | | | After Reading | |
Agree	Disagree		Agree	Disagree
_____	_____	1. When the main character turns 16, he will get a job, a license, and a car.	_____	_____
_____	_____	2. To get a driver's license, he will have to pass three parts or tests.	_____	_____
_____	_____	3. The main character may have trouble passing the vision test.	_____	_____
_____	_____	4. The main character may have trouble parking.	_____	_____
		5. To get a job, he may have to ask friends for suggestions or look for a long time.	_____	_____
_____	_____	6. When the main character turns 16, he will get a lot of advice.	_____	_____
_____	_____	7. When the main character turns 16, people will offer him drugs.	_____	_____
_____	_____	8. When the main character turns 16, he would be trusted when going out on dates.	_____	_____
_____	_____	9. To get a job, he may have to take part-time work.	_____	_____
_____	_____	10. When he gets a car, he will have to not be late on car or rent payments.	_____	_____

Source: Adapted from Mary Morin, Central Junior High School, Kansas City, Missouri (personal communication).

The Student-Generated Anticipation-Reaction Guide helps to ease students past their initial reluctance to engage with text by allowing them to use their own statements. The next guide we discuss also breaks with traditional routines by departing from the usual expectation that students will begin at the beginning and read every word through the end.

Reading Guide-O-Rama

The *Reading Guide-O-Rama* (Cunningham & Shablak, 1975) is another form of reading guide. It is a set of written "prompts" to students as to the best way to read and think about a given reading selection. In constructing a Guide-O-Rama, the teacher should determine which concepts and information he or she expects students to learn from the reading. Next, the teacher should consider how he or she, as an expert reader, would approach the selection. The Guide-O-Rama points out unimportant as well as important information and forwarns the reader about what to expect in class discussion. It may direct students to read portions of the material out of sequence, such as reading a final summary first. It may instruct students to read a short section of the assignment and then summarize the key points or facts. Figure 6.6 presents sample items from a Reading Guide-O-Rama.

Graphic Organizers

Skeletal illustrations for graphic organizers provide another way to guide silent reading comprehension. These may be constructed as specific reading guides (see Figure 6.7) or designed as a generic format, such as Herber's Herringbone Technique (see Figure 6.8) for guiding students through text. They also may be customized to symbolically represent specific ideas and serve as a framework for structuring related information. See the section on pyramiding in Chapter 11 for another example of a graphic aid.

Figure 6.6   Reading Guide-O-Rama

Page 93, paragraphs 3–6: Pay attention to this section. Why do you think Hunter acted in this manner? We will discuss your ideas in class.

Page 94: See if you can rewrite (convert) the boldface print at the top of this page into a question. You should pick up five ideas under this topic very quickly. Jot these down.

Page 179, column 1: The author has provided us with some interesting information here, but it isn't important to our course of study. Just skim it, unless, of course, it is of special interest to you.

Source: Adapted from *Reading Strategies and Practices: A Compendium* by R. Tierney, J. E. Readance, and E. K. Dishner, 2nd ed., 1985, Boston: Allyn and Bacon.

The more generic Herringbone Technique provides a graphic prompt that is quite compelling. It is especially suitable for literature and history.

Notes on Construction and Use of Reading Guides

As suggested in Chapter 1, the act of composing a guide can be an insightful experience for teachers. It draws them into a careful analysis of the textual material and a deeper understanding of the processes the student must call upon to read in a given discipline. It also can get the "creative juices" flowing; teachers often are surprised at the engaging exercises they produce. Furthermore, the former problems of revising and storing guides have been virtualy eliminated with the increasing availability of word processors.

On a more negative note, one must consider the time and energy that necessarily goes into the production of reading guides. Attempts have been made to produce reading guides in department or schoolwide efforts. Each teacher produces guides for portions of the text(s) he or she uses and contributes them to a central file. The complete file of guides can then be accessed by all teachers using that text. Studies of guides produced in such joint efforts, however, tend to indicate that reading guides are more effective in improving comprehension when they are used by their creators. This is understandable when you consider that a teacher who has composed a guide will likely be more attuned to its subtleties and will communicate greater regard for its importance than for a published or peer-produced guide.

On the same note, it is only fair to acknowledge the fact that not all teacher-produced guides are of high quality. The next section describes a way to give students ready access to another kind of guide that offers a greater probability of quality control.

Imbedded Aids: Text Internal

Imbedded Aids to Literacy

A logical alternative to teacher-prepared reading guides would be textbooks with built-in guides: various kinds of aids to the reader inserted directly into the textbook pages for easy access. For many years, educational psychologists studied formats for restructuring textbooks in this way under the descriptor "adjunct aids." However, most of this early research was conducted in nonschool settings, and subjects were military recruits or adults in low-salaried occupations (see the discussion of Rothkopf's work later in the chapter for related details). For most reading specialists, this body of work came to light independently with the development of Imbedded Aids (Manzo, 1977) and Marginal Gloss (Otto & Hayes, 1982), the latter to be discussed shortly.

Imbedded Aids are a collection of formats for built-in guides to silent textbook reading and study. These include help with word analysis, word meaning, basic comprehension, and even thinking beyond the text to greater depth, elaboration,

Figure 6.7   Main Idea and Supporting Details

The first main idea to be dealt with in this chapter may be called "The Thirteen Colonies Decide to Declare Their Independence." If you think of this statement as the rim of a wagon wheel, it will help you find the supporting details or the sequence of important events. These are represented as the spokes. Complete the remaining spokes by discovering the events that led the colonists to seek their independence. (Each of these supporting details will be a major category and will most likely appear in darker print in your text.)

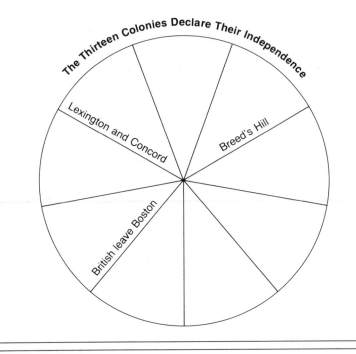

and critical analysis (see Figure 6.9). Imbedded Aids lend assistance at all levels of reading and to readers at all levels.

It may seem unlikely that there can be alterations to a 400-year-old text tradition. Once the thought of adjusting text begins to penetrate your thinking, however, you may be surprised at the number of plausible ideas and innovations that begin to occur to you for revising and modifying text to make it more "user friendly." In a cooperative effort with Houghton Mifflin Company, the first author produced an Imbedded Aids prototype of a chapter from a widely used high school world history text, *Man's Unfinished Journey* (Perry, 1971). This particular chapter employed 11 of 20 Imbedded Aids we had on file at the time:

Figure 6.7 *continued*

Make similar illustrations for the nine spokes, or subtopics. Fill in the supporting details for each (see illustration below). When you are finished finding the supporting details for each main idea (in boldface print), you will have a good outline of this entire chapter.

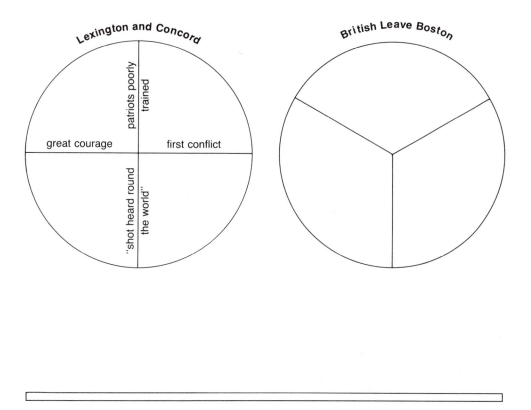

1. Line numbering: for easy reference
2. Reading/study notes: suggestions for reading and studying more effectively
3. Summary notes: for previewing and reviewing important ideas
4. Vocabulary: definitions of terms likely to be unfamiliar
5. In-process comprehension checks: true/false and short-answer questions following text sections
6. To Research: suggestions for independent study
7. Quality writing indicators: symbols mark well-written phrases
8. Deletion-attention device: occasional deletion of words that should be easy to fill in to help signal when attention may be drifting

Figure 6.8 Herringbone
Technique

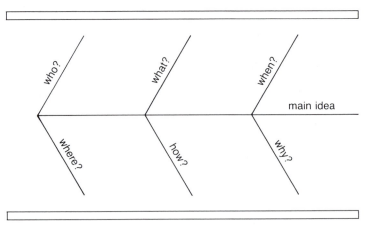

9. To think about: questions with no "right" answers for discussion or composition topics
10. Mininotes: enrichment information related to the text
11. Reader helper notes: additional information and study help keyed to a companion book with extended material (see Figure 6.10)

The illustration in Figure 6.9 was designed to serve as an annotated introduction to the Imbedded Aids chapter of the Perry text.

Imbedded Aids can play a unique role in the educational process: to create a support system for proficient readers who may be unfamiliar with a particular content terrain but would be entirely capable of reading in that realm were assistance available. With such assistance, for example, an English or history major could easily read a medical text. This approach could make almost any book more accessible to virtually anyone requiring its information. In this way, Imbedded Aids could help alleviate some of the problems that render even the best readers functionally illiterate in certain content areas. They can provide near universal access to what is known to those who wish to know it. Despite their cost, Imbedded Aids may turn out to be an inexpensive answer to the question of how to promote higher-order literacy in the nation's schools.

Efficacy of Imbedded Aids

Four studies have been conducted to assess the efficacy of Imbedded Aids materials. The first (Manzo, 1977), a field test of 10th-grade science material with inner-city students, yielded statistically significant findings in support of the Imbedded Aids.

The second study (Manzo, 1979), which used the materials shown in Figures 6.9 and 6.10, was somewhat inconclusive in terms of comprehension gains but was quite positive in terms of student and teacher attitudes. Both teachers and students were enthusiastic about seeing and using such materials. The weaker effect on comprehension in this case seems to have been a by-product of the way the materials were tested. They were mailed to 10 high schools around the nation that were using the Perry text. Teachers were asked to simply have students read the unconventional experimental materials; they were not told to provide any special explanation or orientation. Then students' comprehension scores were compared with those of students who had read the same material in the familiar, unannotated form.

Meeks conducted two follow-up studies (1979, 1980 and 1982). She used aids that stressed metacognitive operations (e.g., students compared their ratings of the relative importance of designated material with those of their teachers and, if there was a considerable difference in the ratings, students were encouraged to reread and reevaluate). The first study yielded no significant differences. The second study, however, in which students were given systematic instruction in how to use the aids, did result in statistically significant findings (Meeks, 1982).

Marginal Gloss

Otto and Hayes (1982) have used the term **Marginal Gloss** to describe built-in reading aids that focus on providing basic assistance to remedial readers (Dana, 1982) as compared with the kinds of assistance that more advanced readers might need. Witte (1982) has shown that like reading guide construction, the construction of this type of aid can serve as an excellent hands-on activity for in-service and teacher training.

Richgels and Hansen (1982) have attempted to produce guidelines for writing Marginal Gloss. Efforts such as theirs have begun to form a specialized field called *text technology*. The additional combination of text technology with computer capabilities to display and retrieve text is provoking speculation about the possibility of a new era of electronic text, called *hypertext*, that would largely replace conventional textbooks. The chief features of hypertext would be (1) availability of the same basic information at varying levels of sophistication; (2) interactive comprehension-checking options; and (3) an opportunity to write critical-constructive reactions for others to consider.

Now that computers have given us the potential to create more flexible and "friendlier" text, we are finding that we need to know more about just *what* makes text more or less "friendly." You should read the next section with an eye toward becoming conversant with the topic rather than expecting immediate application. It is highly likely that many careers will emerge from the joining of text technology and computer and print technology.

TEXT TECHNOLOGY

This section provides an overview of the emerging field of text technology. It briefly details the rationale for the field, outlines two chief competing theories, and reports on relevant findings regarding how text should be structured to achieve different purposes. Next comes a presentation of a unique readability formula that should help you pull together much of this information as it relates to determining text

Figure 6.9 Illustration of Imbedded Aids

The lines of the main text are numbered to provide easy reference.

Notes such as this one give directions for reading and studying the chapter more effectively.

Notes in the right-hand columns summarize the information in the text. Use them to preview and review the main ideas presented.

The notes in the right-hand columns should be read both before and after you read the main text.

Liberal Responses to Industrialization

1   *Liberalism* emerged in England in the seventeenth century during the
2 struggle between Parliament and kings. By the end of the eighteenth cen-
3 tury British liberalism stood for religious toleration, parliamentary govern-
4 ment and the rule of law, freedom of the press, natural right of the individ-
5 ual to life, liberty, and property, and the right to resist arbitrary and
6 *tyrannical* government seeking to interfere with these natural rights. ☐Brit-
7 ish liberals had confidence in human intelligence, supported science, and
8 attacked superstition.☐ In the seventeenth and eighteenth centuries British
9 liberals had been mainly concerned with protecting the rights of the individ-
10 ual against the dangers of oppressive government. But by the beginning of
11 the nineteenth century a new set of problems had arisen in Britain. These
12 problems focused around the plight of the working class and the impact of
13 industrialization.

(a) T or F: Liberalism first appeared in England in the 19th century. (page IV, line I)
(b) Against what dangers were the liberals first concerned with protecting the rights of individuals? (page IV, lines 9-10)

British liberals advocate a laissez-faire policy. British liberals had come
14 to support the doctrine of *laisser faire* (leh-sey fair')—the notion that gov-
15 ernment should not interfere with business. They based their thinking
16 largely on the writings of Adam Smith. In *The Wealth of Nations*, pub-
17 lished in 1776. Smith stated the following: (1) Only when a man is free to
18 operate his business in the way that brings him the most profit can a healthy
19 economy be achieved. (2) By acting in his own self-interest—by trying to
20 achieve a maximum of profit—the businessman benefits the entire commu-
21 nity, for his actions lead to increased production, distribution, and consump-
22 tion of goods. (3) The government harms business and the community when
23 it interferes with the activities of businessmen. (4) The duty of government

17th century liberalism in England stood for
(a) religious freedom;
(b) freedom of the press;
(c) natural rights of individuals;
(d) the right to resist oppressive government;
(e) confidence in human intelligence.

By the 19th century, liberal concerns turned to the plight of the working class.

British liberals supported a *laissez faire* form of government.

This idea was developed by Adam Smith in *The Wealth of Nations*, written in 1776.

Vocabulary:
Terms likely to be unfamiliar are defined in the left-hand columns. The number in parentheses points out the text line where the term is first used.

(1) *Liberalism*: tolerance of the views of others and the willingness to challenge traditions and established institutions.

(6) *tyrannical*: cruel and unjust use of governmental power.

These ☐ symbols mark the beginning and ending of phrases or statements that are especially well written.

TO RESEARCH: Check in an encyclopedia or economics book for further information on Adam Smith's theories.

To Research are suggestions for independent research on related topics.

Questions directly following the text check your comprehension of what you have just read. Questions are of two types: true/false and short answer. Write your answers on a separate piece of paper. The page number and text line supplied after each question give you a quick reference to check your answer.

Occasionally a word is missing from the text. You should be able to fill in the missing word with little trouble. Failure to do so may mean your attention is drifting. The correct word can be found in the lower left-hand margin.

Reader Helper Notes stimulate you to think beyond the basic information covered in the text. Notes at the end of the chapter (pages 32–34) provide additional information and suggest possible answers to the questions raised.

Left margin notes:

Was the liberal idea of laissez faire limited to business? See Reader Helper Note 78.

TO THINK ABOUT: What possible connections can you see between the growth of liberal thinking in Britain and the success of the American Revolution?

MINI NOTE: Adam Smith and T. R. Malthus each had the ability to see things differently from others around them. This is called divergent thinking.

(3) laissez faire

Right margin notes:

Another idea popular with British liberals came from T. R. Malthus in *Essay on the Principles of Population* (1798).

Malthus said excessive population growth was the real cause of poverty, not greedy business practices.

Main text:

1 is to maintain peace and order within the community and not to meddle
2 with the affairs of business.
3 The supporters of _____ insisted that poverty is natural. Since
4 some are meant to be wealthy and some poor, government can do nothing
5 about poverty. Any governmental reforms might hurt business and make
6 things worse.

Malthus blames poverty on overpopulation. Another English thinker
7 who helped shape the liberal attitude in the early days of the Industrial
8 Revolution was T. R. Malthus. In his *Essay on the Principle of Population*
9 (1798), Malthus declared that the population always increases faster than
10 the food supply. As a result mankind is always threatened with starvation.
11 The real cause of poverty, according to Malthus, is overpopulation. Until
12 the poor learn to keep down the size of their families, poverty will never be
13 eliminated. Malthus concludes:

15 When the wages of labor are hardly sufficient to maintain two children, a
16 man marries and has five or six. He of course finds himself miserably
17 distressed. . . . He accuses the [greed] of the rich. . . . He accuses the
18 [prejudiced] and unjust institutions of society. . . . The last person that he
19 would think of accusing is himself.

20 Malthus also argued that as the population increases, the supply of workers
21 becomes greater than the demand. This leads to unemployment, low wages,
22 and perpetual poverty. For Malthus, lowering the birth rate was the only
23 effective way to combat poverty.

24 In effect Malthus was saying that, since the misery of the worker is his
25 own doing, no laws passed by the state can eliminate poverty. Factory
26 owners were delighted with Malthus' view. It soothed their consciences to
27 be told that they were not responsible for the sufferings of workers.

Democratic liberals propose reform legislation. The problems of the
28 working class persisted. Convinced that a laissez-faire policy was not ac-
29 ceptable, a growing number of liberals in England and elsewhere urged the
30 government to introduce reforms to aid the working man. They wanted
31 legislation that would improve conditions of work in the factory, allow the
32 growth of labor unions, eliminate property requirements for voting, and
33 increase educational opportunities for the poor. Whereas the older liberals

---

To Think About are questions which have no one correct answer. They are intended to raise broad generalizations or to provide topics for discussion and debate.

Mini Notes provide enrichment information related to the text.

Source: From the Experimental Edition of Chapter 2 of *Man's Unfinished Journey, A World History* by M. Perry, 1971. Copyright 1971 by Houghton Mifflin Company. All rights reserved.

Figure 6.10   Sample Reader Helper Notes

"Reader Helper Notes"
(A companion soft cover reference
book to the basic textbook)

#78 Was the liberal idea of laissez faire (non-interference) limited to business?

No, the early liberals didn't want interference of any kind from the government, not even in the form of government assistance to the poor. They feared that any interference would lead to interference in business and trade. Adam Smith in Wealth of Nations expressed their views best. He held that all but a helpless few would prosper when men could compete in a free market. T. R. Malthus further argued that those few who would remain poor had only themselves to blame because they had too many children. This philosophy became known as "economic liberalism." Today it would be called conservatism.

In due course a new form of liberalism began to develop which you can more easily understand if you will think of it as "democratic liberalism." Democratic liberals came to believe

that the government had to depart from a laissez faire (non-interference) policy in order to help the poor and ease human suffering.

Reading/Study Suggestion - Go back now to page 526 and read about Malthus (the "economic liberal") and about the rise of the new (democratic) liberalism. After you have read 526 and 527, consider this point: there is a parallel in the differences between the "economic" and "democratic" liberals of 18th Century England and the Republican and Democratic parties of the United States.

You have undoubtedly wondered whether you have understood the differences between the major parties in our country. Stop and think about what similarities and differences there might be between the two.

To clarify your thinking, ask your teacher and/or classmates for their opinions of how these political philosophies compare. Ask your teacher to point out specifically what is meant by the notions "liberal and conservative wings" of political parties.

Source: From the Experimental Edition of Chapter 2 of *Man's Unfinished Journey, A World History* by M. Perry, 1971. Copyright 1971 by Houghton Mifflin Company. All rights reserved.

difficulty. The chapter closes with a brief discussion and review of some of the technological features that make this text more "friendly."

Rationale for Text Technology

Extensive research has shown that schoolbooks often hinder comprehension because they lack appropriate connectives, pronoun referents, and highlighting and signaling devices that help students understand text (Osborn, Jones, & Stein, 1985). This is especially disturbing because research findings indicate that teachers tend to rely quite heavily on the content and organization of the textbooks they use

(Rosecky, 1978; Yarger & Mintz, 1979). Further, research has established that the bulk of students' "productive learning time" is the time spent interacting with textual materials. Hence, improvements in the technology of construction, writing, and display of text are likely to have a great impact on reading and learning (Sari & Reigeluth, 1982). Briefly put, **text technology** addresses an array of means and methods built into the format of the text itself for improving students' processing of text. These include (but are not limited to) the use of overviews, organizers, adjunct questions, and improvements in the actual mechanics of how things are expressed, that is, written and referenced.

A key issue in text technology is whether textual alterations should focus on the content or on the reader. In attempting to shed light on this question, we have drawn from a two-volume work (Jonassen, 1982, 1985a, 1985b) that outlines and critiques progress in text technology from the perspectives of more than 20 authors.

Text-Driven versus Learner-Driven Models of Text Technology

According to Jonassen, two opposing theoretical models underlie efforts to adjust textual material to achieve higher levels of reader comprehension and learning: the *mathemagenic* model and the *generative* model. The distinction between them is most evident in the types of materials each tends to promote. The **mathemagenic,** or text-driven, model underlies most programmed learning and mastery learning materials that emphasize content. The **generative** model is best represented by Anticipation-Reaction Guides and Imbedded Aids, which tend to focus on the reader. The text-driven concept of mathemagenics is largely the brainchild of Ernest Rothkopf (1970), a Bell Laboratory educational researcher. The generative, or learner-driven, model is the synthesis of the work of several educators and theorists.

Before we further examine how the two models differ, it is important to note what they have in common. Both are based on the following three fundamental assumptions:

1. Meaning is *not implicit* in the instructional materials.
2. Material is interpreted to be functional or effective by the *learner.*
3. The effectiveness of material ultimately is determined by the quality of overt *mental manipulations* (or *cognitive transformations*) that the learner must perform on the material.

On the last assumption, namely "How do we get the learner to think about information in a correct way?", the two theories part company. Mathemagenic, or text-driven, theorists seek to control student behaviors related to the attainment of the instructional objectives (Rothkopf, 1970). This amounts to an attempt to elicit identical responses from each learner and, in the process, control student thinking. This supplants the need for metacognitive functioning on the student's part with an external support system. Jonassen calls this type of control over the learner and the learning process a *reductive* approach. The narrowing of student responses, he says, ultimately weakens progress toward independence.

The generative model, on the other hand, seeks to engender strategies of learning from text that are individual and learner generated. It is a constructive rather than reductive approach. Reading and learning are not the passive reception of someone else's organizations and abstractions (Wittrock, Marks, & Doctorow, 1975). Meaning of text and motivation to understand depend on the learner's concept, or frame of reference, and intrinsic need to know. The generative learning model emphasizes not only learner involvement (as does mathemagenics) but learner control (Jonassen, 1985).

The cornerstone of the generative model is implied in the term itself: stimulating deeper, richer, more personal, and more transferable learning. The generative model clearly is more compatible with the broader goals and objectives of the educational process. The mathemagenic model, however, probably has its place as well. It appears to be more oriented toward efficient job training along the lines typically expected in government, business, and industry.

The difference between the two models is also evident in the way each *raises* questions in addition to *answering* them. For example, Rothkopf and associates spent years studying the as yet unresolved "training-based" issue of where to put questions to maximize comprehension: before, during, or after reading. School-based educators, in contrast, have moved on to more practical questions such as "Where, when, and how should questions be posed to increase the likelihood that readers will learn *how* to question and guide their own learning?"

While neither Jonassen nor Rothkopf have said so explicitly, it appears that supporters of the text-driven models also would favor conventional product assessment approaches, such as the Iowa Tests of Basic Skills. In contrast, learner-driven theorists likely would prefer the process-oriented approaches discussed as emerging options in Chapter 3.

One common concern regarding text technology deals with the issue of text structure, which we discussed earlier in this chapter from the standpoint of teaching readers to discern structure. The following section addresses this issue with respect to how textbook writers should structure expository writing to promote effective comprehension.

Text Structuring for Different Objectives

A three-category system has been developed to organize subject matter so that it can be effectively communicated as textual material. This system, according to Sari and Reigeluth (1982), entails checking to see whether the emphasis should be on (1) conceptual organization (or concepts that represent the "what" of the subject), (2) procedural organization (i.e., methods that describe the "how-to"), or (3) theoretical organization (namely principles that represent the "why," i.e., causes and effects, of the subject matter). This information can be used in a variety of ways to structure text for optimal learning. One way would be to ensure that the primary objective becomes the one that drives the structuring of the textual material and that the other two types are used to embellish wherever necessary and appropriate.

It is not entirely clear what types of structuring each category calls for. There are, however, these "rules of thumb" for structuring text:

1. The first chapter of a textbook should "epitomize," or represent, the most general, simple, and/or fundamental aspects of the remainder of the text. In a "how-to" book, it should impart a sense of the "how-to"; in a theoretical book, it should impart the most basic principle of the field. In this text, for example, the first chapter introduced a simple "heuristic" urging you to think and teach along lines advocated by content area reading specialists.
2. The conceptual organization of the text should be sequenced logically so that the main and supportive content within each chapter appear prior to more complex ideas. This chapter, for example, introduces the concept of guiding silent reading first with simple words and activities, then with written guides and aids, and here from the standpoint of text restructuring.
3. To keep the reader apprised of where the text is going, the writer also should use what Pace (1985) calls "self-conscious text." This is where the book "talks about itself," explaining its purposes, design, and rationale. This text employs this device extensively.

Admittedly, at this time such "rules of thumb" do not always constitute a sound formula for writing effective texts any more than the dictum "buy low, sell high" makes one get rich in the stock market. Nonetheless, these efforts are honest, scientifically based beginnings for a time when textbooks perhaps will be constructed to teach as well as expose. Such texts also may put a dent in the growing insecurity that many feel when required to read, absorb, and decide on things about which they may, under current conventions, feel they are "functionally illiterate" (e.g., medical information, tax regulations, warranty options, and political issues). Also, there is the fact that platitudinous-sounding statements, especially when delivered at the right time, can be very influential. The original design for this chapter assumed these more theoretical issues would have been covered first; after all, "theory before practice" is the logic underlying most books and courses of study. While preparing this information, however, the authors were reminded that this basically is a "procedural" text and that more theoretical and pioneering information, while important, should be reserved as embellishments to the text's central question, which clearly is "How do we improve reading, thinking, and content in today's classrooms with today's texts?"

PULLING IT ALL TOGETHER

Having reviewed available means of helping students read silently with effective comprehension, including provision of internal and external types of aids, it is useful to attempt to draw this new-found knowledge together. The Irwin-Davis Readability Checklist (Irwin & Davis, 1980) is based on an interactive model of the reading process and a generative model of text preparation. It invites the teacher to assess the appropriateness of a text from the standpoint of the reader's affective as well as cognitive needs. "Capstone" information and activities of this type can serve to generate the kind of mental manipulations, or cognitive transformations, that both mathemagenic and generative theorists would deem desirable.

The Irwin-Davis Readability Checklist (Figure 6.11) requires that the teacher draw on several crucial factors developed in this chapter for determining the suitability of reading material for students. These factors are grouped under four headings:

1. *Understandability.* Fourteen items addressing the issues of
   a. Compatibility of the text information with students' conceptual and experiential backgrounds
   b. The manner in which concepts are presented and defined
   c. Factors such as syntax, clarity of main-idea statement, presence of irrelevant details, and other elements that researchers have linked to comprehension
   d. Resources that textbook publishers could offer teachers who use their texts.
2. *Learnability.* Six items addressing the degree to which a student is likely to learn and remember what he or she has read and understood.
3. *Reinforcement.* Nine items concerning the availability of supplementary materials for providing sufficient repetitions, practice, and therefore reinforcement of new ideas, facts, and concepts.
4. *Motivation.* Seven items to help the teacher screen the text for its value in tapping into students' motivational resources.

Figure 6.11 Irwin-Davis Readability Checklist

Textbook title: _____

Publisher: _____

Copyright date: _____

Directions: This checklist is designed to help you evaluate the readability of your classroom texts. It can best be used if you rate your text while you are thinking of a specific class. Be sure to compare the textbook to a fictional ideal rather than to another text. Your goal is to find out what aspects of the text are or are not less than ideal. Finally, consider supplementary workbooks as part of the textbook and rate them together. Have fun!

Rate the following questions using the following rating system:

5 = Excellent
4 = Good
3 = Adequate
2 = Poor
1 = Unacceptable
NA = Not applicable

Figure 6.11 *continued*

Understandability

A. _____ Are the assumptions about students' vocabulary knowledge appropriate?

B. _____ Are the assumptions about students' prior knowledge of this content area appropriate?

C. _____ Are the assumptions about students' general experiential backgrounds appropriate?

D. _____ Does the teacher's manual provide the teacher with ways to develop and review the students' conceptual and experiential backgrounds?

E. _____ Are new concepts explicitly linked to the students' prior knowledge or to their experiential backgrounds?

F. _____ Does the text introduce abstract concepts by accompanying them with many concrete examples?

G. _____ Does the text introduce new concepts one at a time with a sufficient number of examples for each one?

H. _____ Are definitions understandable and at a lower level of abstraction than the concept being defined?

I. _____ Is the level of sentence complexity appropriate for the students?

J. _____ Are the main ideas of paragraphs, chapters, and subsections clearly stated?

K. _____ Does the text avoid irrelevant details?

L. _____ Does the text explicitly state important complex relationships (e.g., causality, conditionality, etc.) rather than always expecting the reader to infer them from the context?

M. _____ Does the teacher's manual provide lists of accessible resources containing alternative readings for the very poor or very advanced readers?

N. _____ Is the readability level appropriate (according to a readability formula)?

Learnability

A. _____ Is an introduction provided for in each chapter?

B. _____ Is there a clear and simple organizational pattern relating the chapters to each other?

C. _____ Does each chapter have a clear, explicit, and simple organizational structure?

D. _____ Does the text include resources such as an index, glossary, and table of contents?

E. _____ Do questions and activities draw attention to the organizational pattern of the material (e.g., chronological, cause and effect, spatial, topical, etc.)?

F. _____ Do consumable materials interrelate well with the textbook?

Figure 6.11 *continued*

Reinforcement

A. _____ Does the text provide opportunities for students to practice using new concepts?
B. _____ Are there summaries at appropriate intervals in the text?
C. _____ Does the text provide adequate iconic aids such as maps, graphs, illustrations, etc. to reinforce concepts?
D. _____ Are there adequate suggestions for usable supplementary activities?
E. _____ Do these activities provide for a broad range of ability levels?
F. _____ Are there literal recall questions provided for the students' self-review?
G. _____ Do some of the questions encourage the students to draw inferences?
H. _____ Are there discussion questions which encourage creative thinking?
I. _____ Are questions clearly worded?

Motivation

A. _____ Does the teacher's manual provide introductory activities that will capture students' interest?
B. _____ Are chapter titles and subheadings concrete, meaningful, or interesting?
C. _____ Is the writing style of the text appéaling to the students?
D. _____ Are the activities motivating? Will they make the student want to pursue the topic further?
E. _____ Does the book clearly show how the knowledge being learned might be used by the learner in the future?
F. _____ Are the cover, format, print size, and pictures appealing to the students?
G. _____ Does the text provide positive and motivating models for both sexes as well as for other racial, ethnic, and socioeconomic groups?

Readability Analysis: Summary
Weaknesses

1. On which items was the book rated the lowest?
2. Did these items tend to fall in certain categories?
3. Summarize the weaknesses of this text.
4. What can you do in class to compensate for the weaknesses of this text?

Assets

1. On which items was the book rated the highest?
2. Did these items fall into certain categories?
3. Summarize the assets of this text.
4. What can you do in class to take advantage of the assets of this text?

Source: From "Assessing Readability: The Checklist Approach" by J. W. Irwin and C. A. Davis, 1980, *Journal of Reading, 24,* pp. 129–130. Copyright 1980 by the International Reading Association. Reprinted with permission of Judith W. Irwin and the International Reading Association.

CHAPTER TIE-UPS

Graphic Organizer ◆◆◆

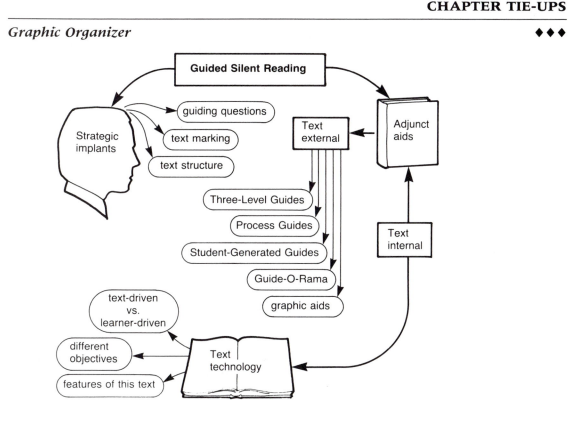

Critique and Anticipation ◆◆◆

Students can be taught to think while they read in essentially three ways: (1) through internalized guiding questions; (2) by use of systems for marking and responding to text; and (3) through study of paragraph patterns. There can also be two types of aids for helping students think more accurately and elaboratively while they read: (1) external adjunct aids, such as reading guides and graphics, and (2) internal Imbedded Aids, such as marginal notes, summaries, and vocabulary aids. Currently all of these devices are being synthesized into a technology of text that is expected to improve the structuring, writing, and display of conventional textbooks and, in all likelihood, create a new form of electronic text that will be programmed to accommodate readers' needs and permit them to react to what they read in a variety of ways.

The next chapter examines postreading instructional strategies that involve verification and further processing of information and ideas acquired from reading. Information and ideas may be clarified, categorized, evaluated, applied, and/or used as models for student compositions. Such postreading processing is the key to effective schema building. Schema enrichment, in turn, leads to increased interest and capacity for further reading and study.

TRADE SECRET

Languaging Your Experiences—Feel Yourself Grow in Wisdom

If you are convinced by now of the value of having youngsters process and articulate, or language-through, their experiences, you will find this next point well worthwhile. What you do, think, and learn as a preservice and in-service teacher—about school, youngsters, and teaching—is highly consequential. It influences the way you feel and the way you will act. Think through your experiences. Express your impressions to yourself. Write them down in a personal journal. Share them with colleagues, course instructors, visiting consultants, and later with yourself in a more reflective mood. In this way, the things you feel, think, and experience will be refined and strengthened into ideas, insights, and solutions. Following this simple formula, you will feel yourself growing in wisdom, and you will contribute to the maturity and respectability of your chosen profession.

One teacher who used this approach in a particularly trying classroom situation came up with this partial solution to getting a class settled and thinking quickly. As soon as the opening bell rang, she asked the class some review questions about the previous day's work—but in an unexpected and clever way. She asked student volunteers to ''take the question'' but not answer it immediately. Instead, they should think about their answer, refer back to the textbook if they wished, and answer when the teacher was ready—after the roll had been taken and paperwork completed. With this simple strategy, impulsive students were given a reason to take a little extra ''think time'' before responding and shy students were given time to compose answers and participate in the ensuing discussion.

Postreading Designs

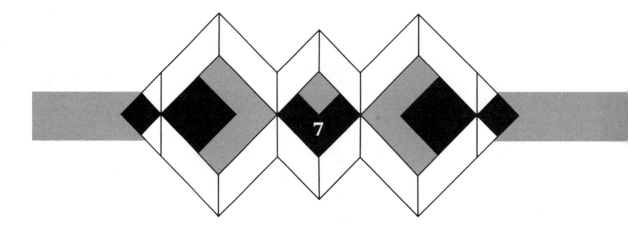

Recitation, Discussion, Writing, and Vocabulary Enrichment for Schema Building

In theory, it is easy to convince an ignorant person; in fact, men not only object to being convinced, but hate those who would convince them.

— Epictetus

FOCUS

Successful comprehension sets the stage for verifying, clarifying, elaborating, embellishing, enhancing, and further exploring. These schema-building processes are impelled through recitation, discussion, writing, and vocabulary enrichment.

CHECKING COMPREHENSION:
RECITATION-BASED APPROACHES

Progress has been likened to a footrace in which reason, knowledge, and invention are pitted against fear, ignorance, and uncertainty. Every classroom teacher coaches a team that will, like it or not, run a leg in this race. This chapter presents some of the equipment and strategies available to teachers for building winning teams through reflective reading.

Figuratively speaking, prereading is planting and cultivating, silent reading is budding and blooming, and postreading is fruit bearing and harvesting. In post-reading, prior energies are transformed into usable products and "seeds" for continuing the process.

The postreading step of the DRA and DR-TA is the point at which students can check comprehension, broaden schema, and extend skills. Most of the tools for nurturing these outcomes are familiar: recitation, discussion, writing, vocabulary building, and exercises in applied and evaluative thinking. This chapter discusses the first four tools; the next chapter covers the last. Box 7.1 demonstrates the importance of postreading reflection and schema building.

Postreading Recitation

Recitation involves simply reviewing, drilling, and quizzing (Dillon, 1984). The dialog in Figure 7.1 illustrates a typical postreading recitation. Notice that teacher

---

BOX 7.1

CONCEPT CLARIFICATION
Schema Building

To get a vivid idea of the powerful role schema plays in constructing meaning from text, consider what meanings, inferences, and conjectures you would make if you examined one week's worth of trash from three different homes. Develop a short description of each family.

Home 1: large white-wine bottle; gourmet frozen dinner boxes; remnants of fresh vegetables; envelopes from Merrill Lynch, Exxon, Dreyfus Fund and American Express; empty laxative and skin moisturizer bottles; *Travel* and *Modern Maturity* magazines

Home 2: frozen french fries package; meat packages; several large soda bottles; chips and cookie packages; gallon-size milk containers; brochures for summer camps and after-school activities; *Time* and *Mad* magazines

Home 3: yogurt containers; bran cereal boxes; packaging from a computer component; two pairs of still usable ladies' shoes; *National Geographic* and *Modern Life* magazines

As you build a schema for each of these families, you draw on your existing schema and prior knowledge. You may feel that you can describe one family easily but need more information on the others. Like the ability to construct meaning from text, your ability to build new schema depends largely on actively comparing your existing knowledge to new information.

Figure 7.1   Postreading Recitation

Students in an eighth-grade health class read a portion of the chapter on poison control the day before the videotaping. In the beginning segment of the transcript, which was typical of the entire lesson, Ms. Sneed quizzed the class on their assigned reading.

Ms. Sneed: All right, Vinny. Would you try to identify the poison for all victims or only the ones that are conscious?
Vinny: All victims.
Ms. Sneed: All victims. Good. Roger? Would you call the poison center for all victims or only the ones that are conscious?
Roger: All of them.
Ms. Sneed: All of them. Good. Lee? Would you treat for shock only those victims who are conscious or all victims?
Lee: All victims.
Ms. Sneed: All victims. Good. Would you watch to be sure that all victims keep breathing, Jeri, or only the conscious ones?
Jeri: All.

Source: From *Using Discussion to Promote Reading Comprehension* (pp. 2–3) by D. E. Alvermann, D. R. Dillon, and D. G. O'Brien, 1987, Newark, DE: International Reading Association. Copyright 1987 by the International Reading Association. Reprinted with permission of Donna E. Alvermann and the International Reading Association.

questioning in recitation tends to be at the text-explicit, or literal, level and focuses on checking and reviewing comprehension. Dolores Durkin (1978–79) claims that this is not comprehension training at all but simply a form of testing. We strongly disagree, however. Simple literal questioning is a perfectly reasonable means of inducing a retrospective analysis of what has been read. It also provides corrective feedback and lays the foundation for further analysis. If every reading and home-work assignment were followed with this much attention, we could expect a fair degree of improvement in students' reading and learning from text.

Support for recitation dates back to Thorndike's (1917) study of comprehension, which demonstrated that reading is an act of *reasoning* and therefore is served better by silent reading and recitation than by oral reading and phonics. As defined above, recitation—reviewing, drilling, and quizzing—is characterized by three literal-level question types: recognition, recall, and translation. Recognition questions require *finding* information; recall questions require *remembering* information; and trans-lation questions require *paraphrasing* information, or converting it from one sym-bolic form to another. Translation questions form a bridge from literal- to higher-level interpretive and applied processing of information. Unfortunately, as noted in Chapter 5 on prereading strategies, studies of classroom practices consistently indicate that teachers tend to ask a very low percentage of translation questions. In the dialog in Figure 7.1, for example, the teacher could say, "Explain the meaning of the chart that shows poisons and their antidotes" and/or "Can someone restate what Mark just said in your own words?"

Peer Recitation

Recitation provides quality *engagement* time between teacher and class. Stating/restating builds a tempo of attention and an aura of activity and learning. Contrary to common belief, bright students do not resent this redundancy, especially if the process is kept brisk and routinely lays a foundation for further, more reflective discussion.

The quality of recitation time can be further enhanced by dividing the class into teams. Each team can be made responsible for leading a postreading, or *Peer Recitation*, session, as we have come to call it. Options and innovations available for Peer Recitation include the following:

1. *Five-question format:* The team leads the class in filling out a "who-what-when-where-why-how" Herringbone-type outline (see Chapter 6 on guiding silent reading).
2. *Question-only:* The class questions the team, and the team responds.
3. *Rapping:* The questions and answers are set to some rhythmic beat or mneumonic device.
4. *Written questions:* Everyone prepares a few questions on the content to be mastered. Going around the room in a certain order (up and down rows or across aisles), students read questions not asked before and the group answers. The teacher might collect the best questions for use on a unit test. This enhances students' motivation to construct quality questions and to listen carefully during recitation.

Handling Incorrect Responses

The most nagging problem in any recitation session is how to handle incorrect responses. Several research-based means of turning incorrect answers into learning experiences have been collected by Collins (1987) and Rakes and Smith (1987); some of these are presented in Figure 7.2. You probably ask most of these questions intuitively, but it is good to have your intuition validated when teaching is your profession.

Collins' 12th strategy, "expand for clarity," begins the conversion of recitation into discussion—our next topic.

EXTENDING COMPREHENSION: DIALECTICAL DISCUSSION STRATEGIES

From Recitation to Discussion

Discussion is distinguishable from recitation in several ways, most notably the following:

1. Different points of view are expressed.
2. Students must interact with one another as well as with the teacher.

Figure 7.2   Fixing Incorrect Answers in Recitation

1. *Think Again.* If you think [students] who gave an incorrect answer [have] the background to answer correctly, ask them to think again: "I'm sure you'll think of it if you just give yourself a little more time."
2. *Give a Prompt.* When students give a partial answer, or need you to provide more structure, offer a small piece of information.
3. *Differential Reinforcement.* Tell the part of the answer that was correct: "You're right, bears are mammals. Do you recall whether mammals are warm blooded? Are human beings warm blooded?"
4. *Paraphrasing the Questions.* If it appears no one knows the answer, yet you judge that they learned the information, rephrase the question.
5. *Expanding the Answer.* Ask [students] to tell why they answered the way they did or why they believe their answer to be correct.
6. *Making Students Accountable.* If a student gives 2 incorrect answers to the same question, or if 2 students answer incorrectly, give the answer and tell them they will need to remember it. (This gives them incentive to remember the question and the answer.) Return to the student(s) again before the period is over and ask the same question.
7. *Asking for Clues.* Ask fellow students to give clues, or ask the student who missed the question to call upon a classmate to help by giving either a clue or the answer.
8. *"Incorrect If" Statements.* If you recognize why the answer was wrong, supply the question for which the answer would have been correct. For example, if you asked, "What is the capital of New Zealand?" and the student answered "Canberra," you could respond "Canberra would be the answer if someone asked what the capital of Australia was. How about the capital of New Zealand?"
9. *Examples of Possibilities.* Use oral multiple choices at the close of a lesson or unit or as a review. "Who was the first European to see the Pacific Ocean? Balboa, Cortez, or Cabeza de Vaca?"
10. *Nonexamples or Opposites.* If students don't raise their hands to answer a question, tell them what the answer is *not*.
11. *One Thing I Learned Today.* Toward the end of class, students are called upon to tell one thing that they learned that day without repeating any item previously stated by another student.
12. *Expand for Clarity.* Ask students to explain the rationale behind their answers.

Source: From "Content Mastery Strategies Aid Class Discussion" by C. Collins, 1987, *The Reading Teacher, 40*, pp. 816–818. Copyright 1987 by the International Reading Association. Reprinted with permission of Cathy Collins and the International Reading Association.

3. Responses should be longer and more elaborate than in recitation.
4. Discussants, including the teacher, are expected to change their minds about what they have read (Alvermann, Dillon, & O'Brien, 1987, p. 13).
5. Discourse should create a dynamic tension, or dialectical interaction, within as well as among individuals.

Meanings shared in class discussion are not merely a collection of individual meanings but a new set of meanings developed as members talk and listen to one another and to themselves (Pinnell, 1984). Classroom discussion differs from social discussion in that its expressed purpose is to orchestrate group-talk, or external languaging. Ideally, external languaging provides a mechanism for fine-tuning *internal talk* so that someone, anyone, and then everyone might reach a higher standard for reflection on the topic discussed.

The backbone of effective discussion, or languaging, is the presence of at least one individual capable of reaching, and thereby modeling, insightful and alternative perspectives. Discussion becomes a *dialectical* analysis when a position or viewpoint is countered by an alternate viewpoint, creating a dynamic tension, or state of "cognitive dissonance" (Festinger, 1957), which must be resolved by reaching a higher level of understanding from which both viewpoints can be considered.

The above point is better illustrated than explained. The first author once observed a group of teachers in a workshop designed to demonstrate the use of reading guides for analysis of poetry. The teachers were asked to read a poem and develop literal-level questions. These easily generated questions drew out the fact that the man in the poem was sitting on a park bench in New York City, watching and reflecting on the innocent play of children. Next, the teachers were asked to create questions that required interpretive-level thinking. These were more difficult to develop, but the teachers finally got help from the two trainers to see how the man's reflections were of the halcyon (happy and carefree) days of youth before we somehow learn to be cross and cunning with one another. Everyone seemed satisfied that this was what the poem was about and that now it had been read with insight and a grasp of its universal truth. This was reconstructive reading, but in short order one person suggested that he saw something else in the poem. As he listened to the group's analysis, he began to think that the man could have wandered out of a nearby office building where he had been caught in a crossfire of office politics. In need of a reprieve, he attributed peace and cooperation to the children's play because he needed to believe that there was a freer time in life. After a long pause, someone else said, "Is there really such a thing as carefree, halycon days?" Then someone else added that only recently she had read about the enormous cruelty that children can bestow on one another and how some seem to derive an innate pleasure from being bullies.

This more cynical bit of counterpoint created the dynamic tension needed to move the discourse from a fairy tale to a slice-of-life insight into the human condition. In another situation, the dynamic tension might have been stimulated by a softer, less cynical view. In either case, however, the "universal truth" may lie not in the author's words or apparent intentions but in some reader's schema, or prior knowledge and experience. In this case, it lay in one reader's insights into stress and its effects on human motivation, perception, and behavior. This was constructive reading.

Notice how the dialectical process—that is, a stated position, followed by an alternate position, followed by further analysis and synthesis—likely enriched the schema of all present. Ideally, when one's schema becomes enriched in this way, it increases one's subsequent ability to activate analogous thoughts independently when confronted with similar material. In this case, participants learned something about how to conjecture about an author's subconscious as well as conscious intentions.

One good question to induce dynamic, or constructive tension is: "What do you suppose prompted the writer to see things as he or she did?" When a dynamic tension is achieved, the teacher can seize the moment to push for fuller reflection and deeper learning. In the situation just described, appropriate follow-up questions might be:

> What do you think of the personal value of a walk in the park as a way to deal
>   with the stress the writer may have been feeling?
> In what other ways might he have dealt with his stress?
> What might business and industry do to reduce stressful conditions?
> Can stress really be avoided, or is it part of the human condition?

And the creative teacher could raise this applied-level question, perhaps as an essay-writing assignment:

> Can anyone tell of a situation that may or has come up in school that might
>   raise one's stress level and how it might be coped with or avoided by the
>   teacher or a change in school policy?

It is this potential to ignite thinking "beyond the lines" and even beyond the author's intended meanings to a more constructive process that is the real promise of dialectical thinking and languaging-based strategies. An early technical report of the Center for the Study of Reading stated it this way:

> The eventual aim [of all reading and content instruction] is to train youngsters to *think
> dialectically,* in the sense of the Socratic teaching method. In the Socratic method, the
> teacher constantly questions the students' basic assumptions and premises, plays devil's
> advocate, and probes weak areas, using such techniques as invidious generalizations,
> and counter-examples. . . . The desired end product is that the student will come to
> perform the teacher's functions for himself via self-interrogation. (Brown & Campione,
> 1977)

The implications of this are clear: The best methods of instruction are those that invite students to think and perform functions that may be even more insightful than the teacher's. Chapter 8 on critical-creating reading exemplifies this attitude by describing several emerging methods for promoting creative/inventive thinking.

Now let us consider several methods for promoting the dynamic tension necessary to ignite such dialectical thinking and discussion. In the same vein, be sure to look carefully at the section on enabling questions in Chapter 9, which focuses on study skills and habits. That section details specific means by which students can be taught to ask questions and make comments that can raise the level of discourse even above what the teacher anticipated.

Three-Question Paradigm for Effective Discussion

Effective discussion is by nature an unpredictable and unwieldy event. It depends in large measure on the leader's willingness to pursue "unplanned" avenues of thought and the accompanying ability to bring them together toward meaningful conclusions. This requires both flexibility and restraint. A simple *Three-Question Paradigm* can be a useful tool for maintaining this balance. This strategy reminds discussion leaders to ask each of the following questions in some way during the course of the discussion:

1. What did you think?
2. What did you read/hear/see?
3. What did you learn?

An example would be "What did you *think* it took to lead a good discussion? What did we say it takes? What did you learn, or have clarified, about leading a discussion in school from what was said above?"

Listen-Read-Discuss

The L-R-D method, which we discussed in Chapter 1, is a simple technique for painlessly initiating a fact-based dialectical discussion. Alvermann et al. (1987) report the following use of the L-R-D in "Ms. Hailey's eighth-grade science class."

The discussion topic was matter. Ms. Hailey had presented the key concepts in a 15-minute lecture guided by a **Structured Overview** on an overhead transparency. Then the students read the corresponding pages of text silently for the next 15 minutes. They were to read to locate information that expanded on the lecture or appeared inconsistent with it. Finally, students and teacher discussed misconceptions and elaborations generated from the comparison. The excerpt from Hailey's class presented in Figure 7.3 shows how this discussion, following the questions suggested for L-R-D postreading, became centered on an examination of some of the unknowns surrounding matter.

Anyone who teaches is almost certain to like this realistic example; it is not particularly rousing, but it is solid and professional. Notice how students in this lesson were (1) informed (lectured to) on a difficult topic; (2) reinforced in their reading; (3) tested in their ability to extend and verify their understandings; (4) permitted to articulate those understandings or possible misconceptions; and (5) redirected to continue their search for verifiable knowledge in their textbooks, in other texts, and implicitly from other sources. Any time a class is structured and kept on target long enough to get this much done, they have run a good leg in the race against ignorance.

Conflict Identification and Resolution

The dialectical process, as mentioned above, is essential to acquisition of critical reading-thinking skills and habits. This process is activated by a phenomenon

Figure 7.3 L-R-D Postreading Discussion

Hailey: What did you understand best about matter from what you heard and read?
Sam: That matter means things that take up space.
Mike: Anything that has mass and takes up space.
Hailey: Okay, that's the definition given in your book. Can you, or someone else, give us some examples? (Various ideas are shared by several students.)
Hailey: What did you understand least about matter?
Julie: I don't get what isn't matter. Like, we can't see air, so it's not matter, right?
Several students (disagreeing with Julie): But air takes up space.
Hailey: Julie, do you agree with that?
Julie: No . . . . at least not if . . . no, I don't agree.
Jenny: All things take up space. Take blowing up a balloon, for example . . .
(interrupted by teacher)
Hailey: What happens to your balloon? What's inside?
Julie: (Thinking, still looking puzzled) Then there's nothing on earth that isn't matter?
Hailey: I can't think of anything, but maybe someone can. (Teacher models a personal uncertainty.)
Sam: Nope. (No one else volunteers a response.)
Hailey: Well, what other questions or thoughts did this lesson raise in your mind about matter?
Mike: I'm still wondering about the matter of certain stuff—like the earth and air—what's it made up of?
Jenny: Yeah, and how do scientists figure out what matter is made of?
Hailey: Those are both good questions. Let's read further to see if the author of our textbook answers them. If not, we'll talk about where we might go to find the answers.

Source: From *Using Discussion to Promote Reading Comprehension* (pp. 36–37) by D. E. Alvermann, D. R. Dillon, and D. G. O'Brien, Newark, DE: International Reading Association. Copyright 1987 by the International Reading Association. Reprinted with permission of Donna E. Alvermann and the International Reading Association.

known as *cognitive dissonance*—psychological discomfort that occurs in the presence of inconsistency (Festinger, 1957). Frager and Thompson (1985) have suggested that teachers collect and share conflicting materials with students as a means of sensitizing them to critical issues and providing them with provocative material with which to develop and hone their critical thinking skills.

Study the general teaching paradigm that follows for teaching conflict identification and resolution. Notice how this activity resembles the dialectical process discussed earlier in the chapter. Examples of "conflict-based" materials for critical reading lessons in music, health, and social studies appear in Figure 7.4.

Teaching Paradigm for Conflict Identification and Resolution

1. Have students read conflicting accounts of the same topic.
2. Increase cognitive dissonance by eliciting from students explanations and arguments supporting each side of the conflict.

Figure 7.4 Content Area Examples of Conflict Identification and Resolution

Content Area Example: Music

Topic: Michael Jackson

Account A. In "Michael Jackson: Junk Culture Triumph" (Johnson, 1984), Jackson is described as a "rather, frail, androgynous creature with a light, genderless voice. . . ." It is reported that "he acts childlike but obviously is a shrewd show-business entrepreneur" and that "it is rumored he had his face modeled to resemble Diana Ross, one of his mentors."

Account B. Johnson (1984) describes Jackson as being as "mystical offstage as he is magical onstage" and as "shy, sensitive, and celibate." The article stresses that Jackson is "pious without pontificating" and that his magic making is motivated by selfless, inner needs.

Content Area Example: Health

Topic: Passive Smoke

Account A. According to an advertisement paid for by the R. J. Reynolds Tobacco Company ("Second-Hand Smoke," 1984), "nothing proves scientifically that cigarette smoke causes disease in non-smokers." The ad explains that it would take nonsmokers four days to inhale the equivalent of one cigarette from the smoke in public places and concludes "our own concerns about health can take an unproven claim and magnify [it] out of all proportion."

Account B. The *Cleveland Plain Dealer* ("Protect Non-Smokers from Smokers," 1984) reports the results of a Japanese study that found "a non-smoker whose family members puff more than two packs a day actually inhales the equivalent of one or two cigarettes." Research recommendations include the warning that "smoking should be restricted in such public places as hospitals, restaurants, meeting rooms, vehicles, and even on sidewalks."

Content Area Example: Social Studies

Topic: Watergate

Account A. In a 1984 newspaper column, Maurice Stans compares Watergate to a witchhunt, causing "wanton injuries on innocent people whose only offense was being a friend or associate of Richard Nixon."

Account B. In *USA Today*, Sam Ervin, Jr. (1984), likens Watergate to an attempt to "rob the American people of the freedom to nominate and elect a candidate for President." Ervin explains that agents of the President "paid hundreds of thousands of dollars to hide the truth."

Source: From "Conflict: The Key to Critical Thinking" by A. M. Frager and L. C. Thompson, May 1985, *Journal of Reading,* pp. 678–679.

3. Model critical reading of the accounts.
4. Extend the lesson to a point where students' dissonance may be resolved by additional reading and by using the critical reading and thinking skills modeled previously.

Resource Materials for Conflict Identification and Resolution
Most examples of conflict must be found in materials other than textbooks. Textbooks tend to defuse even the most controversial topics by presenting them in ways that are more smoothhanded than evenhanded. This may be good for marketing textbooks, but it has a substantial dampening effect on the development of critical thinking. Materials extending the concept of conflict identification and resolution beyond the classroom and into daily life experience can be identified in at least four ways:

• Students can be encouraged to find examples of materials that cry out for a counterpoint (such as newspaper editorials).
• Students can be asked to search in likely places for examples of counterpoints to articles and pieces presented in class.
• Students can be exposed to a strong position just prior to reading a piece that expresses a counterpoint.
• Students can be asked to write their own brief counterpoints as a prelude and/ or follow-up to discussion.

The last example is particularly desirable as a postreading and schema-building activity. It also serves as a good example of how writing—our next topic—can be integrated gracefully into almost any curriculum area. For further discussion of an idea highly related to conflict resolution, see the section on Refutation Text in Chapter 13.

ENHANCING SKILLS: WHOLE LANGUAGE STRATEGIES

There is a growing sense among educators in all fields that effective teaching and learning are more holistic than segmented. One result of this movement has been renewed interest in and emphasis on whole language approaches that combine strategies for improving reading, writing, speaking, and listening into integrated and often cross-disciplinary units of instruction. The postreading strategies presented so far provide for effective development of reading, listening, and speaking skills. Next, we will consider some of the ways to enhance learning in every content area and a basic instructional framework for guiding writing instruction.

Writing across the Curriculum: Rationale and Instructional Framework

Rationale for Writing across the Curriculum
Writing serves at least two practical purposes in improving reading, thinking, and content mastery. Each effort to write a summary of any type following reading

requires considerable reconstruction of text and thereby increases sensitivity to the text's logic and organization. Each effort to write in reaction to or evaluation of text constitutes a plunge into the unknown and therefore is an exercise in using language and thought to discover and organize the "inchoate lump of meanings" (Henry, 1974) we are left with following typical passive reading. Simply put, a routine requirement to write something—almost anything—following reading ignites more active thinking before, during, and following reading.

The following sections present several content-based writing strategies. In general, you will find that these activities conform to the guidelines extrapolated from a review of the modern research on writing by Hittleman (1984) indicating that writing should be:

- Daily rather than infrequent
- Done for real audiences and purposes
- More student than teacher initiated
- Allotted sufficient time for stages of thought and editing to occur
- Set in a writing community environment
- Peer guided, reviewed, and supported
- Done with an initial emphasis on "reacting and responding" to the intended message rather than on "proofreading and editing"

The Writing Process: An Instructional Framework for Writing across the Curriculum

Traditional efforts to teach writing have focused on the final product. More recently, however, an instructional framework for guiding student mastery of the *process* of writing has evolved. This instructional framework follows the process one would reasonably go through in writing. Therefore, it has come to be called simply the **Writing Process.** The Writing Process parallels the Directed Reading-Thinking Activity framework for prereading, guided silent reading, and postreading instruction. This is a useful point to keep in mind, because each of these instructional frameworks serves to remind us of the need to seek out appropriate teaching strategies for each of their phases. In the outline of the Writing Process presented in Figure 7.5, notice that this framework, like the DR-TA, indicates what should be done at each stage in general terms but not how to do it. Six whole language strategies follow, each with a strong emphasis on writing as a means of extending and enriching information and ideas gained from reading.

Why Whole Language Writing?

The strategies for improving writing described next are called *whole language* approaches because they tend to (1) incorporate each of the language arts of reading, writing, listening, and speaking and (2) follow the same natural processes by which language learning most often occurs. This process puts a high premium on relevancy and meaning, the stock in trade of the content teacher. An analysis by Goodman (1986) of when general language learning occurs most naturally is equally descriptive of how and when specific content language proficiency, or "Languaging in the Content Areas," also is best learned. Goodman suggests that language is learned naturally when

- It's real and natural.
- It's whole.
- It's sensible.
- It's interesting.
- It's relevant.
- It belongs to the learner.
- It's part of a real event.
- It has social utility.
- It has purpose for the learner.
- The learner chooses to use it.
- It's accessible to the learner.
- The learner has the power to use it. (1986, p. 8)

Whole Language Strategy 1:
Read-Encode-Annotate-Ponder (REAP)

Read-Encode-Annotate-Ponder, or *REAP* (Eanet & Manzo, 1976), was among the earliest strategies developed to stress the use of writing as a means of improving thinking and reading. REAP does so by teaching students a number of ways to *annotate,* or write short critiques of, what they have read. The various annotations serve as alternative perspectives from which to consider and evaluate information and ideas.

Annotation writing involves the reader in examining the writer's intentions and possible motivations as well as the literal and inferential interpretations of the message. The reader also explores his or her own views and feelings (Manzo, 1985). This meaningful reprocessing of material read helps readers shape the "inchoate lump of meaning" gleaned from reading into a concise and coherent addition to their funds of knowledge and general schema. Research on writing suggests that efforts to develop annotation skills concurrently with reading and content result in enriched factual knowledge, conceptual development, and vocabulary acquisition (Eanet & Manzo, 1976; Cunningham & Cunningham, 1976; Doctorow, Wittrock, & Marks, 1978; Applebee, 1981; Bromley, 1985).

REAP is a two-level strategy: Once students have learned the annotation forms, they can use REAP independently as a "study formula" to guide thoughtful reading, or the teacher can use it as an instructional activity.

Steps in Student Use of REAP

1. R: *Read* to discern the writer's message
2. E: *Encode* the message by translating it into your own language
3. A: *Annotate* by cogently writing the message in notes for yourself or in a thought book to share with others

Figure 7.5   Phases of the Writing Process

Before Writing
Content and Idea Building: "Getting It Out"

In this phase, the teacher tries to prepare students for writing by

1. Raising motivation and interest
2. Encouraging exploration of the topic
3. Calling up relevant prior knowledge and experiences

Content and Idea Clarification and Organization: "Getting It Together"

The teacher's role in this phase is to

1. Encourage idea development by eliciting additional details, reasons, examples, or incidents
2. Provide basic expectations for the final product, usually in the form of a rubric (see Chapter 3 for examples)
3. Assist students in identifying an audience they can keep in mind to guide the form and character of the composition

During Writing
Composing: "Getting It Down"

In this phase, the student attempts to relate the simultaneous din of ideas, purposes, facts, personal feelings, and biases into the linearity of words and structure. This includes finding out what you really think and then whether you can, or dare, say it. Typically the teacher's role in this phase is to

1. Help students express initial thoughts and ideas on paper in sentence-by-sentence form
2. Urge students to use prewriting notes and experiences
3. Encourage the free flow of ideas, even where they seem to contradict one another and raise personal, or cognitive, dissonance

4. P: *Ponder,* or reflect, on what you have read and written, first introspectively and then by sharing and discussing it with others and as a study aid in test preparation

REAP Response to Text Rubric
Figure 7.6 describes and illustrates 10 annotation forms initially developed for teaching the REAP strategy. These forms can be of more general value, however, and taught apart from REAP as a heuristic, or schema, for responding to text. When reading fiction, for example, the rubric offers guidelines for literary analysis and criticism; when reading nonfiction, it provides a set of protocols for thinking about, responding to, and storing new information and ideas.

Figure 7.5 *continued*

4. Build personal conviction that learning and clarity of thinking are desirable and attainable goals

Revising: "Getting It Organized"
This is an appraisal and reconstructive phase. It requires a good deal of introspection and willingness to critique oneself, to be critiqued, and, in several strategies described ahead, to think like an editor and critique the work of others. In this phase, the teacher

1. Encourages students to reorder, rewrite, and revise as needed for fluency and coherence
2. Guides discussions that clarify and thereby point to specific areas of composition that require rewriting
3. Encourages redrafting as needed with an eye toward initial purpose and audience
4. Helps students to learn how well others have understood and interpreted their writing

Editing: "Getting It Right"
In this final phase, the composition is reviewed for correct mechanics such as spelling, grammatical usage, and punctuation. The teacher assists by

1. Encouraging students to fine tune their work
2. Noting common mechanical problems and providing class instruction in these areas

After Writing
Publishing: Going Public

In this phase, a final copy is shared with an audience. The teacher aids in this process by

1. Employing methods that ensure that there will be readers for students' efforts
2. Offering opportunities for the work to serve as a foundation for reading, discussion, or study
3. Offering evaluative feedback based on the rubric for the assignment

If you wish to monitor students' progress toward higher-order literacy, you can refer to the rubric when reviewing student papers. The rubric also can serve as a means of appraising the characteristic way in which a student or group responds to text. To use the rubric for appraisal purposes, as well as in recordkeeping, simply number the annotations in order from 1 to 10. They already are roughly in order of difficulty, so the lower numbers will tend to indicate mechanistic thinking and higher numbers more sophisticated and personal patterns of responding. The examples in Figure 7.6 are based on A. S. Neill's controversial book *Summerhill*. Study them carefully to get a sense of the various perspectives from which text can be viewed and critiqued. A second, briefer set of more typical student-generated annotations is presented ahead.

Figure 7.6   REAP Annotations and Examples

Summerhill **Excerpt**

When we look at an infant, we know there is no wickedness in him—no more than there is wickedness in a cabbage or in a tiger. The newborn child brings with him a life force: his will, his unconscious urge is to live. His life force prompts him to eat, to explore his body, to gratify his wishes. He acts as Nature intended him to act, as he was made to act. But, to the adult, the will of God in the child—the will of Nature in the child—is the will of the devil.

Practically every adult believes that the nature of the child must be improved. Hence, it happens that every parent begins to teach the young child how to live.

The child soon comes up against a whole system of prohibitions. This is naughty and that is dirty and such and such is selfish. The original voice of the child's natural life force meets with the voice of instruction. The church would call the voice of Nature the voice of the devil, and the voice of moral instruction the voice of God. I am convinced that the names should be reversed. I believe that it is moral instruction that makes the child bad. I find that when I smash the moral instruction a bad boy received, he becomes a good boy.

Annotation Examples

1. *Summary annotation*—condenses the selection into a concise form. It is a synopsis of plot and main characters in fiction and an unelaborated statement of significant ideas in nonfiction.

   Example: The child is motivated by natural impulses such as the need to eat or to gratify his or her wishes. This child naturally comes into conflict with a system of prohibitions called "moral instruction." The conflict created by instructing the child in morality is what causes delinquent children.

2. *Heuristic annotation*—a statement, usually in the author's words, that symbolically illustrates the central idea of the selection in an evocative manner.

   Example: "It is moral instruction that makes the child bad. I find that when I smash the moral instruction a bad boy received, he becomes a good boy."

3. *Précis annotation*—an incisive thesis statement of the author's primary proposition, with all unnecessary words removed. The result is an uncluttered, telegramlike message.

   Example: Children have natural needs. Moral instruction conflicts with natural needs. This contradiction causes delinquent behavior.

4. *Organizing question annotation*—converts the author's thesis into a question that the narrative attempts to answer.

   Example: What are the influences that turn boys and girls into sick, delinquent children? Neill says that he knows, and further, he believes that he knows what can be done to correct the situation.

5. *Personal view annotation*—answers the question "How do personal experiences, views, and feelings stack up against the thesis or main idea?"

   Example: I have known at least a few persons who struck me as being inherently troubled and therefore inclined to being delinquent. It seems as if it takes the lives of several other persons to keep them "straight." Modifying education to meet their needs might not be possible, fair, or cost effective in human terms.

Figure 7.6 *continued*

6. *Critical annotation*—a supportive, rejecting, or questioning response to the thesis. The first sentence should restate the author's thesis. The next sentence should state the annotator's position. Additional sentences in the explanation should be kept to a minimum.

   Example: Moral instruction conflicts with "natural needs." Neill is correct, but it is supposed to. Moral instruction is humans' attempt to control their destiny. Clearly some "moralists" have overstated the issue; however, the act of inhibiting certain "natural needs" under certain conditions is essentially a definition of civilization. We don't need less moral instruction; we need more thoughtful moral instruction.

7. *Intentional annotation*—states and briefly explains the annotator's impression of the author's intention, plan, and purpose in writing the selection. This is a variation of the critical annotation.

   Example: Neill's agenda is to preach that children are by nature good and to use this to convince the reader that attempts to improve him or her with moral instruction actually will have the opposite effect.

8. *Motivation annotation*—speculation on the author's likely psychological motive(s) for having created or written the piece. This too is a form of critical annotation, with particular emphasis on introspective, projective, and empathetic thinking.

   Example: Neill seems to have been compelled to create a system of education compatible with his own background, interests, and needs. The value of his approach to American education should be judged against the limited number of people growing up with his privileged background (tony English private schools).

9. *Probe annotation*—identifies practical questions that merit further exploration before a reasoned judgment on the author's points can be reached. Emphasizes verification, consequences, and alternatives.

   Example: Has Neill's system of education been tested against more traditional approaches? What would be the full consequences to schools and students if such a system were adopted, especially in the United States, where this book has created such wide interest? Are there other ways to resolve the dilemma he poses?

   A more typical probe annotation would be the question "What more should we or could we know about the author that would further influence our ability to fairly appraise his or her work?" (This is the question that led to investigating Neill's background.)

10. *Constructive annotation*—offers an intentionally inventive view; may expand and/or suggest an alternative view or resolution.

   Example: Children need both structure and freedom. Replace moral instruction with ethical instruction in the schools. Ethnics flow from a profound understanding of natural human needs rather than from cultural mores and religious beliefs. Fundamental human needs also are more common across time and cultures and therefore are a more appropriate standard for public schooling in a pluralistic and democratic society.

Source: Excerpt from *Summerhill: A Radical Approach to Child Rearing* by A. S. Neill, 1960, New York: Hart.

REAP Teaching Paradigm

This section uses a summary annotation to demonstrate how to actually teach each annotation type. We selected this form because the act of summarizing conforms to the "translation" question in a hierarchy of questioning and thinking, a process that, as stated previously, offers the best way to bridge from literal to higher levels of thinking. Practitioners differ in their opinions regarding when and how to introduce the other annotation types (discussed shortly). The materials needed for REAP instruction are several short, interesting selections written at students' independent to instructional reading levels. The same selections can be used repeatedly in teaching the other annotation forms.

The steps in REAP are as follows:

1. *Recognizing and defining.* Students read a selection. The teacher provides them with a well-written summary annotation and asks them how the annotation parallels what they have read.
2. *Discriminating.* Students read a second selection. This time, the teacher gives them four annotations to consider. One example should be a good summary annotation and the others faulty in some way—too broad, too narrow, and/or tangential to the ideas presented in the selection. In class discussion, students choose the best annotation, logically defend their choice, and explain why the others are unsatisfactory.
3. *Modeling the process.* Students read a third selection. This time, the teacher actually demonstrates to students how to write the summary annotation. This step is most effective when the teacher "thinks aloud," writing and rewriting as necessary to compose a thorough, concise summary.
4. *Practicing.* Students read a fourth selection and individually try writing a summary annotation. A few individual productions are duplicated or put on the chalkboard and compared and evaluated by teacher and class.
5. *Sequencing.* Some students, despite extensive training, will not develop skill in writing quality summaries. Nevertheless, the teacher introduces the other annotations on a suitable schedule to expose these students to the full range of guidelines.
6. *Reinforcement.* The teacher has students exchange annotations and write annotations in response to one another's work. At this point, the teacher can present letters-to-the-editor from newspapers and magazines as examples of dialog centered on text and as models of effective writing from which students can learn incidentally each time they read a newspaper or magazine.

Beyond Summary

In a pilot for her dissertation study, Susan Strode reported the following:

> I tried several different ways of teaching annotations. . . . First, I tried teaching all 10 types of annotations and it just took too much time. Then, I tried teaching all 10 but in less time, and the students came out with only a vague understanding of all 10 types.
>
> Finally, I decided to teach only one type of annotation, but to teach it well. I decided to teach summary annotations because they are the most general and basic. Summary

annotations are like the trunk of a tree and other types branch out in different directions depending on what they ask the annotator to look for. It was my hope that when the students were given a firm understanding and some practice with summary annotations, the skill would easily transfer to other types of annotations. That is exactly what happened.

After teaching summary annotations, a hand-out with brief descriptions of 10 different types of annotations was passed out. The students were each assigned a different type of annotation and instructed to write that type of annotation about a one page article. The students constructed well-written annotations quickly and easily, with no questions and no explanations needed. The results were the same when two other instructors followed the same procedure with their students. When summary annotations are taught well, it does transfer and students are able to write other types of annotations.

Strode's belief is consistent with other researchers' opinions and findings. Bromley (1985), for example, recommends that teachers focus rather exclusively on précis writing (a slightly briefer form of summary) following reading. Her research also supports the transfer value of précis beyond writing to the improvment of vocabulary, comprehension, and study skills such as outlining. The rich tradition of summary writing in European schools further supports this approach.

Personally, however, we continue to support the value of introducing all the annotation variations at an early stage. We believe that even though few students will be able to produce quality critical annotations initially, those who can should receive the opportunity to do so. These "classic underachieving" students, whose ability to think critically and creatively tends to outrun their skill in precise and analytical tasks, have few occasions to shine in typical school curricula. Also, there is some research support for presenting the full range of annotations early. In a review of related research, Hillocks (1987) found that "inquiry"-based methods (which emphasize synthesis and evaluation of information) proved two-and-a-half times more effective in improving writing and thinking than did traditional summarizing and mechanics-based writing. A final reason for this preference relates to student motivation and the low tolerance of many students for rote practice activities. There is a world of difference between being asked to write cogent summaries and being asked to think insightfully and then write. Summarizing has the features of life and thought; reacting/thinking *is* life and thought.

In our experience, the easiest way to teach students to write critical annotations rather than mere summaries is to elicit quick oral reactions to a piece they have read and then work with the class to form these into clear critical annotative responses. Where students' responses differ, cooperative learning groups can be formed to produce annotations representing the various viewpoints.

Following silent reading of a selection on the exploits of Hernando de Soto, an eighth-grade teacher, rather than first seeking a summary of facts, asked the class, "What did you think of de Soto?" Reactions included "sick," "cruel," and "loser." When asked to explain why they felt this way, students recited a litany of facts and events that amounted to a summary. Then the teacher asked them to form their reactions and reasons into personal annotations on the selection. The following annotation is typical of the results:

> Hernando de Soto was a loser. After bringing gold back from Peru, the Spanish king encouraged him to go back to the new world by making him governor of Florida in 1539. He and 550 men looked for more gold. Even though some of them were priests, they mutilated and killed Indians in their search. After three years of this, de Soto died with nothing, and his men returned to Spain emptyhanded.

In this case, students' visceral responses seemed to help them distinguish de Soto from other explorers of his time and recall important information. In this way, the purpose of writing following reading was well served: Information was carefully processed, personalized, and stored for long-term recall. The concept of de Soto and the context of the times replaced a collection of random facts.

Another means of stimulating annotation writing is to refer students to an approximation in the form of letters-to-the-editor in newspapers and magazines. Notice how the following paraphrased letters to the editor can help one get a better grip on one's own and others' thoughts and feelings about the uprising in China in the spring of 1989:

> How tragic it is that to cope with change, China's leaders felt they had to kill their young.

> The people of China will triumph. Deng Xiaoping has forgotten his own history. It is impossible to repress an idea whose time has come!

> China had to crush the democratic resistance. The blood spilled in Tiananmen Square is a small price to pay to prevent a civil war that would consume thousands, if not millions.

Annotations, like letters-to-the-editor, offer a challenge to sift through larger bodies of information to understand and state a position, to refute a position, or to find and examine one's own position. To this extent, such critiques are more valuable than extensive notes, because they align more closely with the purpose of schooling: to teach students how to think for themselves rather than think what others think. As stated above, annotation writing parallels a series of life demands that most everyone faces nearly every day: the need to learn, assess, decide, state, justify, and act. To be taught to annotate is to be shown how to comment on one's journey and, therefore, how to live more purposefully.

With the addition of an annotation exchange feature, REAP can serve as a focal activity for a schoolwide reading program. This feature is discussed further in Chapter 11.

Whole Language Strategy 2: Opinion-Proof

The *Opinion-Proof* strategy requires students to engage in three important higher-order literacy skills:

- *Evaluative thinking*—forming an opinion
- *Verification*—supporting the opinion
- *Persuasive articulation*—writing about the opinion convincingly

Opinion-Proof has a fourth step that promotes cooperative learning, an often neglected dimension of critical analysis.

Santa et al. (1985) recommend using Opinion-Proof as a follow-up to the Free Response text marking system described in the previous chapter. However, it can be used after almost any guided silent reading activity.

Step 1: Provide students with an Opinion-Proof "guide" either written on the chalkboard or as a handout (see the example in step 2).

Step 2: Have students write an opinion and supporting evidence for it from the text.

Following is a guide for the short story "Old Horse," a popular selection about an elderly algebra teacher by Oliver Andresen:

Example   ◆◆◆

Opinion Statement	Evidence to Prove My Opinion
Old Horse was sensitive.	He was patient with Rabbit. He wanted Rabbit to belong. Old Horse forced Rabbit to dislike him. He put himself down for the sake of Rabbit.

Step 3: Students write a connected essay using their opinion and evidence as topic sentence and supporting details, respectively. If further structure is required, the teacher can use "framed paragraphs," a strategy developed by Alder (1974) and Fowler (1982), as illustrated below.

Example   ◆◆◆

Old horse was _____. One reason I feel this way is _____. In addition, _____. Finally, _____.

Here is one possible student response:

> Old Horse was a very sensitive teacher. One reason I feel this way was because of his ability to understand Rabbit. Rabbit was not liked by the other students in his class because he was a friend of Old Horse's. In addition, Old Horse understood Rabbit's need to become a part of a group of friends, and Old Horse knew that he was part of the problem. Finally, Old Horse forced Rabbit to dislike him so much that he could become accepted by the other students. Therefore, Old Horse was a very sensitive man. He even sacrificed himself for the sake of his student.

Step 4: The final step, also developed by Alder (1974), is peer editing. In this step, students (1) develop specific criteria for evaluating their writing (for the above selection, these would include the questions "Does my paragraph contain a main idea statement?" and "Do I have evidence to support my main idea?"); (2) divide up into pairs or small groups and read and react to one another's paragraphs; and (3) edit and/or revise their own paragraphs before submitting a final draft for teacher evaluation.

The Opinion-Proof process seems to provide an excellent sequence for organizing persuasive speeches, another important language art. It accomplishes this by having students state opinions and write out supporting and nonsupporting points. This "reflective turnabout," as Santa et al. refer to it, also makes Opinion-Proof a good framework for the next whole language strategy, Devil's Advocate.

Whole Language Strategy 3: Devil's Advocate

One simple and direct means of improving dialectical thinking is to get students into a discussion that invokes this type of reasoning. *Devil's Advocate* is a method developed by Roby (1983) for doing precisely this via an issues-based discussion. This approach has a rich heritage. It was used by Socrates and Plato and was a common convention at synods of the Roman Catholic Church.

One of three things may happen in a Devil's Advocate discussion: Positions may be strengthened, modified, or abandoned. In any case, students involved in such a discussion do a lot of "growing up." They learn about the enormous complexity of issues that initially appear clear-cut. They learn about the paradoxes involved in trying to solve a problem only to find that one's best solution can sometimes be more disruptive than the existing problem. Finally, they learn how to language an issue through not merely to *state* what they believe but to *discover* what they believe.

The Devil's Advocate strategy entails the following steps (Alvermann et al., 1987):

1. The teacher poses an issue to the class.
2. Students are paired but asked to individually prepare written arguments (using the text for essential information) for each major position on the issue (sometimes there are more than two positions).
3. Students are instructed to describe to their partners their best arguments for each position. They should discuss each argument to determine whether it contains faulty reasoning.
4. Still in pairs, students are asked to discuss with their partners whether the positions they originally supported have changed as a result of this activity and, if so, why and in what way. Then they revise their individual written statements accordingly.
5. A class discussion follows based on students' arguments for each side of the issue, any changes in attitude that occurred as a result of the activity, and sources of further information related to the issue.
6. Students are offered a final opportunity to revise and prepare a final form of their position statements.[1]

Figure 7.7 illustrates the Devil's Advocate strategy. Notice how this method enhances schema by placing heavier emphasis on critical examination of the issue, with the possibility of changing one's mind, than on winning a debate.

---

[1]Step 6 is our own addition. In the sample lesson in Figure 7.7, the teacher would next give students time to add revisions based on points raised in the large-group discussion.

Figure 7.7 Example of Devil's Advocate

Mr. Tennyson, a ninth grade social sciences teacher, used the Devil's Advocate strategy to structure a class discussion on the banning of nuclear testing. His students had read a section of their text that dealt with the horrors of nuclear warfare. As the discussion opens, Tennyson has just finished assigning the students to pairs.

"All right, now, you and your partner find a place where you can talk quietly. Each of you should jot down why you believe the United States should stop testing nuclear weapons. Be sure to support your beliefs with evidence from the text. Then take the opposite stance (why the United States should not stop testing nuclear weapons) and again support your beliefs with evidence from the text."

(The students, working individually in pairs, take about ten minutes to complete this task.)

"Okay, now we're ready for the next step. Choose your best arguments and present them to your partner. Be certain that you discuss your beliefs with your partner; for example, seek your partner's ideas and evaluations of the pros and cons that you took on the issue. Is there evidence of any faulty reasoning on either one's part?"

(After approximately fifteen minutes, the noise level in the room drops, an indication that students have finished presenting the arguments they had with themselves.)

"May I have your attention. . . . There are two more things I would like you to do: (1) Think about how your ideas have changed on banning nuclear testing. For example, has your position shifted from your original one? If so, why? (2) Decide whether you have strengthened your original position, abandoned it completely, or only modified it. Then tell your partner your decision and see if he or she agrees."

After approximately ten minutes, Tennyson drew the students into a whole class discussion by asking them to share some of their ideas on both sides of the issue.

Source: From *Using Discussion to Promote Reading Comprehension* (p. 38) by D. E. Alvermann, D. R. Dillon, and D. G. O'Brien, 1987, Newark, DE: International Reading Association. Copyright 1987 by the International Reading Association. Reprinted with permission of Donna E. Alvermann and the International Reading Association.

The next discussion-based writing strategy furthers many of the same schema-enhancing goals that Devil's Advocate does. It is less structured and, in some ways, more suitable to use with typical content area textual material.

Whole Language Strategy 4: Developmental Discussion

The *Developmental Discussion* strategy encourages further analytical reading, writing, listening, and speaking by providing a focused experience in group problem solving. Attributed to Maier (1963), Developmental Discussion is intended to teach students about the full process of problem solving by involving them in all of its parts: identification and partitioning of the problem, collection of relevant data or information, generation of solutions, and appraisal of solutions. Most important, *it places heavy emphasis on going beyond existing knowledge.*

The steps in Developmental Discussion are as follows:[2]

1. Students are instructed to try to identify certain "conflicting points" or problems inherent in material presented in text and lecture.
2. The teacher initially provides examples that can serve as models of problem identification (this usually requires comparing textual information to prior knowledge and experiences).
3. The teacher assists students in narrowing and partitioning the problem into manageable segments.
4. Students are divided into cooperative learning groups to solve the smaller parts of the problem, using the following questions to guide their analysis:
   a. What do we know about this problem part?
   b. Which parts of the information we have are relevant to the problem?
   c. What more do we need to know to construct a possible solution?
   d. What are some possible solutions given what we now know?
   e. What additional information can we collect—and how—to formulate better solutions? (Each group is asked to jot down notes on individual and group members' answers to these questions.)
5. A large-group discussion is held to illustrate the different ways the problem can be viewed and solutions sought. (Students are reminded to add to their notes during large-group discussion.)
6. The class decides on a solution (usually a synthesis) or—in a significant departure from conventional school practices—may choose to "table" the matter until they can collect additional information (see Figure 7.8 for an anecdotal account).
7. Each student writes out the solution as he or she sees it and in the most convincing way possible. Then students exchange papers and give one another feedback on their essays. The teacher invites students and reviewers to read aloud phrases or sections that they feel were particularly well stated.

Whole Language Strategy 5: Extension of the Guided Reading Procedure

Many reading lessons can fulfill the first step in the Writing Process ("getting it out"), setting the stage for the next step ("getting it down") to follow naturally. Vacca and Vacca (1986) suggest, for example, that writing can be an effective extension of a Guided Reading Procedure lesson:

---

[2]We added step 7 and the parenthetical notes to strengthen writing skills.

Figure 7.8   Anecdotal Account of Developmental Discussion

Mr. Freeble, a high school civics teacher, works with a group of average ability students for fifty minutes each morning. In a previous class session the students had read a five page textbook assignment and had completed the accompanying study guide. The assignment covered information about the Supreme Court—what it is, its purpose and charges, and its relationship to the entire governmental system.

Freeble began the developmental discussion by reviewing the previous textbook assignment for five minutes. From the review, students were reminded of the following key concepts: the Supreme Court is the highest court in the land, the individuals sitting on the Supreme Court are charged with interpreting the Constitution, and members of the Supreme Court may change a previous ruling by another branch of the government.

Next, Freeble asked the students to supply current information about events in the news concerning recent Supreme Court rulings. Elicited were facts about prayer in school and nativity scenes set up on public property. Freeble noted that the seasonal influence (it was close to Christmas) played a large role in students' interest in a local newspaper story about a controversial nativity scene. After ten minutes of discussing that story and its implications for local residents, the class decided on a problem that was text based but of immediate interest to them—should religious groups be allowed to erect nativity scenes on public property?

The teacher guided the students in breaking the larger problem (separation of church and state) into three smaller problems: (1) Does setting up a nativity scene on public property violate the rights of individuals who do not have the same religious beliefs?; (2) What information could the class add that would help solve the problem?; (3) What would be a reasonable way to share what was learned with the people involved in the controversy?

The students broke into smaller groups and began to work on the first part of the problem. Freeble supplied each group with a one page summary of the Pawtucket case involving a Supreme Court ruling on the display of nativity scenes on public property. Freeble circulated among the groups, observing and offering assistance when requested.

During the last fifteen minutes of the period, students participated in a large group discussion in which they reported on their reactions to the Pawtucket case and whether they believed the case had any implications for the local controversy.

Over the next two days, the students worked in small groups to tackle the remaining problem parts. Solutions to the overall problem included working with community leaders to foster improved communication among the dissident groups and writing letters to the editor of the local newspaper on the topic of how the Pawtucket case compared to the local one.

Source: From *Using Discussion to Promote Reading Comprehension* (pp. 40–41) by D. E. Alvermann, D. R. Dillon, and D. G. O'Brien, 1987, Newark, DE: International Reading Association. Copyright 1987 by the International Reading Association. Reprinted with permission of Donna E. Alvermann and the International Reading Association.

As you may recall, after students have read a text passage, they turn their books face down and try to remember everything that was important in the passage. Their recalls are recorded by the teacher on the chalkboard. Seize this opportune moment to show students how to delete trivial and repetitious information from the list of ideas on the board. As part of the procedure, the students are given a "second chance" to return to the passage, review it, and make sure that the list contains all of the information germane to the text.

When this step is completed, the teacher then guides the students to organize the information in outline form. Here is where students can be shown how to collapse individual pieces of information from a list into conceptual categories. These categories can be the bases for identifying or creating topic sentences. The students can then integrate the main points into a summary (Vacca & Vacca, 1986, p. 213).

Another variation on this method, blended from De Composition (Eanet, 1978) and GRASP (Hayes, 1988), is described in Chapter 12.

Whole Language Strategy 6: Semantic Map Retranslation

Following construction and use of a semantic map (or any other type of graphic organizer), an excellent opportunity to enhance whole language development and content mastery arises. *Semantic Map Retranslation* entails converting the map, or portions of it, back into oral and abbreviated written forms. The steps in Semantic Map Retranslation, as we have labeled it, are as follows:

1. The teacher assists students in orally restating some portion of what has been coded into the semantic map by recording the retranslation on the chalkboard, where it can be edited and revised for wording, continuity, and punctuation.
2. Students are directed to individually retranslate another portion of the map in similar written form.
3. Students work in pairs to read and give feedback to one another on the correctness and clarity of their summaries.
4. (Optional) Students are encouraged to add a statement or two of personal reaction.
5. (Optional) The teacher moves about the room looking for examples of good writing that can be shared with the class.

In Semantic Map Retranslation (including steps 4 and 5), students' own summaries and evaluations are used to teach students how to think evaluatively about content material. It emphasizes extending and connecting content-based ideas to information, thoughts, and experiences from students' daily lives. This tends to breathe life and interest into information that otherwise might appear flat and dry.

Figure 7.9 presents a sample Semantic Map Retranslation. Try this strategy yourself using the graphic organizer at the end of the chapter to review and summarize what you have learned.

Figure 7.9   Semantic Map and Sample Retranslation

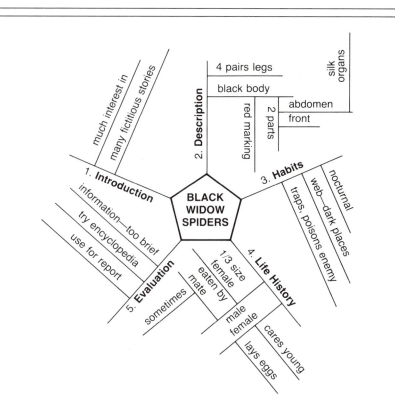

Sample Retranslation
Point 4 tells about the life history of Black Widows, with an emphasis on the differences between males and females. Males are much smaller than females. The female, therefore, can and sometimes does kill and eat the male after being fertilized. The female probably does this because she will need extra nourishment for the eggs she will lay and for caring for the young once the eggs are hatched. This reminds me of how they say pregnant women sometimes go on eating binges and crave unusual foods. I guess the male Black Widow spider who got eaten would have been glad to have brought his mate some pickles and ice cream.

Source: Illustration from "Mapping: A Technique for Translating Reading Into Thinking" by M. Buckley Hanf, January 1971, *Journal of Reading*, p. 228. Reprinted with permission of M. Buckley Hanf and the International Reading Association.

CONCEPT AND VOCABULARY ENRICHMENT

Once comprehension is locked up tight, there are two other aspects of postreading that can be, but seldom are, pursued: concept and vocabulary development. This section presents three word-based activities for enhancing schema along these lines. The first one, Semantic Feature Analysis, provides a paradigm for clarifying and reinforcing concepts. The next two, Vocabulary Self-Collection and Cultural-Academic Trivia, focus on developing cultural literacy and concept bases for subsequent reading.

Concept/Vocabulary Strategy 1: Semantic Feature Analysis

Learning is a process of placing new information into existing schematic categories until a special feature that does not fit is encountered; then a new category must be created to expand schema. *Semantic Feature Analysis* (Johnson & Pearson, 1984) is a method designed to permit students to engage in this process in a conscious and focused way. Semantic Feature Analysis has been found to be significantly more effective than traditional Semantic Mapping for this purpose (Johnson, Toms-Bronowski, & Pittelman, 1984). It also has been shown to effectively improve content area reading vocabulary and comprehension in learning-disabled adolescents (Anders, Bos, & Filip, 1984).

Stieglitz and Stieglitz (1981) describe a version of Semantic Feature Analysis designed specifically for content area use. This variation, called *SAVOR,* or *Subject Area Vocabulary Reinforcement,* proceeds as follows:

1. For demonstration purposes, the teacher first identifies a category of words highly familiar to students; for example, a category of "monsters" would be well within many students' experience (see Figure 7.10). The teacher then elicits words from the pupils that fit in this category (*King Kong, Hulk, Dracula, Cookie Monster, Godzilla*) and has the students list these examples in a column on their own paper.

Figure 7.10   Sample SAVOR Worksheet

	Hairy	Huge	Strong	Mean	Transformation
			"Monsters"		
King Kong	+	+	+	+	−
Hulk	−	+	+	−	+
Dracula	−	−	−	+	+
Cookie Monster	+	−	−	−	−
Godzilla	−	+	+	+	−

2. The students list some features of these monsters (*hairy, huge, strong, mean, transformation*) across the top of the page. Following this, they fill in the matrix by using plus (+) or minus (−) signs to indicate whether a monster has a particular feature.
3. After the matrix is filled in, the teacher leads students to study the different patterns of pluses and minuses and to discover the uniqueness of each word (or, in this case, creature).

Johnson and Pearson (1984), the originators of this activity, state that as pupils gain more experience with Semantic Feature Analysis, the teacher may wish to switch from a plus/minus system to a numerical system (0 = none, 1 = some, 2 = much, 3 = all). Stieglitz and Stieglitz see the method as a culminating activity for reinforcing and expanding concepts introduced in the conventional content area lesson or following reading. The method is particularly suitable for clarifying frequently confused terms (see the example of its use in the science section in Chapter 13).

Concept/Vocabulary Strategy 2: Vocabulary Self-Collection

The *Vocabulary Self-Collection* strategy (Haggard, 1982) requires that each student and the teacher search their television viewing, reading, and home environments weekly and bring to class two content-related words for the entire class to learn. Students are told to write their words on the chalkboard when they enter the classroom. The list is narrowed by eliminating duplications and words that most students know. The student who submitted each remaining word defines that word, and discussion ensues to clarify and extend meaning(s). During this process, students record words in a vocabulary journal along with definitions. Ideally, word manipulation exercises for embedding meanings are employed at this point. Students can develop these exercises for one another, using examples found in conventional vocabulary workbooks.

Concept/Vocabulary Strategy 3: Cultural-Academic Trivia

The *Cultural-Academic Trivia*, or *CAT*, game (Manzo, 1970b, 1985) initially was developed to build the cultural and background knowledge bases of disadvantaged adults entering college. The term *Cultural-Academic Trivia* refers to those lately popularized ''common cultural learnings'' that are stored in our language and are frequently used as metaphors or allusions to explain more difficult facts and concepts. In initial field tests of the strategy, students felt it was quite appropriate that the word *trivia* appeared in the title. In time, however, as their fund of academic information, vocabulary, and allusions expanded, they concluded that it is *minds* that can be trivial, not information. This prompted the idea that the game should be called ''Cultural-Academic Treasures.'' By any name, however, the benefits are the same.

The steps in Cultural-Academic Trivia are as follows:

1. The class is divided into two groups. A chairperson is assigned to each group and given a set of index cards initially prepared by the teacher. On the front of each card is a word or phrase with a number from 1 to 3 designating its relative difficulty. On the reverse side is an explanation or definition of the word or phrase.
2. The chairperson of one group chooses and writes a word or phrase on the chalkboard and then asks students in the other group if they know that word or phrase. (Depending on the age and grade level, points can be given for correct pronunciation.) All the information gained from the members of a group constitutes that group's total response. If that information amounts to merely an identification or recognition of the word or phrase, only the number describing the level of difficulty (from 1 to 3) is awarded to the group. If any worthwhile elaboration (as determined by the teacher) also is contributed, the score is doubled. Conversely, if the students on one team cannot respond successfully, the opposing team is given the opportunity to win points.

◆ ◆ ◆   *Example*

In a high school class, the word *utopia* might be assigned a difficulty level of 2. If one team volunteers that the word means "a perfect political and social system," they gain the two basic points. If team members add that *utopia* is also the title of a book by Sir Thomas More, or that it came from Greek, they receive two additional points.

3. After the first round of the game, students are asked to submit terms they have selected.

Students' contributions are essential if students are to be resensitized to the language they encounter all around them but tend to block out because it is unfamiliar. In the particular setting in which this game was first played, the first author treated the cards as "admission tickets" to class. Students who arrived without one were sent scurrying to the library to find an appropriate term.

Of course, not all words are created equal. The success of this game hinges on the terms used. Well-selected words or phrases should key students to pivotal, or schema-enhancing, academic ideas and allusions (e.g., *hieroglyphics, Communist Manifesto, citizen's arrest, Chaucer*). Such terms can be academically bountiful and should be developed fully. When this game was played by disadvantaged adults preparing for college study, the word *syllogism* was suggested. Recognizing the significance of that term, the first author volunteered a brief discussion of it, thereby giving students a head start on a key concept in a required sophomore course in philosophy. This, of course, is the other important reason to use the CAT game: It helps convert vague terms into working concepts.

If the teacher intends to develop students' sophistication in just one area, the name of the game can be altered accordingly, for example, BAT (Biological-Academic Trivia) or HAT (Historical-Academic Trivia).

"Preppie" Terms

CAT can be used toward some very specialized objectives. We have used it, for example, with inner-city youngsters to teach them some of the shibboleths—identity words and expressions—of the core culture, including such terms as *doffing, frittered, gaffe, scruffy, woozy,* and *guffaw.* Even the best-educated black and white ethnic Americans tend to be uncomfortable using these tony terms. This is because these terms are part of the core culture's social and oral language tradition. Many teachers are from ethnic backgrounds and are among the first members of their families to go on to postsecondary education and therefore could use some shoring up on these terms themselves. Two sources for such terms are television personalities, such as David Letterman, Johnny Carson, and Jane Pauley, and crossword puzzles. A disproportionate number of these terms have a way of appearing on standardized entrance examinations for college and graduate school.

Metaphorical Thinking and Writing

In a recent update article on CAT, the first author (Manzo, 1985) further stressed this strategy's potential for teaching students how to create their own metaphors and allusions to enhance their thinking and writing. This is done by showing students how a fact or event can take on increased significance by the context in which it appears and the meaning we can attach to it. The process of stepping up common facts to metaphorical and allusionary levels can contribute to abstract thinking as well as to vocabulary enhancement and creative writing. The need to do this occurred to me while teaching an 11th-grade American history class. I told the class, anticipating that they would receive the information enthusiastically, that Andrew Jackson carried a hickory stick (actually it was cherry wood) with him everywhere he went, even while he was president. "Yeah, so what?" they responded, at least with their stares. Because they had no schema for this fact, it appeared trivial. It did not occur to me at the time, but I should have drawn upon my background and interest in psychology to suggest other possibilities. This could have had the effect of enhancing the students' schema and showing them how to draw on their own special knowledge and instincts. I might have told them, for example, that the "hickory stick" could have been a sadomasochistic symbol (Jackson once led a brutal raid that wiped out most of the Creek Indian nation), or a phallic symbol (Jackson had fought a dual with another man in a squabble over a woman and killed him), or a power symbol (e.g., as a king's scepter).

Figure 7.11 illustrates how the CAT game can be played to build vocabulary knowledge and allusions. The topic of metaphors, similes, and allusions and their value to comprehension and whole language development is taken up again in the social studies section in Chapter 13.

PUTTING IT ALL TOGETHER

Box 7.2 presents a summarizing activity on prereading, guided silent reading, and postreading instruction.

Figure 7.11   CAT: From Trivia to Metaphor

Item: Geraldine Ferraro

Factual response: A congresswoman from New York; an Italian-American; a vice presidential candidate of the Democratic Party in 1984

Metaphorical response: A person who changed role expectations in an extraordinary way; no little boy will ever see his sister across the sandbox in quite the same way he did before; the American mainstream has again shown its capacity to absorb and be changed by its diverse ethnic and cultural composition.

BOX 7.2

CONCEPT CLARIFICATION
Prereading, Guided Silent Reading, and/or Postreading Assistance

Read the following excerpt from an article in *American Anthropologist.* Answer the questions at the end, and then develop an instructional plan that you feel will be of greatest benefit in helping a class to read and comprehend this material.

(From "'The Body Rituals of the Nacirema' by Horace Miner, 1956, *American Anthropologist, 56,* pp. 503–506.")

The Body Rituals of the Nacirema

The anthropologist has become so familiar with the diversity of ways in which different peoples behave in similar situations that he is apt to be surprised by even the most exotic customs. This point has been expressed with respect to clan organization by Murdock. In this light, the magical beliefs and practices of the Nacirema present such unusual aspects that it seems desirable to describe them as an example of the extremes to which human behavior can go.

Professor Linton first brought the rituals of the Nacirema to the attention of anthropologists twenty years ago, but the culture of this people is still very poorly understood. Little is known of their origin, although tradition states that they came from the east. According to Nacirema mythology, their nation was originated by a culture hero, Notgnihsaw. While much of the people's time is devoted to economic pursuits, a large part of the fruits of these labors and a considerable portion of the day are spent in ritual activity. The focus of this activity is the human body, the appearance and health of which loom as a dominant concern in the ethos of the people. While such a concern is certainly not unusual, its ceremonial aspects and associated philosophy are unique.

The fundamental belief underlying the whole system appears to be that the human body is ugly and that its natural tendency is to debility and disease. Incarcerated in such a body, man's only hope is to avert these characteristics through the use of the powerful influences of ritual and ceremony. Every household has one or more shrines devoted to this purpose. The more powerful individuals in the society have several shrines in their houses and, in fact, the opulence of a house is often referred to in terms of the number of such ritual centers it possesses.

While each family has at least one such shrine, the rituals associated with it are not family ceremonies but are private and secret. The rites are normally only discussed with children, and then only during the period when they are being initiated into these mysteries. The focal point of the shrine is a box or chest which is built into the wall. In this chest are kept the many charms and magical potions without which no native believes he could live. These preparations are secured from a variety of specialized practitioners. The most powerful of these are the medicine men, whose assistance must be rewarded with substantial gifts. However, the medicine men do not provide the curative potions for their clients, but decide what the ingredients should be and then write them down in an ancient and secret language. This writing is understood only by the medicine men and by the herbalists who, for another gift, provide the required charm.

Beneath the charm-box is a small font. Each day every member of the family, in succession, enters the shrine room, bows his head before the charm-box, mingles different sorts of holy water in the font, and proceeds with a brief rite of abulation. The holy waters are secured from the Water Temple of the community, where the priests conduct elaborate ceremonies to make the liquid ritually pure.

In the hierarchy of magical practitioners, and below the medical men in prestige, are specialists whose designation is best translated "holy-mouth-men." The Nacirema have an almost pathological horror of and fascination with the mouth, the condition of which is believed to have a supernatural influence on all social relationships. They also believe that a strong relationship exists between oral and moral characteristics. For example, there is a ritual ablution of the mouth for children which is supposed to improve their moral fiber.

There remains one other kind of practitioner, known as the "listener." This witch-doctor has the power to exorcise the devils that lodge in the heads of people who have been bewitched. The Nacirema believe that parents bewitch their own children. Mothers are particularly suspected of putting a curse on children while teaching them the secret body rituals. The counter-magic of the witch-doctor is unusual in its lack of ritual. The patient simply tells the "listener" all his troubles and fears, beginning with the earliest difficulties he can remember.

In conclusion, mention must be made of certain practices which have their base in native esthetics but which depend upon the pervasive aversion to the natural body and its functions. There are ritual fasts to make fat people thin and ceremonial feasts to make thin people fat. Still other rites are used to make women's breasts larger if they are small, and smaller, if they are large.

◆ ◆ ◆

QUESTIONS
1. What is the focus of the Nacirema ritual? Do you approve?
2. What is the fundamental belief of the Nacirema system?
3. In what ways is the Nacirema culture like or different from your own?
4. In your own words, briefly describe the shrine of the Nacirema.
5. What is the purpose of the font?
6. What group is identified as the second in prestige among magic practitioners?
7. What is the point of the article?

FOR DISCUSSION

What plan of instruction would you use to teach this article? Did you notice that comprehension of the article would be considerably improved simply by the prior knowledge that *Nacirema* is *American* spelled backwards? What further understandings or insights would you wish your students to glean from the passage? Consider the following questions as you determine how you would teach the article:

♦ Which is most important in planning instruction for this material—prereading, guided silent reading, postreading instruction, or some combination of these?
♦ Are there key vocabulary terms that should be introduced?
♦ Is there background information students are likely to have that would aid their comprehension of the passage?
♦ What type of guidance during reading might help students construct meaning from the text as they read?
♦ What postreading assistance might students need to fully comprehend the passage and to provide an intelligent answer to question 7?

CHAPTER TIE-UPS

♦♦♦   *Graphic Organizer*

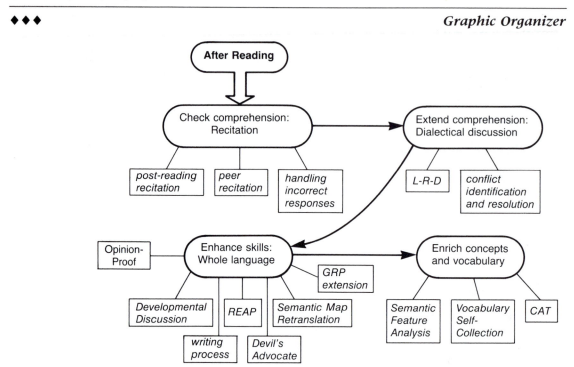

Critique and Anticipation   ◆ ◆ ◆

This chapter focused on the development of precepts and practices that enhance "fruit bearing" and schema—the knowledge structures that permit us to understand and grow from what we read, hear, and experience. It developed four overlapping precepts of schema enhancement: reinforcement of knowledge acquisition through classroom recitation; identification and resolution of conflicting beliefs and information through dialectical discussion; encoding, or restating and mentally manipulating and relating, information through whole language strategies; and enrichment of vocabulary through techniques designed to clarify concepts and/or encourage awareness of words and related facts and associations.

The next chapter is a logical continuation of these concepts. It extends in the direction of critical analysis and creative production—the power to "cull and hybridize" the fruits of earlier learnings.

TRADE SECRET

Favoring One Side of the Class

The brain is very efficient: It forms patterns and habits easily. One such habit of mind is to favor the side of the class that conforms to your handedness. If you're right-handed, you will look at, speak to, and ask more questions of those to your right than you will those to your left. Here are two simple ways to overcome this unrecognized bias:

1. Where desks can be turned easily, make it a point to position yourself at a different side of the classroom periodically, especially when leading recitations and discussions.
2. Write students' names on a set of index cards, shuffle these occasionally, and call on the students whose names come to the top.

Students' hemispheric dominance patterns sometimes are revealed by where they seat themselves. Those who sit to your left as you face the class are likely to be right-brain-dominant. Those to your left are probably left-brain-dominant. Those in the center typically will not have a strong preference. The value of permitting students to sit on the side they prefer is as yet unresolved.

PART THREE

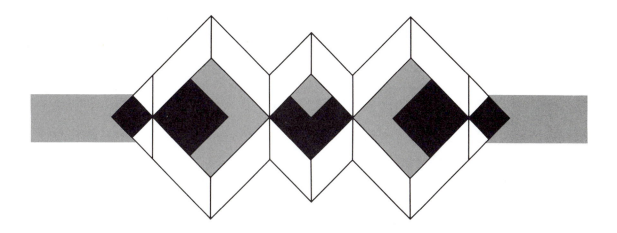

Analytical and
Study Reading

Critical and Creative
Reading and Thinking

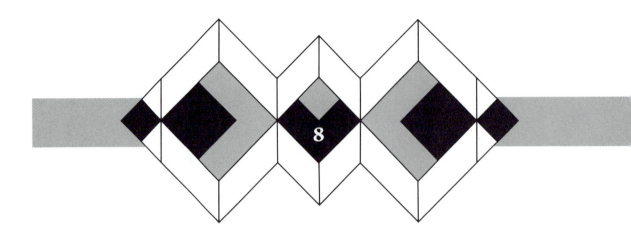

Preface, Traditional Approaches,
and Emerging Options

I am bound by my own definition of criticism: an unbiased endeavor to learn and propagate the best that is known and thought in the world.

— Matthew Arnold

FOCUS

The ultimate purpose of reading is to enhance schema. Reading is an act of culling and synthesizing written ideas and insights into hybrid ones to meet new challenges. There are social disincentives to these acts of critical and creative responding. Fortunately, however, most of these impediments can be overcome quite easily when understood and addressed strategically.

OUTLINE

No sooner does society recognize a need than that need is passed along to our schools to interpret and implement. Society's most recent "discovery" is that the racer's edge in world trade goes to the nation that is the most literate and hard working. Thus, students must be (once again) inculcated with a strong sense of the work ethic, along with an increased capacity to learn, to adapt, and even to create new information, jobs, and industries. One way this need is manifesting itself in the schools is through a renewed interest in teaching critical and creative thinking.

Predictably, this hot "new" thinking movement has generated its share of quick-fix treatments and caustic reactions. Venezuela, for example, has hired Edward DeBono, a self-styled specialist in the art of "lateral" (creative and critical) thinking, to implement his program in all of its schools. California has instituted a graduation requirement in critical thinking on its 19-campus state university system (Paul, 1984). At the same time, educational traditionalists such as Mortimer Adler are trying to explain "why 'critical thinking' programs as such won't work" (Adler, 1987)!

This chapter sets out some of the rudiments of understanding and teaching both critical and creative reading and thinking. As suggested in the opening quote by Matthew Arnold, we have endeavored "to learn and propagate" the best of what we now know about these topics. This includes newer trends such as that reflected in an editorial in the *English Journal*: "The definition of critical thinking should include 'critical viewing': to encourage you and your students to apply your capacity for criticism beyond the conventional study of language and literature to the visual arts, electronic media, and everyday life" (1986, p. 21).

PREFACE TO CRITICAL READING

Definition of Critical Reading

Critical reading is the use of critical thinking in the act of reading (Ennis, 1962). Critical reading and thinking closely parallel the current view of reading as an "interactive" process (Rumelhart, 1984). The reader uses prior knowledge to construct and extend knowledge as well as merely absorb it (Ericson et al., 1987). Such thinking may take place prior to, during, and/or after reading. Critical reading tends, however, to be most easily taught in discussion and writing formats following careful silent reading. Considerable mental training is necessary to think critically during reading, because critical reading involves a certain degree of digression from the "message" into a more reflective mode. Mature readers have developed the ability to return from such digressions with a guiding hypothesis, or sense of "anticipation," of the author's purpose and direction. Immature or unskilled readers and thinkers often return to the printed page with even greater misapprehensions that tend to further distort their understanding of the author's basic message. Although not commonly recognized, there are also readers who follow the author's message so slavishly that they achieve seemingly high levels of accuracy in comprehension by avoiding all digressions. They too are immature readers, for they tend to avoid constructive reading between the lines and almost never read beyond the lines. These are the individuals Chase (1961) had in mind when he coined the term "higher illiterates."

Critical reading has been defined as a "three-factor" ability:

1. An attitudinal factor of effective questioning and suspending judgment
2. A functional factor of logical inquiry and problem solving
3. A judgmental factor based on some set of norms growing out of consensus (Russell, 1961)

The most unfortunate—and misleading—aspect of critical reading and thinking probably is the word *critical* itself. Critical reading and thinking should be considered not a negative process but a constructive one in the sense that it is "inventive." The purpose of criticism is not merely to find flaws but to build toward greater depth and wisdom and insight. Finding flaws in logic or argument is only incidental to this definition of "criticism," while constructive thinking is essential to it.

Another powerful element of higher-order literacy is the concept of metacognition discussed in previous chapters. When students can be taught to be introspective in the sense of contemplating their own thinking and learning, they can be more easily taught how to become effective strategic readers—readers who select the most appropriate reading and study strategy for the task at hand. No doubt this involves being somewhat ingenious with oneself: splitting oneself between pupil and teacher and doer and observer and balancing emotion with discipline.

Impediments to Critical-Creative Thinking

It is no secret that our schools do a relatively weak job of teaching critical reading and metacognitive thinking; but then, while society may give lip service to these skills, it does not welcome them either. There are several reasons for this, and they are difficult to overcome because they are rooted in the way we think, how we feel, what we believe, and the way we conduct commerce. National interest in this problem was confirmed by a recent announcement by the Education Commission of the States of a large "Higher Literacies" project to look into state policies that either "constrain or promote" schools' efforts to teach "writing, problem-solving, critical thinking, argument, analysis, synthesis, interpretation and evaluation" (Tchudi, 1988). We developed a list of likely impediments to these efforts in advance of the commission's report. As an exercise in analytical reasoning, see how many of these you can think of before considering the following list:

1. Textbooks tend to be inane and therefore fail to evoke critical thought.
2. The printed word generates a "halo" effect: Because it is in print, it is true and therefore not worth questioning.
3. Many school administrators and teachers are afraid to broach controversial subjects with students.
4. There is a general emphasis on conformity in almost all aspects of life.

5. Personal emotions and prejudices often tend to disrupt clear thinking.
6. Critical reading-thinking skills are not routinely assessed.
7. There is a lack of models (persons and programs) that epitomize or focus on constructive and critical thinking.
8. Curriculum requirements generally do not include addressing or teaching specific critical reading-thinking skills.
9. There is a pervasive fear among students and teachers that criticism of *anything*, including introspective self-appraisals, ultimately unleashes criticism of *everything*, including schools, teachers, and society.
10. It is a paradoxical fact that classroom questioning is used on the one hand to stimulate curiosity, reinforce knowledge, and ignite discussion and on the other to scold, embarrass, and test.
11. Great ideas often are conceived and forged in passion, and we haven't yet quite figured out how to endure passion in our schools.

A story related by test developer Stanley Porteus (1931) serves as a poignant reminder of how deep and pervasive is our fear of critical thinking and problem solving. When Porteus was working on a test format that used mazes to measure basic IQ, he traveled to Australia to administer the test to aboriginal bushmen. On approaching the leader, Porteus was told that to work with the tribe he had to become an honorary tribe member. Porteus was flattered, and he submitted to a long and complex initiation ritual. When he subsequently began to administer the maze test, the aborigines patiently explained that a problem such as this must be solved by joint council action, not by individuals, and, more important, as an honorary tribe member Porteus was now obliged to help them solve problems rather than identify new ones.[1]

Several of the methodologies and programming ideas discussed in this chapter can reduce some of our inhibitions to critical thinking and problem solving. Before considering these, however, you may wish to know a bit more about students as critical readers.

Stages in Critical Reading-Thinking

Experimental measures of some of the factors involved in "critical comprehending," developed by the authors, (Casale, 1982; Manzo & Casale, 1979, 1983), have helped produce a clearer picture of reader stages, or profiles, such as those found in a typical classroom (see Figure 8.1). Current data based on use of the ALARM battery suggest that about 40% of the school-age population have reached category A, mature comprehenders; that is, these students have achieved compatible growth in comprehension and critical thinking. Categories B (remedial readers), C (higher illiterates), and D (classic underachievers) each constitute between 15% and 25% of a typical school population. These contemporary data are much more optimistic than those yielded by Gray and Rogers in 1956. Those authors claimed that they

---

[1]Thanks to our colleague Henry Berger for suggesting this anecdote.

Figure 8.1   Four Profiles of Critical Reading-Thinking

Type A: Mature Comprehenders—students with solid reading comprehension and a commensurate ability to think critically. These comprehenders could be called "mature comprehenders" for their age and grade levels. They possess high abstract thinking skills and tend to be emotionally well adjusted.

Type B: Remedial Readers—students with weak comprehension and critical thinking skills. These remedial-level readers tend to have lower levels of abstract thinking and show signs of emotional instability, mostly in the form of apathy and emotional dependency (the "I don't know" syndrome).

Type C: Higher Illiterates (Overachievers)—students with high comprehension and weak or intermittently good to poor critical thinking skills. This group seems to personify Chase's term *higher illiterate*. Ironically, these students have fair to good levels of abstract thinking, though average to poor levels of emotional stability, characterized mostly by a desire to be dominant while remaining aloof.

Type D: Classic Underachievers—students with weak comprehension and generally high levels of critical thinking. This group also has fair to good levels of abstract thinking and average to poor levels of emotional stability. They too are immature and tend to epitomize the term *underachiever*.

Source: From "Small Group Approach to the Further Validation and Refinement of a Battery for Assessing 'Progress toward Reading Maturity'" by U. P. Casale, 1982, *Dissertation Abstracts International, 43*, p. 770A.

virtually could not find a single "mature" reader. Current studies, however, have tended to focus on measuring stages of progress toward reading maturity in school-age subjects, while the Gray and Rogers study centered around finding fully mature adult readers in the working world. It seems that it will always be difficult to find a fully mature reader, because reading maturity is a developmental goal that one continually pursues but may never fully achieve. In all likelihood, many more individuals are approximating reading maturity today than ever before due to the increased number of people with a postsecondary education. Additional schooling alone does not ensure intellectual growth, but when combined with simple content area studies it is probably the best single predictor of reading and thinking power. After all, this is the means by which students initially gain "prior knowledge," which enables them to think critically, interactively, and therefore constructively. In other words, content mastery is a legitimate and even necessary contributor to, as well as product of, effective reading and thinking.

Before we examine specific methods designed to improve various aspects of critical reading-thinking, let us consider some of the general ingredients that research and experience have suggested are of value.

General Ingredients of the Prescription

A focused program to promote critical comprehension should contain at least these elements:

1. Training in the ability to answer questions that, as Raphael (1984) describes them, are
   a. Text explicit—"right there on the page"
   b. Text implicit—one must "think and search" the page
   c. Script implicit—derived from thinking on one's own
2. Training in effective thinking while reading, that is, in the ability to digress from the printed page, reflect, regulate emotive responses, and return to silent reading with little disruption in getting the author's message straight
3. Training in thinking and applying knowledge well beyond the immediate context of reading, that is, in developing the entire "structure of intellect" through mastery of a multitude of specific skills (e.g., critical-evaluative thinking, dialectical thinking, metaphoric thinking, divergent thinking, problem solving, and other forms that researchers are just now learning how to delineate and name)
4. Training in social comprehension, or understanding of the rudimentary principles underlying law, ethics, and social structures
5. Training in how to engage in and benefit from critical review
6. Training in acquiring a rich fund of word knowledge, particularly of those words and ideas that serve as common allusions, or metaphors, in written and spoken exposition
7. Training in effective inquiry techniques, both analytical and investigative

A more traditional view of "critical reading" skills would include the following objectives:

1. Investigating sources: searching for, evaluating, and collating viewpoints from several sources
2. Recognizing the author's purpose: identifying the author's bias, accuracy, competence, and viewpoint as well as his or her apparent and hidden purposes in presenting this viewpoint (as exemplified by the "motivation" annotation discussed in the previous chapter)
3. Distinguishing opinion and fact: recognizing omissions, distortion, overgeneralizations, unverified statements, and faulty conclusions drawn from inadequate or misinterpreted facts
4. Making inferences: developing the ability to draw one's own inferences from the material, to recognize the author's inferences, and to discern the inferences implied by the author's choice of words, tone, or mood
5. Forming judgments: judging the author and his or her purpose, beliefs and standards, and presentation; drawing conclusions from the facts, from the inferences, and from the reader's judgments; learning to withhold judgments when emotions or vested interests are involved or information is insufficient
6. Detecting propaganda devices: identifying attempts to influence the reader by appeals to emotions, sheer repetition, distortions or omissions, and faulty logic;

recognizing emotionally toned language, appeals to prejudice, and similar devices (Spache, 1964)

The techniques discussed in the following sections fall into one of three categories: traditional, current, and emerging. You may decide that one of these approaches suits you better than the others, but it is important to commit to doing something tangible to overcome prevailing impediments to effective thinking.

TRADITIONAL TEACHING TECHNIQUES AND ACTIVITIES FOR IMPROVING CRITICAL READING

Propaganda Techniques

Critical reading often involves recognizing an author's use of propaganda techniques. In teaching this aspect of critical reading, it is useful to have a language, or grammar, for thinking about and discussing propaganda, that is, insidious persuasion. Following are eight of the most commonly used terms and ideas that provide useful reference points in any content area:

1. *Bandwagon*: Everyone else is doing a certain thing, so jump on the bandwagon and go along with the crowd. ("More people buy _____ than any other cigarette.")
2. *Testimonial*: A well-known person endorses a certain product or course of action even though he or she is not an authority on the subject. ("Take it from me, _____ acts twice as fast as aspirin.")
3. *Plain folks*: People who appear to be "just plain folks," or "just like you and me," suggest that we think or act in a certain way. ("My family has been in farming for 50 years; you know I won't forget you when I get to Washington.")
4. *Snob appeal*: The opposite of plain folks. ("These beautiful designer jeans were created for the discriminating woman.")
5. *Name calling*: Applying a currently unpopular epithet to a person or movement without examining the evidence. ("That college professor is a radical—perhaps even a communist.")
6. *Glittering generalities*: Words or phrases with favorable connotations that lead us to favor a person or movement without examining the evidence (can also be used with unfavorable words). Such abstract words or phrases (e.g., "public spirit," "patriotic duty," "fiscal responsibility") are used to make us support some person or idea with little further analysis. ("We need a leader who will guide us to greater fiscal responsibility, an improved standard of living, and a more equitable tax structure.")
7. *Transfer*: A symbol that is used to secure allegiance to a program that has no connection with the associated agency. ("Buy Red Cross shoes.")
8. *Scientific slant*: Use of scientific terminology to persuade us to accept something as being more than what it really is. ("The titanium light bulb burns for 7,000 hours"; "Four out of five dentists surveyed . . . ")

It is especially worthwhile to teach these largely advertising techniques because the process of being "sold" on something so closely mimics the process of considering options and candidates under our cherished political system.

Critical Reading Activities

There are several methods for promoting critical reading and thinking that traditionally have been part of the repertoire offered by reading specialists for use in a variety of settings and subjects. Consider the following for your subject and circumstances:

1. Compare two biographies of the same person. Check the facts each source gives, then compare them with those presented in other sources. Which facts are historically true, and which seem legendary?
2. Compare concepts as represented in books with present-day practices in areas such as family relationships, standards of living, ideas about discipline, nutrition, climate, geography, mores, and so on.
3. Read and compare reports of the same event in newspapers from different publishers and/or media sources, and note the variations.
4. Find differing views on a subject. Discuss which are most valid and why.
5. List authorities in specific areas, and discuss whether or not their writings should be accepted. Determine why or why not.
6. Explore several books or articles by the same author to trace the origins of or changes in his or her interests, viewpoints, and feelings.
7. Examine articles from the editorial pages of various newspapers, and discuss each in terms of personal opinion versus facts, biases, radical ideas, and attempts at sensationalism. The same procedures can be used with magazine articles, pamphlets, and books.
8. Develop criteria with the class such as author's background, position, experience with the subject, prejudices, writing style, and date of publication for use in determining the author's competence. (The teacher, as expert reader, should help students learn the following: Who is the author? What are his or interests? Occupation? Experiences? What is the author's background in the subject? How did the author gather his or her information? Why did the author write this book or article? Is his or her reasoning sound? What evidence does the author provide to support his or her conclusions or generalizations? What appears to be the author's intent? Does the author attain this objective?)
9. Develop an idea and have pupils find information for subsequent evaluation and classification as valid or invalid.
10. List facts and opinions offered in a selection, and discuss how they may be distinguished. (Adapted from McKee & Durr, 1966)

CURRENT STRATEGIES FOR TEACHING CRITICAL AND CREATIVE READING AND THINKING

Teaching Strategy 1: Intra-Act

At the heart of most critical thinking is the need to engage in *evaluative thinking*, or value-based reasoning. One of the more representative, and content appropriate, of these methods is called *Intra-Act* (Hoffman, 1977). It is one of the strategies in the recent class of methods that tend to be more finely tuned, tested, and carefully developed as to purpose and rationale.

Intra-Act was designed to develop readers' ability to draw upon a personal-values base or view of the world. Such thinking tends to permeate and color readers' sense of what they read and what they do with it. Intra-Act was influenced by the earlier work of Raths, Harmon, and Simon (1978) on the "valuing process," and the work of Manzo and Sherk (1978) on languaging. Also, it involves group problem solving and cooperative learning. A careful study of the efficacy of the Intra-Act activity conducted by Hoffman (1977) led to these conclusions:

> The results . . . are . . . encouraging. . . . [T]he desired effects were apparent in the subjects' responses. . . . The quality of the verbal interaction and related accuracy of comprehension were sensitive to the structure of the problem-solving task. The study further demonstrated [students'] desire and ability to go beyond the material in projecting and perceiving personal values related to the content of the selections.
>
> . . . Intra-Act offers promise as an alternative to direct methods of instruction so prevalent in content methodology. Given an appropriately structured learning environment . . . students can and do learn from one another. (p. 63)

Steps in the Intra-Act Procedure

1. Students divide into four cooperative learning groups. A chairperson is appointed. (The chairperson's role is rotated each time the activity is performed.)
2. Students read a brief selection, followed by 10 multiple-choice comprehension questions. Students answer the questions within their groups and discuss the reasons for their answers.
3. Valuing exercises are distributed to the student groups.
   a. Four valuing statements are presented. Students decide individually, without sharing their responses, whether they agree or disagree with each statement.
   b. Each student attempts to predict the responses of the other three members of his or her group (see Figure 8.2).
4. Students calculate their accuracy in prediction (number correct divided by number in the group times 100) and record these accuracy ratings over a specified period of time.
5. The teacher leads a whole-class discussion of students' personal judgments about the valuing statements and the accuracy of their predictions of the other students' judgments.

Figure 8.2 Sample Valuing Statement Exercise Sheet

Date: _____

Name: _____

Chairperson: _____

Directions: Circle "A" for "agree" or "D" for "disagree" to indicate your own responses to each statement. Then circle "A" or "D" to indicate how you think each other member of your group responded to each statement.

	Group Members			
	Me	Mary	Jack	Helen
1. Women probably don't make as good legislators as men.	A/D	A/D	A/D	A/D
2. A person should vote according to the wishes of the people he or she represents, not according to personal feelings.	A/D	A/D	A/D	A/D
3. I would have voted the same as Rankin both times.	A/D	A/D	A/D	A/D
4. The writer seems to approve of what Rankin did.	A/D	A/D	A/D	A/D

Working from guidelines developed by Raths, Harmon, and Simon (1978), Schell (1980) developed techniques similar to Intra-Act. These included "rank ordering," "forced choices," "values voting," and the "value sheet." Figures 8.3 and 8.4 describe and illustrate the last two techniques.

A carpenter's hammer has a head and a claw. You already have read about how the next method, the Anticipation-Reaction Guide, can be used to hammer. Now you will see how you can use it to claw up critical analysis.

Teaching Strategy 2: Anticipation-Reaction Guide

Reading Guides: Before and After

The *Anticipation-Reaction (A-R) Guide,* described in Chapter 5 with respect to pre-reading, is an effective strategy for promoting critical reading and responding. This strategy can be extended by using the A-R Guide statements as the basis for pos-treading writing assignments. Figure 8.5 presents an example of an A-R Guide and a related student essay from an advanced economics class.

Figure 8.3 Values Voting

(Based on "The Black Stallion and the Red Mark" in *Moments*, grade 5 [3])

A stallion heads a band of wild horses which "steals" horses from surrounding farms. The farmers band together and capture the herd. The stallion stays with his blind mare rather than running to freedom.

Following reading of the story, the teacher instructs students: "Listen to the following statements. If you agree, raise your hand; if you disagree, turn thumbs down, and if you are undecided, fold your arms."

1. Donald was wrong to tell his father where the wild horses were.
2. The stallion was dumb to stay with the mare and be caught.
3. Donald's father showed good judgment in letting the stallion and the mare stay together in captivity.

Source: From "Value Clarification via Basal Readers" by L. M. Schell, 1980, *Reading Horizons, 20,* p. 218.

Figure 8.4 Value Sheet

(Based on "The Endless Steppe," *Racing Stripes*, grade 6 [5])

A ten-year-old girl and her family live in exile in a labor camp in Siberia in the 1940s. She and her grandmother take a few of the family's belongings to a village market to trade for food.

The teacher has students write responses to the following questions. Then the teacher instructs them to discuss their responses in small groups or reads selected student responses without revealing who wrote them and without comment.

1. If exiled to a labor camp, what five personal belongings (other than clothes) would you take with you?
2. Which would you be willing to trade for food as Esther did?
3. After being on a restricted diet for several weeks like Esther was, what are two or three kinds of food you would trade your belongings for?
4. Is it right for a whole family to be sent to a labor camp when only the father was "guilty?" Why or why not?

Source: From "Value Clarification via Basal Readers" by L. M. Schell, 1980, *Reading Horizons, 20,* p. 219.

Figure 8.5   Anticipation-Reaction Guide: Supply-Side Economics

Directions:
Before reading—Check Agree or Disagree for each statement.
After reading—Write a brief essay on one statement of your choice.

Agree   Disagree

_____   _____   1. Supply-side economics favors the wealthy.
_____   _____   2. You cannot be a Republican and be against supply-side economics.
_____   _____   3. You cannot be a Democrat and be for supply-side economics.

Student Essay
I think that supply-side economics favors the wealthy because it says that when profits go up, the number of suppliers will increase. This also is supposed to increase competition, and therefore reduce prices, since there would be more supply than demand.

The government, under this approach, is dedicated to helping create greater profits for suppliers. This, however, would tend to make the rich richer and leave the poor and middle class to be the perpetual shoppers, looking for oversupplies. In fact, though, whenever supply begins to exceed demand, the rich simply move their assets elsewhere, quickly reducing supply and competition.

Of course, supply-side thinking is basic to free enterprise. Without a profit motive, investors would not take risks. The role of government, however, needs to be balanced carefully so as to avoid unnecessarily crimping profits, but also avoiding measures that virtually guarantee profits. These include big tax breaks for industry or freedom to exploit the environment. When large corporations are legally permitted not to pay tax and/or to leave behind their industrial wastes, this amounts to a hidden surcharge on all the products bought and one that the rest of us, including future generations, eventually must pay.

Benefits to Critical Reading-Thinking

Active interaction of the type generated by Anticipation-Reaction Guides promotes several key ingredients of critical reading-thinking:

1. Conflict identification and resolution (Frager & Thompson, 1985)
2. Metacognition in the form of self-interrogation while reading (Brown, 1980)
3. Relationship of knowledge of the world and comprehension of text (Waern, 1977a, 1977b) among students and between students and teacher (Manzo & Sherk, 1978).

Regarding the last point, Ericson et al. (1987) point out that in the California Academic Partnership Program, in which professors used A-R Guides in working with teachers and junior high school students, students often would leave class at the end of the period still arguing the relative merits of their various points of view.

This act of carrying the classroom out into the student's world may be the most powerful influence of all on learning and thinking. It tends to automatically extend the school day by increasing students' time on task and reducing the sharp line of demarcation that often separates school learning from home and life experiences.

Other Solid Contributors to Critical Reading

Several other key methodologies that contribute directly to the improvement of critical-constructive reading-thinking are discussed in this text. We will briefly describe the most important of these strategies and indicate in which chapters they are discussed so that you can pull them together for a focused paper or program on critical reading-thinking improvement if you wish.

Proverbs Study
Proverbs study (Manzo, 1980a), discussed in Chapter 10, has been shown to be a useful way to build abstract thinking and connect daily experiences to literature and other academic studies.

Reasoning Guides
An early form of Anticipation-Reaction Guide, *Reasoning Guides* (Herber, 1978), described in Chapter 6, have proven a powerful means of teaching students how to generalize and infer from available information.

Text Preview
Text Preview (Graves, Cooke, & LaBerge, 1983), a prereading strategy described and demonstrated in Chapter 12, is a highly effective way to stimulate critical analysis of literature.

Contextual Ignition
Contextual Ignition, illustrated in the science section in Chapter 13, is a powerful approach to a fully integrated strategy for teaching critical reading-thinking through environmental issues. It relies heavily on a certain modicum of what some might consider overzealousness.

Read-Encode-Annotate-Ponder (REAP)
Read-Encode-Annotate-Ponder, or *REAP* (Eanet & Manzo, 1976), introduced in Chapter 7 and developed further in Chapter 9, is a prototypic study-type reading strategy. Generally it is taught at the college level as a study skill technique and at the lower grade levels as a form of postreading writing training. Like most of the concurrent methods described previously, REAP can serve several purposes. It is particularly relevant here, because it provides a logical linkage between critical reading and study skills training, the topic of the next chapter. The contribution of REAP to higher-order literacy is further detailed in Chapter 11 in the context of its unique value in helping to initiate and maintain school- and even district- and community-based reading-thinking programs.

The next section addresses the universal tendency to accept "what is" and teaches us to raise the habit-breaking question "how else might it be?"

EMERGING OPTIONS: MAKING HYBRIDS

If you are adventurous, you will wish to consider joining emerging efforts to use and refine some innovative ideas for teaching and promoting critical-creative reading and thinking. These innovations mark the frontiers of some of the most exhilarating programming efforts in contemporary education. There is a bounty of benefits in teaching for inventive reading-thinking: It naturally puts critical thinking in its proper place; it is contagious; it does not remain confined to the classroom; it is uplifting; it is self-motivating; it stimulates independent reading and library research; it acknowledges and makes a place for our (often battered) divergent-thinking students; it is a mental adventure one can engage in for the rest of one's life; it meets one of the most fundamental purposes of education—creative problem solving; and it can result in the betterment of all humankind, turning every classroom in which it is practiced into a "think tank," or research and development center. No other area of cognitive study, skills development, or social schooling can equal its impact in breadth or depth.

The work reported here represents one of the chief distinctions of the Languaging in the Content Areas (LICA) movement. Recall from Chapter 2 that the LICA thesis stresses teaching students not only to learn how to learn what is known but to learn how to discover and create what is unknown and to be able to effectively speak and write about it.

At this writing, a university-based research and development facility, the Center for Studies in Higher Order Literacy, is being formed to research and promote innovative reading and thinking. Given the time lapse between writing and publishing, the center's work should be further along when you read this. For now, however, consider joining the adventure. You will find most of the strategies discussed ahead defined quite adequately for classroom use. These strategies are referred to as "experimental," not so much because their value is in question but because their place in the schools has been slow to take root. In point of fact, it can be argued that the extent to which creative thinking training improves reading and subject mastery is less important than the degree to which reading and subject study contribute to creative production—which is, after all, the source and the object of all teaching and learning.

Strategy 1: Six Thinking Hats

DeBono's Six Thinking Hats (1985) is a "mindset" approach, similar to those discussed in Chapter 5, that appears to have great promise for improving flexible, and therefore critical-creative, thinking. In brief, the idea is to engage students in reading and discussing various matters under different mental sets. Each set corresponds to a color that symbolically represents it and is figuratively worn as a hat.

The wearer of each hat is expected to consider a problem (or text to be read) from a specified vantage point:

White hat thinking: Considers information from an objective, or "facts-and-figures," point of view

Red hat thinking: Considers information in terms of intuition, feelings, emotions, and hunches

Black hat thinking: Considers information from a critical perspective, that is, one that is fair and logical though essentially negative

Yellow hat thinking: Considers information from a positive point of view ("What about this works or serves some valued purpose?")

Green hat thinking: Considers information from a creative, innovative, "new ideas" point of view

Blue hat thinking: Considers information from the perspective of controlling and recording what the other hats are doing or have done ("Where are we now with this?"; "Let's summarize"; "What are our conclusions?"). This is a form of self-monitoring, or metacognitive, thinking.

Hats can be assigned to students in a variety of ways: by desk row, by the nature of the text, by general topic, or by student choice.

In DeBono's words, "putting on" a hat focuses thinking, while "switching" hats redirects thinking. This strategy initially was designed for use in business and industry with adults; therefore, you may need to modify some of the descriptors for school use.

The best thing about thinking from different mindsets is that it provides real, physical experience of what it feels like to think in alternate ways. Thus, it is a means of breaking up counterproductive habits of thought. It can get the class pessimist to experience positive thinking (yellow hat); the higher-order dysfunctional to think more critically and creatively (black and yellow hats); and the classic underachiever to better adapt to the serial, systematic manner in which things typically are presented in class and in textbooks (white hat).

We think it will be possible to create some new "hats" that are more compatible with the basic mission of schools, such as an "editing hat," an "expert reader hat" (see the characteristics of "effective readers" in Chapter 6 should you wish to try this), a "mature thinker hat," and a "humorist's hat"—the last a valuable lifetime perspective that has lightened many a heavy load for those inclined to use it.

The next section describes several alternative ways that we are currently working on to cue the different thinking approaches.

Strategy 2: Mind Cuing

Mind Cuing parallels DeBono's Thinking Hats. Where it differs is in its heavier focus on students and the context and mission of schooling than on business and industry—where no doubt it also has some value and application.

Instead of using hats and colors figuratively as DeBono does, the teacher puts actual colors where they can be seen and used to cue desired modes of thinking. We are experimenting with several ways of doing this. See if any of these has practical appeal for you:

1. Distribute small, assignment pad–like tablets of colored paper with brief printed descriptors of each mindset a student might be asked to assume.
2. Place large color cards above the chalkboard with key descriptor words embossed on each.
3. Use eyeglasses with tinted lenses that can be easily interchanged to literally alter the way students view things.
4. Use computer screens containing text and programmed to change background color at designated points.
5. Use the Motor Imaging vocabulary strategy described in Chapter 5 to substitute more readily available gestures (or kinesthetic cues) for color cues.

To determine the relative value of these approaches, we plan to compare them to more conventional though also well grounded approaches that emphasize careful training, explanation, and modeling of the various modes of thought.

If the Thinking Hats and Mind Cuing strategies interest you, you might wish to refer to other examples of "mindset" approaches described elsewhere in this text, such as REAP (annotations students can read before, during, and following reading), Note Cue (a means of getting students to contribute to class discussion in specified ways), Communal Poetry (a way to immerse students in imaginative writing—see Chapter 12), and the Parallel Form strategy (which nurtures deeper thinking about complex issues in social studies through personalized role play and use of extended metaphors (see Chapter 13).

The next two "experimental" methods are variations on "getting what you ask for."

Strategy 3: Ask for Invention

Incredibly, one of the easiest ways to instigate inventive thinking in the classroom simply is to ask for it! We can only speculate as to why this is so easily achieved. It appears related to the fact that our brains, while quite capable of creation, are naturally more inclined to see and follow patterns than to mentally venture outside of whatever they deem familiar. It takes a certain degree of "cognitive dissonance," or dissatisfaction with the current situation and knowledge, to prod creation or alternative thinking—hence the common expression "Necessity is the mother of invention." The pleasant surprise in all this is that it doesn't take much "need" to get most minds thinking very creatively very quickly. In many cases, it takes little more than a prompt (see Figure 8.6 for an anecdotal illustration of this point).

Box 8.1 demonstrates the effectiveness of "just asking for" creative thinking. If you feel you really need to build toward it, try the next strategy, a general eight-step paradigm (overall plan) for promoting inventive reading and thinking across the curriculum.

Figure 8.6 Just Ask for It

The first author was having a discussion about creativity over lunch with three graduate students. Two said, modestly, that they tended to be uninventive in their thinking. The third said the same thing, but with the conviction of one who speaks only when necessary.

Violating the social contract all teachers have with the reticent not to challenge their shyness, I said, "No, you are not uninventive, you are *unwilling* to act assertively—to determine where there are problems and to intervene with plausible solutions."

"No," she replied insistently, "I am totally uncreative."

I persisted, "What are we doing right now, and how is it a problem for the shy?" The other two students tried to help but, ironically, could not because they were not self-conscious about the problem I had in mind. Finally, I asked, "Do you like your hot and sour soup?"

"Yes," she replied.

"Why aren't you finishing it?" I asked.

"I did," she murmured.

"No, you didn't, you left some in the bottom."

"Well, I couldn't finish all of it to the bottom!" she snapped back, somewhat annoyed.

"So, then, you have acknowledged a problem! Solve it," I said.

"You mean, how to get the soup out of the bowl without lifting it to your mouth or even tipping the bowl to spoon it out?"

"Yes," I replied.

Overwhelmed with all this attention, she responded in moments, "Well, I suppose the bowl could have been made with an indentation in the shape of a spoon at the bottom. No, wait," she added quickly, "how about simply forming the inside of the bowl at an angle so the soup drains to one side?"

There it was. Despite the fact that pottery has been made in the same way for thousands of years, this shy, "totally uncreative," but prolific-reading student became a creator with two plausible solutions with no more training than a sharp prompt to do so!

**BOX
8.1**

CONCEPT CLARIFICATION
Just Ask for It!

Surely you've worried about how Americans have become couch potatoes. We live sedentary lives, glued to the television set, eathing high-calorie and high-cholesterol foods to excess.

Seat yourself mentally in front of the television set. Now invent some constructive ways to counter this problem without depriving us of the peace and comfort that watching television and munching brings. Think in terms of healthier things people can do while watching television.

We are so certain that you will come up with workable ideas, programs, and products that we have provided no answers for your reference.

Strategy 4: Promoting Inventive Thinking across the Curriculum

The following eight-step procedure can be embellished or abbreviated as age, grade level, and context require:

1. Tell students about invention. Essentially there are four types:
   a. Physical, or product-type, inventions (e.g., the sewing machine)
   b. Social inventions, or ways to better tend to human needs (e.g., democratic government, libraries, social security)
   c. Theoretical renderings, or speculations about how things are related, governed, or otherwise perceivable (e.g., Darwinism; $E = mc^2$; Holmes and Singer's Substrata Factor Theory of Reading)
   d. Artistic renderings, or fresh ways to symbolically represent or highlight, the human experience (e.g., Joyce Kilmer's poem "Trees"; Beethoven's Fifth Symphony; Van Gogh's bright, textural patterns).
2. Read and discuss some previous inventions and how some have failed. (Ask your librarian for help; there are some fascinating books on inventors, inventing, and inventions.)
3. Illustrate for students how inventive thoughts and products have been responsible for advancing your content area (you probably will not have realized yourself how much and how many until you start thinking about it).
4. Have students read in a specific textual area and see how many "new" ideas humankind has had to come up with to understand and produce the few pages of print in that reading assignment.
5. Work with the class to identify what is not known, or as yet solved inadequately, in each content area. (Invite specialists in these areas to class.)
6. Work with students to articulate and write up what is not known into an "Encyclopedia of Our Ignorance" (e.g., how to create full employment and prosperity without inflation). Ask family and friends to identify problems they are having in their lives and for which they desire a creative solution (e.g., living room furniture that can expand—rather than merely convert—to accommodate family get-togethers and the like. We bet you're already thinking about how easily this could be done.)
7. Create. Use SCAMPER (see Figure 8.7) to promote effective problem solving. (You can precede this step by articulating a problem that already has been solved and can be found in texts. Then students can compare their solutions with those discussed in the text.)
8. Reinforce and extend:
   a. Select and use other teaching methods that are compatible with this general paradigm (see the problem-solving approach to study skills in Chapter 9 as an example).
   b. Encourage other teachers and departments to engage in constructive-thinking projects.
   c. Celebrate creativity: Hold Invention and Imagination Conventions in your

Figure 8.7 SCAMPER

S	Substitute?	Who else instead? What else instead? Other ingredient? Other material? Other power? Other place?
C	Combine?	How about a blend, an alloy, an ensemble? Combine units? Combine purposes? Combine appeals?
A	Adapt?	What else is like this? What other idea does this suggest? Does past offer parallel? What could I copy?
M	Modify? Minify? Magnify?	New twist? Change meaning, color, motion, sound, odor, form, shape? What to add? More time? Greater frequency? Higher? Longer? Thicker?
P	Put to other uses?	New ways to use as it? Other uses if modified? Other places to use? Other people to reach?
E	Eliminate?	What to subract? Smaller? Condensed? Miniature? Lower? Shorter? Lighter? Omit? Streamline? Understate?
R	Reverse? Rearrange?	Interchange components? Other pattern? Other layout? Other sequence? Transpose cause and effect? Change pace? Transpose positive and negative? How about opposites? Turn it backwards? Turn it upside down? Reverse roles?

class or school. (See Chapter 11 for examples of materials and services to assist in such projects.)

Box 8.2 offers an application of elaborative thinking.

HOW YOU STACK UP SO FAR

Acquisition of the skills for teaching and promoting higher-order literacy may be as long a process of development as that of achieving maturity in reading. Therefore, before going on to the study skills portion of this text, you may wish to appraise your inclinations and preparedness for promoting critical-constructive reading by completing the inventory in Figure 8.8.

BOX 8.2

CONCEPT CLARIFICATION
Elaborative Thinking

What does it mean to promote elaborative thinking? Simply to go to the next steps, wherever they may lead you. Take the problem of too much television and junk food and too little exercise posed in Box 8.1. Now that you have formulated some creative ways to deal with this problem, ask yourself what would happen if your proposed solutions worked and caught on. Think in terms of economic, social, and personal implications.

Figure 8.8   How Well Do/Would You Teach Critical-Constructive Reading-Thinking?

Directions: Use the numbered scale below to circle the number of your response to each item.

    1   I never do/would
    2   I almost never do/would
    3   I very infrequently do/would
    4   I sometimes do/would when appropriate
    5   I often do/would when appropriate
    6   I always do/would when appropriate

1. I teach students to distinguish between vague and precise words.   1 2 3 4 5 6
2. I lead students to recognize the difference between denotative and   1 2 3 4 5 6
   connotative meanings of words.
3. I help students recognize propaganda devices, such as bandwagon,   1 2 3 4 5 6
   testimonial, plain folks, snob appeal, name calling, glittering
   generalities, transfer, scientific slant.
4. I encourage students to examine the validity of arguments they read   1 2 3 4 5 6
   and judge whether the conclusions are soundly based on the
   premises.
5. I make students aware of the logic of arguments they read and help   1 2 3 4 5 6
   them to reason through those arguments.
6. I design classroom discussions to help students recognize and   1 2 3 4 5 6
   distinguish between objective and subjective information.
7. I have students judge the reliability of information by collecting   1 2 3 4 5 6
   several viewpoints on the same topic from different sources and
   comparing facts and opinions.
8. I ask students to determine the author's qualifications for writing   1 2 3 4 5 6
   about a specific topic.
9. I teach students to determine the author's purpose and to evaluate   1 2 3 4 5 6
   bias, accuracy, viewpoint, and purpose.
10. My instructional activities assure that students identify and evaluate 1 2 3 4 5 6

Figure 8.8 *continued*

the following devices: figurative language, dialogue and authentic
speech, author's style, symbolism, mood, humor, satire and irony,
point of view.

11. I teach students how to recognize and reconcile conflicting   1 2 3 4 5 6
    information and ideas.
12. I ask students to think eventuatively.   1 2 3 4 5 6
13. I urge students to think constructively and creatively as well as   1 2 3 4 5 6
    critically.
14. I teach students to suspend judgment where information is   1 2 3 4 5 6
    inadequate.
15. I train students to think metacognitively: to self-monitor, self-correct,   1 2 3 4 5 6
    and reflect on the appropriateness of their reading/learning
    strategies.
16. I train students to ask for and retrieve additional information where   1 2 3 4 5 6
    this is necessary and proper.
17. I urge students to work cooperatively but to avoid buckling under to   1 2 3 4 5 6
    social pressures where their values and beliefs are concerned.
18. I urge students to accept and to give criticism graciously and   1 2 3 4 5 6
    thoughtfully.
19. I persistently challenge high academic achievers to form and   1 2 3 4 5 6
    express judgments and apply what they learn.
20. I urge students to lead a self-examined and disciplined life.   1 2 3 4 5 6

Analysis and Interpretation: Connect the circled numbers of your responses to form a
profile. To analyze your profile, turn the page(s) horizontally. The more completely your
line is in column 6, the better. Answers in columns 3 or lower indicate possible
weaknesses. Analyze your own weaknesses (if any) according to the following item
analysis: items 1–3, semantics; 4–7, logic; 8–9, authenticity; 10, literary devices; 11–15,
related thinking skills; 16, independent searching; 17–20, personal-social growth and
adjustment.

Source: From "How Well Do You Teach Critical Reading?" by L. M. Clary, 1977, *The Reading Teacher,
31,* p. 144. Copyright 1977 by the International Reading Association. Reprinted with permission by
Linda Mixon Clary and the International Reading Association.

CHAPTER TIE-UPS

◆◆◆   *Graphic Organizer*

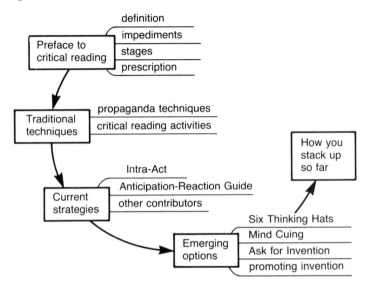

___

◆◆◆   *Critique and Anticipation*

This chapter demonstrated that critical reading involves attitudinal, logical, and judgmental factors. There are at least 11 disincentives to critical reading and thinking that are believed to impede its natural occurrence. Fear of releasing a flood of self-damaging criticism probably is the most powerful impediment.

Broad-spectrum assessment of various factors that bear on "critical comprehending" revealed four profiles of reader types: (1) those with comprehension and critical analysis in good balance (mature readers); (2) those who are low in both comprehension and critical reading (remedial readers); (3) those who are high in comprehension but low in critical reading (higher illiterates, or overachievers); and (4) those with weak comprehension but high critical analysis skills (classic underachievers).

The chapter offered a variety of traditional and emerging options for promoting both critical and creative reading. The strategies holding the greatest promise appear to be those that stress constructive (i.e., creative) responding. These appear to offer the best means of overcoming fear of criticism and the strong biological and socially reinforced disposition to see and follow prescribed paths and patterns rather than pioneer new ones. Fortunately—and contrary to common belief—it appears to take little to coax the mind to think critically and inventively.

The next chapter focuses on study skills and habits. It examines one of the most critical variables in effective learning: the storage of knowledge to make it available for synthesis, application, and other forms of enriched thinking.

TRADE SECRET

Acquiring and Articulating a World View

A teacher is one who can articulate for students and community what others can only vaguely sense. Effective educators often seek books and other sources that can help improve this understanding and articulation of the larger ideas and forces that have shaped our past and are shaping our present and future. Three such sources in particular provide manageable syntheses of vast areas of college education and human experience. You may wish to consider these for your professional library.

The first is *The Great Thoughts*, compiled by George Seldes (New York: Ballantine Books, 1985). This book provides thumbnail sketches of the major ideas that have shaped the history of the world from Abelard (1079–1142), considered the greatest philosopher of his time, to Zola (1840–1902), the French novelist, who wrote optimistically and, we hope, accurately, "Truth is on the march; nothing now can stop it."

The second work is a two-volume set appropriately titled *The Encyclopaedia of Ignorance: Everything You Wanted to Know about the Unknown*, edited by R. Duncan and M. Weston-Smith (Oxford: Pergamon Press, 1978). These volumes attempt to outline what is not known about the physical world and mathematics. It is not light reading, but it is divided into manageable sections that, unless you are a science or math teacher, you probably will need to reread several times.

Finally, there is a small book (117 pages) by Will and Ariel Durant simply titled *The Lessons of History* (New York: Simon & Schuster, 1968). One passage from this book provides a particularly poignant historical perspective on creative thinking, the theme of this chapter. In discussing the many reasons why civilizations rise and fall, they find one common factor:

the presence or absence of *initiative and of creative individuals* with the clarity of mind and energy of will to mount effective responses to new situations. (p. 91)

Study Skills and Habits

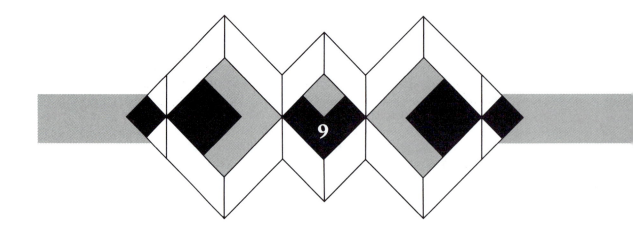

Preface, Notetaking, Memory Training, Test Taking, Speed Reading, and Life Management

Study without reflection is a waste of time; reflection without study is dangerous.
— Confucius

FOCUS

Study skills is a generic term for a class of functions and educational objectives ranging from notetaking to life management skills. Concern for such skills exists in public schools, business, the military, and at the college and graduate school levels. Everyone who teaches needs to be informed to be informative on most aspects of this topic.

PREFACE TO STUDY SKILLS

Advent and Evolution of Developmental Studies ◆ Advice and Orientation Problems ◆ Study Stills Heuristic ◆ Pauk's Eight Learning Principles ◆ SQ3R: A Story unto Itself

CONTENT AREA STRATEGIES FOR IMPROVING LECTURE NOTETAKING AND LISTENING

Palmatier's Unified Notetaking System for Learning (PUNS) ◆ Speedwriting ◆ TQLR for Effective Listening ◆ Enabling Questions ◆ How Not to Listen ◆ Guided Lecture Procedure

CONTENT AREA STRATEGIES FOR MEMORY TRAINING

The Nature and Function of Memory ◆ Seven Memory Training Techniques

CONTENT AREA STRATEGIES FOR TEST TAKING

Taking Multiple Choice Tests ◆ PORPE: A Strategy for Taking Essay Tests ◆ Tips for Avoiding Test Anxiety

SPEED READING: STUDY SKILL OR BLUE SMOKE AND MIRRORS?

CONTENT AREA STRATEGIES FOR LIFE MANAGEMENT

Scheduling ◆ Study Journals ◆ Peer Supplementals for Effective Use of Scheduled Study Periods ◆ PASS ◆ Instant Study Skills ◆ Homilies for Motivation and Life Management

CHAPTER TIE-UPS

Graphic Organizer ◆ Critique and Anticipation ◆ Trade Secret: Underwriters' Assignment Book System

PREFACE TO STUDY SKILLS

The term *study skills* means efficient use of time spent in learning activities. As such, it includes an array of diverse topics such as step-by-step formulas to guide reading, listening, and notetaking; self-directed means for improving memory; principles for stress management; and strategies for improving test preparation and test taking. Study skills may be taught as a short course, as a strand in a regular class, and/or as an integrated function in various content classes. Each approach has merit. The content area approach is gaining in popularity as more teachers are becoming exposed to these strategies in teacher training and in-service programs. The following brief background sketch of the development of study skills provides a perspective for evaluating some of the early study skills strategies and for considering this newly revitalized field as a possible alternative or extra-income dimension of your professional career.

Advent and Evolution of Developmental Studies

The techniques and objectives known as *study skills* have tended to reflect and interact with the educational trends of the times. McMurray wrote the first study skills text for classroom teachers in 1909. It was a "no-frills" book called simply *How to Study and Teaching How to Study.*

World Wars I and II popularized self-directed study techniques. By 1930, books with names like *Outlining as a Study Procedure* (Barton, 1930) were available at the college level. Armed services inductees needed quick training in how to read and master the contents of the manuals that accompanied increasingly sophisticated weapons and machines. Later, returning veterans willingly enrolled in study skills courses to improve their reading efficiency and grades in technical schools and colleges.

The "open admissions" policies initiated in many state and city colleges in the 1960s created a further need to assist underprepared students in meeting college-level reading, writing, and study requirements. A mildly irreverent attitude toward academic life arose in educators' efforts to reach floundering—and resistant—students. This rather offhanded attitude is symbolized in the titles of (otherwise) quality self-help books such as *Study Skills: A Student's Guide to Survival* (Carmen & Adams, 1972) and *Get Your "A" out of College* (McKowen, 1979).

Recently the aura surrounding study practices, especially at the college level, has again grown more conservative and professional. Many colleges and professional schools have departments specializing in what is now called *developmental reading* or, even more broadly, *developmental studies*. As the field of developmental studies has evolved from its initial emphasis on adults and veterans returning to college toward the needs of underachieving college students, its conceptual bases and strategies have become increasingly appropriate for use at high school and intermediate grade levels. Consequently, there has been a gradual but steady trend toward addressing study skills at these levels and in content classes. The logic of introducing study skills at these levels is clear: Study behaviors are habits, and the longer one practices ineffective habits, the more difficult it is to change them.

Currently career opportunities for the content area teacher with study skills specialization are rapidly emerging in colleges and universities, technical schools, and business and industry as well as the public schools. Developmental studies specialists are trained to promote higher-order literacy by assisting learners at all ability levels to maximize their personal reading and learning potential. This relatively new professional role has been acknowledged as a separate area of reading certification by the International Reading Association in its revised (1986) guidelines to professional standards and roles. The study skills techniques discussed in this chapter draw heavily from the developmental reading/studies specialist's stock-in-trade, with the greatest emphasis on those practices that classroom teachers at intermediate and senior high school grade levels can use most conveniently.

Advice and Orientation Problems

There are two big problems in teaching study skills. First, many people resent being given advice, and most study strategies *are* advice. This problem persists even though the formulas are quite effective according to a review of research by Anderson and Armbruster (1982). These authors say that the effectiveness of these strategies rises significantly when taught with "focused attention and encoding"—that is, when teacher and class focus on the strategies as content and students are encouraged to restate and/or recite the steps or basic intent of the study strategy.

Second, both teachers and students tend to get so caught up in the subject matter that neither has the mental reserves to attend to teaching study skills or learning how to learn. Teaching and learning study skills strategies mean adding an additional layer of content to be taught and learned on top of existing demands. The SQ3R strategy, for example, reminds students to survey (S), question (Q), and read, recite, and review (the 3Rs). Teaching students to use study strategies like SQ3R is analogous to teaching teachers to use instructional strategies like the DR-TA. In each case, what is taught is a set of steps that teachers/students are expected to take and apply on their own.

Study Skills Heuristic

The *Study Skills Heuristic* was designed as a paradigm for overcoming some of the advice and orientation problems that tend to arise when teaching study skills in the content classroom. It begins with an orientation step to focus students' attention on the aim of "learning to learn." Next, the study strategy is described. A simulation lesson follows to demonstrate the study strategy and elicit appropriate discussion. The final steps are designed to refine and reinforce the intended study strategy. Note especially the last step, which suggests that students *visualize* themselves using the new approach. We have a sense that this function has great promise as a natural but underutilized tool for amplifying behavior changes following new learnings. To test the personal significance of this technique, try visualizing yourself using the entire Study Skills Heuristic with one of the popular study strategies described ahead, such as SQ3R.

Steps in the Study Skills Heuristic

1. Designate a chunk of content material to be used as a vehicle for teaching study skills (ideally something difficult to learn).
2. Explain to the class that this will be a "simulation" lesson designed to emphasize more effective reading and study skills rather than the content (now both you and your students will be temporarily reoriented). Draw students' attention to a relevant situation that has arisen in class, or raise a study-related question or problem for which the study strategy to be taught might provide assistance.
3. List the steps of the study skills strategy on the chalkboard (subsequently, you can present the method to students in handout form).
4. Present lecture or textbook information with the following requirements: Students are to take notes on the lecture or the reading, study them in class, and take a combined short-answer/essay question test.
5. Model (demonstrate) how each step of the method might "look" when used with the lesson materials. Then provide an opportunity for students to apply the strategy. Before, during, and/or after each step, ask students:
   a. What are you doing or thinking right now?
   b. What could you have done or be doing to improve your (listening, notetaking, reading, study, test-taking, discussion) skills?
   c. What will you do next time?
6. Discuss variations and modifications of the study skills strategy. Encourage students to comment on their perceptions of the strategy's strengths and weaknesses. Ask them to describe how they themselves intend (or would recommend that others do) to employ the method to meet their personal needs.
7. Schedule "refining sessions" to determine whether students have used and practiced the method and what problems and solutions they have discovered in doing so.
8. Try to get at least one other teacher to support and build on the study strategy.
9. Urge students to practice further by visualizing themselves using the study strategy during quiet moments, such as just before falling asleep. (It has been said that restful visualization can teach ice skating in the summer and swimming in the winter.)

Bridging to Peer Models

The Study Skills Heuristic for teaching study strategies emphasizes having students "language-through" their personal thinking so that they can hear themselves and others can hear them. This is an important step in bridging from the teacher as a competent model of language and thinking, as stressed in previous chapters, to fellow students as models of competency. This is particularly desirable because it is easier for students to imitate peer models than teachers. (Many of us could never imitate James Cagney but could easily mimic another person's impersonation of Cagney.)

The next section summarizes additional useful principles of learning and studying.

Pauk's Eight Learning Principles

In one of the early textbooks designed for college students with weak academic skills, Walter Pauk (1974) summarized much of what is known about effective learning and study in his "Eight Learning Principles."[1] These research-based principles provide an excellent orientation to the field of developmental studies and a basis for evaluating the study strategies included in this chapter.

1. *Principle of Motivated Interest.* We remember what interests us. Develop your natural interests, and try to create new interests by reading (e.g., magazine and newspaper articles) in diverse areas.
2. *Principle of Selectivity.* Information must be grouped into units of a manageable size for efficient recall. In the 19th century, Hermann Ebbinghaus, one of the world's earliest experimental psychologists, found that it took 15 times as many trials to memorize 12 nonsense syllables as the number of trials needed to memorize 6 nonsense syllables. One would predict that it would take only twice as many trials.
3. *Principle of Intention to Remember.* Prerequisites to efficient learning include careful attending, getting the facts right the first time, and striving to understand. Recall that this is the basic principle underlying the Guided Reading Procedure, a total reading and study lesson design covered in Chapter 4.
4. *Principle of Basic Background.* What we perceive (see, hear, taste, smell, feel, and *read*) depends in large measure on what we already know. Some intention, if not interest, may be generated by the recognition that introductory-level courses provide the background essential for later courses.
5. *Principle of Meaningful Organization.* George Miller, the eminent Harvard psychologist, found that the immediate memory span of the general population seems fixed at approximately seven "bits" of information, plus or minus two. For effective recall, therefore, information should be categorized into meaningful groups of no more than seven "bits." The telephone company heeded this research when developing the telephone numbering system. The U.S. Postal Service, on the other hand, has challenged it by implementing a nine-digit zip code system.
6. *Principle of Recitation.* Study reading must be an active process. Recitation is analogous to exercising a muscle: It builds and embeds information in long-term memory.

[1]The following description of Pauk's Eight Learning Principles is from Walter Pauk, *How to Study in College*, Fourth Edition. Copyright © 1989 by Houghton Mifflin Company. Adapted with permission.

Pauk reminds us of how H. F. Spitzer's classic study compared the amount of information recalled by students 7 and 63 days after learning. Students who reviewed immediately after learning remembered 83% after 7 days and 70% after 63 days. Those who did not review immediately after learning remembered 33% after 7 days and 14% after 63 days. Control groups of students who also did not review immediately after learning remembered approximately 55% after 1 day, 22% after 14 days, 18% after 21 days, and 1% after 28 days. Obviously recitation-study works!

7. *Principle of Consolidation.* Information must be harbored in the mind for a certain period of time before a temporary memory can be consolidated into a more permanent one. Numerous records of accident victims show that a period of unconsciousness can "erase" the memory of events that occurred from 15 to 5 minutes before the person lost consciousness. Spitzer's study, described in principle 6, further illustrates the effectiveness of an immediate review of new information.

8. *Principle of Distributed Practice.* A number of brief reviews is more effective than one long review session. Short sessions prevent physical and emotional fatigue and help sustain interest and motivation.

The final section in this "preface" to study skills is a critique of one of the earliest study reading strategies, and one that is still widely used. As you review this strategy, it will be useful to compare it with Pauk's Learning Principles as well as with your own study habits.

SQ3R: A Story unto Itself

The *Survey-Question-Read-Recite-Review (SQ3R)* technique is the acknowledged granddaddy of study formulas. However, it appears to have a faulty gene or two. The plain truth is that it does not work quite as well as its billing would suggest. This section should help you form a personal critical judgment of the relative value of SQ3R and determine if, when, and how it might properly be used in its present form or whether it can be fine-tuned to produce better and more consistent results.

SQ3R: A "Universal Strategy"

SQ3R was developed by Francis Robinson (1946), who traced its roots back to 1923. Robinson developed it in response to a need expressed by the U.S. Department of Defense during World War II (Stahl & Henk, 1986). As noted earlier, U.S. troops had much to learn and little time in which to learn it. They needed a rigorous, *self-guided* Directed Reading Activity that they could use with minimal instruction in field training situations. SQ3R stresses meticulous, step-by-step analysis of text, followed by repeated reviews to "overlearn" the material to the point where key information can be recalled and recited with minimal cuing.

Steps in SQ3R

1. *Survey.* Survey a chapter before reading it closely:
   a. Read the title and think about what it says or implies.
   b. Read the headings and subheadings.
   c. Read the summary if there is one.
   d. Read the captions under the pictures, charts, graphs, or other illustrations.
   e. See if there is a bibliography or a list of books related to the content of the chapter.
2. *Question.* Ask yourself questions about what you are going to read:
   a. What does the title of the chapter mean?
   b. What do I already know about the subject?
   c. What did my instructor say about this chapter when it was assigned?
   d. What questions do the headings and subheadings suggest?
3. *Read.* Read actively:
   a. Read to answer the questions you raised while doing the survey/question routine.
   b. Read all the added attractions in the chapter (maps, graphs, tables, and other illustrations).
   c. Read all the underlined, italicized, or boldface words or phrases extra carefully.
4. *Recite.* Go over what you read in step 3 by either orally summarizing what you just read or making notes of some type.
5. *Review.* Periodically survey what you read and learned:
   a. Use your notes or markings to refresh your memory.
   b. Review immediately after reading.
   c. Review again periodically.
   d. Review again before taking an exam on the subject.

Efficacy of SQ3R for Independent and Content Class Use

The consensus among specialists regarding the efficacy of SQ3R as a total formula is positive, albeit not always enthusiastic. Studies reported by Wooster (1958), Willmore (1967), Donald (1967), Diggs (1973), Gurrola (1975), and McNamara (1977) found no significant differences between SQ3R and control (i.e., placebo) treatments. In a widely cited review of the literature on SQ3R, Wark (1964) undertook a point-by-point analysis of each step of the strategy. Only the Recite step was supported in this analysis. Wark aptly concluded, "There is no body of data to demonstrate that any other integrated package of skills could not work just as well [as SQ3R]. Like the legal age for marriage, SQ3R seems to be supported by tradition, rather than a rigorous consideration of the data on productivity" (p. 168).

Thus, despite the popularity of SQ3R, the strategy's value as a winning self-guided reading-study formula still is uncertain. We believe there are at least two reasons why SQ3R does not appear to work. First, many of the students who need it most are too impulsive and undisciplined to fully implement it. Second, there is a lack of effective training and follow-through. Francis Robinson himself observed that SQ3R cannot possibly be effective until it becomes "automatic" and "subordinate to the task of reading" (1946, p. 21). For these reasons, we continue to endorse SQ3R for content classroom use, where each step can be practiced under *teacher guidance*. Used in this way, SQ3R parallels the Directed Reading-Thinking Activity, which has been proven effective. SQ3R can be introduced as the self-study version of the DR-TA, stated in terms that a student, when ready, can begin to apply independently.

CONTENT AREA STRATEGIES FOR IMPROVING LECTURE NOTETAKING AND LISTENING

Palmatier's Unified Notetaking System (PUNS)

Students need instruction in how to learn from lecture as well as from text. *Palmatier's Unified Notetaking System (PUNS)* urges students to review lecture notes immediately after class and supplement them with text information. The notetaking format also provides a built-in study system by separating key words from the body of the notes. PUNS is one of the few notetaking methods that has been validated through empirical research.

In an initial study of four reading and lecture notetaking methods, Palmatier (1971) decided to combine a reading and a lecture notetaking method to see how well students could implement a "multifaceted" approach. He presented one group with the combined lecture and reading method but did not offer it to two other groups. Surprisingly, the group that used the combined method learned the study strategy more easily and made greater gains in classroom content area learning than did the other two groups. Subsequently, Palmatier further studied and refined the combined study technique into the strategy that we call Palmatier's Unified Notetaking System (Palmatier, 1971, 1973, 1976; Palmatier & Bennett, 1974). We have given the strategy his name because we think he deserves special credit for his clearheaded thinking that led to the discovery, if not the creation, of the method.

Steps in PUNS

1. *Record.* Use only one side of 8½" × 11" notebook paper with a three-inch margin on the left side. (Many college bookstores now stock this type of paper for this purpose.) Record lecture notes to the right of the margin. Use a modified outline form to isolate main topics. Leave space where information seems to be missing. Number each page as you record the notes.
2. *Organize.* As soon after the lecture as possible, add two sections to the notes. First, place *labels* inside the left margin. These should briefly describe the information in the recorded notes. Second, insert *important text information* directly into the recorded notes. If you need more space, you can use the back of the notebook paper.
3. *Study.* Remove the notes from the looseleaf binder, and lay them out so that only the left margin of each page is visible. Use the labels as memory cues to recite as much of the information on the right as you can recall. The labels can

be turned into questions stems: "What do I need to know about [insert label]?" Verify your recall immediately by lifting the page to read the information recorded to the right of the label. As you master the material on each page of notes, set that page aside in an "I already know" stack. For objective tests, the labels can be approached at random, simulating the format of multiple choice, true-false, and matching tests. For essay tests, group information into logical units, formulate predicted essay questions, and practice writing answers.

Figure 9.1 presents a sample PUNS format.

Take More Notes! Research Notes on Notetaking

Students often have the mistaken belief that the purpose of taking notes is to briefly record key ideas when in fact they need to be encouraged to write *more,* not less. This may be the chief value of PUNS: It requires students to review and otherwise supplement skimpy lecture notes with text-based information. PUNS also urges the *purposeful* use of text to supplement notes and thus is likely to result in more effective textbook reading.

A recent research review by Kiewra (1985) on student notetaking provides these additional points for your consideration:

* *Notetaking helps.* Thirty-five out of 38 recent studies have demonstrated that taking notes increases attention and learning during lectures.
* *Review makes sense.* Twenty-four out of 32 studies have found that students who review their notes learn and remember significantly more than those who do not.
* *Use the chalkboard.* Locke (1977) found that 88% of students recorded information from the chalkboard but only 52% recorded even the critical ideas when these were stated.
* *Pause briefly.* Providing occasional pauses during a lecture enriches lecture notes and increases recall (Aiken, Thomas, & Shennum, 1975).
* *Take breaks.* There is a 17% decrease in notetaking in the second 20 minutes of a 40-minute class period (Locke, 1977).
* *Vary test formats.* Rickards and Friedman (1978) found that students who expected multiple choice examinations took notes of lower structural importance and recalled more of the details recorded than did students who expected an essay test. On the other hand, students who expected an essay exam took notes of higher structural importance and recalled more concepts.

If we are going to ask students to take more and better notes, students will need to learn to write faster. The next section illustrates a way to teach them how to do this.

Speedwriting

We listen and comprehend speech comfortably at about 500 words per minute; we tend to speak at about 180 words per minute; but we can write only at about

Figure 9.1 Sample PUNS Note Format

Step 1: *Record.* Use the right-hand side of a specially divided page, leaving space to add text notes.

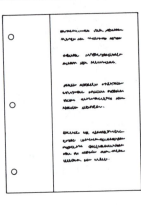

Step 2: *Fill in labels.* Write key word labels in the left margin and text notes in the space provided for lecture notes. Use the back of the previous page if you need more space.

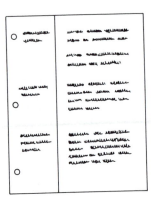

Step 3: *Study key words.* Lay out pages so that only key words show, and try to recite information from your notes. Remove each page as you master its contents.

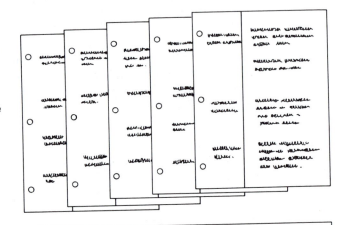

Source: From "Comparison of Four Notetaking Procedures" by R. A. Palmatier, *Journal of Reading, 14,* pp. 235–240, 278.

a third of our normal speaking rate. ∴ (therefore) it pays 2 (to) have a spdwrtg (speedwriting) system. *Speedwriting* is a lubricant that reduces friction and fatigue in notetaking.

Here are some common and useful "spdwrtg" abbreviations:

&	and
c	around, about, approximately
@	at
#	number
w/	with
w/o	without
?	questionable
!	surprising
vs	versus, against, as compared with
=	equals, is, the same as
≠	does not equal
<	is less than, less important than, etc.
>	is greater than, more important than, etc.
∴	therefore
→	causes, results in, produces, yields
eg. or ex.	for example
cf	compare, look this up
i.e.	that is

You can also shorten words by eliminating final letters:

max	maximum
subj	subject
info	information

Another technique is to omit vowels but retain enough consonants to make the word recognizable:

rdg	reading
bkgd	background
gvt	government
clsrm	classroom
lrng	learning

When a word or phrase appears frequently in a lecture, write it out the first time and abbreviate it thereafter:

GNP	gross national product
NDP	National Democratic Party
S/L	standard of living
CW	Civil War

You should recommend abbreviations for words with a high frequency of occurrence in a lecture. Students appreciate practical advice like this and often suggest abbreviations of their own.

The notes students take during lectures are influenced as much by listening skill as by notetaking skill. The next several sections suggest ways to improve attention and active listening.

TQLR for Effective Listening

The most frequent mode of learning is listening. We do *10 times* more listening than than we do reading. Ironically, there has been relatively little research on listening. Most of what we know about it has been learned from studies of reading. *Tune in-Question-Listen-Review (TQLR)* is a simple strategy of unknown origin.

Steps in TQLR

1. *Tune in.* Mobilize your mental processes and be ready to give the speaker your full attention. Get to class a few minutes early so you can quickly review your reading notes or notes from the previous lecture. This will help you anticipate the lecture. Lecturers usually state the point and the approach for that session from the outset. If you are still getting settled and miss the opening, you will be unable to anticipate. You will probably feel like you came in on a TV program five minutes late: confused and mildly annoyed.

2. *Question.* Use questions to aid active listening. The odds are that your instructor has planned what he or she is going to say around a core of important ideas. Each lecture will introduce a few new ideas and provide explanation, examples, or other support for them. Your job is to identify the main ideas. Keep asking yourself these questions:

    a. What is the point of this? What is the important new idea here? What part of this supports the main idea?

    b. What is the purpose of this? Is this an explanation? An example? A generalization? An outline? A sequential development of an idea? A digression?

3. *Listen.* Listen in order to answer your questions. Try to anticipate what is coming next. Make predictions and check them against what the instructor actually says. Your instructor is not going to send up a rocket when stating an important new idea or giving an example but will use signals to telegraph what he or she is doing. For example, the instructor may introduce an example with "for example," as we just did. Here are some other common signals and their meanings:

There are three reasons why . . .   (here they come)

First . . . second . . . third . . .   (there they are)
And most important . . .   (a main idea)
A major development . . .   (a main idea)

The instructor may signal the transmittal of important material with:

On the other hand . . .
On the contrary . . .

As an example . . .
Furthermore . . .
Similarly . . .
In contrast . . .
Also . . .
For instance . . .

The instructor may signal a summary or conclusion with:

Therefore . . .
In conclusion . . .
As a result . . .
Finally . . .
In summary . . .
From this we see . . .

The instructor may even signal very loudly with:

Now this is important . . .
The important idea is that . . .
Remember that . . .
The basic concept here is . . .

Expect signals, and be alert when you receive them.

4. *Review.* You know how quickly memory fades, so take one or two minutes to reinforce your understanding before you leave the classroom. Otherwise, stimuli outside the door will wash out much of what you have learned. After each lecture, on the same day, review your notes briefly (30 to 45 minutes) to note questions or key words in the margins for later self-quizzing reviews. Note the ideas or facts you are not sure you understood and will need to clarify by consulting classmates, the text, or the instructor.

There is no direct evidence on the efficacy of TQLR. Several studies, however (e.g., Cunningham, Cunningham, & Arthur, 1981), have demonstrated that listening can be temporarily improved with direct instruction. For more permanent change to occur, certain steps must be taken to undo lackadaisical, inefficient, and/or self-disruptive habits of listening and to establish the rudiments of more effective strategies for active, mature listening and responding. One way to achieve this is to teach the listener how to get the most out of the speaker and to reduce the "static" that tends to disrupt effective reception of what is being said. The Enabling Questions discussed next can aid listeners in effectively "tuning in" to the speaker.

Enabling Questions

Enabling Questions is a student-initiated heuristic developed by the authors. It is a prepared set of questions that students can use to "tune in" and reduce distraction during lectures. Enabling Questions puts the listener into an active, evaluative thinking mode and urges the teacher or speaker to talk a little less and welcome more discussion.

Following are three sets of interrogatives. The first is designed to improve the organization and clarity of information presented. The second is a means for getting a mental "breather" when information flow seems too rapid to absorb. The third urges the speaker into a "languaging," or give-and-take, discussion characterized by focused listening and collective thinking.

Set 1: Interrogatives for Better Organization and Clarity
Urge students to translate these into their own words:

1. What would you say is/are the chief question(s) you are answering by your lecture (or lesson) today?
2. Which key terms and concepts do you most want us to remember from what you have said (or will say) today?
3. What is most often misunderstood or confusing in the information or position you are presenting today?

Set 2: Interrogatives for Getting a Mental Breather

1. Could you please restate that last point in some other words?
2. Would you please spell _____ and _____ for us?
3. Would you please say which points you particularly want us to note at this time?

Set 3: Interrogatives for Increasing Give-and-Take with the Speaker

1. How does what you have said compare with positions others have taken, and who might these others be?
2. Is there convincing evidence to support your position that you can share with us?
3. What do you think is the weakest part of the position you have taken?
4. How do you think this position (or new information) affects previously held beliefs?
5. What do you suppose would happen if you extended this point another step or two?
6. Would you mind pausing for a moment to see if there are *other views* on this in the class/audience? This would help us better understand and follow your points.

Any one of the latter set of questions likely would put the listener back into an active, evaluative thinking mode and reduce the sometimes excessive dominance of the speaker. It is important that the listener who will learn to use these types of questions do so with an eye toward using them for enriching comprehension, learning, and mature interaction and not as a counteroffensive. One way to help students learn the value and become regular users of Enabling Questions is to write these questions on index cards and distribute a few to each class member. Then urge students to try to use the questions on their card(s) intelligently over a two-to-three-day period. Schedule a day to discuss what happened and what they learned and what might need to be modified to make the Enabling Questions even more enabling.

If this idea appeals to you, you will want to look at three related methods for improving class discussion: Ask-It-Rite (Chapter 10), Note Cue (Chapter 10), and the Response Heuristic (Chapter 12).

How Not to Listen

There are several tips for good listening to be garnered from recognizing "bad" listening habits. The "Nine Worst Listening Habits" include:

1. Calling the subject uninteresting
2. Criticizing the speaker's delivery
3. Getting overstimulated
4. Listening only for the facts (and missing the connective ideas)
5. Faking attention to the speaker
6. Tolerating or creating distractions
7. Evading difficult material
8. Letting emotion-laden words throw you out of tune with the speaker
9. Wasting the differential between speech speed and thought speed

Now let's return to one of our Total Lesson Designs that converts easily into an effective strategy for listening-comprehension training.

Guided Lecture Procedure (GLP)

The *Guided Lecture Procedure (GLP)* is a more teacher-directed method for improving listening. It is the listening counterpart of the Guided Reading Procedure. It was adapted to this form by developmental studies specialists Kelly and Holmes (1979).

Steps in the Guided Lecture Procedure

1. Students are directed to *take no notes* as they listen carefully to the lecture.
2. The teacher writes the objectives of the lecture on the chalkboard along with key technical terms.
3. The teacher lectures for about half the class period, then stops.
4. Students attempt to write down everything they can recall from the lecture.
5. Students form small cooperative learning groups to review and discuss their notes. This discussion, or languaging component, helps build related speaking, writing, and thinking skills.

The Guided Lecture Procedure has been used effectively with classes from middle school to college levels. The small-group activity that forms the second half of the lesson is an excellent cooperative learning activity.

Remember those morphemes—prefixes, suffixes, and roots—that we said are useful in vocabulary acquisition? The next topic will provide several ways to transfer them from Appendix D to your students' minds.

CONTENT AREA STRATEGIES FOR MEMORY TRAINING

The Nature and Function of Memory

One of the cornerstone functions of schooling is to impart and have students learn and remember a wide array of facts. Nonetheless, little thought or effort goes into teaching students efficient and effective ways to recall under pressure. A brief look at the nature of memory reveals that this overlooked area of training may offer a relatively easy means for improving content mastery and student achievement.

There are three types of memory. *Short-term memory* is good for about 30 seconds and is useful in doing simple computations. **Eidetic memory,** which often is forgotten about, is even shorter: It holds the mental image that the mind's eye needs to connect letters into words and words into sentences. Some reading specialists attribute one type of severe reading disability to weakness in eidetic memory. Finally, there is *long-term memory,* where the past resides. It has two functions: episodic and semantic memory. **Episodic memory** keeps track of our real experiences (or autobiographies), while *semantic memory* stores vicarious and school-type learnings.

There are several proven methods for improving semantic memory. These are particularly worthwhile because most people can achieve dramatic improvement in memory with relatively little training. More important, the impact of memory training on content mastery can be substantial and remarkably enduring; most things easily forgotten probably were poorly learned to begin with. Following are seven memory training methods that were derived from diverse sources spanning several centuries.

Seven Memory Training Techniques

Imaging
David Meier, director of the Center for Accelerated Learning, claims that guided *imaging* can create greater "ownership" of study material. Working with a colleague, Owen Caskey, Meier devised an interesting and telling experiment to verify this claim.[2] In the study, material on biology was shown to college students with two different types of videotaped presentation. Half the students were taught via a lively lecture accompanied by attractive props and illustrations. The other half received the identical material on a videotape that guided them to an internal, multisensory experience of the material.

---

[2]Cited in R. J. Trotter, "Better Learning: Imagine That," *Psychology Today,* 19(4), p. 22.

Students in the latter group first were presented with material describing the "elements of a typical brain neuron." Then they were told to imagine that they were floating around in the cytoplasm of a neuron. They were further instructed to conjure up a multisensory image of the cell, in which they would encounter a mild electrical charge, interact with various parts of the neuron, and even poke and play with the things they discovered. Most important, they were told to lock this in mind by realizing that they were inventing a vivid, memorable experience. The students in this group performed 12% better on immediate recall and *26%* better on long-term retention. From this it has been concluded that "There is no device for learning, no matter how sophisticated, that can equal the power, flexibility, and ease of use of the human imagination."

Loci Imaging

Loci imaging, a form of mental imaging, was well known among Greek orators. The idea is to take a familiar location and associate words and ideas with precise locations, or loci points, along the way. Uttero (1988) suggests that youngsters select a familiar spatial layout, such as their homes. Then they are encouraged to mentally place a list of items to be remembered in various rooms. When the items are to be recalled, students need only retrace their steps and retrieve the images from where they deposited them.

Spatial Arrangements

The *spatial arrangements* technique has some of the same characteristics as loci imaging, is equally simple, and lends itself even better to notetaking and conventional study. Words and ideas to be remembered are laid out in any desired simple spatial arrangement, such as an X, a K, or a 2 (see Figure 9.2).

Bellezza (1984) reports that this simple technique proved more effective than another, also ancient form of visual imaging in which one tries to create an unusual mental picture. For example, in trying to remember "baby," "window," and "ship,"

Figure 9.2   Spatial Arrangement Memory Training

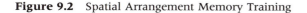

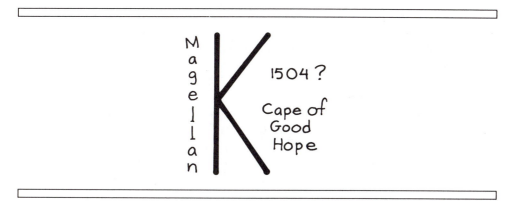

one might first visualize a baby breaking a window and then sailing away in a ship. Apparently the risk in this latter system is the need to remember the unusual, whereas the familiar symbols are more easily recalled even in stressful circumstances.

Clustering

Clustering, or the *progressive parts* approach, involves breaking down longer items to be learned and reorganizing them into parts for individual mastery (e.g., part A, part B, etc.). There is a conventional element of this approach that should be avoided: the tendency to begin study from the same starting point each time. It is better to begin study at different points each time so as not only to learn the initial points, A and B, well but to be fresh and attentive when beginning elsewhere, such as with points C and D. Semantic maps and outlines are good aids for this type of partitioning, because, according to Uttero (1988), they are helpful when studying a middle section (such as C or D) with a sense of its conceptual place in the longer piece.

Acronyms

Acronyms—memory words constructed from the first letter of each word in a list of words to be memorized—can be invaluable aids for life. An example of an acronym that almost every student of geography would be pleased to learn is HOMES, to signify the names of the Great Lakes: *H*uron, *O*ntario, *M*ichigan, *E*rie, and *S*uperior (Uttero, 1988). Another familiar acronym is ROY G. BIV, which represents the colors of the spectrum: *r*ed, *o*range, *y*ellow, *g*reen, *b*lue, *i*ndigo, and *v*iolet.

Read and Recite

It has been said that those who have the best memories for fact-based tests spend 20% of their time *reading* and 80% *reciting* what they want to learn. This is another way of saying that if you spent one hour reading and detailing your notes, next spend four more hours learning them.

Overlearning

Overlearning is the key to remembering. Most forgetting occurs due to poor initial learning; the rest results from fear and interference, often between what one learned initially and what one learned subsequently. The easiest way to overcome all three of these problems is to "overlearn" each section of material before going on to the next.

The power of overlearning was demonstrated by psychologists Paul Foos and Cherie Clark (1984) in a simple study that you can replicate with your own students. Students who were told to get ready for a multiple choice (or recognition-type test) did less well, even on multiple choice questions, than did those who were directed to prepare for an essay (or recall and integration) test. When preparing for unaided recall and recitation, memory will rise to the demand.

CONTENT AREA STRATEGIES FOR TEST TAKING

Taking Multiple Choice Tests

It is difficult to overstate the effects of test taking on the body and the ego. If test taking were a pill, it probably would never pass the Food and Drug Administration guidelines for benefit-to-risk ratio. Here are some ideas and methods, summarized and adapted from Pauk (1974), for use with students from intermediate to graduate school levels. Your students will appreciate your taking the time to share these with them.

Before the Test

Multiple choice examinations call for "recognition learning." In other words, you are given the right or best answer, but you must be able to recognize it. Theoretically, recognition learning does not require as thorough or deep an understanding of the material as an essay test does. However, it requires a familiarity with a broader range of facts and ideas. This leads to study hazards. It is rarely possible to "get by" on a multiple choice test by learning part of the material and "winging it" with the rest. *All* of the material must be reviewed, and because this task seems so large, you naturally tend to postpone it. This leads to last-minute cramming, which leaves you with a head filled with a jumble of facts but no real sense of preparation. You can avoid this pattern by preparing early.

During the Test

1. *Read the directions* for the whole test and each subsection.
   a. Note the number of items, and set a rough schedule for the amount of time you have available. Schedule time to check your work.
   b. Ask about guessing penalties, that is, whether points will be deducted for incorrect or no answers. If not, you should guess when you don't know the answer.
2. Answer the easy items first.
   a. Spending time on difficult questions raises anxiety and may cause you to forget information you knew when the test began.
   b. As you go through the test, you often will encounter information that will help you remember answers to earlier difficult items.
3. Read each question carefully.
   a. Cover the alternatives and read the question; try to state it in your own words. If the question is long and complex, underline the subject and the verb.
   b. With the alternatives still covered, make a guess at the answer. This will enable you to guide the selection instead of letting the alternatives guide you.

   c. Uncover the alternatives one at a time, noting each as "probable" or "not probable" before deciding. (Test constructors often put a correct but not necessarily best alternative at the top of the list.)

4. Use basic reasoning.
   a. If a question is in the negative form—for example, "One of the following is not a cause"—it will be helpful to look for three "true" answers; the one remaining false answer will be the correct one.
   b. Note appropriate grammatical structure from the stem to the alternative.
   c. General statements are more likely to be correct than specific statements, especially if you think of one exception.

5. Keep a positive attitude.
   a. Don't assume that the test is loaded with trick questions. If you adopt a skeptical attitude, you will read too much into the questions and spend too much time in needless internal debate.
   b. As an overall approach, read each question carefully but concentrate on the main point rather than the details.

6. If there is no penalty for guessing, eliminate any choices you know to be incorrect, then guess.

7. Watch yourself for signs of stress.
   a. During the test, pause briefly two or three times to consider whether you are in an overly tense state that could inhibit your performance: Neck muscles contracted? Palms clammy? Weak stomach?
   b. Avoid other anxiety reactions that break concentration: glancing frequently at the clock or the instructor, polishing eyeglasses, examining fingernails, gazing at the wall or ceiling, excessive yawning or stretching.

8. Check your work.
   a. Make sure you answered all questions you had skipped to come back to later.
   b. Check your answer sheet with your question sheet to make sure your numbering corresponds (check just every fifth question or so).
   c. Don't waste time reviewing answers of which you are confident.
   d. Change your answers if you have reason to. Research shows that contrary to common belief, three out of four times your *changes* will be correct. This may be because during a final check, the tension begins to lessen and thought processes are clearer.

After the Test

An excellent way to learn how to take tests is to analyze what you've done on one. When you get your paper back, *go over it,* noting not only what you did wrong but *why.* An hour or two spent in this way may be extremely valuable. See if you detect any point-eating tendencies such as not following directions, bogging yourself down in relatively unimportant items, or mistaking questions entirely. The next time you face an examination, consciously watch yourself for any weaknesses you noted.

Also note what you did *right*. This may spare you hours of worry the next time around. That test question that haunted you for the past several days may be the one you did best on. Often such analysis proves genuinely reassuring.

PORPE: A Strategy for Taking Essay Tests

Michele Simpson (1986) developed *PORPE (Predict-Organize-Rehearse-Practice-Evaluate)* in response to her students' anxiety about taking essay examinations. Her method evolved from a review of the research literature to find practical ideas about how proficient readers prepare for essay-type tests. PORPE's five steps guide students to behave like "effective readers who have some awareness and control of their own cognitive activities while they read and study" (Simpson, 1986, p. 408).

Steps in PORPE

1. *Predict.* Students are asked to predict essay questions which they might be asked. The teacher should make every effort to help students at this stage to raise synthesizing, analyzing, and application questions as well as more literal "what" and "when" types. One way to do this is to introduce them to a glossary of the most common words used in essay questions: *explain, criticize, compare, contrast, react, support, elaborate,* etc. As follow-up, the teacher should model the thought process s/he goes through in preparing (predicting) and phrasing essay questions on a previously studied body of information. Students then should prepare and share their predicted questions with classmates.
2. *Organize.* Students are encouraged to organize the information needed to answer predicted questions. Students are encouraged to use semantic maps and outlines for this purpose. Again, the teacher would do well to model this strategy.
3. *Rehearsal.* This is the conventional "study" or recall and recite step. Students should be encouraged to use appropriate *memory* devices.
4. *Practice.* In this step students practice composing, or answering essay-type questions. They should be reminded of the following in doing so:
   a. Work from an outline.
   b. Make sure your opening sentence rephrases the question and/or takes a clear position.
   c. Make the structure of your answer clear by using transitional words and phrases like "first," "on the other hand," "furthermore," and "finally."
   d. Give examples of major points.
   e. Reread what you wrote, and make appropriate editorial corrections.
5. *Evaluate.* This step continues logically from the latter portion of the last one, but should occur after a brief pause. The idea simply is to consider how a teacher might evaluate your answer. It may be necessary to conduct several sessions where students listen to, read, and discuss the relative merits of various essay

answers before they acquire the ability to get outside of themselves and review their own work.[3]

A recent study of PORPE found the strategy to be significantly more effective than question-answer recitation in improving comprehension and essay writing (Simpson, Hayes, & Stahl, 1988). PORPE also makes a great deal of sense at an intuitive level. It incorporates attention to metacognitive development, content mastery, effective predicting, organizing, and test writing. Structurally, it progresses in logical movements from teacher instruction, modeling, and guidance to total student independence and control—the purpose of all study skills instruction.

Tips for Avoiding Test Anxiety

Some tension at test time is desirable, because it keeps one mentally and physically alert. Too much tension, however, causes mental block. Share these suggestions with students to help them avoid excessive anxiety:

- Get a good night's sleep before the test. Sleep is one of the few activities that do not interfere with learning.
- Eat a good breakfast or lunch. This may calm the nervousness in your stomach and give you energy. (Don't overeat, though—overeating will make you sluggish—and avoid greasy and acidic foods.)
- Allow yourself enough time to get to class without hurrying. If your heart is already pounding, you will be more susceptible to test panic.
- Don't discuss questions at the classroom door. Hearing anything you didn't already know may weaken your confidence and send you into a state of anxiety.
- Leave your books at home. Flipping pages at the last minute will only upset you. If you must take something along, take a brief outline that you know well.
- Skip the difficult questions the first time through the test. Spending time on them will increase anxiety, which could cause you to block on other items. Also, the questions that follow may remind you of information you had forgotten.
- On the day of the test, try to avoid classmates who tend to panic or worry. Interaction with them may pull you into their frame of mind.
- Don't panic if others are busily writing and you are not—your thinking may be more profitable than their writing.
- Don't be upset if other students finish their tests before you do. Use as much time as you are allowed and feel you need. The students who leave early are not always the best students.
- If you still feel nervous during the test, try some emergency first aid: Inhale deeply, close your eyes, hold, then exhale slowly, letting your shoulders drop in

---

[3]From "PORPE: A Writing Strategy for Studying and Learning in the Content Areas" by M. L. Simpson, 1986, *Journal of Reading, 29,* pp. 407–414. Copyright 1986 by the International Reading Association. Reprinted with permission of Michele Simpson and the International Reading Association.

a relaxed manner. Think (very!) briefly about recreational activities that will be your "reward" when the test is over.

Whenever reading and studying are discussed, the topic of speed reading inevitably comes up. Read on to learn more about how much of what you hear about speed reading is true and how much may be a mirage.

SPEED READING: STUDY SKILL OR BLUE SMOKE AND MIRRORS?

Speed reading—or, more correctly, rate of reading—can vary greatly among individuals. On average, however, the rate increases from about 150 words per minute at fourth-grade level to approximately 250 words per minute by twelfth grade. In general, the rate at which one reads tends to be influenced by four factors:

1. The speaking-listening rate to which we all tend to become accustomed (about 180 words per minute)
2. Prior knowledge, or familiarity with the material
3. Personal speed of "central processing," that is, the rate at which one can receive and think about incoming information
4. One's purpose for reading

There is no evidence to suggest that habitually slow readers can be taught to read at super-high rates, although a few individuals quite naturally read up to about 900 words per minute (the upper limit of eye movement). Some individuals, nonetheless, believe otherwise, but they also tend to think that, initial aptitude notwithstanding, almost anyone can become a great ice skater, swimmer, or mathematician with hard work and determination—an unsupportable hypothesis. Such gentle souls are not so much "wrong" in their assertion as they are misguided. It is possible, after all, to control even your heartbeat if you are willing to turn your conscious mind and life energy over to a function that nature has put on automatic pilot. Rate training, like most things, generally comes down to a cost-to-benefit ratio: How much of myself am I willing to put on the line to go just a little faster?

Fortunately, the content teacher can help improve reading rate to a significant degree at small cost. This is possible simply by reminding students to read more rapidly and providing opportunities for them to do so. This is most easily done where there is adequate prior knowledge, such as when silent reading follows lecture and/or discussion (as in the L-R-D Heuristic and the Group Reading Activity). This can be parlayed into a compact and ready "rate-of-reading program" by adding occasional practice in scanning to "survey" before students read and skimming to find specific facts following reading. Further assistance can be provided in the form of a systematic reminder to use Berger's (1972–73) Hand Pacing approach: The hand is quicker than the eye and therefore can be used to sweep across and down the page with eyes following at an increasingly rapid but still comfortable rate. The teacher can keep a record of progress simply by multiplying reading time by the number of words read per minute.

Before leaving this topic, we should say something about commercial "speed reading" courses, since these are marketed in most communities—and to some naive school people. For the most part, these "programs" are like chicken soup: They can't hurt! However, they tend to be based largely on blue smoke and mirrors: The illusion of progress is created by sleights of hand.

One such trick is the typical entry "pretest"; it tends to be more difficult to comprehend than the exit or posttest. Professional speed hucksters will show you how number of words and even "readability estimates" for the pre- and posttests are "comparable." In fact, however, it is the greater idea density and the likelihood of low familiarity with the material that will affect rate the most, and neither of these factors is measurable by current readability formulas.

Another mirror trick is to offer an array of fancy machines such as tachistoscopic devices that flash numbers, words, and phrases at increasingly rapid rates to train rate and breadth of eye fixation. Purveyors of speed-reading courses will say that there is a high positive correlation among fixation time, rate, and reading comprehension. This is true but for two important (but overlooked) facts: The correlations are modest at best, and there is no evidence that more rapid fixations will result in more rapid reading. In fact, the inverse is true: Fixations and rate are more easily improved with comprehension training than comprehension and rate are improved with fixation training.

Another aspect of this mirror trick is accomplished by selling a speed-reading course to high-achieving professionals such as engineers, attorneys, and physicians. This is a mirror trick because focusing the attention of these otherwise high achievers on any factor will markedly improve performance in that area. Also, these individuals have developed the habit of reading materials related to their professions slowly and deliberately; therefore, speed-reading training can easily (but temporarily) boost their reading rates. Finally, these professionals are a volunteer audience—and willingness to pay time and money for anything constitutes high motivation and therefore inflated short-term gains.

The largest puff of blue smoke, however, often persuading even the most skeptical, is the "evidence" the speed kings offer: testimonials from respected people and—the ultimate bit of theatrics—"hard data." The latter typically is built on some kind of "index" based on rate and comprehension of reading. The mirror trick here is just plain "bogus"; rate is multiplied by comprehension on an entry and exit test, and the result is a fictitious spurt in reading speed. To illustrate, if your comprehension score on entry was 85% (probably on a difficult passage) and your "speed" was 275 words per minute, the multiplication of these figures will yield an "efficient reading index" of 23,375. On the other hand, if your exit scores were 70% comprehension (probably on easier material) and your rate was hyped to a mere 500 words per minute, your efficiency index would be a whopping 32,500!

This inflated bit of progress really amounts to a net *loss*. Most of what we read as professionals and as students we need to comprehend at higher, not lower, levels. Seventy percent comprehension is the same as misunderstanding about one-third of what one reads to learn. For most professionals such as pilots, engineers, and surgeons, even a 5% error factor may be too high.

Blue Smoke and Mirrors

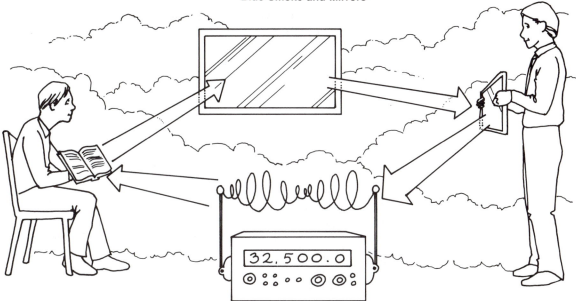

Shazam! You're reading at an effective reading rate of 32,500 WPM!

Finally, the strongest evidence against most commercial speed-reading programs cannot even be calculated, because their purveyors seldom disclose (1) who dropped out of the program; (2) who failed to show improvement despite all the manipulations; and (3) who achieved short-lived rate gains—which probably diminished to near zero by the time the credit card bill came due.

Several reading specialists advocate "flexibility" training over rate training, that is, adjustment of the reading rate to the purpose for reading. This is done by asking oneself, "How important is accuracy, and how fast should I be able to read this and still achieve my purpose, including mere enjoyment?" In summary, to promote rapid reading, urge and train students to

1. Be strategic readers and adapt rate to circumstances
2. Try to read everything about 10% to 20% faster
3. Periodically read something they already know fairly well as rapidly as they can (the L-R-D provides a good opportunity to practice this)
4. Be cautious, if not wary, of packaged speed-reading courses

CONTENT AREA STRATEGIES FOR LIFE MANAGEMENT

The essence of study skills is effective use of time. In fact, much of *life* management amounts to *time* management. Most students can benefit from a careful analysis of the way they typically use out-of-class time.

This section offers several methods for improving life management. Scheduling and use of Study Journals are two valuable strategies for time use analysis and improvement. Peer Supplementals provide a context for students to learn effective self-management habits from one another. PASS, the Problem-Solving Approach to Study Skills, is a teacher-guided strategy for identifying and dealing with personal learning and studying hurdles. The section concludes with a rather "homey" but often useful remedy—homilies.

Scheduling

Pauk (1974) suggests the following guidelines for analyzing study habits:

1. Start with a detailed schedule of how you currently spend your time. Use this to identify good and poor time use habits.
2. Prepare a master schedule by filling in all regularly scheduled activities: meals, classes, work, travel, sleep, and so on. This will show you where blocks of time are available for specific study tasks and recreational activities.
3. Make copies of your master schedule to use each week for planning specific study activities.
4. For each class, schedule a same-day review of notes.
5. Schedule study sessions at times when you are most likely to be alert and in the mood for studying.
6. Plan to do tasks that require the most concentration first, while your mind is fresh. (The tendency is to do the more routine, mechanical tasks first and put off the more difficult ones.)
7. Plan study time in blocks of no more than one hour. It is better to study in four 30-minute sessions than in a crammed 2-hour session.
8. Take time for good meals. Dietary deficiencies can result in irritability and fatigue.
9. Monitor your study time. Some classes will require more time than others. Try to estimate how much time *per week* you need for *each subject*.
10. Monitor your lapses. Which planned activities do you consistently omit? See if you can identify reasons for these omissions and formulate incentives for improvement.
11. Schedule reasonable amounts of time for relaxing. A workable schedule must be a plan for *living*, not merely for studying. Keep working at your schedule until you have developed a system you can live with.
12. Study when you study, and relax when you relax. If you allow thoughts about leisure activities to interfere with your studying, it is likely that worry about all the studying you didn't do will interfere with your leisure.
13. Use your study schedule for one week. Then consider these questions before planning your schedule for the following week:
    a. Did you over- or underestimate the amount of study time you needed?

b. Did you find some scheduled study times particularly inconvenient? How can you rearrange them?

c. Did conflicts arise? How did you deal with them?[4]

As students continue to revise and use their weekly schedules, they should find that they are making more efficient use of their time, are worrying less about getting everything done, and are better able to deal with unexpected events or assignments as they arise.

The next strategy also helps with life management skills. It encourages introspective analysis and personal growth as a student.

Study Journals

Keeping a Study Journal can make students more aware of their present study habits and attitudes. A *Study Journal* is simply a written record of thoughts and feelings about studying and about school. Students should be encouraged to make four or five brief journal entries each week, without undue concern for form or style. Guiding questions should be "What am I doing?" and "How do I feel about it?" Some categories for consideration include the following:

Classes: Participation or lack of it; difficulty paying attention; confidence level

Homework: Difficulty concentrating or "getting started"; organization of materials; strategies for studying

Tests: Thoughts before, during, and after tests; controlling anxiety

Time management: Difficulty getting everything done; setting priorities

Symptoms of stress: Fatigue, headaches, worry, apathy, guilt, problems in interpersonal relationships, insomnia, excessive snacking, and so on

Following are some sample Study Journal entries:

9/10   Algebra class always begins in English, but it soon becomes Greek. There must be something I can do to keep from getting lost about midway???

9/14   When I get home from school, I can't stand to face homework. Soon it's dinnertime, then the good programs are on, then I'm too tired. When are you supposed to do homework anyway?

9/25   I hate tests. I never seem to study the right things.

10/2   I've been having trouble falling asleep, and I wake up two hours early thinking about that darn paper due next week. I also find it impossible to stay awake after lunch.

After students have made several entries in their journals, they should be encouraged to look back over what they have written. Are there noticeable patterns?

---

[4]Walter Pauk, *How to Study in College,* Fourth Edition. Copyright © 1989 by Houghton Mifflin Company. Adapted with permission.

Are there certain kinds of situations that tend to precipitate stress? What coping strategies did students try? How effective were these?

We have found that Study Journals are much more likely to be kept when they are combined with the next strategy, which offers a place and a time for their use and reinforcement.

Peer Supplementals for Effective Use of Scheduled Study Periods

Many youngsters have scheduled "study periods" each day. However, they seldom use this time effectively. The content (or study hall) teacher can help students organize scheduled study periods into *Peer Supplementals*. With this technique, students are assigned certain roles and duties:

- *Note organizer role.* The note organizers are responsible for organizing lecture notes according to the emphasis given in class. They highlight major statements from the lesson and the text for the rest of the class.
- *Test questioner role.* The test questioners develop a series of test-type questions on class notes for all students to practice answering.
- *Resource gatherer role.* The resource gatherers find the information in the text that pertains to class notes, identifies discrepancies between text and class notes, and presents these to the instructor for clarification.
- *Inquirer role.* The inquirers are responsible for finding flaws in the logic and/or information provided in the text and/or in class. They consult other textual and human resources and work with the rest of the unit to raise proper "interrogatives" in appropriate content classes (see the Enabling Questions discussed earlier in this chapter for details on how to do this).

The teacher rotates the student roles periodically.

The basic idea of this approach is to show students how they might work together during study periods to become an efficient training "unit." The teacher first outlines the idea of a study unit and the value of "division of labor." Then the teacher describes the roles to be played by different students and assists students in organizing themselves accordingly.

Peer Supplementals should take up no more than a quarter of scheduled study periods. Content teachers might see fit to use scheduled class time, up to once per week, for this activity.

The next method is also based on group discussion. However, it focuses on identifying and solving individual learning problems.

PASS

The *Problem-solving Approach to Study Skills,* or *PASS* (Manzo & Casale, 1980), is a metacognitive strategy designed to communicate the attitude that school and learning present a series of problems that generally are manageable and often solvable by critical-constructive analysis and personal resolve. PASS was refined and tested with college students in case study fashion by Casale and Kelly (1980).

There is a minor tradition in education of teaching effective problem solving. There are several classic books on problem solving, such as *How to Solve It* (Polya, 1957), and more recent ones such as *The Ideal Problem Solver: A Guide for Improving Thinking, Learning, and Creativity* (Bransford & Stein, 1984). PASS may have a bit of an edge over these, because it does not have to struggle to become a new item in a curriculum; rather, it attempts to teach problem solving *incidentally*, in the context of real-life, student-selected problems. Most other approaches, in contrast, tend to identify and impart the steps of problem solving in some context-suspended state. Arguably, these approaches probably do not teach problem solving as much as they teach *about* it.

Steps in PASS

1. *Count.* The teacher presents students with a list of common study skills problems and asks them to check those that apply to them (see Figure 9.3).
2. *Characterize.* The teacher guides students in defining selected problems, and themselves, in specific terms. (The teacher urges students to take inventories of

Figure 9.3 Common Study Skills Problems

Directions: Check all that apply.

_____ 1. Missing class notes
_____ 2. Incomplete reading
_____ 3. Main idea
_____ 4. Missing details
_____ 5. Poor at inferencing
_____ 6. Poor memory
_____ 7. Text anxiety
_____ 8. Distracting thoughts
_____ 9. Poor attention span in class
_____ 10. Poor attention span while reading
_____ 11. Poor attention span while studying
_____ 12. Weak vocabulary
_____ 13. Poor informational background
_____ 14. Weak mathematical aptitude
_____ 15. Poor writing skills
_____ 16. Poor test-taking skills
_____ 17. Poor outlining skills
_____ 18. Poor library and citation skills
_____ 19. Poor classroom discussion skills
_____ 20. Others: _____

Figure 9.4   Instant Study Skills

1. *Come early to class and leave late.* Important guides to the material and tips on exams frequently are given in the first and last minutes of a lecture.
2. *Sit close to the front of the room.* Studies have shown that students who sit in the front of class make better grades. Perhaps this is true because those who choose to sit closer to the front are the more "motivated" students—but why not assume that a positive feedback loop is at work here; that is, proximity to the instructor increases concentration, which enhances motivation.
3. *Make lecture notes as complete as possible.* The most effective study time may be the actual hour of the lecture. Take extensive notes and concentrate during class, and you will have a good record for thought and home study.
4. *Review lecture notes as soon as possible.* Immediate review probably is the most powerful learning strategy known. Go over the lecture mentally as you walk to your next class. Make it a habit to briefly review class notes each school night.
5. *Preread before reading a section in the textbook.* This gives focus and purpose to reading and a built-in review mechanism.
6. *Underline after you have read a paragraph.* This focuses attention and concentration and avoids "automatic" reading or worse—mindless reading.
7. *On exams, read slowly and answer quickly.* Focus on the question stem instead of the choices. This prevents the frequent and irritating problem of "misreading the question."
8. *On exams, do the easy questions first.* Go through the test quickly. Skip and mark hard questions, and pick those up later. Attempting to do the difficult questions first can be emotionally disruptive, causing you to forget answers that you do know.
9. *Overlearn for exams.* Memorize as many things as you can. Research shows that over 90% of test anxiety can be reduced with better preparation.
10. *To make an A.* There is a relatively easy formula for making an A in any class. Ask yourself, "What is the very *most* the teacher would expect someone to do to get an A on this paper/test/project?" Then do more.

learning style, temperament, skills, abilities, and attitudes in an effort to reach a firmer sense of themselves as learners. The Learning Styles Inventory discussed in Chapter 3 can be helpful here.)

3. *Consider.* Students consider how they typically have dealt with their particular needs and problems and the possible merit in these intuitive coping strategies.
4. *Collect.* The class discusses and judges standard techniques for dealing with reading/study problems on the basis of their compatibility with each student's style and character. Where these appear incompatible, the procedures are dismissed as inappropriate.
5. *Create.* Students seek inventive alternatives that match their personal styles. This step is best handled initially in small groups and then in larger group discussions.

The next strategy tends to conveniently summarize much of what we have so far presented on time management, memory, rate of reading, and personal-social adjustment.

Figure 9.4 *continued*

11. *Hand pace to speed read.* To read faster and with better comprehension, take your hand and begin (right now!) to move it down the page. Gradually increase the speed of movement, and try to read along. "Hand pacing" has been proven effective by Allen Berger, an authority on speed reading.

12. *Spell with the mind's eye.* Spelling accuracy, according to authority Gerald G. Glass, is in "the mind's eye," not in the rules of spelling. Study a word in print (such as *business*) for a moment. Then look up and try to envision the word before you. Try to write the word by copying it from this mental image. Compare your results with the correct spelling. Repeat the process until you have spelled the word correctly three times in a row.

13. *Think "back and forth."* Periodically, try to predict the complete opposite position of a view you now hold or have read about. Giving consideration to the antithesis of a popular viewpoint often stimulates thought about reasonable syntheses, or positions, between the two extremes that otherwise might not occur to you. This back-and-forth reasoning, called *dialectical thinking,* is the foundation of all logical, analytical reasoning.

14. *Learn the "right words."* If you are anxious and unhappy, there is a good chance that you're saying the wrong, or emotionally charged, words to yourself, according to Drs. Ellis and Harper in *A Guide to Rational Living in an Irrational World* (1968). Therefore, use more understated words in everything you say to curb your distracting feelings. Begin by referring to your arch-enemy as a "scoundrel" rather than a "*&$##*@@%." You will be less disrupted, be more stable, and have greater constructive energy.

15. *Your past and present are your future.* Your present level of knowledge, or "personal schema," is the best predictor of how well you will read and learn now and in the future. Build your fund of information by reading an encyclopedia, almanac, or other nonfiction work for 15 minutes a day. You will be surprised at how quickly facts and ideas will begin to repeat themselves: "We find little in a book but what we put there," observed Joseph Joubert in 1842.

Instant Study Skills

To win student commitment to lifelong reading and learning, it is best to begin in an appealing and optimistic way. The content, home room, or study hall teacher can post the *instant study skills* list presented in Figure 9.4 on a bulletin board for students to read at their leisure. After a week or so, the teacher can begin to allude to the list and invite discussion of the relative merit of each skill in different situations. The list was first suggested by Gordon Friedel (1976) strictly for traditional study skills. The authors have adapted and extended it to include several other skills, from how to make an "A" to schema enhancement.

The content teacher's efforts to teach students how to study will be time well spent. Learning is as much attitudinal as it is intellectual. Teaching students how to study tells them that *they* are as important as the *content.* The next section illustrates how this can be done quite informally.

Homilies for Motivation and Life Management

It may sound a little corny, but we all need an occasional *homily*—a short and uplifting lesson—to strengthen faltering motivation and help clarify our values. Every teacher should possess and encourage students to collect a half-dozen or so adages, anecdotes, or fables of deep personal meaning that can serve as homilies to lift spirits and sights as needed.

Homilies can help reduce emotionally disruptive thought patterns and heighten common sense. They are brief forms of the universal truths often sought in great literature. Like proverbs, discussed in the next chapter, homilies provide a powerful way to communicate basic values and life management skills, especially when verbalized at the most "teachable moment." Homilies can reset our "emotional clocks" when they become erratic from the effects of stress or ennui (the feeling that all is meaningless). They are to mental health what vitamin supplements are to diet: great when you need them and harmless otherwise. The value of this little homily to mental hygiene is undoubtable:

> It is told that Frank Lloyd Wright designed a great cathedral in South America early in his career. Once, while at the construction site, he asked a worker, "What are you doing?" "Cutting stone," the worker grudgingly replied. Later Wright put the same question to another worker doing the same job. This time the reply was different: "I'm earning a living to feed my wife and family," said he. Still later, Wright put the same question to yet another stonecutter, who seemed to be much more attentive to his task. The worker paused, looked over at the building site, and said, "I'm helping Frank Lloyd Wright build a cathedral."

It is good to periodically ask ourselves exactly what (in the larger sense) we are doing. The answer might well explain the state and direction of our lives. A good nonsectarian supply of such homilies is Unity Village, Colbern Road, Lees Summit, MO 64063.

CHAPTER TIE-UPS

Graphic Organizer ◆ ◆ ◆

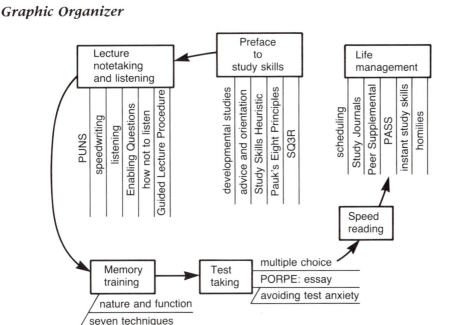

Critique and Anticipation ◆ ◆ ◆

Concern for attention to study skills is spreading. This growing concern offers new career opportunities, but it also represents another area of responsibility for teachers. This responsibility, unlike most others, is shared by students and can lighten the teacher's load by generating significant improvements in notetaking, class participation, and content mastery.

SQ3R is the most widely advocated self-study strategy, but it has not been shown to transfer easily from classroom to independent study. It can, however, be offered to students as a self-study parallel to the classroom Directed Reading Activity instructional framework. Notetaking, on the other hand, can be improved markedly. The Palmatier Unified Notetaking System for Learning effectively combines class and text notes into a single study system. Strategies for listening, memory training, test taking, reading rate flexibility, and life management also are available to content teachers to assist their students in making progress toward reading, thinking, study, and social-emotional maturity.

The next chapter details means for improving the reading, writing, study, and thinking skills of students with special needs.

TRADE SECRET

Underwriters' Assignment Book System

One problem teachers consistently face is getting students to record their home-work and other assignments. Students have elevated variations on the "I don't know" plea to a minor art form. One solution is a monitoring plan designed to underwrite the time-honored assignment pad.

The premise of this plan is that teachers must take time to train students in recording and organizing their schoolwork. Where this has been done consistently, students have been far less likely to resort to the "squeaky wheel" syndrome: working only on the most pressing assignment while ignoring all other work until another wheel (or teacher) squeaks.

A single teacher may employ this monitoring strategy effectively. It works best, however, when it is part of a schoolwide effort spearheaded by homeroom and/or study hall teachers. The plan provides an alternative to telling students to "get organized." Instead, the teacher *shows* students how to become organized and then monitors and grades their progress in doing so. It is important to note that since most students do not seem developmentally ready to assume this responsibility for themselves for some time, this system may realistically need to be kept intact throughout the intermediate and junior high school years, if not through high school.

The core of this approach is a student plan book. The plan book is simply a distinctively colored booklet containing a calendar with spaces large enough for the student to record all assignments for each day and due dates for long-term assignments. Students are required to carry their "blue books," as the students came to call them, to every class. Content teachers call for the plan books to be placed on the desk when they give an assignment. The plan books should be collected and graded by the homeroom or study hall teacher. Grades should reflect students' consistency and neatness in recording assignments. Assignments given but not completed due to absence or illness should be initialed by the student to indicate awareness of missed work. Grading plan books in this way has served as a tangible way to help teachers and students monitor and promote student progress toward effective self-management.

Of course, like any article, plan books can be lost or forgotten. Consequently, some provision for penalizing repeat offenders is necessary. It is wise, however, to avoid a complex process for handling such delinquency; rather, first wait to see how much of a problem it turns out to be. Complex systems of repurchasing and penalties can become counterproductive. Remember, the "blue book" strategy is designed to save valuable instructional time that otherwise would be lost to poor organization and preparation, not to create another bone of contention between teachers and students.

PART FOUR

Compensatory and Content Reading Programs

Special-Needs Students

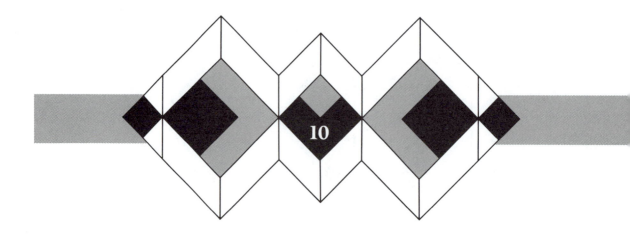

A helping word to one in trouble is often like a switch on a railroad track—an inch between wreck and smooth-rolling prosperity.

— *Henry Ward Beecher*

FOCUS

The methods presented in this chapter can be used by any teacher, but they will be of most interest to a reading resource teacher or a content teacher challenged by a special-needs student. Like the other methods described in this text, these strategies tend to be whole person, whole language oriented and to have a decidedly heuristic bent: They help students and teachers fight boredom by urging discovery of the most fruitful ways to teach and to learn.

OUTLINE

A UNIVERSAL SPECIAL-NEEDS STRATEGY: THE DICTATION METHOD
MOTIVATING THE UNMOTIVATED: STRATEGIES FOR REMEDIAL/
LEARNING-DISABLED/BEHAVIOR-DISORDERED STUDENTS

Encouraging Reading ◆ Improving Classroom Behavior and
Socialization ◆ Personal-Social Adjustment through Bibliotherapy and
Dialogue Journals ◆ Managing Decoding and Comprehension
Disorders ◆ Mainstreaming Strategies

ENGLISH AS A SECOND LANGUAGE (ESL), CULTURAL
HANDICAP, AND MULTICULTURALISM

Strategies for ESL ◆ Improving Oral Language, Comprehension, and Class
Participation: Note Cue Strategy ◆ Improving Comprehension, Dialectical
and Abstract Thinking, Language Skills, and Multicultural Outlook:
Proverbs Mastery Paradigm and Activities ◆ Vocabulary and Second
Language: Motor Imaging Revisited ◆ On the Light Side: Puns and
Parodies ◆ Winning the "Psycholinguistic Guessing Game"

CHAPTER TIE-UPS

Graphic Organizer ◆ Critique and Anticipation ◆ Trade Secret: Catch Them
Being Good

This chapter presents several strategies for teaching special-needs students in the content classroom setting. It focuses on those students who have reading/learning disabilities and those for whom English is a second language (ESL). It also considers at-risk students who have behavior disorders, suffer personal-social adjustment problems, and/or are culturally "different."

Most of the strategies and ideas developed for special-needs students will benefit most "typical" students as well. The reasons are simple. First, people are more alike than different from one another. Second, almost all students are likely to need at some time the kind of extraordinary thought and concern that tends to be reserved for the different, the reluctant, and the dysfunctional.

As you read this chapter, note that we again have tried to select heuristic methods—methods designed to create an environment conducive to teacher/student discovery and learning. You will also find that several of the ideas and practices advocated in this chapter are valuable in promoting a multicultural outlook and tolerance of differences.

We have not included the gifted as a category of special-needs student because too many issues surrounding the definition of "giftedness" are well beyond the scope of this text. However, you will find many methods throughout the text that are useful for challenging the most able students: Chapter 8 on critical-creative reading, for example, offers means of challenging *all* students to their fullest potential. This chapter provides a way to improve the abstract verbal reasoning of the gifted through analysis of proverbs. The next chapter describes several strategies for working with academically gifted students along the lines of enabling them to share their gifts with others; in particular, see the discussions of the Annotation Exchange system and Themed Schools.

A UNIVERSAL SPECIAL-NEEDS STRATEGY: THE DICTATION METHOD

While most of the methods presented in this chapter are appropriate for use in the regular content area classroom, a few are especially universal. The first of these, the *Dictation Method,* is a very old strategy whose benefits have been all but forgotten in contemporary education. To promote renewal of this traditional practice, we offer it here, in a modified form, as one of the closest things to a "one-size-fits-all" method for certain special and regular classroom situations.

The traditional form of the Dictation Method is a bit cumbersome. It calls for the teacher to read a passage aloud to students three times and, in most cases, requires long and sometimes tedious corrections and teacher evaluations. With only a few modifications, however, DiGiacomo (1982), a Florida language arts teacher, and Scarrozo (1983), a Connecticut remedial reading teacher, have independently derived simpler variations. We have combined these and added two "Readiness" and two "Extension" steps to bring traditional dictation up to speed with contemporary research findings and the content reading objectives of this text. Notice how the Dictation Method is designed to improve listening, speaking, reading, spelling, writing, self-correction, and content analysis.

Steps in Content-Based Dictation

Preparation

1. The teacher identifies a section of text of 50 to 250 words for dictation study.

Readiness

2. The teacher asks questions to stimulate a brief discussion of what students already know about the topic to be dictated.
3. The teacher writes key vocabulary words and hard-to-spell words on the chalkboard.

Actions

4. The teacher reads the selection aloud, including punctuation, at about half the normal rate of speech (about 60 to 90 words per minute), while students copy, word for word, everything dictated. On subsequent occasions, punctuation may be omitted so that students can practice punctuating from the length of pauses and other clues.
5. Students compare their work to the original material in the text. Using a simplified rubric, they tally their errors in four categories at the bottom or on the backs of their pages: word omissions or additions; spelling; capitalization; and punctuation.

Extension

6. Students write brief reactions to the dictated text and/or answer a few questions to check their basic comprehension (e.g., "State your feelings about Hamilton's idea of a National Bank. Who opposed it? Why?").
7. The teacher groups students and has them compare their reactions and answers.

This method can be used to good effect as often as once a week for periods of about 30 minutes.

Options and Elaborations

1. Have students keep a running record of their errors over a designated period.
2. Have students count *correct* spellings, punctuation, and capitalization rather than errors and record the number correct over the number possible.
3. Instruct students to read and write a summary, or other form of annotation, on the next portion of the text.
4. Give a brief comprehension test on the portion transcribed from dictation and the next portion read and critiqued.

MOTIVATING THE UNMOTIVATED: STRATEGIES FOR REMEDIAL/LEARNING-DISABLED/BEHAVIOR-DISORDERED STUDENTS

Chapter 5 on prereading defined and developed the role of *engagement theory* in motivation. This section adds a few more thoughts and devices for reaching the reluctant, and occasionally resentful, reader. It begins with ideas for encouraging reading, moves on to means and methods for dealing with disruptive behavior in the classroom, and concludes with several techniques for improving word attack, comprehension, personal-social adjustment problems, and content-based mainstreaming efforts.

Encouraging Reading

Here are several methods designed to encourage reading:

1. Establish an "Uninterrupted Sustained Silent Reading" (USSR) program. Once or twice a week, have students read anything they choose that is content related. Increase the time from 7 to 20 minutes over a few months. This lengthening period of USSR can become an effective management tool as well as a means of teaching students how to read in an increasingly sustained manner. To be sure that everyone has something to read and allay students' sense that this is an idle-time activity, it is best to store USSR materials in class and to periodically invite individual students to discuss what they are reading. This classroom-based activity can be broadened to include the entire school. It is most conducive if teachers, administrators, and *all* other personnel read for a brief sustained period as well.
2. Keep newspapers and magazines available in the classroom for students to read before or after class or during "downtime."
3. Have students fill out a Reading Interest Inventory indicating the types of books they enjoy reading. Invite the school librarian to help you develop a list of suggested book titles related to areas of interest.
4. Encourage students to join a book club and/or subscribe to magazines.
5. Become a reading motivator. Set aside a few minutes of classroom time occasionally to read a poem, newspaper, or magazine article to the class.
6. Let two or more students read the same book for a book report to the class.
7. Use computers to encourage reading. You can buy reading disks or borrow them from libraries to reinforce basic skills and to encourage active reading and responding.
8. Cut out and save the weekly book review section of the newspaper.
9. Ask students to see a movie or television program either before or after reading a book on which one or the other is based.
10. Have students create a Book or Article of the Week poster. Display books and articles with the caption "Read All About It." Invite students to share their books or articles with the class, noting the titles, authors, and sources and providing critiques.
11. Invite local authors or poets to class to discuss their works. (See the Language Shaping Paradigm in Chapter 12 for a "student works" version of this.)
12. Give students incentives to read. Students who read three or more books during a quarter or a semester can be rewarded with a donated gift certificate from a bookstore, record store, clothing store, or food store.
13. Conduct reading conferences with students. Personalized discussion and interest in a student's reading can be deeply motivating.

14. Get students engaged in reading and learning activities *ASAP*—"as soon as possible"—as they enter class, before they become distracted.

To help some reluctant minority-group youngsters settle in ASAP and listen attentively, Mary Morin, a Kansas City teacher, developed an activity that was suited to these students' needs in several ways. She told students that they should check the chalkboard each day as they came into the classroom. A few days each week, they would find a five-minute activity for which they would receive daily credit *if* they completed it within the first five minutes of class. An additional signal for these five-minute activities was that they were done on strips of paper rather than sheets (regular paper cut into strips approximately 8½" × 3"). Morin found that when students had earned class points within the first five minutes of class, she could more easily coax them into continued participation throughout the period—"You don't want to lose those points you just earned, do you?"

Morin's five-minute "ASAPs" often involved media activities. One of the most popular was listening to the audiotaped Lake Wobegon stories by Garrison Keillor. Students were instructed to sketch pictures illustrating the images formed in their minds' eyes as they were listening. When students developed skill in listening and illustrating, Morin added the requirement that they write captions underneath their illustrations. Eventually, she phased out the drawing portion and asked students to summarize the stories in words as they listened.

The next section offers further insights into dealing with behavioral problems.

Improving Classroom Behavior and Socialization

In general, it is good to remember that nothing improves one's hearing more than praise. Having said that, let's be realistic. Some students will misbehave or, in the words of contemporary psychologists, behave "inappropriately." For those occasions you may wish to refer to the Five-Step Response Heuristic, described next, which provides guidelines for direct handling of inappropriate behavior. You may also wish to try several indirect means of influencing student behavior. Ask-It-Rite, Bibliotherapy, and Note Cue are three such strategies and are described ahead. Each provides a way to help students visualize and experiment with more appropriate classroom behaviors. In addition, both Ask-It-Rite and Note Cue are oral language based to facilitate participation by low-achieving readers, who tend to be disruptive and/or apathetic in class.

The thrust of each of these methods is to help teachers and students deal with the sometimes corrosive effects of daily teaching and learning situations more so than the explosive ones—a need poignantly expressed by Chekhov's frequently cited observation that "Any idiot can face a crisis. It is this day-to-day living that wears you out."

Five-Step Response to Inappropriate Behavior
The goal of the *Five-Step Response* procedure is to teach students why they should behave appropriately and how to do so. Punishment need not be an issue unless the problem is very severe. This process begins when the student has general knowledge of the teacher's concerns.

Step 1: *I care about you.* Do not establish an adversary relationship with the student. Avoid getting too clinical or detached when disciplining. Words are not enough—your *actions* must indicate that you care. Begin by making positive comments about the student: "You are a good person/you do good work/there are many wonderful things about you. . . . "

Step 2: *Explain what occurred and why the behavior was inappropriate.* Accept the student, but reject the behavior: "If I ignored this problem, I would be teaching you that what you did was acceptable, and it was not."

Step 3: *Explain what you expect the student to do in the future.* Be specific.

Step 4: *Ask the student to summarize in his or her own words:*
   a. Why what the student did was inappropriate
   b. What the student could do in the future in place of the inappropriate behavior

   Work on item b until the student has a clear picture of what the alternatives are. Then periodically ask whether the student has tried one of the alternatives discussed.

Step 5: *I care about you.* Reaffirm step 1: "Let's move on and grow. Visualize yourself doing the right thing. Yes, I understand that you will lapse, but I will not lose faith in you. Don't lose faith in yourself."

Ask-It-Rite

Ask-It-Rite, or *AIR* (Manzo, 1975), is a simulation activity designed to help students and teachers question and listen more politely to each other. It focuses on the effective use of questioning in the classroom.

AIR requires the assistance of an extra teacher or a guidance counselor. Eight to ten students are selected to represent the class. The remainder of the class serves as a "gallery," making notes to provide objective counterpoint for a postsimulation discussion.

AIR essentially is a "stop action" procedure. The teacher prepares and teaches a typical lesson, and students are expected to respond as they typically do, with one addition: Any member of the class, including the visiting teacher/counselor, may suspend the lesson interaction by simply saying "stop action." During this lapse—which is somewhat like a stage aside—comment is permitted on virtually anything that in the speaker's opinion may be having a strong influence—positive or negative—on learning. The visiting teacher/counselor has the most objective point of view for orchestrating discussion during "stop action."

Both students and teacher tend to take the opportunity to examine their feelings and motivations and to puzzle over mutually acceptable resolutions. Whenever a reasonable resolution is proposed, the "action" is resumed and everyone takes note of whether the suggested change has the desired effect. If it does not, further examination and modification are tried.

Figure 10.1 presents an anecdotal account of AIR. See also Chapter 14 for a discussion of State-It-Rite (SIR), a variation that is especially suitable for vocational education students.

Figure 10.1   Anecdotal Account of AIR

Situation: In a high school English class, a teacher is rushing through a lesson on the parts of speech so that the class can begin certain related exercises in their text. Students appear confused.

The visiting teacher interrupts the lesson. "Stop action," he says. He then asks the class, "Are you understanding what's being said? You all look so confused." The class agrees that most of them are confused. "What can be done?" he asks. After some thought, the class concludes that they should simply tell the teacher they are confused. "How would you tell her?" the visiting teacher asks. "Just tell her," they say. "OK, let's try just telling the teacher and see what happens," agrees the visitor. "Resume action."

A moment later, a student raises his hand. "We don't know what you're talking about," the student says bluntly. The teacher, while fully expecting what the student was going to say, is visibly shaken. She recoils, pulling herself behind a podium, and struggles for something to say.

The visiting teacher again asks for a "stop action." "Well, what have we done?" he asks the class. They have hurt the teacher's feelings, they conclude, and probably shouldn't say anything next time. "Do you mean that you haven't the right to say what you have said?" the visiting teacher queries. "Well, no, but how should it be said?" the class asks. With this cue, a discussion about the distinction between aggressive and assertive statements develops. New, more assertive, but less aggressive wording is formulated. The original lesson is resumed again.

A moment into the lesson, the same student raises his hand. The teacher calls on him. The student says, "Miss Jewel, I've been trying to follow what you've been saying, but my mind sometimes wanders, so I'm not sure I understand."

"Hmmm," she says, moving toward him, "maybe I'd better go over this again." In a single moment, the teacher's body language has changed. She is reaching out to assist a student in need. The class is drawn in by the positive alteration in mood. Now all listen more intently, forgetting that this is only a "simulated" lesson.

The visiting teacher again says, "Stop action" and, in a soft voice, draws the class's attention to the real lesson to be learned: When you take the time to ask or state it properly, everyone benefits and your teacher becomes your able and willing assistant in your efforts to learn.

Personal-Social Adjustment through Bibliotherapy and Dialogue Journals

For students who are inclined to read, Bibliotherapy can be an effective means of dealing with personal-social adjustment problems. *Bibliotherapy* essentially means healing through reading (Edwards & Simpson, 1986). Generally it entails redirecting students' perceptions and attitudes in a healthy direction by getting the right reading material to the right student at the right time. Bibliotherapy has been viewed as a way to trigger an interaction between the reader's personality and the author's story or message.

The sources of problems students encounter as they grow and mature are varied: cultural differences, family relationships, moving, divorce, peer pressure, physical handicaps, racial prejudice, death of loved ones, and many others. Bibliotherapy is a means of "empowering" students to deal with these personal-social adjustment dilemmas. When a student has been "matched" to a book or selection that deals with the situation he or she is facing, three processes are triggered: empathy, catharsis, and insight. *Empathy* is the act of associating some real or fictional character in literature with oneself. *Catharsis* occurs when the reader observes the empathetic character working through a problem to a successful release of emotional tension. Through empathy and catharsis comes further *insight:* the sense of self-discovery that comes with recognizing aspects of oneself and one's situation in a written tale.

Wherever possible, the teacher or counselor who recommends a book to a student should invite the student to retell the story, highlighting incidents and feelings that are relevant to the central situation. Changes in behavior, feelings, and relationships should be looked at closely to permit vivid identification and empathy with the textual characters. Most important, the reader should have an opportunity to form a conclusion about the consequences of certain behaviors or feelings to determine whether or not these behaviors or feelings improve human relationships and happiness (Heaton & Lewis, 1955).

The teacher/counselor may use Bibliotherapy in one of two ways. First, the teacher/counselor can help a student solve an *existing* emotional problem or anxiety by recommending a book that recounts an experience or situation similar to the student's own. By recognizing the problem and its solution in literature, the student may gain new insights about his or her own problem and then can take steps to solve it. Second, the teacher or counselor may use Bibliotherapy for *preventive* assistance. A student who has experienced a situation through literature may be better able to deal with similar situations encountered in real life. This technique can be compared to the process of inoculation against contagious diseases. Use of an instrument such as the Luscher Color Test (Luscher, 1969) or the Manzo Bestiary Inventory (Manzo, 1975b) can help students and teacher to more accurately pinpoint the kinds of problems a student might be having or could encounter.

Bibliotherapy can be enhanced by the addition of a writing component. The easiest way to do this is to have students keep personal journals in which they write brief reactions—at least one sentence—to whatever they read. These can be stored in a box in the classroom where, with students' prior approval, the teacher may read through them and write back personal notes and thoughts. Of course, notes and dialog need not be limited to textual material; they can be extended to anything a student wishes to write. The idea of *Dialogue Journals,* as Staton (1980) calls this process, is as old as conversation between caring friends. Teachers who use this approach regularly report touching insights revealed and warm relationships formed with students who at first appeared apathetic, hostile, or otherwise reluctant to learn (Kirby & Liner, 1981).

Bibliotherapy and Dialogue Journals offer students help in adjustment and progress toward reading, language, thinking, and personal-social maturity by

1. Teaching students to think positively
2. Encouraging students to talk freely about their problems
3. Helping students analyze their attitudes and modes of behavior
4. Pointing out that there are alternative and constructive ways to solve most adjustment problems
5. Helping students compare their problems with others' as a means of lessening internal tension and conflicts in a society that sometimes can appear quite uncaring (Rongione, 1972, as cited in Edwards & Simpson, 1986)

As classroom disruptions begin to diminish and participation starts to rise, it is necessary to simultaneously begin closing gaps in the skill and knowledge levels of remedial students. Failure to do so can inhibit progress and even foster a more embittered and hopeless attitude. The methods described ahead are particularly useful for making quick-paced progress.

Managing Decoding and Comprehension Disorders

The most essential facets of effective reading are decoding and comprehension. Poor readers, by definition, have difficulty with either or both. Previous chapters have described a basic approach to word decoding—Gray's Phonic Elements Paradigm—and comprehension disorders—ReQuest and the Guided Reading Procedure, among others. This section outlines two more teaching methods that are particularly appropriate for addressing these fundamental skills in a relatively direct and explicit way. The Glass Analysis (Glass, 1983) offers students training in a self-help strategy for dealing with word attack problems. The Think Aloud procedure (Davey, 1983) assists students in "self-fixing" perceived comprehension problems. A third "special" method of dealing with comprehension dysfunctions is described in the section on English as a second language. It involves teaching and analyzing proverbs in certain systematic ways.

The Glass Analysis Approach to Teaching the Decoding Aspects of Reading

Some educators believe that word analysis skills need not be taught beyond the sixth grade. They feel that greater emphasis on meaning and comprehension automatically will improve deficient word attack skills. Linguist Nancy Lewkowicz (1987), however, argues convincingly that "decoding is a comprehension skill" and that older students often require and even welcome some explicit instruction in word analysis skills.

Most teachers need not be convinced that many students, particularly the socioeconomically disadvantaged and foreign born, could profit from continuing developmental and corrective training in word analysis. National results on standardized reading tests continue to show a wider spread of reading levels at each successive grade level. This means that if you have a heterogeneously grouped class at any grade level, you are likely to have several students reading at the third-grade level. In most school settings, resources for referring students with decoding deficits for remedial assistance outside the regular classroom will be available. This does not, however, diminish the content teacher's responsibility for these students when they are in his or her class.

Glass Analysis was developed for use with students who have failed to learn basic reading skills through the traditional instructional program. It is a simple procedure that enables virtually anyone who knows how to decode to teach others how to do so. It can be used at opportune times as a whole-class strategy when introducing or reinforcing difficult content terms. Moreover, it takes the mystery out of dealing with the lowest readers. One need not know about diphthongs, digraphs, and other phonic elements and rules. One simply provides occasional assistance when time and circumstances permit.

Glass Analysis is based on two verbal protocols, or "scripts." The scripts are designed to teach students to focus attention on the word and increase their familiarity with the sounds of the most common letter clusters in the English language. The sound for *ing,* for example, has a high frequency of occurrence and is more easily learned as a cluster than as three separate letter sounds that then must be synthesized. Following are the guidelines and steps for using Glass Analysis.

Some Basic Ideas on Teaching Decoding

- Students should continuously look at the word. Never cover part of the word or point to letters when presenting the word.
- Do not include definitions of words in your instruction unless a student asks.
- Reinforce students for correct responses. If a student cannot answer a question, state the answer and return to the question before finishing the word.

Steps in Glass Analysis

1. Write the word to be taught on the chalkboard or a large card.
2. Pronounce the word. Then teach it using as many combinations of letter clusters as is sensible.
3. Use the following questions or verbal scripts:

    "What letters make the ___ ⟨ch⟩ ___ sound?

   After you have used this question with the possible combinations, ask

    "What sound do the letters ___ ⟨c/h⟩ ___ make?

Figure 10.2 illustrates how Glass would use this approach with a new word prior to silent reading. See Figure 10.3 for a listing of common letter clusters, grouped according to difficulty level.

Uses of Glass Analysis. An effective developmental decoding program could use Glass Analysis in three ways:

1. The intermediate and middle school content teacher incidentally uses this simple "letter-clustering" approach each time a new technical or content word is introduced. ("The word is *photosynthesis.* What letters make the *photo* sound? What letters make the *syn* sound? The *thesis* sound? What is the whole word again?")
2. The content teacher occasionally previews textual material assigned for reading and uses Glass Analysis to teach any challenging words, especially foreign-lan-

Figure 10.2 Example of Glass
Analysis

The teacher writes the word *forgetfulness* in large letters on the chalkboard. Then the teacher uses the Glass Analysis script as follows:

In the word *forgetfulness*, what letters make the *for* sound?
The ⟨or⟩ sound?
What letters make the ⟨et⟩ sound?
The ⟨get⟩ sound?
What letters make the ⟨forget⟩ sound?
In the word *forgetfulness*, what letters make the ⟨ful⟩ sound?
The ⟨forgetful⟩ sound?
What letters make the ⟨fulness⟩ sound?
What letters make the ⟨getfulness⟩ sound?

[Notice how many structures can be learned in just one word—all transferable to other words.]

In the word *forgetfulness*, what sound do the letters f/o/r make?
What sound do the letters e/t make?
The g/e/t?
The f/o/r/g/e/t?
What sound do the letters f/u/l make?
What sound does g/e/t/f/u/l make?
What sound does e/s/s make?
n/e/s/s?
In the word *forgetfulness*, what sound do the letters f/u/l/n/e/s/s
   make?
g/e/t/f/u/l/n/e/s/s?
If I took off the letters f/o/r, what sound would be left?
If I took off the *ness* sound, what sound would be left?
What is the whole word?

guage terms, that occur in text. ("This is the Italian word *ciao*. Which letters make the *ch* sound in Italian? Which make the *ow* sound? How is the whole word pronounced again?")

3. All students with serious decoding deficiencies are scheduled for one to five 15-minute sessions per week in which Glass Analysis tutoring is provided. "Decoding stations" are set up in convenient, unobtrusive places throughout the school. These are staffed by a reading specialist, by teachers serving a "duty" period, and/or by paraprofessionals. (Glass Analysis letter cluster kits for such intensive training are available from Easier-to-Learn, Inc., P.O. Box 329, Garden City, NY 11530, 516-475-3803.)

Figure 10.3 contains some of the more popular letter clusters. See the anonymous poem in Figure 10.8 (page 334) for a lively demonstration of the challenges the English language offers to those determined to master its wily ways with words.

Figure 10.3   Glass Analysis Letter Clusters by Difficulty Level

Starters	Medium One	Medium Two	Harder One	Harder Two
1. at	1. ed	1. all	1. fowl	1. er
2. ing	2. ig	2. aw	2. us	2. air
3. et	3. ip	3. el(l)	3. ll(l)	3. al
4. it	4. ud	4. eck	4. ite	4. ied
5. ot	5. id	5. ice	5. es(s)	5. ew
6. im	6. en	6. ick	6. om	6. ire
7. op	7. ug	7. if(f)	7. oke	7. ear
8. an	8. ut	8. ink	8. ore	8. eal
9. ay	9. ar	9. ob	9. tow	9. t̄ēa
10. ed	10. em	10. od	10. ās̄t	10. ēē
11. am	11. up	11. og	11. ane	11. cāre
12. un	12. ate	12. ub	12. eat	12. dēaf
13. in	13. ent	13. uf(f)	13. as(s)	13. ōāt
14. ap	14. est	14. ush	14. ev	14. ue
15. and	15. ake	15. able	15. ind	15. oo
16. ack	16. ide	16. ight	16. oss	16. ou
17. um	17. ock	17. is(s)	17. oem	17. ound
18. ab	18. ade	18. on	18. ost	18. ure
19. ag	19. ame	19. or	19. rol(l)	19. ture
20. old	20. ape	20. ul(l)	20. ōnē	20. ur
21. ash	21. ace	21. ac	21. ale	21. ir
22. ish	22. ang	22. af(f)	22. ave	22. ai
	23. enk	23. ook	23. ove	23. au
	24. ong	24. tion	24. folly	24. oi
			25. āgē	

Comprehension "Fix-up" Strategies

Davey (1983) asserts that the teacher can greatly help students with comprehension problems by periodically modeling the (metacognitive) processes and options available while reading. According to Davey, there are five techniques that poor readers fail to utilize:

1. Poor readers are unable to form good *hypotheses* about the text's meaning before they start reading.
2. They don't reorganize information into *mental images* as they read.
3. They don't use their *prior knowledge* about the subject.
4. They don't always *monitor* their comprehension as they read.
5. If they have a comprehension problem, they don't have the skills to *"fix up"* the difficulty.

Davey suggests that teachers simply need to read difficult text passages aloud to students and model the methods they use to comprehend reading material. Some strategies to be demonstrated during "think-alouds" are as follows:

1. Show students how to *form hypotheses* ("I predict . . . ").
2. Show students how to create visual images ("I have a picture in my mind of . . .").
3. Share an analogy. *Link information* the students already have with the material they are reading.
4. Verbalize a confusing point. *Demonstrate the strategies* you use to monitor comprehension ("This doesn't make sense.").
5. Show students how to *use "fix-up strategies"* ("I'd better reread this"; "Maybe I'll read ahead to see if this gets clearer"; "I'd better look up that word").

To follow up on the last think-aloud strategy, there are basically six "fix-up" strategies to draw upon when comprehension problems arise:

1. Ignore the problem and continue reading.
2. Suspend judgment and continue reading.
3. Form a tentative hypothesis and continue reading.
4. Reread the sentence.
5. Reread the previous sentences.
6. Go to an expert source for further assistance, such as a teacher, friend, or reference book. (Collins & Smith, 1980; Baker & Brown, 1984)

These options can also be called up and modeled in the regular content classroom while using methods such as the ReQuest Procedure, the Oral Reading Strategy, and the Listen-Read-Discuss Heuristic.

Mainstreaming Strategies

Federal Public Law 94-142 mandates that learning-disabled and handicapped youngsters attend school in a "least restrictive environment." This has been taken to mean that wherever possible such students will be "mainstreamed"—expected to attend and be accommodated in regular classes.

Most of the methodology of the content area reading movement is suitable for meeting this requirement. Maring and Furman (1985) have made an especially strong case for seven "whole-class" strategies for helping mainstreamed youngsters "read and listen" better in content area classes:

1. Use Manzo's Oral Reading Strategy (see Chapter 2 for details) at least once a week to increase familiarity and comfortableness with the language of the text.
2. Use the whole-class graphic organizer called *Pyramiding* (Clewell & Haidemos 1983). This activity offers group assistance to learning-disabled students in identifying, classifying, and properly subordinating terms and ideas found in text.
   a. Each student reads silently to identify and write down key facts and ideas.

    b. The teacher leads a discussion, using the chalkboard to "pyramid," or group, facts and phrases into logical categories.

    c. The class decides on a sentence that answers the question "What is the author saying about these ideas?" This sentence forms the base of the triangle (see Figure 10.4.)

3. Enhance and review the Informal Textbook Inventory described in Chapter 3 to help make the course textbook more "user friendly":

    a. How many pages are in the glossary?

    b. Where could you find more information about a term defined in the glossary? (Answer: The index)

    c. What are the first and last page numbers of the index?

    d. Where would you find out about the author's point of view and reasons for writing the text? (Answer: Usually in the preface; sometimes in the introduction)

    e. Where can you most quickly acquire an overview of the major topics addressed in the text? (Answer: The table of contents)

    f. What types of questions are at the end of the chapters? (Answer: Factual questions, questions that involve thinking beyond what is literally stated, vocabulary exercises, and so on)

    g. Of what value and purpose are the introduction and conclusion parts of the chapters? (Answer: They explain what the chapter *will be* about and what it *was* about, respectively.)

    h. What is the purpose of boldface and italics? (Answer: They point out very important terms. Usually these terms are explained in the surrounding context.)

    i. If you were going to read a chapter in three sittings, how would you divide up your study of the chapter? (Answer: Not by dividing the number of pages

Figure 10.4 Whole-Class Strategies for Special-Needs Students

Source: From "Seven 'Whole Class' Strategies to Help Mainstreamed Young People Read and Listen Better in Content Area Classes" by G. Maring and G. Furman, 1985, *Journal of Reading, 28,* p. 696. Copyright 1985 by the International Reading Association. Reprinted with permission of Gerald Maring and the International Reading Association.

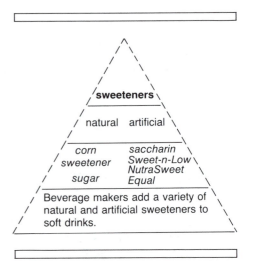

into three equal parts. A chapter should be studied according to the logical divisions indicated by its subheads or sections.)

    j. When your teacher assigns questions at the end of the chapter for homework, should you read them before or after you begin reading the chapter? (Answer: Before—this will make your reading more efficient.)

    k. Why is knowing the parts of the textbook and how to use them important? (Answer: It saves you time when you are looking for information)

    l. Why are some terms in the index indented? (Answer: They are the important components of a larger or broader concept.)[1]

4. Use the Contextual Redefinition strategy (Moore, Readence, & Rickelman, 1982).

    a. Identify words essential to the content but unfamiliar to your students.

    b. Write sentences on the board using these words (use sentences from the text, but if these prove contextually ambiguous, create your own).

    c. Ask the class to attempt to define the words from analysis of sentence context and to explain their conjectures.

    d. Write the meanings they conjecture on the board. Then have them read to verify and/or correct their impressions.

    e. In postreading discussion, have the class reanalyze the terms and conjectured meanings and explain why they stand by or wish to change their impressions of meanings. (Stressing context clues, as discussed in Chapter 5, can be problematic. In this method, however, the teacher guides the process, and immediately corrects any misapprehension.)

5. Use Words on the Wall (Cunningham, Cunningham, & Arthur, 1981) as an uncomplicated means of providing learning-disabled and other students with an easily available set of key words from the text to which they can refer for meaning, significance, spelling, and increased familiarity. Simply write key words with a felt-tip marker on half-sheets of paper and tape them on the walls during a given unit of study.

6. Conduct the Guided Reading Procedure (see Chapter 4 for details) with the following specifications:

    a. Use the procedure every two weeks, and administer a delayed retention test in the intervening week.

    b. Try to get mainstreamed readers to contribute free recalls early in the lesson before the more able students contribute all of the easiest information.

    c. Reread the information on the board as students try to decide which items are main ideas, which are related details, and how to sequence the information.

7. Build "crutches" into reading guides:

    a. Mark with asterisks those questions you feel are most necessary and appropriate for mainstreamed youngsters to answer. Tell them to answer these questions first.

---

[1]List items a through l from "Seven 'Whole Class' Strategies to Help Mainstreamed Young People Read and Listen Better in Content Area Classes" by G. Maring and G. Furman, 1985, *Journal of Reading, 28,* p. 696. Copyright 1985 by the International Reading Association. Reprinted with permission of Gerald Maring and the International Reading Association.

b. Put page, column, and paragraph numbers after certain questions to better guide those students who might have difficulty finding these (Wilkins & Miller, 1983); for example, "92, 2, 2" means page 92, second column, second paragraph.

ENGLISH AS A SECOND LANGUAGE (ESL), CULTURAL HANDICAP, AND MULTICULTURALISM

Strategies for ESL

The role of schema theory, or the importance of background knowledge and experience in reading comprehension, is still a relatively new concept in second-language instruction (Nelson, 1987). However, this construct is now taking a firm hold. ESL specialist Patricia Johnson, for example, has found that the culture of origin of a story has a greater effect on comprehension than does the level of syntactical or semantic complexity (Johnson, 1981). Other ESL specialists are busily replicating and building on other findings that relate reader schema to comprehension (e.g., Carrell, 1984; Obah, 1983). The increasing numbers of youngsters pouring into our schools from foreign and diverse cultural backgrounds are once again hastening the need for all educators to be conversant with the precepts of ESL. Past efforts to accommodate non-Anglo-American youngsters have consistently resulted in a richer, more diverse, and stronger nation.

Many of the methods devised and developed for content area reading have proven especially appropriate for use with linguistically and culturally different students. In many instances, these methods need not even be modified but merely used as described. This certainly applies to strategies such as ReQuest, which a recent study reported to be profoundly effective in ESL classes (McKenzie, Ericson, & Hunter, 1988), as well as to Question-Only, the Cultural-Academic Trivia game, the Subjective Approach to Vocabulary, and most variations on the cloze procedure. See also the Language Shaping Paradigm in the English methods section in Chapter 12. For this chapter, we have selected three strategies we believe are particularly useful with ESL and culturally different students, whether native or foreign born.

The most appealing feature of these methods is that in addressing second-language needs, they simultaneously account for certain universal needs shared by core culture and ethnic Americans. Among the most prominent of these are the need for a multicultural outlook; the need to reconnect ourselves to basic values and wisdom; the need to think abstractly as a requisite to thinking adaptively; and the need to actively participate in class, that is, conduct ourselves in harmony with others while pursuing individual goals. Let us see how the three methods described in this section can help us achieve these and other valued educational goals. We will also see why these methods might also be appropriate for the unmotivated and occasionally disruptive students addressed in the first portion of the chapter.

Improving Oral Language, Comprehension, and Class Participation: Note Cue Strategy

One of the basic but often overlooked problems in achieving effective classroom learning is that students are not taught how to participate in class, that is, to ask, answer, and comment. ESL, at-risk, and culturally different students find these skills especially difficult to acquire. These students often are unfamiliar with the more subtle aspects of the English language, such as tempo, volume, and social protocols.

Note Cue (Manzo & Manzo, 1987a) is a form of strategic parroting designed to show students how a well-orchestrated lesson might occur. In some ways it resembles ''spotting,'' a technique used in physical education to guide initial attempts at tumbling (see Figure 10.5). It is very much a proprioceptive learning experience, like Motor Imaging, and therefore is a form of sensorimotor schema enhancement: The mind *and* the body learn the new routines.

In Note Cue, the student need not think a great deal about *how* to say something, merely *when* to say it. Several field tests of Note Cue suggest that it is an effective means of bringing structure and serenity to discussion that students find comforting and are willing to try to emulate thereafter. (This makes Note Cue a good bet for times when you will be observed and evaluated by a supervisor.)

Note Cue is particularly suitable for ESL and culturally disadvantaged students, because it is a whole language approach that offers opportunities for guided reading, speaking, listening, cooperative interaction, and writing.

Figure 10.5   Note Cue Is Like Acrobatic ''Spotting''

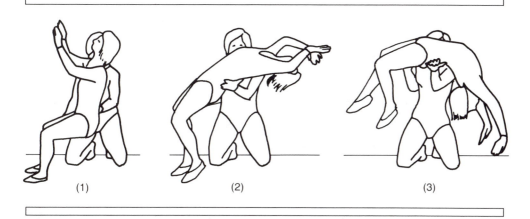

(1)   (2)   (3)

Source: From *Handbook of Gymnastics in the Schools* (p. 166) by J. A. Baley, 1974, Newton, MA.: Allyn and Bacon. Reprinted with permission.

Note Cue: What You See Is What You Say

Prerequisite.   Students should have been taught simple rules for surveying a selection before reading.

Materials.   Textbook selection, trade book, or basal reading story and index cards.

Preparation.   Prepare two sets of cards, one for prereading and one for postreading. On the prereading cards, write prereading (i.e., predictive) questions (one per card), answers (one per card), and comments (one per card). Write the label "Question," "Answer," or "Comment" at the top of each card. Leave a few blank cards (initially just one, then about one more blank each time you use the strategy until only 20% of the cards contain statements). Questions, Answers, and Comments should focus on predicting main topics, important events, and outcomes. Write in pencil, and remember to reread and edit your cards. Prepare the postreading cards the same way, but shift the focus from prediction to verification—what the passage actually states—and related evaluative Questions and Comments.

In preparing both sets of cards, be sure the Answer card is phrased clearly enough to be easily matched to the Question card (e.g., Q: Who followed Abraham Lincoln into the presidency? A: Andrew Johnson followed Abraham Lincoln into the presidency [not simply A: Andrew Johnson]).

Prereading Activity

Step 1: Students are instructed to survey the reading material to try to predict what it will be about. They are told that a brief written test will follow reading and discussion of the selection.

Step 2: While students are surveying, the teacher places one or more random or selected prereading cards on each student's desk.

Step 3: Students are instructed to read their card(s) silently and think about *when* they should read it (them) and about whether they wish to add anything else.

Step 4: Students with blank cards are instructed to think of a Question, Answer, or Comment and, if time permits, write it on their cards.

Step 5: The teacher begins the prereading, or prediction, stage of the discussion by asking who has a Question or Comment that seems to provide a good idea of what the selection will be about. If a Question is read, the teacher asks who has an Answer that seems to fit it. This process continues until the teacher feels that students have a sense of what the passage will be about. (This step should take no more than 10 minutes. The brisk pace and aura of evolving a purpose for reading will convey to students that not all cards need to be read to establish a reasonable purpose for reading).

Step 6: The teacher instructs students to read the selection silently to test their predictions. The teacher also reminds them to read their postreading cards, which will be placed on their desks while they are reading. (The teacher announces that he or she will come to the desk of any student who raises a hand for assistance.)

Postreading Discussion

Step 7: The teacher asks, "Who has a good Question to check comprehension of this selection?"; then "Who has a good Answer to that Question?"; then "Who has a Comment that seems right to state?"; and finally, "Who has reaction(s) or personal Comment(s)?" The last question is intended to encourage extemporaneous statements as well as statements read from cards.

Follow-up

Step 8: Within the same class period, or later if preferred, the teacher gives a test of 5 to 10 questions that require brief written responses. Most questions should be taken directly from the cards to build an appreciation of the cooperative value in reading a cue card for all to hear and profit from.

Amendments and Options.   Several options and amendments to Note Cue have been suggested from our field trials of the method. If initial participation is slow to develop, try these options:

1. Get things going by reading a Question or Comment card yourself.
2. Simply call on someone by name to read his or her card.
3. Stimulate interest by inverting the process slightly: Request that an Answer card be read, then ask, "What is the Question?"
4. Call on at least two students with Question cards to read their cards aloud. Then, rather than immediately requesting an Answer, ask, "Which Question do you think should come first?"
5. Have students write their names in pencil on the back of each card. (Junior high teacher Betty Bennett says this heightens students' sense of "ownership" and accountability for the cards' contents and offers a good way to check afterward which students did not volunteer to read their cards.)

To foster greater independence and transfer of learning, try these options:

1. Reinforce high-quality extemporaneous responses by handing the student a blank card and saying, "That was very good. Would you please write it on this card for future use?"
2. Divide the class into groups, and have them prepare the Note Cue cards for the next selections to be read.
3. Once students are familiar with the activity, prepare some cards with prompts, such as a suggestion that students try to raise a certain kind of Question (e.g., "Try to ask a Question to show that one should doubt what is being said") or an incomplete statement to be completed by students ("Make a Comment by completing this statement: 'I enjoyed reading this story because . . . ' or 'The reaction would have been different in my family or culture. We would have . . .'"). Other types of prompter cards can be personalized ("Come on, Fred, don't you have something you can say about this selection?").

To foster critical thinking, develop evocative Comment cards, preferably ones related to students' experiences. One vivid example of this kind of bridging comes to mind from a lesson observed in an English class. The selection read had been excerpted from a successful book. It described how a 15-year-old boy set out on a solitary voyage across the Pacific in a small craft. The Questions and Answers the teacher had put on the cue cards were primarily from the teacher's manual for the text. One of the Comments that she added, however, raised the class's interest and even indignation: "Where in the world did this young man raise the money and supplies to do this, and why did his parents permit him to risk his life in such a silly venture?" A student might not have worded the Comment quite like that, but such real reactions tend to invite equally real responses and lively discussion.

Finally, Note Cue can be used to foster specific skills development. It permits the teacher to target a variety of learning objectives by incorporating them into the kinds of questions raised, the way answers are written, and the types of Comments offered. For example, Kathleen Youtsey, another field test teacher, chose to stress Raphael's Question Answer Response strategy (1984). Accordingly, her cards tended to include references to whether an Answer to a Question was "right there" (in the text), required "thinking and searching" (needed to be inferred from text), or required the student to think it through "on my own" (since it was not in the text).

Incidental Benefits.   Unlike many conventional lesson designs, Note Cue is cumulative. The cards a teacher composes for today's lesson can be stored for future use. Through cooperative work and sharing, teachers can develop starter sets of Note Cues for virtually every key selection in a text. More important, with each use, previously written cards can be modified following use and new cards generated by students can be added. In this way, lessons can be kept fresh and current.

Finally, Note Cue is another whole language, whole person lesson design. It offers opportunities for reading, speaking, listening, and writing; it gets students doing what their minds and bodies need to learn to do; and it can be very comforting to a teacher who may need to hear and see tangible evidence of progress.

Improving Comprehension, Dialectical and Abstract Thinking, Language Skills, and Multicultural Outlook: Proverbs Mastery Paradigm and Activities

It is difficult to imagine a more productive fountainhead of learning than proverbs. There are books of proverbs for school study dating back to pre–Revolutionary War days. Nonetheless, the value of proverbs has been all but forgotten in contemporary times.

It was the first author's maternal grandmother, a natural teacher, who provided the primary inspiration for the *Proverbs Mastery Paradigm and Activities* (Manzo, 1981b) that follow. Although she had only a single year of formal schooling, she had a rather remarkable education. Like many of her generation, she had received a rich education in the form of the numerous proverbs and aphorisms that permeated her life and time—a tradition that gave her a direct line to the sum of human history, experience, and wisdom. Unfortunately, this centuries-old oral language tradition has been interrupted, and to date there has been no adequate substitute in our schools.

Our own research at the intermediate and junior high levels has shown that skill in interpreting proverbs is strongly related to a number of language skills, including reading comprehension, the ability to deal with complex language patterns, and critical-evaluative thinking. At a lesser but still statistically significant level, proverb interpretation is related to social-emotional stability, vocabulary, analogical (metaphorical) thinking, word recognition, and fund of information (Manzo & Casale, 1981). In short, proverbs are nuggets of commonsense learnings that underlie almost everything written, spoken, heard, and experienced. As Figure 10.6 shows, proverbs speak for themselves quite well.

Steps in the Proverbs Mastery Paradigm

1. *Readiness:* As with any good lesson activity, the teacher first engages students and prepares them to learn. This readiness may be incidental: The teacher capitalizes on a situation, mood, or event that arises naturally. To achieve this, the teacher selects a proverb for discussion that students will likely recognize as compatible with a recent experience. Readiness may also be engineered: The teacher simulates or describes a situation, then uses it as the basis for considering the selected proverb(s).

    A fine example of an engineered readiness activity was provided by a teacher who wrote a proverb (e.g., "Haste makes waste") on a piece of cardboard at the beginning of each week and posted it above the chalkboard. She directed students to copy it into their notebooks in a section labeled "Proverbs." She would say no more about the proverb until later in the week. By that time, when they finally discussed the proverb, students had a great deal to say. All through the week, they had been gathering up possible meanings and applications of the proverb.

2. *Find surface meaning:* The teacher writes a proverb on the chalkboard and asks students to translate it into their own words. It may be necessary to treat the proverb word by word. Recall that translation operations require transferring a word from one symbolic form to another, typically to one more familiar to students. Consider, for example, the difficulties that would arise in teaching the

Figure 10.6 Proverbs Speak for Themselves

Proverbs are the daughters of daily experience. (Dutch)

The genius, wit, and spirit of a nation are discovered in its proverbs. (Bacon)

An old saying, if it comes into use with time, becomes an ordinance. (Plautus)

There is no proverb which is not true. (Spanish)

proverb "He steals a goose and gives giblets in alms." Without a translation of *giblets* and *alms*, it would be impossible to glean the meaning: "Pious and charitable acts cannot undo unjust ones."

3. *Invite application:* The teacher asks students to volunteer real or imaginary situations that illustrate the proverb. Regarding the proverb "He steals a goose . . . ," one student said that he had just learned from a television documentary that the man who instituted the Nobel Peace Prize fund was a dynamite and arms manufacturer and thus a hypocrite who had acted piously.

4. *Seek deep meaning:* Students discuss their individual impressions of the possible meaning(s) of the proverb. (Experience has shown that in an "average" class, prior to instruction, about 15% of students give a totally incorrect response, 10% give an emotive response, 50% give a concrete example, and 25% give an abstract response. Guide students from incorrect, emotive, and concrete responses toward appropriate abstract interpretations of the proverb).

5. *Invite exceptions:* The teacher asks students whether they can volunteer real or imaginary situations that suggest a view contrary to that implicit in the proverb. Initially, students find this difficult to do on their own. Nonetheless, the question should be posed, because it highlights what students are being educated to do. The inclination and ability to consider an alternative proposition are a prerequisite to critical and creative thinking. After the teacher suggests an example or two, students will begin to follow suit.

6. *Raise paradoxes:* The teacher asks students to think of an opposing (and/or alternate-culture) proverb or supplies one personally. If neither can think of an example, the teacher should move on; someone will likely come up with one in a few days. An example might be the proverb "Things are not always as they seem" to cast a different light on the seeming hypocrisy of the Nobel Peace Prize. Another might be the Chinese proverb "If there is something in everyone to be condemned, then too is there something to be pardoned." See Appendix E for additional examples of contrasting proverbs.

7. *Reconcile paradoxes:* The teacher guides students in an attempt to reconcile opposing positions in proverbs with a question to the effect of "If A is true, does that mean B is not?" Most often, this last step has the most profound effect on intellectual growth. Through it students come to realize that most things are set in a dynamic tension to one another. Life and learning are a process of reconciling paradoxes, that is, finding the truth that lies between seemingly contradictory positions.

These seven steps consitute the basic paradigm. Several variations or elaborations are possible and may be necessary in certain situations or to achieve some special effect.

Elaborations

Activity for a Multicultural School Population. The teacher selects proverbs from a wide array of nations and cultures and stresses their "social comprehension" aspects. These multicultural proverbs, for example, suggest the following elements:

Black American: Winter grapes are sour whether you can reach them or not. (The defeatism of slavery)

Greek: What soon grows old? Gratitude. (Independent people who do not want to have to depend on others' goodwill)

African: You do not teach the paths of the forest to an old gorilla. (People close to nature and wise in its ways)

Chinese: Lend to one who will not repay, and you will provoke his dislike. (A sense of caution and concern for unexpected consequences)

Yiddish: Only in the grave is there rest. (Ambitious and industrious people)

Extensive discussion of Anglo-American proverbs can be as important as consideration of alternate-culture proverbs. Study of Anglo-American proverbs can help students from diverse cultural backgrounds and those for whom English is a second language to get a better purchase on American conventions and values:

A stitch in time saves nine. (unknown)

Speak softly and carry a big stick; you will go far. (Theodore Roosevelt)

No government ought to be without censors; and where there is a free press, no one ever will. (Thomas Jefferson)

Every man has his price. (originally Lord Chesterfield)

Activity for Special-Needs Students.   The following activity is appropriate for students with a wide range of special needs: ESL students who are also poor comprehenders or students who are learning disabled, are behavior disordered, or have difficulty grasping underlying abstract concepts. The teacher gives students four possible interpretations of a proverb's meaning. The three "wrong" answers should parallel the major areas of comprehension dysfunction: overly literal thinking, emotive responding, and miscued understanding. The "best" answer should represent an abstract, or "universal," translation of the proverb. Students select and record the statement that best captures the proverb's meaning. Here are two examples:

A. Look before you leap.

    (abstract)   1. Do not act in haste.
    (literal)   2. Watch before you step down.
    (emotive)   3. Do not leap, just look.
    (miscue)   4. We see further in a leap year.

B. You can't judge a book by its cover.

    (abstract)   1. Appearances can be deceiving.
    (literal)   2. You can tell what a book is about by what's on the front.
    (emotive)   3. Don't make judgments.
    (miscue)   4. Judges often deal in undercover work.

Once students have made their choices, discussion should help them see the merit or folly in their decisions. Initial selections can be collected and noted over time for evidence of growth away from emotive, miscued, or literal responding and toward more universal, abstract statements. Used in this way, this activity qualifies as a solid diagnostic-teaching lesson.

Activities for Gifted ESL Students

1. The teacher *begins* instruction with the paradox resolution step of the Proverbs Mastery Paradigm. Students are shown several proverbs that address the same theme. The task is to establish the basic meaning of each, then compare and contrast them to find one or more logical syntheses of the opposing theses. At a deeper level, students can be instructed to look for implied paradoxes within a single proverb. Here are some examples:

    Study the past if you would divine the future. (Confucius)

    History is only a confused heap of facts. (Lord Chesterfield)

    History is bunk. (Henry Ford)

2. Students do a topical study of proverbs, including the proverbs' origins as well as the various forms they may take or be called by: homilies, bromides, adages, maxims, hard-sayings, famous sayings, epigrams, old saws, apothegms, axioms, aphorisms.
3. Students attempt to write some "modern proverbs" of their own that describe their lives and experiences. One way to stimulate this is with incomplete sentences. Two sixth-graders gave us these different views: "Kids who make you laugh in school '. . . have little to laugh about afterwards'; '. . . know what really counts.'"

Activity for Content Area Infusion.   Have students match and explain the relationships of selected proverbs to short stories, characters, events, or terms. The items to be matched should be open-ended to allow for different interpretations. Consider this matching "game" prepared for an English/history unified studies class:

Match the following in a way that suits your thinking. Be prepared to explain your judgments.

Proverbs:

1. Experience is what you get when you are looking for something else.
2. Some folks complain that they don't get what is due them. They should be glad they don't.
3. Every person is a pilot when the sea is calm.
4. The slave who serves only himself is the slave of a slave.

Matching items:

a. Magellan
b. The Iranians
c. "The catbird seat"
d. Narcissus

In this activity, the thoughts provided and views exchanged are more important than the "answers" chosen. A recent National Assessment of Educational Progress report (1988) indicates that American students do most poorly in answering explanation-type questions.

Activity for Improving Evaluative Thinking. Behavior disorders, poor evaluative thinking, and low self-esteem are disabilities that tend to be accompanied by a weak base of understanding of one's own values and those of others. In this activity, the teacher lists three or four proverbs, preferably from different cultural backgrounds, on a handout and discusses the basic meaning of each. Students indicate the extent to which they agree or disagree with each statement. Students' reactions can reveal areas of personal problems and difficulties. The teacher should take the opportunity to discuss these problems with students or refer them to appropriate guidance personnel.

A similar activity can be conducted with small groups in which students try to predict their classmates' responses to the same proverbs. This is a variation on Hoffman's Intra-Act (1977) procedure, discussed in Chapter 8. See Appendix E for a list of proverbs arranged by language and grade difficulty level (Manzo & Manzo, 1987b).

Vocabulary and Second Language: Motor Imaging Revisited

Motor Imaging, described in Chapter 5, deserves additional consideration for ESL students. As mentioned earlier, Motor Imaging is very similar to a method developed for foreign language study by James Asher (1965) called *Total Physical Response.*

Like infants, students who attempt to learn a second language with this approach start their study of the new language by remaining silent but performing a motor act when directed to do so by the teacher. Asher (1981) gives the following example from a lesson script in Japanese. Two students are seated on either side of the teacher. The teacher gives these directions: "Please listen carefully to what I will say and do exactly what I do. Be silent. Don't try to pronounce the words at this time. Just listen and act with me." The teacher then utters a command such as *Tate!* and stands up; the students stand up. Then the teacher says, *Suware!* and sits down, and the class follows suit. Following these one-word utterances, the directions and motor acts rapidly expand to "Stand up, walk to the table, and pick up the red pencil."

Kunihira and Asher (1965) offered evidence to support this approach in teaching adults Japanese. By the third training session, each only 7½ minutes long, subjects were responding to such complicated Japanese directions as *Kamit hon to enpitsu o totte isu ni suware* (pick up the paper, book, and pencil, and sit on the chair.)

This approach to basic vocabulary and language learning seems to further verify the potential value in Motor Imaging for teaching ESL students more esoteric vocabulary as well. It is noteworthy that Asher also attributes the efficacy of this approach to some as yet mysterious ties with brain hemisphere functioning: "The right brain seems to be mute yet able to generate answers through gestures and movements of the body such as pointing, touching, and grasping" (1981, p. 198).

On the Light Side: Puns and Parodies

ESL students typically find themselves having to learn new subjects, a new language, and a new culture simultaneously. Puns and parodies, like proverbs, can be useful in this regard. Unlike proverbs, however, they have an amusing lilt that offers a safe haven for learning the idioms and cultural referents that pepper our language but seldom find focus in school instruction.

Puns are words or phrases used to suggest more than one meaning. *Parodies* mimic and exaggerate more serious works or people in a satirical manner. Longman and Atkinson (1988) recommend the use of both to add a playful dimension to school learning. They suggest these examples of parody and pun in learning the word *numismatist:*

Parody (to the tune of "Four and Twenty Blackbirds"): The numismatist was in his counting house, counting out his money.
Pun: Two numismatists getting together for old dime's sake (p. 194).

See Figure 10.7 for a list of real "groaners" that are packed with word lessons and cultural elements. The book from which these are taken, *The People's Almanac,* and its earlier and later versions are excellent sources of common cultural "trivia" as well.

Winning the "Psycholinguistic Guessing Game"

One of the many reasons why the decoding aspects of reading have been called a "psycholinguistic guessing game" (Goodman, 1967) is that many English words cannot be decoded unless they already are in one's oral language repertoire. How, for example, would one know to say "rōz" for "rose" and for "rows?"—and if one did know that, why would one then think to say "luz" for "lose" rather than "lōz?" The answer is simply that one knows, or comes to know, how to decode words by first learning them aurally or through hearing and speech.

The basis, then, for all ESL programs in reading and content areas must include a good deal of oral language development and some explicit training in word recognition ("This is how this word is pronounced") and word analysis ("This cluster of letters can be pronounced this way, or this way, or even this way"). It is for this reason that the Glass Analysis approach to the decoding aspects of reading described in this chapter for remedial-level readers is equally appropriate for foreign language speakers.

The poem in Figure 10.8, by an author known only by the initials "T.S.W.," illustrates some of the frustration foreign language speakers experience in *learning to read* in English. We can only imagine what their frustration must be in *reading to learn* in English.

Figure 10.7 Puns

1. The Eskimo stabbed himself with an icicle. He died of cold cuts.
2. In his dessert list, a San Antonio restaurateur suggests, "Remember the alamode."
3. There was an advice-to-the-lovelorn editor who insisted, "If at first you don't succeed, try a little ardor."
4. The commuter's Volkswagen broke down once too often. So he consigned it to the Old Volks Home.
5. When a fire chief responded to a call from a lingerie shop, he found no trace of a blaze. His official report read, "Falsie alarm."
6. The wise old crow perched himself on a telephone wire. He wanted to make a long-distance caw.
7. A talkative musician couldn't hold a job. Every time he opened his mouth, he put his flute in it.
8. A farmer with relatives in East Germany heard that a food package he had sent had never arrived. Optimistically, he reassured them, "Cheer up! The wurst is yet to come."
9. When the promoter of a big flower show was told that a postponement was necessary because the exhibits could not be installed on time, he explained to his backers, "We were simply caught with our plants down."
10. There was an unscheduled event in a Baghdad harem. The sultan barged in unexpectedly—and his 62 wives let out a terrified sheikh.
11. A critic declared that he always praised the first show of a new theatrical season. "Who am I," he asked, "to stone the first cast?"
12. Egotist: a man who's always me-deep in conversation.
13. She was unanimously voted the most popular girl in school by the male half of the senior class. They weighed her in the balance and found her wanton.
14. A hen stopped right in the middle of the highway. She wanted to lay it on the line.
15. The husband of a talkative wife sighed, "I've given that woman the best ears of my life."
16. "It's raining cats and dogs," one man remarked. "I know," said another. "I just stepped into a poodle."
17. In Peru, a gallant cavalier fished a drowning maiden out of a lake—and married her before the Inca was dry.
18. An eccentric bachelor passed away and left a nephew nothing but 392 clocks. The nephew is now busy winding up the estate.
19. The baseball pitcher with a sore arm was in the throws of agony.
20. A Turkish salesman promoted an audience with an old-time sultan. "I don't recall your name," said the sultan pleasantly, "but your fez is familiar."

Source: From *The Book of Lists #2* by I. Wallace and D. Wallechinsky, 1980, New York: William Morrow & Co. Copyright 1980 by David Wallechinsky. Reprinted by permission.

Figure 10.8 "Hints on
Pronunciation for Foreigners"

I take it you already know
Of tough and bough and cough and dough?
Others may stumble but not you,
On hiccough, through, laugh, and though.
Well done! And now you wish, perhaps,
To learn of less familiar traps?

Beware of heard, a dreadful word
That looks like beard and sounds like bird,
And dead: it's said like bed, not bead—
For goodness' sake don't call it "deed"!
Watch out for meat and great and threat
(They rhyme with suite and straight and debt.)

A moth is not a moth in mother
Nor both in bother, broth in brother
And here is not a match for there
Nor dear and fear for bear and pear,
And then there's dose and rose and lose—
Just look them up—and goose and choose,
And cork and work and card and ward,
And font and front and word and sword,
And do and go and thwart and cart—
Come, come, I've hardly made a start!
A dreadful language? Man alive.
I'd mastered it when I was five.

— T.S.W.

CHAPTER TIE-UPS

Graphic Organizer ◆◆◆

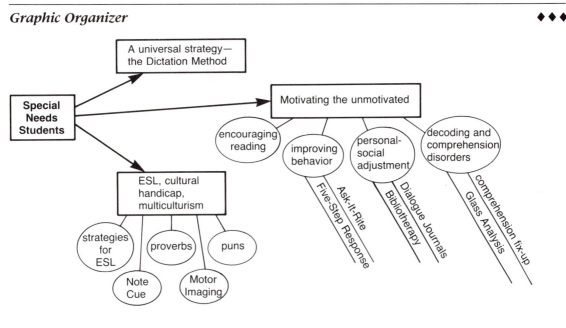

Critique and Anticipation ◆◆◆

This chapter offered an extensive listing of methods to promote personal-social adjustment and improve reading, language, and thinking skills among special-needs students. Eight methods were emphasized: Dictation (to improve listening and writing mechanics); Ask-It-Rite (to improve classroom repartee); Dialogue Journals and Bibliotherapy (to teach writing, introspection, and life management skills); Glass Analysis (to manage decoding problems); comprehension "fix-up" (to improve self-monitoring); Note Cue (to heighten classroom participation); and the Proverbs Mastery Paradigm (to improve aspects of thinking and acculturation). Each of these methods is applicable to broader student groups. Note Cue, for example, can be used to improve class discussion and analysis of any textual material.

The next chapter sets out ways to bring students, faculty, and community together in activities that are beneficial to all.

TRADE SECRET

Catch Them Being Good

Occasionally a teacher and a student, or even an entire class, gets locked into a deadly cycle of misbehavior, criticism, defensive reactions, threats, and punishment—and more misbehavior. One way to break this cycle, educator Pat Wolfe reminds us, is to "catch them being good" and then reward the heck out of them! This simple strategy, though sometimes difficult to mount in a negative atmosphere, is the basis of all behavior modification. As such, it is a great heuristic, or enabling mechanism, for preventing the deadly cycle from occurring as well as clawing your way back to civility if and when it begins.

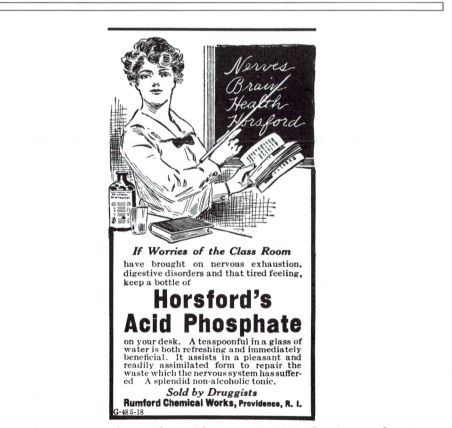

It's never been easy; not then, and certainly not now! (1922 advertisement from *Progressive Teacher*)

If this strategy comes easily to you, we're sorry to say that, according to Wolfe, you still have something else to beware of: turning kids into ''praise junkies.'' But don't worry too much about this, since most of us have trouble finding the opportunity and the will to praise.

Praise, by the way, is most effective when it highlights a specific behavior: ''That was a good idea to write your homework assignment in your notebook, George.'' By matching praise to a specific behavior, you often can buy enough grace to later be able to address some constructive criticism in the same direction without dire consequences: ''You know, George, if you write your assignments from the rear to the front of your notebook, they'll take up only a few pages over the entire semester. They also will be easier to find, and you'll have a record of everything assigned when you need to review for a test.''

Within this teaching tip is an example of another: Address students by name whenever possible. It helps to form a more personal bond.

Schoolwide
Programming

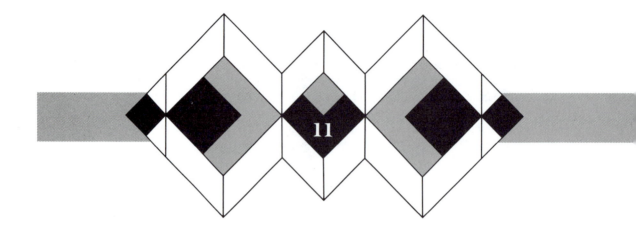

Elements, Hubs, and
Other Catalysts

. . . and that's the big picture!

— *A. Whitney Brown*

FOCUS

This chapter addresses two major points: the importance of the teacher's role in the school-wide reading program and the advantages of forming "hubs"—that is, program heuristics that foster greater and more generative interactions among students, faculty, and community across ages, disciplines, and ability levels.

OUTLINE

THE SCHOOLWIDE CONTENT AREA READING PROGRAM

Day-to-day events may appear random and even fragmented while they are being experienced. For this reason alone, it can be satisfying to get a glimpse of the "big picture." But there is another reason to try to gain such a "top-down" perspective: It offers a solid opportunity to exercise a more assertive role as a professional educator as well as classroom teacher.

Organizing Questions

This chapter is structured to answer two organizing questions that a classroom teacher and/or reading-specialist-in-training would need to understand to be an effective participant in a school's content reading program:

1. What do schoolwide CAR programs typically look like? This question contains two other implicit questions:
   a. What help can I expect, and from whom?
   b. What is expected of me as a teacher?
2. What more can be done?

The term *program* here means any plan targeted at a stated goal or objective.

Key Elements of Vital Reading Programs

Vital reading programs, in our judgment, are built around seven key elements:

- An ideology
- Clear roles and responsibilities
- Special services for various segments of the student body
- Ongoing needs assessment and program evaluation
- A curriculum implementation plan
- A staff development program that provides consultation, in-service, and sharing opportunities
- Heuristic activities that promote collaboration

The following sections show how some of these elements might be or are being implemented in actual school programs. The examples and discussions include optional as well as essential elements. Several of these elements may overlap in practice; therefore, the discussion does not parallel the above points in every case.

IDEOLOGY

An ideology usually is expressed in the form of a unifying theme or focus that serves as the conceptual basis for guiding programming. Examples of focus themes that are compatible with the content of this text might include

1. Promoting progress toward reading-language-thinking-content-social/emotional maturity as opposed to mere reading competence
2. Promoting higher-order literacy, or working to diagnose and remedy shortfalls in critical-constructive thinking, among the academically proficient as well as remedial readers
3. Languaging, or whole language, approaches to improvement in reading, writing, speaking, listening, and thinking
4. Concurrent methods, or teaching strategies that simultaneously teach reading and "trace elements" such as inquiry skills, self-examination, and personal-social effectiveness—or the whole person
5. Cooperative versus competitive reading and learning, namely operating the school as an ideal community

Realistically speaking, these themes may not always play well in a particular school, even though they should be an integral part of the school's philosophical or ideological goals. In such situations, it is more practical to express the focus for the school program in more conventional terms, such as

- Effective comprehension and vocabulary
- Efficient reading and study skills
- Reading and writing to learn

In most cases, the ideology of the school program will be expressed in a combination of the above terms with some locally recognized need, such as functional literacy for job flexibility, college preparation, or effective reading and proper classroom decorum.

CLEAR ROLES AND RESPONSIBILITIES

The chief element in translating program ideals into practice is the assignment of role responsibilities. Following are the most commonly acknowledged responsibilities of the school administrator, reading specialist, and classroom teacher.

School Administrator

The school administrator

1. Initiates and supports development of goals and objectives and means of evaluation for the reading program
2. Commissions and acts on schoolwide survey testing
3. Supports in-service and other reading-related faculty development programs
4. Directs program evaluation

Reading Specialist

As a rule of thumb, a secondary school should have one full-time reading specialist for every 250 students. The reading specialist

1. Serves as resource person and arbitrator in development of goals and objectives and means of evaluation for the reading curriculum
2. Coordinates schoolwide survey testing and evaluates results
3. Administers additional diagnostic tests as dictated by survey testing and/or referrals
4. Provides remedial-corrective instruction as necessary
5. Provides ongoing assistance to teachers as program structure permits in a variety of forms: in-service activities, preparation of materials, demonstration lessons, evaluation of materials, and so on
6. Assists in ongoing evaluation of the reading program
7. Elicits and coordinates the contributions of other support services such as the library, counselors, parents, and so forth
8. Coordinates and assists the efforts of outside consultants as needed

Content Teachers

Intermediate-grade classroom teachers and content teachers at all subsequent levels

1. Participate in developing goals and objectives and means of evaluation for the reading program
2. Identify students with possible reading difficulties as soon as possible
3. Assist in ongoing evaluation of the reading program
4. Teach in ways that support a shared responsibility for promoting reading progress
5. Initiate discussions and goals with reading/resource specialists

SPECIAL SERVICES COMPONENT

In the context of this discussion, *special services* means assistance available for students with special needs. This typically involves "pull-out" programs, elective or minicourses, and centers.

Pull-out Services

In *pull-out programs,* a reading specialist offers diagnostic and/or remedial/corrective tutoring for youngsters who cannot be adequately provided for in regular classes. This component is intended to ensure that

1. No remedial-level reader "falls between the cracks" and leaves school only quasi-literate after 12 years
2. Foreign-born and other language-handicapped students receive special attention where this appears necessary

3. Diagnosis and treatment are provided for other difficult, different, or sometimes overlooked problems (e.g., higher-order literacy dysfunctions, cultural differences, study skills deficiencies, and reading-related writing, grammar, and spelling dysfunctions)
4. Consultation is provided for all teachers in selecting and using appropriate methods and materials

Elective Courses

Reading specialists in upper elementary, middle, and high schools frequently offer exploratory minicourses or full elective courses on topics such as study skills, speed reading, critical reading, and vocabulary enrichment. This type of short-term, focused instruction reinforces and builds on the ongoing content reading instruction provided daily in content classrooms.

Learning Centers

The learning center usually is the hub out of which the reading department operates. Bernice Bragstad, an International Reading Association award-winning content area reading specialist and consultant, says that her former high school's learning center provided these three services:

1. Individualized or small-group tutoring in any subject, provided by a select cadre of proficient student-tutors or the reading specialist
2. Individualized help with writing, provided by several English teachers who served their "duty" periods in this way
3. A preventative biweekly summer tutoring program conducted by high school students for middle and junior high students

In addition to the above services, learning centers can offer "walk-in" assistance with almost any pressing homework or academic problem. The Kansas City Public School District has extended this concept to a "homework hotline." The hotline is available after school hours and staffed by volunteer teachers.

NEEDS ASSESSMENT: THE SCHOOL AUDIT

The *school audit,* that is, information about the effects of schooling, is essential to determining what needs to be done and how to best do it. This type of information should be collected regularly by the school reading specialist(s) and cross-verified by an independent audit from an outside team of consultants every three to five years. Surveys guided by outside consultants help identify problems that have a way of cropping up in virtually every operation in which day-to-day pressures erode educators' sensitivity to flaws in policy and procedure. Most effective businesses routinely budget for such periodic surveys and reviews. It is a fundamental form of quality control.

The school survey should be guided by a comprehensive model that avoids unnecessary disruption of the basic school program. Such disruption can be prevented by

• Using as much existing data as is available from standardized testing
• Collecting data informally and regularly from informal diagnostic-teaching systems and instruments (e.g., the Informal Textbook Inventory)
• Using stratified random sampling of students rather than testing all students (typically a 20% sampling of students from different age, grade, and IQ levels and from different feeder schools is more than adequate to yield an evaluative picture of a school's needs)

To aid in the selection of instruments and eventual interpretation of data, we suggest Wiener and Cromer's (1967) Diagnostic, or Assessment, Model. The Wiener-Cromer Model guides assessment into four possible problem areas that hamper reading success. Problem areas are represented by the "4Ds": *defect, deficiency, disruption*, and *difference*.

Defect.   A reading problem may be due to an innate problem such as mental inadequacy, physiological problems such as vision and hearing defects, and other possible constitutional problems that hamper a student's ability to benefit from instruction and/or extracurricular experiences. Basic assessment instruments include IQ tests, hearing and eye examinations, and medical records, as well as often-overlooked clues to problems such as absentee data and/or other indications of intermittent and nonevident handicapping conditions (e.g., allergies, hypersensitivity, and organ problems).

Deficiency.   Reading problems sometimes arise from some specific weakness such as poor phonics skills or inadequate vocabulary, low fund of general information, and/or poor abstract thinking. Generally, most standardized reading tests assess these types of problems adequately. The exception occurs in the areas of abstract and critical-evaluative thinking. Such problems are rarely assessed and therefore tend to go unnoticed and unattended.

Disruption.   Reading difficulties may arise from long-term or recurring interruptions in the educational process. Such interruptions may result simply from absence from school or from an internal state of affective distress that interferes with one's ability to sustain attention and learning. Assessment instruments in this category include prior years' attendance records and measures of personal-emotional adjustment, personality, and temperament factors. This nonintellective category, as we expressed strongly in Chapter 3 on assessment, is often overlooked, thus leaving one of the four wheels on the school vehicle completely unattended.

Difference.   Another cause of reading difficulties lies in the degree of difference between individual or selected groups of students and the expectations of teachers and the basic assumptions of the school. Such differences typically involve language, experiential, or cultural and informational background. They can result in mismatches between what students can do and what the school expects them to do.

At a language and informational level, Wiener and Cromer note, "A psychologist reading a physics book, or a physicist reading a psychology book, would be slowed down, and show more errors . . . with less comprehension than when each reads in his own field." At another level, "difference" can be thought of more broadly as any mismatch arising out of poor understanding of student backgrounds, cognitive style characteristics, life experiences, and cultural orientations. This category often is overlooked, particularly in relatively white, homogeneous environments. We have seen circumstances in which the oversight has had devastating effects. In one case, disregard for differences between the school's expectations and the characteristics of its student population (in this case, Italian) led to the highest dropout rate in the city, even though students' IQs and achievement scores had been slightly higher than national norms. In another case, an entire small city (of largely German descent) had an extremely low proportion of graduates going on to postsecondary education despite the fact that the student population had much higher than average IQs and achievement scores. School officials responsible for educating these youngsters clearly needed a more careful school audit to determine the source of the mismatch between schooling and students.

CURRICULUM IMPLEMENTATION PLAN

Apart from the obvious effort to infuse each course with the necessary reading-related skills, each discipline can be designated, by common agreement, to give special attention to specific features of the content reading curriculum. Distribution and assignment of reading and reading-related skills to each subject area proceeds best when school units volunteer to play a role. This horizontal distribution also can be detailed vertically by age/grade level.

Here is an example of possible distribution by major disciplines of the content reading curriculum:

English
1. Story comprehension
2. Poetry comprehension
3. Language patterns
4. Creative writing
5. Summary writing
6. Systematic vocabulary
7. Literary reference books

Social studies
1. Analytical discussion
2. Critical reading
3. Metaphorical thinking
4. Critique and reaction writing
5. Notetaking
6. Social studies vocabulary
7. Almanac, encyclopedia, and related reference skills
8. Reading maps, charts, graphs, and cartoons

Science
1. Inquiry training
2. Thesis and detail writing from expository material and observation
3. Cooperative reading-learning
4. Accurate recall
5. Science vocabulary
6. Hypothesis formulation and testing
7. Abstract thinking

Mathematics
1. Recitation
2. Translation skills
3. Test taking
4. Mathematics vocabulary
5. Expository writing: What did this problem ask, and why did I solve it as I did?
6. Cooperative problem solving

STAFF DEVELOPMENT

A well-planned staff development program is an important means of ensuring that programs endure and evolve over time in an institutional setting that undergoes frequent changes in administration and staff. An effective plan for staff development should include three basic components:

1. A means of enlisting teacher support in program development and an ongoing sense of program ownership
2. A way to provoke program review and renewal
3. A means of fine-tuning a program and accommodating individual teacher's needs.

This section offers means for addressing each of the above components. First, it describes action research as a way to enlist teacher support and ownership. Next, it discusses in-service training as a means of providing ongoing training. Finally, it describes the role of the reading resource teacher as a source of individualized support and training.

Action Research

Classroom experimentation is a sensitive and successful way to change instructional routines, according to Carol Santa. She and her colleagues (Santa, Isaacson, & Manning, 1987) point out that by involving teachers in planning, conducting, and reporting classroom research, they greatly increased teacher "ownership" of ideas while providing "hands-on" evidence of the value of several basic content area reading strategies.

The process of involving teachers in action research projects is more manageable today than ever before. Assistance with research design and statistics usually can be had for a small fee or even free from a school district's own office of research, from advanced degree-seeking teachers, from doctoral-level central office staff, and/ or from nearby university campuses. The idea of "teacher scholars" has a rich history in education (Chall, 1986). No doubt you have noticed that several of the methods and ideas presented in this text were suggested by classroom teachers and other school practitioners.

In-service

In-service, or staff informing and training, is a key feature of successful school programming. This can take several forms. The action research model just discussed is one means of broadening horizons. The most practical methods, however, involve direct in-service training.

There are no clear formulas for conducting in-service teacher training. Nonetheless, there has been a good deal of research on the efficacy of various "generic" approaches. Ruth Wade (1984), in a "meta-" (broad-summary) analysis of 91 well-documented studies, reached these conclusions:

1. In-service training that includes both elementary and secondary teachers often is more effective than in-service training for either group separately.
2. In-service training is most successful when participants are given special recognition for their involvement, selected on a competitive basis, or designated to participate.
3. Regardless of who conducts in-service sessions (trainers come under many different job classifications), teachers are more likely to benefit when they learn on their own. Similarly, of all the diverse types of training structures, independent study is the most effective.
4. There is no magical combination of methods for successful in-service. Nevertheless, in-service programs that use observation, microteaching, auditory and visual feedback, and practice, either individually or in some combination, are more effective than programs that do not use these methods.
5. There is no evidence that "coaching," or advice giving, greatly enhances instructional effectiveness. At best it is moderately effective.
6. In-service is less successful when participants are regarded as major contributors. Programs are more effective when the leader assumes the role of "giver of information" and the participants are "receivers of information." (Wade, 1984)

In-service training can be greatly enhanced by indirect means such as newsletters and professional libraries. One of the finest newsletters we have seen is the *RICA* (Reading in the Content Areas) *Newsletter* published by the Secondary Reading Office of the Orange County Public Schools in Orlando, Florida (Joy Monahan, program consultant). A typical edition features a practical idea or strategy. Figure 11.1, taken from one issue, nicely outlines the RICA concept of "Secondary School Reading" while illustrating the idea of Semantic Mapping.

We ourselves believe that in-service education proceeds best through a combination of the above options. In our judgment, it is most important to have teacher-

Figure 11.1 Reading in the Content Areas Newsletter Excerpt: Semantic Map of Secondary School Reading

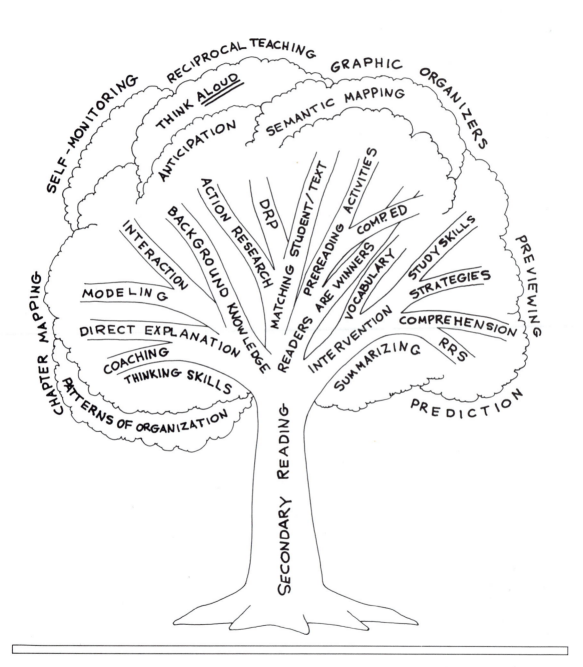

Source: Used by permission of Joy Monahan, artist and editor of *Reading in the Content Areas Newsletter*, published by the Orange County, Florida Reading Department.

led workshops following those led by outside consultants. The teacher-led presentations should review and constructively critique information provided by consultants. Teacher presentations of this type aid in adaptation and adoption of new ideas. They also help relieve somewhat the sense of isolation many teachers feel, while allowing for the emergence of intellectual leadership in each school (see the section on Teacher Advocates later in the chapter).

Reading Resource Teacher

More friendly than the idea of a reading specialist-consultant is that of the reading resource teacher. This notion, which is used in many school districts, focuses on informing teachers of the services available to them and having them request these as they see fit. Figure 11.2 offers a good example of how Alice Woods and Mary Topping (1986) have done this in survey form for the Polk County, Florida, schools.

HUBS AND OTHER HEURISTICS

The L-R-D Heuristic and the universal strategies were offered in earlier chapters as selected means of getting schoolwide reading going. Then the Informal Textbook Inventory and broad-based assessment were offered as systems to keep reading from becoming random or too narrow in focus. Now we need ways to coordinate and sustain these efforts and to keep reading growing. For this purpose, a **hub**, or unifying strategy, is desirable—one that can serve as a heuristic for stimulating relevant interactions among faculty, between faculty and students, and, ideally, between *both* faculty and students and "thinkers-at-large" in the community. These nonprofessional educators, or "extant teachers," as they may more properly be called, can provide an inexpensive and valuable additional resource for improving the social and intellectual lives of students, staff, and the host community. One way to tap all of this brainpower is to institute a school- or districtwide Annotation Exchange system.

Annotation Exchange: Collaborative Critiquing and Creating

The idea for an Annotation Exchange system emerged some years ago as part of a series of other potential innovations for libraries (Manzo, Sherk, Leibert, & Mocker, 1971). Some of these are described later in the section on Living Libraries. The technology of that time did not easily permit the Annotation Exchange system to work. Inexpensive computers were needed but not yet available. The basic idea, however, was preserved and has attained popularity in the form we now know as REAP (Eanet & Manzo, 1976), the reading-writing-study strategy described in Chapter 7 on postreading designs.

Simply put, the *Annotation Exchange*, or *AnX, system* is a means of providing readers with a constructive, or "talk-back," mechanism—one that offers an option to write a brief, personalized annotation in response to what they have read. AnX would

Figure 11.2   Sample Survey

Name: _____

Planning Hour: _____

Planning Room: _____

Dear Faculty of _____ High School:

Attached is a list of my duties as a Reading Resource Specialist for your school. Please note that I will be serving all areas of academics including ESL and vocational programs. In addition, I plan to conduct a school-wide inventory of reading materials that I hope will further assist you once our program is under way. Below is a list of services that I can offer you. Please check those that interest you. If I have omitted an area of interest or need, please add it. Be sure that you have indicated the time and location of your planning period so that I may contact you.

I am excited about working with all of you in this program. Please be patient with me, as it may take me a little while to get the program under way, but rest assured that I'll make every effort to meet your expectations.

_____ Make presentations to classes on specific study skills, test-taking strategies or study strategies.

_____ Make presentations to classes on the reading skills of a content area.

_____ Plan programs on college entrance test-taking for accelerated students (Polk Community College).

_____ Assist by teaming with content teacher to present vocabulary and reading comprehension skills. (Teacher must be present.)

_____ Work with small groups of problem readers for a few class periods to provide additional help.

extend this mechanism such that "responses" could be stored on a computer and made available to users of the system. Then subsequent users would write different types of annotations on the same selection or reactions to a previous annotation.

The AnX system establishes a network that gives students access to the best thoughts of our best thinkers. As such, it provides an immediately available form of assistance with basic comprehension and offers poignant examples of critical and creative reading and thinking. It does this by providing a net with which to catch and then showcase the potentially valuable, and sometimes fleeting, insights of previous readers. This may take the form of "debunking" a popular myth, such as Margaret Mead's impressions of the innocence and sexual freedom of natives described in *Coming of Age in Samoa*, or some insight on how to solve a particularly difficult problem. There is every reason to believe that a national, or even international, network of school systems, universities, and public libraries could be linked to one another in such a collaborative effort.

Figure 11.2 *continued*

_____ Make class presentations on organizational skills.

_____ Review new test materials to determine readability span and/or reading skills needed.

_____ Locate materials on study skills, critical thinking, etc.

_____ Do diagnostic testing for areas of student strengths and weaknesses.

_____ Determine readability span of texts and related reading materials.

_____ Arrange for taping of chapters for very poor readers.

_____ Prepare study guides for chapters from your text with exercises that include major concepts, technical vocabulary, and comprehension skills.

_____ Locate relevant articles in professional journals.

_____ Write publishers for teaching guides.

_____ Provide inservice in the area of reading to assist you in recertification.

_____ Additional areas

Thanks so much for your cooperation.

Sincerely,

Room _____

Source: From "The Resource Specialist: A Model" by A. R. Woods and M. H. Topping, 1986, *Journal of Reading, 29,* p. 735. Copyright 1986 by the International Reading Association. Reprinted with permission of Alice Woods and the International Reading Association.

The national need for such a system was expressed by Edgar Dale (1984) when he observed, "Knowledge is increasing faster than we can distribute it. We increase knowledge at electronic speed, but continue to distribute it with a horse and buggy" (p. 46). The real justification for such a modern-day contrivance, however, is provided in the history of art and ideas. In every period of expansion of substance or style, creative people have been brought together by fortune or design. Thus, we have had Pericles' Athens, the Medicis' Florence, Elizabeth's London, Goethe's Weimar, and Beethoven's Vienna (Bacon, 1963). The AnX system can bring minds together across greater distances and circumstances than has ever been possible in human history.

Establishing a Schoolwide AnX System

It is no easy matter to initiate a schoolwide AnX program. This and other ideas described ahead, however, might be ideal proposals for some of the "excellence in education" funds that many states and districts are offering for inventive programming:

1. Each department identifies a set of seminal, or core, books and materials. These are placed on reserve in the library and/or in classrooms. Alternate textbooks and other supplementary course materials may be included as well.
2. Students are taught the REAP reading-study method. This is best initiated by the English and/or reading department. Subsequently, it is extended to and reinforced in all other disciplines. When extended to external or public library users, a manual explaining and illustrating the REAP/AnX system may be necessary. General library users are quite willing to contribute annotations on "bestsellers," classics, or books in areas of special interest to them.
3. An AnX committee made up of a coordinator and volunteers should serve as "referees" and "consulting editors" for reviewing annotation submissions. Based on reviewers' judgments as to quality, originality, and need, an annotation could be approved for inclusion in either spiral-bound or computer-based collections. Annotations also could be returned with editorial suggestions and encouragement to resubmit. This review system resembles the format followed by scholarly journals with peer review boards.

AnX as a Content Area Reading Hub: The World Writes a Book

The process of undertaking and operating an AnX hub provides a catalyst for students and teachers to begin to read, write, and think more deeply. In so doing, the connections among fields become more apparent and the lines between them less clear. An AnX hub also provides students with a tangible reason to seek assistance from teachers with their thoughts and the wording of these into acceptable annotations.

Infusions of annotations from teachers of different disciplines, as well as from students, cooperating businesspeople, scholars, and persons from diverse cultural and ethnic backgrounds, can be expected to commingle and incubate creative disbelief, or constructive analysis, in contrast to the more typical "one-upmanship" of critical review and debunking. School-based efforts to use and extend REAP into an AnX system contain elements of a vision for peace and understanding as much as for educational progress: At each stage of development, there is a bounty for students, teachers, communities, and even nations. As fully operating systems, hubs started humbly in different schools and different lands could begin to collaborate as the people of the world write their first book (see Figure 11.3).

Other Programming Catalysts

Earlier in the chapter, we outlined the roles and responsibilities of school administrators, reading specialists, and content teachers. As suggested above, however,

Figure 11.3   From REAP Annotations to AnX Systems

1. When used independently, REAP is a self-guided, study-type reading method.
2. When reviewed by teacher and returned to students, REAP is a teacher-guided method for improving writing, reading, and content acquisition.
3. When discussed and compared in class with other students' annotations and perspectives, REAP is a peer-oriented method for improving comprehension, written and oral communication, and content knowledge.
4. When selected annotations of varying types are taught and compared, REAP provides a method for improving general and specific thinking skills.
5. When selected annotations are accessible for "prereading," REAP becomes an AnX—a peer-generated system of adjunct aids.
6. When teacher annotations are added to the system, AnX is a professional helping hand that is extended into silent reading at a most teachable moment, when the student is experiencing difficulty and insight.
7. When annotations are solicited from the community, AnX is a cross-age program that also extends educational services to adults.
8. When annotations are sought from specialists and authorities, AnX is an inexpensive and high-quality program for the gifted: Masters of each art become the teachers of that art.
9. When AnX crosses district, regional, and national boundaries, the educational level—and the value of education—is elevated wherever it reaches (intellectual comradeships are formed).
10. When AnX is further extended across national boundaries, opportunities for broader multicultural views, cross-cultural understandings, and reductions in world tensions increase. Empathy tames the egocentric beast.
11. When AnX is fully operative, there will be a more rapid creation and evolution of poignant ideas even as less poignant ones are successfully challenged. Insights do not add up; they multiply.

purposeful, catalytic ideas and functions are necessary to ignite growth and maintenance of effective programming.

The following sections describe some other purposeful and potentially program-enhancing heuristics in the same vein as the AnX system. See if any of these ideas strike you as worthy of a proposal to a local PTA, foundation, or government agency seeking to fund innovations in education.

Living Libraries
A *Living Library* is a library that simultaneously is being consumed and is swelling from use. The initial collection should wear thin while new productions by students, faculty, and community enrich the library and swell it out of its plant. WeWriters, Inquiry Books, and Certificators are examples of ways to increase library appeal even for reluctant readers.

WeWriters

The AnX system is only one means of adding students' collected thoughts to the library. Another is to actively support development of a *WeWriters* section of the library to house student essays, plays, poetry, and other literary productions. Faculty and community also can be invited to contribute. This program component can begin at the *elementary*, or *Wee*Writer, level.

Selected student literary works and reactions to various contemporary and school issues could be woven into school yearbooks as another means of capturing the "spirit of the times." Again, a standing committee composed of a librarian, an English teacher, a content area teacher, elected students, and perhaps an interested community member could collectively serve as an editorial board. At least two categories of student production should be accommodated: one in which almost all contributions could be included (here the author would be responsible for the preparation of the manuscript) and one in which school funds would be used for typing, printing, and binding to add an aura of quality and permanence to the collections.

Inquiry Books

The faculty and library staff can actively stimulate curiosity through *Inquiry Books*. These are created by inviting students to submit index cards with written questions for which they have discovered or desire precise references. Again, teachers and community could submit these as well. Periodically, questions could be categorized in different ways, printed, and bound.

Books of questions could be placed in conspicuous locations in the library and study halls, and selected questions could appear in newsletters, bulletins, and other school publications (see Figure 11.4). Periodically students could receive assignments to locate and write out answers to questions of their own choosing.

Instigator and Certificator

It has been said that selective reading in any field for 15 minutes a day over a 4-year period will produce a specialist in that field. Whether or not this is true is irrelevant. The point is that the school library can easily instigate and certify planned independent study, ideally with the cooperation of content area specialists. Specialists could outline courses of study, guide independent reading with adjunct aids and private conferences, and, through sound assessment, certify that serious learning has occurred. Organized topics of study could include many special-interest areas outside the realm of strict academics, such as the often exciting avocations of professional staff members (e.g., sailing, coin collecting, photography).

The incidental benefits from the latter approach are considerable. Students and teachers get to know one another through their mutual interests rather than only in their school roles, and the school itself becomes less one-dimensional and more reflective of a broader community of human interests and abilities. Together these activities also tend to create a gravitational force that gently pulls students, staff, and community into the school's reading and other programming efforts.

Figure 11.4   Sample Inquiry Book
Questions

Where was basketball invented? (You'll be surprised!)
[Reference: *World Book*, vol. __, p. __]

What exactly is a predicate?
[Reference: *Warriner's Grammar*, p. 82]

What is meant by the String Theory of the Universe?
[Reference: *Discover*, April 1, 1988, p. 62]

Teacher Advocates: A Life-Support Plan

Teacher Advocates provide the glue that holds a reading program together during rough times. The objective of this purposeful idea is for each teacher to become a booster for a designated area: to demonstrate it, stay abreast of it, and generally watch over and guide it on an as-needed basis. The idea grew out of our work in the small rural community of Colby, Kansas, nearly 100 miles from the nearest college. For rural America, self-reliance is more a necessity than a moral objective. In an effort to sustain a junior high school reading program through difficulties such as unavailability of a reading coordinator, the informational technology for operating the junior high school's reading program was parceled out carefully to each teacher on staff.

Under the Colby Plan, each teacher worked to become an expert in a designated area, typically a single instructional methodology. The process began with an intensive in-service workshop. Teachers formed liaisons with us, and we then became their personal resource consultants. The school principal served as the primary intermediary in establishing the agenda for consultant visitation days, though correspondence by phone and mail with each teacher was the primary means by which this plan was held together.

ThemedSchool: Free Enterprise and Invention Convention

ThemedSchool (see Figure 11.5) is a schoolwide or districtwide simulation of a significant aspect of real life. ThemedSchool fosters a sense of the relevance of school subjects while putting academics in perspective. It is built around a simulation that (1) takes place throughout the year; (2) requires participation by practically every department and student in the school; (3) culminates in some tangible product or event; (4) rehearses students for meeting real-life demands; and (5) involves the community as Extant Teachers. Quality themes can be repeated on an appropriate cycle, such as every fourth year in a typical three-grade middle school.

ThemedSchool simulations are heuristics on a broad scale. They require extraordinary planning and care. The lessons learned, however, are equally extraordinary. Students gain new respect for one another's talents and abilities while in school and come to appreciate the importance of effective communication and social skills.

Figure 11.5   Sample ThemedSchools

Free Enterprise

The final product is a trade fair held in the spring at which students would sell various goods and products that they either manufactured or purchased for resale. The fair should follow the rules and regulations of state and local governments. Students would be urged to find and study these, seeking the assistance of teachers, parents, friends, attorneys, and participating businesspeople. They would form companies and bid for contracts (e.g., construction, maintenance, and security of fairgrounds). Students could keep money earned, or it could go toward some worthwhile charitable or common goal.

Invention Convention

Throughout the year, students work with one another, friends, parents, teachers, and senior citizens to identify everyday problems. Typical problems might range from catching pesky flies to meeting catastrophic health care needs that may befall a family.

Students, working either in self-formed groups or individually, attempt to solve at least one problem. The proposed solutions are written up and screened by a faculty and student team. The most promising solutions are selected for presentation at an Invention Convention. At the convention, a panel of judges determines further levels of distinction and selects prizewinners.

For further particulars and materials on operating an Invention Convention, contact Invent America!, 510 King Street, Suite 420, Alexandria, VA 22314; Weekly Reader, Field Publishing, 245 Long Hill Road, Middletown, CT 06457; InVenture, Inventors Council of Dayton, 140 E. Monument Avenue, Dayton, OH 45402; or our own Foundation for Better Ideas (providing a Registry for Better Ideas), c/o A. V. Manzo, University of Missouri–Kansas City, Kansas City, MO 64110.

They also establish working ties with their community and respect for its industry and problems.

Other Themes might include

- "Personal Expression—from Cartooning to Music"
- "Our Physical World" (Where are we geographically? What is physically under, above, around, and even in us? For example, it has been noted that our blood has the same proportion of salt as that of the sea.)
- "Fitness" (Our mental and physical fitness needs; developing a personal program to meet them)
- "Leisure" (Exploration of hobbies, games, volunteer work, and other healthy outlets)

Shortcourses

A grant or special-project monies can be sought to fund a *Shortcourse* program. In such a program, teachers and community members are offered stipend and material funds to develop a variety of Shortcourses to provide brief but intensive instruction in a focused area. Shortcourses can be used to fill academic and personal needs that fall between the cracks of existing programming. Sample Shortcourses might include Test Taking; College Preparation; Oral Vocabulary Development; The Newspaper (its parts and uses); Personal Computing; Creative Thinking; Discussion Seminars on "Important Books" and "Significant Ideas"; and focused exposure to a particular culture.

Shortcourses may be offered during the school day or before or after school. Before- and after-school Shortcourses should require a minimal fee. It is a good precedent for students and parents to pay for certain "school-like" information. Nearly 70% of current U.S. business is classified primarily as information services, yet schools continue to try to give such services away. One of the ironies of our Information Age is the loss of prestige of institutions that provide low-cost information accompanied by a huge rise in prestige for individuals, professions, and institutions that charge dearly for it. We hope that this book will lead you to more highly value your informational products and pedagogical skills.

Two features of contemporary school programming currently are serving as valuable catalysts to reading and content objectives. They are *media*—a sleeping giant—and *microcomputing*—a growing one.

Media: A Sleeping Giant

As used here, the term *media* refers primarily to television but is meant to include radio, magazines, and newspapers. Media bashing has become a popular sport, even within media circles. This heavy assault, especially on nonprint media, clearly needs reevaluation. A school's entire curriculum can be enhanced by the judicious use of film, broadcast television, and access to videotape libraries. These, after all, are powerful sources of information and, as such, potentially painless means of building a fund of knowledge, cultural literacy, schema, and world view.

A recent cable news network story reported that adults are watching $3\frac{1}{2}$ to $4\frac{1}{2}$ hours of television per day and children much more. It is difficult to see why this is considered inherently bad. In a typical day's offerings, one easily can be exposed to quick news and thorough news; entertainment and educational programs for children; documentaries and docudramas; financial and medical programs; foreign language programming; multicultural and multiracial stories, news, and outlooks; courses for college credit; discussions and perspectives on many of life's pleasures and woes; and a good deal of sports and entertainment. Obviously, not all of these offerings are of the highest quality, nor are they always very highminded. But the same can be said of the print media.

As a general rule, most of the procedures described in this text for use with textbooks are applicable, with slight modification, to radio, television, magazines, and newspapers. Think, for example, about how easily the Listen step of the Listen-Read-Discuss Heuristic could be provided through a television or radio presentation on a text-related topic. Realize too how readily students could be taught how to annotate in response to what they have viewed or heard as well as read. Following viewing and writing, pertinent portions of a story, speech, or documentary could be rerun to verify, refute, or simply further analyze the information and/or presentation. In general, provisions can be made for the previewing, viewing, and postviewing of television and radio almost as readily as is now being done with print media.

Even more powerful than the role of media as a receptive function is a growing interest in communications as a theme base for school curricula. In this environment, youngsters from elementary through high school are being taught how to plan, write, and produce radio and television broadcasts as well as how to watch them analytically. Several such programs already are operating around the nation, the Cincinnati and Kansas City public schools being among the more progressive.

Microcomputing: A Growing Giant

Microcomputers can add cohesiveness to a reading program and relieve a staff of some otherwise tedious chores. In several places throughout this text, we have made passing reference to microcomputer usage. In view of the decisions many face as to whether to purchase computers for home or school use and why, it seems appropriate to comment briefly on the potential value of computers in the content area reading program. Courses on computer literacy, now being offered by most institutions, will answer more technical questions.

Let's first consider the question of whether computers are a justifiable expense from the standpoint of content and reading training. Clearly they are, but there are some nagging problems. The biggest problem is the lack of compatibility of equipment and software, or programs. The computer industry could help us all if they would sit down and agree to a standard language and compatible components. At the moment this is difficult, because so much computer technology is in a state of growth and flux. From a user's point of view, however, the situation can be exasperating. It's as though each maker of audiotape and record players required a different size and speed of recording and playback equipment. The problem is magnified by rigorous training requirements for most word processing programs and huge manuals of "documentation" that can make a pencil look very attractive.

Having said all this, it is worth considering what can be done with microcomputers, which, while still expensive, now rival the power and flexibility of the million-dollar machines of only a generation ago. Microcomputers are wonderful electronic exercise books. There are software programs that present and even generate vocabulary reinforcement and mathematics practice exercises. Best of all, the machine doesn't get tired, bored, or ill; it provides immediate feedback; and some programs actually keep score and provide printouts of patterns of responses. There also are more inventive programs that teach active reading, allow the student to write or choose different endings to stories, and provide simulation activities in science, social studies, and economics. The most ambitious effort by far is a growing interest in developing textbooks that contain "hypertext"—that is, imbedded aids and other loop-out material to supplement and support the basic text.

For the most part, however, the greatest potential benefit of computers has yet to be realized. It is not only in computer-assisted instruction for students but in computer-managed instruction for teachers. As a rule, teachers have not yet been given desktop computers. Where these are readily available, they can be used to

- Quickly and easily spot-check readability of text and supplementary materials
- Manage grades
- Store and generate tests
- Store teaching strategies
- Score and even interpret tests
- Store and retrieve written responses to books in a classroom, school-based, or larger Annotation Exchange program

A word of caution is in order. As useful as computers can be, there is nothing vital to the school reading program that can be done with them that cannot be done without them. Further, any aspect of program development begun in earnest without computers will help justify their future purchase.

CHAPTER TIE-UPS

Graphic Organizer   ◆◆◆

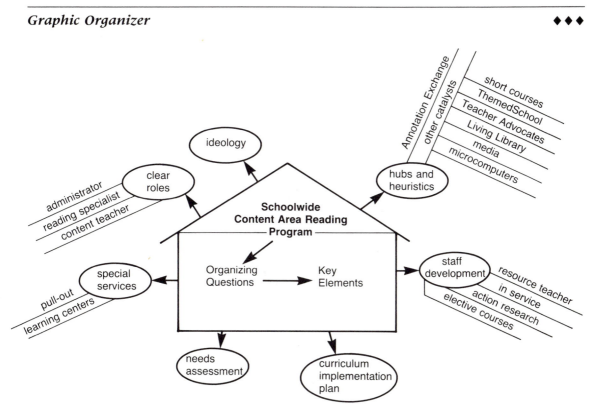

◆ ◆ ◆   *Critique and Anticipation*

This chapter identified seven necessary features of a quality content area reading program. Then it gave examples of these as well as of several optional features. The chapter stressed and elaborated on the value and significance of one feature that is often overlooked in school programming: hubs, or places and operations designed to ignite and keep the programs going and growing. Several hubs were suggested—some grand and some modest, but all capable of raising the value and status of reading, language, and thinking skills.

The next chapter offers some specialized content reading methods for English and math teachers. It asks teachers to consider their common ground as teachers of language: one verbal, the other notational. The expectation is that this will further reduce some of the artificial walls separating interdisciplinary learning and functioning.

TRADE SECRET

Reduce "Parent Involvement"

As educators, we sometimes tend to overdo our efforts to enlist "parental involvement." In your own efforts to involve parents, keep in mind that parents don't work for us—we work for them. Several common practices deserve to be rethought. Most of them turn out either to be assignments for parents rather than for students or to exceed our authority. Here are some examples:

- Requiring that parents sign students' homework
- Requiring that parents sign students' assignment pads each day
- Requiring students with no means of transportation to go to a public library on their own time
- Requiring students to order and purchase books or special supplies
- Requiring students to view a certain television program
- Requiring rather than inviting parents to pick up student report cards, meet teachers, or attend school functions

In all likelihood, there are many evenings spoiled and dinners ruined because students must bring up homework and other obligations and school problems to their parents. Evenings and dinnertimes ought to be a time for family members to interact with one another in personal ways. Even a seemingly small assignment can be brought to a parent on the heels of a long and stressful day or a difficult home situation. Instead of demands, consider offering options, invitations, and help to parents. In this way, you can satisfy parents who wish to help students with homework and such without presuming to tell all parents what to do and when to do it regardless of what they have planned or is happening on a particular evening in their lives. If we can reduce the "help" we ask of parents and increase the "help" we provide them, it is a good bet that they will value us and what we have to offer more fully.

PART FIVE

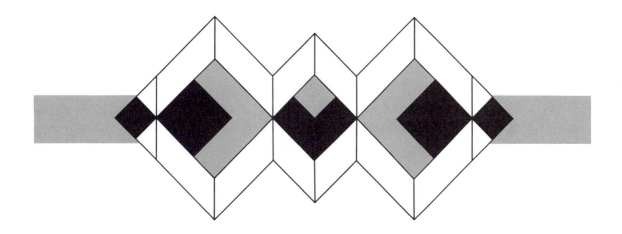

Content Area
Applications

English and Mathematics

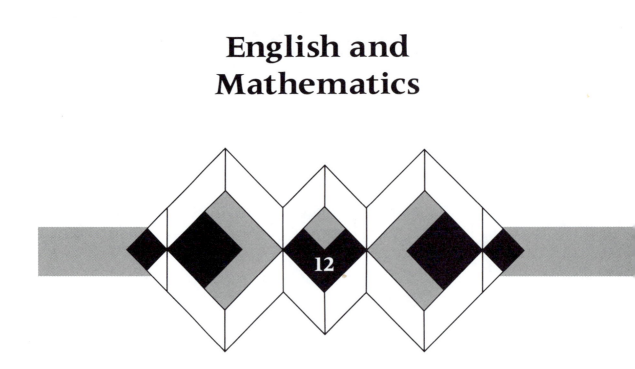

Writing and Notation

Reading maketh a full man; conference a ready man; and writing an exact man.
— Francis Bacon

FOCUS

English and mathematics are methods of coding. Both contribute naturally to the reading process in their own ways, and both benefit from it. English and mathematics are best improved through whole language, whole person approaches.

OUTLINE

ENGLISH

Reading and English ♦ Teaching English and Reading ♦ Writing: A Leitmotif ♦ Prose Reading, or The Odd Pursuit of Teaching Books ♦ Poetry Comprehension and Appreciation ♦ Looking Back ♦ Mathematics

MATHEMATICS AS A SECOND LANGUAGE

Five Languaging-Based Teaching Strategies ♦ Looking Back

CHAPTER TIE-UPS

Graphic Organizer ♦ Critique and Anticipation ♦ Trade Secret: Teachers as Ethnic Groups

Although seldom discussed in the same context, English and mathematics are fraternal in many ways. Both are systems of language used to probe, identify, and code the realities around us. Both have complex rules of grammar and usage. Both lend themselves to creative expression, although this feature of mathematics is not widely realized. The greatest difference between English and mathematics probably is that English tends to be a left-brain function and a way to talk about our subjective relationship to the world, while mathematics tends to be right-brain-centered and offers an abstract means of seeing the world in more spatial terms. To master both subjects is, quite literally, to be bilingual and bicultural and therefore able to conduct a more insightful dialectical examination of the human experience. It also appears to be a major means of igniting deeper thinking, more rapid transfer of training, and creativity.

ENGLISH

The English curriculum is the focal point for teaching language mastery. The term is a quaint reminder of our colonial and cultural past. In fact, our language is Anglo-American and the discipline is Language Arts, or effective listening, speaking, reading, and writing, in both formal and informal circumstances.

Reading and English

Student progress in reading receives its greatest emphasis in the English curriculum. English is the only discipline that traditionally has designated reading improvement as a key objective. It also provides direct and systematic instruction in vocabulary, writing, cultural literacy, and literary appreciation. As such, it lays the linguistic and cultural foundations for effective comprehension in all realms and ensures that at least some explicit attention is given to receptive and expressive language in school. There are sound reasons for continuing this focus on language up to and through graduate education. The most obvious is the fact that oral, written, and spoken language, like reading, are developmental processes one can refine and enhance throughout one's lifetime.

Even greater than the contribution of the English curriculum to reading progress are the requirements that reading in English places on students. The most difficult of these is the requirement to read anthologies of prose and poetry that often span hundreds of years in origin, context, and style.

This chapter addresses several means and methods for teaching the core "English" curriculum while contributing to and benefiting from the reading curriculum. Curricular requirements addressed include textbook usage, grammar, writing, reference skills, and literary appreciation. These are considered primarily from the perspective of meeting the needs of developmental and corrective readers in a standard English classroom situation.

Teaching English and Reading

Informal Textbook Inventory Specifications

The first—and simplest—way to benefit reading and English objectives concurrently is to construct and use an Informal Textbook Inventory of the type described and illustrated in Chapter 3. Figure 12.1 presents some illustrations and examples of English-specific question types that can be added to the basic Informal Textbook Inventory format.

Grammar: The Cloze Talking Procedure

A most efficient means of teaching grammar is with a specialized application of the cloze procedure that we have come to call the *Cloze Talking* procedure. A cloze passage worksheet is prepared by deleting random words from a text passage. Students work individually or in pairs to fill in the deleted words. A whole-class Cloze Talking procedure follows. This discussion, or languaging through, of correct and incorrect choices of replacement words provides a painless way to teach grammar. In the process of conducting the discussion, the teacher offers his or her knowledge of grammar and terminology incidentally as students work to label their thoughts.

Example   ◆◆◆
So, then, what Frank is saying is that a "modifier" word needs to go in this space. Well, there are two kinds of modifiers. One is called an *adjective*—it modifies nouns, or persons, places, and things. The other is called an *adverb*—it modifies actions or verbs or other adverbs. Which kind of modifier do you suppose is needed here, an adjective or an adverb? Can you see any easy way to tell adverbs from adjectives?

   With this approach, grammar is taught and learned contextually, by self-discovery. More important, it is taught when and where the need arises, much as most other concepts and labels are learned in natural language development. Note, however, that this should not *replace* traditional instruction. Some grammar should be taught directly and systematically as well, especially to college-bound students. Grammar lends consistency and stability to language; thus, all literate citizens should have a working knowledge of its principles. Cloze Talking can turn rote knowledge of grammatical definitions and facts into working knowledge of a living language.

Writing: A Leitmotif

Strictly speaking, reading and writing are less highly correlated than many people believe, although each surely benefits the other in a reciprocal way. Together they describe a "literate" person as opposed to one who is simply "not illiterate." Good writing dignifies the human experience. To teach youngsters to write is to provide

Figure 12.1   Informal Textbook Inventory Questions for English

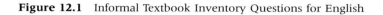

I. Use of Text Aids to Locate Information
   Construct 10 to 15 questions which assess students' ability to use parts of the textbook, such as:
   A. What is the title of the book?
   B. When was it published?
   C. Who wrote the book?
   D. How many chapters are in the book?
   E. How are the chapters arranged or grouped?
   F. On what page does Chapter 8 begin?
   G. In which chapter can you find something about Langston Hughes?
   H. In which chapter can you find "Types of Humor in Modern American Literature"?

II. Rate of Reading and Levels of Comprehension
   Choose a passage from the textbook which has not been read by students. Have students read the passage and record the time when they finish it. Help them to compute their rate of reading, or words per minute (number of words read divided by number of minutes spent = words per minute). Have students answer questions about the passage which require comprehension at literal, interpretive, and applied levels.

III. Vocabulary Skills
   A. *Contextual Analysis:* Choose sentences from the textbook which contain words which may be difficult for students. List these sentences, with the difficult words underlined. Have students predict the meaning of the underlined words, using clues from the context to make reasonable predictions (evaluate student responses in terms of "reasonableness" of prediction rather than accuracy of definition).
   B. *Structural Analysis:* Select words from the textbook which are made up of affixes and recognizable English root words. Have students identify and explain the meaning or function of the root word, prefix, and/or suffix in each of these words.
   C. *Dictionary Use:* Choose sentences from the textbook which contain a word or

them with the tools necessary for defining and describing their lives and circumstances for others to understand and consider. It is for this reason that it is so important to teach those least likely to write—the disenfranchised—how and why to do so.

There are many ways and no one way to teach writing. Any reasonable approach that draws attention to words, phrasing, and punctuation will result in some improvement, but no single method is likely to impart all the nuances of this complex craft. The writer's personal commitment, inclination to practice and revise, and intellectual development are just a few of the many factors involved in growth toward maturity in this aspect of language mastery. Writing is the most difficult skill to teach because it entails a profound paradox: It is not simply a matter of

Figure 12.1 *continued*

words that have multiple meanings. List these sentences, with the multiple-meaning word(s) underlined. Have students check a dictionary to select and write the appropriate meaning of each underlined word according to its use in the sentence. (From a term paper by Fengfang Lu, UMKC, 1986)

IV. Use of Reference Sources to Locate Information
    A. In our classroom dictionary, locate the origin of the word ("bonfire").
    B. Using the library card catalog, find the names of two books written by (Judy Blume). Who is the author of (*The Great Gilly Hopkins*)?
    C. In the *Reader's Guide to Periodical Literature,* locate the journal and the year and month in which you find the short story entitled ("Down the Down Staircase: A Sequel").
    D. In the *Essay and General Literature Index,* find the titles for three stories related to the theme of (family conflict).
    E. In the *Current Biography,* locate information about Ernest Hemingway's life.
    F. In Bartlett's *Familiar Quotations,* locate the person credited with having written: "Go, sir, gallop, and don't forget that the world was made in six days. You can ask me for anything you like, except time."
    G. A thesaurus is a book of words grouped by ideas and used to locate precise words to express your idea. In *Roget's International Thesaurus,* locate at least three nouns which could be used instead of *cheerfulness.*

V. Use of Graphic Aids to Interpret Meaning
    A. Study the cartoon on page _____ of your text. Describe what you believe to be the message of the cartoon.
    B. Examine the time line of major English literary periods on page _____ of your text. What years are considered to encompass the neo-classical literary period? List three prominent writers of this period.
    C. The diagram on page _____ depicts the plot structure of Jackson's "The Lottery." After reading the story, briefly discuss the conflict, rising action, climax, and denouement of "The Lottery."

Source: Sections IV and V from Criscoe/Gee, CONTENT READING: A Diagnostic/Prescriptive Approach, © 1984, pp. 83–84. Reprinted by permission of Prentice-Hall, Inc., Englewood Cliffs, N.J.

clearly and cleverly saying what one thinks but also a way to *discover* what one is thinking. It is a tool for introspection.

All of the remaining methods covered in this section have writing as their primary theme or leitmotif. Nevertheless, writing will never be easy to teach or to learn. It is a habit of mind and always hard work. The prolific writer and economist John Kenneth Galbraith has said it most profoundly: "[T]here are days when the result is so bad that no fewer than five revisions are required. In contrast, when I'm greatly inspired, only four revisions are needed."

The Language Shaping Paradigm

There are two fundamental problems encountered in improving writing. The first is to get students to write sufficiently to generate an adequate sample for editing, or shaping. The second is to win students' cooperation in a critical review of the personal patterns of language and thought that their writing reveals.

The basic idea of the *Language Shaping Paradigm* (Manzo, 1981a) is to connect students to the printed page through their own writing. More important, the method urges students to value and profit from personal thoughts and experiences and to lead more "examined" lives. In these respects, the Language Shaping Paradigm resembles two other methods: the traditional elementary-school-oriented Language Experience Story and a method well described by its title, Read and Meet the Author, or RAMA (Santeusanio, 1967).

The efficacy of the Language Shaping Paradigm is inferred from a study of its parent, RAMA, and from experience and anecdotal accounts. Santeusanio (1967) found RAMA to be significantly more effective than a control treatment in improving the reading comprehension and writing of college freshmen. Our own experience with the Language Shaping Paradigm has tended to support and extend the generalizability of this approach to other levels, including adult basic education students.

The basic teaching strategy entails having students read essays written (or dictated) by classmates. Each time the method is used, someone's essay is treated as an important work. The essay is edited (by both the teacher and the student-author) and reproduced with accompanying exercises designed (by the teacher) to improve reading comprehension, language usage, and creative writing.

Steps in the Language Shaping Paradigm

1. The teacher begins with a *provocative discussion* to establish a purpose for writing.
2. *Students write themes* in a conventional way (or the teacher writes as the student dictates his or her essay).
3. The teacher selects a student story or essay and edits it jointly with the student-author, informing the student that his or her work will be used for class study.
4. The teacher prepares comprehension questions and language improvement exercises for the material.
5. The teacher duplicates the theme and exercises for the class to read and discuss. The student-author is urged to maintain a "low profile" during the initial discussion.
6. The teacher invites the student-author to participate more openly as the discussion moves to the language improvement exercises. This is the student-author's greatest learning opportunity in terms of writing, speaking, and learning to benefit from constructive criticism.

The theme shown in Figure 12.2 is the product of a nearly illiterate adult named Frank who had enrolled in a high school equivalency program. The story was stimulated by a discussion of dream interpretation. The instructor worked individually with Frank, writing his story for him as Frank dictated it. The other class members wrote their own stories. Frank and the instructor edited the theme together until it was to Frank's liking. Frank took the editorial suggestions in good spirits. The forthcoming "publication" of the written piece seemed to offer its own justification for such straightforward editing and correcting of the more glaring grammatical and logical inconsistencies.

Frank's essay was reproduced for the other students. After an oral comprehension check, using a set of *who, what, where, when, how,* and *why* questions, the students did the Language Improvement Exercises (arranged in order of increasing difficulty) illustrated in Figure 12.2.

The next two strategies also are designed to shape *language* as a means of improving writing.

Reducing/Expanding Sentences

Bill Martin, Jr., an enthusiastic supporter of children's writing, suggests several other means of improving writing, two of which are appropriate here: Reducing Sentences and Expanding Sentences. A description of Reducing Sentences (see Figure 12.3) shows by inference how Expanding Sentences (adding words) is done.

Reducing/Expanding Sentences is especially useful when done as a whole-class activity using samples from students' own writing. It concentrates attention on the main ideas of sentences and the subtle changes of meaning evoked by slight changes of words and punctuation.

De-Composition and GRASP

Marilyn Eanet (1983) and David Hayes (1988) have independently designed methodologies that expand the Guided Reading Procedure (GRP) into a flexible method for teaching writing and reading in combination.

Eanet's idea uses the GRP to urge students to learn how textual material is composed by decomposing it into component parts and then recomposing it in their own words. Hayes's Guided Reading And Summarizing Procedure, or GRASP, also follows the Guided Reading Procedure by having students use the student-generated information as the basis for composing their own summaries of the material. The following strategy synthesizes Eanet's De-Composition and Hayes's GRASP:

1. *GRP lesson.* The teacher conducts a conventional Guided Reading Procedure lesson up through the outlining step.
2. *Decomposing.* The teacher asks students, "Can you describe how the author put this information together?"
3. *Recomposing.* The teacher asks the class, "Can you think of other logical ways by which this selection could have been composed?"
4. *Summarizing.* The teacher has students write their own summaries, following these guidelines:
   a. Include only important information (leave out unimportant details).
   b. Where possible, compress information by combining it.
   c. Add information needed to achieve coherence

Figure 12.2   Language Shaping Paradigm: Student Theme and Language Improvement
Exercises

I Dreamed I Was Green
Author: Frank Xxxxxx, Age 31
Kansas City, Missouri

1   I fell asleep late last night on the couch in front of my TV.
I was watching an old movie called the "Boy with the Green Hair." My
body ached from another long day. My stomach was now working on the
cornbeef and cabbage, Dynamite! The combination made me dream a
5   strange dream. I dreamed that I woke up and had turned green. God,
it was so real! At first I thought it was the light. Then I thought
someone was playing a practical joke on me. But none of these things
made sense. The kids were fast asleep and my wife had not yet come
home from her part-time job. She is a ticket girl at the Waldo. I
10   called the doctor. The answering service wanted to know what was
wrong. I told them. He never called back. I went next door to my
neighbor, Bud. He was shocked. He brought me to the hospital. His
wife watched our kids.
The doctors said there is nothing wrong with you that we can
15   tell, except that you are definitely green!
Now the dream gets all crazy. All I know is that I find myself
planted in the backyard and beginning to look more and more like a
tree. Then a lot of time passes. And the house is old and my wife
and kids are gone, but I'm still in the backyard. No one seems to
20   notice me. I'm not unhappy. I'm not happy. I'm nothing. I'm just
there.
Well, that's not really true, about me just being there, I mean.
There are moments when I'm very happy, like when squirrels and birds
are playing on my branches. And I really feel good when I turn
25   beautiful colors in the fall. And even though I don't like the
winter, it's kind of nice to be covered with blue-white snow.
February is the worst. Dark and sad. But then in March I begin to
swell on the inside. I feel life stirring inside me, like a woman
does long before anyone even knows she is pregnant. Then April
30   showers and then in May I bust-out of myself and turn beautiful green.
I woke up at about that time. This may sound crazy, but I was a
little disappointed that I was not green.

Level I: Choosing More Appropriate Words

Sometimes replacing or modifying a few words in a paragraph can greatly enhance the
clarity and sharpness of an essay. Carefully study the paragraph below. Decide which
of the underlined words you would replace from the list of words in the left column.

Figure 12.2 *continued*

---

1   2
I called the doctor. The answer service wanted to know what was wrong. I told them.
3   4
He never called back. I went next door to my neighbor, Bud. He was shocked. He
  5   6
brought me to the hospital. His wife watched our kids.

Replacement Words

spoke to	I (1) _____ the doctor. The answering service (2) _____ what
phoned	was wrong. I told them. (3) _____ never called back. I went next
asked	door to my neighbor, Bud. He was shocked. (4) _____
the doctor	(5) _____ me to the hospital. His wife (6) _____ our kids.
Bud	
drove	
looked after	
told	

Level 2: Improving Style/Mood

"I Dreamed I Was Green" is written in a half-humorous, half-serious vein; that is to say, the language is quite casual. Decide which of the sentences below best matches the mood of "I Dreamed I Was Green." Underline the words, phrases, and/or punctuations that seem to contribute to, or take away from, that mood. Write "I" for improved, "N" for not improved. (Number 1 is done as an example).

___N___ 1. I asked the doctor's answering service if they might have an opinion on why I was green.
_____ 2. I called the doctor. Naturally, I got some corny answering service.
_____ 3. You got it! The doc never called back.
_____ 4. I went next door to consult with my neighbor, Bud. He was shocked.
_____ 5. Bud's wife, Martha, volunteered to look after the children while I was at the hospital.

Level 3: Rewriting or Reorganizing

Do *either* A or B:

A. Pretend that you are the author of the article, and rewrite the paragraph between lines 16 and 21 in a way that you believe would improve it.

_____

_____

_____

_____

B. Reorganize: Can you see any means by which this piece can be re-ordered so that the basic story remains the same but the effect is more imaginative or stylish? (You may rewrite small sections, if necessary, to show what you mean.)

Figure 12.3   Reducing Sentences

Reducing Sentences is highly useful in helping students figure out how sentences work. When a person reduces a sentence, he or she eliminates all unnecessary words, phrases, and clauses. This is done by underlining the words to be taken out. The danger in reducing a sentence is that one is apt to alter or destroy the sentence meaning or to tamper with the author's style of writing. Now let's reduce a few sentences and analyze the results.

A bird also has another way to help keep himself warm in winter.

By seeing to it that the birds near your home have plenty to eat, you can "keep their furnaces roaring" and their bodies warm in winter.

The bird's outer feathers are staggered like shingles on a roof to keep out the rain and snow.

— from "How Birds Keep Warm in Winter,"
Sounds of Mystery

Discussion: In the first sentence, the reducing sharpened the sentence. The eliminated (underlined) words are truly unnecessary. In the second sentence, the meaning is preserved but the aesthetics seem to suffer. In the third sentence, the basic sentence is unchanged, but an important conceptual detail is eliminated.

Source: Bill Martin, Jr., lecture, Kansas City, Missouri.

(Note: Hayes suggests that the teacher demonstrate how the first cluster of information can be written into a single sentence, explaining why certain information is omitted, how other information can be combined, and the purpose[s] served by the changes. Then students are directed to write the next sentence while the teacher does the same on the chalkboard, preferably at the rear of the room. Students then share their sentences and comments about how their renditions compare with the teacher's. The teacher should be prepared to revise his or her sentence, writing changes above or below the original sentence to leave a visible record of the revision process. Teacher and students compose the next sentence or two together [see Figure 12.4].)

5. (Optional) The teacher encourages students to write a brief reaction to the material read, analyzed, and summarized. Refer to the REAP Response Rubric (Chapter 7) for examples of possible means by which to react.

Prose Reading, or the Odd Pursuit of Teaching Books

Teachers of literature essentially are tour guides to Proust, Austen, Donne, Faulkner, and Joyce—to the great authors who, after all, were teachers themselves. This section recommends several "tour guide" strategies. The first method offers a link between responsive reading and motivated writing.

Figure 12.4   Development of the Prose Summary

A. The first group of details converted to prose:

The Rosetta stone provided the key for reading the ancient ~~language of Egypt. The~~ ~~ancient~~ Egyptian language *which* had been a riddle for hundreds of years.

B. Addition of the second group of details:

The Rosetta Stone provided the key for reading the ancient ~~language of Egypt. The~~ ~~ancient~~ Egyptian language *which* had been a riddle for hundreds of years. An officer in Napoleon's engineering corps ~~found~~ The Rosetta stone *was found in 1799* ~~half buried in the mud~~ near *the Egyptian city of* Rosetta., → by

C. The completed summary:

The Rosetta stone provided the key for reading the ancient ~~language of Egypt. The~~ ~~ancient~~ Egyptian language *which* had been a riddle for hundreds of years. An officer in Napoleon's engineering corps ~~found~~ The Rosetta stone *was found in 1799* ~~half buried in the mud~~ near *the Egyptian city of* Rosetta. *by* The black basalt stone bore inscriptions in ancient Egyptian hieroglyphics, *in*

Demotic, and *in* Greek. The inscriptions were deciphered by Jean Champollion, who with

knowledge of Greek and Coptic (the last stage of the Egyptian language), compared ~~Greek~~ words *in the Greek texts* with ~~Egyptian~~ words *in the Egyptian texts*. The inscriptions ~~were~~ *had been* carved by Egyptian priests to

commemorate the crowning of Egyptian king Ptolemy Epiphanes, 203–181 B.C. In 1822

Champollion described the decipherment in a pamphlet, which has since been used as

a tool for translating ancient Egyptian literature. The Rosetta stone is *preserved* ~~kept~~ in the British

Museum.

Source: From *Guided Reading and Summarizing Procedure* by D. A. Hayes, 1988, Manuscript, University of Georgia, Athens, GA.

Literature Response Journals

Middle school teacher Kris Myers (1988) reports that she generates student interest in reading literature assignments by having them keep running *Literature Response Journals* of their reactions to literary pieces. She uses Bleich's (1975) Response Heuristic, which suggests how most readers wish to respond to literature. Bleich shows a profound insight into typical human behavior when he suggests that readers first wish to give their personal perceptions of a work (what it means to them); then they are better able to analyze the reasons for their associations and affective responses.

Myers developed "Twenty (Better) Questions" (see Figure 12.5) based on Bleich's ideas. Students seem more willing to write in response to these questions, Myers suggests, because otherwise they are seldom asked what they think about what they read and, even less often, *why* they think what they think.

Emphasis on the "why" questions raises this teaching strategy to the level of a concurrent method for improving metacognitive thinking as well as reading and writing. It also helps address a previously noted major instructional shortfall reported by a recent national assessment of educational progress: Students routinely did poorly in answering "explanation" questions (Applebee & Langer, 1983).

Myers has her middle school students respond to any one question of their choice or, occasionally, asks that they all respond to one particular question. She expects at least a half-page-long reaction and occasionally grades these papers. Students' grades are determined by the "seriousness of intent and obvious knowledge of the story" (1988, p. 65).

Another literature response system, called *Correlative Thinking,* invites use of analogies.

Correlative or Analogical Thinking

The value of analogies, or co-relating one thing to another, in reading has been frequently noted (Bean, Searles, Singer, & Cowen, 1987; Hayes & Tierney, 1982; Manzo, 1977). Independent use of analogies, however, has remained a difficult thinking skill to inculcate in students.

High school English teacher Elizabeth McGonigal (1988) has described a method for helping students learn how to create and use analogies independently in two situations: while reading literature and as a prewriting activity for responding to literature.

Steps for Using Analogies to Teach Correlative Thinking

1. Explain the concept of analogies and show examples of the different ways these can be constructed as equations. The two most popular ways are as follows:
    a. mother : daughter :: father : _____
       (a. uncle b. cousin c. son d. brother-in-law e. aunt)
    b. doctor : lawyer :: _____ : _____
       (a. client : illness b. client : ailment c. patient : litigation d. patient : client)

Figure 12.5 Twenty "Better" Questions

1. What character(s) was your favorite? Why?
2. What character(s) did you dislike? Why?
3. Does anyone in this work remind you of anyone you know? Explain.
4. Are you like any character in this work? Explain.
5. If you could be any character in this work, who would you be? Explain.
6. What quality(ies) of which character strikes you as a good characteristic to develop within yourself over the years? Why? How does the character demonstrate this quality?
7. Overall, what kind of a feeling did you have after reading a few paragraphs of this work? Midway? After finishing the work?
8. Do any incidents, ideas, or actions in this work remind you of your own life or something that happened to you? Explain.
9. Do you like this piece of work? Why or why not?
10. Are there any parts of this work that were confusing to you? Which parts? Why do you think you got confused?
11. Do you feel there is an opinion expressed by the author through this work? What is it? How do you know this? Do you agree? Why or why not?
12. Do you think the title of this work is appropriate? Is it significant? Explain. What do you think the title means?
13. Would you change the ending of this story in any way? Tell your ending. Why would you change it?
14. What kind of person do you feel the author is? What makes you feel this way?
15. How did this work make you feel? Explain.
16. Do you share any of the feelings of the characters in this work? Explain.
17. Sometimes works leave you with the feeling that there is more to tell. Did this work do this? What do you think might happen?
18. Would you like to read something else by this author? Why or why not?
19. What do you feel is the most important word, phrase, passage, or paragraph in this work? Explain why it is important.
20. If you were an English teacher, would you want to share this work with your students? Why or why not?

Source: From "Twenty (Better) Questions" by K. L. Myers, 1988, *English Journal, 77,* pp. 64–65. Copyright 1988 by the National Council of Teachers of English. Reprinted with permission.

2. Present completed analogies from literature for discussion:

   Macbeth : Lady Macbeth :: Adam : Eve
   (In this activity, students discover that Lady Macbeth, like Eve before her, controlled the fate of her mate. Also, like Eve, it was Lady Macbeth's greed and pride that caused her to manipulate a gullible man.)
3. Encourage additional analogies arising from the discussion:

   Macbeth : Lady Macbeth :: indecisive : decisive
   or

   Macbeth : Lady Macbeth :: Ollie North : William Casey

4. Write incomplete analogies on the board and elicit several possible completions:

(from *The Adventures of Huckleberry Finn*)
river : shore :: _____ : _____
(from "The Love Song of J. Alfred Prufrock")
women : mermaids :: _____ : _____

5. Once students no longer find analogies intimidating, have them attempt to construct their own.[1]

The carryover of analogy construction into writing, according to McGonigal, is predictable: Students feel "ownership" of the basic idea and write with greater authority and power. It is notable that where there has not been careful, guided, and direct instruction in analogy construction, students seldom are able to generate analogies. For further discussion of analogies, see the Parallel Form Strategy in the social studies section in Chapter 13.

Cooperative Glossaries

Many great books contain quite erudite language, which can pose a considerable obstacle to comprehension and appreciation for immature readers. Erudite language by definition is uncommon: It can contain unfamiliar words, archaic language forms, and difficult, phonetically represented dialect. A simple *Cooperative Glossary,* however, can serve as a useful tour guide on such incursions into unfamiliar surroundings.

Here is an approach to Cooperative Glossary construction that phases in an increasing measure of student independence and fosters a spirit of responsible cooperative learning:

1. The teacher constructs a simple vocabulary guide to a few pages of a longer selection or book.
2. Students are urged to use the Cooperative Glossary whenever they feel the need to do so.
3. Students are urged to read a few pages beyond those covered by the guide.
4. Discussion develops about how the guide helped and which additional words and/or phrases might need definition.
5. Each student is assigned to prepare a Glossary for a few pages of the remainder of the text. Students should be told to note the page number for each word they select and to record *only* the dictionary definition that applies to the way the word is used in the selection.
6. Glossaries are compiled and reproduced for the entire class.
7. (Optional) The teacher adds a pronunciation guide. This step is optional because it is difficult to do; however, most students would desire—and need—one.

Figure 12.6 presents an example of a Cooperative Glossary.

---

[1]From "Creative Thinking: Writing Analogies about Literature" by E. McGonigal, 1988, *English Journal,* 77, pp. 66–67. Copyright 1988 by the National Council of Teachers of English. Reprinted with permission.

Figure 12.6 Cooperative Glossary for *A Tale of Two Cities*

Page	Chapter	Word	Definition	Pronunciation
67	3	inscrutable	cannot be understood	in-screw-ta-ble
68		lamentation	cry out	la-men-ta-shun
70		opiate	a drug to help a person sleep	o-pee-ut
71		perpetuation	continuing	per-pet-chu-a-shun
72		specter	ghost	speck-tur
81	4	consignment	delivery	cun-sine-ment
83		disconcerted	confused	dis-cun-sir-ted
84		oblivion	complete forgetfulness	o-bli-vee-un
85		sonorous	loud praise	sah-nore-us
87		supplicatory	begging	sup-pli-cu-tory

Text Preview Guide

The *Text Preview Guide,* developed by Graves et al. (1983), is a teacher-constructed guide with three sections: one to build interest, one to provide a synopsis, and one to define key vocabulary and guiding questions. Previews should be about 400 words long (see Figure 12.7).

Because Text Preview Guides require considerable preparation time, it is recommended that they be constructed only for difficult selections that will be taught several times (Ericson et al., 1987). They resemble, but are more comprehensive than, the Advance Ideational and Literal Organizers described in Chapter 5 on prereading.

Teaching poetry is even more difficult than teaching prose. The next strategy takes a creative process approach to this problem.

Poetry Comprehension and Appreciation

Communal Poetry

At least three factors prevent most youngsters from relating to poetry: The language form is foreign, students lack knowledge of typical poetic allusions, and, most important, students tend to lack specific knowledge of poetry and empathy with the poetic process; that is, they do not see poetry as a useful medium for languaging through thoughts and feelings.

Communal Poetry was developed by Manzo and Martin (1974) to counter these elements and enable students to better understand and relate to poetry. We found the method to be unusually stimulating of comprehension and appreciation of poetry as well. Communal Poetry initially was field tested with a group of 10th-grade inner-city youngsters who had failed English at least once before. The benefits

Figure 12.7   Text Preview Guide

I. Build Interest

Many adults read fairy tales to their children. Did any adult ever read fairy tales to you? Which ones do you remember?

Many fairy tales have a princess who falls in love. The young man she falls in love with must often prove himself worthy to her father, the king. Perhaps he must slay a dragon or survive other dangerous experiences. In some fairy tales, the young man even saves the princess from some horrible beast.

Stories like this are not only for children, however. Stories for teenagers and adults may have many similarities with fairy tales. For example, there are many stories in which modern day parents disapprove of the boy their daughter loves, but they change their minds about him when he does something wonderful, and everything ends happily. Can you think of examples from television or the movies which are modern day fairy tales?

Sometimes in a story or television program something happens that you don't expect. Maybe there is a sad ending instead of a happy ending, or the thief turns out to be a king in disguise. Another unexpected ending might involve having the ugly woman turn out to be a beautiful fashion model working under cover for the police. Can you think of other examples?

II. Synopsis

In "The Lady or the Tiger," a king has an unusual way of deciding if a man accused of a crime is guilty or innocent. The accused man is forced to walk into an arena and must open one of two doors. Behind one door is a ferocious tiger who immediately tears the man to pieces as punishment for being guilty. Behind the other door is a beautiful woman who immediately marries him as a reward for his innocence. All the people of the kingdom are required to attend this trial.

---

of the method are best illustrated by the poem this group composed (see Figure 12.8).

Steps in Communal Poetry

1. The teacher asks questions designed to elicit fresh language and personal sensory responses about a chosen subject.
2. Responses are recorded on the chalkboard. Clichés and other prosaic or hackneyed phrases are edited out as they occur.
3. Once the board is filled with "raw material," students are asked to choose a beginning line from the material on the board.
4. The teacher writes the line and then aids students in selecting other phrases, helping them to establish rhythm and/or continuity of thought.

Figure 12.7 *continued*

III. Review of Characters, Vocabulary, and Guiding Questions

Now it happens that a common man falls in love with the king's daughter. She loves him in return. But the king finds out about their love and the young man's fate is to be decided in the arena. The princess knows which door hides the tiger and will be able to give her lover a signal. But she is very jealous of the beautiful young woman behind the other door.

What signal does she give her lover? You will have to read to find out.

Before you read the story, we want to tell you again the three most important people in it. They are the king, the princess, and the young man.

There are also some words we would like to define:

The king is "semibarbaric" and "authoritarian." "Semibarbaric" means that he is only half civilized. The other half of the king enjoys bloody shows in the arena. "Authoritarian" means that he demands that everything be done his way.

The princess is "fervent" and "imperious." "Fervent" means that she openly shows her feelings. "Imperious" means that she demands her own way, just as her father does.

As you read, be thinking of these questions:

1. What signal does the princess give her lover?
2. What does the young man find behind the door he opens?
3. Why did the princess choose that door?
4. If you were writing this story, how would you have ended it?

Source: From "Increasing Critical Reading in Junior High Classrooms" by B. Ericson, M. Hubler, T. W. Bean, C. C. Smith, and J. V. McKenzie, 1987, *Journal of Reading*, 30, p. 436. Copyright 1987 by the International Reading Association. Reprinted with permission of Bonnie Ericson and the International Reading Association.

5. The teacher reads the recorded lines aloud again and asks students for additional choices from the board, allowing changes as the group indicates need.
6. When students are satisfied with the product, the leader reads the finished poem aloud.
7. A final copy is prepared with the names of the student participants, and copies are presented to the class.

Conceptual Readiness. Once a topic has been selected, the teacher decides how much preparation appears necessary to construct a communal poem. If the topic lends itself to unit study, the teacher may wish to spend days or weeks perusing the available literature with the class. The poem "Somebody's Missing" in Figure 12.8 was preceded by an entire unit on "death and dying." A valuable aspect of this approach is that students discover that their own experiences and thoughts

Figure 12.8   Example of Communal Poetry

Somebody's Missing

Take a look around.
somebody's missing.
    the dogs are howling
    somebody's going to sleep.

The grandfathers know
    what's going on:
    the air is polluted with grief.

Down on the corner, in the grocery store,
he's about to touch you on the arm
    with a silver knife
    a black guillotine
    a .38 pointed at your head.

Even the tough people are scared.

There I was slipping in the dark,
smelling the dumpyard,
    the wrinkled dirt,
    feeling so low I felt like getting high.

It's time
    to let life into this poem!
Time to take a bath,
    to pay death back with babies,
    to make even a policeman cry.

It's true
    not only an undertaker knows bodies,
Let's touch one another
    and send Death Nowhere.

generated while studying a topic often resemble those expressed in literature. They also enrich their fund of general information and, therefore, of cultural literacy.

Perceptual Readiness.   *Perceptual readiness* refers to the choosing of a set of lenses through which to observe reality. This approach is a forerunner of Pichert and Anderson's (1977) finding, mentioned in Chapter 5 on prereading, on the influence of mindset on selective comprehension. There are several types of set: posture set, question set, and continuity set. These are not mutually exclusive.

In the *posture set,* a way of perceiving the subject is suggested: "You are a minister; describe the new clothing styles" or "Pretend you have a bucket over your head; what do you hear as you sit in class?"

In the *question set,* a variety of prepared questions are asked through which the subject can be filtered. Some of the questions asked in the inner-city situation alluded to above were as follows: "What kind of costume does death wear?"; "If death were coming through the door, what would it look like?"; "How can you tell when death has been somewhere?"; "Who knows death best?"

In the *continuity set,* a pattern or tone is established by reading certain types of poems or catchy phrases. One third-grade class heard poems that were rather irreverent, such as Dave Etter's "As You Travel, Ask Us." In response, the third graders produced "Ronald":

Ronald

Ronald took his fork
  and went wump
    to Miss Moore
right in the rear end.
  The fork got bent.
Three cheers for Ronald!
  (Hurrah!!!)

It is valuable to pause and have students reflect on how "set," or anticipation, influences what we produce and comprehend. This "metacognitive" step improves comprehension and expression by heightening students' awareness of their own thought processes and increasing ability and inclination to monitor and correct misapprehensions.

Cloze-Plus for Poetry

Cloze-Plus was developed as an alternative to reading guides and conventional analyses of poetry. Blanc, the developer of Cloze-Plus (1977), says that guides and conventional questions place a screen between the student and the poem. Guides in particular tend to encourage substitution of familiar words for the poet's, effectively altering the meaning of the poem.

Cloze-Plus deals directly with the poem. It also encourages peer teaching, urges students to generate their own guiding questions, and serves as a readiness step for poetry writing activities.

Steps in Cloze-Plus

1. The teacher deletes every fifth word of a poem, beginning with the title.
2. The teacher tells students that although they have not read the poem, they are to try to recreate it as closely as possible to the exact words of the original. The teacher points out that the activity will be difficult and students should rely on whatever clues they can find.
3. Students organize into groups to discuss their word choices. The teacher stands back and "lets it happen."
4. Once the groups have reconciled their choices, the teacher resumes a leader role, explaining terms such as *context, syntax,* and *rhyme* and asking students to

Figure 12.9 Example of Cloze-Plus

Richard Cory

Whenever Richard _____ 1 _____ went down town,
We _____ 2 _____ on the pavement looked _____ 3 _____ him;
He was a _____ 4 _____ from sole to crown,
_____ 5 _____-favored and imperially slim.

_____ 6 _____ he was always quietly _____ 7 _____.
And he was always _____ 8 _____ when he talked;
But _____ 9 _____ he fluttered pulses when _____ 10 _____ said,
"Good-morning," and _____ 11 _____ glittered when he walked.

_____ 12 _____ he was rich,—yes, _____ 13 _____ than a king—
And _____ 14 _____ schooled in every grace;
_____ 15 _____ fine, we thought that _____ 16 _____ was everything
To make _____ 17 _____ wish that we were _____ 18 _____ his place.

So on _____ 19 _____ worked, and waited for _____ 20 _____ light,
And went without _____ 21 _____ meat, and cursed the _____ 22 _____,
And Richard Cory, one _____ 23 _____ summer night,
Went home _____ 24 _____ put a bullet through _____ 25 _____ head.
—Edwin Arlington Robinson

(1. Cory; 2. people; 3. at; 4. gentleman; 5. clean; 6. And; 7. arrayed; 8. human; 9. still;
10. he; 11. he; 12. And; 13. richer; 14. admirably; 15. In; 16. he; 17. us; 18. in; 19. we;
20. the; 21. the; 22. bread; 23. calm; 24. and; 25. his)

express how they might have used these to fill in the blanks. (Further class discussion might include comments on poetic license, grammar, vocabulary, and style.)

5. The teacher reads the poem aloud, pausing at the previous blanks to give students time to correct their initial responses.

Figure 12.9 presents an example of Cloze-Plus.

Looking Back

Several other valuable methods for use in English class were described in previous chapters. Among the more relevant strategies are all of the cloze exercises; rubrics and other means for assessing writing; REAP; ReQuest; Intra-Act; the Directed Reading-Thinking Activity; and particularly the very versatile Story Mapping. Students can develop the Story Map after they have read and analyzed a selection, or the Map can be presented to the class and used to guide reading (see Figure 12.10).

Figure 12.10 Story Map for John Steinbeck's "The Pearl"

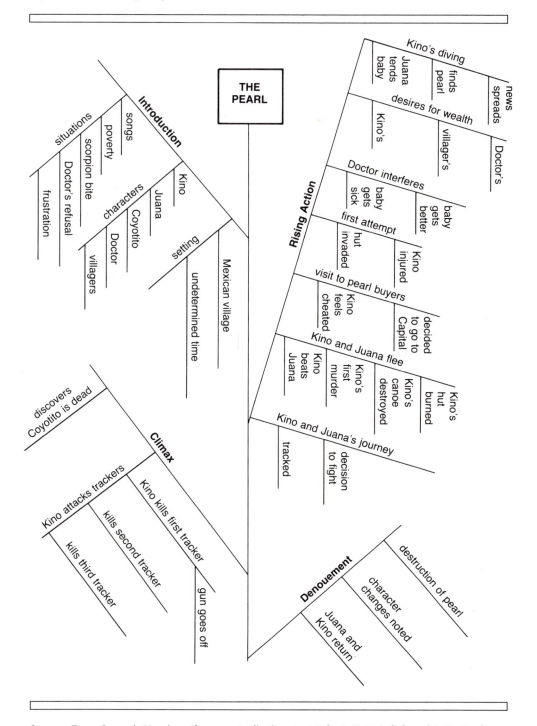

Source: From *Semantic Mapping: Classroom Applications* (p. 13) by J. E. Heimlich and S. D. Pittelman, 1986, Newark, DE: International Reading Association. Copyright 1986 by the International Reading Association. Reprinted with permission of Joan Heimlich and the International Reading Association.

MATHEMATICS

A contemporary publication titled "The Mathematics Report Card—Are We Measuring Up?" (1986) could just as easily have been called "Are We Messing Up?". The article reports a study conducted by the National Assessment of Educational Progress. Among its findings are the following dismal facts about the state of mathematics proficiency in the United States:

- More than 25% of 13-year-olds cannot handle elementary school arithmetic.
- One-third of 11th graders agree that they don't even know what their math teacher is talking about.
- Only 6% of 17-year-olds can handle algebra or multistep math problems.
- Scores for Blacks and Hispanics, despite modest gains, lag 7% to 11% behind those of Caucasians.
- The average Japanese high schooler does better at math than does the top 5% of American high school students.

James Stigler, a University of Chicago behavioral scientist who has studied patterns of math instruction across cultures, has reported, "In U.S. elementary schools, teachers don't know mathematics. They assign basic problems but skip word problems because word problems are harder to teach" (*Time*, June 20, 1988, p. 79). Stigler goes on to note that the "shakers and makers of testing must share low marks for math along with the pupils and teachers."

The difficulties students experience in dealing effectively with "word problems" and related mathematical concepts is unparalleled among current educational dilemmas. Clearly there are more "math illiterates" than there are people who cannot read; many can read and language effectively but are relatively incompetent to deal with simple mathematical concepts, fundamental computations, and even the simplest practical problems requiring mathematics. Until recently, however, this problem has been among the lowest-ranked national priorities. Weakness in dealing with math concepts, computation, and word problems is so pervasive that it tends to pass for a "fact of life."

Mathematics instruction in its current form contributes very little to the reading and language arts curriculum, even though Thorndike (1917) likened reading comprehension to solving a problem in mathematics. In turn, most current forms of reading and language arts instruction contribute very little to mathematics.

Mathematics as a Second Language

Improvement of mathematics and reading instruction undoubtedly must begin with the reconstruction of math books to conform more closely to conventional conversational language. Math itself is a system of reality coding that can benefit from a languaging, or conversational, approach. Students can be taught to listen to and speak the language of mathematics in settings and situations that closely parallel the ways in which people successfully learn second languages. Using the principles of second-language instruction, the reason, purpose, and value of mathematical systems can be more easily imparted, reinforced, and internalized.

The following section details six languaging-based teaching strategies. These include specifications for an Informal Textbook Inventory; a special application of Semantic Feature Analysis to mathematical terms; three procedures for improving reading and processing of word problems; and one method for increasing sensitivity to extant problems to be articulated as well as solved.

Languaging-Based Teaching Strategies

Informal Textbook Inventory
Math books can be most intimidating to the non-math-oriented person. One way to help students overcome the helpless, sinking feeling that tends to accompany their incursions into mathematics is to give them a glimpse of the friendlier features of the mathematics book. The Informal Textbook Inventory is ideally suited to this purpose.

The math teacher should plan on spending a minimum of three days on this activity and giving two one-day refresher and extender sessions about two months apart. As students' skills and knowledge base in mathematics grow, so will their perceived need for, and therefore receptivity to, the "helping" features and value of the text.

The teacher should make an extra effort to conduct all sessions in a relaxed and supportive atmosphere. The Informal Textbook Inventory experience can be a nonthreatening, math-teacher-generated means of desensitizing and counterconditioning math anxiety. The examples in Figure 12.11, especially questions 2, 5, 6, and 7, offer useful ways to help students converse in conversational terms about mathematical systems.

Semantic Feature Analysis
The previously discussed method called Semantic Feature Analysis (Pearson & Johnson, 1978) is especially useful in teaching mathematics (see Figure 12.12). It is based on the Frayer Model, in which concepts are formed from knowing what something *is* and what it *is not*. It is important to note that it is best to introduce terms that have much in common separately until students can identify each term with nearly total accuracy. See the section on science applications in Chapter 13 for a more thorough discussion of this teaching-learning paradox, called *proactive* and *retroactive inhibition.*

The Dahmus Method
The *Dahmus method* for teaching word problems (Dahmus, 1970) emphasizes the translation of English statements into math statements. Recall from previous chapters that translation questions provide a bridge from literal to higher-order thinking skills.

Figure 12.11   Mathematics Informal Textbook Inventory

Part 1: Using Your Text Effectively

See how quickly you can answer the following questions using the parts of your book to their best advantage.

1. Locational Skills

Directions: Terms used in the book can be found in one of several places; preface, contents, appendix, and glossary/index. You will be able to locate each term on the right in one of the places on the left. Locate the term and then mark the place where you found it. Do this as quickly as you can.

Book Section	Term
A. Preface	_____ Using your income
	_____ Axes
B. Contents	_____ Individual differences
	_____ 4 pecks = 1 bushel
C. Appendix	_____ Cubic units
	_____ Objectives
D. Glossary/index	_____ Tables and graphs
	_____ 1,760 Yds = 1 mile
	_____ Dividing fractions
	_____ Hourly wage
	_____ Measure your progress
	_____ Inch
	_____ Lesson organization
	_____ Overtime
	_____ Review

2. Practice in Reading the Mathematics Book

Directions: When the signal to begin is given, read page 69. As soon as you have finished, close the book. Write after the word "TIME" below the number of minutes you spent reading this selection.

TIME: _____

When you have finished reading, answer all of the following questions. Remember, once you have closed the book you may not open it to look for any answers.

Vocabulary: Mathematical and General

a. Define *prime* first in the words of the text, then in your own words.

_____

b. What did the author mean when he said, "a simple hunting and fishing existence . . ."?

_____

c. What does *signified* mean?

_____

Figure 12.11 *continued*

Main Ideas

d. How did the author explain that early humans needed a method of counting things?

_____

e. Why did the author include information about early counting methods in this chapter?

_____

3. **Interpreting Graphs**

Directions: Turn to page 259 and read the section entitled "Reading Bar Graphs." Study figure 199 and answer the following questions:

a. How many students (total number) are represented on the bar graph? _____

b. Circle the two categories below in which the same number of students is found:
   Poor   Fair   Good   Excellent   Superior

c. Use the graph to determine an approximate answer to the following questions:

   How many students received "poor" grades? _____
   How many students received "good" grades? _____
   How many students received "excellent" grades? _____
   How many students received "superior" grades? _____

d. Would you say that this test was a good test or a poor test? (Explain your answer.)

_____

4. **Seeing and Using Text Markers**

Directions: Read pages 119, 120, and 121. When you finish, close your book and fill in the missing parts of the following outline. Do this in pen.

I. Units of Measurement
   A. Direct: measuring height with ruler
   B. _____
      1. Measuring temperature—thermometer
      2. _____ _____ _____
      3. _____ _____ _____
      4. Measuring air pressure—barometer
II. Ancient Measurement Devices
   A. _____
      1. thumb
      2. foot
      3. hand
      4. forearm
      5. _____
   B. Difficulties of Ancient Measuring Devices
      1. _____
      2. _____

Figure 12.11 *continued*

_____

Directions: Now that you have written in your first set of responses in pen, open your book and try to complete the outline in pencil.

5. Summarizing

Directions: You are going to read the section "The Metric System of Weights and Measures," p. 202. When you have finished this section about the consistency of the metric system, close your book. Write a summary of what you have read in four complete sentences.

_____
_____
_____
_____

6. Where I Need Help!

Directions: Think back to all that you just read and the answers you gave. Indicate in no fewer than two sentences where you think you need help in understanding the information presented.

_____
_____

7. What More?

Directions: Think again about what you have read. What are you most curious about? Write at least one sentence telling what you would like to learn more about.

_____

_____

Steps in the Dahmus Method

1. The statements and their parts in the translation must be in the same order as the verbal form.
2. No operations or substitutions should be performed until the translation is completed.
3. Students should read slowly and translate each idea and fact in the verbal form as it appears before reading. Dahmus recommends that students *not* read the entire problem beforehand.
4. All other facts suggested by the verbal form and required for the solution should be stated mathematically on students' papers. There should be no verbal forms of translation, only math notation.
5. Students should use deductive reasoning on the translated and implied facts to obtain a solution.

Figure 12.13 provides an example of the Dahmus method.

Dahmus describes three student requirements that are essential to the success of this method:

Figure 12.12   Semantic Feature Analysis in Mathematics

	Four Sided	Curved or Rounded Lines	Line Segment	All Sides Equal in Length	Right Angles
Triangle	−	−	+	+	+
Rectangle	+	−	+	−	+
Parallelogram	+	−	+	+	+
Circle	−	+	−	−	−
Trapezoid	+	−	+	−	−
Semicircle	−	+	+	−	−
Square	+	−	+	+	+

Shapes appears as a centered heading spanning the columns above.

Source: From "SAVOR the Word to Reinforce Vocabulary in the Content Areas" by E. L. Stieglitz and V. S. Stieglitz, 1981, *Journal of Reading, 25,* p. 48. Copyright 1981 by the International Reading Association. Reprinted with permission of Ezra L. Stieglitz and the International Reading Association.

- Students must be able to translate English expressions into mathematical symbols.
- Students must be able to solve equations.
- Students must be able to solve systems of equations.

The next two methods provide means of teaching students the requisite skills for analyzing and translating verbal problems into mathematical notation.

R/Q Procedure

R/Q essentially is an adaptation and extension of ReQuest (Manzo, 1969a, 1969b) and Reciprocal Teaching (Palincsar & Brown, 1984) to mathematics: It adds a reciprocal, or "talking and listening," component to setting up and solving word problems. This encourages students to ask as well as answer questions, allows them to acquire needed information without social risk, and reveals subtle learning needs to the teacher as well as to students themselves.

Figure 12.13   Example: The Dahmus Method

Mark is twice as old as John. In two years, the sum of their ages

$$M = 2X \qquad J. \qquad (M + 2) + (J + 2)$$

will be five times as much as John's age was four years ago.

$$= 5X \qquad (J - 4)$$

How old is each now?

$$M = ? \quad J = ?$$

Steps in the R/Q Procedure. The R/Q procedure is a three-stage process:

Stage 1

1. Four similar problems are selected. One problem is used in each of the three distinct stages of the R/Q procedure, with the fourth problem used for follow-up reinforcement.
2. Students are told to silently read and attempt to solve problem 1.
3. The correct answer to problem 1 is revealed. Whether their answers are correct or not, students proceed to the next step.

Stage 2

4. a. Both teacher and students silently read the first sentence of problem 2.
   b. Students are told that they will be permitted to ask the teacher all the questions they wish about a word problem, but no more than two questions at a time, after which the teacher may ask students two questions. The teacher should answer all questions fully, avoiding the inclination to tell students too much more than they wish to know at that time and also be careful not to answer too cursively or literally. The teacher should try to grasp what students are trying to understand and help them frame their questions so that they contain some mathlike language and are more easily answerable.
   c. Once students have asked their questions, the teacher may ask two questions about the first sentence, including the same questions just asked to determine if his or her answers were understood.
   d. A reciprocal interaction of this type continues until students have asked all the questions they wish. At that point, students must attempt to solve the problem. The teacher's questions should be carefully articulated and directed so as to provide a good guide to systematic inquiry. Questions should be directed toward answering these generic questions:
      (1) What does the problem say?
      (2) How is the problem best organized—translated into math notation—to be solved?
      (3) What computations need to be done, and in what order?
      (4) How is each computation done?
      (5) How can the answer be verified?

Stage 3

5. All students who have erred in problem 1 attempt to correct their errors; those who correctly completed problem 1 proceed to problem 3.
6. Students check their work against the corret answers for problems 1 and 3.
7. Students who have attempted problems 1 and 3 form into small groups. The groups include some students who still made errors in problem 1 and some who have solved both problems 1 and 2 but may be erring (usually only computationally) on problem 3.
8. An R/Q interaction (as above) is conducted within each group between students who have not solved problem 1 and those who have.

9. A second R/Q interaction takes place, this time between those who have not solved problem 3 and those who have.
10. The teacher does a fourth problem with the entire class in the same fashion as that previously employed.

Peer Teaching in Mathematics (PTM): To Teach Is to Learn Twice

It is a well-established fact that the mind, within limits, will tend to meet the demands placed on it. A student who is asked to teach something will struggle harder to understand and rehearse it than one who expects to merely sit through it. Teaching also creates social incentives, especially with regard to a sense of dominance and importance.

Peer Teaching in Math (PTM) is another "house wine" device we developed for this text. Essentially it is a learning-through-teaching strategy. It has students present a playful mind-problem to the class in their own words. Peer Teaching tends to utilize and improve students' ability to articulate and follow a mathlike problem and solution; involves critical-creative thinking; and builds some subtle social skills (such as addressing a group, getting help with solving and presenting a challenging concept, and feeling empathy with the teacher regarding the difficulty of teaching mathematical systems).

Steps in Peer Teaching

1. The teacher collects a set of "mind-bender"-type problems and their solutions. Two excellent sources are *Discover* magazine's monthly feature (see Figure 12.14) and Martin Dudeney's book *536 Puzzles and Curious Problems* (Scribner, 1975, paperback).
2. The teacher distributes a different "mind-bender," with the answer, to each student.
3. Students study their problems and solutions, seeking help from the teacher or some other source in understanding the problems/solutions.
4. The teacher has a student explain his or her problem to the class.
5. The teacher directs the class to try to solve the problem, individually or in groups.
6. The student whose problem is being addressed leads a discussion of proposed solutions.
7. The student attempts to explain the solution to the class's satisfaction.
8. The class continues this process on an occasional basis over the term, each time using a different student's "mind-bender."
9. (Optional) Students rate their peer teacher on a point scale for quality of presentation.

Unsolved Problems

Most of us are intrigued by unsolved mysteries. Mathematics is filled with unsolved problems. Share some of these with students, and then have them read about them. Figure 12.15, for example, is an account of Fermat's last theorem. It makes for interesting reading, telling, and re-telling to friends and family—that is, languaging in mathematics.

Figure 12.14 "Mind-Bender" Problems and Solutions

Problem: A man went into a bank with a thousand dollars, all in dollar bills, and ten bags. He said, "Place this money, please, in the bags in such a way that if I call and ask for a certain number of dollars you can hand me over one or more bags, giving me the exact amount called for without opening any of the bags." How was it to be done? We are, of course, only concerned with a single application, but he may ask for any exact number of dollars from one to one thousand.

Solution: The contents of the ten bags (in dollar bills) should be as follows: 1, 2, 4, 8, 16, 32, 64, 128, 256, 489. The first nine numbers are in geometrical progression, and their sum, deducted from 1,000, gives the contents of the tenth bag. With these amounts, any dollar total between $1 and $1,000 can be delivered without opening the bags or subdividing their contents.

Problem: A correspondent informs us that on Armistice Day (November 11) in 1928, he had lived as long in the twentieth century as he had lived in the nineteenth. This tempted us to work out the day of his birth. Perhaps the reader may like to do the same. We will assume he was born at midday.

Solution: The man must have been born at midday on February 19, 1883, and at midday on November 11, 1928, he had lived 10,176½ days in each century. Of course, the century ended at midnight on December 31, 1900, which was not a leap year, and his age on November 11, 1928, was 55 years and nearly nine months.

Source: *Discover, 4* (9), September 1983, pp. 82, 98.

Looking Back

Each of the methods described in this section puts heavy emphasis on having students talk, write, react, and become socialized in mathematics terms. This languaging-based approach to math seems to be a prerequisite to effective reading and thinking in mathematics. Other methods described previously also may be used effectively with math. Most notable among these are the Question-Only and Oral Reading Strategies. Other more explicitly reading-centered approaches applicable to mathematics include the Guided Reading Procedure and use of Advance Organizers and reading guides. The Note Cue method, described in the second-language section in Chapter 10, can be used to help reluctant learners take a "safe tumble" into greater participation in math class as well.

Figure 12.15   Fermat's Last Theorem

In Porges's 1954 short story "The Devil and Simon Flagg," Simon taunts the devil to solve an odd puzzle that is the legacy of Pierre de Fermat (fer'-maz). Fermat, a 15th-century mathematician, died before he was able to leave a record of the proof of his last theorem.

Around 1630, Fermat jotted down a fleeting insight in the margin of a book. Cramped for space, however, he began his notation by writing, "I have discovered a truly marvelous demonstration which this margin is too narrow to contain." He went on to write out the theorem but did not have room to follow it with its proof.

Fermat's last theorem was inspired by the fact that there are triplets of numbers in which the square of one number equals the sum of the squares of the other two. This property, for example, is evident in the Pythagorean Theorem of right triangles. The square of the long side always equals the sum of the squares of the shorter sides. Thus, if the shorter sides are 3 and 4, the longest must be 5, because 3 squared (9) plus 4 squared (16) equals 5 squared (25). There are other triplets of numbers that are nonsequential for which this also is true. For example, 13 squared equals 12 squared plus 5 squared.

Fermat's last theorem, however, says that this property cannot be extended beyond squares to any other power. No triplets exist, for example, where the cube of one number equals the sum of the cubes of the other two. In the language of mathematics, $x + y = z$ never has a solution where n is greater than 2.

Now, several hundreds of years later, no one has yet found an exception to this rule, up to 125,000. Nor, however, has anyone been able to provide the proof for the theorem. Paul Hoffman, writer for *Discover* magazine (January 1989), reports that a savvy character had scribbled Fermat's last theorem on the wall of a New York City subway station near New York University, along with the words "I have discovered a truly remarkable proof of this, but I can't write it now because my train is coming."

CHAPTER TIE-UPS

◆◆◆   *Graphic Organizer*

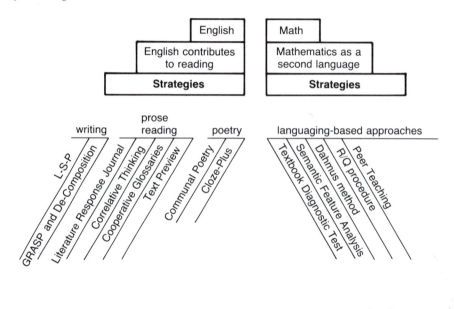

◆◆◆   *Critique and Anticipation*

This chapter addressed two subjects that are treated distinctly but in fact are connected in a fundamental way: Both are systems of language and analysis. The English section stressed several whole language methods, with particular emphasis on writing. The mathematics section also stressed whole language approaches, but with a special focus on languaging. The union of mathematics and language arts clearly would support the best interests of both disciplines. While many people are functionally illiterate in reading, countless more are ''illiterate'' in mathematics and computation even though they are competent in other realms.

The next chapter applies the principles of whole language and content area reading to the social and biophysical sciences.

TRADE SECRET

Teachers as Ethnic Groups

Although we do not always realize it, as content teachers we tend to form ourselves into ethnocultural groups. We speak our own language, have our own cultural referents, and share similar goals and a certain kinship. For students, going to English and math classes can be like going to "Englishland" and "Math-land"; they are embarking on a world trip with bewildering changes in language, culture, and orientation required at the sound of a bell. We should keep this in mind and try to be more thoughtful and accommodating hosts when our guests arrive.

One way to be a good host is to physically walk up close to your "guests" as they enter your classroom and greet them. Another is to ask questions outside the strict course of study, such as "What do you find most curious or different about this subject and the way you typically think and do?"; or "What would you most like to know about or be able to explore in this subject?" They will probably want to know what the choices are, which will offer an excellent opportunity to give an enlightened overview of your field and its way of answering, or probing, the human experience. In other words, show them around your house.

Biological-Physical and Social Sciences

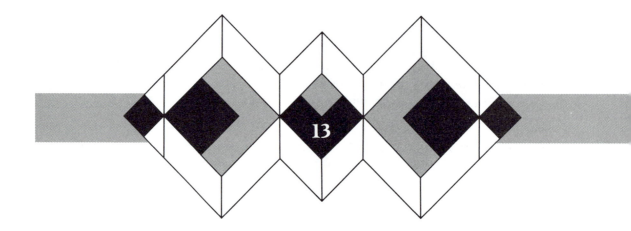

Scientific and Executive Thinking

There is but one bond of peace that is both permanent and enriching: the increasing knowledge of the world in which experiment occurs.

— *Walter Lippman*

FOCUS

Science and social studies are richly schema enhancing and therefore naturally promote more effective reading. Similarly, quality reading and instruction greatly enhance scientific and critical-evaluative, or executive, thinking—the privilege and obligation of every voting citizen.

OUTLINE

BIOLOGICAL-PHYSICAL SCIENCES

Contribution of Science to Reading ◆ Problems in Reading Science ◆ Big Solutions: Ideology and Curriculum ◆ Smaller Solutions: Text Writing and Reading ◆ Looking Back

SOCIAL STUDIES

Executive Training ◆ Contribution of Social Studies to Reading ◆ Obstacles to Reading and Studying in Social Studies ◆ Overcoming Problems ◆ Adjunct Aids Revisited ◆ Looking Back

CHAPTER TIE-UPS

Graphic Organizer ◆ Critique and Anticipation ◆ Trade Secret: Student Monitors

This chapter extends and tests the application of languaging in the content areas to science and social studies. These sciences are highly compatible with the Languaging in the Content Areas (LICA) thesis: Each is driven by the importance to human development of deep processing, or thinking beyond the surface levels of what is known to what remains to be discovered and understood.

BIOLOGICAL-PHYSICAL SCIENCES

For over 30 years, science education has called for science to be taught as a "narrative of inquiry" with emphasis on self-discovery and hands-on learning. In point of fact, science education remains largely textbook dominated. On the plus side, a good deal of the influence of this revisionist view is now being reflected in published science materials and in a revised and more socially sensitive science curriculum in teacher training institutions. Accordingly, the stated goals of science education now include understanding self, appreciating technology, preparing for college, advancing modern culture, and understanding local issues.

Contribution of Science to Reading

The typical science curriculum, whether textbook or experiment based, already contributes naturally to growth in reading. Simply by teaching science well, the science teacher helps students to better grasp the fundamentals of systematic observation, scientific thinking, problem solving, science vocabulary, science concepts, and the physical world. These elements promote progress in reading by enhancing student schemas as well as important related linguistic and thinking skills.

The characteristics of a "mature reader," such as those described in Chapter 1, strongly resemble and therefore are greatly compatible with the characteristics of a "scientifically literate person" as defined by the National Science Teachers Association:

> The scientifically literate person has a substantial knowledge base of facts, concepts, conceptual networks, and *process skills* which enable individuals *to continue to* learn and think logically. [Emphasis added]

Problems in Reading Science

The problems students encounter in reading science material stem in large measure from five problem areas:

- Inadequate background of information
- Misconceptions about the physical world
- Inconsiderate (assumptive or inadequately explained and technically overwhelming) text

- Difficulty in handling esoteric terms
- Inadequate preparation of teachers, particularly at the elementary level, in the basic sciences.

Let us now consider some solutions to these problems as they bear on effective reading and study.

Big Solutions: Ideology and Curriculum

Using New-Generation Science Texts

There is a new generation of science materials that offer great promise but have some rough spots that are not easily overcome. Their promise lies in their basis in compelling issues, their stress on scientific thinking, and the opportunities they offer for developing integrated reading, writing, and science skills. The problem they pose is that "issues"-based materials tend to exceed the mental and social maturity levels of most students and can be quite controversial in some communities. Also, real issues cannot be easily disassembled and reassembled to meet a typical learning sequence. However, this effort must be supported if we are to engage and build student interest and commitment.

The Stipes Publishing Company (Champaign, Illinois), for example, offers a junior high series that stresses independent environmental research. In the mid-1970s, a period of high social consciousness, the modules contained in this series were chosen as an outstanding innovative science program by the National Science Teachers Association. By the company's own admission, however, the materials have had many critics. Some teachers anticipated that 12- and 13-year olds simply could not do the things expected of them in the independent research and that loss of discipline, if not chaos, would follow.

From what we have observed, however, these fears are largely unfounded. In fact, many typically unmotivated students appear to be drawn into the problem-centered approach this program offers. They investigate issues (such as deer hunting) from different perspectives. They write letters to environmental groups, state agencies, and gun and hunting organizations for further information. They weigh and evaluate their own knowledge, beliefs, and values against those of the "major players" in each environmental issue. In so doing, they learn a good deal about science while doing a great deal of reading, writing, and thinking.

Again, this approach does not follow a comfortable scope and sequence chart in science or reading and language arts, and it tends to perhaps prematurely engage young minds in very complex, controversial, and even "scary" issues. However, it also follows a prescription for learning that is more ancient than formal didactic teaching: It deals with *life*. As such, it tends to impel the learner to read, think, write, acquire information, and form concepts as an extension of a value-driven issue rather than as a hollow ritual of schooling.

Let us now look at a less ideological and more curriculum-based approach to improving science and reading.

Cognitive Processing Approach to Reading in Science

Three precepts form the bases for several programs designed to improve science and reading. These essentially are restatements of the cognitive processing model of reading discussed in Chapter 4:

1. There is a strong and well-documented relationship between effective reading and effective analytical reasoning, or cognitive processing.
2. Questions appearing on comprehension tests strongly resemble those on standard tests of verbal intelligence (Whimbey, Carmichael, Jones, Hunter, & Vincent, 1980).
3. Reading and science can best be improved by strengthening thinking skills.

Robert Karplus (1974) provided the major impetus for this approach to science education. The central feature of this training approach was to have students carefully work through Piagetian-based laboratory experiments. Whimbey et al. (1980) borrowed Karplus' basic plan and incorporated it into a reading and science improvement program at their institution, Xavier University in New Orleans. Their summer program, SOAR (Stress on Analytical Reasoning), resulted in significant gains in reading comprehension and vocabulary among its predominantly Black participants. Certain aspects of their program would be difficult to replicate; others, however, can be easily duplicated or reasonably substituted for.

The program essentially had two components:

1. Piagetian-based laboratory exercises each morning
2. Cognitive process instruction and vocabulary training in the afternoon

The Piagetian tasks were developed and conducted by faculty from biology, chemistry, mathematics, computer science, and physics. Each morning session was organized around a "learning cycle" format (Karplus, 1974). The learning cycle contained an exploration, invention, and application phase.

The cognitive processing component had two thrusts. One centered on problem-solving exercises in control of variables, proportional reasoning, "combinatrics," probability, and correlation. The second stressed critical reading and analytical reasoning but had several other distinctive features. Chief amomg these were problem-solving and vocabulary classes conducted by former Xavier students who were attending medical schools during the regular academic year. A workbook guided the tutors' efforts—problem solving and comprehension (Whimbey & Lochhead, 1979). The crux of the teaching approach was threefold. First, students attempted to solve problems by thinking aloud; then they were shown "think-aloud" responses from academically successful people; finally, they again applied "think-aloud" in peer pairs. Figure 13.1 presents two examples of the type of analytical reading and reasoning problems used in these classes.

Figure 13.1 Think-Aloud-Type Reasoning Exercises

1. Cross out the letter after the letter in the word *pardon*, which is in the same position in the word as it is in the alphabet.
2. *Pot* is to *soup* as _____ is to _____.
   a. vacuum cleaner : rug
   b. automobile : carry
   c. food : ice
   d. dishwasher : dishes

The Xavier program had one other noteworthy feature. Each Friday there was a "Quiz Bowl Competition" among five member teams. The teams were presented with problems and vocabulary covered during that week. The competition generated a good deal of cohesiveness among the groups and strong motivation to continue academic work outside of regular class hours.

Smaller Solutions: Text Writing and Reading

Use of Science Texts
One ready means of learning how effectively students are using their science text while helping them improve their use is to prepare an Informal Textbook Inventory on the basic text. Here are some examples of science-oriented items to add to an ITI:

Using Resource Materials

- The book *Through the Magnifying Glass* will tell you many ways to use scientific tools:
  a. How could you find who wrote the book?
  b. What is its library call number?
- Where in the library could you locate the titles of filmstrips that deal with ecology?
- In what library index could you locate the title of an article by Asimov?

Applying Theoretical Information

- How can the law of "centrifugal force" be proven?
- Describe an example of inertia which you might see everyday.

Formulas and Symbols

- List the meaning of the symbols *F* and *C*.
- What do *cm* and *ml* stand for in measurement? (Criscoe & Gee, 1984, pp. 124–125)

Using Graphics and Visual Aids

◆ What does the illustration on page 202 (see below) say about the current flow in electricity?

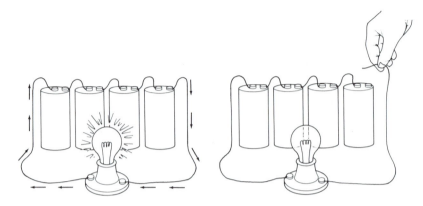

(Answer: Current flow requires a closed path)

Avoiding Confusion of Related Terms

When teaching a new term, teachers often attempt to make the term conceptually clearer by introducing related terms that are similar or opposite in form or meaning. For example, the cellular processes of meiosis (larger cell division) and mitosis (divisions occurring within the nucleus of a dividing cell) often are taught in close proximity to each other or even as contrasting points. The problem is that within minutes—and certainly after just a few hours following such a lesson—these words and concepts have melded together into an indistinguishable partnership. This is an extremely troublesome problem, because it is not like confusing Laurel and Hardy in a movie in which the names are largely irrelevant. Rather, it is more like confusing Laurel and Hardy in a written account, in which the reader has no physical clues and soon will intertwine almost every element of their personalities into one amorphous lump.

One simple way to overcome this problem is to select one of the two confusing elements and focus on it alone: teach it, have students recite it, and reinforce it with pictures and gestures (as in Motor Imaging). The teacher continues this process until students can define, describe, spell, and say the term with 100% accuracy and confidence. Then the teacher moves on to the second, related element. In all likelihood, the potentially interfering term already will have established a beach-head for itself incidentally, since both terms probably appear together in the class text and also will have to be used alternately as needed in class lectures and discussions. In class lectures, the teacher should remember to repeat and stress the meaning of only one of the two terms each time they arise for a few days.

When instruction is not carried out in this way, the learning of the second term can lead to the unlearning of the first. This phenomenon is known as **retroactive**

inhibition in theories of learning. The confusion created between the two terms can produce so much internal static that it can further result in poor reading and learning of all subsequent related terms and material—a condition known as **proactive inhibition.** It is a good idea to share these concepts with students as a "study tip" in science class.

The problems of retroactive and proactive inhibition can be resolved with the Frayer model for teaching concept words described in Chapter 5. The Frayer model, illustrated in Figure 13.2, will work best if (1) all aspects of the concept are explored—essential and nonessential examples and nonexamples—and (2) if the teacher makes every effort to avoid discussing the confusing terms during this tender period of learning.

Anticipation and Reiteration: Using Media and Magazines

One effective way to build your own as well as students' background knowledge in science is to read lay science magazines and watch public television. A new breed of lay-technical writers are turning out articles on such mind-boggling topics as quantum physics and string theory in crystal-clear language—which is not to say that these topics are easily comprehended even then. *Discover* and *Omni* are among the best written of these publications. *Science World*, a Scholastic Inc. product, offers a school version that can only be called brilliant: The writing is crisp, and the illustrations are as engaging and informative as any we have seen. Various forms of reading guides on selected articles can be prepared. These can be used with the articles prior to or following textbook coverage.

Public interest in science is at a high-water mark. This makes it easy to find television programs that either form a foundation for or provide elaboration on much of the basic science curriculum. Cable television regularly features programs

Figure 13.2 Frayer Model

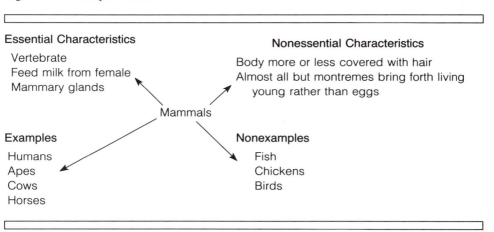

such as ''Science International,'' ''Nova,'' ''Wild Kingdom,'' and ''Mr. Wizard.'' These can be taped and replayed at an appropriate time during a course of study. Viewing guides, similar to reading guides, can be prepared to accompany the tapes.

Overcoming Preconceptions and Misconceptions in Science

Extensive observations of science classes by Anderson and Smith (1984) led these authors to conclude that the greatest source of difficulty in reading and interpreting science material arises from students' faulty preconceptions about the physical world. Failure to take students' preconceptions into account prevented nearly one-third of the students they tested from properly conceptualizing the science principles they were being taught. From their observation of teaching, Anderson and Smith also suspected that the teachers themselves had never fully grasped key scientific concepts such as how light permits us to see and therefore were ill prepared to guide effective teaching and learning on certain topics.

One means Anderson and Smith designed for overcoming the problem of student preconceptions appears to be an effective heuristic for clarifying possible misconceptions that the teacher holds as well. The method consists of constructing a transparency that asks a question that the class first tries to answer from prior or existing knowledge. Responses are recorded on the chalkboard or transparency. Then the question is repeated with the expectation that students will look up the answer offered in the textbook and/or in related materials (see Figure 13.3).

Working on this same problem, Alvermann and Hynd (1987) offer an alternative solution. They have used *refutation texts*—materials written in such a way as to ''refute'' or explicitly tell students ahead of time that they are reading ideas that are at odds with popular (mis)conceptions (see Figure 13.4). The same basic strategy seems well suited to incorporation into a Guide-O-Rama (Cunningham & Shablak, 1975) or as an adjunct aid. Boldface print could say, ''PAUSE HERE: Consider or record your current thoughts about motion theory. In all probability, the information that follows will differ greatly from what you now think or believe.''

In Figure 13.4, the first selection is set up to compare Newtonian mechanics with the popular misconception of impetus theory, while the second one is written in straightforward expository with reference to the theory it is refuting. Again, the refutation approach tends to result in greater comprehension—although, of course, not always.

Adjunct aids of all kinds, whether advance organizers, embedded aids, or reading guides, seem to work best with science materials. This probably is due to the fact that these materials are the most overly assumptive and inconsiderate. As such, science materials also are the most likely to be improved and to result in heightened comprehension. This point was revalidated recently in a study of comprehension of biology material using several text-based learning aids, including one that employs analogies (Bean et al., 1987). The potential value in using analogies in text writing is developed more fully in the social studies applications discussed later.

Use of Reciprocal Teaching

Using the content area version of Reciprocal Teaching as described in Chapter 5, Palincsar and Brown (1986) reported that student comprehension of science ma-

Figure 13.3 Preconception Transparency

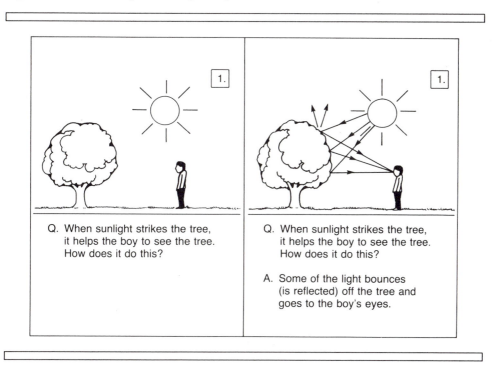

Q. When sunlight strikes the tree, it helps the boy to see the tree. How does it do this?

Q. When sunlight strikes the tree, it helps the boy to see the tree. How does it do this?

A. Some of the light bounces (is reflected) off the tree and goes to the boy's eyes.

Source: From *Comprehension Instruction: Perspectives and Suggestions* by Gerald Duffy, Laura Roehler, and Jana Mason. Copyright © 1984 by Longman Inc. Reprinted by permission.

terial improved 20% in 20 days. Each day students were given portions of text to read. Using headings as clues, students were to write two statements indicating what they thought they would be learning about. The teacher elicited these statements from the group and compared predictions. Then students read a segment (usually four paragraphs) and wrote two questions and a summary reflecting the information presented in that segment. Students also noted in writing any information they felt required further clarification. Then they discussed their questions, summaries, and points of clarification.

Adaptations of the Guided Reading Procedure

Two adaptations of Manzo's Guided Reading Procedure have been fashioned by Spiegel (1980) for pre- and postreading activities using science material. Spiegel's GRP-based Prereading Procedure has students identify clear purposes for study, become aware of specific gaps in their knowledge, and build the "scaffolding" necessary for forming new concepts. Spiegel's approach appears to use the idea of establishing preconceptions and using refutations in an easy classroom format. She achieves this by having students bring to mind what they already know about a topic and then organizing this information into an "advance outline" prior to

Figure 13.4   Examples of Refutation and Nonrefutation Text

Refutation Text

Selection 1

Newtonian Mechanics vs. Impetus Theory

A central point to be made is that the medieval impetus theory is incompatible with Newtonian mechanics in several fundamental ways. . . . To get a sense of some of the motion studies mentioned, imagine the following situation. A person is holding a stone at shoulder height while walking forward at a brisk pace. What will happen when the person drops the stone? What kind of a path will the stone follow as it falls? Many people to whom this problem is presented answer that the stone will fall straight down, striking the ground directly under the point where it was dropped. A few people are even convinced that the falling stone will travel backward and land behind the point of its release. In reality, the stone will move forward as it falls, landing a few feet ahead of the release point. Newtonian mechanics explain that when the stone is dropped, it continues to move forward at the same speed as the walking person, because (ignoring air resistance) no force is acting to change its horizontal velocity.

Nonrefutation Text

Selection 2

Newtonian Mechanics

We certainly learn from our experiences. From repeated exposures to particular events, we learn to induce principles which guide our expectations for future events. . . . Newtonian mechanics can also be used to predict what path a stone will follow when it is dropped from shoulder height by a person walking forward at a brisk pace. Assuming no air resistance, the stone will move forward as it falls to the ground, coming to rest a few feet ahead of the point at which it was released. That is, the stone continues to move forward at the same speed as the person who is walking. Why? Because no force is acting upon it to change its horizontal velocity. Of course, as the stone falls forward it also moves downward at a steadily increasing speed. The forward and downward motions result in a path that closely approximates a parabola.

Source: Adapted from *Overcoming Misconceptions in Science: An On-line Study of Prior Knowledge Activation* by D. E. Alvermann and C. R. Hynd, 1987, paper presented at the annual meeting of the National Reading Conference, St. Petersburg, FL.

reading. Then students read to test their preconceptions. The same basic idea operates in the postreading variation described next. However, that procedure contains more options to accommodate weaker readers.

Steps in the Prereading GRP

1. The teacher identifies a unit or topic of study that is fairly narrow in scope, such as photosynthesis or spiders.

2. The teacher has students tell peer recorder(s) at the chalkboard everything they know about the topic prior to lecture or reading.
3. The class identifies conflicting information and areas in which no information has been provided ("Hey, we don't know what spiders eat!"; "Are very large spiders insects or animals?").
4. Students construct an outline with conflicting information listed side by side ("Spiders have six legs/eight legs[?]"). Areas in which no information is known are listed by headings in the outline.
5. The outline is displayed in the classroom throughout the unit of study.
6. The class is told to read to fill in or alter the outline (see Figure 13.5).

Steps in the Postreading GRP

1. Students are given different books to read on the same topic (these can be at varying levels of difficulty so that slower students can read materials closer to their reading levels).
2. Following the regular steps of the GRP, recalls and outline are expanded to include different perspectives and wider information sources.

Spiegel (1980) points out that since not everyone has read precisely the same material, each student can contribute something unique to the outline. Usually each student can attain the status of contributor to such a lesson because the material he or she reads, regardless of its level of difficulty, is likely to contain a unique piece of information. It has been suggested that once a GRP outline is constructed, sudents can be taught how to language in science by having them write a paragraph or two of reconnected prose from the outline. (See GRASP and De-Composition in the previous chapter for tips on how to achieve this.)

Figure 13.5 GRP Prereading Outline

```
                        Spiders
  I. How they look
     ?A. Have six legs/eight legs
      B. Have two body parts
     ?C. Antennae
 II. How they live
     ?A. What they eat
      B. Spin webs
         1. Made of silk
         2. Lots of different kinds of webs
         3. Sticky
            ?a. What makes them sticky
            ?b. Why doesn't the spider get stuck
```

Figure 13.6   Example of Student-Generated Mapping in Biology

Step 1: Read the title of the chapter, for example, "The Cell: The Basic Unit of Life."
Illustrate that subject with a drawing that appeals to you. Next, print the chapter
title in capital letters.

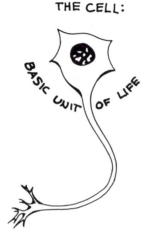

Step 2: Try to predict what major concepts the author will present. Then check the
headings. This chapter has four: (1) cells as building blocks; (2) cell structure
and function; (3) cell chemistry; (4) movement of molecules. Print these and
connect them to the topic, adding a question mark to each one.

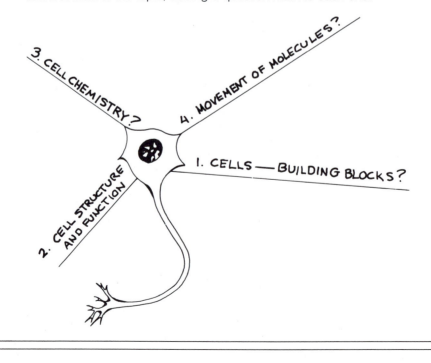

Figure 13.6 *continued*

Step 3: Actively read the material under the first heading. Then pause. Immediately recall what you just learned. Draw lines to link supportive details to the heading. Making this visual structure clarifies understanding. Now check your map against the book. Did you record the most important information from this section of the chapter?

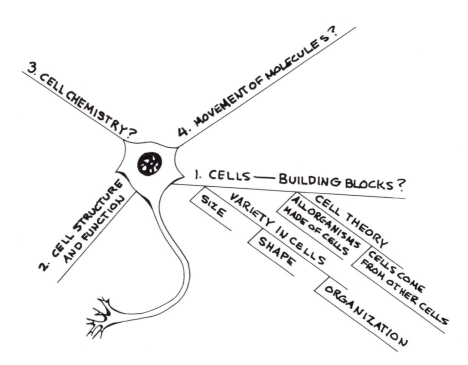

Step 4: After studying and mapping each section, you now have a one-page map of the whole chapter. One more procedure is necessary to move this knowledge into long-term memory. Take a few minutes each day to review this map.

Step 5: Keep your chapter maps in a special section of your notebook so you can review them frequently.

Looking Back

Several methods covered in previous chapters have excellent application to science. Chief among these are the Question-Only Strategy, which offers an effective means of inquiry training; the Oral Reading Strategy for giving direct assistance with science words and phrasing; and mapping for imparting a "conceptual set" for numerous easily confounded details. Figure 13.6 shows how Bragstad used a chapter in biology to modify teacher-directed mapping into a student-generated form.

SOCIAL STUDIES

Executive Training

According to Peters (1982), social studies consists not merely of traditional fields like history, government, sociology, and geography but fields such as psychology and philosophy and several conceptual approaches that can be applied across these fields, such as social inquiry, moral education, and values clarification.

The Constitution gives enormous executive power to every citizen. Social studies is the fundamental school-based source of the executive training that every citizen needs in order to read, interpret, and act on the streams of raw and prepared information emanating from newspapers, magazines, and broadcast media. The awesome responsibility facing all citizens with such executive power increases the responsibility of those of us who must agonize over what and how to teach them.

Contribution of Social Studies to Reading

The principles, precepts, and actual content of social studies underlie almost everything written. This may explain why social studies as a discipline is so highly correlated with general reading comprehension (Artley, 1944; Adams, 1982). Also for this reason, the social studies teacher is especially well situated to enhance students' understanding of how best to read and think about nearly all things written. This is done naturally as the teacher and textbook report to students how others think and feel about a variety of issues such as economics, politics, and culture and the consequences of these beliefs on individual liberties. Most important from the standpoint of reading progress, social studies is synonymous with schema enhancement: It imparts a rich fund of general information, a specialized vocabulary, refined critical-evaluative thinking skills, and the rudiments of cultural literacy.

Obstacles to Reading and Studying in Social Studies

The major problems students encounter in reading in social studies stem in large measure from the very elements to which social studies ultimately contributes in general reading. Reading in social studies often requires conceptual and informational preparation. It also requires considerable training and assistance with objective reasoning and in connecting loose factual elements into a structure, or schema base, that subsequently can be used to read, grasp, and interpret still more. Because social studies is the fountainhead of citizenship, there has been concern about effective reading in this discipline from the earliest days of the Republic. In an early observational study of the difficulties experienced by students in reading in social studies, John Dewey lamented that the average eighth grader appeared to

- Be ignorant of significant word meanings
- Act with disregard for certain parts or unfamiliar phrases of key sentences

♦ Show a tendency to consider social studies reading as a process of memorization, or mindless retelling for test purposes (Dewey in Hafner, 1977)

We now acknowledge that several of these problems can be traced to the poor quality of writing and organization of social studies textbooks. Dreher, Singer, and Letteer (1987) have delivered some sad news in this regard. In their study, which compared the friendliness, or considerateness, of social studies texts from the early 1970s with those of the 1980s, they found no significant improvement in the quality of texts on any of seven factors used in their assessment.

Generally there are two types of poor writing found in social studies. One type is characterized as being ambiguous, assumptive, or poorly explained. This form, which also might be called "inconsiderate text," is difficult to overcome but not as devastating to students' interest and willingness to learn as the second source of the problem: accounts that are banal, depressingly dull, and wordy. The latter is especially disturbing because it need not be the case. Social studies, after all, is the collected stories of human foibles and exploits. It is the story of humans' "unfinished journey." As such, social studies brims with engaging cross-currents of human motivation and bold deeds. It needs only to be told in an unencumbered way to be engaging to almost every student.

The first teaching method described in this section, the Parallel Form Strategy, addresses this problem immediately and directly. It offers a way to overcome some of the problems of dull accounting by connecting the reader to the story on the page in some very personal ways. Other methods covered include means of helping students with weak literal-level reading, such as Dewey observed, and helping all students to think more analytically and evaluatively.

Chapter 2 contains a complete example and format for constructing Informal Textbook Inventories that can be used to guide students in effective use of their social studies text.

Overcoming Problems

Parallel Form Strategy

An effort to get youngsters to read a difficult and distant "current events" book led to the development of the *Parallel Form*, or "It-takes-some-to-know-some," Strategy (Manzo, 1977). The students, who came from a poor, Black, ex-urban location (outside the city and suburbs), were required to read and study current events spanning the period between 1955 and 1961. The time is worth noting to follow the illustration in Figure 13.7.

Relevant research on this general approach has been conducted by Bean et al. (1987), Gentner (1983), and Hayes and Tierney (1982). Using a method similar to Parallel Form, Hayes and Tierney reported that "specific analogous information" provided to students prior to and during reading had a significant positive effect on both their *motivation* to read and their *comprehension* of what they read.

The Parallel Form Strategy basically is a prereading strategy. It can be quite helpful in sorting out disruptive thought patterns and replacing them with a common, more rational, and experiential base for reading.

Figure 13.7 Parallel Form Strategy

The class was asked to pretend they were sixth graders attending a progressive elementary school that held an annual prom for its graduates. (There was such a school nearby.) An attractive new girl in class was said to have two boys vying for her attention. Their names were written on the proverbial love triangle: Alpha at the top, Donnie Ray and Osceola at either angle of the base. A situation was provided to stir the pot: Donnie Ray's father owned a florist shop, and Osceola's father was a candy maker.

The simulated scene was a schoolyard at recess some days before the prom. Donnie Ray's friends, the teacher said, were gathered about him demanding, "How will you win a date with Alpha?" To which he responded, "First I've got to let her know I exist." Suiting action to words, he proposed to dash past her several times to display his blazing speed.

Osceola was asked to suggest a countermove. He got on the athletic high bar and began to chin as his friends loudly counted, proclaiming his awesome strength to all within earshot.

Not very subtle, but it stirred Donnie Ray to suggest a persuasive countergesture: "In the morning, I will send Alpha a single rose" (by emissary).

Osceola immediately countered, "I will send candy" (in the same manner).

"Tomorrow," Donnie Ray returned, "I will bring a bouquet."

But Osceola matched and surpassed his rival: "And I'll bring a box of candy and a cozy sack lunch for two."

The vying continued, to the cheers and jeers of the class, until Alpha was asked to choose her date. "Couldn't I wait another day or two?" she coyly asked.

"No way!" Donnie Ray snapped. "In fact, you're not deciding nothing!"

"Right" Osceola volunteered. "Me and this turkey are going to settle this thing right here and now!"

While the class was still laughing and jabbering at that macho proposal, the teacher began to slowly erase each name from the triangle and write in new ones. The class grew quiet and perplexed as they observed these changes on the chalkboard:

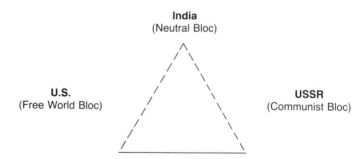

"You won't believe this," they were told, "but if you read pages 29 to 36 in your current events books, you will find a story very much like the one you 'sixth graders' just made up." This was true enough. Between 1955 and 1961, the United States and the Soviet Union were wining and dining India and the neutral nations to get their support in the General Assembly of the United Nations. When the giveaway programs appeared to be faltering, both countries began to test bigger and bigger hydrogen bombs while seemingly chanting the macabre refrain "My bomb's bigger than your bomb." In fact, the kids had anticipated, by a few months, the near catastrophe at the Berlin Wall, where the world learned a new word: *brinkmanship.*

Steps in Parallel Form

1. The teacher identifies an analogy that might serve as an extended metaphor, or parallel, for material to be read and studied.
2. The teacher discusses and/or acts out the analogy.
3. The teacher tells students that they are about to read or study a parallel situation.
4. Students read the textbook account.
5. The class discusses the points of similarity and difference.
6. The teacher asks, "What have you learned today (about the topic, yourself, and/ or effective reading and studying)?"

A Variation.   The greatest limitation of Parallel Form is that it can require a good deal of teacher inventiveness and hard work in finding strong and personal analogies to the textual material to be covered. One variation on this approach, however, can shift creative responsibility to students by calling for student- or teacher-orchestrated dramatizations. In this version, students are grouped and asked to read introductory biographical information on selected leading figures in a given area of study. Then a situation is defined for each group and students are expected to extemporaneously act out a brief drama (or comedy) for five minutes.

In one such dramatization, about which we have firsthand knowledge, civil rights figures whose biographies had been studied were presented as young people attending a high school dance. The boy playing Martin Luther King dramatized, in a lighthearted way, King's teenage brashness when asking girls to dance. Apparently King was one of the school's leading "jitterbuggers." The simulation-dramatization revealed a little-known and very humanizing fact about the sometimes somber-looking civil rights leader. The students in this primarily white private school subsequently read and studied the unit on the civil rights movement with greater empathy than they otherwise might have mustered. Similarly Rosa Parks, Ralph Abernathy, and many others were revealed as having been real people, capable of great joy and gaiety—people forced by grim circumstances into a maelstrom of conflict.

Another Variation (Which Probably Won't Work).   If you think it might be a good idea to have students identify and develop their own analogies, think again. Bean et al. (1987) tested this approach with science material and found that it just doesn't work. Apparently students need to know a great deal about an analogy, or be able to easily conjure it up, for it to be a worthwhile guide to new learning. But don't be discouraged. Most likely we simply have not found the best way to do this yet. Give it some thought, and you may be the creative mind that solves this problem. As a guide, see McGonigal's (1988) apparently successful solution in the section on English methodology.

Adjunct Aids Revisited

Adjunct aids to text study, such as built-in Imbedded Aids and teacher-developed reading guides to be used alongside text, seem especially well suited to social studies.

Surprisingly, for reasons not quite understood, it has been difficult to support the cost-to-benefit ratio for using Imbedded Aids and reading guides in published social studies materials. A typical finding regarding reading guides is that of Estes (1969), who found that while guides help with social studies comprehension, they do so only to a small degree.

The "face validity," or positive look and feel, of Imbedded Aids and reading guides in social studies remains strong nonetheless. Confidence in internal and external adjunct aids stems from the fact that they tend to address improvements in aspects of critical-evaluative thinking that to date have been inadequately measured. For this and related reasons alluded to in Chapter 7, we continue to recommend and use them.

This section presents three adjunct aid formats not illustrated previously: All That Apply, Reasoning Guides, and Critical Judgments Exercises.

Guiding Questions: All That Apply

A simple, albeit quite specialized, social studies reading guide format, *All That Apply,* is similar to the Herringbone and Cartwheel Graphics formats. The authors developed it for trouble-free current events student research and study. The teacher specifies words, and students use the All That Apply questions just as the name indicates: They refer to class notes and assigned readings related to the specified words to answer all questions that apply. The All That Apply questions can be posted on a bulletin board, or students can write them on the inside covers of their notebooks.

Here are some examples of All That Apply questions:

1. Who are they (is s/he)?
2. How is it spelled and pronounced?
3. Where is it (are they) from?
4. What does it mean?
5. What happened?
6. Why is it important?

Figure 13.8 presents a sample assignment and student answers.

The terms used for All That Apply assignments can be added to the deck of cards used in playing Cultural-Academic Trivia.

Reasoning Guides

A *Reasoning Guide* is a specialized form of reading guide that strongly emphasizes interpretive and applied levels of reading and thinking (Herber, 1978). Reasoning Guides are constructed as follows:

1. The teacher constructs a guide that draws focused attention to the key portions of a longer section (see Figure 13.9).
2. Students read the longer selection first before using the guide.

Figure 13.8   Sample "All that Apply" Lesson: Assigned Terms and Student Responses

Terms:

A. Azerbaijanis
B. Nagorno-Karabakh

Sample answers:

A. Azerbaijanis—questions 1, 2, 3
   (As-er-by-zhah-nee): Over 7 million people who live in Russia and northern Iran.
   They are ethnically related to the Turks.
B. Nagorno-Karabakh—questions 1, 2, 3, 5, 6
   (Nay-gor-no Kah-rah-bah): An Azerbaijanis-controlled mountain city within the
   U.S.S.R. that is inhabited largely by Armenians. The Armenians rioted and
   demonstrated in late 1988 following mistreatment by the Azerbaijanis. The place and
   event are important because the long-standing hatred between the Azerbaijanis and
   the Armenians is adding to Russia's fear that she will be unable to maintain control
   over the more than 100 ethnic groups within her borders.

3. Students complete the Reasoning Guide, rereading the key portions of the text as necessary.
4. A class discussion in which students compare their answers and their reasons follows.
5. Students further discuss what they learned about their own thinking and about thinking in general, for example:
   a. In what way(s) can we discover what attitudes we and others hold other than by what we/they say? (By our/their actions)
   b. Is there really any value in trying to form generalizations without all the facts? (Life requires that we do, but any new piece of information may change all previous thoughts and conclusions)

Critical Judgments Exercises
An interesting format for promoting critical-evaluative thinking in social studies was developed by ninth-grade teachers Susan Tarwater and the late Phyllis McConnel as part of their education specialist degree project at the University of Missouri–Kansas City. The *Critical Judgments Exercise* follows the format of one of the critical judgments subtests of the ALARM battery discussed in Chapter 3. McConnel and Tarwater used these formats in a team-taught core curriculum program combining social studies and English. The team approach permitted team members to relieve one another from classroom teaching duties to enable them to develop the necessary materials.

Figure 13.9   Reasoning Guide

Part I

Directions: Reread the sentences below taken from John F. Kennedy's inaugural address, which you just read in its entirety in your textbook. Then complete the exercises called for below.

A. The world is very different now.
B. For man holds in his mortal hands the power to abolish all forms of human poverty and all forms of human life.
C. . . . [T]he rights of man come not from the generosity of the state but from the hand of God.
D. United there is little we cannot do in a host of cooperative ventures.
E. To those people in huts . . . we pledge our best efforts . . . not because the communists are doing it, . . . but because it is right.
F. We dare not tempt them with weakness.
G. So let us begin anew, remembering on both sides that civility is not a sign of weakness, . . .
H. Let both sides explore what problems unite us instead of belaboring those problems which divide us.
I. And so, my fellow Americans, ask not what your country can do for you; ask what you can do for your country.

Part 2

Directions: Consider the statements below, and decide based on the statements above whether JFK would have approved or disapproved of each. In column A, answer yes or no. In column B, write the letter indicating the quotation from JFK that influenced your decision.

In the Critical Judgments Exercise, students first decide and then discuss their judgments of the relative values of certain pieces of information. The format can be used with general or background information or with items selected from a section of text that students read in class. Figure 13.10 presents examples of both general-information and text-based items.

Figure 13.9   *continued*

For number 10, write an original statement that you think JFK might have made. Quote some part of the address (in your text) other than the quotations listed above as evidence.

A   B

1. The problems we are facing today are not much different than those that faced our forefathers.
2. The oriental world is immensely different from our own.
3. Our rights are given to us out of the goodness of humans' love for humankind.
4. If we are to win over the threat of world communism, we must give money, supplies, and help to underdeveloped nations of the world.
5. Let us demonstrate our goodwill to the world by disarming.
6. Only the federal government can solve the complex problems of our society.
7. We will never resort to violence.
8. The events of the past have helped us to realize the truth of Washington's policy of isolationism. We should continue to heed the advice of our president.
9. The greatest threat to humankind is not famine and sickness but the threat of world communism.
10. _____
    _____
    _____
    _____

Looking Back

Several of the teaching methods and designs covered in previous chapters are particularly suitable for social studies. These include Graphic Aids, the Guided Reading Procedure, Mapping, ReQuest, REAP, the Directed Reading-Thinking Activity, Intra-Act, the Listen-Read-Discuss Heuristic, Palmatier's Unified Notetaking System for Learning, the Cultural-Academic-Trivia game, and all of the universal strategies covered in Chapter 2.

Figure 13.10   Critical Judgments Exercise

Part 1: General-Information Items

Directions: Using your best judgment, decide what you think would be the value to society in knowing each of the statements listed below. *Consider each statement to be true.* We shall discuss these momentarily.

  1 = of no use
  2 = of little use
  3 = of moderate use
  4 = very useful
  5 = extremely useful

1. Mary Queen of Scots inherited the throne at the age of six days.
2. Simplicity and elegance in writing are more desirable than length or vocabulary.
3. The first European to sail into New York Harbor was Henry Hudson.
4. The tomato is not a vegetable but a fruit.
5. Lefthandedness is a recessive genetic trait.
6. Mary Goddard was the only woman to have her name on the Declaration of Independence.
7. Diamond dust is black.
8. Red meats are high in fat content.

Part 2: Text-Based Items

Directions: Indicate your judgment of the relative values of the statements below taken from your text. Use the five-point scale—1 = lowest, 5 = highest value—that we have used previously.

A. 1. The Nobel Prize is given at least once every five years.
    2. The Nobel Prize is awarded for important discoveries or inventions in the five categories of knowledge.
    3. No Nobel Prizes were given in 1940–1942.
    4. The Nobel Prize was founded by Alfred Nobel, a Swedish chemist and philanthropist.
    5. Women as well as men have been awarded the Nobel Prize.

B. 1. Oliver Cromwell was called "The Protector."
    2. Cromwell was born in 1599.
    3. Cromwell was a violent and persuasive speaker.
    4. Cromwell expanded England's territories and increased her commerce.
    5. Cromwell's court was frugal but dignified.

Graphic Organizer   ◆ ◆ ◆

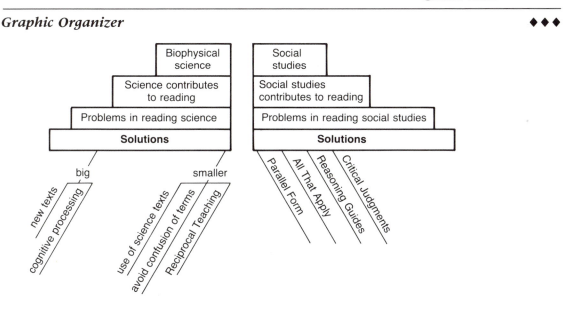

Critique and Anticipation   ◆ ◆ ◆

Research has shown that effective reading and effective scientific thinking are nearly synonymous. Further, the goals of modern science education are highly coincidental with many of the objectives of maturity in reading, language, thinking, and personal-social growth. Research has also demonstrated that the goals and functions of social studies education are highly compatible with virtually all aspects of the content area reading curriculum, particularly the improvement of critical-evaluative thinking, a fundamental requirement of good citizenship.

This chapter presented several teaching methods that have particular applicability in science and social studies but are valuable in other areas as well. These included Spiegel's Guided Reading Procedure variations, the Parallel Form Strategy, and the three reading guide formats: All That Apply, Reasoning Guides, and Critical Judgments Exercises.

The next chapter continues in the same vein but focuses on what traditionally have been called the "minor area" subjects—a term you will come to reappraise after thoughtful reading of that chapter.

TRADE SECRET

Student Monitors

Veteran teachers will tell you that students often don't know just what constitutes "correct" behavior. Even when they do know what is "right," they lose sight of it in the complex interplay of school life.

One means of helping you communicate to students what constitutes good and correct behavior is to construct self-monitoring checklists for them. These can be made up from those tedious drawn-up lists of behavioral objectives found in curriculum guides or from lists such as those of the characteristics of mature readers presented in this text. These objectives merely need to be written more simply. Figure 13.11 is a checklist we constructed for self-monitoring and improving classroom decorum.

Figure 13.11 Classroom Monitor

Name _____

Directions: Check (√) all that apply to today's class. If you feel an explanation is necessary for a certain response, mark it with a plus sign (+) and write your comments below or on the back.

Yes	No	
____	____	1. I was on time for class.
____	____	2. I came ready for class (with paper, book, pencil/pen, eyeglasses, other: _____.)
____	____	3. I did my homework and had it ready to turn in.
____	____	4. I settled down quickly and was ready to listen and learn.
____	____	5. I avoided talking to others once class began.
____	____	6. I did not leave my desk without permission.
____	____	7. I did not disrupt the class in any way.
____	____	8. I answered thoughtfully when called upon.
____	____	9. I raised my hand to participate.
____	____	10. I asked a thoughtful question.
____	____	11. I followed directions.
____	____	12. I kept good notes.
____	____	13. I had my books and other materials stored safely out of the aisles.
____	____	14. I listened when others spoke.
____	____	15. I acted with respect toward my classmates and teacher.
____	____	16. I sat with good posutre and took interest in the class.
____	____	17. I completed course work assigned to be done in class.
____	____	18. I wrote down any out-of-class assignments in a proper place.
____	____	19. I was cheerful and cooperative.
____	____	20. I intend to be ready and work hard in our next class.

Comments: _____
_____

Physical Education, Vocational Education, Art and Music

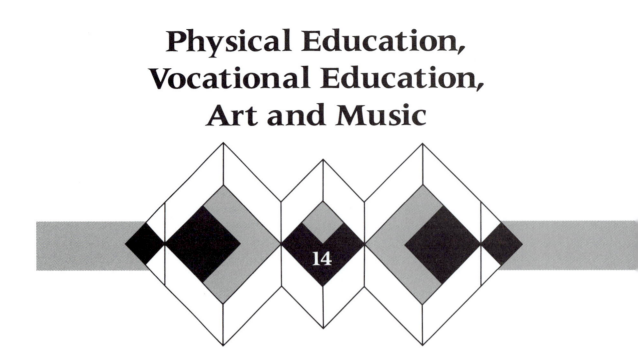

14

Reading for Application and Life Enrichment

Man reaches fulfillment . . . in books, or work, or healthful play.

— *Isaac Watts*

FOCUS

The term ''minor subject'' needs reappraisal. These subjects have been deeply affected by the information explosion. As a result, they require as much reading and analysis as the major subjects do. Further, they are essential to a full, integrated, and dignified life. They are important ''trace elements'' in educational and personal nourishment.

OUTLINE

CONTENT AREA READING IN THE SUPPORT SUBJECT AREAS

The Dignity of the ''Average Guy'' ◆ Two Programming Approaches

PHYSICAL EDUCATION

The Physical Domain ◆ Ten P.E. Strategies for Buttressing Higher-Order Literacy

VOCATIONAL EDUCATION

Problems and Goals ◆ Services and Strategies

ART AND MUSIC

The Challenge ◆ Meeting the Challenge

CHAPTER TIE-UPS

Graphic Organizer ◆ Critique ◆ Trade Secret: Acquiring and Using New Methods

CONTENT AREA READING IN THE SUPPORT SUBJECT AREAS

The contemporary forces that have led to the information explosion in the core areas of the curriculum have profoundly influenced the support subjects as well. The evidence for this is readily apparent in even a casual inspection of any support area syllabus. In music, students now study jazz and rock as well as choral, orchestral, and symphonic works. Physical education now encompasses physiology and less popular sports such as badminton and soccer. In industrial arts, particularly automotive technology, there now is a strong emphasis on electronics. Home economics now addresses complex issues in nutrition, parenting, and family relationships. Business education, which formerly meant typing and shorthand, now means word processing, inventory control, and purchasing. In short, the traditional separation between academic subjects and ''minor'' area subjects has all but vanished. These support areas involve complex technologies and require considerable and ongoing reading, research, and critical analysis.

Today teachers associated with support area subjects rarely need to be convinced that their subjects, at least in part, contain a heavy academic component. Thus, the support area teacher has a heavy investment in nourishing reading, writing, studying, language, and thinking skills.

The Dignity of the "Average Guy"

Quite apart from their role as contributors to the major subject area curricula, the support area subjects enhance the dignity of the ''average'' person. Art, music, sports, and crafts can belong to everyone irrespective of levels of education and income. Regrettably, however, the United States has tended to lag behind the rest of the civilized world in teaching the values of these special features of life to the common working person. The first author once heard a European house painter humming the music from the opera *La Bohème*. When I asked—with somewhat more surprise than intended—if he liked opera, he responded, ''Of course'' and went on to say that he thought it very strange that Americans regarded higher culture as the property of the upper classes. Given that the ideal of a quality education is to equip us to lead a full life, the importance of the support area subjects perhaps can be likened to that of those factors previously referred to as ''trace elements'' in progress toward reading maturity: smaller but absolutely essential ingredients for a full, integrated, and dignified life.

It is rather ironic that we do not put more stock in the value of the support area subjects. American students, after all, are more affluent and powerful than most youngsters. At 18 years of age, they inherit an ennobling legacy: the power to vote on an equal footing with every other American citizen on all official issues governing the nation.

Working within some obvious space constraints, this chapter attempts to offer some poignant and practical suggestions to support area teachers for meeting several academic objectives while simultaneously promoting the curricula and values of their particular courses of study.

Two Programming Approaches

In reviewing the strategies and activities offered ahead, keep in mind that the teacher of support area subjects would be wise to coordinate new demands on students with the rest of the faculty. Many of the strategies and activities suggested will entail a marked departure from conventional expectations and practices in support area subjects. Failure to communicate and coordinate the goals of these activities could result in a backlash from overburdened students and unsympathetic core curriculum teachers.

Two previously mentioned "Languaging in the Content Areas" programming ideas are suitable across all of the support areas: the Community of Language approach and ThemedSchools.

Community of Language Approach

One of the easiest and most effective things that any teacher—and particularly one in the support area subjects—can do to improve reading and language is to elevate the quality of language used in his or her subject. We know of at least one such situation. All the teachers in a junior high school adopted a list of 30 difficult words from a test preparation manual. Rather than teaching these words explicitly or assigning them to students, each teacher made a conscious daily effort to use the words whenever and wherever possible. Teachers watched for opportunities to use the words in appropriate contexts and sometimes even created contexts as an excuse to use the words. Throughout the spring semester, students heard these 30 words in math class, science lab, shop, art, and gym. In only a few weeks' time, students could be heard using the words in casual conversations in the hallways and cafeteria. The teachers effectively had created an elevated community of language.

The impact of a simple plan like this cannot be exaggerated. It builds student respect for teachers, reinforces reading vocabulary, raises word consciousness and precision in thinking, and boosts standardized test scores, making youngsters more competitive on college admissions and scholarship examinations. It can have even more far-reaching effects: Students may take their new language home and incidently share it with family and friends. This can elevate the levels of language and precision in thinking in both families and community, thereby reaching children who have not yet started school and parents who have long since left it.

ThemedSchool

The idea of a ThemedSchool, as discussed in Chapter 11 on schoolwide programming, is to create a year-long emphasis on a special topic or subject area. ThemedSchools typically involve cooperation among students from various grade and ability levels and culminate in a lifelike opportunity for collaboration on a product. The support area subjects can sponsor themes such as "Ways to Express Yourself," "The Sporting Life," or "Hobbies."

PHYSICAL EDUCATION

"Reading is sport," wrote Gentile (1980). "It requires mastering of fundamental skills, sufficient practice, a well-balanced diet of literary experiences, and a lifetime of development" (p. 4). The artificial separation of physical and academic edu-acation that exists in most schools is unfortunate, unnecessary, and uncaring. Plato placed gymnastics at the highest level for training his philosophers. Gentile offers the diagram in Figure 14.1 to illustrate the many shared characteristics of reading and sports.

The Physical Domain

Linking Physical and Academic Development
The relationship between physical and academic development is more than co-incidental. As we noted in earlier chapters, all learning enters through and takes place in the body as well as in the mind. The linking of motor involvement with language and academic learning can be a "natural" for the P.E. class, as illustrated in a recent news report:

> In the gymnasium at the Jackson Avenue Elementary School in Mineola, New York, 8-year-olds ran through the pathways of a human circulatory system drawn on the parquet floor.
> Pretending they were blood cells, they grabbed oxygen molecules (bean bags) from a bucket, raced through the heart chambers (red and blue Hula-Hoops) and completed the circuit by exchanging the oxygen for carbon dioxide (crumpled waste paper). Their warm-up finished, the panting pupils checked their pulse rates.
> Watching them, Kathleen Kern, the school's physical education teacher, said, "You can't teach kids about aerobic fitness until they understand the circulatory system."

In the same vein, Gentile (1980) suggests an interesting "metacognitive" activity involving reading, appreciation of the physical domain, and provocative discussion: In gym class, have students read and discuss statements, such as one from Michener's *Sports in America,* which says, in effect: "If I had a child determined to be a writer, I'd expect that child to take two courses: one in ceramics so that he or she could feel form emerging from inchoate clay and a second in eurhythmic dancing so that child could feel within his or her own body the capacity for movement, form, and dramatic shifts in perspective."

A Word of Caution
Recently (July 25, 1988) *Time* magazine reported some very telling figures on the American "health craze." Health club membership is up to $5 billion per year; athletic shoes have reached an even higher annual gross of $6 billion; and "diet"

Figure 14.1   Shared Characteristics of Reading and Sports

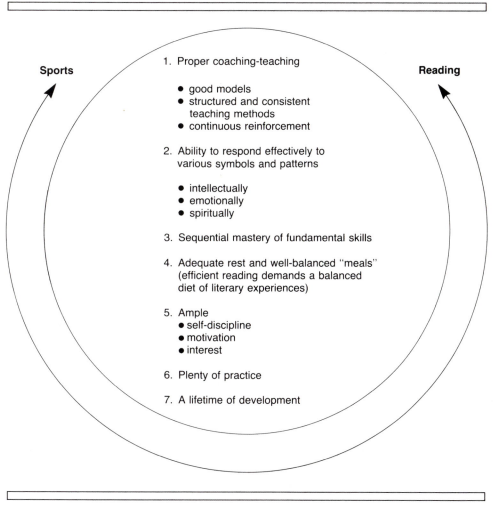

Sports   Reading

1. Proper coaching-teaching

   • good models
   • structured and consistent
     teaching methods
   • continuous reinforcement

2. Ability to respond effectively to
   various symbols and patterns

   • intellectually
   • emotionally
   • spiritually

3. Sequential mastery of fundamental skills

4. Adequate rest and well-balanced "meals"
   (efficient reading demands a balanced
   diet of literary experiences)

5. Ample
   • self-discipline
   • motivation
   • interest

6. Plenty of practice

7. A lifetime of development

Source: From *Using Sports and Physical Education to Strengthen Content Area Reading Skills* (p. 7) by L. M. Gentile, 1980, Newark, DE: International Reading Association. Copyright 1980 by the International Reading Association. Reprinted with permission of Lance M. Gentile and the International Reading Association.

foods account for $74 billion per year—one-third of the nation's food bill. Some observers have begun to see psychological dangers in these statistics.

Several recent books address these potential dangers, and the P.E. teacher should read these and invite students to read and report on them. The most poignant of these books is by Arthur Barsky, a Harvard psychiatrist (*Worried Sick: Our Troubled Quest for Wellness*, Little, Brown, 1988). Barsky says, in effect, that Americans live not "exhuberantly" but "apprehensively," as if our bodies were dormant adversaries, programmed to betray us at any moment. If this is true, it is rather frightening to think that we, as guardians of our nation's youngsters, may be falling prey to a potentially dangerous national obsession. We must be thoughtful and a little cautious even as we champion healthier, more active living. During a period of awakening, there often is a tendency to exaggerate and overdo.

Let us now turn to some *balanced* means of combining the goals of P.E. with those of general literacy.

Ten P.E. Strategies for Buttressing Higher-Order Literacy

The highest goal of the reading curriculum, as noted several times previously, is not merely to teach youngsters to read but to promote language, thinking, and social-emotional maturity. Here, in slightly paraphrased form, are several strategies recommended by Maring and Ritson (1980), professors of reading and physical education, respectively, for fostering "reading maturity" in gym classes.

Strategy 1: Reading to Reinforce Instruction
Make up one-page handouts that summarize and reinforce the physical education content and skills that have just been taught via lecture-explanation, demonstration, or charts and diagrams. Type key terms in all-capital letters, and underline portions of the text that explain their meanings. On the bottom or back of each handout, include a set of questions that relate to the main ideas in the lesson. After students have read the handout, have them form small groups to answer the questions (see Figure 14.2).

Strategy 2: Read and Do
Prepare "Read and Do" instruction sheets so that students will learn required content and at the same time improve their ability to follow written directions (see Figure 14.3).

Strategy 3: Book Checkout
In the locker room or near your office, place a revolving book rack displaying high-interest paperbacks (with checkout cards pasted inside the back covers) that relate to aspects of your physical education curriculum. Consult the school librarian and reading specialist for assistance in book selection. (See also Gentile [1980] for book lists in each sports area.) Have the class or team elect a librarian to be responsible for the lending and returning of the books.

Strategy 4: Interest Grabbers
Place a large bulletin board near the locker room to display current magazine and newspaper clippings. (The informative displays used in most health clubs can provide some sources.) Once or twice a week, take a minute at the beginning or end of the period to say a word or two to highlight some of the clippings.

Figure 14.2   Reading to Reinforce
Instruction

The Basic Rules of Basketball

Directions: Review the underlined information about the capitalized key terms below. Then answer the questions that follow.

Key Terms
1. Each team is composed of five MEMBERS *who play the entire court area.*
2. A team scores *2 points when the ball passes through the hoop during regular play* (FIELD GOAL).
3. A team may score additional points by means of free throws when a member of the opposing team commits a PERSONAL FOUL (*hacking, pushing, holding, etc.*).

Questions
1. Where on the court do team members play?
2. Explain in your own words what a field goal is.
3. Name two kinds of personal fouls.

Strategy 5: Team Teaching

Encourage colleagues in your English department to adapt and teach a unit on sports literature in some of their classes. While the unit is being taught, informally discuss unit content with members of your classes who are participating in the project. See strategy 2 for another example of team planning and teaching.

Strategy 6: Vocabulary Reinforcement

Give students opportunities to review the major physical education concepts and points you have been teaching by having them do vocabulary reinforcement exercises. These might include simple exercises, Semantic Feature Analysis exercises

Figure 14.3   Read and Do

Motor Development Exercise

Single-heel click: Jump into the air, click heels together once, and land with feet apart (any distance). This can be turned into an amusing exercise in which students try to write out totally unambiguous expository directions for their peers to follow. You might invite an English teacher to cooperate with you on this project.

(see Chapter 7 for details), or crossword puzzles generated by microcomputer programs designed for teacher use in this manner.

Strategy 7: Learning Packets

As an extension of strategy 2, work up a number of student-guided unit packets so that students will read and do rather than listen and watch and then do. These packets will add variety to your presentation of content and also will free you for individualized instruction while students are busy carrying out their assignments (see Figure 14.4).

Figure 14.4   Learning Packet: Rolls, Balances and Stunts

Directions: All of the following skills are to be worked on with a partner (a different partner in each class session). Each person progresses at his or her own pace. You may work on one skill from each of the following three sections. Before you begin, though, make sure you understand the proper warmups from your instructor's demonstration in the first session. Develop a new flexibility exercise of your own, and fit it into your warmup pattern. For reference information, consult the pages indicated in your text.

Section 1: Rolls
1. Forward roll—p. 10
2. Backward roll—p. 11
3. Forward roll to a cross-legged stand and then a backward roll—p. 19
4. Side roll—p. 16
5. Cartwheel—pp. 42–43
6. Kip (neck spring)—pp. 46–47
7.
8.
9.

Section 2: Balances
10. Tripod—p. 26
11.
12.
13.
14.
15.

Section 3: Partner Stunts
16. Hand balance pullover—pp. 32–33
17.
18.
19.
20.

Strategy 8: "Testlets"
Evaluate students' performance skills and knowledge by giving short tests that require students to read and follow directions (see Figure 14.5). Each test can be presented on an individual card. Students should be familiar with this format before being tested.

Strategy 9: Junk Mail
When pamphlets or brochures describing "new games" such as Dutch korfball, hocker, and archery golf are routed to your mailbox because the address reads "Attention: PE Teacher," assign a group of student volunteers—some of whom may be less able readers—to study the descriptions and diagrams of the games and demonstrate to the class how they are played. This gives students practice in following directions and in reading at interpretive and applied levels of comprehension.

Strategy 10: Student Reports
Have students read and write a brief (half-page) report on any person making news in sports. Invite different students to give these reports in the opening five minutes of class. Tack up the best reports on a cork display board (Gentile, 1980).

Figure 14.5 Testlets

Grapevine Test
Stand with heels together. Bend trunk forward, extend both arms down between legs and behind ankles, and hold fingers of hands together in front of ankles. Hold this position for five seconds. Failure: (a) to lose balance; (b) to not hold fingers of both hands together; (c) to not hold the position for five seconds.

Three-Dip Test
Take a front leaning-rest position. Bend arms, touching chest to the floor, and push body up again until forearms are in a straight line with upper arms. Execute three performances in succession. Do not touch the floor with legs or with abdomen. Failure: (a) to not push body up three times; (b) to not touch chest to floor; (c) to touch the floor with any part of the body other than hands, feet, and chest.

Full-Left-Turn Test
Stand with feet together. Jump upward, making a full turn to the left. Land at approximately the same place from where the test was started. (Feet may be separated when landing.) Do not lose your balance or move feet after they have touched the floor. Failure: (a) to not make a full turn to the left; (b) to move feet after they have returned to the floor; (c) to lose your balance.

VOCATIONAL EDUCATION

Problems and Goals

> [T]he daily struggle of making a living in America is more difficult to cope with than all of the events we went through in prison and at sea. The reason is that there is nothing "heroic" about surviving the never-ending problems of daily life.
> —Vietnamese boat person Vu Thanh Thuy, at Marist College graduation ceremony, Poughkeepsie, NY, in *Time,* June 13, 1988, p. 74.

Federal Public Law 98-524, also known as the Carl D. Perkins Vocational Act of 1984, has as one of its main purposes the goal of improving the academic foundations of vocational education students. Simply put, the objective is to create a work force able to adjust to the "changing content of jobs." This act contains provisions to support schools willing to develop quality programming in reading and vocational areas.

The justification for such programming is well supported by several studies that have shown that the average workday for nonprofessional workers requires between 24 minutes and 4 hours of reading per day (Rush, Moe, & Storlie, 1986). Related research indicates that workers themselves underestimated by an average of 45% the amount of time they spent reading (Mikulecky, 1982). Furthermore, job-related reading is by no means easy. The materials essential to job competency in 11 fields, ranging from account clerk to welder, have readability levels that rarely dip as low as 9th grade and typically reach as high as the 16th grade level. Secretarial reading is the most difficult, ranging from l6th to college graduate levels (Diehl & Mikulecky, 1980).

Not surprisingly, one of the nagging problems of vocational education has been the difficulty level of school texts. While this situation is changing, there still are plentiful examples of "inconsiderate" text. Derby (1987) offers these examples from one vocational education textbook:

> This chapter is devoted to a study of the various ways in which the basic engine theory and parts are utilized to produce multicylinder engines of several types.

This, Derby explains, is an awkward way of saying,

> This chapter is about the different kinds of engines that are used in today's cars.

In a second example, the same textbook states:

> Although a number of three-rotor and four-rotor experimental engines have been built, common usage at this time employs either a one-rotor or a two-rotor engine.

A more "considerate text" version would read:

> Although a number of experimental engines have been built with three or even four rotors, most engines being built today have just one or two rotors.

It is difficult to understand how such fuzzy language routinely gets published without professional editing. Part of the problem is that textbooks are still being prepared by subject specialists and English-major editors without the input of text technology specialists. Textbooks simply need to be constructed as teaching tools rather than reference devices. In the meantime, there are a few things the vocational technology teacher can provide for students whose training and livelihood will depend on reading technical texts and service manuals.

Services and Strategies

Seven Services Vocational Technology Teachers Can Provide

1. Work with students to use, and where necessary create, text aids such as Advance Organizers, pivotal questions, glossaries of terms, and concept maps.
2. Use the Oral Reading Strategy (see Chapter 2) frequently. Remember to ask many translation questions.
3. Follow the simple steps of the Listen-Read-Discuss Heuristic so that students will be better ''empowered'' for reading inconsiderate text.
4. Using the Informal Textbook Inventory, give students practice and instruction in using basic texts and reference books. For students of electricity, teach the use of the *National Electrical Code;* for health assistants, demonstrate the *Physician's Desk Reference* on diseases; and for automotive students, develop familiarity with the *Chilton Repair Manual* and other motor company services manuals (Derby, 1987).
5. Use the Question-Only procedure as a prereading and prelecture strategy: Instead of merely announcing a topic, show the class a vital engine part and have them conduct a systematic inquiry into its nature, functions, and most frequent failure points.
6. Vocational technology subjects offer abundant opportunities to use the Typical to Technical Vocabulary Approach (Pearson & Johnson, 1978). This strategy also can be used to concurrently improve abstract thinking (see the explanation ahead). Here are some examples of automotive terms, suggested by Piercy (1976), for which students might have culled meanings from everyday life:

differential	a set of gears that permit rear wheels to revolve at different speeds
differential	peculiarity; distinction; feature; earmark
governor	a device for automatically controlling the speed of an engine by regulating the intake of fuel
governor	the elected head of any state in the United States
distributor	a mechanical device for distributing electric current to the spark plugs of a gas engine
distributor	a business firm that distributes goods to customers
drum	a metal cylinder
drum	a percussion instrument
shoe	the curved part of a brake that presses against the wheel rim

shoe	an outer covering for the foot
muffler	a device for deadening the sound of escaping gases of an internal combustion engine
muffler	a heavy neck scarf

Abstract thinking can be improved by urging students to see and express the common element in the everyday and technical meanings. This may involve looking up the origins and root meanings of a word as expressed between the brackets of a dictionary definition.

7. Guiding a pre- and postreading analysis of diagrams and illustrations is a powerful way to promote strategic reading. This can be done in a survey fashion prior to reading and in a very careful way following silent reading. Where this procedure is followed routinely, students will be keyed into the supportive graphic material as they begin to read and anticipate further analysis following reading. This combination should increase the probability that they will use the illustrations, like the one in Figure 14.6, to grasp and clarify meanings when they read silently. It also should help them become better strategic readers for the time when they must read independently in school and on the job.

Career-Oriented Literature (COL)

Quite apart from textbooks and manuals, the vocational education teacher needs a ready and readable supply of career-oriented literature (COL). *Career-oriented literature* refers to articles and stories about jobs and career areas. It tends to reflect how real people feel about their jobs and vocations.

COL materials tend to touch on matters that textbooks and manuals rarely address, such as apprenticeship programs and various employee benefit options. A few publishers offer other special, hard-to-find, human elements:

- The Globe Book Company has two books (*All in a Day's Work* and *It Happened on the Job*) containing true, brief anecdotal accounts of work situations which are unusual and sometimes humorous.
- Pitman Learning offers *Pacemaker Vocational Readers,* a set of ten high interest, controlled vocabulary books describing young trade-type people in challenging situations.
- *Scholastic Magazine* has an *Action Series* that has a number of job-related storybooks like *The Plumber's Line, Rosina Torres, L.P.N., Demolition Man,* and *Paramedic Emergency.*
- Vocational Biographies, Inc. offers *Project Earth and Project Explore* describing jobs and careers in the context of scientific principles and actual Vocational Biographies highlighting real individuals.
- *Career World* (formerly *Real World*) is a color newspaper, written in the vein of *USA Today.* It addresses the work-a-day world and contains actual reading skill exercises. (Derby, 1987)

Figure 14.6

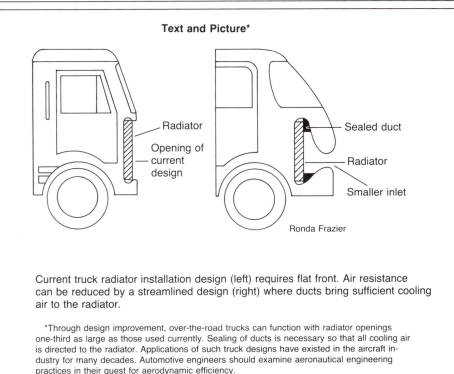

Text and Picture*

Ronda Frazier

Current truck radiator installation design (left) requires flat front. Air resistance can be reduced by a streamlined design (right) where ducts bring sufficient cooling air to the radiator.

*Through design improvement, over-the-road trucks can function with radiator openings one-third as large as those used currently. Sealing of ducts is necessary so that all cooling air is directed to the radiator. Applications of such truck designs have existed in the aircraft industry for many decades. Automotive engineers should examine aeronautical engineering practices in their quest for aerodynamic efficiency.

Source: From *Occupational Literacy Education* (page 43) by T. Rush, A. Moe, and R. Storlie, 1986, Newark, DE: International Reading Association. Copyright 1986 by the International Reading Association. Reprinted with permission of R. Timothy Rush and the International Reading Association.

Language Experiences

Most activities undertaken in career and vocational education can be performed better with student input. Language Experience Activities (LEAs) provide such opportunities. Here are a few LEA-type activities that are especially suitable for the vocational education class.

1. *"Celebrity" Interview:* Have students interview working people as though the latter were celebrities. Ask concerned questions such as might be asked of celebrities: "How did you first get into this business?"; "Has this work been fulfilling for you?"; "Have you ever wished that you could have done something else?"; "Can you tell me an interesting or amusing experience that you have had in this line of work?" Students could be instructed to watch television

interview shows to get some ideas for "people questions." Discuss the questions they might ask before they ask them.

2. *Dialogue Journal:* Have students keep a journal (a notebook kept in class) in which they write a sentence or two every other day regarding their career interests and experiences. Periodically, read and write a brief reaction to these: "Charlie, I didn't realize that your father is an electrician!"; "Mary, if you will see me after class, I can tell you where to get more information on summer jobs with the city."

3. *Vocabulary from the Workplace:* To help build respect and support for the vocational program throughout the school, have students interview friends and family about words and expressions that they use on the job but laypeople would be unlikely to know. Ask English teachers, for example, to use Haggard's (1978) Vocabulary Self-Selection Strategy to include some of these words on English vocabulary lists. Vocabulary collections of this type can contribute to students' sense of accomplishment and make English teachers realize that many students who might not know what *onomatopoeia* means probably do know what a *rocker-panel* is (the name for the narrow shelf beneath all car doors). Terms such as these, which the English teacher probably doesn't know and which rarely can be found in most standard dictionaries, constitute a wider and richer language system than most academically oriented teachers have considered. For a comprehensive listing of the most frequently encountered terms in 11 fields, see Rush et al. (1986).

4. *Language Shaping Paradigm:* Collect essays and other personal stories from students. Edit these with students, and select a few to be reproduced and read with the rest of the class. For further details on the LSP, see the English section in Chapter 12.

5. *Magazines:* Have students subscribe to a few quality news and trade magazines. These can be read in class or for homework. Assign groups to give well-organized reports on different articles, or have students lead discussions as recommended in Reciprocal Teaching.

Reading and Consumer Decision Making

There is a strong resemblance between effective reading and consumer decision making, according to Peck and Laughlin (1982). Working from this premise, these authors concluded that both can be improved by confronting students with "consumer dilemmas." The dilemma is written and presented to students in short-story form. An authentic consumer document, such as a charge account or security agreement and/or a selection from a consumer magazine, may accompany the dilemma.

Prior to reading, students try to estimate the difficulty level of the material to "crank up" their metacognitive thinking. Question sheets are provided to guide their reading and the decision-making process. Finally, students evaluate their decisions.

State-It-Rite: Simulated Language Experience

The vocational education student is likely to be heading toward the workplace sooner than the academic student. An essential element of success in the workplace is captured in a quaint old phrase, "proper decorum": The way you look and speak can be as important as what you say. It is a concern that President Bush set out for the entire nation when he called for a "kinder and gentler America." To promote this essential "trace element," try an extension of Ask-It-Rite called *State-It-Rite (SIR)*.

SIR activities are simulations disguised to elicit class reactions to different ways of handling workplace situations. The scenarios can be drawn from actual student experiences and from reading selections. One means of guiding student interactions in these "stop-action, discuss, and resume-action" activities is to ask students to think of how someone whom they admire might handle each situation. This activity ties in nicely with career-oriented literature: reading brief biographies of famous and ordinary people who have demonstrated wisdom, grace, and humor in facing life's daily challenges.

Here are some heuristics, or guidelines for behavior, to share with students prior to or following SIR simulations:

* Everyone looks better with a smile.
* Answer anger not with anger but with concern.
* If you've messed up, it often is best to apologize, offer a brief explanation, and indicate that you would value another chance.
* Listen when others speak.
* Remember that those whom you can help to like themselves better will like *you* better.
* Even if you are fired, don't burn bridges. Say you are sorry that you disappointed your employer and that you plan to try harder in your next job.
* Try all these things at home with your parents. You will be surprised at the positive power you can exert in family life.
* Again, listen when others speak. Most problems spring from failure to do so.

Decorum Journal: Reprocessing and Writing

Evaluate and discuss what students have learned following each simulation, and have them record key actions and phrases in a *Decorum Journal*. Activities of this type are compatible with languaging, metacognitive, and motivational theories: They tend to induce more careful processing of experiences, heighten self-monitoring, and provide a reason for reading further as well as more carefully observing effective models of effective behavior.

Example

2/19: We noticed that whenever people open their eyes just a little bit wider when someone is talking to them, they say they can actually hear better. The person talking also gets the feeling that you are listening better.

3/4:   From what I've seen today, I'd better learn to say "Sir" and "Ma'am." It probably will stick in my throat at first. But I think Mr. Wilson is right—it seems to make you bigger, not smaller.

ART AND MUSIC

The Challenge

Art and music teachers are important advocates of cultural literacy in the schools. Studies in art and music contribute to progress toward reading maturity in a variety of ways. They raise students' level of cultural literacy, or schema, and therefore contribute to effective comprehension. They offer a sheltering and enriching alternative to the everyday challenge and drone of life and therefore can enhance personal-social adjustment. They reflect diverse perspectives and historical periods and therefore contribute to a broad, multicultural outlook. Most important, they provide *pleasure* and offer an outlet for expression to those who need an alternative to writing and reading alone. For these reasons, it is important to consider ways to gently weave content area reading objectives into the art and music curricula in a manner that will benefit both.

Writing in art and music almost by nature tends to be esoteric. Sentences often contain complex syntax, unusual phrasings, assumptive references, sophisticated ideas, and names and words of foreign origin: "One does not really read a music theory book . . . one grapples with it" (Duke, 1987). A typical passage even from a lay book on music reads like this:

> In all of art's best periods, creative people were brought together, and thus we had Pericles' Athens, the Medici's Florence, Elizabeth's London, Goethe's (and later Liszt's) Weimar, Beethoven's (and later Brahms') Vienna, Emerson's Concord, Lowell's Boston and Monet's Paris. These were by no means smooth waters, but they were lively. (Bacon, 1963, p. 130)

One would need to be quite well informed in the areas of art, music, literature, and history and in the characteristics of several different cultures to take in the full significance of this almost casual observation by Ernest Bacon, pianist and teacher.

Meeting the Challenge

The art and music teacher can help students meet and profit from the challenge of "inconsiderate text" in several ways:

1. Use the Oral Reading Strategy to familiarize students with syntax, phrasing, and usual pronunciations.

2. Ask frequent translation questions: "Can you say this in your own words?"

3. Add information as needed to enhance schema: "Have you read or heard about the Medici family in world history class yet? They were a wealthy and influential Italian family in medieval Florence—a thriving seaport city in Italy. They were great patrons of the arts."

4. Teach mini-lessons on foreign pronunciation and cultural literacy as time and opportunity permit. When coming across a name like Goethe, you might say, "This name is pronounced *GER-tuh*. It is a German name. Johann Wolfgang von Goethe was a writer who had a powerful influence on art in his time and down to this day. He felt that art should be natural, sincere, and simple. He lived at about the time the French and American Revolutions were occurring."

5. Use the Listen-Read-Discuss Heuristic and Note Cue to guide reading and discussion in art and music.

6. Have students use the Subjective Approach to Vocabulary with illustrations: Divide a page into quarters, and have students write the new word in quadrant I, write its dictionary meaning in II, draw a pictorial representation in III, and write out the subjective association in IV. Then the class discusses these and stores them in their notebooks.

7. The same basic matrix can be used to teach art history and appreciation. A miniature artwork is pictured (or named) in quadrant I; a brief background and description of the work are given in quadrant II; a published or teacher critique goes in quadrant III; and a student critique, or personal evaluation, appears in quadrant IV (see Figure 14.7). This process results in students creating a personal art collection while developing aesthetic sense, critical-evaluative thinking, and critical writing skills. (Note: Reproductions of artworks of about 2" × 2," with sticky backs, can be purchased from the Metropolitan Museum of Art in New York City.)

8. Work with science, literature, and social studies teachers to have students produce various forms of artistic representations of significant ideas. Permit freedom of expression (see Figure 14.8).

9. Work with the school principal to use music in appropriate settings. Music has been shown to facilitate creative writing, mathematics, spelling, and art (Taylor, 1980; Greenhoe, 1972; Maor, 1979). While music sometimes can be distracting during reading, classical music has been found to be conducive to comprehension gains (Mullikin & Henk, 1985). The classical music played in the latter study was Pietro Mascagni's *Cavalleria Rusticana "Intermeggio."* A no-music condition produced better performance than did rock music, which is to say that rock is disruptive. Apparently something soft, slow, and with methodical cadence is necessary to foster reading.

The second author found this to be true while using taped music during "free reading" time with urban junior high school reading classes. Music was played during the first 10 minutes of class, during which time students who were caught up with class work had the privilege of reading anything of their choosing. I began the year with a few classical and "easy-listening" instrumental selections that I used for free reading time. Not knowing about Mullikin and Henk's finding, I succumbed several times to students' pleas to use rock music instead. It never worked: With a rock music background, students were more distracted than they would have been otherwise. Even when I eliminated rock music, however, they appreciated the more traditional melodic pieces enough to hush one another rather than lose the privilege.

Figure 14.7   Art History Matrix

I. Artwork

Toulouse-Lautrec, *Russian Woman*, 1891,
30¾″ x 23½″, private collection.

II. Background and Description

A painting by Toulouse-Lautrec (1891) in pale brown and tan with a splash of blue. It resembles a drawing viewed from a strangle angle to give it a candid-camera realism. It can be found in the Albi museum in France.

III. Critique

This painting is taken from the perspective of the artist—a near-midget with poor vision, unattractive features, and an aristocratic background. Like many artists of his time, Lautrec was inspired by Japanese prints. He learned from them how to dramatize a composition by eliminating detail.

IV. Subjective Response

This picture strikes me as capturing a certain essence of femininity. Like most things simple, it would be easy to live with.

Figure 14.8   How a Bill Becomes a Law (Lenny's Rendition)

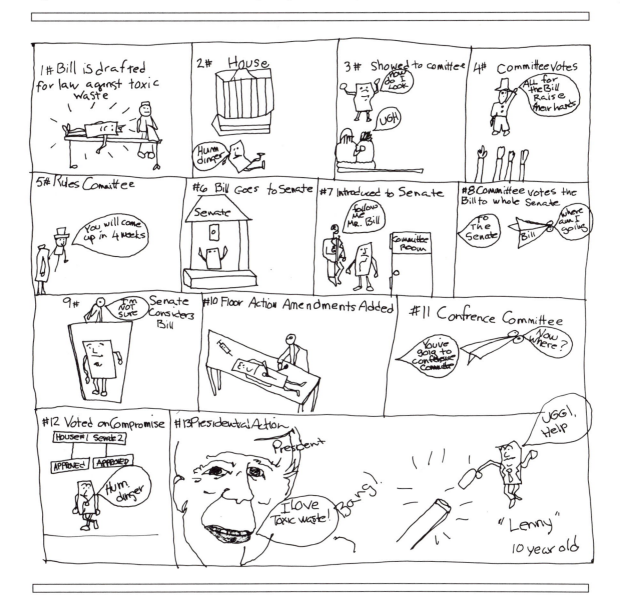

10. Television shows such as "L.A. Law" and "Hill Street Blues" are dramatized with music. Work with the English teacher to have students think through and try to score selections of literature with appropriate musical pieces. This takes a good deal of thinking and analysis. If you feel daring, ask students to select or compose theme tunes for the school and/or individual teachers.

CHAPTER TIE-UPS

◆◆◆   *Graphic Organizer*

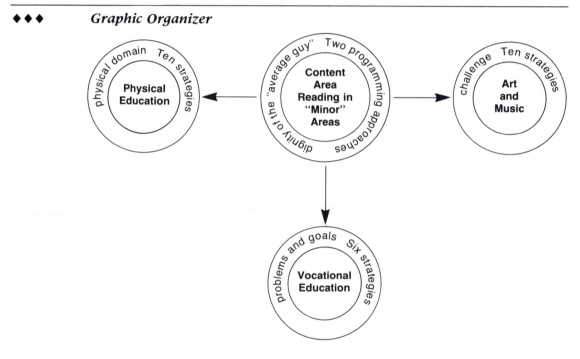

◆◆◆   *Critique*

This chapter offered several examples and illustrations of applications of previously discussed methods, along with several that are unique to each of the support area subjects covered. Most of the methods presented urged cooperation with core subject teachers. This cooperation will likely strengthen the contribution of the support areas to whole person education as well as augment the contribution of the core subjects to support area study.

TRADE SECRET

On Acquiring and Using New Methods

Whether you are a preservice or veteran teacher, the value and credibility of new methods often are reduced initially by certain predictable inhibitions to your performance. This may be one of the darkest and best-kept secrets of teacher education. The reasons are basic and human.

As preservice or in-service teachers, our dissonance level tends to rise to a point of distraction when we first use a new method, and especially so when we will be observed or evaluated. There also are things we may think about that can be counterproductive: "If this really works, why didn't I think of it?"; "I thought of this, but I won't get credit for it even if I use it"; "What if this is a better way to go but I can't make it work?"

As we suggested in Chapter 1, early attempts to do anything new are bound to raise some self-doubt, ego defensiveness, and performance anxiety. This tends to narrow our focus and flexibility and thus limit our ability to attend to students and their individual needs. However, this scenario is less discouraging than it may appear. Consideration of an analogous situation—learning how to drive a car—suggests that we can overcome many of these problems through simple awareness and practice.

When we first learn how to drive, we dare not play the radio, carry on a conversation, or take in the scenery. As our driving becomes more habitual, both from actual practice and from visualizing, we can do all of these things and more. So it is with a new teaching method: It is important to continue to use a new method until dissonance is reduced, comfort is increased, and we once again can become sensitive and aware of student needs. A new methodology generally needs to be employed no more than two to four times for the benefits to begin to outweigh the initial drawbacks. Unfortunately, there is a strong tendency to abandon new ideas and methods before completing even a single full trial.

Keep this in mind, and make a commitment to yourself to try a new method at least three times before you reach a firm conclusion. To further ensure your continued growth as a professional, remember to make some lesson prompters. Having the summarized steps of the new method handy and easily visible can raise your security and confidence levels and help keep you from losing your way in the whirl of classroom cross-currents.

Appendix A
Pivotal Questions and Brief Answers

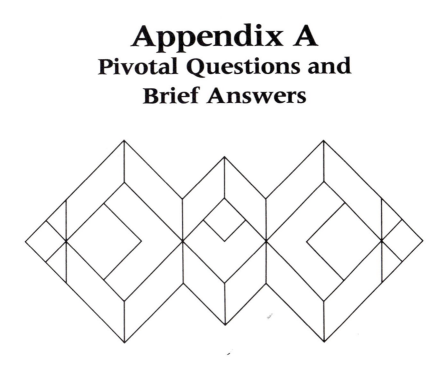

1. *Haven't students learned to ''read'' by the time they finish grade school?* Yes, about as well as third-year students play a musical instrument: They've got basic technique, can read music, and play a tune. But reading, like playing an instrument, is a lifelong, *developmental* learning process. To play the wide variety of musical types with poignant interpretation and style takes practice and coaching. Of course, a few individuals can go it alone. They practice on their own and coach themselves. But they, as the great violinist Itzak Perlman once noted, are in danger of becoming misguided or developing bad habits. And yes, Perlman too occasionally schedules a class with a master teacher!

2. *In the past, few students were taught ''reading'' after grade school. Doesn't reading improve naturally and, more or less, as a result of reading?* For *most* students, the answer is no—reading skills are not acquired ''naturally.'' We tend to *think* that reading improves naturally because we, as secondary teachers, probably had very little ''coaching'' ourselves in how to read in content areas. Our teachers were not trained to provide this assistance.

For the most part, learning to read content materials has tended to be a ''sink-or-swim'' challenge: You figured out how to do it, or you failed to learn the subject. Today's educational policies have put increased demands on the teacher to ensure that students learn. The following chain of events tends to unfold: Students have trouble learning what they must learn from the text; the teacher begins to present the material in other ways; students are required to read less; eventually even those students who might have developed reading skills no longer are doing so as well as they might.

3. *If reading instruction is still needed, why can't it just be taught in a separate class by a reading teacher?* It was, at the beginning of the CAR movement, and sometimes still is. The most serious problem with the separate-class approach is that it tends to be effective only for able students who already are adept at transfer of training: application of skills learned in one context to meet challenges in other contexts. Average and poor students, in contrast, have difficulty in transferring training; therefore, isolated training in reading and study skills does not help them in their other classes. These students need coaching in *every* type of reading—and who is better able to provide it than the content teachers, who are experts in how to think, talk, question, and explore in their particular subject fields?

4. *How can content teachers be expected to have time to teach reading when most school districts have stringent policies that mandate teacher responsibility for students' (including mainstreamed students') mastery of content objectives?* The fact that content teachers are held responsible for student learning—more so today than ever before—is the strongest argument for the need for content area reading. Coaching of content area reading is not done *in addition to* teaching content; it is done *while* teaching content. When such coaching accompanies the teaching of content, students (including mainstreamed ones) become more capable of independent learning.

Two principles of instruction tend to characterize effective and efficient strategies for coaching content reading. First, *concurrent* teaching strategies are designed to permit one to teach toward several objectives at a time. Second, *heuristic* strategies are designed so as to remove obstacles from effective teaching and learning while reinforcing positive effects. These concepts are exemplified throughout this text.

5. *Some content areas, such as physical education, art, music, and math, involve little or no reading. What should teachers in these disciplines know about content area reading, and why? What* they should know are the basics and some specifics: something about the nature of the reading process and a variety of teaching strategies for implementing guidance in developmental reading in their subjects in their classrooms.

Why they should know and do these things relates to two concepts that are central to effective schools. First, every teacher is responsible for the overall goals of the school, not simply for his or her own classes. Accordingly, every teacher can contribute to the schoolwide reading program by developing merely a few lessons that involve some student reading and are carefully designed to permit even poor readers to have successful reading experiences. Second, the purpose of school is not so much to teach "subjects" as it is to introduce subjects and strategies for pursuing them through school and in the future. The serious student of any subject will need effective reading strategies and habits: It is impossible to teach students all they will need to know into the future.

There is an interesting sidelight on this issue. Content teachers have pointed out to us that some good readers have trouble in classes that require little reading. These students tend to be language-oriented visual learners and are somewhat at a loss in classes geared toward auditory learning. The addition of a few reading-oriented lessons often can help these students feel more comfortable in these courses.

6. *What skills and abilities can content teachers expect students to bring to class? How can these be assessed?* In general, the higher the grade, the wider the range of students'

reading abilities. This is because after elementary school, poor readers usually get very little reading instruction and therefore make slower progress. A seventh-grade class may have reading levels ranging from fourth to ninth, while a tenth-grade class is likely to range from fifth to college level.

Another point to keep in mind is that students' reading abilities will vary according to their interests and backgrounds of information in different subjects. Standardized test scores from students' files are a place to start, but these should be supplemented with information collected by the content teacher.

7. *How can students of varying ability levels be helped to read and learn content from a common classroom text? Are there practical alternatives to the single-text model?* There are several alternatives, but none are very practical. A frequent suggestion, for example, is to vary or even individualize reading materials. But this takes an extraordinary amount of preparation and continuous monitoring. A better strategy is to vary the instructional approach, starting with some basic information about individual students' reading abilities and the difficulty level of the text. Then concurrent strategies can be used to present content from the text while showing students how to read and remember the information. Even poor readers can be empowered to read difficult text when prereading activities draw out and extend their funds of information, identify and explain difficult vocabulary terms, and provide clear purposes for reading.

8. *How can students' independent reading and learning strategies be improved?* Different theories of reading have different implications for the best way to approach instruction. This text takes the perspective that the best way to guide students toward reading maturity is to demonstrate, or model, effective study-reading behaviors and provide ample opportunities and incentives for practicing these under the teacher's observation and guidance. This ''languaging'' approach parallels the process by which language and thinking are learned naturally. It is a key ingredient of many of the teaching procedures described in the text.

9. *What does a content area reading program look like?* An effective reading program must begin with teachers who are informed about content area reading concepts and strategies. Initial training should be maintained by quality in-service programs that rekindle interest and motivation. Effective programs for special-needs students should be in place to support content teachers' efforts in cases where student needs exceed what can be provided in the context of a conventional classroom setting. Finally, knowledgeable and supportive administrative leadership is essential to a strong and ongoing schoolwide reading program.

Appendix B
Educator's Personal Recorder
and Professional Planner

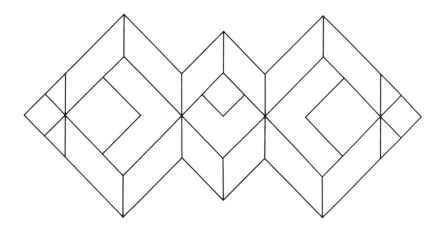

Materials needed: looseleaf or other binder, paper, cardboard sleeves

Section I: Guiding Thoughts

A. Thoughts and Perspectives on Careers in General

Examples ◆ ◆ ◆

1. Successful careers don't just happen; they are the result of vision, planning, and effort.
2. Most successful careers are beset by occasional setbacks. Expect these, and be ready to push on.
3. When truth stands in your way, you are headed in the wrong direction.

B. Thoughts and Perspectives on Teachers and Teaching

Examples ◆ ◆ ◆

1. The art of teaching is the art of assisting discovery.
2. The enthusiastic teacher is a lifelong student.
3. The finer the instruction, the more it invites; the poorer it is, the more it compels.

C. Thoughts and Perspectives on Schools and Schooling

Examples ◆ ◆ ◆

1. Nowadays school heads are chosen to *run* a school rather than lead it (Bacon, 1963).
2. The school's task is to take a lot of live wires and see that they get well grounded.

Section II: Employment Record

A. Nonteaching job experiences

B. Educational job experiences

C. Other

[Sleeve: current resume, constructed from all other parts]

Section III: Personal History (Birth to High School)

A. Family background

B. Medical/health factors

C. Social, athletic, religious affiliations

D. Academic record, K–12

E. Hobbies and interests

F. Significant memories

[Sleeve: birth certificate, school records, early photos, letters, memorabilia]

Section IV: Personal History (Postsecondary)

A. Academic (degrees, majors, minors)

B. Activities (extracurricular, organizational, religious, athletic)

C. Social life (personal and family)

D. Intellectual development (books, magazines, ideas)

[Sleeve: transcripts, letters of references, other records]

Section V: Material Accounting

A. Gifts, trusts, support

B. Income history

C. Loan history

D. Assets (stocks, car, furniture, property)

E. Approximate net worth

F. Prospects (likely legacies and/or opportunities)

[Sleeve: records, photos, memorabilia, papers]

Section VI: Professional History

A. Certificates

B. Evaluations/recommendations

C. Memorable teachers and colleagues

D. Teaching experiences: subjects, grade levels, situations

E. Related nonteaching roles and experiences

F. Memorable inservice, conferences, sabbaticals

G. Memorable articles, books, papers

H. Membership and roles in committees and professional organizations

I. Grants, travel, awards

J. Summer activities and employment

[Sleeve: related letters, certificates, and papers]

Section VII: Self-Appraisals

A. Attitudes

B. Interests and abilities

C. Temperament/personality

D. Teaching/learning style

E. Personal assessment of strengths and weaknesses as a person and as a teacher

[Sleeve: records]

Section VIII: Occasional Notes

A. Notes on memorable personal events (marriage, deaths, births, friendships)

B. Notes on memorable professional experiences (significant mentor relationships, special students)

[Sleeve: appropriate records]

Section IX: Blueprints

A. Set out some personal career objectives.

B. Collect and/or set out some objectives that might contribute to your professional education.

[Sleeve: related articles and notes]

Section X: Teaching Competence

A. List the teaching methods you have mastered.

B. List the teaching methods you intend to try.

[Sleeve: related articles and notes on each method]

Appendix C
ALARM Subtest Descriptions and Sample Items

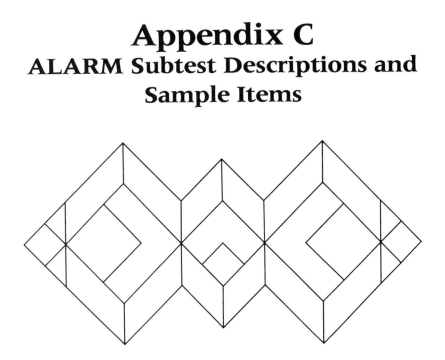

Test 1: (Basic) Word Recognition

A word-opposites test made up of words with regular and irregular elements (10 items).

Sample items

A. black:	1. red	2. whole	3. blue	4. green	5. white
B. sweat:	1. dry	2. bitter	3. neat	4. nit	5. score

Test 2: (Basic) Vocabulary

A word-similarities test of high-frequency words that should be known by the junior high school level (20 items).

Sample items

A. congress:	1. President	2. parliament	3. board	4. color	5. Washington
B. nimble:	1. dumb	2. numb	3. agile	4. gifted	5. negative

Test 3: (Basic) Analogies

A word reasoning test that requires a word or phrase to complete an analogy. Vocabulary is controlled and estimated at fifth-reader level (10 items).

Sample items

A. *Shelves* are to books as *cartons* are to:
   1. floors   2. ceilings   3. eggs   4. pickles   5. boxes
B. *Eight* is to *ten* as *thirteen* is to:
   1. eighteen   2. twelve   3. fifteen   4. zero   5. five

Test 4: Complex Sentences

Requires translation of a sentence of relatively easy words but complex syntax into component parts.

Sample items

Sentence: About the palace the curious citizens watch, through the iron-grilled fence, the merchants with gold-covered purses walking in the courtyard with an air of their importance.

A. "about the palace" means:
   1. around the palace
   2. the merchants are talking about the palace
   3. there will be a bout, or fight, at the palace
   4. where the merchants are going

B. "Ernest had been her favorite" is the same as:
   1. Her favorite had been Ernest.
   2. Ernest had been favorite.
   3. Her Ernest had been favorite.
   4. Favored had been her Ernest.

Test 5: Modified Cloze

A measure of language redundancy patterns found in prose. Deletions are on a nonfixed schedule ranging between 3 and 9 words (25 items).

Sample items

         were   know

There (56)   are many tests in which the Indian boy had to (57)   that

         are   show

he could bear pain.

Test 6: Reading Comprehension

Students read two relatively brief, high-interest passages, which are followed by multiple choice questions of a main idea, detail, and inferential nature (15 items).

Test 7: Fund of Information (or Cultural Literacy)

Students are required to rapidly process the best answer to questions designed to tap a diverse pool of commonly held information (33 items).

Sample items

A. Each of these presidents was first a vice-president except:
1. Lyndon Johnson
2. Gerald Ford
3. Richard Nixon
4. John Kennedy

B. The "Golden Age" of Greece was about the year:
1. 7000 B.C.
2. 500 B.C.
3. 1500 A.D.
4. 1800 A.D.

C. Which number cannot be divided evenly by 3?
1. 16
2. 15
3. 18
4. 36

Test 8: Proverbs (or Abstract) Comprehension

Students decide which of four statements best represents the most abstract version of a proverb. Reading level and idea load are controlled. The subtest also could be scored for tendency to choose answers that tend to indicate a high degree of emotionality (tendency to have one's thoughts disrupted by extraneous elements). Two forms are available: elementary and secondary (15 items each).

Sample items

A. The squeaking wheel gets the grease.

(emotional) 1. Silence is best.
(concrete)   2. The loud child gets the love.
(abstract)   3. Things attracting attention tend to be taken care of first.
(incorrect)   4. Greased wheels rotate more easily.

B. Clothes make the man.
(abstract)   1. The way one presents oneself is the way one tends to behave.
(incorrect)   2. Don't judge a book by its cover.
(concrete)   3. Clothes and such can make you feel good.
(emotional) 4. A man is what he is no matter how he dresses.

Test 9: Critique Preference

A measure of "elaborative thinking"—a brief selection is presented, followed by five critiques of varying degrees of sophistication. The student is asked to order these from least to most preferred. Points are awarded on the supposition that preferences for more sophisticated critiques indicate an inclination to think more elaboratively, or "dialectically."

Examples illustrate three levels of critique of the same passage, which was taken from the A. S. Neill book *Summerhill.*

1. The child is motivated by natural impulses such as the need to eat or to gratify wishes. This child naturally comes into conflict with a system of prohibitions called moral instruction. The conflict created by instructing the child in morality is what causes delinquent, "bad" children.
2. Children have natural needs. Moral instruction conflicts with natural needs. This contradiction causes delinquent behavior.
3. Neill is correct. Moral instruction does conflict with "natural needs": It is supposed to. Moral instruction is humankind's attempt to control our destiny. Clearly, some "moralists" have overstated the issue; however, the act of inhibiting certain reactions is virtually a definition of civilization. We don't need less moral instruction, we need more thoughtful instruction.

Test 10: Self Construct Test

Students construct a social-psychological protrait of themselves by expressing different levels of identification with or rejection of 33 animals on a 5-point scale. The subtest has the potential to yield several possible indices of affective factors. The factors surveyed most frequently are general emotional stability and level of achievement motivation (adapted from the Bestiary Inventory [Manzo, 1975]).

Test 11: Teaching/Learning Range

A measure of adaptability—10 methods are described, and students express their general level of preference for each on a 5-point scale. The broader a student's range, the greater his or her maturity and adaptability. The information acquired from this subtest also can be used in much the same manner as most other cognitive or learning styles inventories.

Sample items

Lecture learning: The teacher does most of the talking. Questions are permitted, but there generally is little discussion.

Tutoring: The teacher works with one student (or a small group) while the remainder of the class is engaged in another activity.

Test 12: Cultural Compatibility

This is a "difference" inventory designed to determine the extent to which there is a "shared context" between students and curriculum. Students indicate whether their self-concepts, attitudes, experiences, and opportunities are equal to assumptions about the "average" American student and, therefore, the expectations of schools.

Sample items

A. I like being the way I am.
B. I believe that I will become better at almost everything I do as I grow older.
C. When I become frustrated in school, I double my effort.
D. Some of my relatives have graduated from college.
E. Members of my family have owned their own business(es).

Test 13: Critical Judgments—Useful Information

Students are asked to reflect their view of the world in judging the "value to society" of information contained in each of several sentences. They are to assume that the information is correct (18 items).

Sample items

A. Adolf Hitler once owned 8,960 acres of land in Colorado.
B. Two things cannot occupy the same place at the same time.

Test 14: Critical Judgments—Reasonability

Students are again asked to reflect their views of the world in judging how "reasonable" they believe each of several sentences to be (9 items).

Sample items

A. It is okay for parents to hit young children when it appears necessary.
B. Men appear to be more naturally aggressive than women.

Test 15: Critical Judgments—Appreciation

Students are asked once more to reflect their world views in making a range of judgments, some of the type required in tests 13 and 14, plus estimations of an aesthetic nature—"Does this word or phrase seem balanced—not too flat, or emotional, or biased?"—and logic—"Does this seem logical within the framework of the story?" Together these are taken as an index of students' maturity in appreciation of what they read.

Appendix D
Morphemes: Prefixes, Suffixes, and Roots

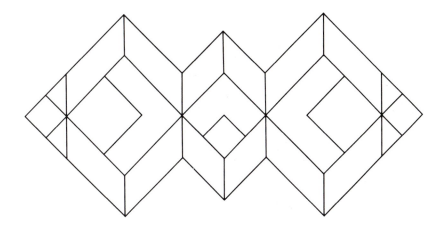

I. Prefixes, five categories

A. Negative Connotation

	Meanings	*Example*
in-		*in*sensitive
im-		*im*possible
ir-	not, non-, un-	*ir*responsible
il-		*il*legal
un-	not, in-, non-, contrary, removal or privation of	*un*necessary
non-	not, un-, in-	*non*sense
dis-	separation, reversal, depriving, negation	*dis*suade
mis-	amiss, wrong, ill	*mis*spell
anti-	opposite, against, instead, counter	*anti*toxin

B. Indicating Direction, Time, or Occurrence

ex-	out of, off, from beyond, away from, without, thoroughly, formerly—but not now	*ex*it

---

Source: From *Comprehensive High School Reading Methods* (pp. 35–42) by David L. Shepherd, 1982, Columbus, Ohio: Merrill Publishing Company. Copyright by David L. Shepherd. Reprinted by permission.

	Meanings	*Example*
in-	in, within, into, toward, on	*in*fuse
per-	throughout in space or time, away or over, completely, perfectly, extremely, very; largest or relatively large, highest, or relatively high (chem.)	*per*mit
re-	back, backwards, back from advancing, again	*re*trace
de-	down; separation, off; away; out of; intensification, completely; reversing, undoing, depriving, freeing from	*de*face
circum-	round, about, on all sides, revolving about, surrounding	*circum*spect
sub-	under, below, beneath, lower; next lower than, subordinate to; forming a further division, a repetition, continuation of below the category of but above the category which follows (biol.); situation on ventral side or under (anat.); having less than normal amount (chem.); near base of, bordering upon (geog., geol.); inversely (math.)	*sub*terranean
syn-, sy-, sym-	with, along with, at the same time	*syn*chronize
trans-	over, across, beyond, through, transcending	*trans*port
retro-	backward, back, situated behind	*retro*active

C. Indicating Relationship

auto-	self	*auto*mobile
co-	with, together, in conjunction, jointly; corresponding function of the complement of an arc or angle (math.); complement of the delination, latitude (astron.)	
com-	with, together, in conjunction, very	*com*mit
con-	equal to *com-* before consonants except b, h, l, m, p, r, w	*con*form
col-	assimilated form of *com-*	*col*lude
cor-	assimilated form of *com-*	*cor*respond
counter-	opposite or contrary, reciprocal, retaliatory, complementary	*counter*act
contra-	against, contrary, in opposition	*contra*dict
hyper-	over, above, beyond, beyond the norm; super; extra; denoting position above (anat., zool.); equal to *per-* (chem.)	*hyper*active
super-	above, over; on or at the top of, over and above, more than; that surpasses all or	*super*cilious

Meanings	Example
most others of its kind; exceeding, in excess; in addition, extra; secondarily; situated over, on upper part or dorsal side (biol.); having the ingredient in large proportion (chem.)	

D. Time and Number

	Meanings	Example
pro-	priority in place, or time, or order; before	*pro*ceed
pre-	before in time, previously, previous, in advance, in front of, ahead of, prior to	*pre*cede
post-	after, subsequent, later; behind or posterior (biol.)	*post*pone
uni-	one, single, have but one	*uni*form
bi-	two, twice, double; relation to each of two symmetrically paired parts (biol.)	*bi*ennial
tri-	having three, into three, thrice, every third; denoting presence of three atoms, groups, or equivalents of that signified by the term to which it is attached (chem.)	*tri*ennial
quadr-	four	*quadr*ilateral
tetra-	four	*tetro*meter
penta-	five	*penta*gon
quin-	five	*quin*tet
sex-	six	*sex*tet
hexa-	six	*hexa*gonal
sept-	seven	*sept*ennial
oct-	eight	*oct*agon
dec-	ten	*dec*ade
centi-	one hundred	*centi*meter
milli-	one thousand	*milli*gram
kilo-	one thousand	*kilo*gram
hemi-	half	*hemi*sphere
semi-	half; approximately half, partly; precisely half; halved or bissected; coming twice; in one half, in some particular; in low degree, no more than half; little more than, little better than	*semi*circle
multi-	many, much; having many; many times over; more than two	*multi*ply

E. Additional (Misc.)

ante-	before, preceding, in front of, prior, anticipatory, anterior, fore	*ante*dote

	Meanings	*Example*
inter-	among, between, together; mutual, mutually, reciprocal, intervening	*inter*cede
intra-	within, inside, into	*intra*mural
intro-	to, into, within, inward	*intro*duce
fore-	in front, as forerunner, beforehand, preceding, before	*fore*cast

II. Suffixes: Noun and Adjective

A. Noun Suffixes

	Meanings	*Example*
-ion	result of	fus*ion*
-sion	the act, quality, condition or result of	explo*sion*
-ation	the act of	form*ation*
-ity	state or condition	dens*ity*
-ty		plen*ty*
-ance	quality or state of being	disturb*ance*
-ence	quality or state of being	pres*ence*
-ment	result of or a means, agency, or instrument	govern*ment*
-ness	conditon, state of being	good*ness*
-hood	condition, state of being	neighbor*hood*
-ship	condition, state of being or ability as in penmanship, friendship; or rank as in lordship	partner*ship*
-dom	rank of, position of, state of being one who has to do with; one of a size, capacity, value, date; resident of; agent	free*dom*
-or	state, quality, agent, doer	elect*or*
-ant	person or thing acting as agent	attend*ant*
-less	lacking or without	worth*less*
-most	the most	fore*most*
-able	able to, able to be	formid*able*
-like	similar	life*like*
-ward	in the direction of	for*ward*
-itis	inflammation	appendi*citis*
-ize	to subject to, to render; to impregnate, treat, or combine with (chem); practice or carry on	minim*ize*
-fy	to make, to form into	rati*fy*
-ate	combine, impregate, treat with (chem.)	agit*ate*

	Meanings	*Example*

B. Adjective Suffixes

-able (-ible)	implication of capacity, fitness, worthiness to be acted upon; tending to, given to, favoring, causing, able to, liable to	service*able*
-ive	having the nature or quality of, given or tending to	dece*ive*
-al or -ial	belonging to, pertaining to, indicating the presence of the aldehyde group (-al, chem.)	remed*ial*
-ful	full of, abounding in, characterized by; able to or tending to	master*ful*
-ish	of the nature of, belonging to	mann*ish*
-less	without, destitute of, not having, free from; beyond the range of; unable or without power	self*less*
-ary	pertaining to, connected with; a person or thing belonging to or connected with; a place for	residu*ary*
-ous (-ious)	full of, abounding in, having, possessing the qualities of, like; denotes valence lower than that denoted by -ic (chem.); used to form adjectives corresponding to nouns of classification (biol.)	grac*ious*

III. Common Roots: Latin and Greek

A. Latin

Root	*Meaning*	*Derivatives*
-aud-, -audit-	hear	auditorium
-avi-	bird	aviation
-caput-	head	capital
-ced-, -cess-	move, yield	recede
-clar-	clear	clarify
-clin-	lean	incline
-clud-, -claud-, -clus	shut	seclude
-cord-	heart	cordial
-corp-	body	corporal
-cred-	to believe	credible
-curr-, -curs-	run	current
-dic-, -dict-	say	predict
-domin-	master	dominate
-duc-, -duct-	lead	conduct
-fac-, -fic-, -fact-, -fect-	to make, do	factory

Root	Meaning	Derivatives
-fer-	bear, carry	transfer
-fin-	end	finish
-fort-	strong	fortitude
-jun-, -junct-	join	junction
-laud-, -laudat-	praise	applause
-let-, -lect-	gather, choose, read	collect
-legis-, -lex-	law	legislature
-lux-, -luc-	light	elucidate
-magn-	great	magnificent
-mal-	bad	malevolent
-man-	hand	manual
-mit-, -miss-	send	missile
-mov-, -mot-	set in motion	motor
-nov-, -novus-	new	renovation
-pac-	peace	pacific
-pel-, -puls-	urge, drive	propel
-pend-, -pens-	hang, weigh	pensive
-plic-, -plex-	bend, fold	plexiglas
-pon-, -pos-	place, put	postpone
-sci-	know	science
-scrib-, -script-	write	describe
-solv-, -solut-	loosen	solution
-sepec-, -spect-	look	spectator
-sta-	stand firm	stable
-stru-, -struct-	build	construct
-tend-, -tens-	stretch	tendency
-tort-	to twist	distort
-ven-, -vent-	come	convention
-ver-	true	veritable
-vert-, -vers-	turn	reverse
-viv-, -vit-	live, life	vitality
-vid-, -vis-	see	evident
-voc-	call	vocation

B. Greek Roots

Root	Meaning	Derivatives
-anthrop-	man	anthropology
-arch-	first, chief	monarch
-aster-	star	astronomy
-bibl-	book	bibliography
-bio-	life	biology
-chrom-	color	chromatic
-chron-	time	chronological
-crypt-	secret	cryptic

Root	Meaning	Derivatives
-dem-	people	democracy
-derm-	skin	epidermis
-dox-	opinion	paradox
-dynam-	power	dynamic
-gam-	marriage	polygamy
-gen-	birth	eugenics
-geo-	earth	geography
-gyn-	woman	gynecology
-graph-, -gram-	write, written	photograph
-hetero-	different	heterogeneous
-homo-	same	homogeneous
-hydr-	water	hydrometer
-lith-	stone	monolith
-log-, -logy-	speech, word, study	astrology
-metr-	measure	thermometer
-micro-	small	microscope
-path-	feeling, suffering	sympathy
-phil-	love	philosopher
-phon-	sound	dictaphone
-photo-	light	photogenic
-physio-	nature	physics
-pod-	foot	tripod
-polis-	city	metropolis
-psych-	mind	psychology
-scop-	see	microscope
-tele-	far	telescope
-the-	god	atheist
-tom-	cut	anatomy
-zo-	animal	zoology

Appendix E
Proverbs for Instructional Use

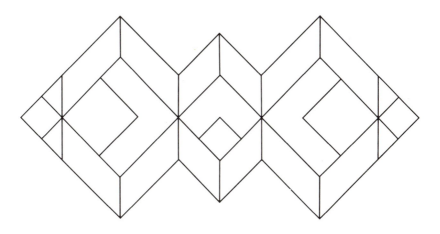

CODING KEY

Language Difficulty Level	Age/Grade Difficulty
1 primary	A 5 to 7 years old
2 intermediate	B 8 to 12 years old
3 secondary	C 13 to 16 years old
4 archaic or otherwise unusual language form	D 17 to 21 years old
	E adult life

1 D HE WHO MAKES NO MISTAKES MAKES NOTHING. The person who is afraid of making mistakes never does anything of value.

2 C Compare: A BURNED CHILD DREADS THE FIRE.

2 C A MISS IS AS GOOD AS A MILE. Failure by however little is still failure.

3 C Contrast: OMELETS ARE NOT MADE WITHOUT BREAKING EGGS.

4 E MONEY BEGETS MONEY. Money that's put to use earns more money.

2 B Contrast: A PENNY SAVED IS A PENNY EARNED.

2 D THE LOVE OF MONEY IS THE ROOT OF ALL EVIL. People's drive to acquire money and things causes them to do evil things.

2 E Compare: POVERTY IS THE ROOT OF ALL EVILS.

3 C Compare: MONEY IS A GOOD SERVANT BUT A BAD MASTER.

2 D   REVENGE IS SWEET. It feels good to get back at someone who has wronged you.

2 B   Contrast: TWO WRONGS DON'T MAKE A RIGHT.

2 C   THERE IS NO ROSE WITHOUT A THORN. There is nothing good that doesn't have negative aspects as well.

2 C   Contrast: EVERY CLOUD HAS A SILVER LINING.

4 A   WHAT IS SAUCE FOR THE GOOSE IS SAUCE FOR THE GANDER. What applies to one person applies equally to another.

3 D   Contrast: CIRCUMSTANCES ALTER CASES.

1 A   OUT OF SIGHT, OUT OF MIND. When someone or something is not immediately present, our thoughts turn to other things.

2 C   Contrast: ABSENCE MAKES THE HEART GROW FONDER.

2 E   SILENCE GIVES CONSENT. Have the courage of your convictions, or live with the consequences.

2 D   Contrast: THERE IS TIME TO SPEAK AND TIME TO BE SILENT.

2 D   Contrast: SPEECH IS SILVER BUT SILENCE IS GOLDEN.

4 D   Contrast: DISCRETION IS THE BETTER PART OF VALOR.

1 A   SPARE THE ROD AND SPOIL THE CHILD. Love means being critical, at times, of the ones you love.

1 A   Contrast: BOYS WILL BE BOYS.

2 E   THREATENED FOLK LIVE LONG. People who must struggle learn how to survive.

2 E   Compare: A CREAKING GATE HANGS LONG ON ITS HINGES.

3 C   NEVER TROUBLE TROUBLE TILL TROUBLE TROUBLES YOU. Don't spend your time imagining difficulties which may never come about.

2 C   Compare: DO NOT CROSS THE BRIDGE TILL YOU COME TO IT.

2 C   Contrast: PREVENTION IS BETTER THAN CURE.

3 D   Contrast: FOREWARNED IS FOREARMED. If you have anticipated trouble, you'll be better able to deal with it when it comes.

1 C   IT IS BETTER TO WEAR OUT THAN TO RUST OUT. It is better to act than to live in fear.

1 C   Contrast: A LIVING DOG IS BETTER THAN A DEAD LION.

1 C   Contrast: IT'S BETTER TO BE SAFE THAN SORRY.

2 C   WHERE THERE'S A WILL THERE'S A WAY. If you are determined to do something, you will find a way to do it no matter how difficult this might be.

2 C   Compare: NECESSITY IS THE MOTHER OF INVENTION.

3 D   Contrast: WHAT CAN'T BE CURED MUST BE ENDURED.

Glossary

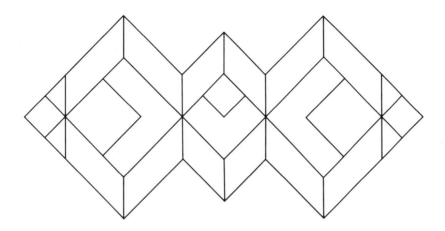

accommodation: Learning that involves reorganization or change of schema, or prior knowledge structures. *See also* assimilation; schema.

adjunct aids: All written aids to text reading and study, including external reading guides and internal embedded aids. *See also* reading guides, embedded aids, Marginal Gloss.

affective: Having to do with feelings and emotions.

assimilation: Learnings that conform to prior knowledge and therefore can be received and stored easily. *See also* accommodation.

broad-spectrum assessment: Testing of a wide array of factors that contribute to overall reading effectiveness, such as thinking and language skills and emotional maturity, rather than testing of reading effectiveness alone.

cloze teaching/testing: Written exercise formats in which some words are omitted and students are directed to "fill in the blanks" by analyzing the remaining context.

cognitive: Having to do with the intellect and thinking.

cognitive mapping: *See* graphic organizer.

collaborative teaching: Classroom and schoolwide practices that develop from common concerns and planning efforts by more than one teacher.

comportment: Behaviors, bearing, and attitudes that mark one's conduct with respect to social conventions; deportment.

concurrent methods: Teaching procedures that address more than one objective at a time, especially those that address affect and attitudes as well as cognitive concerns.

constructive reading: An interactive process that intentionally draws on prior knowledge to build elaborated meanings, as opposed to reconstructive reading, in which the author's meaning is the primarily concern. *See also* creative reading.

content area reading: A field of study dealing with the process of learning from text in the various academic disciplines.

cooperative learning: Learning that takes place in an environment in which emphasis is placed upon group achievements rather than individual ones. Once students are familiar with this new emphasis and with basic procedures for small group work, cooperative learning activities tend to result in emphasizing and strengthening the processes as well as the products of learning.

creative reading: . Constructive, inventive responding to text, typically arising from combining non-text-based knowledge with text-based information, resulting in insights or problem solving beyond that found in the text.

decoding: The act of deciphering words, usually through analysis of phonetic elements, configuration clues, and/or recognition from repeated practice and exposure.

defensive/responsive teaching: Opposing modes of teaching. Defensive is marked by rigid adherence to practices developed in reaction to real or anticipated classroom problems; its primary purpose is to avoid negative outcomes. Responsive, or strategic, teaching is marked by flexible classroom practices developed to meet the needs of particular groups of students; its primary purpose is to achieve positive outcomes despite problems and disruptions.

developmental literacy: The aspect of reading education that deals with the typical maturation process through which one learns to read materials of increasing difficulty and sophistication.

direct explanation: Explicit, teacher-led instruction in a particular skill or body of information.

disruptive thinking: *See* emotive thinking.

eidetic memory: Short-term recall of visual stimuli. *See also* episodic memory; semantic memory.

embedded aids: A generic term referring to all classes of assistance to readers built into textual material, including adjunct aids, Imbedded Aids, and Marginal Gloss.

emergent literacy: The aspect of reading education that deals with the initial processes and stages of learning to read.

emotive thinking: emotional overresponding to text, resulting in a disruption of accurate comprehension.

empowerment: Activities and procedures that raise student preparedness and capacity to read, write, and learn at higher levels than they characteristically are able to achieve.

encoding: Restating something in other ways or terms; paraphrasing what one has read or heard into a verbal statement or written account.

engagement: Attainment of student attention and positively motivated participation in a lesson or activity.

episodic memory: Recall of biographical or real-life events. *See also* eidetic memory; semantic memory.

fading: The gradual release of teacher support until the student can do it for him/herself.

frustration level: The difficulty level (usually stated in grade-level units) at which one is unable to learn from textual material, even with instructional assistance.

functional literacy: The aspect of reading education that deals with issues and concerns related to processes and problems of learning to read well enough to negotiate life's everyday activities and demands.

generative learning: Processes that result in learning beyond the immediate requirement, interest in learning, and learning how to learn.

graphic organizer: Any pictorial display of verbal material; typical forms include Structured Overviews, Story Mapping, Semantic Mapping, Semantic Organizers, and Cognitive Mapping. *See also* Semantic Mapping.

hearing capacity: *See* listening level.

heuristic approaches/heuristics: Guidelines for teaching that tend to cause teachers and students to perform and discover elements of effective teaching and learning; self-educating, or learn-by-doing, methods.

higher-order literacy: The aspect of reading education that deals with processes and problems of learning to read beyond the lines to critical, applied, and creative levels and to speak and write accordingly.

hubs: Places and activities that draw together diverse student populations and interdisciplinary functions; a programming catalyst.

Imbedded Aids: Specialized adjunct aids to higher-level comprehension in text reading and study that are built into the margins or body of textbook pages. *See also* adjunct aids, Marginal Gloss, and embedded aids.

independent level: The difficulty level (usually stated in grade-level units) at which one is able to learn from textual material with no instructional assistance.

instructional level: The difficulty level (usually stated in grade-level units) at which one is able to learn from textual material with instructional assistance.

languaging: A dialog between a teacher and student(s), or an internal dialectical examination, in which a line of reasoning is pursued and each party or position permits the contributions of the other(s) to influence their perspective and developing understanding of a difficult idea, concept, or position.

Languaging in the Content Areas (LICA): Application of the principles of languaging and dialectical thinking to instruction in the various disciplines; places high value on concept formation, discovery teaching, and creative production.

listening level: The difficulty level (usually stated in grade-level units) at which one is able to learn from textual material read to one; also known as *hearing capacity.*

Marginal Gloss: Adjunct aids printed or written in the margins of text, primarily to aid basic comprehension and vocabulary meaning. *See also* adjunct aids, Imbedded Aids.

mastery learning: An instructional approach based on the assumption that learning occurs in sequential steps, that a curriculum can be broken down into testable objectives; and that frequent testing is necessary because students who do not learn initially must be retaught before proceeding to more difficult objectives. Opposes the idea that students should stretch to achieve higher-order skills as a means of facilitating learning of basic skills.

mathemagenics: A theory of instruction and text technology that emphasizes controlled and appropriate responding to text (primarily at a literal and inferential but not a critical-creative level).

metacognition: Ability to think about, monitor, and, where necessary self-correct one's own reading-thinking processes; the basis of strategic reading. *See also* strategic reading.

modeling: A visible and/or audible demonstration of a particular behavior by a competent user of that behavior; often an externalized version of a behavior that otherwise would be internal and unobservable.

paradigm: A working plan, or model, containing all known essential elements of a particular process.

prior knowledge: All background information that in some way is related to a particular set of "new" information.

proactive inhibition: The negative effect on new learning due to the influence of previously taught information that is similar and therefore easily confused due to look (e.g., the letters *b, d, p*) or concept (the terms *homogeneous* and *heterogeneous*). *See also* retroactive inhibition.

proprioceptive learning: Sensory-motor, or visceral, learning that is registered in the nervous system and therefore can be easily triggered.

readability: An index, usually in grade equivalency units, of the difficulty level of printed material.

reading expectancy level: The level (usually stated in grade-level units) at which a student should be proficient in reading, based on a combination of measured intellectual level and age or grade in school and/or listening level.

reading guides: Written questions and/or activities, usually teacher prepared, based on a selection from a textbook to be completed before, during, or after reading. Various forms include Three-Level Guides, Anticipation-Reaction Guides, Process Guides, and Reasoning Guides.

reading readiness: Calling up of an appropriate mindset and/or giving of relevant facts, concepts, and word meanings necessary to undertake successful (empowered) reading of a particular piece of material.

reciprocity: A give-and-take between parties permitting them to influence one another; a critical element in inducing students to observe and emulate teacher modeling.

recitation: A classroom practice in which students orally restate previously presented information in response to factual questions or other stimuli.

retroactive inhibition: The confusion and possible loss of previously learned responses due to premature introduction of similar ones. For example, a student may know the word *gore,* then be taught *gorge* and *gourd,* resulting in confusion of all three and therefore in a net loss of learning.

schema: A mental organization or structure of information, facts, ideas, experiences, and sensory-motor learnings that influences what and how one understands; known in classical psychology as *apperceptive mass.*

scope and sequence: An organization of learning objectives that indicates what is to be learned and when it is to be addressed; an instructional management system.

Semantic Mapping: A graphic organization and representation of relationships among concepts and terms; used primarily in vocabulary study. *See also* graphic organizer.

semantic memory: recall of conceptual information which has been coded in language. *See also* eidetic memory; episodic memory.

Story Mapping: *See* graphic organizer.

strategic reading: The flexible use of various procedures to self-regulate, direct, and otherwise enhance silent reading, study, and thinking; e.g., prediction; rereading to correct faulty predictions; translating and relating to prior knowledge.

strategic teaching: The flexible use of instructional approaches, methods, and procedures to enable students to acquire and independently use effective and flexible strategies for

reading and learning; usually marked by a preparatory phase, modeling, reciprocity, feedback, practice, and fading.

Structured Overviews: *See* graphic organizer.

synergism: An effect in which the sum is greater than would be expected by simple addition of the parts involved.

teachable moment: The moment of greatest felt need to learn; propitious moment; moment of greatest receptivity.

text technology: The field of study related to effective means of organizing, writing, and displaying text to maximize reading and learning; primarily recent innovations in adjunct aids, electronic text, and text rewriting systems.

trace elements: Subtle, though potentially highly empowering elements in reading progress, e.g., ability to think metaphorically and elaboratively and to criticize and be criticized.

whole language: An instructional approach that emphasizes the integration and full use and enrichment of reading, writing, speaking, and listening in ways that are interesting and, where possible, real.

Writing Process: An instructional framework for writing instruction that parallels the process of effective writers; includes getting it out, getting it down, getting it straight, and going public.

References

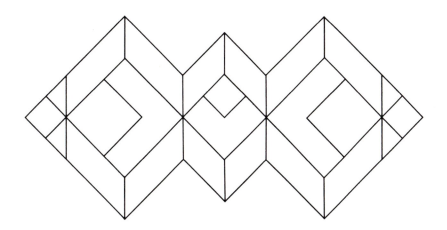

Adams, E. K. (1982). What research says to the disciplinarian. In G. H. McNinch (Ed.), *Readings in the disciplines. Second yearbook of the American Reading Forum* (pp. 109–111). Athens, GA: American Reading Forum.

Adler, M. J. (1987). "Critical thinking" programs: Why they won't work. *The Education Digest, 52,* 9–11.

Aiken, E. G., Thomas, G. S., & Shennum, W. A. (1975). Memory for a lecture: Effects of notes, lecture rate, and information density. *Journal of Educational Psychology, 67,* 439–444.

Alder, J. (1974). *Individualized language arts.* Weehawken, NJ: Weehawken School District.

Allen, R. Van. (1976). *Language experiences in communication.* Boston: Houghton Mifflin.

Alley, G., & Deshler, D. (1980). *Teaching the learning disabled adolescent: Strategies and methods.* Denver, CO: Love.

Alvermann, D. E., & Boothby, P. R. (1983). A preliminary investigation of the differences in children's retention of "inconsiderate" text. *Reading Psychology, 4,* 237–246.

Alvermann, D. E., Dillon, D. R., & O'Brien, D. G. (1987). *Using discussion to promote reading comprehension.* Newark, DE: International Reading Association.

Alvermann, D. E., & Hynd, C. R. (1987). *Overcoming misconceptions in science: An on-line study of prior knowledge activation.* Paper presented at the annual meeting of the National Reading Conference, St. Petersburg, FL.

Anders, P. L., Bos, C. S., & Filip, D. (1984). The effect of semantic feature analysis on the reading comprehension of learning-disabled students. In J. A. Niles & L. A. Harris (Eds.), *Changing perspectives on research in reading/language processing and instruction. Thirty-third yearbook of the National Reading Conference* (pp. 162–166). Rochester, NY: National Reading Conference.

Anderson, C. W., & Smith, E. L. (1984). Children's preconceptions and content-area text-books. In G. G. Duffy, L. R. Roehler, & J. (M.) Mason (Eds.), *Comprehension instruction: Perspectives and suggestions* (pp. 187–201). New York: Longman.

Anderson, R. C. (1970). Control of student mediating processes during verbal learning and instruction. *Review of Educational Research, 40,* 349–369.

Anderson, T. H., & Armbruster, B. B. (l982). Reader and text: Studying strategies. In W. Otto & S. White (Eds.), *Reading expository material* (pp. 219–235). New York: Academic Press.

Andresen, O. (l970). Old Horse. In E. E. Sargent, H. Huus, & O. Andresen, *How to read a book* (pp. 33–35). Newark, DE: International Reading Association. (Short story reprinted from *Luther Life,* November 1959, 71. Philadelphia, PA: Luther League of America.)

Ankney, P., & McClurg, P. (1981). Testing Manzo's Guided Reading Procedure. *The Reading Teacher, 34,* 681–685.

Applebee, A. N. (1981). *Writing in the secondary school.* Urbana, IL: National Council of Teachers of English.

Applebee, A. N., & Langer, J. A. (1983). Instructional scaffolding: Reading and writing as natural language activities. *Language Arts, 60,* 168–175.

Armstrong, D. P., Patberg J. (P.), & Dewitz, P. (1988). Reading guides: Helping students understand. *Journal of Reading, 31,* 532–541.

Artley, A. S. (1944). A study of certain relationships existing between general reading comprehension and reading comprehension in a specific subject-matter area. *Journal of Educational Research, 37,* 464–473.

Aschner, M. J., Gallagher, J. J., Perry, J. M., Afsar, S. S., Jenné, W., & Farr, H. (1962). *A system for classifying thought processes in the context of classroom verbal interaction.* Champaign: University of Illinois, Institute for Research on Exceptional Children.

Asher, J. J. (1965). The strategy of the total physical response: An application to learning Russian. *International Review of Applied Linguistics in Language Teaching, 3,* 291–300.

Asher, J. J. (1981). Comprehension training: The evidence from the laboratory and classroom studies. In H. Winitz (Ed.), *The comprehension approach to foreign language instruction* (pp. 187–220). Rowley, MA: Newbury House.

Atkinson, J., & Raynor, J. O. (1978). *Personality, motivation, and achievement.* New York: John Wiley and Sons.

Au, K. H. (1979). Using the experience-text-relationship method with minority children. *The Reading Teacher, 32,* 678–679.

Ausubel, D. P. (1960). The use of advance organizers in the learning and retention of meaningful verbal material. *Journal of Educational Psychology, 51,* 267–272.

Bacon, E. (1963). *Notes on the piano.* Syracuse, NY: Syracuse University Press.

Baker, L., & Brown, A. L. (1984). Metacognitive skills and reading. In P. D. Pearson (Ed.), *Handbook of reading research* (pp. 333–394). New York: Longman.

Baker, R. L., & Schutz, R. E. (Eds.). (1972). *Instructional product research.* New York: Van Nostrand.

Baldwin, R. S., & Kaufman, R. K. (1979). A concurrent validity study of the Raygor readability estimate. *Journal of Reading, 23,* 148–153.

Bandura, A., & Walters, R. (1963). *Social learning and personality development.* New York: Holt, Rinehart and Winston.

Barrett, T. C. (1967). *The evaluation of children's reading achievement.* Newark, DE: International Reading Association.

Barron, R. F. (1969). The use of vocabulary as an advance organizer. In H. L. Herber & P. L. Sanders (Eds.), *Research in reading in the content areas: First year report* (pp. 29–39). Syracuse, NY: Syracuse University, Reading and Language Arts Center.

Barsky, A. J. (1988). *Worried sick: Our troubled quest for wellness.* Boston: Little, Brown.

Barton, W. A. (1930). *Outlining as a study procedure.* New York: Columbia University, Teacher's College.

Bean, T. W., & Pardi, R. (1979). A field test of a guided reading strategy. *Journal of Reading, 23,* 144−147.

Bean, T. (W.), Searles, D., Singer, H., & Cowen, S. (1987). *Acquiring concepts from biology text: A study of independent generation of procedural knowledge versus the use of text-based procedural knowledge.* Paper presented at the annual meeting of the National Reading Conference, St. Petersburg, FL.

Behle, P. (Ed.). (l982). *The double helix: Teaching the writing process.* Florissant, MO: Ferguson−Florissant Writers Project.

Bellezza, F. (1984). The spatial-arrangement mnemonic. *Journal of Educational Psychology, 75,* 830−837.

Berger, A. (1972−1973). Increasing reading rate with paperbacks. *Reading Improvement, 9,* 78−84.

Berget, E. (1973). Two methods of guiding the learning of a short story. In H. L. Herber & R. F. Barron (Eds.), *Research in reading in the content areas: Second year report* (pp. 53−57). Syracuse, NY: Syracuse University, Reading and Language Arts Center.

Berget, E. (1977). The use of organizational pattern guides, structured overviews, and visual summaries in guiding social studies reading. In H. L. Herber & R. T. Vacca (Eds.), *Research in reading in the content areas: Third year report* (pp. 151−162). Syracuse, NY: Syracuse University, Reading and Language Arts Center.

Berliner, D. C., & Rosenshine, B. V. (1976). *The acquisition of knowledge in the classroom.* San Francisco: Far West Laboratory for Educational Research and Development.

Betts, E. (1946). *Foundations of reading instruction.* New York: American Book.

Bjork, L. (1984). [Review of *Teaching reading study skills in content areas* by D. Rubin]. *Journal of Reading, 27,* 472−473.

Blanc, R. A. (1977). Cloze-plus as an alternative to ''guides'' for understanding and appreciating poetry. *Journal of Reading, 21,* 215−218.

Bleich, D. (1975). *Readings and feelings: An introduction to subjective criticism.* Urbana, IL: National Council of Teachers of English.

Bloom, B. S. (Ed.). (1956). *Taxonomy of educational objectives: The classification of educational goals. Handbook 1. Cognitive domain (Handbook 2. Affective domain* edited by D. R. Krathwohl, B. S. Bloom, & B. B. Masia). New York: Longman, Green.

Bloom, B. S. (1971). Mastery learning. In J. H. Block (Ed.), *Mastery learning: Theory and practice* (pp. 47−63). New York: Holt, Rinehart and Winston.

Bloom, B. S. (1976). *Human characteristics and school learning.* New York: McGraw-Hill.

Bloom, B. S., Hastings, J. T., & Madaus, G. F. (1971). *Handbook on formative and summative evaluation of student learning.* New York: McGraw-Hill.

Boothby, P. R., & Alvermann, D. E. (1984). A classroom training study: The effects of graphic organizer instruction on fourth graders' comprehension. *Reading World, 23,* 325−339.

Bormuth, J. (R.) (1963). Cloze as a measure of readabiity. In J. A. Figurel (Ed.), *Reading as an intellectual activity. International Reading Association Conference Proceedings, 8* (pp. 131−134). Newark, DE: International Reading Association.

Bormuth, J. R. (1965). Validities of grammatical and semantic classifications of cloze test scores. In J. A. Figurel (Ed.), *Reading and inquiry. International Reading Association Conference Proceedings, 10* (pp. 283−286). Newark, DE: International Reading Association.

Bormuth, J. R. (1966). Readability: A new approach. *Reading Research Quarterly, 1(3),* 79−132.

Bormuth, J. R. (1967). Comparable cloze and multiple choice comprehension test scores. *Journal of Reading, l0,* 291−299.

Bormuth, J. R. (1968). Cloze test readability: Criterion reference scores. *Journal of Educational Measurement, 5,* 189–196.

Bormuth, J. R. (1969). Factor validity of cloze tests as measures of reading comprehension. *Reading Research Quarterly, 4,* 358–365.

Bourne, L. E., Ekstrand, B. R., & Dominowski, R. L. (1971). *The psychology of thinking.* Englewood Cliffs, NJ: Prentice-Hall.

Bragstad, B. (l985, March). *Mapping: Using both sides of the brain.* Lecture handout, International Reading Association State Council Meeting, Orlando, FL.

Bransford, J. D., & Stein, B. S. (l984). *The ideal problem solver: A guide for improving thinking, learning, and creativity.* New York: W. H. Freeman.

Bromley, K. D. (1985). Précis writing and outlining enhance content learning. *The Reading Teacher, 38,* 406–411.

Brown, A. L. (1980). Metacognition development and reading. In R. J. Spiro, B. C. Bruce, & W. F. Brewer (Eds.), *Theoretical issues in reading comprehension* (pp. 453–481). Hillsdale, NJ: Erlbaum Associates.

Brown, A. L., & Campione, J. C. (1977). *Memory strategies in learning: Training children to study strategically* (Technical Report No. 22, p. 36). Champaign: University of Illinois, Center for the Study of Reading.

Brown, A. L., Campione, J. C., & Day, J. D. (1981). Learning to learn: On training students to learn from texts. *Educational Researcher, 10*(2), 14–21.

Bruner, J. C. (1971). *Toward a theory of instruction.* New York: Norton.

Buckley, H. (1971). Mapping: A technique for translating reading into thinking. *Journal of Reading,* 228.

Bush, W., & Waugh, K. W. (l982). *Diagnosing learning problems* (3rd ed.). Columbus, OH: Merrill.

Cambourne, B. (1977, August). *Some psycholinguistic dimensions of the silent reading process: A pilot study.* Paper presented at the annual meeting of the Australian Reading Conference, Melbourne.

Campione, J. C. (1981). *Learning, academic achievement and instruction.* Paper presented at the Second Annual Conference for Reading Research and the Study of Reading, New Orleans, LA.

Carmen, R., & Adams, R. (1972). *Study skills: A Student's Guide to Survival.* New York: John Wiley and Sons.

Carney, J. J. (1973). An investigation of the effects of separate vs. content-integrated reading training on content mastery and social studies reading ability of junior high school social studies students (Doctoral dissertation, Syracuse University, Syracuse, NY). *Dissertation Abstracts International, 34,* 6249A.

Carr, E. (M.), Dewitz, P., & Patberg, J. (P.) (1989). Using cloze for inference training with expository text. *The Reading Teacher, 42,* 380–385.

Carr, E. (M.), & Ogle, D. (1987). K-W-L Plus: A strategy for comprehension and summarization. *Journal of Reading, 30,* 626–631.

Carrell, P. L. (1984). Schema theory and ESL reading: Classroom implications and applications. *The Modern Language Journal, 68,* 332–343.

Carver, R. P. (l975–1976). Measuring prose difficulty using the Rauding Scale. *Reading Research Quarterly, 11,* 660–685.

Carver, R. P. (1985). Is the Degrees of Reading Power test valid or invalid? *Journal of Reading, 29,* 34–41.

Casale, U. P. (1982). Small group approach to the further validation and refinement of a battery for assessing "progress toward reading maturity" (Doctoral dissertation, University of Missouri–Kansas City). *Dissertation Abstracts International, 43,* 770A.

Casale, U. P. (1985). Motor imaging: A reading-vocabulary strategy. *Journal of Reading, 28,* 619–621.

Casale, U. (P.), & Kelly, B. W. (1980). Problem-solving approach to study skills (PASS) for students in professional schools. *Journal of Reading, 24,* 232–238.

Casale, U. P., & Manzo, A. V. (1983). Differential effects of cognitive, affective, and proprioceptive approaches on vocabulary acquisition. In G. H. McNinch (Ed.), *Reading research to reading practice. Third yearbook of the American Reading Forum* (pp. 71–73). Athens, GA: American Reading Forum.

Chall, J. S. (1967). *Learning to read: The great debate. An inquiry into the science, art, and ideology of old and new methods of teaching children to read, 1910–1965.* New York: McGraw-Hill.

Chall, J. S. (1983). *Learning to read: the Great Debate* (updated edition). New York: McGraw-Hill.

Chall, J. S. (1983). Literacy: Trends and explanations. *Educational Researcher, 12*(9), 3–8.

Chall, J. S. (1986). The teacher as scholar. *The Reading Teacher, 39,* 792–797.

Chase, F. (1961). In the next decade. *Supplementary Educational Monographs, 91,* 7–18. Chicago: University of Chicago Press.

Clary, L. M. (1977). How well do you teach critical reading? *The Reading Teacher, 31,* 142–146.

Clewell, S. F., & Haidemos, J. (l983). Organizational strategies to increase comprehension. *Reading World, 22,* 314–321.

Collins, A., & Smith, E. E. (1980). *Teaching the process of reading comprehension* (Technical Report No. 182). Champaign: University of Illinois, Center for the Study of Reading.

Collins, C. (1987). Content mastery strategies aid class discussion. *The Reading Teacher, 40,* 816–818.

Conley, M. W. (1986). Teachers' conceptions, decisions, and changes during initial classroom lessons containing content reading strategies. In J. A. Niles & R. V. Lalik (Eds.), *Solving problems in literacy: Learners, teachers, and researchers. Thirty-fifth yearbook of the National Reading Conference* (pp. 120–126). Rochester, NY: National Reading Conference.

Crafton, L. K. (1983). Learning from reading: What happens when students generate their own background information? *Journal of Reading, 26,* 586–592.

Crane, S. (1962). The open boat. In N. Foerster & R. Falk (Eds.), *American poetry and prose* (pp. 866–867). Boston: Houghton Mifflin. (Original work published 1919)

Criscoe, B. L., & Gee, T. C. (1984). *Content reading: A diagnostic/prescriptive approach.* Englewood Cliffs, NJ: Prentice-Hall.

Critical thinking, critical viewing. (1988). *English Journal, 77*(1), 21.

Crowder, R. G. (1982). *The psychology of reading.* New York: Oxford University Press.

Culver, V. I. (1975). The guided reading procedure: An experimental analysis of its effectiveness as a technique for improving reading comprehension skills (Doctoral dissertation, University of Missouri–Kansas City). *Dissertation Abstracts International, 36,* 7062A.

Culver, V. I., Godfrey, H. C., & Manzo, A. V. (1972). A partial reanalysis of the validity of the cloze procedure as an appropriate measure of reading comprehension [Research report summary]. *Journal of Reading, 16,* 256–257.

Cunningham, J. W., Cunningham, P. M., & Arthur, S. V. (1981). *Middle and secondary school reading.* New York: Longman.

Cunningham, P. M., & Cunningham, J. W. (1976). SSSW, better content-writing. *The Clearing House, 49,* 237–238.

Cunningham, P. M., Moore, S. A., Cunningham, J. W., & Moore, D. W. (1983). *Reading in elementary classrooms: Strategies and observations.* New York: Longman.

Cunningham, D., & Shablak, S. L. (1975). Selective Reading Guide-O-Rama: The content teacher's best friend. *Journal of Reading, 18,* 380−382.

Dahmus, M. E. (1970). How to teach verbal problems. *School Science and Mathematics, 70,* 121−138.

Dale, E. (1984). *The educator's quotebook.* Bloomington, IN: Phi Delta Kappa.

Dale, E., & Chall, J. S. (1948). A formula for predicting readability. *Educational Research Bulletin, 27,* 11−20, 37−54.

Dana, C. (1982). Gloss in action: Gloss used in remedial reading classes to improve comprehension of expository text. In G. H. McNinch (Ed.), *Reading in the disciplines. Second yearbook of the American Reading Forum* (pp. 25−27). Athens, GA: American Reading Forum.

Davey, B. (1983). Think aloud—Modeling the cognitive processes of reading comprehension. *Journal of Reading, 27,* 44−47.

Davidson, J. L. (1970). The relationship between teachers' questions and pupils' responses during a directed reading activity and a directed reading-thinking activity (Doctoral dissertation, The University of Michigan, Ann Arbor). *Dissertation Abstracts International, 31,* 6273A.

Davis, F. B. (1944). Fundamental factors of comprehension in reading. *Psychometrika, 9,* 185−197.

DeBono, E. (1985). *Six thinking hats.* Boston: Little, Brown.

Derby, T. (1987). Reading instruction and course related materials for vocational high school students. *Journal of Reading, 30,* 308−316.

Deutsch, M. (1962). Cooperation and trust: Some theoretical notes. In M. R. Jones (Ed.), *Nebraska Symposium on Motivation, 1962. Current Theory and Research in Motivation, 10* (pp. 275−319). Lincoln: University of Nebraska Press.

Dewitz, P., Carr, E. M., & Patberg, J. P. (1987). Effects of inference training on comprehension and comprehension monitoring. *Reading Research Quarterly, 22,* 99−121.

Diehl, W. A., & Mikulecky, L. (1980). The nature of reading at work. *Journal of Reading, 24,* 221−227.

Diggs, V. M. (1973). The relative effectiveness of the SQ3R method, a mechanized approach, and a combination method for training remedial reading to college freshmen (Doctoral dissertation, West Virginia University, Morgantown, 1972). *Dissertation Abstracts International, 33,* 5964A. (University Microfilms No. 74−4,786)

DiGiacomo, G. (1982, October). The teacher as dictator. *NEA Today,* p. 12.

Dillon, J. T. (1984). Research on questioning and discussion. *Educational Leadership, 42*(3), 50−56.

Doctorow, M., Wittrock, M. C., & Marks, C. (1978). Generative processes in reading comprehension. *Journal of Educational Psychology, 70,* 109−118.

Donald, M., Sr. (1967). The SQ3R method in grade seven. *Journal of Reading, 11,* 33−35, 43.

Dreher, M. J., Singer, H., & Letteer, C. A. (1987). Explicitness in sixth-grade social studies textbooks. In J. E. Readence & R. S. Baldwin (Eds.), *Research in literacy: Merging perspectives. Thirty-sixth yearbook of the National Reading Conference* (pp. 177−185). Rochester, NY: National Reading Conference.

Duffelmeyer, F. A., Baum, D. D., & Merkley, D. J. (1987). Maximizing reader-text confrontation with an Extended Anticipation Guide. *Journal of Reading, 31,* 146−150.

Duffy, G. G., & Anderson, L. M. (1982). *Final report: Conceptions of reading progress* (Research Series No. 111). East Lansing: Michigan State University, Institute for Research on Teaching.

Duffy, G. G., & Roehler, L. R. (1982). Direct instruction of comprehension: What does it really mean? *Reading Horizons, 23,* 35−40.

Duffy, G. G., Roehler, L. R., & Mason, J. (M.) (Eds). (1984). *Comprehension instruction: Perspectives and suggestions.* New York: Longman.

Duffy, G. G., Roehler, L. R., Meloth, M. S., Vavrus, L. G., Book, C., Putnam, J., & Wesselman, R. (1986). The relationship between explicit verbal explanations during reading skill instruction and student awareness and achievement: A study of reading teacher effects. *Reading Research Quarterly, 21,* 237–252.

Duke, C. R. (1987). Integrating reading, writing, and thinking skills into the music class. *Journal of Reading, 31,* 152– 157.

Durkin, D. (l978–1979). What classroom observations reveal about comprehension instruction. *Reading Research Quarterly, 14,* 481–533.

Dykstra, R. (1968). Summary of the second-grade phase of the Cooperative Research Program in primary reading instruction. *Reading Research Quarterly, 4,* 49–70.

Eanet, M. G. (1978). An investigation of the REAP reading/study procedure: Its rationale and efficacy. In P. D. Pearson & J. Hansen (Eds.), *Reading: Disciplined inquiry in process and practice. Twenty-seventh yearbook of the National Reading Conference* (pp. 229–232). Clemson, SC: National Reading Conference.

Eanet, M. G. (1983). Reading/writing: Finding and using the connection. *The Missouri Reader, 8,* 8–9.

Eanet, M. G., & Manzo, A. V. (1976). REAP—A strategy for improving reading/writing/study skills. *Journal of Reading, 19,* 647–652.

Edwards, P. A., & Simpson, L. (1986). Bibliotherapy: A strategy for communication between parents and their children. *Journal of Reading, 30,* 110–118.

Ellis, A., & Harper, R. A. (1968). *A guide to rational living in an irrational world.* Englewood Cliffs, NJ: Prentice-Hall.

Ennis, R. H. (1962). The concept of critical thinking. *Harvard Educational Review, 32,* 81– 111.

Erickson, L. G., Stahl, S. A., & Rinehart, S. D. (1985). Metacognitive abilities of above and below average readers: Effects of conceptual tempo, passage level, and error type on error detection. *Journal of Reading Behavior, 17,* 235–252.

Ericson, B., Hubler, M., Bean, T. W., Smith, C. C., & McKenzie, J. V. (1987). Increasing critical reading in junior high classrooms. *Journal of Reading, 30,* 430–439.

Ervin, S., Jr. (1984, August 8). Don't forgive Nixon unless he repents. *USA Today,* p. 12A.

Estes, T. H. (1969). Use of prepared guide material and small group discussion in reading ninth grade social studies assignments: Pilot study report. In H. L. Herber & P. L. Sanders (Eds.), *Research in reading in the content areas: First year report* (pp. 64–70). Syracuse, NY: Syracuse University, Reading and Language Arts Center.

Estes, T. H. (1970). Use of guide material and small group discussion in reading ninth grade social studies assignments (Doctoral dissertation, Syracuse University, Syracuse, NY). *Dissertation Abstracts International, 31,* 5930A.

Estes, T. H. (1973). Guiding reading in social studies. In H. L. Herber & R. F. Barron (Eds.), *Research in reading in the content areas: Second year report* (pp. 58–63). Syracuse, NY: Syracuse University, Reading and Language Arts Center.

Estes, T. H., & Vaughn, J. L., Jr. (1978). *Reading and learning in the content classroom.* Boston: Allyn and Bacon.

Farnan, N. J. (1987). All the language arts for reading comprehension. *Journal of Reading, 31,* 274–275.

Feathers, K. M., & Smith, F. R. (1987). Meeting the reading demands of the real world: Literacy based content instruction. *Journal of Reading, 30,* 506–511.

Festinger, L. (1957). *A theory of cognitive dissonance.* Evanston, IL: Row, Peterson.

Foos, P. W., & Clark, C. (1984). Testing multiple study choices. *Human Learning, 2,* 86–94.

484   REFERENCES

Fowler, G. L. (1982). Developing comprehension skills in primary students through the use of story frames. *The Reading Teacher, 36,* 176–179.

Frager, A. M., & Thompson, L. C. (1985). Conflict: The key to critical reading instruction. *Journal of Reading, 28,* 676–683.

Frayer, D. A., Frederick, W. C., & Klausmeir, H. J. (1969). *A schema for testing the level of concept mastery* (Working Paper No. 16). Madison: University of Wisconsin, Wisconsin Research and Development Center for Cognitive Learning.

Friedel, G. (1976, September). *Instant study skills.* Workshop handout, University of Missouri–Kansas City.

Fry, E. (1968). A readability formula that saves time. *Journal of Reading, 11,* 513–516, 575–578.

Fry, E. (1977). Fry's readability graph: Clarification, validity, and extension to level 17. *Journal of Reading, 21,* 242–252.

Gee, T. C., & Rakow, S. J. (1987). Content reading specialists evaluate teaching practices. *Journal of Reading, 31,* 234–237.

Gentile, L. M. (1980). *Using sports and physical education to strengthen content area reading skills.* Newark, DE: International Reading Association.

Gentner, D. (1983). Structure-mapping: A theoretical framework for analogy. *Cognitive Science, 7,* 155–170.

Geyer, J. J. (1972). Comprehensive and partial models related to the reading process. *Reading Research Quarterly, 7,* 541–587.

Glass, G. G. (1973). *Teaching decoding as separate from reading.* Garden City, NY: Adelphi University Press.

Goodman, K. S. (1967). Reading: A psycholinguistic guessing game. *Journal of the Reading Specialist, 6,* 126–135.

Goodman, K. S. (1984). Unity in reading. In A. Purves & O. Niles (Eds.), *Becoming readers in a complex society. Eighty-third yearbook of the National Society for the Study of Education. Part 1* (pp. 79–114). Chicago: University of Chicago Press.

Goodman, K. S. (1986). *What's whole in whole language?* Portsmouth, NH: Heinemann.

Goodman, K. (S.), & Goodman, Y. (1983). Reading and writing relationships: Pragmatic functions. *Language Arts, 60,* 590–599.

Gough, P. B., & Cosky, M. J. (1977). One second of reading again. In N. J. Castellan, Jr., D. Pisoni, & G. Potts (Eds.), *Cognitive theory, 2* (pp. 271–288). Hillsdale, NJ: Erlbaum Associates.

Graves, M. F., Cooke, C. L., & LaBerge, M. J. (1983). Effects of previewing difficult short stories on low ability junior high school students' comprehension, recall, and attitudes. *Reading Research Quarterly, 18,* 262–276.

Gray, W. S. (l925). Summary of investigations related to reading. *Supplementary Educational Monographs, 28.* Chicago: University of Chicago Press.

Gray, W. S. (1948). *On their own in reading.* Chicago: Scott Foresman.

Gray, W. S., & Rogers, B. (1956). *Maturity in reading.* Chicago: University of Chicago Press.

Greenewald, M. J., & Wolf, A. E. (1980). Professional journals in secondary education: Which ones do teachers recommend most? *The Clearing House, 53,* 349–350.

Greenhoe, M. L. (1972). Parameters of creativity in music education: An exploratory study (Doctoral dissertation, The University of Tennessee, Knoxville). *Dissertation Abstracts International, 33,* 1766A.

Grobler, C. Van E. (1971). Methodology in reading instruction as a controlling variable in the constructive or destructive channeling of aggression (Doctoral dissertation, University of Delaware, Newark, 1970). *Dissertation Abstracts International, 32,* 6197A.

Gunning, R. (1979). Fog index of a passage. *Academic Therapy, 14,* 489−491.

Guralnik, D. B., & Friend, J. H. (Eds.). (1968). *Webster's new world dictionary of the American language.* New York: World.

Gurrola, S. (1975). Determination of the relative effectiveness and efficiency of selected combinations of SQ3R study method components (Doctoral dissertation, New Mexico State University, 1974). *Dissertation Abstracts International, 35,* 6938A. (University Microfilms No. 75−10,822)

Guszak, F. J. (1967). Teacher questioning and reading. *The Reading Teacher, 21,* 227−234.

Hafner, L. E. (1977). *Developmental reading in middle and secondary schools: Foundations, strategies, and skills for teaching.* New York: Macmillan.

Haggard, M. R. (1978). The effect of creative thinking-reading activities (CT-RA) on reading comprehension. In P. D. Pearson & J. Hansen (Eds.), *Reading: Disciplined inquiry in process and practice. Twenty-seventh yearbook of the National Reading Conference* (pp. 233−236). Clemson, SC: National Reading Conference.

Haggard, M. R. (1982). The vocabulary self-collection strategy: An active approach to word learning. *Journal of Reading, 27,* 203−207.

Hanf, M. B. (1971). Mapping: A technique for translating reading into thinking. *Journal of Reading, 14,* 225−230, 270.

Harker, W. J. (1972−1973). An evaluative summary of models of reading comprehension. *Journal of Reading Behavior, 5,* 26—34.

Harker, W. J. (Ed.). (1977). *Classroom strategies for secondary reading.* Newark, DE: International Reading Association.

Harris, A. J., & Sipay, E. R. (1985). *How to increase reading ability: A guide to developmental and remedial methods* (8th ed.). New York: Longman.

Harste, J. (1978). Instructional implications of Rumelhart's model. In W. (A.) Diehl (Ed.), *Secondary reading: Theory and application. The 1978 Lilly Conference on Secondary Reading* (Monographs in Teaching and Learning No. 1, pp. 21−23). Bloomington: Indiana University, School of Education.

Hash, R. J. (1974). The effects of a strategy of structured overviews, levels guides and vocabulary exercises on student achievement, reading comprehension, critical thinking and attitudes of junior high school classes in social studies (Doctoral dissertation, State University of New York at Buffalo). *Dissertation Abstracts International, 35,* 3574A.

Hayes, D. A. (1988). *Guided reading and summarizing procedure.* Manuscript, University of Georgia, Athens.

Hayes, D. A., & Tierney, R. J. (1982). Developing readers' knowledge through analogy. *Reading Research Quarterly, 17,* 256−280.

Head, M. H., & Readence, J. E. (1986). Anticipation guides: Enhancing meaning through prediction. In E. K. Dishner, T. W. Bean, J. E. Readence, & D. W. Moore (Eds.), *Reading in the content areas: Improving classroom instruction* (2nd ed., pp. 229−234). Dubuque, IA: Kendall/Hunt.

Heaton, M. M., & Lewis, H. B. (1955). *Reading ladders for human relations* (3rd ed.). Washington, DC: American Council on Education.

Heimlich, J. E., & Pittelman, S. D. (1986). *Semantic mapping: Classroom applications.* Newark, DE: International Reading Association.

Henderson, E. H. (1963). A study of individually formulated purposes for reading in relation to reading achievement, comprehension and purpose attainment (Doctoral dissertation, University of Delaware, Newark). *Dissertation Abstracts, 24,* 5529.

Henry, G. H. (1974). *Teaching reading as concept development: Emphasis on affective thinking.* Newark, DE: International Reading Association.

Herber, H. L. (1978). *Teaching reading in content areas* (2nd ed.). Englewood Cliffs, NJ: Prentice-Hall.

Hesse, H. (1949). *Magister ludi* (M. Savill, Trans.). New York: Holt. (Original work published as *Das Glasperlenspiel,* 1943)

Hillocks, G., Jr. (1987). Synthesis of research on teaching writing. *Educational Leadership, 44*(8), 71–76, 78, 80–82.

Hittleman, C. (1984, Spring/Summer). Peer response groups: The writing process in action. *Language Connections: Hofstra University Newsletter, 4.*

Hittleman, D. K. (1978). Readability, readability formulas, and cloze: Selecting instructional materials. *Journal of Reading, 22,* 117–122.

Hoffman, J. V. (1977). Intra-Act: A languaging in the content areas teaching procedure (Doctoral dissertation, University of Missouri–Kansas City). *Dissertation Abstracts International, 38,* 3248A.

Holbrook, H. T. (1984). Prereading in the content areas. *Journal of Reading, 27,* 368–370.

Holmes, J. A. (1953). *The substrata-factor theory of reading.* Berkeley: California Book.

Holmes, J. A., & Singer, H. (1961). *Substrata factor differences underlying reading ability in known-groups.* Washington, DC: United States Office of Education.

Hori, A. K. O. (1977). An investigation of the efficacy of a questioning training procedure on increasing the reading comprehension performance of junior high school learning disabled students. Unpublished master's thesis, University of Kansas, Lawrence.

Horowitz, R. (1985). Text patterns. Part I. *Journal of Reading, 28,* 448–454.

Hunter, M. (1980). Altering the "alterable variables." *The Educational Forum, 45,* 121–122.

International Reading Association, Professional Standards and Ethics Committee. (1986). *Guidelines for the professional preparation of reading teachers.* Newark, DE: International Reading Association.

Irwin, J. W., & Davis, C. A. (1980). Assessing readability: The checklist approach. *Journal of Reading, 24,* 124–130.

Jason, M., & Dubnow, B. (1973). The relationship between self-perceptions of reading abilities and reading achievement. In W. MacGinitie (Ed.), *Assessment problems in reading* (pp. 96–100). Newark, DE: International Reading Association.

Johnson, D. D., & Pearson, P. D. (1984). *Teaching reading vocabulary* (2nd ed.). New York: Holt, Rinehart and Winston.

Johnson, D. D., Pittelman, S. D., & Heimlich, J. E. (1986). Semantic mapping. *The Reading Teacher, 39,* 778–783.

Johnson, D. D., Toms-Bronowski, S., & Pittelman, S. D. (1982). *An investigation of the effectiveness of semantic mapping and semantic feature analysis with intermediate grade students* (Program Report 83–3). Madison: University of Wisconsin, Wisconsin Center for Education Research.

Johnson, D. W., Johnson, R. T., Edythe, A., Holubec, J., & Roy, P. A. (1984). *Circles of learning: Cooperation in the classroom.* Alexandria, VA: Association for Supervision and Curriculum Development.

Johnson, D. W., Maruyama, R. T., Johnson, R. T., Nelson, D., & Skon, L. (1981). Effects of cooperative, competitive and individualistic goal structures on achievement: A meta-analysis. *Psychological Bulletin, 89,* 47–62.

Johnson, P. (1981). Effects on reading comprehension of language complexity and cultural background of a text. *TESOL Quarterly, 15,* 169–181.

Johnson, R. E. (1984, May). Michael Jackson: The world's greatest entertainer. *Ebony,* pp. 163–170.

Johnson, R. T., & Johnson, D. W. (1985). Student-student interaction: Ignored but powerful. *Journal of Teacher Education, 46,* 22–26.

Jonassen, D. H. (Ed.). (1982). *The technology of text: Principles for structuring, designing, and displaying text* (Vol. 1). Englewood Cliffs, NJ: Educational Technology Publications.

Jonassen, D. H. (1985a). Generative learning vs. mathemagenic control of text processing. In D. H. Jonassen (Ed.), *The technology of text: Principles for structuring, designing, and displaying text* (Vol. 2, pp. 9−45). Englewood Cliffs, NJ: Educational Technology Publications.

Jonassen, D. H. (Ed.). (1985b). *The technology of text: Principles for structuring, designing, and displaying text* (Vol. 2). Englewood Cliffs, NJ: Educational Technology Publications.

Karlin, R. (1984). *Teaching reading in high school: Improving reading in content areas* (4th ed.). New York: Harper and Row.

Karplus, R. (1974). *The science curriculum improvement study*. Berkeley: University of California Press.

Kay, L., Young, J. L., & Mottley, R. R. (1986). Using Manzo's ReQuest model with delinquent adolescents. *Journal of Reading, 29,* 506−510.

Kelly, B. W., & Holmes, J. (1979). The Guided Lecture Procedure. *Journal of Reading, 22,* 602−604.

Kierwa, K. A. (1985). Students' note-taking behaviors and the efficacy of providing the instructor's notes for review. *Contemporary Educational Psychology, 10,* 378−386.

Kintsch, W. (1977). *Memory and cognition*. New York: John Wiley and Sons.

Kirby, D., & Liner, T. (1981). *Inside out: Developmental strategies for teaching*. Montclair, NJ: Boynton/Cook.

Kirsch, I., & Guthrie, J. T. (1977−78). The concept and measurement of functional literacy. *Reading Research Quarterly, 13,* 485−507.

Krathwohl, D. R., Bloom, B. S., & Masia, B. B. (Eds.). (1956). *Taxonomy of educational objectives: The classification of educational goals. Handbook 2. Affective domain (Handbook 1. Cognitive domain* edited by B. S. Bloom). New York: Longman, Green (or McKay).

Kunihira, S., & Asher, J. J. (1965). The strategy of the total physical response: An application to learning Japanese. *International Review of Applied Linguistics in Language Teaching, 3,* 277−289.

Langer, J. A. (1981). From theory to practice: A prereading plan. *Journal of Reading, 25,* 152−156.

Langer, J. A., & Nicolich, M. (1981). Prior knowledge and its relationship to comprehension. *Journal of Reading Behavior, 13,* 373−379.

LaPray, M., & Ross, R. (1969). The graded word list: Quick gauge of reading ability. *Journal of Reading, 12,* 305−307.

Legenza, A. (1978). Inquiry training for reading and learning improvement. *Reading Improvement, 15,* 309−316.

Lehr, F. (1984). Cooperative learning. *Journal of Reading, 27,* 458−460.

Leong, C. K. (1980). Laterality and reading proficiency in children. *Reading Research Quarterly, 15,* 185−202.

Leong, C. K., & Haines, C. F. (1978). Beginning readers' analysis of words and sentences. *Journal of Reading Behavior, 10,* 393−407.

Levin, T., & Long, R. (1981). *Effective instruction*. Alexandria, VA: Association for Supervision and Curriculum Development.

Lewkowicz, N. K. (1987). On the question of teaching decoding skills to older students. *Journal of Reading, 31,* 50−57.

Lipson, M. Y. (1982). Learning new information from text: The role of prior knowledge and reading ability. *Journal of Reading Behavior, 14,* 247−261.

Lipson, M. Y. (1983). The influence of religious affiliation on children's memory for text information. *Reading Research Quarterly, 18,* 448−457.

Locke, E. A. (1977). An empirical study of lecture note taking among college students. *Journal of Educational Research, 71*, 93–99.

Longman, D. G., & Atkinson, R. (1988). *College learning and study skills.* St. Paul, MN: West.

Lordon, J. (1981). Small group instruction: To make it work. *The Clearing House, 54*, 265–266.

Lovett, M. B. (1981). Reading skill and its development: Theoretical and empirical considerations. In G. MacKinnon & T. Waller (Eds.), *Reading research: Advances in theory and practice* (Vol. 3, pp. 1–37). New York: Academic Press.

Lscher, M. (1969). *The Lscher color test* (I. A. Scott, Ed. and Trans.). New York: Random House. (Original work published as *Psychologie der Farben*, first published as *Psychologie der Farben: Textband zum Lscher-Test*, 1949)

Maier, N. R. F. (1963). *Problem solving discussions and conferences: Leadership methods and skills.* New York: McGraw-Hill.

Manzo, A. V. (1969a). Improving reading comprehension through reciprocal questioning (Doctoral dissertation, Syracuse University, Syracuse, NY, 1968). *Dissertation Abstracts International, 30*, 5344A.

Manzo, A. V. (1969b). The ReQuest procedure. *Journal of Reading, 13*, 123–126.

Manzo, A. V. (1970a). CAT—A game for extending vocabulary and knowledge of allusions. *Journal of Reading, 13*, 367–369.

Manzo, A. V. (1970b). A theoretical model of the teaching-learning factors believed to be interacting in the development of reading comprehension. In G. B. Schick & M. M. May (Eds.), *Reading: Process and pedagogy. Nineteenth yearbook of the National Reading Conference* (Vol. 2, pp. 125–127). Milwaukee, WI: National Reading Conference.

Manzo, A. V. (1973). CONPASS English: A demonstration project. *Journal of Reading, 16*, 539–545.

Manzo, A. V. (1974a). The Ask-It-Rite procedure. *Forum for Reading, 4*(1), 22–27.

Manzo, A. V. (1974b). The group reading activity. *Forum for Reading, 3*(2), 26–33.

Manzo, A. V. (1975a). Guided Reading Procedure. *Journal of Reading, 18*, 287–291.

Manzo, A. V. (1975b). Manzo's Bestiary Inventory. Monograph of the Center for Resources Development in ABE, University of Missouri–Kansas City.

Manzo, A. V. (1977). *Recent developments in content area reading.* Keynote address, Missouri Council of Teachers of English, Springfield, MO.

Manzo, A. V. (1979). "Imbedded aids" to readers: Alternatives to traditional textual material. *The New England Reading Association Journal, 14*(1), 13–18.

Manzo, A. V. (1980a). The astrobasics; or, Why have I been permitted to come thus far? *The Missouri Reader, 5*, 17–18.

Manzo, A. V. (1980b). Three "universal" strategies in content area reading and languaging. *Journal of Reading, 24*, 146–149.

Manzo, A. V. (1981a). The Language Shaping Paradigm (LSP) for improving language, comprehension, and thought. In P. L. Anders (Ed.), *Research on reading in secondary schools: A semi-annual report* (Monograph No. 7, pp. 54–68). Tucson: University of Arizona, College of Education, Reading Department.

Manzo, A. V. (1981b). Using proverbs to teach reading and thinking; or, Com faceva mia nonna (the way my grandmother did it). *The Reading Teacher, 34*, 411–416.

Manzo, A. V. (1983). "Subjective approach to vocabulary" acquisition (Or ". . .I think my brother is arboreal!"). *Reading Psychology, 3*, 155–160.

Manzo, A. V. (1984, December). *A comparison of two methods of improving abstract verbal reasoning in remedial readers.* Paper presented at the annual meeting of the American Reading Forum, Sarasota, FL.

Manzo, A. V. (1985). Expansion modules for the ReQuest, CAT, GRP, and REAP reading/study procedures. *Journal of Reading, 28,* 498−502.

Manzo, A. V., & Casale, U. P. (1979). *Toward defining and assessing reading maturity.* Paper presented to the Secondary Reading Research Group of the National Reading Conference, San Antonio, TX.

Manzo, A. V., & Casale, U. (P.) (1980). The five C's: A problem-solving approach to study skills. *Reading Horizons, 20,* 281−284.

Manzo, A. V., & Casale, U. P. (1981). A multivariate analysis of principle and trace elements in mature reading comprehension. In G. H. McNinch (Ed.), *Comprehension: Process and product. First yearbook of the American Reading Forum* (pp. 76−81). Athens, GA: American Reading Forum.

Manzo, A. V., & Casale, U. P. (1983). A preliminary description and factor analysis of a broad spectrum battery for assessing "progress toward reading maturity." *Reading Psychology, 4,* 181−191.

Manzo, A. V., & Casale, U. P. (1985). Listen-read-discuss: A content reading heuristic. *Journal of Reading, 28,* 732−734.

Manzo, A. V., & Legenza, A. (1975). Inquiry training for kindergarten children. *Journal of Educational Leadership, 32,* 479−483.

Manzo, A. V., & Manzo, U. C. (1987a). *Asking, answering, commenting: A participation training strategy.* Paper presented at the annual meeting of the International Reading Association, Anaheim, CA.

Manzo, A. V., & Manzo, U. C. (1987b). Using proverbs to diagnose and treat comprehension dysfunctions. *Rhode Island Reading Review, 3*(2), 37−42.

Manzo, A. V., & Martin, D. C. (1974). Writing communal poetry. *Journal of Reading, 17,* 638−643.

Manzo, A. V., & Sherk, J. K. (1971−1972). Some generalizations and strategies for guiding vocabulary acquisition. *Journal of Reading Behavior, 4,* 78−89.

Manzo, A. V., & Sherk, J. K. (1978). Reading and "languaging in the content areas": A third generation approach. *The New England Reading Association Journal, 13*(1), 28−32.

Manzo, A. V., Sherk, J. K., Leibert, R. E., & Mocker, D. W. (1971). *Re: Reading and the library* (Improvement of Learning Monograph Series No. 1). Kansas City: University of Missouri–Kansas City, Reading Center.

Maring, G. H., & Furman, G. (1985). Seven "whole class" strategies to help mainstreamed young people read and listen better in content area classes. *Journal of Reading, 28,* 694−700.

Maring, G. H., & Ritson, R. (1980). Reading improvement in the gymnasium. *Journal of Reading, 24,* 27−31.

Martin, D. C., Lorton, M., Blanc, R. A., & Evans, C. (1977). *The Learning Center: A Comprehensive Model for Colleges and Universities.* Grand Rapids, MI: Central Trade Plant.

Martin, R. W. (1968). Transformational grammar, cloze, and performance in college freshmen (Doctoral dissertation, Syracuse University, Syracuse, NY). *Dissertation Abstracts International, 30,* 70A.

Mason, G. E., & Blanchard, J. S. (1979). *Computer applications in reading.* Newark, DE: International Reading Association.

Mason, G. E., Blanchard, J. S., & Daniel, D. (1987). *Computer applications in reading* (3rd ed.). Newark, DE: International Reading Association.

Mason, J. M. (1980). When do children begin to read: An exploration of four year old children's letter and word reading competencies. *Reading Research Quarterly, 15,* 203−227.

Mason, J. (M.), Stewart, J., & Dunning, D. (1986). What kindergarten children know about reading. In T. E. Raphael (Ed.), *The contexts of school-based literacy* (pp. 97–114). New York: Random House.

Maxon, G. A. (1979). An investigation of the relative effectiveness between questions and declarative statements as guides to reading comprehension for seventh grade students. In H. L. Herber & J. D. Riley (Eds.), *Research in reading in the content areas: Fourth year report* (pp. 66–78). Syracuse, NY: Syracuse University, Reading and Language Arts Center.

McCallister, J. M. (1964). Using paragraph clues as aids to understanding. *Journal of Reading, 8,* 11–16.

McGonigal, E. (1988). Correlative thinking: Writing analogies about literature. *English Journal, 77*(1), 66–67.

McKee, P., & Durr, W. K. (1966). *Reading: A program of instruction for the elementary school.* Boston: Houghton Mifflin.

McKenzie, J. V., Ericson, B., & Hunter, L. (1988). *Questions may be an answer.* Manuscript, California State University at Northridge.

McKowen, C. (1979). *Get your A out of college.* Martinez, CA: Northernaire Publications.

McLaughlin, G. H. (1969). SMOG grading—A new readability formula. *Journal of Reading, 12,* 639–646.

McNamara, L. P. (1977). A study of the cloze procedure as an alternate group instructional strategy in secondary school American government classes (Doctoral dissertation, Northern Illinois University, DeKalb). *Dissertation Abstracts International, 39,* 216A.

McNeil, J. D. (1987). *Reading comprehension: New directions for classroom practice* (2nd ed.). Glenview, IL: Scott Foresman.

Meeks, J. W. (1979). Imbedded aids to readers: An alternative textbook approach. *Reading Improvement, 16,* 95–98.

Meeks, J. W. (1980). Effects of imbedded aids on prose-related textual material. *Reading World, 19,* 345–351.

Meeks, J. W. (1982). Adjunct aids and teacher regulation of learning from text. In G. H. McNinch (Ed.), *Reading in the disciplines. Second yearbook of the American Reading Forum* (pp. 36–37). Athens, GA: American Reading Forum.

Meeks, J. W., & Morgan, R. F. (1978). Classroom and the cloze procedure: Interaction in imagery. *Reading Horizons, 18,* 261–264.

Meichenbaum, D., & Asarnow, J. (1979). Cognitive-behavioral modifications and metacognitive development. In P. C. Kendall & S. D. Hollan (Eds.), *Cognitive-behavioral interventions: Theory, research and procedures* (pp. 11–35). New York: Academic Press.

Meyer, B. J. F. (1975). *The organization of prose and its effect on memory.* Amsterdam: North-Holland.

Michael Jackson: Junk culture triumph. (1984, May). *Working Woman,* p. 192.

Mikulecky, L. (1982). Job literacy: The relationship between school preparation and workplace actuality. *Reading Research Quarterly, 17,* 400–419.

Miller, W. E., & Dollard, J. (1941). *Social learning and imitation.* New Haven, CT: Yale University Press.

Missouri Department of Elementary and Secondary Education. (1986). *Core competencies and key skills for Missouri schools: For grades 2 through 10.* Jefferson City, MO: Author.

Misuse of grade equivalents. (1982). Resolution passed by the Delegates Assembly of the International Reading Association, April 1981. *The Reading Teacher, 35,* 464.

Mitchell, D. C. (1982). *The process of reading: A cognitive analysis of fluent reading and learning to read.* Somerset, NJ: John Wiley and Sons.

Moore, D. W., Readence, J. E., & Rickelman, R. J. (1982). *Prereading activities for content area reading and learning.* Newark, DE: International Reading Association.

Mullikin, C. N., & Henk, W. A. (1985). Using music as a background for reading: An exploratory study. *Journal of Reading, 28,* 353–358.

Muth, K. D. (1987). Teachers' connection questions: Prompting students to organize text ideas. *Journal of Reading, 31,* 254–259.

Myers, K. L. (1988). Twenty (better) questions. *English Journal, 77*(1), 64–65.

National Assessment of Educational Progress. (1986). *Mathematics Report Card.* Princeton, NJ: Educational Testing Service.

National Assessment of Educational Progress. (1988). *Reading Report Card.* Princeton, NJ: Educational Testing Service.

Neill, A. S. (1960). *Summerhill: A radical approach to child rearing.* New York: Hart.

Nelson, G. L. (1987). Culture's role in reading comprehension: A schema theoretical approach. *Journal of Reading, 30,* 424–429.

Niles, O. (1965). Organization perceived. In H. L. Herber (Ed.), *Developing study skills in secondary schools* (pp. 57–76). Newark, DE: International Reading Association.

Obah, T. Y. (1983). Prior knowledge and the quest for new knowledge: The third world dilemma. *Journal of Reading, 27,* 129–133.

Osborn, J., Jones, B. F., & Stein, F. (1985). The case for improving textbooks. *Educational Leadership, 42*(7), 9–16.

Otto, W., & Hayes, B. (1982). Glossing for improved comprehension: Progress and prospect. In G. H. McNinch (Ed.), *Reading in the disciplines. Second yearbook of the American Reading Forum* (pp. 16–18). Athens, GA: American Reading Forum.

Pace, A. J. (1985). Learning to learn through text design: Can it be done? In D. H. Jonassen (Ed.), *The technology of text: Principles for structuring, designing, and displaying text* (Vol. 2, pp. 1–25). Englewood Cliffs, NJ: Educational Technology Publications.

Padak, N. D. (1986). Teachers' verbal behaviors: A window to the teaching process. In J. A. Niles & R. V. Lalik (Eds.), *Solving problems in literacy: Learners, teachers, and researchers. Thirty-fifth yearbook of the National Reading Conference* (pp. 185–191). Rochester, NY: National Reading Conference.

Palincsar, A. S., & Brown, A. L. (1984). Reciprocal teaching of comprehension monitoring activities. *Cognition and Instruction, 1,* 117–175.

Palincsar, A. S., & Brown, A. L. (1986). Interactive teaching to promote independent learning from text. *The Reading Teacher, 39,* 771–777.

Palmatier, R. A. (1971). Comparison of four note-taking procedures. *Journal of Reading, 14,* 235–40, 258.

Palmatier, R. A. (1973). A notetaking system for learning. *Journal of Reading, 17,* 36–39.

Palmatier, R. A., & Bennett, J. M. (1974). Notetaking habits of college students. *Journal of Reading, 18,* 215–218.

Pauk, W. (1974). *How to study in college.* Boston: Houghton Mifflin.

Paul, R. W. (1984). Critical thinking: Fundamental to education for a free society. *Educational Leadership, 42*(1), 4–14.

Pearce, D. L. (1983). Guidelines for the use and evaluation of writing in content classrooms. *Journal of Reading, 27,* 212–218.

Pearce, D. L. (1987). Works covered in graduate reading research courses: Two surveys. *Reading Horizons, 28,* 39–48.

Pearson, P. D. (Ed.). (1984). *Handbook of reading research.* New York: Longman.

Pearson, P. D., & Johnson, D. D. (1978). *Teaching reading comprehension*. New York: Holt, Rinehart and Winston.

Peck, M. P., & Laughlin, M. A. (1982). Critical reading, reasoning, and consumer decision making. In G. H. McNinch (Ed.), *Reading in the disciplines. Second yearbook of the American Reading Forum* (pp. 101–105). Athens, GA: American Reading Forum.

Pepitone, E. A. (1980). *Children in cooperation and competition*. Lexington, MA: D. C. Heath.

Perry, M. (1971). *Man's unfinished journey*. Boston: Houghton Mifflin.

Peters, C. W. (1982). The content processing model: A new approach to conceptualizing content reading. In J. P. Patberg (Ed.), *Reading in the content areas: Application of a concept* (pp. 100–109). Toledo, OH: University of Toledo, College of Education.

Petre, R. M. (1970). Quantity, quality and variety of pupil responses during an open-communication structured group directed reading-thinking activity and a closed-communication structured group directed reading activity (Doctoral dissertation, University of Delaware, Newark). *Dissertation Abstracts International, 31,* 4630A.

Phelps, S. (l979). The effects of integrating sentence combining activities and guided reading procedures on the reading and writing performance of eighth grade students. In H. L. Herber & J. D. Riley (Eds.), *Research in reading in the content areas: Fourth year report* (pp. 99–112). Syracuse, NY: Syracuse University, Reading and Language Arts Center.

Pichert, J. W., & Anderson, R. C. (1977). Taking different perspectives on a story. *Journal of Educational Psychology, 69,* 309–315.

Piercy, D. (1976). *Reading activities in content areas*. Boston: Allyn and Bacon.

Pinnell, G. S. (1984). Communication in small group settings. *Theory into Practice, 23,* 246–254.

Polya, G. (1957). *How to solve it*. New York: Doubleday Anchor.

Porteus, S. D. (1931). *The psychology of a primitive people*. New York: Longmans, Green.

Postman, N., & Weingartner, C. (1969). *Teaching as a subversive activity*. New York: Delacorte Press.

Protect non-smokers from smokers. (1984, September 27). *Cleveland Plain Dealer*, p. 7A.

Rabow, G. (1988, January). The cooperative edge. *Psychology Today,* pp. 54–58.

Rakes, S. K., & Smith, L. J. (1987). Strengthening comprehension and recall through the principle of recitation. *Journal of Reading, 31,* 260–263.

Raphael, T. E. (1984). Teaching learners about sources of information for answering comprehension questions. *Journal of Reading, 27,* 303–311.

Ratekin, N., Simpson, M. L., Alvermann, D. E., & Dishner, E. K. (1985). Why teachers resist content area reading instruction. *Journal of Reading, 28,* 432–437.

Raths, L. E., Harmon, M., & Simon, S. B. (1978). *Values and teaching* (2nd ed.). Columbus, OH: Merrill.

Raygor, A. L. (1977). The Raygor readability estimate: A quick and easy way to determine difficulty. In P. D. Pearson (Ed.), *Reading: Theory, research and practice. Twenty-sixth yearbook of the National Reading Conference* (pp. 259–263). Clemson, SC: National Reading Conference.

Readence, J. E. (1984). Fostering meaning-making in reading and writing. In D. W. Protheroe (Ed.), *Reading-writing connections* (pp. 202–206). Storrs: University of Connecticut, Reading and Language Arts Center.

Reeve, R. A., Palincsar, A. S., & Brown, A. L. (1985). *Everyday and academic thinking: Implications for learning and problem solving* (Journal of Curriculum Studies Technical Report No. 349). Champaign: University of Illinois, Center for the Study of Reading.

Richgels, D. (J.), & Hansen, R. (1982). Guidelines for writing gloss notations with a focus on comprehension skills and strategies. In G. H. McNinch (Ed.), *Reading in the disciplines*.

Second yearbook of the American Reading Forum (pp. 18–23). Athens, GA: American Reading Forum.

Richgels, D. J., & Hansen, R. (1984). Gloss: Helping students apply both skills and strategies in reading content texts. *Journal of Reading, 27,* 312–317.

Rickards, J. P., & Friedman, F. (1978). The encoding versus the external storage hypothesis in note taking. *Contemporary Educational Psychology, 3,* 136–143.

Riley, J. D. (1979a). The effect of reading guides upon students' literal, interpretive, and applied level comprehension of word problems. In H. L. Herber & J. D. Riley (Eds.), *Research in reading in the content areas: Fourth year report* (pp. 113–131). Syracuse, NY: Syracuse University, Reading and Language Arts Center.

Riley, J. D. (1979b). The effects of reading guides and a directed reading method on word problem comprehension, problem solving ability, and attitude toward mathematics. In H. L. Herber & J. D. Riley (Eds.), *Research in reading in the content areas: Fourth year report* (pp. 79–98). Syracuse, NY: Syracuse University, Reading and Language Arts Center.

Robinson, F. (1946). *Effective study.* New York: Harper Brothers.

Roby, T. (1983, April). *The other side of the question: Controversial turns, the devil's advocate, and reflective responses.* Paper presented at the annual meeting of the American Educational Research Association, Montreal.

Roehler, L. R., & Duffy, G. G. (1984). Direct explanation of comprehension processes. In G. G. Duffy, L. R. Roehler, & J. (M.) Mason (Eds.), *Comprehension instruction: Perspectives and suggestions* (pp. 265–280). New York: Longman.

Rongione, L. A. (1972). Bibliotherapy: Its nature and uses. *Catholic Library World, 43,* 495–500.

Rosecky, M. (1978). Are teachers selective when using basal guidebooks? *The Reading Teacher, 31,* 381–384.

Rosenshine, B. V. (1984). Content, time, and direct instruction. In P. L. Peterson & H. J. Walberg (Eds.), *Research on teaching: Concepts, findings, and implications* (pp. 102–106). Berkeley, CA: McCutchan.

Roser, N. (1984). Teaching and testing reading comprehension: An historical perspective on instructional research and practices. In J. Flood (Ed.), *Understanding reading comprehension: Cognition, language, and the structure of prose* (pp. 48–60). Newark, DE: International Reading Association.

Rothkopf, E. Z. (1970). The concept of mathemagenic activities. *Review of Educational Research, 40,* 325–336.

Rumelhart, D. E. (1977). Toward an interactive model of reading. In S. Dornic (Ed.), *Attention and performance VI: Proceedings of the Sixth International Symposium on Attention and Performance, Stockholm, Sweden, July 28–August 1, 1975* (pp. 573–603). Hillsdale, NJ: Erlbaum Associates.

Rumelhart, D. E. (1984). Understanding understanding. In J. Flood (Ed.), *Understanding reading comprehension: Cognition, language, and the structure of prose* (pp. 1–20). Newark, DE: International Reading Association.

Rush, T., Moe, A., & Storlie, R. (1986). *Occupational literacy education.* Newark, DE: International Reading Association.

Russell, D. (1949). *Children learn to read.* New York: Ginn.

Russell, D. (1961). *Children learn to read* (2nd ed.). New York: Ginn.

Salisbury, R. (1934). A study of the transfer effects of training in logical organization. *Journal of Educational Research, 28,* 241–254.

Samuels, S. J. (1977). Introduction to theoretical models of reading. In W. Otto, N. A. Peters, & C. W. Peters (Eds.), *Reading problems: A multidisciplinary perspective* (pp. 7–41). Reading, MA: Addison-Wesley.

Samuels, S. J., & Turnure, J. E. (1974). Attention and reading achievement in first-grade boys and girls. *Journal of Educational Psychology, 66,* 29–32.

Sanacore, J. (1984). Metacognition and the improvement of reading: Some important links. *Journal of Reading, 27,* 706–712.

Sanders, P. L. (1969). Teaching map reading skills in grade 9. *Journal of Reading, 12,* 283–286, 337.

Santa, C. M., Dailey, S. C., & Nelson, M. (1985). Free-response and opinion-proof: A reading and writing strategy for middle grade and secondary teachers. *Journal of Reading, 28,* 346–352.

Santa, C. M., Isaacson, L., & Manning, G. (1987). Changing content instruction through action research. *The Reading Teacher, 40,* 434–438.

Santeusanio, R. (1967). RAMA: A supplement to the traditional college reading program. *Journal of Reading, 11,* 133–136.

Sari, I. F., & Reigeluth, C. M. (1982). Writing and evaluating textbooks: Contributions from instructional theory. In D. H. Jonassen (Ed.), *The technology of text: Principles for structuring, designing, and displaying text* (Vol. 1, pp. 53–90). Englewood Cliffs, NJ: Educational Technology Publications.

Scarrozo, S. (1983). Dictation: A technique in need of reappraisal. *Educational Leadership Training, 37,* 121–126.

Schatz, E. K., & Baldwin, R. S. (1986). Context clues are unreliable predictors of word meanings. *Reading Research Quarterly, 21,* 439–453.

Schell, L. M. (1980). Value clarification via basal readers. *Reading Horizons, 20,* 215–220.

Schell, L. M. (1988). Dilemmas in assessing reading comprehension. *The Reading Teacher, 42,* 12–16.

Schmuck, R. A., & Runkel, P. J. (1985). *The handbook of organizational development in schools* (3rd ed.). Prospect Heights, IL: Waveland Press.

Schwarz, J., & Goldberg, M. (1962). *New York State in story.* Phoenix, NY: Frank E. Richards.

Second-hand smoke: The myth and the reality. (1984). Advertisement by the R. J. Reynolds Tobacco Co.

Shablak, S. (L.), & Castallo, R. (1977). Curiosity arousal and motivation in the teaching/learning process. In H. L. Herber & R. T. Vacca (Eds.), *Research in reading in the content areas: Third year report* (pp. 51–65). Syracuse, NY: Syracuse University, Reading and Language Arts Center.

Shanahan, T. (1986). Predictions and limiting effects of prequestions. In J. A. Niles & R. V. Lalik (Eds.), *Solving problems in literacy: Learners, teachers, and researchers. Thirty-fifth yearbook of the National Reading Conference* (pp. 92–98). Rochester, NY: National Reading Conference.

Shepherd, D. (1982). *Comprehensive high school reading methods* (3rd ed.). Columbus, OH: Merrill.

Simpson, M. K. (1986). A teacher's gift: Oral reading and the reading response journal. *Journal of Reading, 30,* 45–50.

Simpson, M. L. (1986). PORPE: A writing strategy for studying and learning in the content areas. *Journal of Reading, 29,* 407–414.

Simpson, M. L., Hayes, C. G., Stahl, N. (A.), Connor, R. T., & Weaver, D. (1988). An initial validation of a study strategy system. *Journal of Reading Behavior, 20,* 149–180.

Singer, H. (1975). The SEER technique: A non-computational procedure for quickly estimating readability level. *Journal of Reading Behavior, 7,* 255–267.

Singer, H. (1976). Theoretical models of reading. In H. Singer & R. B. Ruddell (Eds.), *Theoretical models and processes of reading* (2nd ed., pp. 634–654). Newark, DE: International Reading Association.

Singer, H., & Dolan, D. (1980). *Reading and learning from text.* Boston: Little, Brown.

Singer, H., & Ruddell, R. B. (1976). *Theoretical models and processes of reading* (2nd ed.). Newark, DE: International Reading Association.

Smith, D. E. P. (1967). *Learning to learn.* New York: Harcourt Brace Jovanovich.

Smith, F. (1978). *Understanding reading: A psycholinguistic analysis of reading and learning to read* (2nd ed.). New York: Holt, Rinehart and Winston.

Smith, F. (1979). *Reading without nonsense.* New York: Teachers College Press.

Smith, N. B. (1964a). Patterns of writing in different subject areas: Part I. *Journal of Reading, 8,* 31–37.

Smith, N. B. (1964b). Patterns of writing in different subject areas: Part II. *Journal of Reading, 8,* 97–102.

Smith, R. J., & Dauer, V. L. (1984). A comprehension-monitoring strategy for reading content area materials. *Journal of Reading, 28,* 144–147.

Spache, G. D. (1953). A new readability formula for primary grades reading materials. *The Elementary School Journal, 53,* 410–413.

Spache, G. D. (1964). *Reading in the elementary school.* Boston: Allyn and Bacon.

Spiegel, D. L. (1980). Adaptations of Manzo's Guided Reading Procedure. *Reading Horizons, 20,* 188–192.

Stahl, N. A., & Henk, W. A. (1986). Tracing the roots of textbook study systems: An extended historical perspective. In J. A. Niles & R. V. Lalik (Eds.), *Solving problems in literacy: Learners, teachers, and researchers. Thirty-fifth yearbook of the National Reading Conference* (pp. 366–374). Rochester, NY: National Reading Conference.

Stans, Maurice H. (1984, August 8). Watergate witchhunt injured this country. *USA Today,* p. 12A.

Staton, J. (1980). Writing and counseling: Using a dialogue journal. *Language Arts, 57,* 514–518.

Stauffer, R. (1969). *Directing reading maturity as a cognitive porcess.* New York: Harper and Row.

Steinley, G. (1983). In the works: A new model of content reading? *Journal of Reading, 27,* 238–244.

Stevens, K. C. (1982). Can we improve reading by teaching background information? *Journal of Reading, 25,* 326–329.

Sticht, T. G., Beck, L. J., Hauke, R. N., Kleiman, G. M., & James, J. H. (1974). *Auding and reading: A developmental model* (Air Force Contract No. F41609-73-C-0025, Project 1121). Alexandria, VA: Human Resources Research Organization.

Stieglitz, E. L., & Stieglitz, V. S. (1981). SAVOR the word to reinforce vocabulary in the content areas. *Journal of Reading, 25,* 46–51.

Strode, S. (1988). Unpublished predissertation report, University of Missouri–Kansas City.

Taylor, G. C. (1980). Music in language arts instruction. *Language Arts, 58,* 363–367.

Taylor, W. L. (1953). "Cloze procedure": A new tool for measuring readability. *Journalism Quarterly, 30,* 415–433.

Tchudi, S. (N.) (1988). Invisible thinking and the hypertext. *English Journal, 77*(1), 22–30.

Tchudi, S. N., & Huerta, M. C. (1983). *Teaching writing in the content areas: Middle school/junior high.* Washington, DC: National Education Association.

Thelen, J. N. (1969). Use of advance organizers and guide material in viewing science motion pictures in ninth grade: Pilot study report. In H. L. Herber & P. L. Sanders (Eds.), *Research in reading in the content areas: First year report* (pp. 59–63). Syracuse, NY: Syracuse University Reading and Language Arts Center.

Thelen, J. N. (1977). Use of advance organizers and guide material in viewing science motion pictures in ninth grade. In H. L. Herber & R. T. Vacca (Eds.), *Research in reading in the content areas: Third year report* (pp. 179–189). Syracuse, NY: Syracuse University, Reading and Language Arts Center.

Thorndike, E. L. (1917). Reading as reasoning: A study of mistakes in paragraph reading. *Journal of Educational Psychology, 8,* 323–332.

Tierney, R. (J.), Readence, J. E., & Dishner, E. K. (1985). *Reading strategies and practices: A compendium* (2nd ed.). Boston: Allyn and Bacon.

Tonjes, M. J., & Zintz, M. V. (1987). *Teaching reading, thinking, study skills in content classrooms* (2nd ed.). Dubuque, IA: William C. Brown.

Uttero, D. A. (1988). Activating comprehension through cooperative learning. *The Reading Teacher, 41,* 390–395.

Vacca, R. T. (1973). An investigation of a functional reading strategy in seventh-grade social studies classes (Doctoral dissertation, Syracuse University, Syracuse, NY). *Dissertation Abstracts International, 34,* 6278A.

Vacca, R. T., & Vacca, J. L. (1986). *Content area reading* (2nd ed.). Boston: Little, Brown.

Valencia, S., & Pearson, P. D. (1987). *Reading assessment: Time for a change.* The Reading Teacher, 40, 726–732.

Wade, R. K. (1984–1985). What makes a difference in inservice teacher education? A meta-analysis of research. *Educational Leadership, 42*(4), 48–54.

Waern, Y. (1977a). Comprehension and belief structure. *Scandanavian Journal of Psychology, 18,* 266–274.

Waern, Y. (1977b). On the relationship between knowledge of the world and comprehension of texts. *Scandanavian Journal of Psychology, 18,* 130–139.

Walker, A., & Parkman, M. (1924). *The study readers: Fifth year.* New York: Merrill.

Wallace, I., Wallechinsky, D., Wallace, A., & Wallace, S. (1980). *The people's almanac: Book of lists 2.* New York: William Morrow.

Wark, D. M. (1964). Survey Q3R: System or superstition? In D. M. Wark (Ed.), *College and adult reading. Third and fourth annual yearbook of the North Central Reading Association* (pp. 161–170). St. Paul: University of Minnesota, Student Counseling Bureau.

Weaver, W. W., & Kingston, A. J. (1963). A factor analysis of cloze procedure and other measures of reading and language ability. *Journal of Communication, 13,* 252–261.

Weinstein, C. E. (1987). Fostering learning autonomy through the use of learning strategies. *Journal of Reading, 30,* 590–595.

Welker, W. A. (1987). Going from typical to technical meaning. *Journal of Reading, 31,* 275–276.

Whimbey, A., & Lochhead, J. (1979). *Problem solving and comprehension: A short course in analytical reasoning.* Philadelphia, PA: Franklin Institute Press.

Whimbey, A., Carmichael, J. W., Jr., Jones, L. W., Hunter, J. T., & Vincent, H. A. (1980). Teaching critical reading and analytical reasoning in Project SOAR. *Journal of Reading, 24,* 5–10.

Wiener, M., & Cromer, W. (1967). Reading and reading difficulty: A conceptual analysis. *Harvard Educational Review, 37,* 620–643.

Wilkins, G., & Miller, S. (1983). *Strategies for success: An effective guide for teachers of secondary-level slow learners.* New York: Teachers College Press.

Williams, J. P. (1973). Learning to read: A review of theories and models. *Reading Research Quarterly, 8,* 121–146.

Willmore, D. J. (1967). A comparison of four methods of studying a college textbook (Doctoral dissertation, University of Minnesota, 1966). *Dissertation Abstracts, 27,* 2413A.

Witte, P. L. (1982). Glossing content area texts: A vehicle for inservice training. In G. H. McNinch (Ed.), *Reading in the disciplines. Second yearbook of the American Reading Forum* (pp. 23–25). Athens, GA: American Reading Forum.

Wittrock, M. C., Marks, C., & Doctorow, M. (1975). Reading as a generative process. *Journal of Educational Psychology, 67,* 484–489.

Wixson, K. K., Peters, C. W., Weber, E. M., & Roeber, E. D. (1987). New directions in statewide reading assessment. *The Reading Teacher, 40,* 749–754.

Wood, K. D. (1985). Free associational assessment: An alternative to traditional testing. *Journal of Reading, 29,* 106–111.

Wood, K. D. (1987). Fostering cooperative learning in middle and secondary level classrooms. *Journal of Reading, 31,* 10–19.

Woods, A. K., & Topping, M. H. (1986). The reading resource specialist: A model. *Journal of Reading, 29,* 733–738.

Wooster, G. F. (1958). Teaching the SQ3R method of study: An investigation of the instructional approach (Doctoral dissertation, The Ohio State University, 1953). *Dissertation Abstracts, 18,* 2067–2068.

Yarger, G. P., & Mintz, S. L. (1979). *A literature study related to the use of materials in the classroom.* Washington, DC: U.S. Office of Education, National Diffusion Network.

Author Biographies

Anthony Manzo received his B.A. in history and philosophy from St. John's University, his M.Ed. from Hofstra University, and his Ph.D. in Education from Syracuse University. He has taught social studies and English at the junior and senior high levels and reading at the K–college levels. He has chaired the Division of Reading and Special Education of the University of Missouri–Kansas City. Currently he serves as Director of the Center for Studies in Higher Order Literacy at the University of Missouri–Kansas City as well as Professor of Education and Coordinator of College Reading. Professor Manzo has served on the publications board or as consulting editor to several professional journals, including the *Journal of Reading, Reading Psychology,* and the *Journal of Research and Development in Education.* He has published numerous articles, received awards for writing and research, and chaired several important efforts, including the work of the International Reading Association committee that produced the current Guidelines for the Preparation of Reading Professionals and the reading research advisory group to the Assistant Secretary of Education for Educational Research and Improvement. His personal research and development interests are in reading comprehension, creative thinking, teacher empowerment, and educational reform.

Ula Casale Manzo received her B.A. in English and secondary education with honors from Park College and her M.A. and Ph.D. in reading education from the University of Missouri–Kansas City, graduating Summa Cum Laude. She has taught reading and language arts from the elementary to college levels, served as Assistant Professor of Education at Northwest Missouri State University, and served as a developmental studies specialist at both the University of Kansas and the University of Missouri–Kansas City Schools of Medicine. Currently she serves as Curriculum Coordinator of Language Arts, K–12, for the School District of Kansas City, Missouri. In this position, she also coordinates the development of a new K–12 communications/writing magnet school program. As teacher, professor, and administrator, her interests and work include writing and instructional processes, teacher training, and the administrative and urban conditions that bear on student, teacher, and community affairs.

Nested Chapters Index

VOCABULARY ACQUISITION

Ideally, every teacher should be trained and committed to promoting vocabulary growth across grades and disciplines. In fact, this remains an area to which more lip service is given than effort. When you have thought it through and are ready to make a commitment to this area of programming, this nested chapter on vocabulary should be of considerable assistance. It stresses actual methods of teaching vocabulary, in contrast to most texts that stress the importance of vocabulary acquisition and simply give examples of various word manipulation, or workbook-type, exercises. To put it bluntly, anyone can hand out exercise books. Professional teachers, however, whatever their subject or grade specialization, should be equipped to teach words and how to learn words in any situation.

QUESTIONING

Questions drive focused reading, thinking, listening, and speaking. They are the chief means of testing and teaching and the most effective means of manifesting curiosity. Both teachers and students need to be taught to question in the most effective ways possible.

WRITING

Writing takes courage and discipline—that is why it is difficult but very worthwhile.

7. Content-based, whole language methods for teaching writing, speaking, listening, and reading: Opinion Proof (pp. 228–230); Devil's Advocate (pp. 230–231); Developmental Discussion (pp. 231–232); Extension of the Guided Reading Procedure (pp. 232–234); Semantic Map Retranslation (pp. 234–235)

8. Increasing sensitivity to text structure (pp. 179–183)

9. Study Journal writing (pp. 297–298)

10. Dialogue Journals—in mental health (pp. 313–315); Decorum Journal for vocational technology (pp. 437–438)

11. The Language Shaping Paradigm for reluctant writers (pp. 368–371)

12. De-Composition and GRASP (pp. 369–372)

13. Writing Communal Poetry (pp. 377–381)

14. Writing from Guided Reading Procedure in science (pp. 405–409)

15. Annotation Exchange (pp. 349–352)

16. WeWriters (p. 354)

LIFE MANAGEMENT

Mature comprehension requires emotional stability and, in turn, builds emotional maturity. If we haven't taught students to deal with the inevitable throes of life, we haven't taught them much.

1. As part of reading maturity (p. 39)

2. Why assess affect? (pp. 82–84)

3. Effect on anticipation (pp. 126; 129)

4. Disruptive thinking defined (p. 344)

5. Instant Study Skills, numbers 13, 14, 15 (pp. 301–302)

6. Reducing misapprehension before reading—ReQuest (pp. 136–141); Mind Set Approaches (pp. 146–147); Student Generated Anticipation-Reaction Guides (pp. 188–190)

7. Through Cooperative Learning, Group Reading Activity, Cooperative DR-TA (pp. 112–120)

8. Creative thinking as a life management skill: Thinking Hats and Mind Cuing (pp. 260–262)

9. Trace elements theory (p. 100)

10. As part of vocabulary development—in SAV (pp. 158–161); "Preppie" terms (p. 239); Motor Imaging for behavioral reconditioning (pp. 160–163)

11. In evaluative reading—IntraAct (pp. 255–256); DR-TA (pp. 104–106); GRP (pp. 107–111); science—Refutation Text (p. 404); social studies—Parallel Form strategy (pp. 411–413)

12. Critical Judgments exercises (pp. 415–416; 418)

13. Through writing—Decorum Journal (pp. 437–438); Communal Poetry (pp. 377–381); Dialogue Journal (pp. 313–315); Study Journal (pp. 297–298)

14. Homilies for life management (p. 302)

15. As part of study skills training—Problem-Solving Approach to Study Skills (pp. 298–300); scheduling (pp. 296–297)

16. Through bibliotherapy (pp. 313–315)

17. In class—Behavior Paradigm (pp. 311–312); Note Cue (pp. 323–326); Ask-It-Rite (pp. 312–313); Question-Only (pp. 49–50)

18. Proverbs study—remedy for emotive, or disruptive, thinking (pp. 326–331)

19. In the school and workplace—State-It-Rite (p. 437)

20. ThemedSchools (pp. 355–356)

21. Building self-worth—dignity of the "average guy" (pp. 424–425); anecdote on interpreting experience and literature (pp. 214–215)

Author Index

Subject Index